Communications
in Computer and Information Science 201

Honghua Tan Mark Zhou (Eds.)

Advances in Information Technology and Education

International Conference, CSE 2011
Qingdao, China, July 9-10, 2011
Proceedings, Part I

Springer

Volume Editors

Honghua Tan
Wuhan Institute of Technology
Xiongchu Road 693
Wuhan, China
E-mail: honghua_tan@yahoo.cn

Mark Zhou
Education Society
The Sherwood No.8 Fuk Hang Tsuen Road
Tuen Mun, Hong Kong
E-mail: zhoumarkhk@sina.com

ISSN 1865-0929 e-ISSN 1865-0937
ISBN 978-3-642-22417-1 ISBN 978-3-642-22418-8 (eBook)
DOI 10.1007/978-3-642-22418-8
Springer Heidelberg Dordrecht London New York

Library of Congress Control Number: 2011931540

CR Subject Classification (1998): I.2, D.2, H.4, I.4, F.1, H.3

Typesetting: Camera-ready by author, data conversion by Scientific Publishing Services, Chennai, India

Printed on acid-free paper

Springer is part of Springer Science+Business Media (www.springer.com)

Preface

The present book includes extended and revised versions of a set of selected papers from the 2011 International Conference on Computer Science and Education (CSE 2011), held during July 9–10, 2011, which was jointly organized by Springer and the International Science and Engineering Center, Hong Kong.

Qingdao, located in the southeastern part of Shandong province, is a beautiful seaside city with clean air and enchanting sea views. This city, bordered by the Yellow Sea on two sides, has the largest bathing beach in Asia and produces the mellow Qingdao Beer. To the east of Qingdao, a short distance across the Yellow Sea, lie Korea and Japan, making the city an important port for international trade. For 33 years, up to 1949, Qingdao was a colony of Germany and Japan. Thus, Qingdao has a great deal of European architecture. This foreign architecture—a remnant of the colonial past—now beautifies this seaside city. The red roofs, green trees, blue sea, and azure sky form a bright and colorful scene. The city is sometimes known as the Switzerland of the Orient.

Surrounded by the sea on three sides, Qingdao attracts many tourists with its charming seascape. Sights like the Eight Passes Villas, Wusi Square, Zhan Bridge, Mt. Laoshan, No.1 Bathing Beach, Badaguan Scenic Area make Qingdao unforgettable. Just walking on the sand and listening to the surf breaking on the beach becomes enjoyable.

The goal of CSE 2011 was to bring together researchers from computer science and education as well as practitioners to share ideas, problems and solutions relating to the multifaceted aspects of computers and education.

Being crucial for the development of computer science and education, our conference encompasses a large number of research topics and applications: from artificial intelligence to computers and information technology; from education systems to methods research and other related topics. Our expert reviewers from home and abroad ensure we have high-quality international conference through their rigorous reviewing process. All accepted papers are published the *Communications in Computer and Information Science* series by Springer.

Have been possible without the help of the Program Chairs, organization staff, and the members of the Program Committee. We thank them for their hard work.

We are confident that the conference program provided attendees with detailed insight into the new trends in this area, and we look forward to meeting you at future events.

Honghua Tan

Organization

General Chairs

Honghua Tan	Wuhan Institute of Technology, China
Junwu Zhu	Yangzhou University, China

Program Chairs

Chang Wen	Chienkuo Technology University, Taiwan
Chris Marry	Harokopio University of Athens, Greece

International Program Committee

Lizhe Wang	Virginia Polytechnic Institute and State University, USA
Benmei Chen	Gwangju Institute of Science and Technology, Korea
Dehuai Zeng	Shenzhen University, China

Publication Chairs

Honghua Tan	Wuhan Institute of Technology, China
Xiaolong Wang	Wuhan Insititue of Technology, China

Table of Contents – Part I

Table of Contents – Part II

Optimality Conditions for Nondifferentiable Vector Optimization Problems under Invexity

Hai Sun[1] and Ling Lin[2]

[1] College of Mathematics and Information
[2] Land and Resource College, China West Normal University, Nanchong, Sichuan, 637002, People's Republic of China
cwnush@126.com

Abstract. In this paper, we introduce two new classes of invexity functions, i.e., pesudoinvex-I and pesudoinvex-II. The relationships among invexity, pesudoinvexity-I and pesudoinvexity-II are shown by some examples. Further, the optimality conditions for nondifferentiable vector optimization problems are established. The results presented in this paper generalized some results in the literature.

Keywords: Invexity, Optimality condition, Nondifferentiable vector optimization problem.

1 Introduction

The optimality conditions for vector optimization problems play an important part in optimization theory. Some authors investigated this problem under different conditions. On the other hand, convexity also plays a key role in some areas of mathematics. And many authors extended the concept of convexity. Hanson [1] introduced the concept of invex functions for scalar-valued functions. Chen et al. [2] used η -approximation method for solving a differentiable multiobjective optimization problem and gave some dualities results. Arana-Jimenez et al.[3] proposed the concept of pseudoinvexity for differentiable functions, and established relationships between these new classes of functions. Arana-Jimenez et al. [4] obtained some characterizations to efficient solutions of multiobjective optimization problems under some generalized pseudoinvexity assumptions. Jabarootian and Zafarani [5] introduced the concept of nondifferentiable invex function.

Motivated and inspired by the above mentioned works, we introduce two new classes of invexity functions, i.e., pesudoinvex-I and pesudoinvex-II. The relationships among invexity, pesudoinvexity-I and pesudoinvexity-II are shown by some examples. Further, the optimality conditions for nondifferentiable vector optimization problems are established. The results presented in this paper generalized some results in the literature.

Throughout this paper, without other specifications, Let R^n be the n-dimensional Euclidean space, $S \subset R^n$ be an nonempty open set and

H. Tan and M. Zhou (Eds.): CSE 2011, Part I, CCIS 201, pp. 1–6, 2011.

$R_+^n = \{x = (x_1, \ldots, x_n)^T : x_i \geq 0, i = 1, \ldots, n\}$, where the superscript T denotes the transpose. Let $f = (f_1, \ldots, f_k)^T : S \to R^k$, and let f_i be locally Lipschitz, $i = 1, \ldots, k$.

We consider the following nondifferentiable vector optimization problem (for short, (VOP)):

$$\min_{x \in S} f(x).$$

Definition 1.1. A point $x_0 \in S$ is said to be a weakly efficient solution of (VOP) if,

$$f(x) - f(x_0) \notin -\operatorname{int} R_+^k, \forall x \in S.$$

Definition 1.2. A point $x_0 \in S$ is said to be an efficient solution of (VOP) if,

$$f(x) - f(x_0) \notin -R_+^k, \forall x \in S.$$

Definition 1.3. A real-valued function $\ell : R^n \to R$ is said to be locally Lipschitz if for any $z \in R^n$ there exist a positive constant κ and a neigborhood N of z such that, for each $x, y \in N$,

$$|\ell(x) - \ell(y)| \leq \kappa \|x - y\|,$$

where $\|\bullet\|$ denotes any norm in R^n. The Clarke [4] generalized subgradient of ℓ at z is denoted by

$$\partial \ell(z) = \{\xi : \ell^0(z; d) \geq \xi^T d, \forall d \in R^n\}.$$

Definition 1.4. Let the mapping $f : S \to R^k$. The generalized subgradient of f at $z \in S$ is the set

$$\partial f(z) = \partial f_1(z) \times \partial f_2(z) \times \ldots \times \partial f_k(z).$$

Where $\partial f_i(z)$ is the generalized subgradient of $f_i, (i = 1, 2, \ldots, k)$ at $z \in S$. Every element $\zeta = (\zeta_1, \ldots, \zeta_k) \in \partial f(z)$ is a continuous linear operator from R^n to R^k and $\zeta y = (\zeta_1 y, \ldots, \zeta_k y)$, for all $y \in R^n$.

Definition 1.5. A point $x_0 \in S$ is said to be a vector critical point of (VOP) if there exists $\lambda \in R_+^k$ such that

$$\lambda^T \xi = 0, \forall \xi \in \partial f(x_0).$$

Definition 1.6. The function $f : S \to R^k$ is called invex if there exists a vector function $\eta : S \times S \to R^n$ such that for all $x, \hat{x} \in S, \xi \in \partial f(\hat{x})$,

$$f(x) - f(\hat{x}) - \xi\eta(x,\hat{x})^T \in R_+^k .$$

Definition 1.7. The mapping $f : S \to R^k$ is called pseudoinvex-I if there exists a vector function $\eta : S \times S \to R^n$ such that for all $x, \hat{x} \in S, \xi \in \partial f(\hat{x})$,

$$f(x) - f(\hat{x}) \in -\mathrm{int}\, R_+^k \Rightarrow \xi\eta(x,\hat{x})^T \in -\mathrm{int}\, R_+^k .$$

Definition 1.8. The mapping $f : S \to R^k$ is called pseudoinvex-II if there exists a vector function $\eta : S \times S \to R^n$ such that for all $x, \hat{x} \in S, \xi \in \partial f(\hat{x})$,

$$f(x) - f(\hat{x}) \in -R_+^k \Rightarrow \xi\eta(x,\hat{x})^T \in -\mathrm{int}\, R_+^k .$$

Remark 1.1. It is easy to see that invexity and pseudoinvexity-II imply pseudoinvexity-I.

2 Main Results

In this section, we give some examples to illustrate the relations among invexity, pseudoinvexity-I and pseudoinvexity-II. Further, the optimality conditions for (VOP) are established under appropriate assumptions.

Example 2.1. Let $f = (f_1, f_2) : R \to R^2$ be defined as $f(x) = (|x|, -|x|)$.
Firstly, we verify that f is pseudoinvex-I. For any $\hat{x} \in R, \eta \in R,$ we have

$$\hat{x} > 0, \partial f(\hat{x}) = (1,-1), \xi \in \partial f(\hat{x}), \xi\eta = (\eta, -\eta) \notin -\mathrm{int}\, R_+^k ;$$
$$\hat{x} < 0, \partial f(\hat{x}) = (-1,1), \xi \in \partial f(\hat{x}), \xi\eta = (-\eta, \eta) \notin -\mathrm{int}\, R_+^k ;$$
$$\hat{x} = 0, \partial f(\hat{x}) = [-1,1] \times [-1,1].$$

Taking $\xi = (-1,1) \in \partial f(\hat{x})$, we have

$$\xi\eta = (-\eta, \eta) \notin -\mathrm{int}\, R_+^k .$$

For any $x, \hat{x} \in R,$

$$f_1(x) - f_1(\hat{x}) = |x| - |\hat{x}| < 0 \Leftrightarrow f_2(x) - f_2(\hat{x}) = |\hat{x}| - |x| > 0,$$

that is,

$$f(x)-f(\hat{x}) \notin -\operatorname{int} R_+^2.$$

Thus f is pseudoinvex-I with respect to η.

Secondly, taking $x=1, \hat{x}=0, \xi=(0,0)$, one has

$$f(x)-f(\hat{x})=(1,-1)-\xi\eta=(1,-1)-(0,0)\notin R_+^2.$$

Therefore, f is not invex with respect to η.

Example 2.2. Let $f=(f_1,f_2):R\to R^2$ be defined as $f(x)=(|x|,1)$. Firstly, we verify that f is invex and pseudoinvex-I. For any $\hat{x}\in R$, we have

$$\partial f(\hat{x})=\begin{cases}(1,0), \hat{x}>0,\\ (r,0), r\in[-1,1], \hat{x}=0,\\ (-1,0), \hat{x}<0.\end{cases}$$

Taking

$$\eta(x,\hat{x})=\begin{cases}|x|-|\hat{x}|, \hat{x}>0,\\ \frac{|x|}{2}, \hat{x}=0,\\ |\hat{x}|-|x|, \hat{x}<0.\end{cases}$$

One has

$$f(x)-f(\hat{x})=(|x|-|\hat{x}|,0)=\begin{cases}(|x|-|\hat{x}|,0), \hat{x}\neq 0,\\ (|x|,0), \hat{x}=0.\end{cases}$$

It can be check that

$$f(x)-f(\hat{x})-\xi\eta(x,\hat{x})^T\in R_+^2$$

and so, f is invex and pseudoinvex-I with respect to η. Secondly, taking $x=1, \hat{x}=2$, one has

$$f(x)-f(\hat{x})=(1,-1)-\xi\eta=(-1,0)\in -R_+^2.$$

From $\xi=(1,0)\in\partial f(\hat{x})$, it follows that

$$\xi\eta=(\eta,0)\notin -\operatorname{int} R_+^2.$$

Therefore, f is not pseudoinvex-II with respect to η.

Remark 2.1. Remark 1.1 and Examples 2.1 and 2.2 illustrate that invexity and pseudoinvexity-II imply pseudoinvexity-I, but the converse is not true.

Theorem 2.1. Every vector critical point is a weak efficient solution of (VOP) iff f is pseudoinvex-I.

Proof. Assume that $\hat{x}$ is the vector critical point of (VOP), then there exists a vector $\lambda \in R_+^k$ such that

$$\lambda^T \xi = 0, \xi \in \partial f(\hat{x}).$$

Therefore the system

$$\lambda^T \eta < 0, \eta : \mathrm{R}^n \times \mathrm{R}^n \to \mathrm{R}^n$$

has no solution. By the pseudoinvexity-I of f, there does not exist $x \in S$ such that

$$f(x) - f(\hat{x}) \in -\operatorname{int} R_+^k.$$

Thus $\hat{x}$ is the weakly efficient solution of (VOP).

Conversely, assume that $\hat{x}$ is the vector critical point of (VOP), then there exists a vector $\lambda \in R_+^k$ such that

$$\lambda^T \xi = 0, \xi \in \partial f(\hat{x}).$$

Therefore the system has no solution η, $\lambda^T \eta < 0$. By the assumptions, $\hat{x}$ is the weakly efficient solution of (VOP), then the following system has no solution :

$$f(x) - f(\hat{x}) \in -\operatorname{int} R_+^k.$$

Therefore f is pseudoinvex-I with respect to η. This completes the proof.

Theorem 2.2. Each vector critical point is an efficient solution of (VOP) iff f is pseudoinvex-II.

Proof. It can follow the lines of the previous proof. This completes the proof.

3 Conclusions

In this paper, two new classes of invexity functions, i.e., pesudoinvex-I and pesudoinvex-II. Further, the relationships among invexity, pesudoinvexity-I and pesudoinvexity-II are shown by some examples. Finally, the optimality conditions for nondifferentiable vector optimization problems are established. Further research, we can apply our results to study optimization, computational algorithms, management, building mathematical model, economics, variational inequalities, and complementary problems and so on.

References

1. Hanson, M.A.: On sufficiency of the Kuhn-Tucker conditions. Journal of Mathematical Analysis and Applications 80, 544–550 (1981)
2. Chen, J.W., Cho, Y.J., Kim, J.K., Li, J.: Multiobjective optimization problems with modified objective functions and cone constraints and applications. Journal of Global Optimization 49, 137–147 (2011)
3. Arana-Jimenez, M., et al.: A characterization of pseudoinvexity in multiobjective programming. Mathematical and Computer Modelling 48, 1719–1723 (2008)
4. Arana-Jimenez, M., et al.: Pseudoinvexity, optimality conditions and efficiency in multiobjective problems, duality. Nonlinear Analysis 68, 24–34 (2008)
5. Chen, J.W., Zou, Y.Z.: Existence of solutions of F-implicit variational inequalit problems with extended projection operators. Acta Mathmatica Sinica Chinese Series 53(2), 375–384 (2010)
6. Chen, J.W., Qi, Y.: Solvability of set-valued vector optimization problem. In: Proceedings of the 1st International Workshop on Education Technology and Computer Science, ETCS, vol. 3, pp. 934–938 (2009)
7. Jabarootian, T., Zafarani, J.: Generalized invariant monotonicity and invexity of nondifferential functions. Journal of Global Optimization 36, 537–564 (2006)
8. Fukushima, M.: Equivalent differentiable optimization problems and descent methods for asymmetric variational inequality problems. Mathematical Programming 53, 99–110 (1992)
9. Taji, K., et al.: A globally convergent Newton method for solving strongly monotone variational inequalities. Mathematical Programming 58, 369–383 (1993)
10. Peng, J.M.: Global method for monotone variational inequality problems with inequality constraints. Journal of Optimization Theory and Application 95(2), 419–430 (1997)
11. Solodov, M.V.: Some Methods Based on the D-Gap Function for Solving Monotone Variational Inequalities. Computational Optimization and Applications 17, 255–277 (2000)

A New Service Mining Method Based on Semantic Process

Xin-wei Zhai[1,2,*] and De-gan Zhang[1,2]

[1] Tianjin Key Lab of Intelligent Computing & Novel software Technology, Tianjin University of Technology, 300381, China
[2] Key Laboratory of Computer Vision and System (Tianjin University of Technology), Ministry of Education, 300381, China
zxw9908@eyou.com

Abstract. Service mining is the important research field in universal environment. Locating a network service or a device on demand is a challenging task for pervasive computing. We introduce a new approach that explores the use of Semantic Web language in building architecture for service mining in mobile environment in this paper. We propose a Web Ontology Language based ontology for service description, and for supporting logic-based service matchmaking. We introduced a semantic process algorithm according to the ontology. The algorithm takes the semantic meaning of service into account, enable interact between between device and device. It improves the veracity of service process, and paves the way for fuzzy process and service composition.

Keywords: Service mining, semantic, Ontology, Web Ontology Language.

1 Introduction

Service mining is the important research field in universal environment [1]. Locating a network service or a device on demand is a challenging task for pervasive computing [2]. In order to match user expectations, service mining need consider the functional and non-functional aspects. Non-functional aspects include QoS and User Preferences etc. Meet the functional process services may not meet the performance requirements of user expectations. But how to match functional expectations is the most basic requirements of functional expectations, process algorithm in high-performance functions is based on non-functional factors on the results of matches. Semantic web service description language OWL-S does not describe the QoS ontology [3]-[7]. If we want to match the introduction of non-functional, we need to expand on the OWL-S [8]-[11]. So we propose adding a semantic process algorithm for process QoS, design and comply with semantic web services process model in this paper.

2 Service Description

The overall structure of the ontology is shown in Figure 1. Space and Time are semantic description of the service locations and service time, Person is used to describe the

* Corresponding author.

H. Tan and M. Zhou (Eds.): CSE 2011, Part I, CCIS 201, pp. 7–14, 2011.

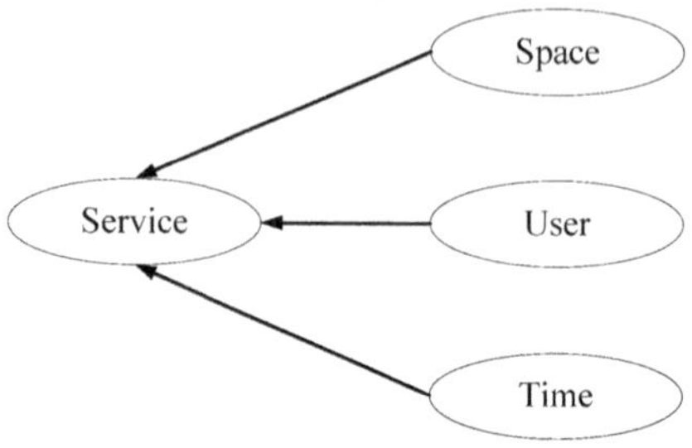

Fig. 1. Basic structure of the ontology

user's personal information, is mainly used for service process. The ontology model simplifies a number of other features such as security, user privacy, etc.

2.1 Description of Location

In the ubiquitous environment, services are varied, as shown in Figure 2. Description of spatial information services possible methods include:

1. An Internet address, description of services offered by the network, URI Uniform Resource Locator used to describe, such as http ://www. sun code. cn / services/ Weather Report .
2. Real-life address, description of services, from life, such as hospitals, schools, location, and so on.
3. A coordinate system can be used for local area or a small environment, the location and orientation in the description of the equipment.

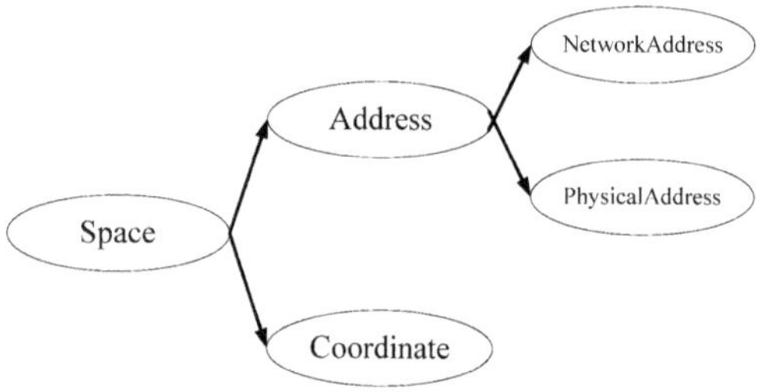

Fig. 2. Space Description

In the description of spatial information, the first need to define the namespace description.

```
<rdf:RDF
    xmlns =http://www.titucs/pc/space#
    xmlns:owl =http://www.w3.org/2002/07/owl#
    xmlns:rdf =http://www.w3.org/1999/02/22-rdf-syntax-ns#
    xmlns:rdfs=http://www.w3.org/2000/01/rdf-schema#
    xmlns:xsd ="http"//www.w3.org/2001/XMLSchema#">
```

Where, xmlns = http://www.suncode.cn/sapce #, define the default namespace, that is, when the document appears when the label is not prefix the namespace reference. xmlns: xsd = http://www.w3.org/2000/10/ XML Schema #,defined in the document to appear as a prefix xsd namespace entries, this is the introduction of XML Schema to define vocabulary. xmlns: owl = http://www.w3.org/2002/07/owl #, defines the term there should be looking for owl prefix namespace. OWL is a common statement in the document to add OWL vocabularies, such as owl: Object Property.

Class constraints include setting the definition of the class type ID, to determine the logic between class and class relations, and so on.

Complete class definition is as follows:

```
<owl:Class rdf:ID="Space"/>
<owl:Class rdf:ID="Address">
    <rdfs:subClassOf rdf:resource="#Space">
</owl:Class>
<owl:Class rdf:ID="Coordinate">
    <rdfs:subClassOf rdf:resource="#Space">
</owl:Class>
<owl:Class rdf:ID="NetworkAddress">
    <rdfs:subClassOf rdf:resource="#Address">
</owl:Class>
<owl:Class rdf:ID="PhysicalAddress">
    <rdfs:subClassOf rdf:resource="#Address">
</owl:Class>
```

2.2 Description of Time

Figure 3 is a reference model of Time ontology Description.

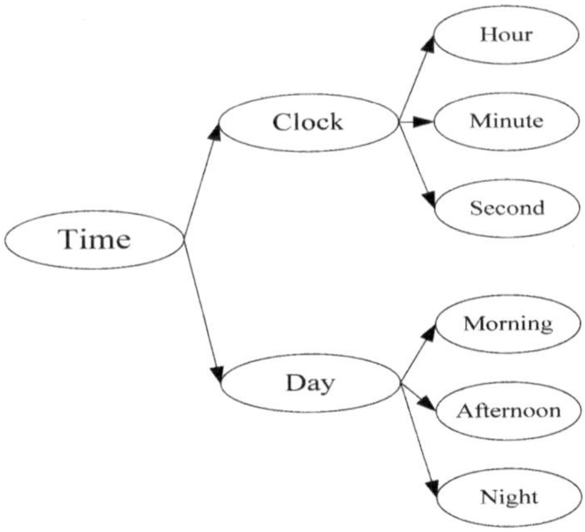

Fig. 3. Time Description

Time ontology namespace using xmlns = http://www.suncode.cn/space #.

Time Ontology property includes:

1. startTime（Used to describe the properties of the service start time）

2. endTime（Used to describe the properties of the service end time）
3. That the relationship between class attributes, such as before, after, withen, equals, etc.

Example, attributes can be defined, said after Morning Afternoon classes and relations between classes, defined as follows:

```
<owl:ObjectProperty rdf:ID="after">
    <rdfs:domain rdf:resource="#Afternoon">
    <rdfs:range rdf=resource="#Morning">
</owl:ObjectProperty>
```

2.3 Description of User

User information can be divided into two categories, one for the common information such as user name, phone number, email address, etc.; another feature for the user information, such as personality, body shape, hobbies and so on. Class hierarchy shown in Figure 4.

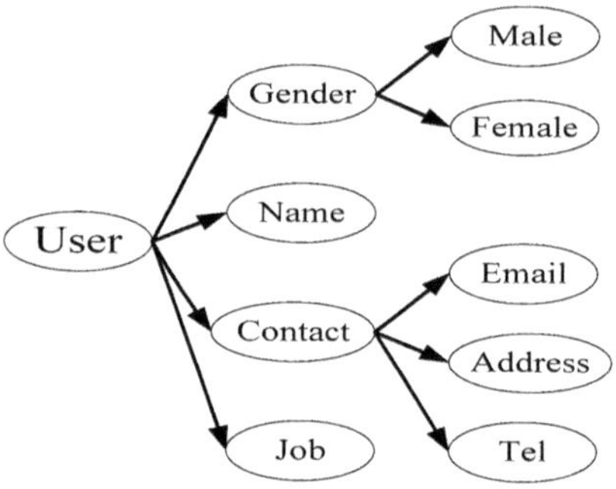

Fig. 4. User Information

User ontology namespace using xmlns=http://www.suncode.cn/userInfo#. Defined as follows:

```
<owl:Class rdf:ID="User">
 <rdfs:subClassOf>
 <owl:Restriction>
   <owl:onProperty rdf:resource="#Name"/>
    <owl:cardinality
rdf:datatype="http://www.w3.org/2001/XMLSchema#nonNegativeInteger">1</owl:cardinalit
y>
 </owl:Restriction>
 </rdfs:subClassOf>
 <rdfs:subClassOf>
 <owl:Restriction>
```

```
        <owl:onProperty rdf:resource="#gender"/>
        <owl:cardinality
rdf:datatype="http://www/w3/org/2001/XMLSchema#nonNegativeInteger">1</owl:cardinalit
y>
       </owl:Restriction>
       </rdfs:subClassOf>
      </owl:Class>
```

3 Semantic Service Process Algorithm

Semantic Web services may be a collection of concept and not a single, thus the concept of process between a set of process is the basis of research services.

3.1 BGM Algorithm

Through the field of information analysis and comparison of various algorithms, integrated semantic Web service process has above characteristics. Semantic process algorithm is based on BGM (Balance Genealogy Measure) algorithm. Set process algorithm on the premise that the concept to be matched leaf nodes and are defined in the concept of spanning tree [10]-[11]: A concept set to the lowest common parent node, each node in the concept of set paths constitute this set of concepts of the "spanning tree". In Figure 5, T1 is the concept of set (6,13,14,15) spanning tree, T2 is the concept of set (9,13) of the spanning tree.

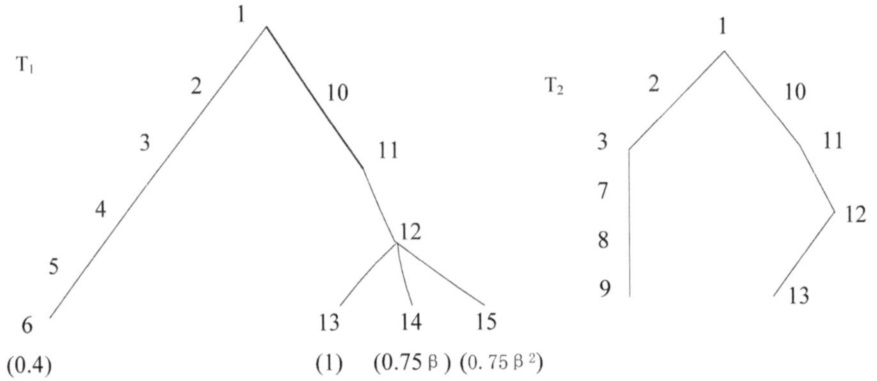

Fig. 5. GM algorithm

BGM algorithm main idea is that if there is more than the first tree in a leaf node and a node in the second tree is the best match, then reduce the duplication of the similarity process. BGM checks interval parameter p [0, 1], is used to control the repetition rate of decline in the similarity process.

As shown in Figure 6, the final value and match the order of the relevant match, such as process the order if it is 14, 13,15, then the process value will become 0.75, β, 0.75β2, smaller than the above results. In order to make the final value obtained is the best match, BGM of nodes in T1 sequence can be obtained using the following matches to the maximum similarity, in that order known as the "best order ":

1. Find the absolute process leaf node.
2. Find the match with a common parent node of leaf node.
3. Find process nodes with a common grandfather leaf node.

If you want to calculate the similarity of two sets C1, C2, assuming that they correspond to the tree T1 and T2, the step of BGM algorithm is as follows: For each leaf T1 in 11, with the optimal sequence for a visit. Find 11; in a few of the best process node 12. If there are multiple leaves T2 and 11 is the best match, then pick a match had been the least number of nodes, that is, count (12) is minimized. count (12) + +; continue to step (l), until the T1 in each leaf are matched before. Defined LCATI, T2 (ll) that any element of Tl 11 and T2 in the match that the highest elements of a common minimum ancestors. The d is for the depth of the root definition. There is the following computing formula:

$Sim(C_1, C_2)=\Sigma l_1 \in c_1 leafsimT_1,T_2(l_1)/\|C_1\|$	(1)
$leafsimT_1, T_2(l_1)=optleafsimT_1,T_2(l_1)*\beta^{match\_count(l2)-1}$	(2)
$optleafsimT_1, T_2(l_1)=depth(LCAT_1,T_2(l_1))/depth(l_1)$	(3)

3.2 QoS Matchmaking

In order to meet the requirements of seamless service based on the above algorithm by adding a QoS process.

Considering the advantages and disadvantages of a variety of QoS models, based OWL ontology language, In this paper, OWL-S service ontology to extend, define a semantic QoS model-OWL-QoS ontology. Ontology of this model includes QoSProfile, QoSAtribute, QoSMetric and QoSValue four classes.

Shown in Figure 6, which corresponds to all the web services ommonQosAttribute need to have the Qos parameters, such as price, response time, reliability, reputation and so on..

Both from the semantic and numerical analysis of the characteristics of Qos parameters, combined with general semantic similarity model is proposed for Qos comprehensive information process similarity model, the specific algorithm see [8]. This model can solve the different concepts of information as described in the process of heterogeneous Qos.

4 Test

We have done many experiments and tests. Now here we give some examples of them.

Program A: Based on previous similarity calculation service process algorithms and filters to study the output sequence of the three services that most closely matches the performance indicators.

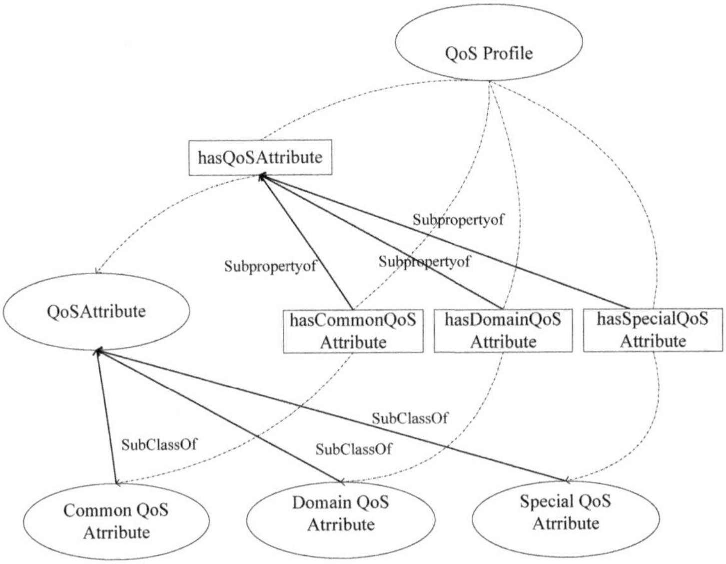

Fig. 6. QoSProfile

Program B: Set the threshold on the process (take 0.7), filtered through the threshold, the output sequence.

Program C: Adding QoS to use the proposed service mining after process algorithm, process the highest QoS services.

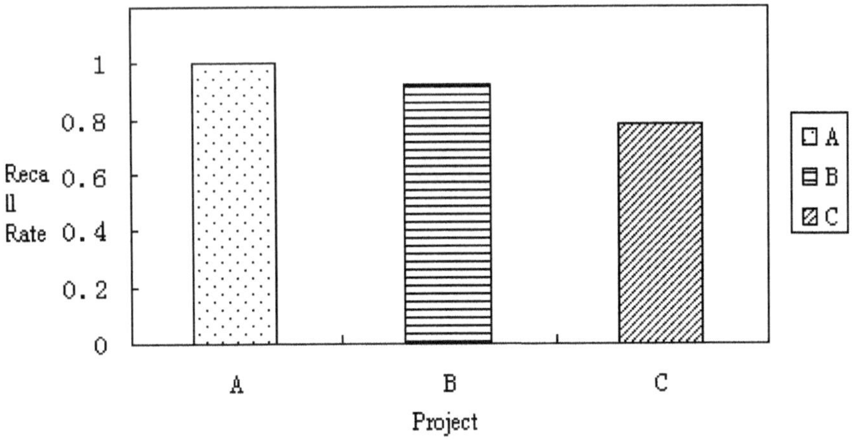

Fig. 7. Recall Rate

From three process system to assess the performance of Web services, including system response time and precision and recall. System response time which means the system from a user submits a request to return to the time sequence process service; precision refers to the process system to find out the results and the results given by experts in the field of coincidence degree.

Examine the recall of three programs, the programs B and C are set to the threshold, so the recall is lower than that of Option A. Program by adding C. The QoS process, so the recall rate is the lowest of three, shown in Figure 7.

5 Conclusion

We propose a Web Ontology Language-based ontology for service description, and for supporting logic-based service matchmaking. Besides service description, service matchmaking is another important problem in service mining. We introduced a semantic process algorithm according to the ontology. The algorithm takes the semantic meaning of service into account, enable interact between device and device. The experiment and tests can be seen that semantic based service mining model has a faster response time, and precision, and can output to the user the best service to meet the requirements of pervasive computing service requirements.

References

1. Weiser, M.: The computer for the twenty-first century. Scientific American 265(3), 94–104 (1991)
2. Zhang, D.G.: Web-Based Seamless Migration for Task-oriented Nomadic Service. International Journal of Distance Education Technology (JDET) 4(3), 108–115 (2006)
3. Zhang, D.G.: A kind of new decision fusion method based on sensor evidence. Journal of information and Computational Science 5(1), 171–178 (2008)
4. Zhang, D.G.: A Kind of new approach of context-aware computing for ubiquitous application. International Journal of modeling, Identification & Control 8(1), 10–17 (2009)
5. Bakhouya, M., Gaber, J., Koukam, A.: Service mining and composition in ubiquitous computing. In: Proceedings of 2004 International Conference on Information and Communication Technologies: From Theory to Applications, pp. 489–490 (2004)
6. Dogac, A., Kabak, Y., Laleci, G.B.: Enriching ebXML registries with OWL ontologies for efficient service mining. In: Proceedings of 14th International Workshop on Research Issues on Data Engineering: Web Services for e-Commerce and e-Government Applications, pp. 69–76 (2004)
7. Masuoka, R., Labrou, Y., Parsia, B., Sirin, E.: Ontology-enabled pervasive computing applications. Intelligent Systems 18(5), 68–72 (2003)
8. Zuo, Z., Zhou, M.: Web Ontology Language OWL and its description logic foundation. In: Proceedings of the Fourth International Conference on Parallel and Distributed Computing, Applications and Technologies, PDCAT 2003, pp. 157–160 (2003)
9. Wang, X.H., Zhang, D.Q., Gu, T., Pung, H.K.: Ontology based context modeling and reasoning using OWL. In: Proceedings of the Second IEEE Annual Conference on Pervasive Computing and Communications Workshops, pp. 18–22 (2004)
10. Kopena, J., Regli, W.C.: DAMLJessKB: a tool for reasoning with the Semantic Web. Intelligent Systems 18(3), 74–77
11. Helal, S.: Standards for service mining and delivery. IEEE Pervasive Computing 1(3), 95–100 (2002)

A New Method for Solving Variational Inequalities Problem

Hai Sun

College of Mathematics and Information, China West Normal University,
Nanchong, Sichuan, 637002, People's Republic of China
cwnush@126.com

Abstract. In this paper, some properties of the filled function are given without Lipchitz continuity. Further, we propose a new algorithm by filled function method. The implementation of the algorithm on several test problems is reported with numerical results.

Keywords: Nonlinear complementarity, Variational inequality, Algorithm, Gap function, Monotone mapping.

1 Introduction

Let X be a nonempty closed convex set in R^n and $F: R^n \to R^n$ be a given continuously differentiable mapping. The variational inequality problem (for short, VIP(X, F)) is to find a vector $x^* \in X$ such that

$$\langle F(x^*), x - x^* \rangle \geq 0, \forall x \in X. \tag{1.0}$$

It is well known that, if $X = R_+^n$, the nonnegative orthant in R^n, the VIP(X, F) is reduced to the Nonlinear Complementarity Problem: find $x^* \in X$ such that

$$x \geq 0, F(x) \geq 0, x^T F(x) = 0.$$

The VIP(X, F) have been widely studied and many algorithms have been proposed to solve it, such as SOR method, projection method, generalized gradient method, implicit method ,and non-linear Jacobi (diagonalization) methods (see,[3-6]). Another approach is to transform the VIP(X, F) into an equivalent minimization problem based on the optimization technology (see [6-11]). An obvious advantage of this approach is that the minimization problem can be solved by some algorithms which possess a global convergence property. At present, the filled function method is one of the determinate global optimization methods, and it can find the global solution of the minimization problem. The filled function method only needs to use the mature local minimization algorithm, so it's popular with the scientific and technical workers in recent years. The basic idea is to use the auxiliary function, and minimize the original function constantly to find the global minimum. So considering the advantages of the above mentioned methods, we proposes a filled function method to

H. Tan and M. Zhou (Eds.): CSE 2011, Part I, CCIS 201, pp. 15–22, 2011.

solve the monotone variational inequalities. The filled function was firstly introduced by GE in [12]. The main aim of this paper is to develop a novel method for solving the monotone variational inequalities.

Let X be a nonempty closed convex subset of R^n. The metric projection $P_X(x)$ from x onto the closed convex set X, is defined as the solution of the problem: $\min \|y-x\|$, subject to $x \in X$.

Firstly, we recall some definitions and basic results.

Definition 1. Suppose x^* is a current local minimizer of $f(x), P(x,x^*)$ *is* said to be a filled function of $f(x)$ at x^*, if it satisfies the following properties:

(1) x^* is a strict local maximizer of $P(x,x^*)$ over X;

(2) $\nabla P(x,x^*) \neq 0$, $x \in S_1$, where $S_1 = \{x \mid f(x) \geq f(x^*), x \in X \setminus \{x^*\}\}$,i.e. $P(x,x^*)$ has no minimizers or saddle points in S_1;

(3) If x^* is a local minimizer and $S_2 = \{x \in X : f(x) < f(x^*)\} \subset \operatorname{int} X$ is nonempty, then there exists $x_1^* \in S_2$ such that x_1^* is a local minimizer of $P(x,x^*)$.

Definition 2. The mapping $F : X \to R^n$ is called monotone on X if

$$\langle F(x) - F(y), x - y \rangle \geq 0 \ , \forall x, y \in X \tag{1.1}$$

and strictly monotone on X if strict inequality holds in (2.1) whenever $x \neq y$. F is called strongly (or uniformly) monotone with modulus $\mu > 0$ on X if

$$\langle F(x) - F(y), x - y \rangle \geq \mu \|x - y\|^2 \ , \forall x, y \in X \tag{1.2}$$

Lemma 1. If F is the gradient of a differentiable function $\theta: R^n \to R$, VIP(X, F) can be reformulated as an optimization problem: *min* $\theta(x)$, *subject to* $x \in X$.

Lemma 2. (1) F is strictly monotone on X if the Jacobian matrix $\nabla F(x)$ is positive definite for all $x \in X$, i.e., $\langle x - y, \nabla F(x)(x - y) \rangle > 0 \ , \forall x, y \in X$.

(2) F is strongly monotone on X if and only if $\nabla F(x)$ such that

$$\langle x - y, \nabla F(x)(x - y) \rangle \geq \mu \|x - y\|^2 \ , \forall x, y \in X \tag{1.3}$$

Lemma 3. (1)The projection operator $P_X(\bullet)$ is nonexpansive, i.e., $x, y \in R^n$

$$\|P_X(x) - P_X(y)\| \leq \|x - y\| \tag{1.4}$$

(2) for each $x \in R^n$, $P_X(x)$ satisfies, *for all* $y \in X$,

$$\langle x - P_X(x), y - P_X(x) \rangle \le 0.$$

Lemma 4. x^* solves VIP(X, F) iff $x^* = P_X(x^* - F(x^*))$, i.e. iff x^* is a fixed point of the mapping $H : R^n \to R^n$ defined by $H(x) = P_X(x - F(x))$.

2 Properties of Filled Function

Assumption 1. (1) The set $X \subseteq R^n$ is nonempty, closed, convex and bounded.

(2) The map $F : X \to R^n$ is monotone on X.

(3) The montone variational inequalities has at least a solution.

If F is monotone, the VIP(X, F) is called the monotone variational inequality problem, denoted by MVI(X, F).

Definition 3. A gap function for the MVI(X,F) is a nonnegative function $\theta : D \to R_+$ such that x^* is a solution of the MVI(X,F) iff $x^* \in D$ and $\theta(x^*) = 0$.

$$f(x) = \max_{y \in X}(\langle F(x), x - y \rangle - \frac{1}{2}\|y - x\|^2) = \langle F(x), x - H(x) \rangle - \frac{1}{2}\|H(x) - x\|^2 \tag{2.1}$$

Lemma 5. The function $f(x)$ defined by (2.1) is a gap function for MVI(F,X).

Lemma 6.([9]) The function $f(x)$ defined by (2.1), then $f(x) \ge 0, \forall x \in X$, and x^* solves VIP(X,F) iff $x^* \in X$ and $f(x^*) = 0$. Hence, x solves the VIP(X,F) iff it solves the optimization problem (OP): $\min_{x \in X} f(x)$.

Lemma 7. ([9]) If the mapping $F : R^n \to R^n$ is continuous, then the function $f : R^n \to R$ defined by (2.1) is also continuous. If F is continuously differentiable, then f is also continuously differentiable and its gradient is given by

$$\nabla f(x) = F(x) - [\nabla F(x) - I](H(x) - x). \tag{2.2}$$

Lemma 8. ([9]) Assume that $F : R^n \to R^n$ is continuously differentiable and its Jacobian matrix $\nabla F(x)$ is positive definite for all $x \in X$. If x is a stationary point of (OP), i.e., $\langle \nabla f(x), y - x \rangle \ge 0$ for all $y \in X$, then x is a global optimal solution of (OP), and hence it solves the VIP(X, F).

Consider the one parameter filled function for the MVI(X,F) (see [24])

$$F(x, x^*, \rho) = -\rho\|x - x^*\|^2 + \min[0, f(x) - f(x^*)] \tag{2.3}$$

where $\rho>0$ is a parameter and x^* is a current local minimizer of (OP)

Lemma 9. **([10,11])** If x^* is a local minimizer of (OP) , then x^* is a strict local maximizer of $F(x,x^*,\rho)$.

Lemma 10. **([10,11])** If x^* is a local minimizer of problem (2.2) and x_1 is a point such that $f(x^*)\le f(x_1)$, $x_1\ne x^*$, then it holds $\nabla F(x_1,x^*,\rho)\ne 0$ .i.e. if $x_1\in \operatorname{int} X$,then x_1 is not a stationary point of $F(x,x^*,\rho)$.

Lemma 11. **([10,11])** Assume that x^* is a local minimizer of problem (2.2), x_1 and x_2 are two points in X such that $\|x_1-x^*\|<\|x_2-x^*\|$ and $f(x^*)\le f(x_1)$, $f(x^*)\le f(x_2)$, we have $F(x_2,x^*,\rho)<F(x_1,x^*,\rho)<0=F(x^*,x^*,\rho)$.

Lemma 12. **([10,11])** If x^* is a local minimizer of problem (2.2), $x_1\in \operatorname{int} X$ such that $f(x^*)\le f(x_1)$, $x_1\ne x^*$, then for any small $\varepsilon_1>0$, there exists d_1 such that

$$0<\|d_1\|\le\varepsilon_1, x_1-d_1, x_1+d_1\in X\ ,\ \|x_1-d_1-x^*\|<\|x_1-x^*\|\le\|x_1+d_1-x^*\|,$$

Lemma 13. **([10,11])** If x^* is a local minimizer of problem (2.2), then any local minimizer or saddle point of $F(x,x^*,\rho)$ in the set $S_2=\{x\in X: f(x)<f(x^*)\}$

Lemma 14. **([10,11])** If x^* is a local minimizer of problem (2.2) but not a global minimizer, i.e., $S_2=\{x\in X: f(x)<f(x^*)\}\subset \operatorname{int} X$ is nonempty, then there exists x_1^* *in* S_2 such that x_1^* is a local minimizer of $F(x,x^*,\rho)$ when $\rho>0$ small enough.

Lemma 15. If x^* is a global minimizer of (2.2), then $F(x,x^*,\rho)<0, x\in X$

3 Algorithm for MVI(X,F)

The development in this section is to suggest an efficient algorithm. Two search directions are investigated first such that one can start an initial point $x_1\in X\setminus N(x_1^*,\sigma)$ for some $\sigma>0$ to escape from the current local minimum x_1^* and minimize the proposed filled function along the search directions so as to get a point x_k with $f(x_k)<f(x_1^*)$. Then, one can use x_k as an initial point in a local search to find a better local minimizer x_k^* of $f(x)$ with $f(x_k^*)<f(x_1^*)$. Let x^* be the current local minimum, x^i is the current iterative point. d^i is the current iterative direction.

Lemma 16. For given constants λ_L and λ_U with $0<\lambda_L<\lambda_U$, let $x^i \in X$ and $x^{i+1}=x^i+d^i \in X$ where d^i is a search direction at x^i such that $\lambda_L \le \|d^i\| \le \lambda_U$. Let θ^i be the angle between x^i-x^* and d^i. Then the following formulas are equivalent:

(1) $\|x^{i+1}-x^*\| > \|x^i-x^*\|$;

(2) $2(x^i-x^*)^T d^i + \|d^i\|^2 > 0$;

(3) $(x^i-x^*)^T d^i + (x^{i+1}-x^*)^T d^i > 0$;

(4) $\cos\theta^i > -\dfrac{\|d^i\|}{2\|x^i-x^*\|}$

If $(x^k-x^*)^T d^k \ge 0, \forall k=0,1,\ldots,i-1$, then $\|x^i-x^*\|^2 \ge \lambda_L{}^2 + \|x^0-x^*\|^2$.

Theorem 1. Let $d \neq 0$ be a search direction at $x\in X$ where $f(x)\ge f(x^*)$, then

$$\nabla F(x,x^*,\rho)^T d<0 \Leftrightarrow (x-x^*)^T d>0.$$

Search direction D_1 and its property: Let $D_1=-\nabla F(x,x^*,\rho)$ be a search direction at X, where $f(x)\ge f(x^*), x\neq x^*$. Then $D_1 \neq 0$, $D_1^T\nabla F(x,x^*,\rho)<0$.

Search direction D_2 and its property: Let $D_2=-\dfrac{\nabla f(x)}{\|\nabla f(x)\|}-\dfrac{\nabla F(x,x^*,\rho)}{\|\nabla F(x,x^*,\rho)\|}$ be a search direction at $x\in X$, where $f(x)\ge f(x^*)$, $x\neq x^*$, $\|\nabla f(x)\|\neq 0$, $\|\nabla F(x,x^*,\rho)\|\neq 0$.

If $D_2\neq 0$, then $D_2^T\nabla f(x)<0$ and $D_2^T\nabla F(x,x^*,\rho)<0$.

Now we construct the following algorithm 3.1.

Step0: Choose a tolerance $\varepsilon>0$, a fraction $\bar{\rho}>0$, a lower bound of ρ such that $\rho_L>0$, (e.g. $\varepsilon:=10^{-4}$, $\bar{\rho}:=10^{-1}$, set $\rho_L:=10^{-6}$). Choose an initial point $x_1\in X$. Set k := 1.

Step 1: Starting from an initial point $x_1\in X$, minimize $f(x)$ and obtain the first local minimizer x_1^* of $f(x)$.

Step 2: Choose a set of initial points $\{x_{k+1}^i : i=1,2,\cdots,m\}$ such that $x_{k+1}^i\in X\setminus N(x_k^*,\sigma_k)$ for some $\sigma_k>0$.

Step 3: Let $\rho=10$.

Step 4: Set $i := 1$.

Step 5: If $i \leq m$, then set $x := x_{k+1}^{i}$ and go to Step 6; Otherwise, go to Step10.

Step 6: If $f(x) < f(x_k^*)$, then use x as an initial point for a local minimization method to find x_{k+1}^* such that $f(x_{k+1}^*) < f(x_k^*)$, set $k := k+1$ and go to Step2; Otherwise, go to Step7.

Step 7: Select $D_2 = -\frac{\nabla f(x)}{\|\nabla f(x)\|} - \frac{\nabla F(x, x_k^*, \rho)}{\|\nabla F(x, x_k^*, \rho)\|}$ as the search direction. If all the following conditions hold: (a) $\|\nabla f(x)\| \geq n\varepsilon$; (b) $\|D_2\| \geq n\varepsilon$; (c) $D_2^T (x - x_k^*) \geq 0$; (d) $\nabla^T f(x) \nabla F(x, x_k^*, \rho) > 0$, then go to Step8; Otherwise, go to Step9 .

Step 8: Find a new x in the direction D_2 such that both $F(x, x_k^*, \rho)$ and $f(x)$ can reduce to certain extents. If x attains the boundary of X during minimization, then set i := i + 1 and go to Step5; Otherwise, go to Step6.

Step 9: Let $D_1 = -\nabla F(x, x_k^*, \rho)$ and find a new x in the direction D_1 such that $F(x, x_k^*, \rho)$ can reduce to certain extent. If x attains the boundary of X during minimization, then set i := i + 1 and go to Step5; Otherwise, go to Step 6.

Step 10: Decrease ρ by setting $\rho := \bar{\rho} \times \rho$. (a) If $\rho \geq \rho_L$, then go to Step4. (b) Otherwise, the algorithm is incapable of finding a better minimizer starting from the initial points $\{x_{k+1}^{i}\}$. The algorithm stops and x_k^* is taken as a global minimizer.

4 Numerical Test

In this section, we give an example of numerical test. The numerical test is implemented in Microsoft Visual C++. In my programs, we obtain local minimizers of the objective function by Quasi-Newton Method, and $\|\nabla f(x)\| \leq 10^{-6}$ is the terminate condition. The symbols used in the tables are given as follows: x_1 denotes the initial point which satisfies $x_1 \in X$, x_k^* denotes the k th local minimizer, $f(x_k^*)$ denotes the function value of the k th local minimizer, T_f denotes the CPU time in seconds to obtain the final results for the algorithm, and throughout our computational experiments, the parameters in Algorithm 3.1 are set as $\varepsilon := 10^{-4}$, $\hat{\rho} := 10^{-1}$, $\rho_L := 10^{-6}$, $\rho := 10$. Problem. (see [10]) Computational results for problem 1 are shown in Table 1.

Table 1. Numerical results of Example

x_1	x_k^*	$f(x_k^*)$	$x_k^{*T} f(x_k^*)$	T_f (ms)
$(1,1,1,1,1)^T$	$\begin{pmatrix} 5.799380 \\ 0.000000 \\ 0.000001 \\ 0.000000 \\ 1.730698 \end{pmatrix}$	$\begin{pmatrix} 0.000000 \\ 14.159839 \\ 30.675194 \\ 39.683727 \\ -0.000001 \end{pmatrix}$	0.000021	343
$(1,0,0,0,1)^T$	$\begin{pmatrix} 5.799379 \\ 0.000001 \\ 0.000000 \\ 0.000000 \\ 1.730698 \end{pmatrix}$	$\begin{pmatrix} -0.000001 \\ 14.159839 \\ 30.675187 \\ 39.683720 \\ -0.000000 \end{pmatrix}$	0.000015	281
$(1,0,1,0,1)^T$	$\begin{pmatrix} 5.799378 \\ -0.000000 \\ -0.000000 \\ 0.000002 \\ 1.730694 \end{pmatrix}$	$\begin{pmatrix} -0.000000 \\ 14.159865 \\ 30.675184 \\ 39.683747 \\ -0.000000 \end{pmatrix}$	0.000061	140
$(0,0,100,0,0)^T$	$\begin{pmatrix} 5.799379 \\ 0.000000 \\ -0.000000 \\ 0.000001 \\ 1.730696 \end{pmatrix}$	$\begin{pmatrix} 0.000000 \\ 14.159848 \\ 30.675186 \\ 39.683731 \\ 0.000001 \end{pmatrix}$	0.000039	281

References

1. Chen, J.W., Cho, Y.J., Kim, J.K., Li, J.: Multiobjective optimization problems with modified objective functions and cone constraints and applications. Journal of Global Optimization 49, 137–147 (2011)
2. Chen, J.W., Zou, Y.Z.: Existence of solutions of F-implicit variational inequalit problems with extended projection operators. Acta Mathmatica Sinica Chinese Series 53(2), 375–384 (2010)
3. Pang, J.S., Chan, D.: Iterative methods for variational and complementarity problems. Mathematical Problemming 24, 284–313 (1982)
4. Fukushima, M.: A relaxed projection method for variational inequalities. Mathematical Programming 35, 58–70 (1986)
5. Xiao, B., Harker, P.T.: A nonsmooth Newton method for variational inequalities, I: theory. Mathematical Programming 65, 151–194 (1994)
6. Harker, P.T., Pang, J.S.: Finite-Dimensional variational inequality and nonlinear complementarity problems: a survey of theory, algorithms and applications. Mathematical Programming 48, 161–220 (1990)
7. He, B.S.: Inexact implicit methods for monotone general variational inequalities. Math. Program., Ser. A 86, 199–217 (1999)
8. Fukushima, M.: Equivalent differentiable optimization problems and descent methods for asymmetric variational inequality problems. Mathematical Programming 53, 99–110 (1992)

9. Taji, K., et al.: A globally convergent Newton method for solving strongly monotone variational inequalities. Mathematical Programming 58, 369–383 (1993)
10. Peng, J.M.: Global method for monotone variational inequality problems with inequality constraints. Journal of Optimization theory and Application 95(2), 419–430 (1997)
11. Solodov, M.V.: Some Methods Based on the D-Gap Function for Solving Monotone Variational Inequalities. Computational Optimization and Applications 17, 255–277 (2000)
12. Ge, R.P.: A filled function method for finding a global minimizer of a function of several variables. Mathematical Programming 46, 191–204 (1990)

An Empirical Comparison of Two Boosting Algorithms on Real Data Sets with Artificial Class Noise

Xiaowei Sun[1,*] and Hongbo Zhou[2]

[1] Software College, Shenyang Normal University, Shenyang 110034, China
junyaomail@163.com
[2] Liaoning SG Automotive Group CO., LTD., Shenyang 110027, China

Abstract. Boosting algorithms are a means of building a strong ensemble classifier by aggregating a sequence of weak hypotheses. In this paper, multiple TAN classifiers generated by GTAN are combined by a combination method called Boosting-MultiTAN is compared with the Boosting-BAN classifier which is boosting based on BAN combination. We conduct an empirical study to compare the performance of two algorithms, measured in terms of overall test correct rate, on ten real data sets. Finally, experimental results show that the Boosting-BAN has higher classification accuracy on most data sets, but Boosting-MultiTAN has good effect on others. These results argue that boosting algorithms deserve more attention in machine learning and data mining communities.

Keywords: boosting, combination method, TAN, BAN, Bayesian network classifier.

1 Introduction

Classification is a fundamental task in fault diagnosis, pattern recognition and forecasting. In general, a classificr is a function that chooses a class label (from a group of predefined labels) for instance described by a set of features (attributes). Learning accurate classifiers from pre-classified data is a very active research topic in machine learning and data mining. In the past two decades, many classifiers have been developed, such as decision trees based classifiers and neural network based classifiers.

Boosting[1-4] is a general method for improving the performance of any "weak" learning algorithm. In theory, boosting can be used to significantly reduce the error of any "weak" learning algorithm that consistently generates classifiers which need only be a little bit better than random guessing. Despite the potential benefits of boosting promised by the theoretical results, the true practical value of boosting can only be assessed by testing the method on "real" learning problems. In this paper, we present such experimental assessment of two new boosting algorithms.

* Fund Support: Liaoning Province Education and Science "Eleventh Five-Year Plan " research topic (JG10DB032).

H. Tan and M. Zhou (Eds.): CSE 2011, Part I, CCIS 201, pp. 23–30, 2011.

The first provably effective boosting algorithms were presented by Schapire and Freund[1] in 1995. Boosting works by repeatedly running a given weak learning algorithm on various distributions over the training data, and then combining the classifiers produced by the weak learner into a single composite classifier. The first provably effective boosting algorithms were presented by Freund[3] and Schapire[5]. More recently, we described and analyzed AdaBoost, and we argued that this new boosting algorithm has certain properties which make it more practical and easier to implement than its predecessors.

TAN[6] and BAN[7] are augmented Bayesian network classifiers provided by Friedman and Cheng J. They treat the classification node as the first node in the ordering. The order of other nodes is arbitrary; they simply use the order they appear in the dataset. Therefore, they only need to use the CLB1 algorithm, which has the time complexity of $O(N^2)$ on the mutual information test (N is the number of attributes in the dataset) and linear on the number of cases. The efficiency is achieved by directly extending the Chow-Liu tree construction algorithm[8] to a three-phase BN learning algorithm: drafting, which is essentially the Chow-Liu algorithm, thickening, which adds edges to the draft, and thinning, which verifies the necessity of each edge.

In this paper, multiple TAN classifiers generated by GTAN are combined by a combination method called Boosting-MultiTAN is compared with the Boosting-BAN classifier which is boosting based on BAN combination. We conduct an empirical study to compare the performance of two algorithms, measured in terms of overall test correct rate, on ten real data sets. Finally, experimental results show that the Boosting-BAN has higher classification accuracy on most data sets, but Boosting-MultiTAN has good effect on others. These results argue that boosting algorithm deserve more attention in machine learning and data mining communities.

2 Learning Bayesian Network Classifiers

Learning Bayesian network classifiers involves two steps: structure learning and parameter (conditional probability tables) learning. We will focus on structure learning methods for different Bayesian network classifiers in the subsections below.

2.1 Tree Augmented Naive-Bayes (TAN)

Letting $X=\{x_1,\ldots,x_n, c\}$ represent the node set (where c is the classification node) of the data. The algorithm for learning TAN classifier first learns a tree structure over V\{c},using mutual information tests. It then adds a link from the classification node to each feature node in the manner as we construct a Naïve-Bayes (i.e., the classification node is a parent of all other nodes.) A simple TAN structure is shown in Figure 1.(note that features x_1, x_2, x_3, x_4 form a tree.)

The learning procedure can be described as follows.

1. Take the training set and $X\backslash\{c\}$ as input.
2. Call the modified Chow-Liu algorithm. (The original algorithm is modified by replacing every mutual information test $I(x_i,x_j)$ with a conditional mutual information test $I(x_i,x_j/\{c\})$).

3. Add c as a parent of every x_i where $1 \leqslant i \leqslant n$.
4. Learn the parameters and output the TAN.

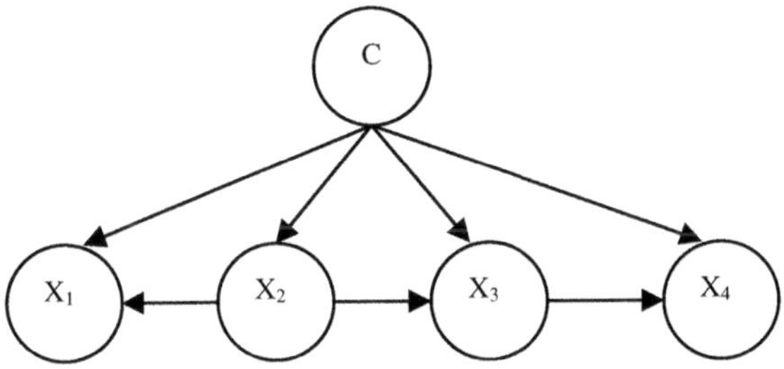

Fig. 1. A simple TAN structure

This algorithm, which is modified from the Chow-Liu algorithm, requires $O(N^2)$ numbers of conditional mutual information tests. This algorithm is essentially the first phase of the BAN-learning algorithm. TAN classifier is stable that can not be combined with a quite strong learning algorithm by boosting.

2.2 BN Augmented Naive-Bayes (BAN)

BAN classifier has been studied in several papers. The basic idea of this algorithm is just like the TAN learner of Section 2.1, but the unrestricted BN-learning algorithm instead of a tree-learning algorithm (see Figure 2).

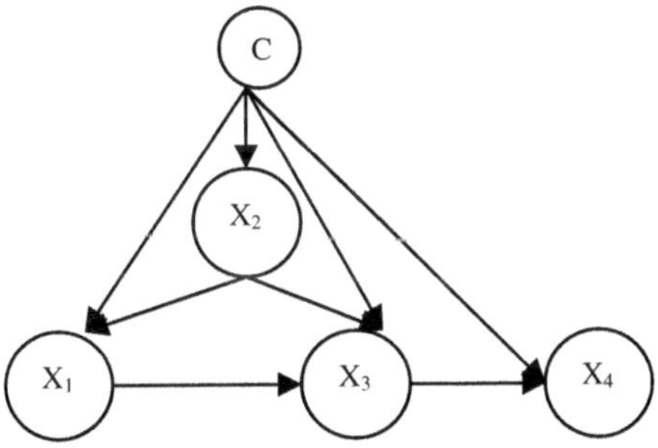

Fig. 2. A simple BAN structure

Letting $X=\{x_1,\ldots,x_n, c\}$ represent the feature set (where c is the classification node) of the data, the learning procedure based on mutual information test can be described as follows.

1. Take the training set and $X\backslash\{c\}$ (along with the ordering) as input.
2. Call the modified CBL1 algorithm. (The original algorithm is modified in the following way: replace every mutual information test $I(x_i,x_j)$ with a conditional

mutual information test $I(x_i,x_j/\{c\})$; replace every conditional mutual information test $I(x_i,x_j/Z)$ with $I(x_i,x_j/Z+\{c\})$, where $Z \subset X \backslash \{c\}$.
3. Add c as a parent of every x_i where $1 \leqslant i \leqslant n$..
4. Learn the parameters and output the BAN.

Like the TAN-learning algorithm, this algorithm dose not require additional mutual information tests, and so it requires $O(n^2N)$ (where n is the number of node attributes; N is the number of training examples) mutual information tests. The longest time spent in the algorithm is to calculate mutual information. In BAN structure, the second step in the three-phase is used ε to sort mutual information. The ε is a given small positive threshold, it is not fixed, and can be changed in many times. By setting different thresholds ε can construct many BAN classifiers. BAN classifier is unstable that can be combined with a quite strong learning algorithm by boosting.

3 Two New Boosting Algorithms

3.1 Boosting-MultiTAN Algorithm

GTAN[9] is proposed by Hongbo Shi in 2004. GTAN used conditional mutual information as CI tests to measure the average information between two nodes when the statuses of some values are changed by the condition-set C. When $I(x_i,x_j/\{c\})$ is larger than a certain threshold value ε, we choose the edge to the BN structure to form TAN. *Start-edge* and ε are two important parameters In GTAN. Different *Start-edges* can construct different TANs. GTAN classifier is unstable that can be combined with a quite strong learning algorithm by boosting.

The Boosting-MultiTAN algorithm may be characterized by the way in which the hypothesis weights wi are selected, and by the example weight update step.

Boosting-MultiTAN (Dataset, T) :
Input: sequence of N example Dataset=$\{(x_1,y_1),\ldots,(x_N,y_N)\}$ with labels $y_i \in Y=\{1,\ldots,k\}$, integer T specifying number of iterations.

Initialize $w_i^{(1)} = 1/N$ for all i, TrainData-1=Dataset
Start-edge=1;t=1;l=1
While((t≤T)and (l≤2T))

1. Use TrainData-t and start-edge call GTAN, providing it with the distribution.
2. Get back a hypothesis $TAN^{(t)} = X \rightarrow Y$.
3. Calculate the error of TAN(t):

$$e^{(t)} = \sum_{i=1}^{N} w_i^{(t)} I(y_i \neq TAN^{(t)}(x_i))$$

If e(t)≥0.5, then set T=t-1 and abort loop.

4. Set μ(t)=e(t)/(1-e(t)) .
5. Updating distribution $w_i^{(t+1)} = w_i^{(t)} (\mu^{(t)})^s$,

```
    Where
```
$$s = 1 - I(y_i \neq TAN^{(t)}(x_i))$$

```
6. Normalize
```
$w_i^{(t+1)}$, to sum to 1.

```
7. t=t+1,l=l+1,start-edge=start-edge+n/2T.
8. end While
Output the final hypothesis :
```

$$H(x) = \arg\max_{y\in Y}(\sum_{t=1}^{T}(\log(\frac{1}{\mu^{(t)}}))*I(y = TAN^{(t)}(x)))$$

3.2 Boosting-BAN Algorithm

Boosting-BAN works by fitting a base learner to the training data using a vector or matrix of weights. These are then updated by increasing the relative weight assigned to examples that are misclassified at the current round. This forces the learner to focus on the examples that it finds harder to classify. After T iterations the output hypotheses are combined using a series of probabilistic estimates based on their training accuracy.

The Boosting-BAN algorithm may be characterized by the way in which the hypothesis weights wi are selected, and by the example weight update step.

```
Boosting-BAN (Dataset, T) :
Input: sequence of N example Dataset={(x1,y1),…, (xN,yN)}
       with labels yi∈Y={1,…,k}, integer T specifying
       number of iterations.
```
Initialize $w_i^{(1)} = 1/N$ for all i, TrainData-1=Dataset

```
Do for t=1,2,…,T
1. Use TrainData-t and threshold ε call BAN, providing
   it with the distribution.
```
2. Get back a hypothesis $BAN^{(t)} = X \rightarrow Y$.

```
3. Calculate the error of BAN(t):
```

$$e^{(t)} = \sum_{i=1}^{N} w_i^{(t)} I(y_i \neq BAN^{(t)}(x_i)).$$

```
   If e(t)≥0.5, then set T=t-1 and abort loop.
```
4. Set μ(t)=e(t)/(1-e(t)) .

5. Updating distribution $w_i^{(t+1)} = w_i^{(t)}(\mu^{(t)})^s$,

where $s = 1 - I(y_i \neq BAN^{(t)}(x_i))$.

6. Normalize $w_i^{(t+1)}$, to sum to 1.

```
Output the final hypothesis :
```

$$H(x) = \arg\max_{y\in Y}(\sum_{t=1}^{T}(\log(\frac{1}{\mu^{(t)}}))*I(y = BAN^{(t)}(x)))$$

4 The Experimental Results

We conducted our experiments on a collection of machine learning datasets available from the UCI[10]. A summary of some of the properties of these datasets is given in Table 1. Some datasets are provided with a test set. For these, we reran each algorithm 20 times (since some of the algorithms are randomized), and averaged the results. For datasets with no provided test set, we used 10-fold cross validation, and averaged the results over 10 runs (for a total of 100 runs of each algorithm on each dataset).

In our experiments, we set the number of rounds of boosting to be $T=100$.

Table 1. Dataset used in the experments

No.	Dataset	Instances	Classes	Attributes	Missing values
1	Iris	150	3	4	×
2	Kr-rs-kp	3169	2	36	×
3	LED	1000	10	7	×
4	Mushroom	8124	2	22	√
5	Promoters	106	2	57	×
6	Segment	2310	7	19	×
7	Soybean Large	683	19	35	√
8	Tic-Tac-Toe	958	2	9	×
9	Wine	178	3	13	×
10	Zoology	101	7	16	×

The results of our experiments are shown in Table 2. The figures indicate test correct rate averaged over multiple runs of each algorithm. The italic in the table show that the classification is superior than another one obviously. From Table 2 in the 10 datasets, Boosting-BAN did significantly and uniformly better than Boosting-MultiTAN.

On the data sets "Iris" and "LED", the Boosting- MultiTAN was inferior to the Boosting-BAN. The Boosting-BAN correct rate was better than the Boosting-MultiTAN correct rate in another 7 datasets. The reason is, in these cases the rate of attributes and classes are less than other Datasets. This reveals that the features in the three datasets are most dependent to each other. These weak dependencies can improve the prediction accuracy significantly, as we see from Table 2. These experiments also indicate that when the dataset is small and data loss ,the boosting error rate is worse.

Table 2. Experimental results

No.	Dataset	Boosting-MultiTAN	Boosting-BAN
1	Iris	***93.8***	90.5
2	Kr-rs-kp	93.3	*99.3*
3	LED	***73.9***	72.3
4	Mushroom	99.9	*100*
5	Promoters	89.3	*91.7*
6	Segment	94.3	*96.4*
7	Soybean Large	92.6	*93.7*
8	Tic-Tac-Toe	74.7	*79.2*
9	Wine	97.3	*98.5*
10	Zoology	96.8	*97.7*

5 Conclusions

GTAN and BAN classifiers are unstable, by setting different parameters, we can form a number of different TAN and BAN classifiers. In this paper, multiple TAN classifiers generated by GTAN are combined by a combination method called Boosting-MultiTAN is compared with the Boosting-BAN classifier which is boosting based on BAN combination. Finally, experimental results show that the Boosting-BAN has higher classification accuracy on most data sets.

When implementing Boosting classifiers, we were able to calculate the value of ε directly given our prior knowledge. Of course, in a real situation we would be very unlikely to know the level of class noise in advance. It remains to be seen how difficult it would prove to estimate ε in practice.

References

1. Freund, Y., Schapire, R.E.: A decision-theoretic generalization of on-line learning and an application to boosting. In: Vitányi, P.M.B. (ed.) EuroCOLT 1995. LNCS, vol. 904, pp. 23–37. Springer, Heidelberg (1995)
2. Schapire, R.E., Freund, Y., Bartlett, Y., et al.: Boosting the margin: A new explanation for the effectiveness of voting methods. In: Fisher, D.H. (ed.) Proc of the 14th Int' 1 Conf. on Machine Learning, pp. 322–330. Morgan Kaufmann, San Francisco (1997)
3. Freund, Y.: Boosting a weak learning algorithm by majority. Information and Computation 121(2), 256–285 (1997)
4. Quinlan, J.R.: Bagging, Boosting, and C4.5. In: Ben-Eliyahu, Rachel (eds.) Proc of the 13th National Conf. on Artificial Intelligence, pp. 725–730. AAAI Press, Menlo Park (1996)

5. Schapire, R.E.: Schapire, The strength of weak learnability. Machine Learning 5(2), 197–227 (1990)
6. Friedman, N., Geiger, D., Goldszmidt, M.: Bayesian network classifiers. Machine Learning 29(2/3), 131–163 (1999)
7. Cheng, J., Greiner, R.: Comparing Bayesian network classifiers. In: Laskey, K.B., Prade, H. (eds.) Proc. of the 15th Conf. on Uncertainty in Artificial Intelligence, pp. 101–108. Morgan Kaufmann, San Francisco (1999)
8. Cheng, J., Bell, D.A., Liu, W.: An algorithm for Bayesian belief network construction from data. In: Proc. of AI &STAT, Lauderdale, Florida, pp. 83–90 (1997)
9. Shi, H., Huang, H., Wang, Z.: Boosting-Based TAN Combination Classifier. Journal of Computer Research and Development 41(2), 340–345 (2004)
10. UCI Machine Learning Repository, `http://www.ics.uci.edu/~mlearn/MLRepositoryhtml`
11. Freund, Y., Schapire, R.E.: Experiments with a new Boosting algorithm. In: Saitta, L. (ed.) Proc of the 13th Int'l Conf. on Machine Learning, pp. 148–156. Morgan Kaufmann, San Francisco (1996)
12. Sun, X.: Augmented BAN classifier. In: International Conference on Computational Intelligence and Software Engineering (2009)

Response Surface Methodology Analysis of Biodegradation of Acrylonitrile in Bioreactor

Qi Wang

School of Life and Environmental Sciences, Wenzhou University, 325035, China
victor527@126.com

Abstract. Response surface methodology (RSM) was used to study the biodegradation effect of the various parameters namely, initial acrylonitrile(AN) concentration, pH, temperature and to optimize the process conditions for the maximum degradation of acrylonitrile by implementing the Box-Behnken statistical design in bioreactor. The analysis of variance (ANOVA) of the quadratic model demonstrates that the model was highly significant. Using this methodology, the optimal values of pH, temperature, initial AN concentration were 6.54, 26.22 ℃and 424.32mg/L, respectively. The experiment results showed that the RSM based on Box-Behnken design was useful for optimizing the biodegradation process.

Keywords: Response Surface Methodology, Acrylonitrile, Biodegradation.

1 Introduction

Acrylonitrile(AN) is an raw material that has been extensively used for manufacturing acrylic fiber, synthetic chemistry and synthetic rubber. It is the priority pollutant in many countries [1] including the United States, China and Germany for its toxicity. AN wastewater, with high strength chemical oxygen demand (COD) and AN, was treated by techniques including activated sludge treatment [2-4], wet air oxidized and activated carbon treatment [5],ect. Treatment techniques of refractory biodegradation organic pollutants are hot point to current water pollution control due to its serious pollution and hazardousness to people's health in water, soil and sediments.

Response surface methodology (RSM), an experimental approach for finding the optimum conditions, is an efficient graphical statistical technique to identify different factors that produce the best operation or process. RSM was first used for optimizing machining techniques [6]. Recently, it has been successfully applied to a different process for achieving its optimization using RSM, which included bioremediation studies [7, 8], enzyme optimum reactions[9-15], wastewater treatment progress[16-18], production of activated carbon and xylose [19, 20], ect. Physicochemical methods have high treatment costs and may cause secondary pollution; hence this study attempts to investigate AN removal by the biological method. In the present study, response surface methodology was used to study the biodegradation effect of the various parameters to optimize the process conditions for the maximum degradation of acrylonitrile by implementing the Box-Behnken statistical design in bioreactor.

H. Tan and M. Zhou (Eds.): CSE 2011, Part I, CCIS 201, pp. 31–36, 2011.

2 Materials and Methods

2.1 Materials

Original mixed bacteria were obtained from soil samples polluted by nitriles for long period of time. Rice husk was supplied by Dalian food storage and transportation industrial company, Dalian, China.

2.2 Microorganism Medium and Culture Conditions

Microorganisms were collected and accumulated in rice husk biofilm culture equipment. Cultures were maintained at 25℃and 150 rpm for the duration mentioned in the experiment design. More than 90% AN degradation after 24 h was obtained and this indicated that the rice husk carrier for immobilized microbial could treat AN wastewater at normal operational condition.

2.3 Analytical Methods

The AN concentration was analyzed by using pyridine colorimetric analysis method. The pH was measured by glass microelectrode numerical pH-meter (Shanghai Precision Instruments, China).

2.4 Design of Experiments by Response Surface Methodology

Response surface methodology is a combination of statistical and optimization technique used to evaluate the relationship between a set of controllable experimental factors and observed results. This optimization process involves three major steps: (i) performing statistically designed experiments, (ii) estimating the coefficients in a mathematical model, and (iii) predicting the response and checking the adequacy of the model[21].

A design matrix comprising of 17 experimental runs was constructed. The non-linear computer-generated quadratic equation model for predicting the optimal point can be expressed according to Eq. (1):

where y is the measured response associated with each factor level combination; b_0 is an intercept;b_1 to b_{33} are regression coefficients computed from the observed experimental values of y; and x_1, x_2 and x_3 are the coded values levels of independent variables. The terms x_{12}, $x_{13,}$ x_{23} and x_i (i=1, 2or 3) represent the interaction and quadratic terms, respectively[22].

Box-Behnken design was specifically selected since it requires fewer runs than a central composite design(CCD) in cases of three or four variables. Data were processed using Design-Expert (version 7.0, Stat–Ease, Minneapolis, USA) program including ANOVA to obtain the interaction between the process variables and the response. The quality of the fit of polynomial model was expressed by the coefficient of determination R^2, and its statistical significance was checked. From three-dimensional plots, the simultaneous interaction of two factors on the response was studied.

3 Results and Discussion

To find the optimum conditions for degradation of AN in bioreactor, the experimental design as a function of the selected main factors has to be determined. The most important parameters that affect the efficiency of AN degradation are temperature, pH and initial AN concentration. In order to study the combined effect of these factors, experiments were performed at different combinations of the physical parameters using statistical experiments. Temperature, pH and initial AN concentration were chosen as independent variables and the efficiency of AN degradation as dependent output response variable. Table 1 represents the coded and nature values of the experimental variables.

Table 1. The Level and Range of Independent Variables Chosen for AN Degradation

Variable	Unit	Coded value	nature value	Range and level of actual and coded values		
				-1	0	+1
pH	-	x_1	X_1	5.0	6.5	8.0
Temperature	℃	x_2	X_2	10	25	40
Initial AN concentration	mg/L	x_3	X_3	100	500	900

The design and results of experiments carried out with the Box–Behnken design are given in Table 2.

Regression analysis of the data was performed for testing the adequacy of the proposed quadratic model and the following second-order polynomial equation was derived (Eq. (2))

$$y=96.882+1.22x_1+2.05x_2-5.1075x_3-23.43475x_1^2-14.86475x_2^2 \\ -13.46975x_3^2+0.2475x_{12}-0.2475x_{13}-1.4325x_{23} \quad (2)$$

where, y is the predicted response(AN degradation rate), x_1, x_2 and x_3 are the coded values of pH, temperature and initial AN concentration, respectively.

Analysis of variance (ANOVA) was important in determining the adequacy and significance of the quadratic model. ANOVA for the fitted quadratic polynomial model is summarized in Table 3. Excellent co-efficient of determination R^2 value of 0.9944 indicated the suitability of the fitted second order polynomials to predict these response variables. The smaller the magnitude of the p-value the more significant is the corresponding coefficient. It is shown that a probability value for the multiple regression is very small ($p < 0.0001$; $p < 0.01$ when significant). Fisher's test for the analysis of variance done on the experimental data indicated that the model was highly significant with and F-value of 138.52.

Table 2. Box-Behnken Experimental Design Matrix with Experimental and Predicted Values of AN Degradation Rate

Run	x_1	x_2	x_3	X_1	X_2	X_3	AN degradation rate /%	
							Observed	Predicted
1	-1	-1	0	5.0	10	500	57.73	55.56
2	1	-1	0	8.0	10	500	58.45	57.51
3	-1	1	0	5.0	40	500	58.22	59.17
4	1	1	0	8.0	40	500	59.93	62.10
5	-1	0	-1	5.0	25	100	62.35	63.62
6	1	0	-1	8.0	25	100	66.51	66.55
7	-1	0	1	5.0	25	900	53.94	53.90
8	1	0	1	8.0	25	900	57.11	55.84
9	0	-1	-1	6.5	10	100	69.27	70.17
10	0	1	-1	6.5	40	100	79.35	77.14
11	0	-1	1	6.5	10	900	60.61	62.82
12	0	1	1	6.5	40	900	64.96	64.06
13	0	0	0	6.5	25	500	97.26	96.88
14	0	0	0	6.5	25	500	96.74	96.88
15	0	0	0	6.5	25	500	96.95	96.88
16	0	0	0	6.5	25	500	97.14	96.88
17	0	0	0	6.5	25	500	96.32	96.88

Table 3. Analysis of Variance(ANOVA)for the Fitted Quadratic Polynomial Model

Source	Squares	DF	Square	Value	Prob > F
Model	4699.85	9	522.21	138.52	< 0.0001
x_1	11.91	1	11.91	3.16	0.1188
x_2	33.62	1	33.62	8.92	0.0203
x_3	208.69	1	208.69	55.36	0.0001
x_1^2	2312.37	1	2312.37	613.36	< 0.0001
x_2^2	930.36	1	930.36	246.78	< 0.0001
x_3^2	763.93	1	763.93	202.63	< 0.0001
x_1x_2	0.25	1	0.25	0.06	0.8061
x_1x_3	0.25	1	0.25	0.06	0.8061
x_2x_3	8.21	1	8.21	2.18	0.1836

The interactive influences of temperature, pH and initial AN concentration on AN degradation rate are illustrated in Fig.1-3. All the relationships among the three variables are non-linear. The effect of initial AN concentration was found to be highly significant ($p = 0.0001$) on percentage removal of AN. Although the bioreactor are effective, over certain AN concentration it inhibits the biodegradation efficiency. Therefore optimization of initial AN concentration is essential for the successful biodegradation. Activated sludge growth was inhibited by 150 mg/L acrylonitrile. Rice husk is probably the most abundant and low-cost natural commercially available. It is a good carrier of bacteria and buffer medium of high strength AN, that the cultivated acrylonitrile-degrading bacteria can be used to effectively remove AN and tolerate high strength AN. From the Fig.1-3 it can be interpreted that maximum and minimum AN degradation rate of 97.5% and 78.3% can be obtained by conducting experiment after 24h reaction time.

These types of 3D plots are useful in study of the effects of two factors on the response at one time. The optimization problem given in Eq.(2) is solved using constrained optimization program supplied in the Matlab optimization toolbox. Optimal values of pH, temperature, initial AN concentration were 6.54, 26.22℃and 424.32mg/L, respectively.

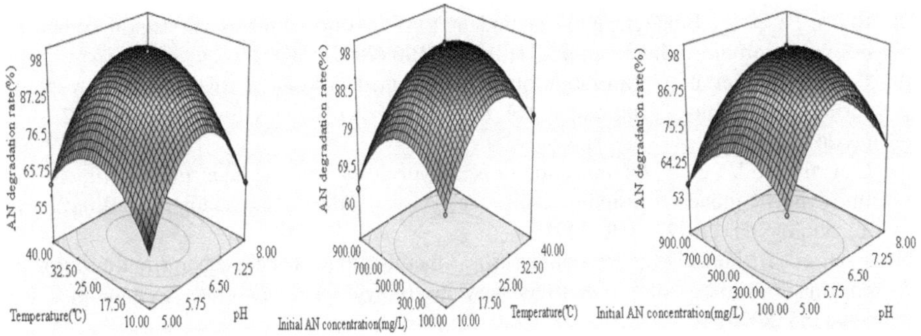

Fig. 1. Effect of Initial AN Concentration, Temperature and pH on AN Degradation Rate n

As a result of employing response surface methodology to optimize parameters of biodegradation of AN in bioreactor, therefore, it was shown that the variables, temperature, pH and initial AN concentration, all affected biodegradation efficiency.

4 Conclusion

The statistical analysis proved to be a useful and powerful tool in developing optimum biodegradation conditions. ANOVA of the quadratic model demonstrates that the model was highly significant. RSM based on Box–Behnken design showed that optimal values of pH, temperature, initial AN concentration were 6.54, 26.22 ℃ and 424.32mg/L, respectively.

References

1. Tong, Q.Y., Zhang, G.W.: Rapid synthesis of a superabsorbent from a saponified starch and acrylonitrile/AMPS graft copolymers. Carbohydrate Polymers 62(1), 74–79 (2005)
2. Wyatt, J.M., Knowles, C.J.: Microbial-Degradation of Acrylonitrile Waste Effluents - the Degradation of Effluents and Condensates from the Manufacture of Acrylonitrile. International Biodeterioration & Biodegradation 35(1-3), 227–248 (1995)
3. Abdel-Aal, S.E., Gad, Y.H., Dessouki, A.M.: Use of rice straw and radiation-modified maize starch/acrylonitrile in the treatment of wastewater. Journal of Hazardous Materials 129(1-3), 204–215 (2006)
4. Huang, S., Quail, K., Moss, R.: The optimization of a laboratory processing procedure for southern-style Chinese steamed bread. International Journal of Food Science and Technology 33(4), 345–357 (1998)

5. Kumar, P., Mishra, H.N.: Optimization of mango soy fortified yogurt formulation using response surface methodology. International Journal of Food Properties 6(3), 499–517 (2003)
6. Choudhury, I.A., El-Baradie, M.A.: Machinability assessment of inconel 718 by factorial design of experiment coupled with response surface methodology. Journal of Materials Processing Technology 95(1-3), 30–39 (1999)
7. Rigas, F., et al.: Bioremediation of a soil contaminated by lindane utilizing the fungus Ganoderma australe via response surface methodology. Journal of Hazardous Materials 140(1-2), 325–332 (2007)
8. Rigas, F., et al.: Biodegradation of lindane by Pleurotus ostreatus via central composite design. Environment International 31(2), 191–196 (2005)
9. Demirkol, S., et al.: Optimization of enzymatic methanolysis of soybean oil by response surface methodology. Journal of the American Oil Chemists Society 83(11), 929–932 (2006)
10. Canettieri, E.V., et al.: Optimization of acid hydrolysis from the hemicellulosic fraction of Eucalyptus grandis residue using response surface methodology. Bioresource Technology 98(2), 422–428 (2007)
11. Jeong, G.T., Park, D.H.: Response surface methodological approach for optimization of enzymatic synthesis of sorbitan methacrylate. Enzyme and Microbial Technology 39(3), 381–386 (2006)
12. Sin, H.N., et al.: Optimization of enzymatic clarification of sapodilla juice using response surface methodology. Journal of Food Engineering 73(4), 313–319 (2006)
13. Kunamneni, A., Singh, S.: Response surface optimization of enzymatic hydrolysis of maize starch for higher glucose production. Biochemical Engineering Journal 27(2), 179–190 (2005)
14. Sharma, A.K., Sarkar, B.C., Sharma, H.K.: Optimization of enzymatic process parameters for increased juice yield from carrot (Daucus carota L.) using response surface methodology. European Food Research and Technology 221(1-2), 106–112 (2005)
15. Kumar, G.V., Rao, M.N.: Enzymatic synthesis of butyl butyrate using response surface methodology. Journal of Food Science and Technology-Mysore 41(5), 560–562 (2004)
16. Ahmad, A.L., Ismail, S., Bhatia, S.: Optimization of coagulation-flocculation process for palm oil mill effluent using response surface methodology. Environmental Science & Technology 39(8), 2828–2834 (2005)
17. Ravikumar, K., et al.: Optimization of process variables by the application of response surface methodology for dye removal using a novel adsorbent. Dyes and Pigments 72(1), 66–74 (2007)
18. Zinatizadeh, A.A.L., et al.: Process modeling and analysis of palm oil mill effluent treatment in an up-flow anaerobic sludge fixed film bioreactor using response surface methodology (RSM). Water Research 40(17), 3193–3208 (2006)
19. Bacaoui, A., et al.: Optimization of conditions for the preparation of activated carbons from olive-waste cakes. Carbon 39(3), 425–432 (2001)
20. Rahman, S.H.A., et al.: Optimization studies on acid hydrolysis of oil palm empty fruit bunch fiber for production of xylose. Bioresource Technology 98(3), 554–559 (2007)
21. Box, G.E.P., Hunter, W.G., Hunter, J.S.: Multifactor experimental design for exploring the response surfaces. Ann. Math. Stat. 28, 195–242 (1957)
22. Box, G.E.P., Behnken, D.W.: Some new three level designs for the study of quantitative variables. Technometrics 2, 455–475 (1960)

Research and Practice of Digital Signal Processing Experimental Platform Based on Network

Chengbo Yu and Rumin Yang

Chongqing University of Technology
Chongqing, China, 400050
yuchengbo@cqut.edu.cn, yangrumin@163.com

Abstract. Aiming at the actualities in experiment teaching of digital signal processing, this paper introduces a virtual experiment platform based on network, discusses some key techniques and shows its feasibility through several examples. The remote teaching can be realized in order to extend student's study space through this experiment platform.

Keywords: network, experiment platform, virtual, digital signal processing.

1 Introduction

The rapid development of technology and the gradual intensification of system change and teaching in higher education have profound effects on the personnel training of institutions of higher education. Currently, various institutions of higher education are facing a same issue of importance, i.e., how to improve the traditional education and teaching method by using modern educational technology, to create diversified educational techniques suitable for the studying features of different college students, and to establish a new-type experimental teaching platform. Especially for general institutes of higher education, how to effectively use modern educational technology is extremely important for changing the actualities in the shortage of skilled teachers and the present teaching structure that is not very reasonable, for culturing highly talented person with initiative spirit and practical ability, and for gradually developing unique features for running the university with improved quality and benefit. On the basis of discussing the features of digital signal processing and the present experimental teaching, this paper introduces a LabVIEW based virtual experiment platform on network, and carries on some useful exploration and practice, with favorable teaching effects.

2 Necessities of Developing the Experimental Platform of Digital Signal Processing Based on Network

With the development of technology, this world has come into a digitized age. Computer has already become an indispensable tool in signal acquiring, analyzing and processing. Signal analyzing and processing have been infiltrating almost every engineering field, leading to great expansion of the connotation and extension of

H. Tan and M. Zhou (Eds.): CSE 2011, Part I, CCIS 201, pp. 37–44, 2011.

digital signal processing. The theory and its application of signal processing has been paid more and more attentions, as a result, this kind of courses is widely set up in domestic institutions of higher education. The digital signal processing is a key course of signal processing, with extremely abundant content that are playing more and more important role in many scientific and technological fields. This course not only emphasizes college students' understanding and handling of theory and basis concepts, but also pays attention to cultivation of engineering practical ability in order to develop creativity. The experimental course offered by college is an efficient way to improve college students' abilities, but for a long time, the experimental teaching method of digital signal processing is very traditional. Generally, experimental teaching is only regarded as a supplementation of theoretical teaching, with a subsidiary status. For the designing of experimental projects, basic and demonstrative experiments, always with single content and only to verify what the college students have learned in classroom, are given first priority. Generally, these experiments adopt an almost fixed mode, that is, in certain time, with the instructions of teacher and according to certain methods and instruments, letting the students accomplish the overall experimental process.

In the traditional experimental process, what the students really do is three items: getting familiar with the relative content of experimental instruction, performing the experiment according to the instruction, and finishing experimental report. The experimental instruction, carefully compiled by the teacher, generally has the following content: experimental principle and method, experimental procedures, record form of experimental data, experimental curve required to plot, standard form of experimental report, etc. In this traditional teaching mode, majority students study very passively. If things go on like this, it will result in student's strong dependence on teacher and lack of ability to deal with practical problems, let alone innovation ability. In the past, the experimental course of digital signal processing offered by our university is mainly performed by setting up hardware circuit using analog instrument. The limitation of hardware circuit and electronic component performance has obvious effect on the flexibility and real-time performance of the experiments. The students are limited to do experiments only in the laboratory. In addition, because of the shortage of teacher and experimental site and the limitation of opening hours of laboratory, the openness of experiment hasn't been realized in an all-round way, and the practical opportunities provided to students cannot be guaranteed. So it's difficult to motivate the student's learning interest, initiative spirit and creativeness.

Therefore, taking the computational practice as a basic tool, it's of great significance to promote the application of network information technology in digital signal processing, to develop virtual experiments based on remote computer, and to provide college students opportunities to do experiments based on network in order to improve teaching efficiency.

3 The Key Techniques of Experimental Platform

This experimental platform, based on LabVIEW environment, adopts C/S mode based DataSocket technique to realize signal's network transmission, and is composed of three submodules, including registration information submodule, help submodule, and submodule of signal analyzing and processing. This platform involves the following key techniques, such as real-time transmission of signal, data storage, data playback, registering of student information, generation of independent application program, etc. In the below, the realization of each key technique will be introduced, respectively.

3.1 DataSocket Technique to Realize Signal's Network Transmission

The DataSocket technique is based on highly encapsulated TCP/IP protocol, realizing the real-time data exchange and sharing between Server and Multiuser during the measurement process. Before carrying on positive communication, it's necessary to deploy the DataSocket Server Manager and run the DataSocket Server. DataSocket Server Manager is an independent run program, with the following main functions: setting up the maximum number of client programs connected by DataSocket Server and establishing the maximum number of data items, establishing user group and users, setting up user authority to create, read and write data items, restricting unidentified user to visit and attack the Server. DataSocket Server is a program that must run on the Server end, supervising the data exchange between programs on the Client end and user group with different authorities set up by Manager. The block diagram program of Server's data acquiring and transmitting in C/S mode is shown in Figure 1.

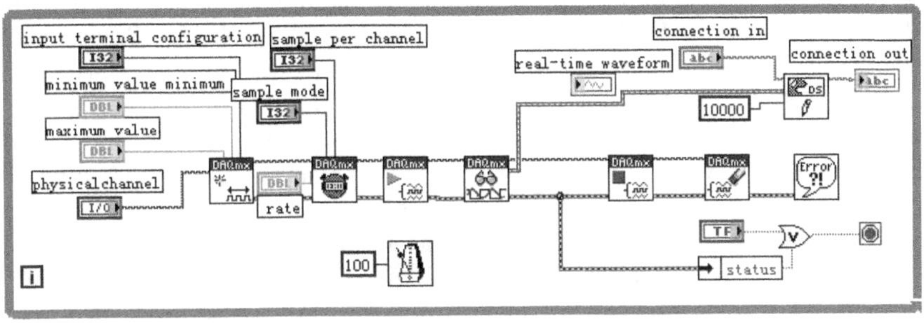

Fig. 1. The block diagram program of Server's data acquiring and transmitting in C/S mode

Corresponding to the block diagram program of the Server, by using the uniform resource locator (URL) generated on the Server and the programs compiled by DataSocket Read functions, the Client can realize the real-time reading of the data transmitted from the Server. It's worth noting that, after running the programs on the Client and Server, when the indicator light in the top right corner of oscillogram exhibits green, it is showed that the data transmitting or accepting is correctly connected; when the indicator exhibits red, it is showed that the connection between the data and DataSocket Server fails.

3.2 The Module of Data Storage and Playback

LabVIEW provides users abundant functions for data storage. According users' requirement, the data can be stored as text file (txt or xls), binary file, or wave file.

In order to conveniently examine the stored data from files, this system chooses to store the dada in text file mode, and the block diagram program of data storage is shown in Figure 2.

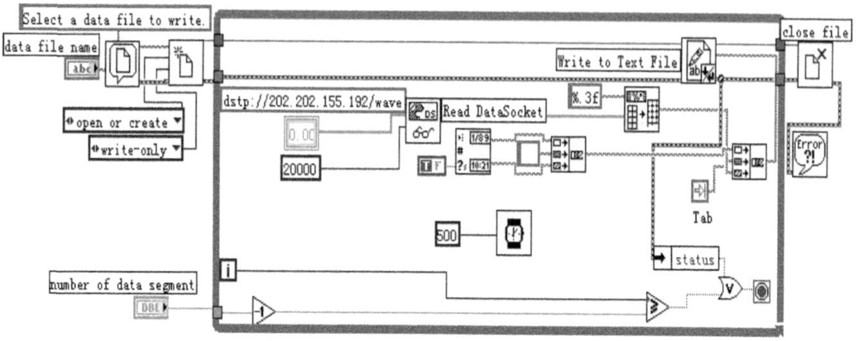

Fig. 2. The block diagram program of data storage

Here are some notes about the block diagram program of data storage: (1) the number of data segment can be set up, and every data segment possesses time information; (2) before running the program, the data file name must be determined (txt file or xls file); (3) DSTP in the program is: dstp://202.202.155.192/wave, which is the basis for the Client to accept the data transmitted from the Server, here, 202.202.155.192 is the IP address of the Server; (4) the 20000 of the program is the maximum value of network time delay, an error will be reported by the program if the Client and the Server cannot be connected in 20000ms. The maximum time delay, with a default value of 10000, can be set according to the network situation and how many data will be transmitted. Corresponding to the data storage program, the data playback program is compiled by the functions such as file opening/ creating/ replacing, file reading, file closing, index array, etc., and can playback data from the data storage file (qqq.xls in this program). The operation interface of data storage and playback is shown in Figure 3.

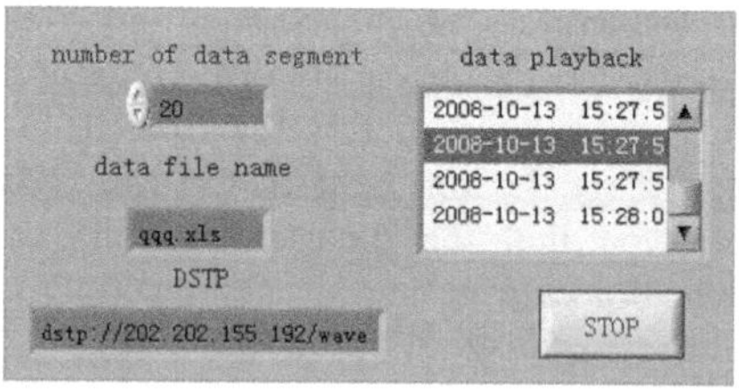

Fig. 3. The operation interface of data storage and readback

3.3 The Submodule of Registration Information

In order to better registration information, this platform develops a special registering submodule of student information, storing these basic informations (such as name, number, login date, operating time) into given txt file. The block diagram program and front panel are shown in Figure 4 and Figure 5, respectively.

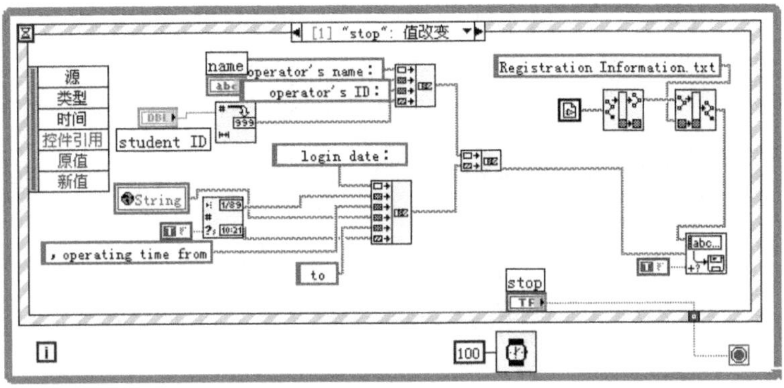

Fig. 4. The block diagram program of registration information

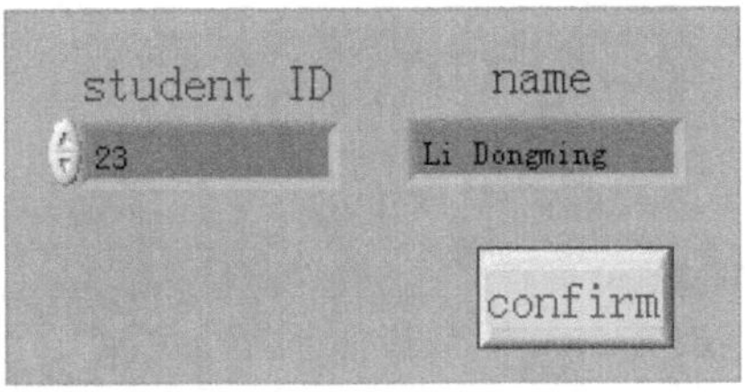

Fig. 5. The front panel of registraton information

On the running state, after verifying the inputted number 23 and name "Li Dongming", the operator information is inputted into "registration information.txt", shown as "operator name: Li Dongming, operator number: 23, login date: 8-18-2007, operating time: from 10:59:08 to 11:23:12".

4 Examples

The login interface of this platform is shown in Figure 6, including some buttons like login, registration, help, logout. After clicking the button of "logint", the student can enter the main interface of experimental module, as shown in Figure 7. This experimental module can process two kinds of signal resource: one is the real physical signal transmitted from acquisition card (in the experimental platform introduced in this paper, the model number of data acquisition card is PCI-MIO-16E-4), the other one is the analog signal generated by LabVIEW. In this module, Student can carry on many traditional experiments, such as spectrum analyzing, wave filtering, windowing experiment, self-correlation and cross-correlation, etc. In the following, two examples will be given to make a brief introduction to this platform.

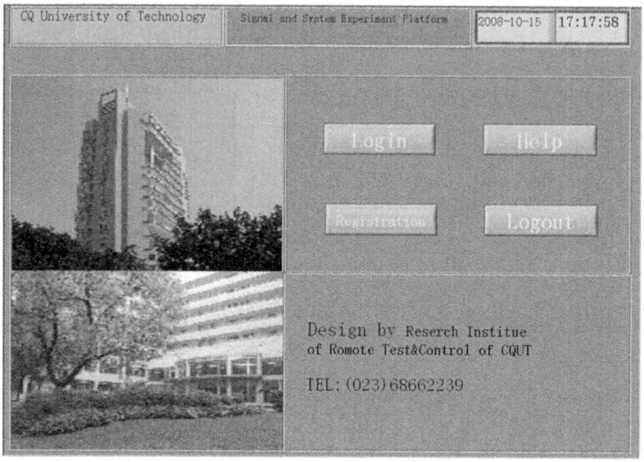

Fig. 6. The login interface of experimental platform

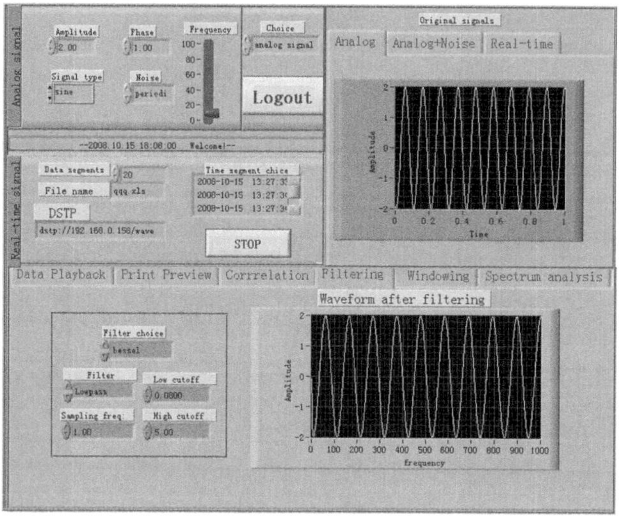

Fig. 7. The interface of experimental module

4.1 Signal Generating and Spectrum Analyzing

After entering the main experimental interface, student can enter the interface of experimental module by clicking the button of “login”. Then choose the “analog signal” from the optional column of “choice”, and set the relative parameters in the parameter setting region corresponding to the analog signal (signal type: "square signal": amplitude: 2: duty cycle: 50%; frequency: 20Hz). Figure 8 (a) is the square signal generated by LabVIEW, whose amplitude spectrum is recorded in Figure 8 (b).

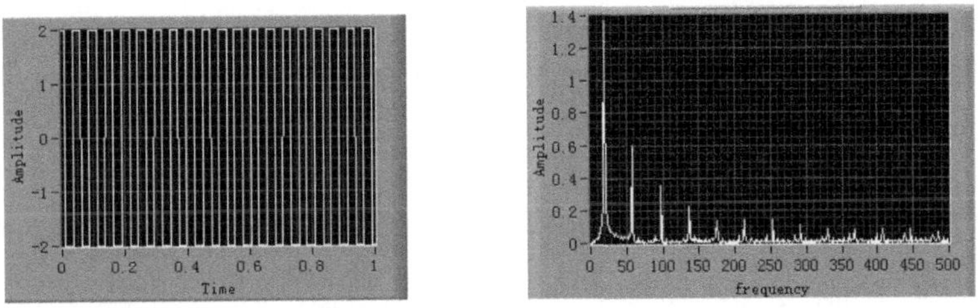

(a) Square signal (b) Amplitude spectrum

Fig. 8. Square signal and its amplitude spectrum

4.2 Self-correlation Processing of Signal

Similarly, after login the experimental module, choose "analog signal superimposed with noise" from "operating options" and "Gauss white noise" from noise type, and set the relative parameters in the parameter setting region corresponding to the analog signal, then the corresponding wave shapes can be obtained. The sine wave signal superimposed with Gauss white noise and its wave shape after self-correlation processing is shown in Figure 9 (a) and (b), respectively. From Figure 9 (b), it could be concluded that the self-correlation processing can effectively detect the periodic signal submerged in the noise signal.

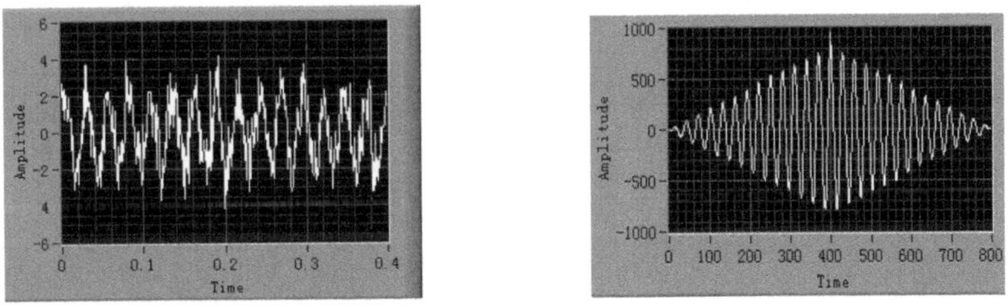

(a) Sine wave signal superimposed with Gauss white noise (b) After self-correlation processing

Fig. 9. The sine wave signal superimposed with Gauss white noise and its wave shape after self-correlation processing

5 Conclusion

After being released on web network, this experimental platform can be applied to remote teaching. The experimental platform is mainly composed of virtual electronic instruments, realizing remote measurement and experiment by integrating software with computer network. On the basis of this platform, the theoretical and experimental teaching with fixed time and site can be extended to the on-line teaching at anytime and anywhere. In summary, this platform fully utilizes the network resources to serve the experimental teaching, and can motivate students' learning interest and inquisitiveness, gradually changing students' learning method and thinking mode.

Acknowledgment. This article belongs to the key project of higher education teaching reform of Chongqing (No. 0824077) and the project of higher education research of Chongqing University of Technology (No. 2007013).

References

1. Lepin, Y., Haitao, L.: Advanced programming. Tsinghua University Press, Beijing (April 2003)
2. Qirong, L.: Construction of personal Laboratory based on virtual instrumental technology. Electronic Industry Press, Bingjing (October 2006)
3. Chengbo, Y.: Signal and system, 2nd edn. Tsinghua University Press, Beijing (June 2003)
4. Guopin, H., Kun, W.: Programming and designing of virtual instruments based on LabVIEW7.1. Tsinghua University Press, Beijing (February 2003)
5. Oppenheim, A.V., Willsky, A.S.: Signals and System. Publishing House of Electronics Industry, Beijing (March 2007)

The Correlation Study Based on VAR Model between Major Financial Risk Indicators and Economic Growth

Zheng Qin*, Lihua Cheng**, Juan Du***, and Bo Tian

Shanghai University of Finance and Economics Information Management and Engineering
Room103, Ningyuan Building, No777, Guoding Road, Shanghai, China 200433
huachengli2003@163.com

Abstract. This paper based on GDP of 1992-2009 year dates and related factors, constructed three risk indicators model of money、 bank、 asset, analyze correlations between three indicators and GDP growth, which reflected risk in those years. And this paper selected the key factors about economic growth-money index by using linear regression. Established VAR model by using money index and GDP growth, by making per unit test、Co integration、Grange and pulse, which reflected the correlations about some financial index and economic growth in china, forecasted the risk in next year. Instructed that money risk make some pulse power to china economic, but with time disappear, the pulse power disappear.

Keywords: Economic Growth, Financial Risk Indicators, VAR model.

1 Introduction

Economists may disagree about that the role of the financial sector in economic growth. Robert Lucas (1988, p.6) dismisses finance as an "over-stressed" determinant of economic growth. Joan Robinson (1952, p. 86) famously argued that "where enterprise leads finance follows." From this perspective, finance does not cause growth and finance responds to changing demands from the "real sector." At the other extreme, Merton Miller (1988, p.14) argues that financial markets contribute to economic growth is a proposition too obvious for serious discussion. Drawing a more restrained conclusion, Bagehot (1873), Goldsmith (1969), and McKinnon (1973) and some other studiers reject the idea that the finance-growth relation can be safely ignored without substantially limiting our understanding of economic growth.

Financial systems may influence saving rates, investment decisions, technological innovation, and hence long-run growth rates. A comparatively less well-developed theoretical literature examines the dynamic interactions between finance and growth by developing models where the financial system influences growth, and growth transforms the operation of the financial system.

* Supported by National Natural Science Foundation of China .NO.70971083.

** Support by National Natural Science Foundation of China. NO.7105003.

*** Support by Specialized Research Fund for the Doctoral Program of Higher Education. NO.20100078120001.

H. Tan and M. Zhou (Eds.): CSE 2011, Part I, CCIS 201, pp. 45–54, 2011.

Furthermore, an extensive theoretical literature debates the relative merits of different types of financial systems. Some models stress the advantages of bank-based financial systems, while others highlight the benefits of financial systems that rely more on securities markets.

Many learners do this research, for example, Shou jun Ma selected 13 economic indicators and make early warning mechanism, Guo shi Wang's statistics on the financial risk monitoring and early warning indicator system. Dao ping Huang、Zhen Hui Li、Bo Wang considered China's financial risk evaluation index system. In order to better consider the relation. We select some financial risk indicator to index finance sector. And set GDP to Eviews5.0, And made a theoretical correlation analysis with financial risk indicators, to explore the Eviews5.0, And made a theoretical correlation analysis with financial risk indicators, to explore the opportunities for economic growth and financial crisis characteristics.

2 Analyses

This paper will use Eviews5.0 software, Estimated by OLS, analyze by VAR model.

2.1 Model Explaining and Variables Instructing

2.1.1 Select Variables

When many factors influent economic, for example , exchange rate, interest rate, foreign exchange store、credit rate、money supply、shares price index、house price index and etc.; When those indicators change, the economic may be change. And the economics of risk or opportunities maybe find by analyzing indicators which influent economic growth, risk variables as gene variable; and function relation represent relation between economic index and risk index.

Table 1. Risk variables

sort	Detail name	Simple name	value
Money indicator CC	Fact exchange rate	RER	
	Fact interest rate	RIR	$\sum_{i=1}^{3} a_i w_i$
	Foreign exchange store	FES	
Bank indicator BC	Credit rate	RLD	
	Money supply	MS	$\sum_{i=1}^{3} b_i w_i$
Asset indicator FB	Shares price index	SR	
	House price index	HR	$\sum_{i=1}^{2} c_i w_i$

The economic index function is:

$$INDEX=f1 \ (RER, \ RIR, \ FES, \ RLD, \ MS...) \tag{1}$$

And the indicator is Gross National Product, RER as fact exchange rate, RIR as fact interest rate, FES as foreign exchange store, RLD as credit rate, MS as money supply, SR as shares price index, HR as house price index.

2.1.2 Data Sources

In order to reflect the economic performance in recent years, this paper selects 1992-2009 quarterly dates as economic indicators and economic index etc. Data sources are 2009 statistical yearbook and relation webs. Economic indicators and some other infect dates in Schedule1.

2.1.3 Constructed Index

Any economic variable cannot enough on behalf of a whole process in economic fluctuations. So the paper uses many indicators to construct risk index.

1. The currency indicators index constitutes by real exchange rate, real interest rate, and foreign exchange reserves. And the formula is:

$$CC_t = \omega_{RER}\left(\frac{RER_t - RER_{t-1}}{RER_{t-1}}\right) + \omega_{RIR}\left(\frac{RIR_t - RIR_{t-1}}{RIR_{t-1}}\right) - \omega_{FES}\left(\frac{FES_t - FES_{t-1}}{FES_{t-1}}\right) \tag{2}$$

the weight ω_{RER}、 ω_{RIR} and ω_{FES} is every variable actual accuracy. The formula is:

$$\omega_t = \left(\frac{1}{SD_t}\right) / \left(\frac{1}{SD_{RER}} + \frac{1}{SD_{RIR}} + \frac{1}{SD_{FES}}\right) \tag{3}$$

2. The bank indicator index. We use the ratio of loan to deposit、 real interest rate and money supply construct the bank risk index. The formula is :

$$BC_t = \omega_{RLD}\left(\frac{RLD_t - RLD_{t-1}}{RLD_{t-1}}\right) + \omega_{RIR}\left(\frac{RIR_t - RIR_{t-1}}{RIR_{t-1}}\right) + \omega_{MS}\left(\frac{MS_t - MS_{t-1}}{MS_{t-1}}\right) \tag{4}$$

the weight ω_{RLD}、 ω_{RIR} and ω_{MS} is every variable actual accuracy. The formula is:

$$\omega_t = \left(\frac{1}{SD_t}\right) / \left(\frac{1}{SD_{RLD}} + \frac{1}{SD_{RIR}} + \frac{1}{SD_{MS}}\right) \tag{5}$$

3. The asset indicator index. Using stock price index and house price index construct financial bubble pressure. The asset indicator index formula is :

$$FB_t = \omega_{SR}\left(\frac{SR_t - SR_{t-1}}{SR_{t-1}}\right) + \omega_{HR}\left(\frac{HR_t - HR_{t-1}}{HR_{t-1}}\right) \tag{6}$$

The weight ω_{SR} and ω_{HR} is every variable actual accuracy. The formula is :

$$\omega_t = \left(\frac{1}{SD_t}\right) / \left(\frac{1}{SD_{SR}} + \frac{1}{SD_{HR}}\right) \tag{7}$$

Three indicators calculate by the data, we can get the weight. And three indicator index equations are:

$$CC_t = 0.71\left(\frac{RER_t - RER_{t-1}}{RER_{t-1}}\right) + 0.28\left(\frac{RIR_t - RIR_{t-1}}{RIR_{t-1}}\right) - 0.01\left(\frac{FES_t - FES_{t-1}}{FES_{t-1}}\right) \tag{8}$$

$$BC_t = 0.938\left(\frac{RLD_t - RLD_{t-1}}{RLD_{t-1}}\right) + 0.061\left(\frac{RIR_t - RIR_{t-1}}{RIR_{t-1}}\right) + 0.001\left(\frac{MS_t - MS_{t-1}}{MS_{t-1}}\right) \tag{9}$$

$$FB_t = 0.003\left(\frac{SR_t - SR_{t-1}}{SR_{t-1}}\right) + 0.997\left(\frac{HR_t - HR_{t-1}}{HR_{t-1}}\right) \tag{10}$$

From three equations, we can see that, the major factor is that real exchange rate (RER), loans ratio (RLD), house price index (HR).

Table 2. Indexes and main Factors

Three indicators	Currency indicator（CC）	Bank indicator(BC)	Asset indicator(FB)
Main factor	real exchange rate（RER）	loans ratio（RLD）	House price Index（HR）

According to the equation and using the known data in Table 2 we can calculated three indicators values and trends changes between 1993 and 2009. As shown below:

Table 3. The values of the risk variables and GDP% *above* the tables

year	GDP%	CC	BC	FB
1993	0.142	0.106783	0.008763	0.002208
1994	0.131	0.337656	−0.10504	−0.01265
1995	0.109	0.001231	−0.04023	0.024823
1996	0.1	−0.05337	−0.05626	0.002942
1997	0.093	−0.0454	0.01011	0.014685
1998	0.078	−0.0742	−0.02102	−0.01274
1999	0.076	−0.0244	−0.04904	−0.01319
2000	0.084	−0.0007	−0.06416	0.012517
2001	0.083	−0.00293	−0.0239	0.010229
2002	0.091	−0.02935	−0.0221	0.014108
2003	0.1	−0.00408	−0.00466	0.010884
2004	0.101	0.009095	−0.02877	0.046153
2005	0.104	−0.01073	−0.07627	−0.01934
2006	0.116	0.005015	−0.00252	−0.01555
2007	0.13	−0.03709	0.000629	0.022745
2008	0.09	−0.06426	−0.02956	−0.01215
2009	0.08	0.006309	0.01896	−0.00066

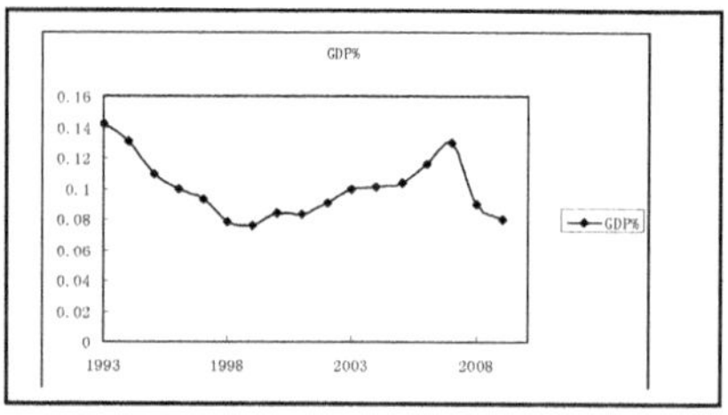

Fig. 1.1. GDP growth rate changes trends

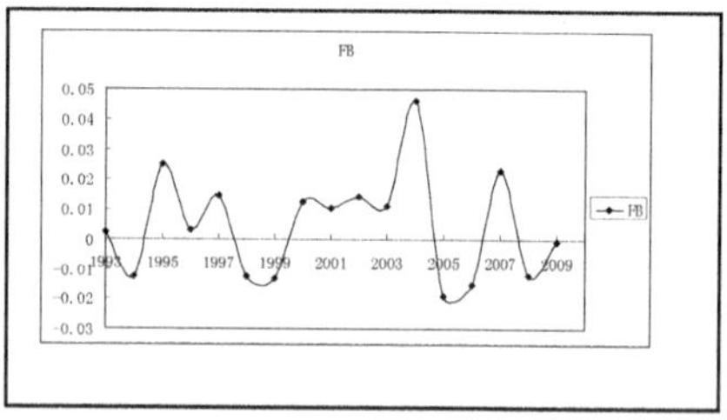

Fig. 1.2. Asset indicator index

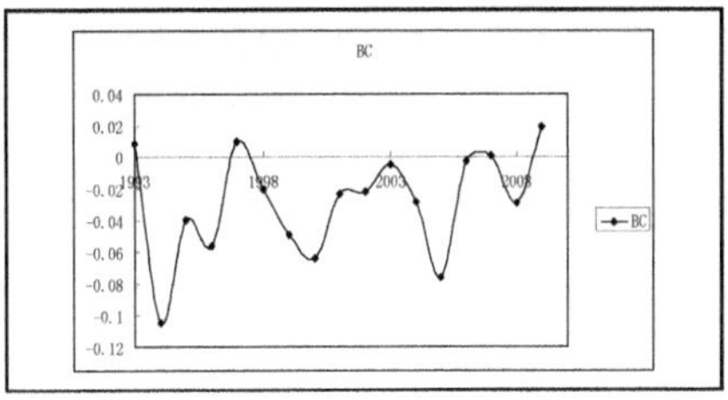

Fig. 1.3. Bank indicator index

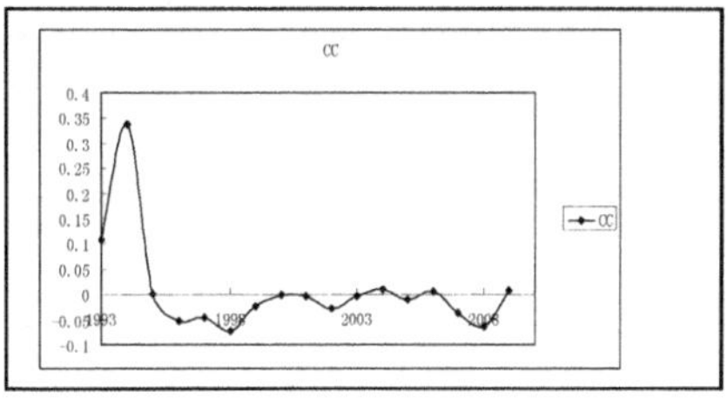

Fig. 1.4. Currency indicator index

Can be roughly seen from Figure 1.1 to Figure 1.4, between the trends of GDP growth change and currency indicator have the same change trend. But it also showed some positive correlation. GDP growth rate in the last two or three years to decline, FB and BC have big volatility, very smooth, explain that they have a greater risk of volatility. BC basically following zero value, CC's value has been relatively stable after 1995 years, basically around zero.

2.2 The Relationship between GDP Growth and Three Risk Indicators

2.2.1 Using OLS Regression to Estimate

In Eviews5.0, using the classical method of linear regression do OLS by above data.GDP growth rate as explained variable, three indicators CC、BC、FB as explanatory variables. As can be see Fig. 2

Variable	Coefficient	Std. Error	t-Statistic	Prob.
C	0.102527	0.005842	17.55066	0.0000
CC	0.143206	0.047083	3.041544	0.0095
BC	0.161233	0.142660	1.130274	0.2788
FB	0.118341	0.244182	0.484641	0.6360
R-squared	0.420306	Mean dependent var		0.100471
Adjusted R-squared	0.286530	S.D. dependent var		0.019701
S.E. of regression	0.016641	Akaike info criterion		-5.151559
Sum squared resid	0.003600	Schwarz criterion		-4.955509
Log likelihood	47.78825	F-statistic		3.141873
Durbin-Watson stat	1.074030	Prob(F-statistic)		0.061809

Fig. 2. The result of regression equation

$$\hat{GDP}\%_t = 0.102527 + 0.143206CC_t + 0.16233BC_t + 0.118341FB_t \qquad (11)$$

Compare each variable t-statistics and critical values (critic value) $t_{17.5\%}$=2.11, found that in addition to foreign currency risk indicators CC, the statistical values of the other variables BC, and FB are significantly less than 95% of under Degrees of freedom at the critical value of 2.11 so can be considered in addition to foreign currency risk indicators CC. The remaining variables on the annual growth rate of GDP were not significant. From the output result, we can see that both R^2=0.42and $\overline{R}^2$ =0.286 are much smaller than 0.9.thus the fitted regression equation is not satisfied. This paper eliminates assets FB indicators, banks BC indicators those two indicators. And only discuss the relevance of CC and GDP%. Re-Linear

Variable	Coefficient	Std. Error	t-Statistic	Prob.
C	0.098842	0.004060	24.34762	0.0000
CC	0.115335	0.041720	2.764502	0.0145

R-squared	0.337528	Mean dependent var	0.100471
Adjusted R-squared	0.293363	S.D. dependent var	0.019701
S.E. of regression	0.016561	Akaike info criterion	-5.253376
Sum squared resid	0.004114	Schwarz criterion	-5.155351
Log likelihood	46.65369	F-statistic	7.642470
Durbin-Watson stat	1.117381	Prob(F-statistic)	0.014458

Fig. 3. The result of regression equation

Regression, we can get the result:

$$\hat{GDP\%_t} = 0.098842 + 0.115335CC_t; R^2 = 0.34 \quad (12)$$

As can be seen from the fitting results, although it has some positive correlation between annual GDP growth rate and monetary indicators CC. Smaller coefficients of regression equation and $R^2 = 0.34$, well below the 0.9, Shows that the result of fitting equation is not very satisfactory, this may be a great relationship about few dates. Because the researcher dates are between 1993 and 2009. But the least squares must have much dates, can we get more accurate results. However, due to the inconvenience of various aspects, this paper has resulted at too few data collected. So only do linear regression to illustrate the problem, we cannot obtain a credible result。 Therefore we use the following VAR model to explain the change。 As GDP% mainly have a strong correlation with CC, That is the main change in GDP which may have caused changes in CC。 Therefore, following mainly use those two variables to analysis.

2.3 Empirical Analysis Based on VAR

In accordance with the following steps, we research the relationship between the change of annual GDP rate and currency indicator index.

2.3.1 Vector Autoregressive (VAR) Model Introduced、Construction and Testing

Tradition regression model is based upon economic theory. Using model appropriately descript economic entities, analyze how exogenous variables influent endogenous variables. But this model has some defects. One defect is that it considers some variables as endogenous, but considers other variables as exogenous. This decision is often subjective. Because those two variables maybe reinforce each other; another defect is that when construct simultaneous equation model. To make the model identifiable, this paper must round some of the variables in equation. The core ideology of VAR model is that no considerate economic theory, but direct considerate time series relationship between various economic variables.

VAR General Form:

$$Y_t = \alpha + \sum_{i=1}^{p} \beta_i Y_{t-i} + \varepsilon_t \quad (13)$$

Among $E(\varepsilon_t)$=0, $E(\varepsilon_t, Y_{t-i})$=0, i=1, 2, … p ; Y_t Is the variance of stationary linear random process composed by (n×1) Vector. β_i Is (n×n) Coefficient matrix. Y_{t-i} is Y_t vector i Order lagged variables, ε_t is errors. In this model, it can be seen as Random interference terms.

2.3.2 Unit Root Test and Select Lag Order

Because of the existence of false regression problems, the stationary of sequence must be tested firstly when fitting dynamic regression model. Considering the sample period is short, and sample data are quarterly data, in order to maintain a reasonable degree of freedom, strong interpretability of the model, and eliminate the error of the autocorrelation, this paper set the maximum lag to 2.

Because many economic variables are originally unstable, their stationary must be tested. First do unit root test on the time series of GDP growth rate and monetary indicators (CC) respectively, to ensure that the two time series are stationary. Common unit root tests have PP test and ADF test. In this paper we will use ADF test to judge whether the time series exist unit root effect.

Table 4 shows the ADF test results of the variables of GDP% and CC, as well as their first-order difference. Initial setup is with intercept and time trend, and with first-order difference. We can find that, both the two time series of GDP% and CC are not stationary

Table 4. Risk variables *above* the tables

Variable	Inspection Type (c, T, d)	ADF statistic	Critical value (5%)	P value	Conclusion
GDP%	(c, T, 0)	-2.109496	-3.791172	0.4791	Unstable
D (GDP%)	(c, 0, 0)	-2.95551	-1.96627	0.0061	stable
CC	(c, T, 0)	-3.490943	-3.828975	0.083	Unstable
D (CC)	(c, 0, 0)	-3.948056	-1.974028	0.0009	stable

Note: (c, T, d) represent intercept, time trend and the lag order in the test of equation . The lag order select by minimum AIC criterion. D (X) represent as The first difference of X.

2.3.3 Co Integration Test and Granger (Granger) Causality Test

By Johansen co integration test, including the Johansen trace test and the Johansen rank test. Two result show that two Variable

We do Granger (Granger) causality test with ΔGDP% and ΔCC, can get causality between china year GDP growth rate and currency indicator.

The result shows that, at the 5% significance level, ΔGDP% isn't Granger cause of ΔCC. This show that CC is not GDP growth rate. On contrary, GDP growth rate change isn't cause of CC Change .of course, the sample is too small. So the conclusion credibility is not high. Only have some reference value.

Unrestricted Cointegration Rank Test (Trace)

Hypothesized No. of CE(s)	Eigenvalue	Trace Statistic	0.05 Critical Value	Prob.**
None *	0.935187	47.90135	15.49471	0.0000
At most 1 *	0.366934	6.857709	3.841466	0.0088

Fig. 4.1. Race Test results

Unrestricted Cointegration Rank Test (Maximum Eigenvalue)

Hypothesized No. of CE(s)	Eigenvalue	Max-Eigen Statistic	0.05 Critical Value	Prob.**
None *	0.935187	41.04364	14.26460	0.0000
At most 1 *	0.366934	6.857709	3.841466	0.0088

Fig. 4.2. Rank Test results

Null Hypothesis:	Obs	F-Statistic	Probability
DCC does not Granger Cause DGDPPER	15	0.07348	0.79095
DGDPPER does not Granger Cause DCC		0.26164	0.61827

Fig. 4.3. Lag1 Granger causality test result

2.3.4 VAR Model Result

In Eviews5.0, according the result by estimated between DCC and DGDP% equation. we can get equation between DGDP% and DCC on the VAR vector auto regression. The lag orders all are the first order lag. The VAR equation:

$$\begin{pmatrix} GDP\%_t \\ CC_t \end{pmatrix} = \begin{pmatrix} 0.065 \\ 0.063 \end{pmatrix} + \begin{pmatrix} 0.725 & 0.021 \\ -0.735 & 0.172 \end{pmatrix} \begin{pmatrix} GDP\%_{t-1} \\ CC_{t-1} \end{pmatrix} + \begin{pmatrix} -0.413 & 0.030 \\ -0.066 & -0.049 \end{pmatrix} \begin{pmatrix} GDP\%_{t-2} \\ CC_{t-2} \end{pmatrix} + \begin{pmatrix} \varepsilon_{1t} \\ \varepsilon_{2t} \end{pmatrix} \quad (14)$$

1. All factors which affect GDP change rate don't included in VAR model.
2. Lag order selected may affect the result estimated by VAR model.
3. Statistical data itself due to various reasons, there is a certain error. So the fitting results of the VAR model have some affected. And because the paper selected dates start from 1992, dates are few, thus may affect the result accuracy.
4. Indeed have no relationship between GDP and CC.

2.3.5 Impulse Response Analysis

In practice, As the VAR model is a non -theoretical model .its Coefficient is difficult to explain. When analysis VAR model, we never analysis one variable affect another variable ,but using the impulse response function analysis affection by a standard deviation of information impact with random disturbance term .on according with the need of practical analysis, following shows that ,get GDP growth rate、 currency indicator a positive impact of unit size ,we can get following:

From figure5.1.1, we can see that, GDP change with the response is the same direction. In section 4 reach minimum points. And slow convergence in subsequent period. Figure 5.1.2 shows that, in current issue, give currency risk a position positive impact, the impact of GDP in current issue have a larger role. And the impact have

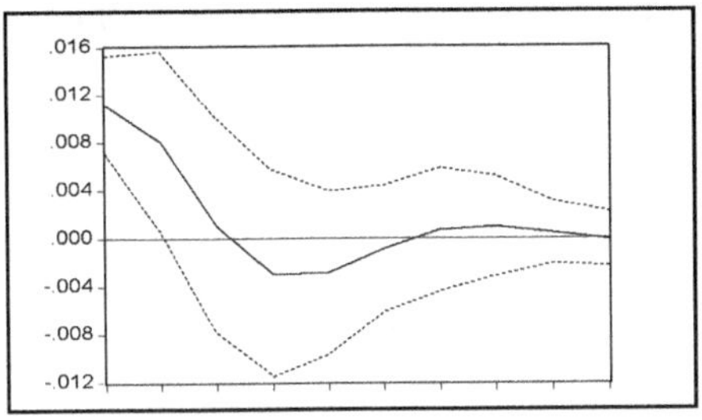

Fig. 5.1.1. Gross domestic product impacts of them

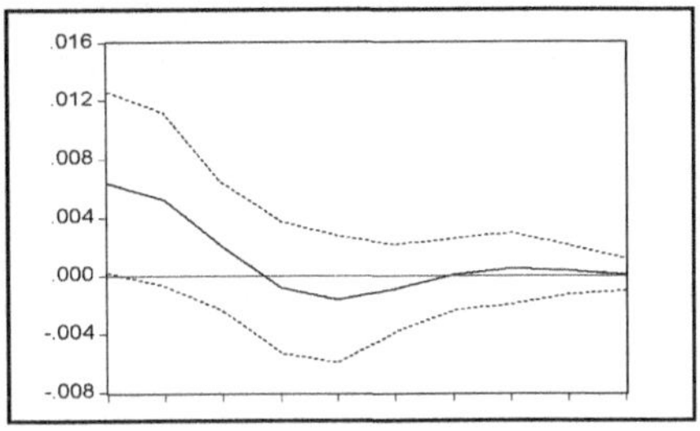

Fig. 5.1.2. The currency indicator impact on Gross Domestic product

significant role in promoting short-term impact, the impact gradually weakened after 2 periods. It showed that the impact of currency risk give the same direction impact, this impact has a significant role in promoting and short-term impacting. That the currency risk have a certain impact on GDP in short time.

3 The Main Conclusion

The paper do Co integration、Granger causality test between the sequence of variables of GDP growth and currency risk indicators. And we do impulse response analysis at same time, this paper get those main conclusions.

1. Analyzed to currency risk indicators and target asset bubbles, we do early warning for China's financial risk profile in 2009.the results reflected that the currency risk indicators, bank risk indicators and target asset bubbles all issued low risk early warning signals.
2. GDP growth and currency risk indicators don't have the simple linear relationship, it cannot descript the accurate relation in each other by using traditional OLS estimation method, at the same time, the GDP% and the other factors, for example, linear relationship between bank indicators and asset indicators is not clear. These factors are not very significant impact On the GDP growth rate.
3. Through the unit root test results, GDP % growth and currency indicator are Non-stationary time series, but through co integration, we can find that it exits a co integration relationship. There is a long-term dynamic equilibrium relationship between them.
4. From Granger causality test and VAR equation, we can see that GDP growth rate and the currency risk have some Correlation, but the Correlation is not large. Currency risk indicators cannot lead to change at GDP growth rate. That cannot explain change at GDP. At same time, the GDP growth rate cannot lead to change at the currency risk indictors.

5. Through further analyze impulse response ,it demonstrated that currency risk have significant role in boosting short-term for China's economic development. But this influence will disappear over time.

References

1. De Gregorio, J.: Inflation, Taxation and Long Run Growth. Journal of Monetary Economics 31(3) (1993)
2. Frankel, J.A., Rose, A.K.: Currency crashes in emerging markets: an empirical treatment. Journal of International Economics 41, 35–66 (1996)
3. Liu, Z.: System of Early Warning Indicators of Financial Crisis. World Economy (April 1999)
4. Liu, Z.: Model Review about Oversea Early Warning of Financial Crises. World Economy (July 2000)
5. Tang, X.: Establishing An Early Warning System of Financial Crisis. Economics Information (June 2002)
6. Feng, Y., Wu, C.: Currency Crisis Early Warning System. Systems Engineering-Theory Methodology Application (January 2002)
7. Zhang, Y., Sun, G.: Theoretical Analysis and Empirical Analysis on Financial Crisis Early Warning System. Studies of International Finance (October 2003)
8. Shi, Z., Mu, X.: Research on China's foreign exchange risk warning———UsingThree Logic Models. Studies of International Finance (July 2005)
9. Chen, S., Yang, Y., Ma, H.: Early Warning of Financial Risks in China. Quantitative Economics (July 2006)
10. Hou, L.: Investigate Relationship on Between GDP and Shanghai Composite Index. Economic Perspective (October 2009)
11. Wang, S.: Study Based on VAR Model between inflation and economic growth. Economic Theory and Business Management (January 2009)
12. Taboga, M.: Macro-finance VARs and Bond Risk Premia: A Caveat. Review of Financial Economics (July 2009)
13. Li, Y., Huo, H.: Correlation Analysis on Stock Market and Real Economy. Forward Position in Economics (June 2009)
14. Shoudon, Ma, C., Ma, C.: Study on China's Financial Risk Early Warning Based on MS-VAR Model and State of The Region. Jilin University Journal (Social Science) (January 2009)
15. Chen, F., Chai, J., Chen, T.: Empirical Study Based on VAR Model between Foreign Trade and Economic Growth. Journal of Xiamen University
16. Jeanne, O., Masson, P.: Currency crises, Sunspots and Markov-switching régimes. Journal of International Economics 50, 327–350 (2000)
17. Chen, Z., Wang, Y.: Two-sided coherent risk measures and their application in realistic portfolio optionzation. Journal of Banking & Finance (June 2008)
18. Levine, R.: Finance and Growth: Theory and Evidence (September 3, 2004)

Research on Professional Talent Training Plan and the Course System of Electric Information Engineering Specialty

Cheng-bo Yu, Ruming Yang, and Rui Li

Research Institute of Remote Test and Control,
Chongqing university of Technology,
400050 Chongqing, China
yuchengbo@cqut.edu.cn, yangrumin@gmail.com,
ruirui881123@yahoo.cn

Abstract. With the development of information technology, the demand of the professional talent of electronic information is higher, and the scientific and reasonable training plan is significant for talents foster. In this paper, the talent training goal and feature for electric information engineering specialty are introduced, the modularizing course system and reform measures are discussed, and the guarantee system on new training plan implementation is proposed.

Keywords: electric information engineering specialty, talent training plan, course system.

1 Introduction

As a kind of information science, the electric information engineering specialty is a new specialty after the ministry of education readjusting the undergraduate specialty of the common colleges, it is the combination of the electronic and computer science specialty. It contains the teaching content of electronic engineering, application of electronic technology, information engineering, wireless technology and information system. This specialty has an extensive applicability and the talent demand is big. In the 21st century, the information infrastructure construction is the key construction of each developed country, and it occupies an important position in China's national economy. With the development of the information technology and related industry, the demand of the professional talent of electronic information is higher. Therefore, we should take measures in widening specialty scope, reforming the personnel training mode, improving the quality of talent training, enlarging professional connotation and strengthening the students' adaptive capacity when make new professional talent training plan. We need to train more high quality electronic information technology talent in the demands of the new situation. According to our school's actual situation and existing advantage, we revised the professional talent training plan and the course system of electric information engineering specialty with the joint efforts of professional teachers in order to make the new talent training plan more scientific and reasonable.

H. Tan and M. Zhou (Eds.): CSE 2011, Part I, CCIS 201, pp. 55–61, 2011.

2 The Specialty Characteristics and Training Objective

The electronic information engineering takes "strengthening basic, broaden the diameter, paying attention to quality and prominent ability" for the principle. According to cultivate students' knowledge, ability, and quality coordinated, they are required to know the basic theory and professional knowledge in the area of electronic technology, computer, information acquisition, transmission, processing, storage and application. Meanwhile, students are received the basic training by electronic technology and engineering practice, then they are equipped with the basic skills of designing, researching, applying and developing the electronic equipment and information system. The training plan pays attention to practice, strengthening the transverse cooperation of factories and research institutes, establishing practice bases, cultivating students' ability of linking theory with practice. In order to improve students' innovation ability and scientific research ability, we use "tutorial system" to guide students to participate in teachers' scientific research. Cultivating the advanced application-oriented engineering and technical personnel with system design ability and manufacturing capability who have solid professional basis and master the knowledge of the latest electronic technology, information processing and storage, information acquisition and processing, information transmission, etc.

The professional training target of electronic and information engineering is: cultivate the talents adapted to the all-round development in the 21st century and make them grasp the basic theory, the professional basic theory, specialty knowledge and practical skills of the electronic technology and information systems, and also make them be engaged in researches, design, manufacturing, application and development of various kinds of electronic equipment and information systems. Therefore, the graduate students should be equipped with the following knowledge and ability: (1)know the professional basic theory, specialty knowledge and practical skills well to be adapt to the needs of this specialty; (2)grasp the basic concept and practice skills of electronic circuit and have the basic ability to analyze and design the electronic equipment;(3)grasp the basic theory and application of the information acquisition, transmission and processing, then have the basic skills to analyze, design and apply the information system; (4)have the fundamental ability to track new theories, new knowledge and new technology in the field of electronic information engineering, and also have the practical ability of scientific research; (5)have the preliminary ability of researching, developing new systems and new technology; (6)grasp the way of literature retrieval and material inquiring, and master a foreign language.

From the above we can see that the electronic information engineering specialty has a widely engineering application background and prospect, the graduates must have the ability of engineering application background. At present the enterprises and research units in China have no conditions to retrain the graduates, so universities should provide students with engineering training opportunities in order to make the graduates have a strong ability to work in a certain field. For this reason, exploring the cultivating of students in the new situation is of great importance.

3 The Basic Framework of Talents Training Plan

Our new revision of the electronic information engineering personnel training plan is made of three platforms and eight curriculum module as shown in table 1. The eight curriculum module system is made of the module included in the three platform, the practice teaching module and the quality education implementation plan.

Table 1.

Serial number	Teaching module	Credit hour	Credit proportion	Class hour	Class hour proportion
1	Public required course module	65.5	33.8%	910	41.7%
2	Public optional course module	8	4.1%	128	5.9%
3	Discipline required course module	28	14.4%	448	20.5%
4	Discipline optional course module	12	6%	192	8.8%
5	Professional required course module	16.5	9.2%	264	12.1%
6	Professional optional course module	15	8.3%	240	11%
7	Centralization practice teaching module	35	17.7%	(560)	—
8	Quality education implementation plan	14	7.2%	—	—
Total		194	100%	2182	100%

3.1 Public Course Platform

Public course platform is opened to the entire school students and offered to cultivate students' comprehensive quality and establish students' comprehensive development. This platform contains the public required course module and the public optional course module.

The public required course module is made of ideological and political theory course, sports, foreign language, mathematics, computer, physics, etc. It aims to cultivate students' application ability of political quality, scientific quality, psychological quality, physical quality, foreign language strengthening and computer application.

Some students have known the basic computer knowledge before they entered the university as the popularity of the computer. So we take layered teaching aim at students in different levels. For example, we organize a test for Fundamentals of Computer in the beginning of one semester and then we depart students into 3 levels: qualified(A), good foundation(B)and bad foundation(C).

Then the students A can achieve this course's credits directly; the students B enter into the class of Fundamentals of Computer A to learn computer hardware and software foundation, website construction, web design and network application knowledge; the students C enter into the class of Fundamentals of Computer B to learn the basic computer overview, operating system based on the Windows XP, office 2003, web design based on FrontPage 2003, multimedia technology foundation and introduction of common software, information system's safety management and social responsibility. We do this can teach students according to their aptitude.

The public optional course module is made of social sciences, natural sciences and literature and art. Every public optional course's credits are less than 2.

3.2 Discipline Course Platform

The discipline course platform is offered to achieve the broad caliber training target and it opens to the most students in this specialty. Its curriculum system construction is a process of optimizing professional structure, widening specialty caliber, integrating the teaching resource and regulating the knowledge system. This platform includes the discipline (professional) required course module and discipline optional course module of the electrical and information engineering.

The discipline (professional) required course module mainly includes discipline foundation courses, technological foundation courses and related discipline foundation courses. And it mainly has the courses of complex-variable function and integral transform, engineering drawing, circuit principle, analog electronic technology, digital electronic technology, electronic experiment, experiment of electrical engineering and electronics, principle and interface technique of micro-computer, principle and interface technique of micro-computer experiment, electrical information professional English.

The discipline optional course module further widens the specialty caliber, enlarges the scope of knowledge and makes students understand the development forefront and other professional courses in this specialty. The total credit score is 1.5 to 2 times multiple of the credit score should be learned. In this module, we set up the courses of field theory and vector analysis, EDA technology, object Oriented Programming, EMC, theory and Application of SCM, DSP techniques and application, the design and application of embedded systems, electronics synthesis experiment. And considering the capacity of a class and making students choose their class more convenient according to their own actual situation, we roll over some of the classes, such as EDA technology, EMC, theory and Application of SCM, DSP techniques and application and the design and application of embedded systems.

3.3 Professional Course Module

The professional course platform is offered to realize the training objectives of this specialty and it opens to the students in this specialty. It contains the professional required course module and the professional optional course module. The curriculum settings should both complying with the request of the ministry of education according to the undergraduate subject catalogues, and should reflect the characteristics and advantages of electronic information engineering. We emphasize high quality selected when setting up the professional required courses and cutting-edge and characteristic when in the professional optional courses.

The professional required course module mainly offers the most important courses in the field of the automation major and reflects the characteristic of this specialty best. It sets up the courses of high-frequency electronic circuit, signal and system, information and coding, communications theory, digital signal processing, electronic measurement and transducers and electronic information comprehensive professional experiment. This module integrates the experiment courses and opens up the verification, comprehensive and designing experiments.

The professional optional course module mainly offers the courses which can make students grasp the latest knowledge with professional characteristics. It contains the courses of information science and technology introduction, electromagnetic field and wave, automatic control theory, computer network, optoelectronic technology, optical fiber communication technology, digital communication principle, the optical fiber sensing technology, communication protocol development and application, access network and intelligent network technology, mobile communication, electronic information system modeling and simulation, embedded operating system and application, database principle and application, the algorithm and the data structure, the development and practice of electronic information system. We offer the courses of IST information science and technology in the second semester. Several teachers combine their research and teaching with them to introduce the development of the IST information science and technology, the basic situation and research fields of electronic and information engineering specialty, the application of IST information science and technology in each area, the characteristic of this specialty and questions the students should pay attention to through the form of lectures. And it makes students have a preliminary and comprehensive understanding to this specialty. Moreover, other professional optional courses are offered at the 6th and 7th semester in order to make students can widen their specialty knowledge on the basis of ensuring their study on the professional required courses.

3.4 Centralization Practice Teaching Module

The centralization practice teaching module is set up to cultivate students' analytical and solving ability to the practical engineering problems or real-life problems, and it also cultivate students' project practice ability, analysis and comprehensive ability, cooperation spirit and innovative consciousness in a strong way. The detailed setting includes a military training, engineering training, course exercise in electronic technology, production practice, the integrated application design of SIP, the integrated design of electronic information engineering and graduation design (including the graduation fieldwork). The segment of engineering training includes the basic training of machinery manufacturing and electronic skill training, and it is designed to cultivate students' practical engineering skills and improve their practical ability. In addition, in order to realize the consistency and practicability, we reform the teaching link of curriculum design in the centralization practice teaching module. After the computer courses, there are two weeks' segments of the integrated application design of SIP at the 7th semester and it mainly consolidate students' hold on knowledge of micro computer systems' work principle, interface technology and programming method and can also use these knowledge synthetically. Then we set up three weeks' segments of the integrated design of electronic information engineering to apply the computer knowledge to digital signal processing and electronic equipment with the basics of computer application, and then complete the design, analog, execution and test. It can form the foundation for the graduation design and make the curriculum design to implement.

3.5 Quality Education Implementation Plan

This module offers the optional courses which can promote students' comprehensive quality development through their individual difference, individuality and specialty. It takes the way of "rolling opened and dynamic management" and can lift life quality and personality taste. This module mainly includes three types: A. social sciences (such as history and culture, philosophy and ideology, economic management and law); B. natural sciences (such as engineering and general technology); C. literature and art (such as literature and appreciation, art and sport).

4 The Safeguard Measures of Talent Training Plan

(1)In the new talent training plan, we take the tutorial system and let tutors guide students to take the course and learn the professional knowledge, thus can avoid the blindness of the students. At the same time, they will guide students to join some scientific research, cultivate students' learning ability, practice ability and scientific research ability and then increase students' comprehensive quality.

(2)Reform the traditional teaching module and study the suitable teaching module which can combine IT with the course. For example, the visual teaching mode for the combination of multimedia and real object, the inquiry teaching mode for the combination of virtual experiment and theory, the interactive teaching mode for the combination of network environment and classroom teaching", etc. At present, the ongoing research projects are "the research on the new mode of the network information technology's teaching and learning" which belongs to the research (key) project of Chongqing higher education teaching reformations, "the research and practice on the virtual experiment teaching platform of information processing course group" which belongs to the experimental technology development fund project of Chongqing University of Technology, "the research and practice on the teaching mode of the integration of IT and courses" which belongs to the higher education research project of Chongqing University of Technology.

(3)In order to provide an important guarantee to the teaching, we pay attention to textbooks' construction, writing, and then choose the suitable textbooks for the IT environment. The textbook sensor and automatic detecting technology is the research achievements of education science "the 15th" national planning research, and it won the first prize in the national university of excellent textbooks and the first prize in college's excellent textbooks. Then signal and system, the key to exercises and experiment guidance of signal and system (the second edition), digital signal processing with the MATLAB and information theory and coding were written. These textbooks provide examples and experimental subjects for the MATLAB.

5 Conclusions

As electronic information technology is developing with each passing day and the talent demands of the society is also changing, these put forward higher requirement for the undergraduate education of electronic information which undertake the tasks of cultivating talents. Only should we keep pace with the times, reform the teaching mode of electronic information engineering specialty continually, construct the teaching system which combine the theory teaching and practical teaching, coalesce the theory teaching, practical teaching and engineering teaching and strengthen the cultivation of students' engineering practice skills, can we convey more excellent electronic information technology talents to our country's economic construction.

Acknowledgmet. This article belongs to educational reform research key project of Chongqing higher education(No.0824077).

References

1. Xiong, Q., Chen, H., et al.: The exploration and practice for the construction of electronic engineering information. Journal of Wuhan University of Science and Technology 10(2), 69–72 (2008)
2. Zeng, X., Sun, K.: The exploration and practice to cultivate scientific students' innovation ability. Higher Science Education 65(1), 97–99 (2006)
3. Liu, W., Huan, X., Chen, A.: The research and practice for the training mode of electronic information engineering specialty. Journal of Hunan Engineering College 16(1), 80–81, 87 (2006)

A Secure Network Access Approach Based on Heterogeneous Key Exchange Protocol

Yingjie Xia, Li Kuang, and Kuang Mao

Hangzhou Institute of Service Engineering, Hangzhou Normal University,
310012 Hangzhou, P.R. China
{xiayingjie,kuangli,mbill}@zju.edu.cn

Abstract. This paper proposes an efficient and secure inner network access approach which is based on a heterogeneous Diffie-Hellman key exchange protocol in an unsecured network. The inner and outer network structure is commonly applied in various areas, such as different departments of government, enterprises. As the wireless communication network boosts up, the users in outer network try to use PDA, smart phone to access the inner network to acquire necessary information. Due to the limitation of the storage and computational capability of these mobile terminals, traditional secure inner network access approach which uses special cable to do the access is not suitable for this case. Therefore, we design a heterogeneous key exchange protocol for the mobile terminal in outer network and application server in inner network to negotiate the communication shared key. The gateway between inner and outer network can be protected from the third party attack by the trusted computing. The experimental results show that the heterogeneous key exchange protocol is efficient and secure for inner network access.

Keywords: Heterogeneous Diffie-Hellman key exchange protocol, network access, ECC, ElGamal.

1 Introduction

Nowadays, many enterprises and departments of government have already built their inner network security infrastructure based on public key infrastructure (PKI) or privilege management infrastructure (PMI). The secure authentication to the users who request to access the inner network can effectively prevent different kinds of access intrusion and malicious attack. Along with the development of wireless communication network, more and more mobile applications require terminals like PDA or smart cell phone as the nodes for information acquirement from inner network. However, the PKI/PMI-based security infrastructure used in special cable network can not easily be transplanted to the wireless communication network, because of its limitations of small bandwidth, wide data openness and little storage capacity of the terminal. However, most of current inner network access technologies are based on the special cable network. Therefore, in order to make various mobile terminals securely and efficiently access the resources on the application server in inner network, it is significant to design a secure, trusted and high-efficiency inner network access approach.

H. Tan and M. Zhou (Eds.): CSE 2011, Part I, CCIS 201, pp. 62–69, 2011.

The encryption of the data communication is a key approach to ensure the security of the communication between the inner and outer network. Many algorithms can be used to encrypt the communicated data, such as RSA, Elliptic Curve Cryptography [1], Diffie-Hellman key exchange [3], etc. They can be chose according to different trade-off between efficiency and security. Diffie-Hellman protocol can generate a new key through the secure exchange of keys in unsecured network. Thus, the mobile terminal and application server can negotiate their public shared key through their own private key and public key transmitted by the gateway between inner and outer network. Traditional isomorphic Diffie-Hellman requires both key exchange sides to use the same secret key pair generation algorithm. In our mobile terminal application, since the transmission medium of inner and outer networks are different, the secret key pair generation algorithm used in inner network does not fit for the mobile terminal in outer wireless communication network due to its limitations on computation capability and storage capacity. In this paper, we design a heterogeneous Diffie-Hellman key exchange protocol which allows the two key exchange sides to use different key generation algorithm. Because ECC has the advantages of high security, small storage capacity and low computation complexity, the mobile terminal use ECC to generate the key pair while the application server uses the ElGamal [2].

The authentication of the mobile terminal and the application server is another key mechanism to determine the accessibility on the application server in inner network. In wireless communication network, the mobile terminal usually initiates the key exchange process and aims at the application server in inner network. However, in the Diffie-Hellman key exchange process, block attack by sending a mass of key exchanges requests, such as distributed denial of service (DDoS), can cause the application server wasting a lot of resources doing useless work. Therefore, in our inner network access approach, we choose proper types of public key certificates for the mobile terminal and application server respectively, and use an authentication system which regards wireless gateway as a medium to authenticate the mobile terminal and application server.

This paper demonstrates an inner network access approach based on a heterogeneous Diffie-Hellman (HD-H) key exchange protocol and a public key certificate authentication technology. The rest of the paper is organized as follows. Section 2 introduces our network structure including inner network, network boundary and outer network, and the general communication sequence among the mobile terminal, trusted gateway and the application server. Section 3 describes the heterogeneous Diffie-Hellman key exchange protocol. Section 4 introduces the authentication and authorization process for the mobile terminal. In section 5, we draw a conclusion on our inner network access technology and plan some future work.

2 Network Structure and Communication Sequence

In this section, we demonstrate the main framework of our inner network access technology, as depicted in Fig. 1. Our network structure is based on the combination of wireless network and wired network. According to different roles, the network structure consists of three parts: outer network, network boundary and inner network.

The trusted gateway [9] in network boundary is responsible for the transmission of the keys, the authentication of the certificates and the authorization of the mobile terminal.

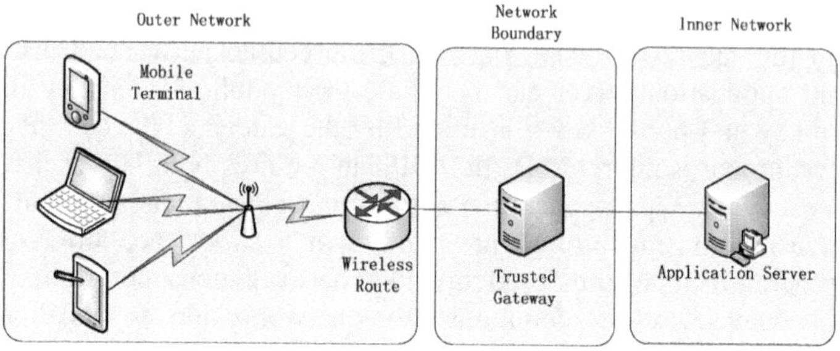

Fig. 1. Framework of inner network access approach

Fig. 2 shows the communication between mobile terminal and application server by trusted gateway. Every legal mobile terminal needs to request a digital signature from the trusted gateway as part of its certificate. The mobile terminal integrates ECC algorithm to generate the public-private key pair *(C_{pu}, C_{pr})* and the application server in inner network uses ElGamal algorithm to generate the public-private key pair *(S_{pu}, S_{pr})*. Both public keys are used in the Diffie-Hellman key-distribution algorithm.

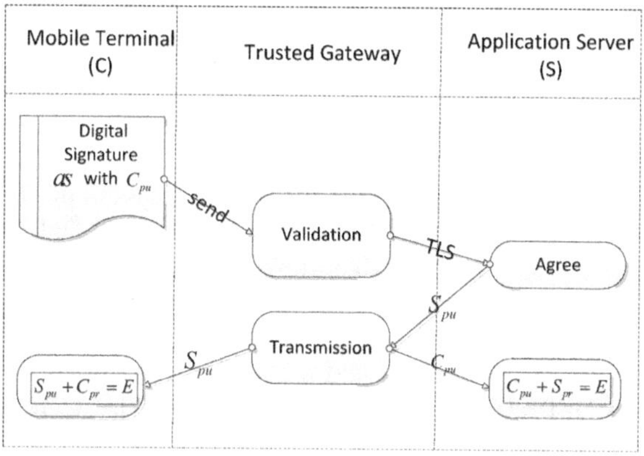

Fig. 2. Communication between mobile terminal and application server by trusted gateway

The mobile terminal sends its certificate which contains the public key and digital signature to the trusted gateway. The trusted gateway validates the digital signature to determine the validity of the mobile terminal. If the terminal is legal, a secure data communication channel will be built between the mobile terminal and trusted gateway. After that, the trusted gateway sends a TLS connection request to the application server and begins to use Diffie-Hellman key exchange protocol. When the application server agrees with the trusted gateway, it sends its public key S_{pu} to the trusted gateway and receives the mobile terminal's public key C_{pu} from the trusted gateway. S_{pu} is directly sent to the mobile terminal. In the end, according to the Diffie-Hellman key exchange protocol, the mobile terminal and application server can negotiate a shared key E which can be used to encrypt the communication data between them.

3 Heterogeneous Diffie-Hellman Key Exchange Protocol

In this section, the details of HD-H key exchange protocol will be introduced. In HD-H, the two public keys used in generating the shared key are created by the ECC and ElGamal algorithms respectively. Since both cryptographies use the same cyclic group, the shared key can be generated using the Diffie-Hellman shared key generated process. Therefore, these two sides can successfully generate the same shared key to encrypt the communication data between them.

3.1 ECC Key Pair Generation Protocol

Elliptic Curve Cryptosystems (ECC) is a famous public-key cryptography based on the algebraic structure of elliptic curves over finite fields. The mobile terminals such as PDA, cell phones have the limitation on computational capability and storage. And ECC only needs less storage but can get high security performance. Therefore, ECC is well fit for the mobile terminal as the key generation algorithm on one side of HD-H.

The following describes the process of generating the public and private key pair for mobile terminal:

(a) Choose a finite field $F(q)$ and an elliptic curve $E_p(a,b)$, and randomly select a base point g;
(b) Randomly generate a bit sequence C_{pr} as the private key;
(c) Calculate the public key $C_{pu}= C_{pr}*g$.

where C_{pr} is private information and $E_p(a,b)$, C_{pu}, g are the public information known by everyone. g and $E_p(a,b)$ will be sent together with the digital signature containing C_{pu} to the trusted gateway, and finally reaches the application server in the inner network.

3.2 ElGamal Key Pair Generation Protocol

The ElGamal encryption system is an asymmetric key encryption algorithm in public key cryptography. It can be defined over any cyclic group and the public and private key generation is one of its parts. The application server in inner network use ElGamal key generator to generate the public and private key pair. Since the cyclic group of ECC is also Decisional Diffie-Hellman (DDH) hardness, the cyclic group of ECC can be used in ElGamal.

The following describes the process of generating the public and private key pair for application server:

(a) Receive the mobile terminal's $E_p(a,b)$ and g;

(b) Use the same cyclic group as ECC through generator g;
(c) Randomly choose a number sequence S_{pr} as the application server's private key;
(d) Compute $S_{pu}= S_{pr}*g$, $S_{pu} \in E_p(a,b)$ as the application server's public key;

where S_{pu} is the public information and S_{pr} is the private information kept by the application server itself. S_{pu} will be sent to the mobile terminal.

3.3 Generation of Shared Key

After the key exchange process between mobile terminal and application server, they need to establish a shared key to encrypt the communication data. Since the key pair generation process of the two different encryption algorithms are under the same cyclic group, the two key pairs are well suitable for the generation of shared key. The mobile terminal's key pair is (C_{pr},C_{pu}) and the application server's secret key pair is (S_{pr},S_{pu}). Each side has the public key of the other side. We can generate the shared key S as follows:

(a) Mobile terminal: $S= C_{pr} * S_{pu} = C_{pr} * S_{pr} *g$;
(b) Application server: $S= S_{pr} * C_{pu} = S_{pr} * C_{pr} *g$;

where both sides have the same generator g, and they will generate the same shared key. The generation process is secure because nothing is disclosed. In the following section, we will analyze the security of this key exchange protocol in detail.

3.4 Security Analysis

The heterogeneous Diffie-Hellman key exchange protocol is based on the traditional Diffie-Hellman key exchange protocol. It is currently considered difficult for the eavesdropper to solve the traditional Diffie-Hellman problem to obtain C_{pr} and S_{pr} which can be used to calculate the shared key. Though the discrete logarithm problem makes the computation of the C_{pr} and S_{pr} easily, it is more difficult to get the C_{pr} and S_{pr} in our heterogeneous Diffie-Hellman key exchange protocol due to the private and public key pair generation process not only uses ElGamal encryption system but also performs ECC to generate the key pair. This heterogeneous key generation approach is far more difficult to crack.

However, the communication between mobile terminal and application server is still vulnerable to a man-in-the-middle attack. A malicious person in the gateway may establish two distinct key exchanges, thus the third party is able to get the communication data. This problem can be solved by the trusted gateway.

4 Mobile Terminal Authentication and Authorization

Before the trusted gateway transmits the information of mobile terminal, it is necessary to validate its legality. This validation prevents DDoS attack that the illegal mobile terminal request a mass of key exchange behavior with the application server, causing the legal mobile terminal unable to accomplish the key exchange process.

Along with the development of Wireless Public Key Infrastructure (WPKI) [4], wireless network environment begins to form a standard certificate and key management framework. WPKI is the optimization and extension of public key infrastructure in order to adapt for the wireless environment [5]. Since WPKI always uses WTLS [6] as its authentication protocol, we replace the traditional X509 certificate with the WTLS certificate for mobile terminal [7, 8]. The advantages of less storage and less computation match the features of mobile terminal.

The trusted gateway takes the responsibility of Certificate Authority (CA) and authorizes all legal mobile terminals. When CA authorizes a mobile terminal a, it requires a to generate a public-private key pair (C_{pr},C_{pu}) using ECC algorithm. The CA uses a's public key and its identity information to generate a digital certificate *ac*. This digital certificate *ac* is public and held by a.

After the generation of ECC key pair(C_{pr},C_{pu}), the mobile terminal a uses its private key C_{pr} to encrypt the digital certificate *ac* and get a digital signature *as*. Then a sends the *as* together with the public key C_{pu} to the trusted gateway. Trusted gateway decrypts the *as* with C_{pu}. If the result is the same as the identity information in *ac*, the mobile terminal is proved as a legal terminal. Then, the trusted gateway can transmit a's public key C_{pu} to the application server to begin the Diffie-Hellman key exchange process described in section 3.

5 Experimental Results

In this section, we demonstrate the effectiveness using the trusted gateway to prevent the block attack such as DDos. The experiment is setup under the real inner and outer network structure. Our mobile terminal is a PDA installed Windows Mobile 6 System where we implement the ECC key pair generation algorithm. The mobile terminal contains the certificate signed by the trusted gateway. ElGamal encryption system is implemented on the application server of a 2.93GHz CPU and 2GB memory desktop computer in the inner network. The trusted gateway is responsible for the authentication and authorization of the mobile terminal. It also takes charge of transmitting the communication data and keys.

Through the certification of the mobile terminals, DDoS attack can be avoided by preventing a large amount of key exchange between illegal mobile terminals and application server. However, the trusted gateway will still receive a large amount of key exchange requests from legal mobile terminals which will affect its response. We just use a common desktop computer as our trusted gateway. In Fig. 3 (a), the authentication response time of the trusted gateway, the key exchange duration with and without trusted gateway which begins from the key exchange request sending by the mobile terminal and end with the shared key generated moment is shown while the number of the legal and illegal visitors of mobile terminal increases. The authentication response time increases due to the concurrent access to the trusted gateway, but it increases slower. The key exchange duration is similar as the authentication response time of the trusted gateway, because for one mobile terminal the key exchange duration is mostly affected by the response time of the trusted gateway. In addition, the big gap between the key exchange duration with and without trusted gateway shows that the trusted gateway successfully prevents the DDoS attack by refusing a large amount of illegal mobile terminals' requests.

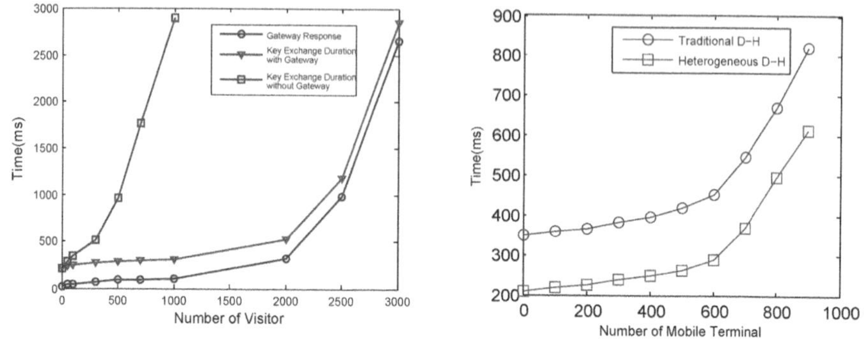

(a) Authentication response time and key exchange duration

(b) Key exchange duration of traditional and heterogeneous Diffie-Hellman

Fig. 3. Experimental results

We also simulate to experiment the relationship between the legal mobile terminals and the key exchange duration time. Fig. 3 (b) illustrates the key exchange duration of traditional Diffie-Hellman key exchange protocol using RSA and the heterogeneous Diffie-Hellman key exchange protocol using ECC and ElGamal as the number of legal mobile terminal increases. The results show that the heterogeneous Diffie-Hellman key exchange process is more efficient than the traditional Diffie-Hellman key exchange process for the reason that the mobile terminal uses ECC instead of the more-time-consuming algorithm RSA. Furthermore, it can still afford to deal with a large amount of mobile terminals' key exchange requests using one application server.

6 Conclusion and Future Work

In this paper, we propose a novel inner network access approach for the heterogeneous network structure. The approach is based on heterogeneous Diffie-Hellman key exchange protocol, which uses ECC and ElGamal to generate the key pairs on the mobile terminal and application server respectively. Since both sides generate the keys under the same cyclic group, the shared key is negotiated to encrypt the communication data. We also build a CA on the trusted gateway for the authentication and authorization to prevent the attacks like DDoS. The experimental results show that the trusted gateway can greatly prevent the block attack and the heterogeneous Diffie-Hellman key exchange process is also more efficient than the traditional Diffie-Hellman key exchange process.

In the future work, we plan to use identity-based encryption (IBE) to take the place of certificate-based encryption because IBE can help save storage and make authentication and authorization more secure. Moreover, we will also try to extend heterogeneous Diffie-Hellman key exchange protocol to use some other cryptography methods besides ECC and ElGamal.

Acknowledgments. This research work is supported by Science and Technology Planning Project of Zhejiang Province under grant number 2010C31018, and Scientific Research Fund of Hangzhou Normal University under grant number HSKQ0042. The authors also do appreciate the helpful assistance from Fubiao Xia in University of Birmingham.

References

1. Koblitz, N.: Elliptic curve cryptosystems. Mathematics of Computation 48, 203–209 (1987)
2. ElGamal, T.: A Public-Key Cryptosystem and a Signature Scheme Based on Discrete Logarithms. IEEE Transactions on Information Theory 31(4), 469–472 (1985), doi:10.1109/TIT.1985.1057074
3. Hellman, D.: http://en.wikipedia.org/wiki/Diffie%E2%80%93Hellman_key_exchange#cite_note-0
4. WAP Forum: WAP 2.0 Technical White Paper, http://www.wapforum.org/what/WAPWhite_Paper1.pdf
5. WAP Forum: WAP public key infrastructure definition, http://www1.wapforum.org/tech/documents/WAP-217-WPKI-20010424-a.pdf
6. WAP Forum: WAP certificate and CRL profiles, http://www1.wapforum.org/tech/documents/WAP-211-WAPCert-20010522-a.pdf
7. WAP Forum. Wireless Transport Layer Security Specification, http://www1.wapforum.org/tech/documents/WAP-199-WTLS-20000218-a.pdf
8. Trask, N.T., Jaweed, S.A.: Adapting public key infrastructures to the mobile environment. BT Technology Journal 19(3), 76–80 (2001)
9. Berger, B.: Guide to Trusted Computing. Computer Technology Review (May 2008)

Algorithm for Inverse Kinematics Model Based on Projection Method

Liangji Chen and Huiying Li*

Zhengzhou Institute of Aeronautical Industry Management
450015 Zhengzhou, China
{chenjiaxiclj,lihuiying.lhy}@163.com

Abstract. In order to implement the five-axis high-speed and high-accuracy machining on a computer numerically controlled (CNC) machine tools, the cutter location and orientation data need to be converted to the 5 coordinates of machine by CAD/CAM system. These data to be converted are defined with respect to the coordinate system of work-piece, and they need to be converted to the machine's control commands in machine coordinate system. The kinematics chain of a typical five-axis milling machine of table rotating and tilting type has been introduced in this paper, and then an inverse kinematics model and an efficient algorithm for the model have been presented finally. The real use has been demonstrated to validate the feasibility of the proposed method.

Keywords: CNC, 5-axis, kinematics model.

1 Introduction

At present, five-axis machining, which has high efficiency and quality, is the more widely adopted technology for manufacturing valuable parts of complex 3D sculptured surfaces, such as in aerospace, automotive, and die/mold industries. In order to manufacture the machined surface correctly, the cutter location (CL) data which includes the position and orientation of the cutter, must be transformed to the CNC codes. Since these CL data are defined with respect to the work-piece coordinate system, they need converting for machine control commands defined in machine coordinate system, through a processing so called as a NC post-processing. It can be accomplished through a series of transformation among coordinate systems at machine elements, which are similar to arms of robot.

Essentially, the NC machine requires its own special postprocessor which is designed according to the kinematics model of that NC machine. Various studies have addressed the issue of developing post-processors for machine tools. Suh et al. [1] developed a program for simultaneous motion of five-axis machine. Kruth and Kelwais [2] developed a program of interference free with the modification of the CL by simulating NC data that are post-processed. Sakamoto and Inasaki[3] classified the

* Corresponding author.

H. Tan and M. Zhou (Eds.): CSE 2011, Part I, CCIS 201, pp. 70–77, 2011.

configuration of commercial five -axis machines into three types. Lee and She [4] derived analytical equation of inverse kinematics for generating NC data of the models by Sakamoto and Inasaki.

The five-axis machines have operation limits in more than one rotating axis. Any post-processor that is able to handle the operation limit is not available in the above works. Mean-while, most commercial CAD/CAM software vendors who are capable of generating tool path data for five-axis machining provide these post-processors for several types of five-axis machines. However, they may cause some erroneous operation during phase reverse process that is due to unsymmetrical operation limits about rotating axes. This work aims to develop efficient algorithms for NC post-processor for five-axis milling machine.

2 Kinematics Model of Machine

Fig.1 shows a typical five-axis milling machine of table-rotating/tilting type that is widely adopted for machining small and medium size parts. A generalized five-axis kinematics model will be developed here to deal with most of the common five-axis machining problems. The kinematics elements of the machine consist of the work-piece, the C-axis rotational disc, the B-axis rotational table, the Y-axis linear table, the machine fixed bed, the X-axis linear table, the Z-axis linear table, the spindle, and the cutter.

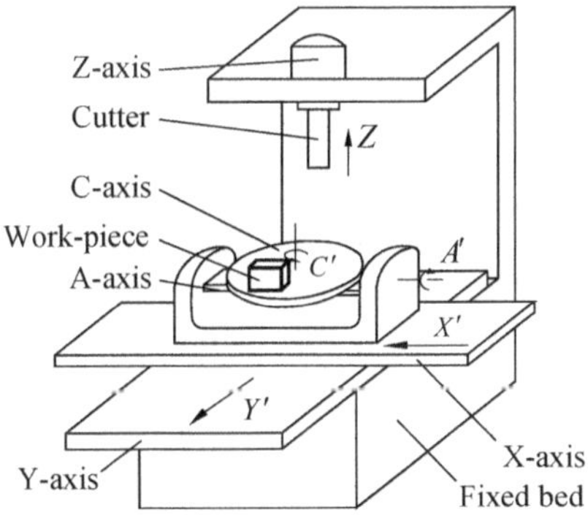

Fig. 1. A five-axis milling machine of table rotating/tilting type

The five-axis machine shown in Fig.1 can be seen as two open kinematics chains, including the side of cutter and the side of the work-piece. The chain of cutter side is sequentially composed of machine fixed bed, Z-axis and the cutter and the chain of work-piece side is orderly including fixed bed, Y-axis, X-axis, A-axis, C-axis and the work-piece. As shown in Fig.2, the coordinate systems of m, y, x, a, c, w and t are established on the fixed bed, Y-axis, X-axis, A axis, C-axis, the work-piece and the cutting tool, respectively.

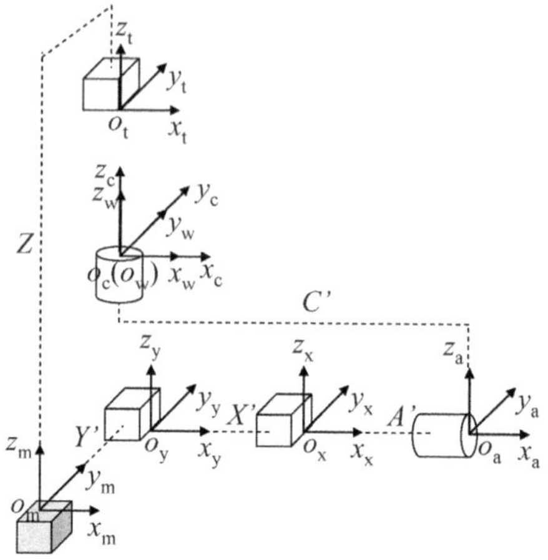

Fig. 2. Kinematics chains and coordinate systems

The D-H matrix of the chain of cutter side, that is, the coordination transformation matrix between the t coordinate system and the m coordinate system can be represented as

$$ {}^{\mathrm{m}}_{\mathrm{t}}\boldsymbol{T} = \begin{pmatrix} 1 & 0 & 0 & 0 \\ 0 & 1 & 0 & 0 \\ 0 & 0 & 1 & a+b+Z \\ 0 & 0 & 0 & 1 \end{pmatrix}, \tag{1} $$

where Z is control command of Z axis of machine, a and b be the distances from tool-tip point and intersection point of A and C axis to the plane of work-table at the initial time, respectively. Assumed that the origin point of the m coordinate system is the intersection point of A and C axis, so, the tool-tip point and the tool-axis vector in the m coordinate system can be respectively calculated as

$$ \boldsymbol{O}_{\mathrm{m}} = {}^{\mathrm{m}}_{\mathrm{t}}\boldsymbol{T} \cdot (0 \quad 0 \quad 0 \quad 1)^{\mathrm{T}} = (0 \quad 0 \quad a+b+Z \quad 1)^{\mathrm{T}} \tag{2} $$

and

$$ \boldsymbol{L}_{\mathrm{m}} = {}^{\mathrm{m}}_{\mathrm{t}}\boldsymbol{T} \cdot (0 \quad 0 \quad 1 \quad 0)^{\mathrm{T}} = (0 \quad 0 \quad 1 \quad 0)^{\mathrm{T}}. \tag{3} $$

The coordination transformation matrix between the m coordinate system and the w coordinate system can be represented as follows

$$ {}^{\mathrm{w}}_{\mathrm{m}}\boldsymbol{T} = {}^{\mathrm{w}}_{\mathrm{c}}\boldsymbol{T} \cdot {}^{\mathrm{c}}_{\mathrm{a}}\boldsymbol{T} \cdot {}^{\mathrm{a}}_{\mathrm{x}}\boldsymbol{T} \cdot {}^{\mathrm{x}}_{\mathrm{y}}\boldsymbol{T} \cdot {}^{\mathrm{y}}_{\mathrm{m}}\boldsymbol{T} \tag{4} $$

Through the above calculation, the matrix ${}^{\mathrm{w}}_{\mathrm{m}}\boldsymbol{T}$ has the following expression

$$ {}^{\mathrm{w}}_{\mathrm{m}}\boldsymbol{T} = \begin{pmatrix} \cos C' & -\cos A' \sin C' & \sin A' \sin C' & X' \cos C' - Y' \cos A' \sin C' \\ \sin C' & \cos A' \cos C' & -\sin A' \cos C' & X' \sin C' + Y' \cos A' \cos C' \\ 0 & \sin A' & \cos A' & Y' \sin A' - b \\ 0 & 0 & 0 & 1 \end{pmatrix} \tag{5} $$

where *X'*, *Y'*, *A'* and *C'* are control commands of X, Y, A, and C axes of machine, respectively.

After giving a set of D-H parameters(*X'*, *Y'*, *Z*, *A'* and *C'* here), Eqs.6 can be used to compute the position and direction vectors of t relative to w coordinate system as follows

$$\boldsymbol{O}_{\mathrm{w}}={}^{\mathrm{w}}_{\mathrm{m}}\boldsymbol{T}\cdot\boldsymbol{O}_{\mathrm{m}} \tag{6}$$

and

$$\boldsymbol{L}_{\mathrm{w}}={}^{\mathrm{w}}_{\mathrm{m}}\boldsymbol{T}\cdot\boldsymbol{L}_{\mathrm{m}}\,. \tag{7}$$

However, the postprocessor should compute the D-H parameters from the input CL data ($\boldsymbol{O}_{\mathrm{w}}$ and $\boldsymbol{L}_{\mathrm{w}}$ here) relative to w coordinate system. This is the problem of the inverse kinematics.

3 Postprocessor of the Machine

Let the CL data to be calculated be

$$(o_{\mathrm{x}},o_{\mathrm{y}},o_{\mathrm{z}},l_{\mathrm{x}},l_{\mathrm{y}},l_{\mathrm{z}}),$$

where $(o_{\mathrm{x}},o_{\mathrm{y}},o_{\mathrm{z}})$ and $(l_{\mathrm{x}},l_{\mathrm{y}},l_{\mathrm{z}})$ denote the tool-tip point coordination and the tool-axis orientation vector in the w coordinate system respectively. Apparently, we have the following eqution

$$\sqrt{(l_{\mathrm{x}})^2+(l_{\mathrm{y}})^2+(l_{\mathrm{z}})^2}=1.$$

That is,

$$\boldsymbol{O}_{\mathrm{w}}=\begin{pmatrix} o_{\mathrm{x}} \\ o_{\mathrm{y}} \\ o_{\mathrm{z}} \\ 1 \end{pmatrix}={}^{\mathrm{w}}_{\mathrm{m}}\boldsymbol{T}\cdot\begin{pmatrix} 0 \\ 0 \\ a+b+Z \\ 1 \end{pmatrix}=$$

$$\begin{pmatrix} (a+b+Z)\sin A'\sin C'+X'\cos C'-Y'\cos A'\sin C' \\ -(a+b+Z)\sin A'\cos C'+X'\sin C'+Y'\cos A'\cos C' \\ (a+b+Z)\cos A'+Y'\sin A'-b \\ 1 \end{pmatrix} \tag{8}$$

and

$$\boldsymbol{L}_{\mathrm{w}}=\begin{pmatrix} l_{\mathrm{x}} \\ l_{\mathrm{y}} \\ l_{\mathrm{z}} \\ 0 \end{pmatrix}={}^{\mathrm{w}}_{\mathrm{m}}\boldsymbol{T}\cdot\begin{pmatrix} 0 \\ 0 \\ 1 \\ 0 \end{pmatrix}=\begin{pmatrix} \sin A'\sin C' \\ -\sin A'\cos C' \\ \cos A' \\ 0 \end{pmatrix}. \tag{9}$$

A' and *C'* must fulfill the limitation angles of the corresponding machine rotational axes, i.e. $-90° \leq A' \leq 90°$, and $-360° \leq C' \leq 360°$. Note that, by comparing the sign of l_x, l_y and l_z, the value of *A'* and *C'* are taken into account which quadrant the tool-axis direction vector is in.

According to the structure of five-axis machine tool shown in Fig.1, there are the following cases about the sign of l_x, l_y and l_z ($l_z > 0$ for any CL data).

Case1: if l_x and l_y are equal to zero, l_z must be equal to 1, that is, the cutter's axis is parallel to the Z-axis and the projection line of the axis to the XY-plane is a point as shown in Fig.3;

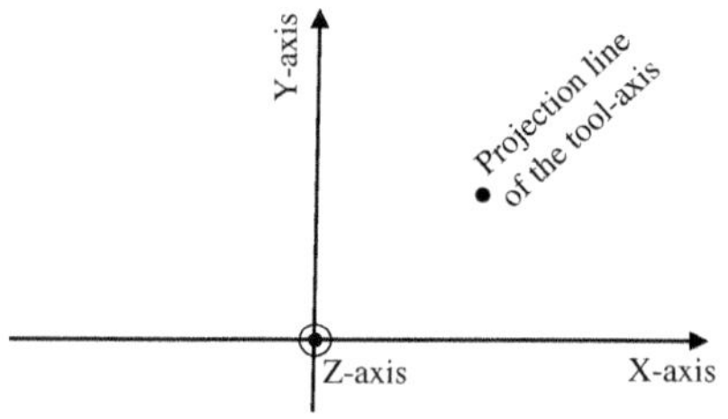

Fig. 3. Projection line of the tool-axis in case 1

Case2: if l_x is equal to zero, the cutter's axis should be parallel to the YZ-plane and the projection line is as depicted in Fig.4;

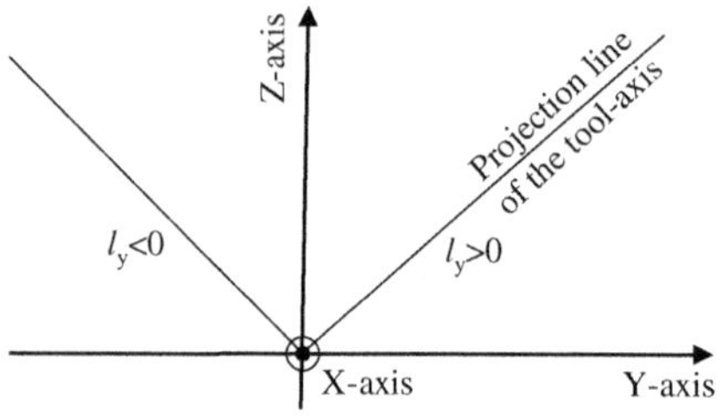

Fig. 4. Projection line of the tool-axis in case 2

Case3: if l_y is equal to zero, the cutter's axis is parallel to the XZ-plane (Fig.5);

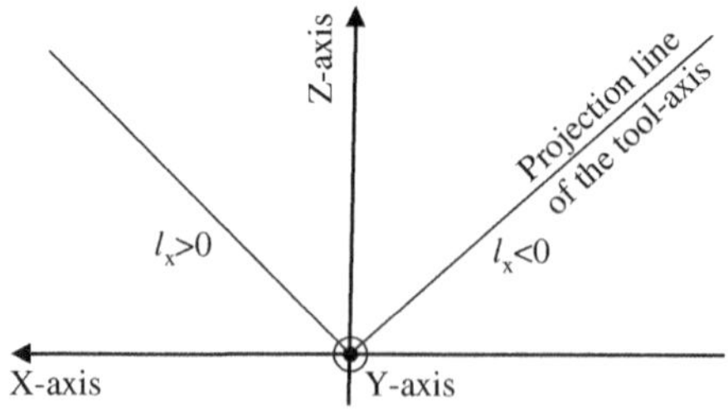

Fig. 5. Projection line of the tool-axis in case 3

Case4: the others is that l_x and l_y are all not equal to zero(Fig.6);

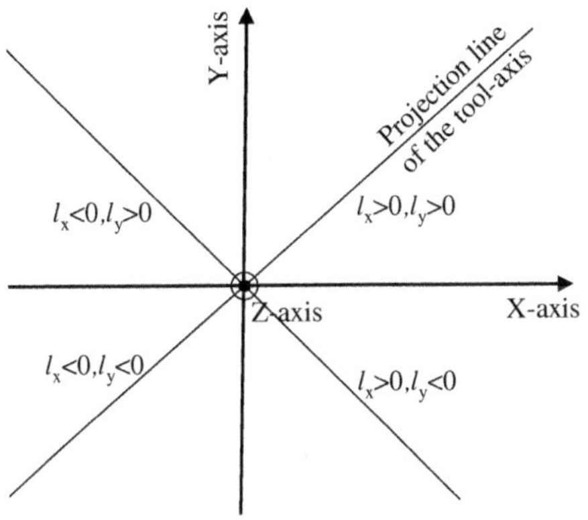

Fig. 6. Projection line of the tool-axis in case 4

At first, the rotating and tilting angles will be taken into account:

(a) For case 1, the cutter's direction vector coincides with Z-axis of the five-axis machine, so, the A-axis and the C-axis tables need not rotate or tilt. We will have

$$A' = 0, C' = 0 \tag{10}$$

(b) For case 2, the cutter's axis has already been parallel to the YZ-plane, accordingly, the C-axis need not rotate and only the A-axis has a tilting angle. We have the following result according to Eq.(9)

$$A' = \arcsin(-l_y), C' = 0 \tag{11}$$

(c) For case 3, in order that the cutter's axis is parallel to the YZ-plane, there should be a rotating angle about Z-axis. Thus, the C-axis need rotate a right angle and the A-axis has a tilting angle. The following result can be obtained

$$A' = \arcsin(\pm l_x), C' = \pm 90^\circ \tag{12}$$

(d) For case 4, rotating a C' angle around Z-axis and then tilting an A' angle around A-axis, we will yield

$$\begin{aligned} A' &= \arccos(l_z) \\ C' &= \begin{cases} \arccos(-l_y / \sin A') & \text{if } l_x > 0 \\ 360^\circ - \arccos(-l_y / \sin A') & \text{if } l_x < 0 \end{cases} \end{aligned} \tag{13}$$

For the three translational axes, X-, Y- and Z-axis, the following equations can be obtained according to the Eq.(8)

$$\begin{cases} Y' = (o_z + b)\sin A' - o_x \cos A' \sin C' + o_y \cos C' \sin A' \\ Z = -(a+b) + (o_z + b)\cos A' + o_x \sin A' \sin C' - o_y \sin A' \cos C' \\ X' = [o_x - (a+b+Z)\sin A' \sin C' + Y' \cos A' \sin C'] / \cos C' \end{cases} \tag{14}$$

After substituting *A'* and *C'* into Eq.(14), the distances *Y'*, *Z*, and *X'* can then be obtained. *Y'*, *Z*, and *X'* must fulfill the limitation of the translational axes, and otherwise a cutter retraction is needed. According to the obtained values from Eq.(14), the postprocessor can generate the corresponding NC codes for the table-tilting type five-axis NC machine tool. The realization algorithm for the postprocessor can be depicted as follows.

Algorithm for postprocessor:

Reading and inputting CL data file, recording the following useful data information:

CL data($o_x, o_y, o_z, l_x, l_y, l_z$ *) and geometric parameters of the five-axis machine(a and b);*

If l_z *is equal to 1, then* $A' = 0, C' = 0$;

Else if l_x *is equal to 0, then* $A' = \arcsin(-l_y), C' = 0$;

Else if l_y *is equal to 0, then* $A' = \arcsin(-l_x), C' = 90$;

Else calculating A' and C' with Eq.(13);

Substituting A' and C' into Eq.(14) to get the three translational distances of Y-, Z-, and X-axis, that is, Y', Z, and X' respectively.

Output the five control commands and writing to the NC Files.

The kinematics models and the inverse kinematics models for other types of five-axis machines can be formulated in the same way and will not be shown in this paper.

4 Example

There are two CL data ($\boldsymbol{O}_1,\boldsymbol{L}_1$) and ($\boldsymbol{O}_2,\boldsymbol{L}_2$) in work-piece coordinate system as shown in Fig.7. Assumed that the main parameters of the five-axis machine in Fig.1, *a* and *b*, are 450mm and 150mm respectively, then the CNC codes depicted in machine coordinate system can be obtained by the postprocessor presented in this paper:

For CL data ($\boldsymbol{O}_1,\boldsymbol{L}_1$), the corresponding CNC code is X_1=50, Y_1=50, Z_1=−340.2, A_1=30°, C_1=90° and for CL data ($\boldsymbol{O}_2,\boldsymbol{L}_2$), X_1=36.607, Y_1=229.461, Z_1=−563.75, A_1=45°, C_1=240°.

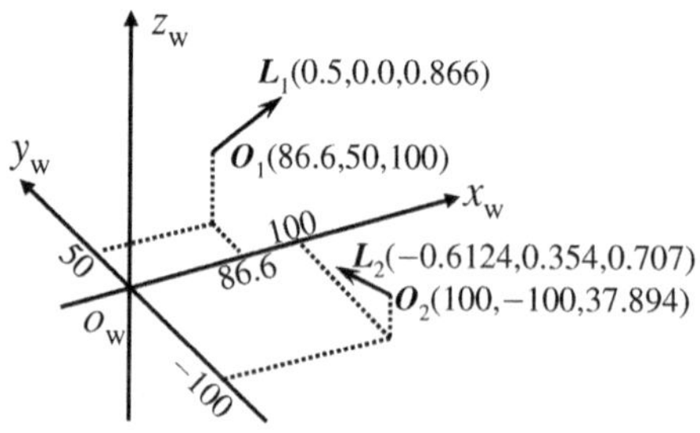

Fig. 7. The two CL data to be post-processed

Acknowledgments. This research is wholly supported by the the National Natural Science Foundation of China (No.50905168) through Zhengzhou Institute of Aeronautical Industry Management. The author thanks for their support for this research.

References

1. Suh, S.H., Lee, J.J., Kim, S.K.: Multi-axis Machine with Additional-axis NC System: Theory and Development. Int. J. Adv. Manuf. Technol. 14, 865–875 (1998)
2. Kruth, J.P., Kelwais: NC Post-processing and NC-simulation for Five-axis Milling Operations with Automatic Collision Avoidance. In: Proceedings of the International Manufacturing Engineering Conference (1996)
3. Sakamoto, S., Inasaki, I.: Analysis of Generating Motion for Five-axis Machining Centers. Trans. Jpn. Soc. Mech. Engr. Ser. C 59, 1553–1559 (1993)
4. Lee, R.S., She, C.H.: Developing a Postprocessor for Three Type of Five-axis Machine Tools. Int. J. Adv. Manuf. Technol. 13, 658–665 (1997)
5. Denavit, J., Hartenberg, R.S.: A Kinematics Notation for Lower-pair mechanisms based on Matrices. ASME J. Appl. Mech. 22, 215–221 (1955)
6. Cheng, M., Tsai, M., Kuo, J.: Real-time NURBS Command Generators for CNC Servo Controllers. International Journal of Machine Tools & Manufacture 42, 801–813 (2002)
7. Tsai, M., Cheng, C., Cheng, M.: A Real-time NURBS Surface Interpolator for Precision Three-axis CNC Machining. International Journal of Machine Tools & Manufacture 43, 1217–1227 (2003)

Pruning Search Space for Heuristic Planning through Action Utility Analysis

Ruishi Liang*, Hui Ma, and Min Huang

School of Computer, Zhongshan Institute,
University of Electronic Science and Technology of China
Zhongshan 528402, China
liangruishi@gmail.com

Abstract. This paper studies how to prune search space under the Relaxed Planning Graph heuristic framework which is firstly proposed in FF. Based on the observation of relations between action and proposition layers, we present a new and high-quality domain-independent pruning strategy for forward-chaining heuristic planning through Action Utility Analysis. The proposed strategy extracts so-called directly-used actions from relaxed planning graph as promising successors. Its pruning result is in general better than the helpful actions strategy. Our strategy can be used in any progression state space search framework. Experiments in the STRIPS benchmarks of International Planning Competitions (IPC) show that our pruning strategy along with algorithms decreases the search space effectively, and can outperform helpful action strategy of FF.

Keywords: AI planning, heuristic search, pruning strategy, action utility analysis.

1 Introduction

AI Planning is known to be PSPACE-complete [1] even in the simple STRIPS set [2]. Over the last few years a significant increase of the efficiency of planning system has been achieved with the evolution of biennial International Planning Competitions (IPC) [3].

Heuristic search-based planners were introduced by Bonet & Geffner [4] and are now very popular. They perform a heuristic forward or backward search in the space of world states to find a path from the start state to a goal state. Several of them entered the International Planning Competitions, including HSP [4], FF [5], LPG [6] and Fast Downward [7]. FF was in particular awarded for outstanding performance at IPC-2 and was the top performance planner in the STRIPS track of IPC-3.

FF is a progression heuristic planner, searching the space of world states of a planning task in the forward direction, guided by Relaxed Planning Graph (RPG) heuristic functions. As a side effect of RPG, a pruning technique named helpful action

* This work was supported by the Scientific Research Foundation of Zhongshan Institute, University of Electronic Science and Technology of China under Grant No. 410YKQ03, 05jpk06, 2009JXTD11 and 409YKQ04.

H. Tan and M. Zhou (Eds.): CSE 2011, Part I, CCIS 201, pp. 78–86, 2011.

can be obtained. The search process of FF is guided by enforced hill climbing algorithm which combines local and systematic search. Although solving STRIPS-style planning problems efficiently, FF spends much running time on evaluating lots of candidate successors.

This paper studies how to prune search space more exactly. We analyze the weakness of helpful action pruning strategy of FF. Then we present a new and high-quality domain-independent pruning strategy for forward-chaining heuristic planning through Action Utility analysis. The strategy tries to partition all candidate actions into three different utility types, useless actions, indirectly-used actions and directly-used actions, based on the observation of "Too Early Applied Actions" in relaxed planning graph. Only the kind of directly-used actions is preserved for further pruning forward search space. Finally, we apply our pruning strategy in enforced hill climbing search algorithm, which combines local and systematic search.

We implemented the ideas in our planner HQFF and evaluate the performance in the STRIPS benchmark domains of IPC. The results show that our planner leads to a significant reduction in search effort as well as high quality solution plans.

2 Preliminary

To introduce the background and notations of our work, we first briefly review STRIPS planning task definitions. Then the relaxed planning graph heuristic is presented. The helpful action pruning strategy is also illustrated in this section. Further details and examples can be found in the literatures [2] [5] [8].

2.1 STRIPS Planning Task

In propositional STRIPS planning, all construct are based on logic propositions. Given a set of propositions F, a world state s is a set of (true) propositions. An action a is given as a triple of proposition sets, $a = (pre(a), add(a), del(a))$, where $pre(a) \subseteq F$ is the preconditions of a, and $add(a) \subseteq F$ and $del(a) \subseteq F$ are the add list and the delete list, respectively. Given a world state s and an action a, the result of executing a in s, namely $result(s, a)$, is $result(s, a) := s \cup add(a) \setminus del(a)$, if the action is applicable in s, i.e., $pre(a) \subseteq s$. Otherwise, $result(s, a)$ is undefined. The set of all applicable actions in state s is denoted as $App(s)$. The result of executing an action sequence $<a_1, a_2,\ldots, a_N>$ in a state s is recursively defined by $result(s, <a_1, a_2,\ldots, a_N>) := result(result(s, a_1), <a_1, a_2,\ldots, a_N>)$, and $result(s, <>) := s$.

Definition 1. A STRIPS planning task $T = (F, A, I, G)$ is a tuple where F is the set of logic propositions, and A is the set of grounded actions, and I and G are initial state and goal state, respectively.

An action sequence $<a_1, a_2,\ldots, a_N>$ is a plan for T if and only if $G \subseteq result(I, <a_1, a_2,\ldots, a_N>)$.

2.2 Relaxed Planning Graph Heuristic

Relaxed Planning Graph (RPG) heuristic estimates the goal distance of search state through defining a relaxation of original planning task by ignoring the delete effects of the actions in A. A planning graph for the relaxed planning task will be constructed by the GraphPlan [9] algorithm first. Then a non-optimal relaxed plan, a solution to the relaxed task, can be extracted from the planning graph in polynomial time.

Definition 2. Given a STRIPS task $T = (F, A, I, G)$. The relaxation a^+ of an action $a \in A$, $a = (pre(a), add(a), del(a))$, is defined as $a^+ = (pre(a), add(a), \varnothing)$. Accordingly, the relaxation T^+ of T is (F, A^+, I, G), where $A^+ = \{ a^+ \mid a \in A \}$.

An action sequence $<a_1, a_2, \ldots, a_N>$ is a relaxed plan for T if $<a_1^+, a_2^+, \ldots, a_N^+>$ is a plan for T^+.

Definition 3. Given a STRIPS task $T = (F, A, I, G)$. Let s be a search state in T. The relaxed planning graph (RPG) for the relaxed task (F, A^+, I, G) is a layered graph alternating between proposition levels and action levels, which is represented as a sequence $P_0, A_0, \ldots, P_i, A_i, \ldots, A_{k-1}, P_k$.

$$P_i := \begin{cases} s & , if\ i = 0 \\ P_{i-1} \cup \{add(a) \mid pre(a) \subseteq P_{i-1}\}, & if\ 1 \le i \le k \end{cases}$$

$$A_i := \{a \in A^+ \mid pre(a) \subseteq P_i\}, 0 \le i < k.$$

where k is the final layer of the relaxed planning graph.

After constructing the RPG for a search state s, FF starts at the final layer of RPG and uses a backtrack-free procedure that extracts a sequence of actions that correspond to a successful relaxed plan for s. During the extraction process, two kinds of sets are maintained: the sequence of sub-goal sets $G_1, \ldots, G_k$ that represent the sub-goals first appearing in the respective levels $P_1, \ldots, P_k$; the sequence of solution action set $O_0, \ldots, O_{k-1}$ that represent the actions achieving the sub-goals in $G_1, \ldots, G_k$. Actually, the sequence $< O_0, \ldots, O_{k-1}>$ is the relaxed plan for s, and the total number of actions in the sequence is the heuristic value for s, i.e.,

$$h(s) = \Sigma_{i=0}^{t-1} \mid O_i \mid$$

If no relaxed plan can be extracted, the heuristic value of s is set to ∞.

Based on RPG and relaxed plan, a pruning strategy called helpful actions is proposed in FF. Formally, the set of helpful actions to s is defined as

$$HPA\ (s) := \{a \in A \mid pre(a) \subseteq s \wedge add(a) \cap G_1 \neq \varnothing\}$$

where G_1 is the set of sub-goals constructed at layer P_1 of RPG.

2.3 Weakness of Helpful Action Pruning Strategy

Although the set of helpful actions provides promising successors for heuristic search, it still contains too many actions which are somewhat harmful to latter search process.

As an example, consider a typical transportation planning task from Depots domain in Figure 1: The postal service must deliver a number of crates to their respective destinations using its vehicle fleet of cars and trucks. There are two trucks t0 and t1, and two crates c0 and c1 in the task.

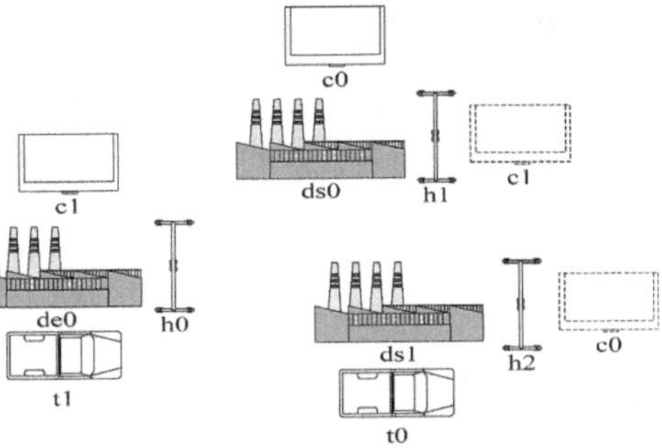

Fig. 1. A typical transportation planning task

Initially, t0 and c1 are in de0, c0 is in ds0 and t0 is in ds1. The goal of the task is to deliver c0 to ds1 and c1 to ds0. The relaxed planning graph for initial state I is depicted in Figure 2.

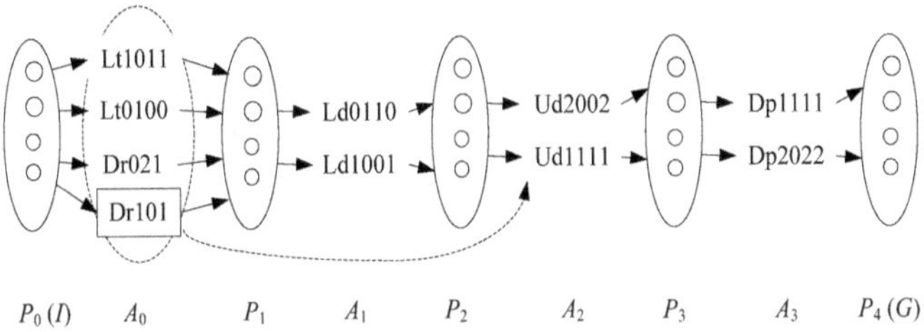

Fig. 2. Layer Membership of Relaxed Plans for initial state I

After relaxed plan extraction procedure, a set of help actions are obtained according to the definition of helpful action, which corresponds to action layer A_0 in Figure 2. Exactly, the set of helpful actions are as follows:

HPA (I) := { Lift(hoist1 crate0 pallet1 distributor0), Lift(hoist0 crate1 pallet0 depot0), Drive(truck0 distributor1 distributor0), Drive(truck1 depot0 distributor0)}.

Consider the action Drive(truck1 depot0 distributor0), denoted as a. Although it is considered as a helpful action, its positive effects do not support any precondition of actions in neighbor action layer A_1. Indeed, it supports some precondition of action Unload(hoist1 crate1 truck1 distributor0) in layer A_2. Suppose the successor state after executing a in state I is s. By computing its heuristic value, we can see that $h(s) > h(I)$. So it is easy to see that the action a is not real "helpful" for current state I.

Theoretically, for an action a in the action layer A_i of a relaxed planning graph G_T, if the positive effects of a do not support any precondition of actions in neighbor action layer A_{i+1}, neither support any goal in G, we call a "*Too Early Applied Actions*".

Obviously, helpful action pruning strategy does not the side effect of too early applied actions into account. As a result, the pruning result seems to be imperfect in many planning problems. Take the planning task Depots-p5 in Depots domain as an example, following helpful action pruning, the number of search states is 220433 while the plan length is only 72. That is to say, 6889 states are evaluated in each search iteration.

3 Pruning Search Space through Action Utility Analysis

We have analyzed the phenomenon of too early applied action in relaxed planning graph, which motivates us to develop a high quality pruning strategy to overcome this phenomenon. As mentioned in last section, the action Drive(truck1 depot0 distributor0) is a too-early-applied action that is not real helpful for further search. It only provides indirect utility for actions layer A_1 and should be pruned from candidates. Other three actions provide direct utility for action layer A_1 because some of their positive effects are preconditions of some actions in layer A_1. Finally, actions not in the set of helpful actions contribute no utility for action layer A_1 and thus should be pruned.

For the sake of discussion, we partition all actions that are applicable in state s into three types according to their utility. They are useless actions, indirectly-used actions and directly-used actions.

Useless actions are those actions whose positive effects have no intersection with sub-goals layer G_1 and goal set G.

$$L(s) := \{a \in A \mid pre(a) \subseteq s \wedge add(a) \cap G = \varnothing \wedge add(a) \cap G_1 = \varnothing\}$$

Indirectly-used actions are those actions whose positive effects have no intersection with sub-goals layer G_1 but intersect with goal set G, some of them are too-early-applied actions of action layer O_1.

$$R(s) := \begin{cases} \{a \in A \mid pre(a) \subseteq s \wedge add(a) \cap G \neq \varnothing \wedge add(a) \cap G_1 = \varnothing\}, \text{ if } t = 1; \\ \{a \in A \mid pre(a) \subseteq s \wedge ((add(a) \cap G \neq \varnothing \wedge add(a) \cap G_1 = \varnothing) \vee \\ \quad (add(a) \cap G_1 \neq \varnothing \wedge add(a) \cap G_1 \cap (G \cup pre(O_1)) = \varnothing))\}, \text{ if } t > 1. \end{cases}$$

The set of directly-used actions excludes all too-early-applied actions. Indeed, it is the difference set of $App(s)$ with $L(s)$ and $R(s)$, i.e.,

$$U(s) := App(s) - L(s) - R(s). \quad (1)$$

The formal definition is as follows.

Definition 4. Given a STRIPS task $T = (F, A, s, G)$ and its relaxed planning graph RPG. The set of *directly-used actions* for state s is defined as follows:

$$U(s) := \begin{cases} \{a \in A \mid pre(a) \subseteq s \wedge add(a) \cap G_1 \neq \varnothing\}, \text{ if } t = 1; \\ \{a \in A \mid pre(a) \subseteq s \wedge (add(a) \cap G_1 \cap (G \cup pre(O_1)) \neq \varnothing)\}, \text{ if } t > 1. \end{cases} \quad (2)$$

where t is the final layer of RPG, and G_1 and O_1 are the set of sub-goals and the set of solution actions constructed at layer P_1 of RPG, respectively.

If the final layer of RPG is 1, directly-used actions are those actions whose positive effects have intersection with G_1; otherwise, directly-used actions are those actions whose positive effects have common intersection with G_1 and G, or have common intersection with G_1 and the preconditions of O_1, according to the above definition.

It is not easy to prove that the formula 1 is equivalent to formula 2.

Theorems 1. The formula 1 is equivalent to formula 2.

Proof sketch: Since the set *App*(*s*) is definite, we only need to prove that every action in *App*(*s*) is also in the above three sets, i.e., *L*(*s*), *R*(*s*) and *U* (*s*). □

Now take the planning task in Figure 1 as an example again. The set *R*(*I*) and *U* (*I*) for initial state *I* are as follows:

R(*I*) ={ Drive (truck1 depot0 distributor0)},
U(*I*) ={ Lift (hoist1 crate0 pallet1 distributor0), Lift (hoist0 crate1 pallet0 depot0), Drive (truck0 distributor1 distributor0)}.

Our pruning strategy always maintains the set of directly-used actions *U* (*I*) as promising successors. In other words, the set of useless actions and the set of indirectly-used actions are pruned from search space, which reduces whole search space and results in better search efficiency. For example, following our pruning strategy, the planning task Depots-p5 in Depots domain searches total 1847 states to achieve the goal state from initial state. Compared to helpful action pruning strategy, our strategy saves 99.2% search time.

4 Experiments

All the ideas are implemented in our planning system HQFF (High Quality Fast Forward planning system), which is a forward-chaining heuristic planner based on our new pruning strategy in conjunction with relaxed planning graph heuristic and enforced hill climbing search algorithm.

We compare our planner with the state-of-the-art planner FF verion2.3. The test suites are all derived from the benchmark domains of the third recent planning competitions IPC-3. The selected two propositional domains are: Depots and Satellite. Each domain provided a sequence of problems, roughly ordered by increasing hardness. All tests have been performed on an Intel Core Duo T2450 2.00GHz machine with 1 GB of memory running Fedora Release-8 / Linux kernel 2.6. Each test is limited to 180s of CPU time.

Summaries of the results obtained are presented in Table 1 and Table 2. Table 1 indicates the results of 22 problems in Depots domain, while Table 2 shows the results of 20 problems in Satellite domain.

In Depots domain, both HQFF and FF fail to solve all 22 problems guiding by heuristic search. Focusing on the solved problems, it can be seen with reference to the tables I that in most problems HQFF performs much better than FF, not only in terms of planning time but also in terms of plan quality.

In Satellite domain, both HQFF and FF solve 20 problems successfully. Compared to FF, HQFF outperform FF in 19 problems, except in problem No. 19.

Overall, across the two domains, it can be seen that HQFF exhibits strong performance. This indicates that our pruning strategy provides better performance in those evaluation domains than helpful action pruning strategy of FF.

Table 1. Comparison results in Depots domain

	HQFF			FF		
	N	T	L	N	T	L
1	20	0.00	10	20	0.00	10
2	26	0.00	15	33	0.00	15
3	272	0.04	38	318	0.03	37
4	--	F		--	TO	--
5	1847	0.56	82	220433	67.2	72
6	94668	47	92	--	TO	--
7	151	0.03	27	148	0.01	27
8	--	F		856	0.15	37
9	1411	0.91	75	2356	1.36	75
10	--	F		1519	0.22	34
11	206	0.11	60	574	0.29	63
12	1053	1.12	86	5008	5.14	94
13	51	0.02	25	79	0.02	26
14	222	0.1	35	427	0.2	37
15	6925	7.98	88	22421	22.67	85
16	273	0.11	36	108	0.04	28
17	505	0.33	38	1600	1.15	38
18	651	0.84	69	533	0.72	60
19	--	F		430	0.25	47
20	2610	4.24	88	6927	11.22	98
21	77	0.12	32	104	0.19	32
22	--	F		4524	37.29	102

Keys: N. - Expanded Nodes, T. – Running Time, L. – Solution Length, TO - Time Out (180 seconds)

Table 2. Comparison results in Satellite domain

	HQFF			FF		
	N	T	L	N	T	L
1	11	0.00	9	15	0.00	9
2	16	0.00	13	24	0.00	13
3	15	0.00	11	19	0.00	11
4	20	0.00	18	27	0.00	18
5	20	0.00	16	28	0.00	16
6	29	0.00	20	47	0.00	20
7	39	0.00	22	54	0.00	22
8	33	0.01	28	54	0.01	28
9	54	0.01	35	73	0.02	35
10	52	0.01	35	87	0.03	35
11	45	0.02	34	91	0.04	34
12	57	0.03	43	91	0.05	43
13	116	0.09	61	243	0.2	61
14	49	0.03	42	84	0.05	42
15	108	0.1	52	182	0.18	52
16	86	0.11	53	180	0.23	53
17	82	0.12	48	152	0.23	48
18	40	0.02	35	75	0.04	35
19	469	0.35	77	365	0.28	73
20	1007	0.78	105	5889	5.19	107

Keys: N. - Expanded Nodes, T. – Running Time, L. – Solution Length, TO - Time Out (180 seconds)

5 Conclusion and Future Work

We have proposed a new and high quality pruning strategy based on the partition of all applicable actions according to their utility for non-optimal STRIPS heuristic planning. The pruning strategy always maintains the set of directly-used actions as promising successors, which reduces whole search space and results in better search efficiency. Comparison again a leading state-of-the-art STRIPS planner shows that our strategy is competitive with the state-of-the-art planner based on helpful action pruning technique. Exploring our method more deeply and improving the performance in more classes of problems, for example the ADL problems [10], are major directions for future work.

References

1. Helmert, M.: Complexity results for standard benchmark domains in planning. Artificial Intelligence 143(2), 219–262 (2003)
2. Fikes, R., Nilsson, N.: STRIPS: A new approach to the application of theorem proving to problem solving. Artificial Intelligence 2, 189–208 (1971)
3. International Planning Competition Archives official website, `http://ipc.icapsconference.org/`
4. Bonet, B., Geffner, H.: Planning as Heuristic Search. Artificial Intelligence 129, 5–33 (2001)
5. Hoffmann, J., Nebel, B.: The FF planning system: Fast plan generation through heuristic search. Journal of Artificial Intelligence Research 14, 253–302 (2001)
6. Gerevini, A., Saetti, A., Serina, I.: Planning Through Stochastic Local Search and Temporal Action Graphs in LPG. Journal of Artificial Intelligence Research 20, 239–290 (2003)
7. Helmert, M.: The fast downward planning system. Journal of Artificial Intelligence Research 26, 191–246 (2006)
8. Liang, R.S., Jiang, Y.F., Bian, R.: Ordered Hill Climbing Search for Heuristic Planning. In: Proc. 2009 International Conference on Information Engineering and Computer Science, pp. 3264–3267 (2009)
9. Blum, A., Furst, M.: Fast Planning Through Planning Graph Analysis. Artificial Intelligence 90, 281–300 (1997)
10. Koehler, J., Nebel, B., Hoffmann, J., Dimopoulos, Y.: Extending planning graphs to an ADL subset. In: Proc. 4th European Conf. on Planning, pp. 275–287 (1997)

Generation and Enumeration of Implication Sets

Xiaodong Wang* and Daxin Zhu

School of Mathematics and Computer Science,
Quanzhou Normal University,
362000 Quanzhou, China
{wangxiaodong,dex}@qztc.edu.cn

Abstract. This paper studies the problem on generation and enumeration of accurate implication sets. Based on the backtracking search algorithm, an efficient recursive construction algorithm is presented for the problem. The new techniques suggested improve the time and space complexities of the backtracking search algorithm dramatically.

Keywords: monetary system; implication sets; generating algorithm.

1 Introduction

Suppose $C(k)$ is a monetary system that divides the currency denomination into $k+1$ decimal levels:

$$\{1,2,5\};\{10,20,50\};\cdots;\{10^i,2\times 10^i,5\times 10^i\};\cdots;\{10^k\}.$$

For example, China's currency system (RMB) can be classified as $C(4)$.

We denote $c(i,j), 0\le i\le k, 0\le j\le 2$ the levels of monetary values.

The monetary value of level i can be written as $c_i=(c(i,0),c(i,1),c(i,2))^\top$, $0\le i\le k$. In particular, when $i=k$, $c_k=(10^k,0,0)^\top$.

For any integer $n\in I^+$ we can obviously express n by the above currency system as follows

$$n=\sum_{i=0}^{k}\sum_{j=0}^{2}a(i,j)c(i,j) \tag{1}$$

where $a(i,j)\in I^+, 0\le i\le k, 0\le j\le 2$.

Denote $a_i=(a(i,0),a(i,1),a(i,2))^\top, g(a_i,c_i)=a_i^\top c_i, 0\le i\le k$ and $a=(a_0,a_1,\cdots,a_k)^\top$.

Then, the integer n can be expressed by

$$n=\sum_{i=0}^{k}a_i^\top c_i=\sum_{i=0}^{k}g(a_i,c_i)\triangleq f(k,a) \tag{2}$$

* Supported by the Natural Science Foundation of Fujian under Grant No.2009J01295 and the Haixi Project of Fujian under Grant No.A099.

H. Tan and M. Zhou (Eds.): CSE 2011, Part I, CCIS 201, pp. 87–92, 2011.

For a given $n \in I^+$, the above representation is obviously not unique in general. The different values of a satisfying (1) will give different representations of the positive integer n. Set $A(k,n) = \{a \mid f(k,a) = n\}$ constitutes all representations of a positive integer n in the given currency system.

Let a and b be two-dimensional arrays. $b \leq a$ if and only if $b(i,j) \leq a(i,j)$, $0 \leq i \leq k$, and $0 \leq j \leq 2$; $b < a$ if and only if both $b \leq a$ and $b \neq a$.

Let

$$s(k,a) = \{f(k,b) \mid f(k,a) = n, 0 < b \leq a\} \tag{3}$$

The set $s(k,a)$ is defined as an implication set of the positive integer n, which is the collection of all the money under the representation a.

Set

$$R(k,n) = \bigcap_{a \in A(k,n)} s(k,a) \tag{4}$$

is defined to be an accurate implication set of the positive integer n in the given currency system.

For any $x \in R(k,n)$, regardless of the kind of par value of the currency that composes the positive integer n, it certainly contains x.

The main problem concerned in this paper is for the given positive integers k and n, how to find the corresponding accurate implication set $R(k,n)$ efficiently.

2 Generating Algorithm

2.1 A Simple Algorithm

By definition, the accurate implication set of the given positive integers k and n in the currency system $C(k)$ can be formulated as (4). In the following algorithm description, we use operations + and - for a set U and a positive integer v defined as follows

$$U + v = \{x + v \mid x \in U\},\ U - v = \{x - v \mid x \in U \text{ and } x \geq v\}$$

Based on this formula we can design a simple backtracking algorithm [1,2,3] to find $R(k,n)$ as follows.

Initially, $R = \{1, 2, \cdots, n\}$ and $S = \emptyset$. A function call **Backtrack**(n) will compute the set $R = R(k,n)$.

2.2 Pruning Technique

If par value 1, 2, and 5 are used to compose the money, then positive integer 10 can be one of the following 10 different representations.

Let $E = \{e_i, i = 1, \cdots, 10\}$.

For the positive integers $m = 10$, $m = 12$ and $m \geq 14$, if $m = g(a_0, c_0) = \sum_{j=0}^{2} a(0,j)c(0,j)$, then there must be an integer $d \in E$ such that $d \leq a_0$.

Algorithm 1. Backtrack(t)

```
if t = 0 then
    R ← R ∩ S;
    return;
else
    foreach c(i, j) ∈ C(k) do
        if c(i, j) ≤ t then
            S ← S + c(i, j);
            Backtrack(t − c(i, j));
            S ← S − c(i, j);
        end
    end
end
```

When $m < 10$, there must be no $d \in E$ such that

$m = g(a_0, c_0) = \sum_{j=0}^{2} a(0,j)c(0,j)$ and $d \leq a_0$.

When $m = 11$, we can take $a_0 = (0, 3, 1)$, then there is no $d \in E$ such that $11 = g(a_0, c_0)$ and $d \leq a_0$. The value for a_0 is unique.

When $m = 13$, we can take $a_0 = (0, 4, 1)$, then there is no $d \in E$ such that $13 = g(a_0, c_0)$ and $d \leq a_0$. The value for a_0 is also unique.

Let $n = f(k,a) = \sum_{i=0}^{k} a_i^{\top} c_i = \sum_{i=0}^{k} g(a_i, c_i)$ and $D(a,i) = \{d \leq a_i \mid d \in E\}, 0 \leq i \leq k$.

The integer transformation $\sigma(a,i)$ can be defined as follows.

(1) If $D(a,i)$ is not empty, then for any $d \in D(a,i)$, $\sigma(a,i) = (a_0, \cdots, a_i - d, a_{i+1} + (1,0,0), \cdots, a_k)$.

(2) If $D(a,i)$ is empty, then $\sigma(a,i) = a$.

For any $a \in A(k,n)$ we have, $\sigma(a,i) \in A(k,n), 0 \leq i \leq k$ and $s(k, \sigma(a,i)) \subseteq s(k,a), 0 \leq i \leq k$.

Theorem 1. *Let*

$$\begin{aligned} S_0 &= \{1, 2, 3, 4, 5, 6, 7, 8, 9, 11, 13\} \\ B(k,n) &= \{a \in A(k,n) \mid \sigma(a,i) = a, 0 \leq i \leq k\} \\ F(k,n) &= \{a \in B(k,n) \mid a_i^{\top} c_0 \in S_0\} \end{aligned}$$

Then,

$$R(k,n) = \bigcap_{a \in A(k,n)} s(k,a) = \bigcap_{a \in B(k,n)} s(k,a) \bigcap_{a \in F(k,n)} s(k,a)$$

Proof. Omitted.

By making use of the constraints of $F(k,n)$ in Theorem 1, we can add pruning condition in the backtracking algorithm to improve the searching speed as follows [5].

Algorithm 2. Backtrack(t)

```
if t = 0 then
    R ← R ⋂ S;
    return;
else
    foreach c(i, j) ∈ C(k) do
        if c(i, j) ≤ t and a_i^T c_0 ∈ S_0 then
            S ← S + c(i, j);
            Backtrack(t − c(i, j));
            S ← S − c(i, j);
        end
    end
end
```

3 Recursive Construction and Enumeration

Let

$$\mathrm{div}(x, y) = \left\lfloor \frac{x}{y} \right\rfloor ; \mathrm{mod}(x, y) = x - y \left\lfloor \frac{x}{y} \right\rfloor .$$

$$G_1(k, n) = \{a \in F(k, n) \mid a_0^T c_0 = \mathrm{mod}(n, 10)\}$$
$$G_2(k, n) = \{a \in F(k, n) \mid a_0^T c_0 = 10 + \mathrm{mod}(n, 10)\}$$

Then we have,
If $\mathrm{mod}(n, 10) \notin \{1, 3\}$, then $F(k, n) = G_1(k, n)$;
If $\mathrm{mod}(n, 10) \in \{1, 3\}$, then $F(k, n) = G_1(k, n) \bigcup G_2(k, n)$.

Theorem 2. *If* $\mathrm{mod}(n, 10) \notin \{1, 3\}$, *then*

$$R(k, n) = \bigcap_{a \in G1(k,n)} s(k, a);$$

If $\mathrm{mod}(n, 10) \in \{1, 3\}$, *then*

$$R(k, n) = \left(\bigcap_{a \in G1(k,n)} s(k, a) \right) \bigcap \left(\bigcap_{a \in G2(k,n)} s(k, a) \right) .$$

Proof. Omitted.
Let U and V be two sets of integer. The circle plus operation for sets U and V is defined as

$$U \oplus V = \{x + y \mid x \in U, y \in V\}.$$

The multiplication of a set U by an integer m is defined as

$$m \times U = \{mx \mid x \in U\}.$$

$$
\begin{aligned}
T_0 &= R(k, \text{mod}(n, 10));\\
T_1 &= 10 \times R(k-1, \text{div}(n, 10));\\
T_2 &= \bigcap_{a \in G_2(k,n)} s_0(k, a);\\
T_3 &= 10 \times R(k-1, \text{div}(n, 10) - 1);\\
T_4 &= R(k, 10 + \text{mod}(n, 10)).
\end{aligned}
$$

Theorem 3. *If* $\text{mod}(n, 10) \notin \{1, 3\}$, *then* $R(k, n) = T_0 \bigcup T_1 \bigcup (T_0 \oplus T_1)$*;*
If $\text{mod}(n, 10) \in \{1, 3\}$, *then*

$$R(k, n) = (T_0 \bigcup T_1 \bigcup (T_0 \oplus T_1)) \bigcap (T_3 \bigcup T_4 \bigcup (T_3 \oplus T_4));$$

$R(0, n) = \{1, 2, \cdots, n\}$.

Proof. Omitted.
According to Theorem 3, we can design a recursive generating algorithm **RecurGern**(k, n) for computing $R(k, n)$ as follows [4].

Algorithm 3. RecurGern(k, n)

if $k = 0$ **or** $n < 14$ **then**
    return `Direct`(k, n);
end
$T_0 \leftarrow$ `Direct`$(k, \text{mod}(n, 10))$;
$T_1 \leftarrow$ `RecurGern`$(k-1, \text{div}(n, 10))$;
$R \leftarrow T_0 \bigcup T_1 \bigcup (T_0 \oplus T_1)$;
if $\text{mod}(n, 10) \in (1, 3)$ **then**
    $T_3 \leftarrow$ `Direct`$(k, 10 + \text{mod}(n, 10))$;
    $T_4 \leftarrow$ `RecurGern`$(k-1, \text{div}(n, 10) - 1)$;
    $R \leftarrow R \bigcap (T_3 \bigcup T_4 \bigcup (T_3 \oplus T_4))$;
ond
return R;

In the algorithm description above, the sub-algorithm **Direct**(k, n) compute the set $R(k, n)$ directly by a pre-computed solution table.

4 Conclusions

We have suggested efficient techniques for constructing the accurate implication sets of a given monetary system. We also give exact solutions for computing the maximal elements of e accurate implication set. The proposed combinatorial problem was solved completely.

References

1. Bird, R.: Pearls of Functional Algorithm Design. Cambridge University Press, New York (2010)
2. Bitner, J.R., Reingold, E.M.: Backtrack programming techniques. Communications of the ACM 18(11), 651–656 (1975)
3. Cormen, T.H., Leiserson, C.E., Rivest, R.L.: Introduction to Algorithms. MIT Press, Cambridge (2001)
4. Kleinberg, J., Tardos, E.: Algorithm Design. Addison Wesley, Massachusetts (2005)
5. Kreher, D.L., Stinson, D.: Combinatorial Algorithms: Generation, Enumeration and Search. CRC Press, New York (1998)

Research on the Share and Service Technology of Hebei Resources and Environmental information

Leigang Sun, Jianfeng Liu, and Quanhong Xu

Institute of Geographical Sciences, Hebei Academy of Sciences,
Shijiazhuang, China, 050011
sunlgyuyn@163.com

Abstract. With the intensive study on Resources and Environmental issues and the leaping of data product, the demand for the geospatial information sharing between the various departments is going strong. The paper designs the geospatial information network services architecture based on the Caringorm, the Spring and the iBATIS after lucubrating Flex technology and ArcGIS Server technology, and realizes the Resources and Environmental Data Sharing Platform of Hebei province using this architecture. The study proves that this Tech development Form has better UI performance, interactive capability, reusability and scalability, and also cuts way back on application development cycle. This system, of high practical value, will be able to provide the public, scientists, and administration with convenient and rapid access to Resources and Environmental information.

Keywords: Information sharing, Resources and Environmental information, Flex, ArcGIS Server.

1 Introduction

The waste and depletion of resources and the environmental destruction and deterioration make resources and environmental problems as the biggest confusion in the process of economic and social development. Resources and environmental data becomes an important part of the national data resources. For a long time, since the separation of departments and industry independent, there is no mechanism for data sharing, which makes scientific research and business development difficult obtain the basic data required, and the existing resources can not be used efficiently.

With the development of network technology, more and more desktop application turn to web platform, however, the user experience is not ideal, especially for the large amount of spatial information data[3]. The existing geospatial information network services still have some limitations, such as: the poor interaction and user interface display which can not meet the user requirements and reduce the availability of the system, excessive pressure on the server side and do not taking full advantage of the client processing which will greatly increased the demands on network bandwidth. Through the integration of Caringorm, Spring and iBATIS and lucubrating the Flex and ArcGIS Server technology, the paper designed the geospatial

H. Tan and M. Zhou (Eds.): CSE 2011, Part I, CCIS 201, pp. 93–100, 2011.

information network services architecture and implemented the Resources and Environmental Data Sharing Platform of Hebei province, which makes full use of the client-side processing and balances the calculated load of the client and server, and also the resources and environmental data from different sources gets be integrated.

The rest of this paper is arranged as follows. We introduce related key technologies in Section 2. The details of this system architecture is presented in Section 3. The system function design and implementation are presented in Section4. Finally, we draw conclusions and point out the future work.

2 Key Technologies

2.1 RIA and Flex

RIA(Rich Internet Application) is a kind of technological innovation on the presentation layer, which is integrated with the advantages of fast response and better interactive in desktop application and the characteristic of wider spread and low-cost deployment in web application. Providing the richer, more interactive and responsive user experience, The RIA improves greatly the disadvantages of traditional web application[7,8,4]. The RIA migrates most of the business logic from the server to the client and retains only a little on the server side, which is different from the traditional web application concentrated the most of interactive applications on the server side[2]. Nowadays the Flex/Flash, Silverlight, JavaFX, Ajax and so on are the more mature products in the RIA area. Backing from Flash platform, the Flex technology possesses the unique advantage.

This system development uses the Flex technology, which is a high-efficiency product set of RIA development based on standard programming model, makes up for the missing elements of traditional web application, reduces the number of communication with the server, and shows the data details at length[9]. Developers may compile the RIA programs into Flash files, which could be accepted by the Flash Player. this means that the programs developed using the Flex technology do not install additional client plug-in components for most browsers, which is also characteristic of the Flex technology. ArcGIS API for Flex, Integrated with Flex technology and developed by ESRI company, bring GIS application the new opportunity.

2.2 ArcGIS Server

As ESRI's latest products, ArcGIS Server 10 is an Enterprise Level GIS Application Platform which centrally manages and supports multi-user, and provides users with rich GIS functionality, including spatial data management, mapping, geoprocessing, spatial analysis, data modeling, browser-based data editing, 3D visualization and so on. It also provides many management tools used to configure, publish and optimize GIS services, which can meet the various needs of the client. ArcGIS API for Flex, as extended development components of ArcGIS Server, can be used to develop the RIA on the basis of constructing GIS services[1]. ArcGIS API for Flex Version 2 is based on Flex 4 and Flash Builder 4, by which we can create easy responsive applications possessing of intuitive user interface and rich visual effects, and make full use of the series of ArcGIS's powerful mapping, geocoding, geoprocessing and other functions.

3 System Architecture Design

This system architecture choose B/S(Browser/Server) three-layer of network system structure, including Presentation Layer, Application Layer and Data Layer. The Application Layer includes J2EE Application Server and ArcGIS Server. Figure.1 shows the system architecture of this prototype system.

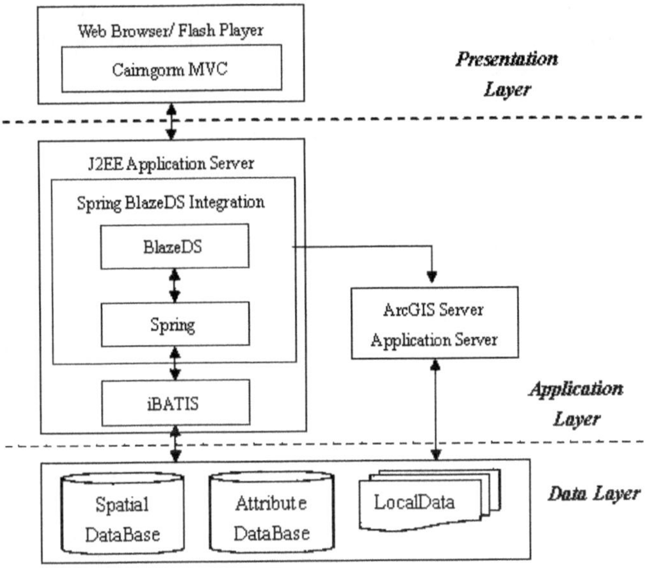

Fig. 1. System Architecture

3.1 Presentation Layer

Based on ArcGIS API for Flex and Flex Technology and designed using Cairngorm framework, the Presentation Layer presents a rich, highly interactive visual interface configured and managed by specialized components for users, and displays spatial information and attribute information by the way of integrated graphics. The Presentation Layer is divided into the three components of View, Model and Controller using MVC model as the main design. The View component is responsible for showing user interface; the Model component focuses on the preservation of data, maintains the data consistency between the Flex client and the server-side, and the consistency of reference to the same data in different views; And the Controller component is responsible for event handling, maps events to the Command, completes cross-platform remote calls using agent services, displays the data in Model to the View, and also provide a packaging mechanism for event handling and service calling. In asynchronous communication and event-driven Flex platform, Cairngorm can provide fast and reliable method for business applications.

The Presentation Layer, possessing the characteristics of high cohesion and low coupling, will free developers from the complicated design patterns and make them focus more on the implementation of business logic. This will greatly improve the program's reusability, scalability and maintainability.

3.2 Application Layer

As the core of the whole architecture, the Application Layer provides Spatial Information Map Services and Remote Business Services. ArcGIS Server, the Map Server, provide raster map services, vector map services, geocoding services, geoprocessing services, property inquiry services and other spatial information services for clients, and connects with the background spatial database through ArcSDE. The Remote Business Services, provided by J2EE Server and designed by the way of integrating Spring and iBATIS framework, will interact with the background database for business data exchange with Flash Remoting technology.

3.2.1 Spatial Information Services

The Spatial Information Map Services will be published by the way of combining dynamic map rendering with map slicing technique. Choosing the new map slicing technique for those bottom spatial data which do not often change, and choosing the dynamic rendering method for those real-time data or those data to be returned according to the needs of the client user, which will greatly reduce the pressure on the server and improve the response speed of the map with a better user experience. All spatial information services are REST-style web services. Just using the URL, we can easily create, publish and use these services, and achieve the seamless interoperability of GIS, which has the scalability, stateless, better performance, caching support and other advantages over complex soap-based services. For example, we can easily access to those server-side spatial information services by specifying the URL path, <esri:ArcGISDynamicMapServiceLayer url="http://localhost:8399/arcgis/rest/services/zyhj/MapServer" />.

3.2.2 Remote Business Services

Flex can implement the communication with Java and other server through three components: HTTPService, WebService and RemoteObject. This architecture chooses RemoteObject, the most flexible and common way, to achieve remote access to business data and database queries. The RemoteObject method is based on the binary AMF protocol for data exchange, whose greatest feature is the ability to complete automatically data type conversion from client to server side when carrying out information exchange. For these reasons, its transmission efficiency is much higher than that of the HTTPService and WebService, especially for large data. BlazeDS is a RemoteObject implementation technology when using Java as the server-side technology, and also is an open source, free project published under the LGPL v3 license. The remote access technology of BlazeDS uses call-response model, which allows Flex or Adobe Flash applications access server-side Java objects the same as access to local objects. The BlazeDS technology can integrate Java security strategy existing in the server-side, provide transparent, high-performance data conversion and transmission services between ActionScript and Java for those fast response applications, and also support Message Services based on publish/subscription mode by extending the existing Message Services structure. Figure.2 shows the whole process of remote service call via BlazeDS.

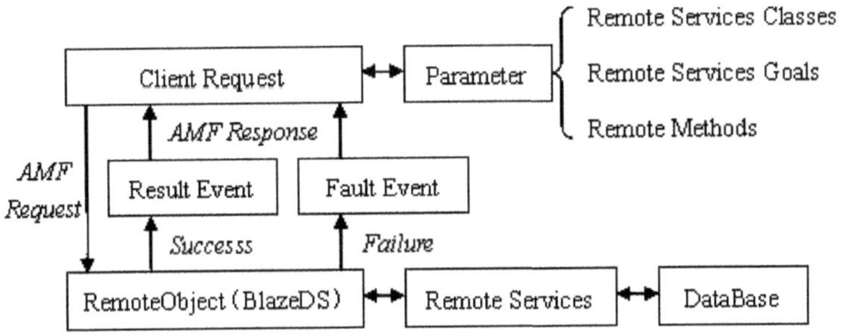

Fig. 2. Remote Service Call

In order to simplify the management of business objects, this architecture integrate BlazeDS and Spring using the Spring BlazeDS Integration component. MessageBroker, the core component of BlazeDS, is configured as spring managed bean. Through integrating Spring, a lightweight IoC(Inversion of Control) and AOP(Aspect-oriented Programming) container framework, it will avoid over-coupling caused by hard-coded program. We will get be freed from the monotonous and boredom management codes and carry out transaction management flexibly through declaration, which greatly improves the efficiency and quality of development. Thanks to Spring providing the direct support for excellent frameworks (such as Structs, iBATIS, Hibernate, etc.), this architecture introduces the flexible and compact iBATIS framework and achieves the separation with spring-managed business logic. Thereby reducing the coupling and improving the cohesion, and minor modifications to this framework will meet new applications, which improves the scalability of the system to some extent.

3.3 Data Layer

The Data Layer includes ArcSDE and the Relational DataBase used to store spatial data , metadata and associated business data. Spatial data will be visual managed and operated through ArcCatalog and organized by the way of large classification and small stratification. That is to say, the data is first divided into basic geographic information, thematic information, image data and other categories, and each category also includes different geographical elements, such as the thematic information category is divided into land use, topography, ancient rivers, geology, soil, environment, disaster and other sub-categories. Metadata is data about dada, and in the geospatial database is the description of data content, quality, presentation, data sources, spatial reference and other relevant characteristics. Because of its characteristics, metadata has become an important tool for data management, data sharing and data use[5,6]. These metadata information, user information and other business data are stored in large Oracle database and managed effectively through the special background management system.

4 System Function Design and Implementation

This system are functionally divided into five modules: the Information Publishing module, Statistical Analysis module, Metadata Directory Service module, Data Retrieval module and System Management module. ①System Management module, which is the basis of the whole system, provides support for user management, data management and privilege management. Data management includes metadata management, data editing, data conversion, layer management, multimedia information maintenance, etc. ②Information Publishing module, open to all users, provides basic operation on spatial information, including zoom in, zoom out, pan, full extent, eagle eye, location, label, measure, etc. ③Statistical Analysis module, the core module of the system and mainly for intermediate and advanced users, provides online spatial query, spatial analysis, statistical mapping, thematic analysis and other advanced functions of resources and environmental information. ④ Metadata Directory Service module provides the discovery, positioning and navigation of information resources and services, which will implement the sharing and exchange

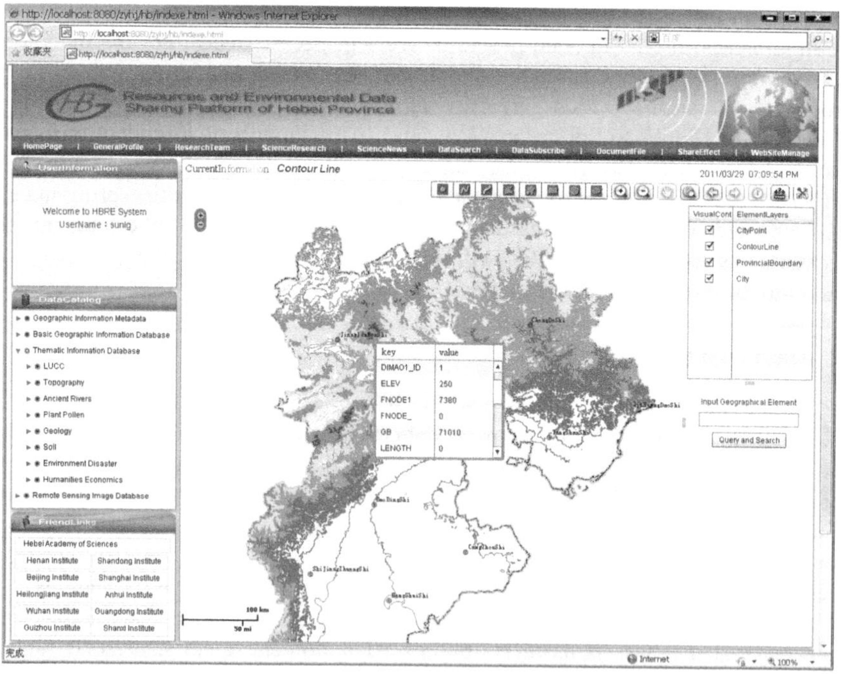

Fig. 3. Effects of System Operation

of distributed resources and environmental information and make the government departments, research universities, public understand the contents of a variety of resources and environmental information. ⑤Data Retrieval module will achieve the access to the text, tables, audio, video and other types of data, including the full text retrieval and classification retrieval of all data resources.

In view of the professional features of the system and network operating environment, only registered uses can log in the system with the purpose of limiting the available system functions according to different levels of users. The user level is divided into general users, professional users, advanced users and administrators. The system administrator will distribute the corresponding system functions according to the user level after examining its authenticity. Figure.3 shows the effect of system operation.

5 Conclusions and Future Work

Currently, interaction speed and interface expression are the severe test that geospatial information network sharing has to face. However, the emergence of RIA technology provides a good solution. Through the integration of Caringorm, Spring and iBATIS and lucubrating the Flex and ArcGIS Server technology, the paper designed an Enterprise Application Architecture for the field of geospatial information sharing, which has better reusability, scalability and maintainability and facilitates the modification and addition of functional modules. Based this architecture, the paper developed and implemented the Resources and Environmental Data Sharing Platform of Hebei province, which achieves multi-source data integration and sharing, greatly improves the utilization of data outcome, breaks information barriers between departments, eliminates information silos and promotes the process of information resources development and utilization. The system is currently running stable, overcomes the poor interaction and slow response of original system and has a richer user interface. In the future work, we will improve the current system and use this architecture in other professional spatial information systems.

Acknowledgments. The authors wish to thank the independent reviewers for the manuscript, Hebei Academy of Sciences important support Project(Grant No. 11104), Hebei Academy of Sciences Youth Fund Project(Grant No. 11128) for finance support and the Program Committee of CSE 2011 for opportunity.

References

1. ArGIS API for Flex On-line Help, `http://www.resources.esri.com/arcgisserver/apis/flex`
2. Chen, Q., She, J.F., Pan, S., Xiao, K., Jiang, H.D.: RIA-based Way of Building WebGIS. J. Remote Sensing Information 104, 89–94 (2009)
3. Lan, X.J., Duan, B.X., Peng, J.W.: Research and Application on WebGIS Based on Ajax. J. Science of Surveying and Mapping 2, 214–218 (2009)
4. Long, M., Li, T., Wang, Q.S., Qi, D.S.: Storage and Search of WebGIS multimedia data based on RIA. J. Science of Surveying and Mapping 2, 173–174 (2010)

5. Pan, D., Shen, J.Y.: Research on Soft Architecture for Real-Time Metadata Management. Journal of Xi An JiaoTong University 6, 566–569 (2005)
6. Shao, X.J., Shi, H.J., Li, X.Y., Zhao, X.B.: Research and Design of Meta Data Integration Architecture Based on Model-driven. J. Computer Engineering and Applications 15, 173–174 (2006)
7. Wang, L.L., Hu, D.H., Wang, Z.C., Song, H.: Research and Realization of RIA WebGIS based on Flex. J. Computer Application 12, 3257–3260 (2008)
8. Wu, T., Qi, M.R., Li, Y., Yan, H.W.: Research on the Application of RIA Technique in WebGIS Development. J. Bulletin of Surveying and Mapping 6, 34–37 (2006)
9. Zhou, B.X., Zhou, J.H., Wang, K.: Research on Grid Power Enterprise Information Visualizaion System Based on ArcGIS Flex API. J. Geomatics and Spatial Information Technology 2, 123–126 (2010)

Traffic Accidents Prediction Model Based on Fuzzy Logic

Hao Wang[1], Lai Zheng[2], and Xianghai Meng[2]

[1] Heilongjiang Province Highway Construction Bureau, Harbin 150076, China
alanwh1972@tom.com
[2] School of Transportation Science and Engineering, Harbin Institute of Technology, Harbin 150090, China
zhenglai1985@163.com, mengxianghai100@126.com

Abstract. Traffic accidents prediction has an important meaning to the improvement of traffic safety management, and urban traffic accidents prediction model which based on fuzzy logic is taken forward in this paper by contrasting to traditional traffic accidents prediction models. This model is trained and tested by the traffic and traffic accident data of 133 Harbin city roads, and finally gets a fuzzy logic prediction model which has 41 effective rules. The test result shows that there is a good relationship between the observed numbers and predicted numbers. Thus, prediction of the urban traffic accidents by fuzzy logic is viable. Besides, the concept of safety improvement factor is taken forward, which can be used to find out the prominent influence factors of high risk road and then to improve the safety of these roads.

Keywords: traffic accident, prediction, fuzzy logic, control rules, prominent influence factors.

1 Introduction

Traffic safety is not only a social problem, but also a technical problem. The result and reliability of traffic accident prediction has an important meaning to the improvement of the traffic safety management.

Traditional traffic accidents prediction methods have their respective advantages and disadvantages. Time-series method makes use of former traffic accidents data to extrapolate the future, which is fit for steady-going roads or area road systems, but the problem is that it needs a long time traffic accidents data. Empirical model is a prediction model based on given road at given area, thus this model has better pertinence and applicability as well as inferior transplantable ability. Regression analysis establishes function relationship between traffic accidents and influence factors by statistics theory, and then predicts traffic accidents by the function. This method is in common use, however, because it fulsome depends on the history data, so the extrapolation and sensitivity is not very good. Gray prediction finds information from the accidents data themselves, and then seek after its immanent disciplinarian. This method can be used to do rapid and short-time prediction when the data partial lost or the datum is not integrity.

In recent years, some scholars find that generalized linear models such as negative binominal distribution and Poisson distribution accord better with the actual condition

H. Tan and M. Zhou (Eds.): CSE 2011, Part I, CCIS 201, pp. 101–108, 2011.

[1-5], and they have done some researches on its transplantable ability[6, 7]. With the development of ITS and GIS, these technologies have been used more and more in traffic accidents prediction. In China, lots of researches have been done to predict accidents based on gray theory, neural network, and fractal theory [8-10].

The essence makes the occurrence of traffic accidents have randomicity, at the same time, inducing factors of accidents have obvious fuzziness and uncertainty, and how to deal with all of these is always a hard subject to traditional accidents prediction methods. Thus, accident prediction method based on fuzzy logic is brought forward.

1.1 Fuzzy Logic Accidents Prediction Model

According to the characteristics of traffic and traffic accidents, annual average daily traffic (AADT), driving difficulty (DD), velocity (V) and lane width (LW) can be used as input variables of accidents prediction system. Obviously, driving difficulty has very distinct fuzziness. The output variable is the number of accidents per kilometer (AF) at each artery road. Accidents prediction system and its fuzzy inference model's structure are shown in Fig. 1, and the key is to ensure the effective control rules.

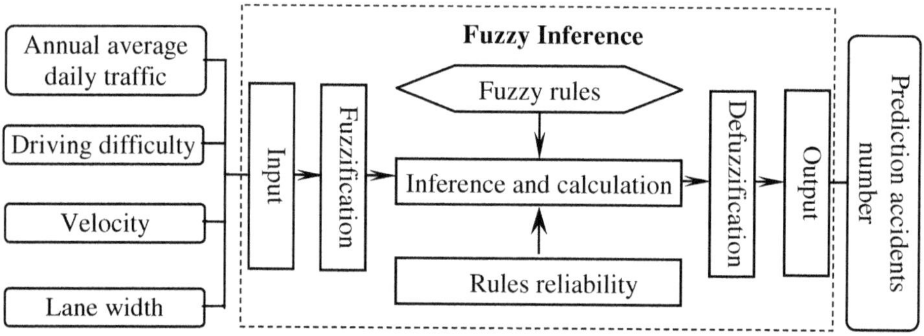

Fig. 1. Accidents prediction system & fuzzy inference model

1.2 Fuzzification

To fuzzify input and output domain, the number and quantification levels of each variables have to be estimated. In this paper, fuzzy statistics theory and 133 Harbin arteries accidents data are used to ensure the fuzzy sets of each variable and its corresponding membership functions. Annual average daily traffic is fuzzified into three fuzzy sets: low, medium and high. Driving difficulty is fuzzified into easy, medium, less difficult and difficult. Velocity has low and high two fuzzy sets. Lane width is fuzzified into three sets: narrow, medium and wide. To get better prediction precision, the output variable is fuzzified into five sets: few, less, medium, more and many. Membership functions of input and output variables are shown as Fig. 2 and Fig. 3.

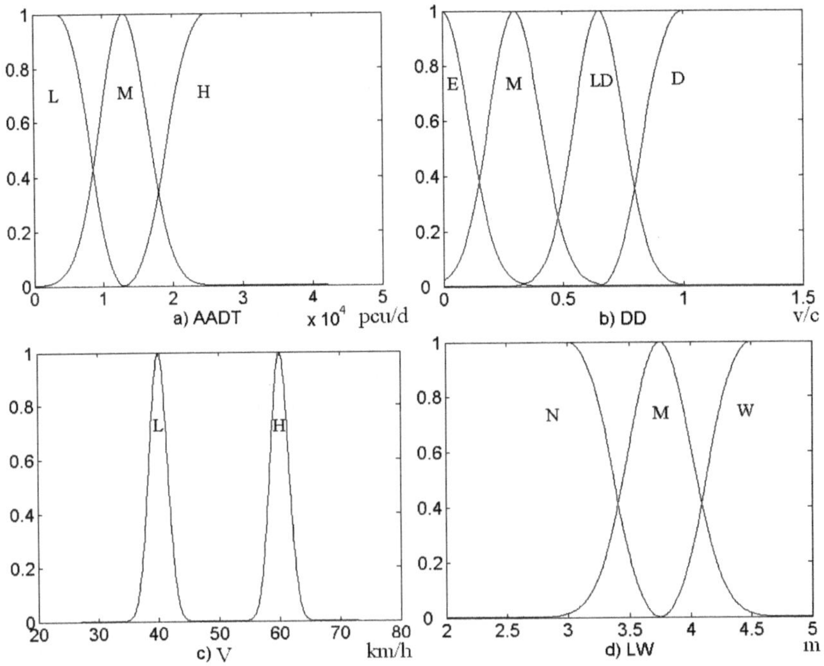

Fig. 2. Membership functions of input variables

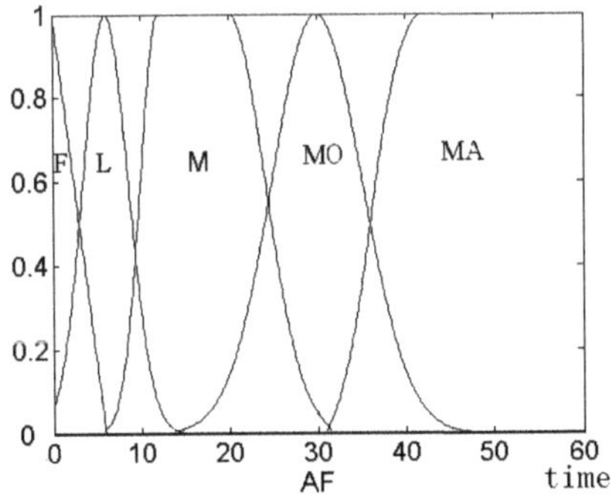

Fig. 3. Membership functions of output variable

1.3 Fuzzy Control Rules

The procedure for deriving a fuzzy control rule is as follow. For the ith test site, a rule can be constructed, e.g., if annual average daily traffic is high, driving difficulty is difficult, velocity is high, and lane width is narrow, then the number of accidents per kilometer is many. The weight of this rule is:

$$w_i = \mu_{AADT_i} \wedge \mu_{DD_i} \wedge \mu_{V_i} \wedge \mu_{LW_i} \wedge \mu_{AF_i} \tag{1}$$

Where: w_i is the weight of the ith rule, based on the data of the ith test site. μ_{AADT_i} is the highest degree of membership of annual average daily traffic among all fuzzy sets at the ith test site. μ_{DD_i} is the highest degree of membership of driving difficulty among all fuzzy sets at the ith test site. μ_{V_i} is the highest degree of membership of velocity among all fuzzy sets at the ith test site. μ_{LW_i} is the highest degree of membership of lane width among all fuzzy sets at the ith test site. μ_{AF_i} is the highest degree of membership of the number of accidents per kilometre among all fuzzy sets at the ith test site.

In this paper, fuzzy control rules are developed based on two data sets that were collected at 133 sites during 1999-2004 in Harbin. The first data set contain 78 sites, which is numbered 1-78, is used in training; the other data set has 55 sites, which is numbered 79-133, is the testing data.

After reviewing data from every site, a total of 78 rules are obtained. If the antecedences of several rules are the same, then the rule, which has the largest weight, is kept. Finally, 41 rules are obtained, shown as Table 1.

Table 1. Fuzzy control rules

IF				THEN
AADT	DD	LW	V	AF
H	H	NA	H	MO
M	M	NA	H	M
H	EH	NA	H	MA
:	:	:	:	:
:	:	:	:	:
L	L	W	L	F
M	H	N	H	MO

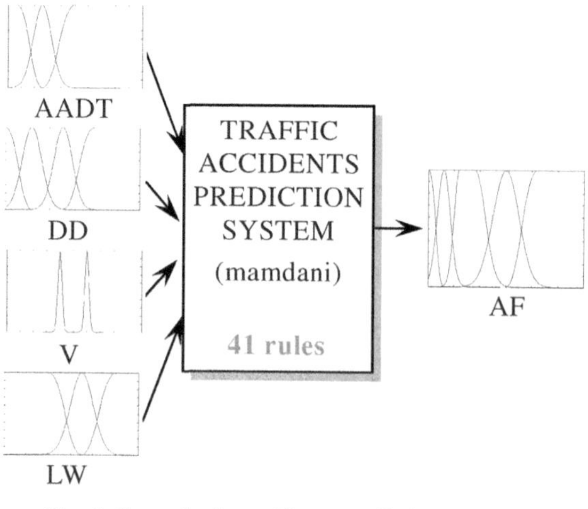

Fig. 4. Fuzzy logic accidents prediction model

1.4 Accidents Prediction Model

According to input variables, theirs membership functions, and 41 effective control rules, the number of prediction accidents per kilometer can be obtained by defuzzification. The final fuzzy logic accident prediction model is shown as Fig. 4.

2 Test and Analysis of the Model

Put the test data set into the fuzzy logic model can get the prediction accidents number per kilometer and the result is shown in Table 2. For testing the precision of the model, two error formulas are used, the first is used to test the precision of single sample, and the second is used to the precision of the whole sample. Table 2 display the predicted numbers of accidents per kilometer corresponding to the observed numbers of accidents per kilometer. Figure 5 shows the predicted and observed numbers of accidents per kilometer at each location, and there is a compositor of the whole sample by the number.

Table 2. Contrast among test data

No.	Observed (accidents/km)	Predicted (accidents/km)	Absolute error	No.	Observed (accidents/km)	Predicted (accidents/km)	Absolute error	Total error
79	21.60	21.9	0.30	107	1.65	3.20	1.55	0.08
80	13.41	15.9	2.49	108	2.84	3.00	0.16	
81	30.01	35.6	5.59	109	3.43	3.20	0.23	
82	2.72	3.2	0.48	110	0.35	0.60	0.25	
83	18.18	19.9	1.72	111	6.50	7.20	0.70	
84	17.54	15.9	1.64	112	1.62	1.50	0.12	
85	15.50	16.2	0.70	113	2.36	3.20	0.84	
86	14.49	15.9	1.41	114	12.67	12.20	0.47	
87	39.10	35.6	3.50	115	6.39	6.90	0.51	
88	6.95	8.1	1.15	116	3.00	6.60	3.60	
89	17.86	15.9	1.96	117	3.32	3.00	0.32	
90	11.58	21.9	10.32	118	12.81	15.90	3.09	
91	16.97	15.9	1.07	119	4.83	0.00	4.83	
92	20.45	21.9	1.45	120	19.80	21.90	2.10	
93	13.74	15.9	2.16	121	8.10	7.20	0.90	
94	10.06	21.9	11.84	122	0.73	0.60	0.13	
95	0.54	0.6	0.06	123	11.39	34.03	22.64	
96	15.75	15.9	0.15	124	0.67	0.00	0.67	
97	4.44	1.2	3.24	125	1.02	0.60	0.42	
98	3.43	7.5	4.07	126	0.26	0.60	0.34	
99	6.19	6.9	0.71	127	12.27	12.20	0.07	
100	26.85	21.9	4.95	128	20.48	15.90	4.58	
101	10.02	8.9	1.12	129	10.31	7.20	3.11	
102	8.35	6.6	1.75	130	1.28	0.00	1.28	
103	7.99	6.9	1.09	131	4.82	6.90	2.08	
104	15.99	15.9	0.09	132	5.77	0.00	5.77	
105	7.77	6.9	0.87	133	1.68	2.10	0.42	
106	4.45	6.9	2.45					

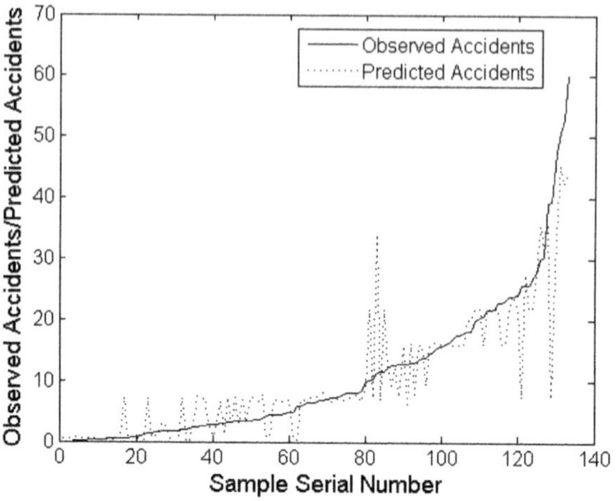

Fig. 5. The predicted and observed number at each location

The error shows that the predicted numbers of accidents per kilometer have a relatively good correlation with the observed numbers of accidents per kilometer, and the total error is only 8%. However, for some points, there are still have some biggish error, and this is caused by the randomicity of traffic accidents. Of course, how to construct a consummate control rules and resolve the randomicity problem is still a job need more research.

3 Identify the Prominent Influence Factors of High Risk Artery

The effective control rules not only express the relationship between the input and output, but also clearly show the mechanism of occurrence of traffic accidents. Thus, it is not difficult to use this model to ensure the prominent influence factors of high risk artery. So a safety improvement factor (SIF) is introduced [11].

$$SIF = \frac{|N_0 - N_1|}{N_0} \times 100\% \tag{2}$$

Where: N_0 is the observed number of traffic accidents at the high risk artery, and N_1 is the predicted number of traffic accidents at the high risk artery after changing a influence factor.

In order to see how each input variable affects the safety of the artery, three steps are followed. Firstly, a location is selected that is likely to have more traffic accidents than other sites. Then, one roadway or traffic condition is varied in a certain range at each time, and the SIF is calculated. The prominent influence factor can be ensured by SIF, and the principle is the bigger the SIF is after the changing, the more it influences the occurrence of traffic accidents.

Take the number 4 site for example, the AADT, DD, V, and LW are 44320, 1.09, 60, and 3.25, respectively, and the observed accidents is 60.09 time/km. When the AADT changes down to 13000, the SIF is 84.91%, and when DD changes down to

0.1, the SIF is 98.11%, but when change the other two variables, the variety of SIF is not obvious. All the concrete varieties are shown in Fig 6. Thus, annual average daily traffic and driving difficulty are the prominent influence factors to site 4.

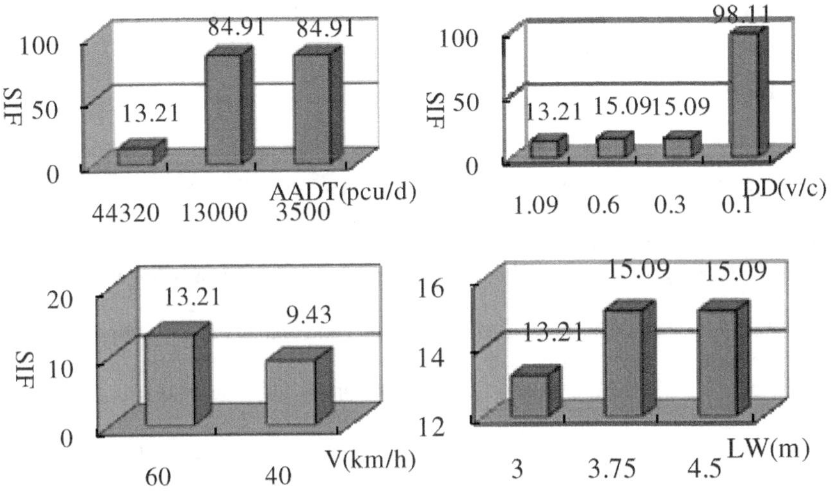

Fig. 6. Safety improvement factor vs. input variables

4 Case Analysis

This paper take a part of road network from 2010 Harbin program road network as a case and do the case analysis by the fuzzy logic model. This area locates in the center of the city, divided into 42 traffic zones, and the road network contains 44 arteries. The vehicle trip gross in 2010 is 411150 pcu/d, from which the annual average daily traffic can be got by weighted average method. Driving difficulty is determined by traffic load and cross section, and the velocity and lane width have been given in the program. Input the four variables into the model can get the number of prediction accidents at each artery. In this area there will be 787 traffic accidents in 2010, and 2.16 per day.

5 Conclusion

Modeling a traffic accidents prediction system has proven to be a very difficult task. Traffic accidents are caused by complex interactions among many roadway, vehicle, human, and environmental factors. But, they also occur because of random variables such as inattentiveness, misjudgment, drivers, recklessness and other unforeseeable events that may contribute significantly to the modeling error. The ultimate objective of this paper is to develop a model that can predict the city artery traffic accidents, and find the prominent influence factors of high risk artery. Because of the random character of traffic accidents, it cannot be realistically expected the developed methodology will be efficient in predicting the exact number of traffic accidents. It has been proved the fuzzy logic model is viable in predicting city artery traffic accidents. However, there are still further researches to do to improve the reliability and efficiency of the fuzzy logic model. In addition, new extensive data sets will be necessary to provide the basis for constructing a high quality model.

References

1. Milton, J., Mannering, F.: The relationship among highway geometrics, traffic-related elements and motor-vehicle accident frequencies. Transportation 25, 395–413 (1998)
2. Abdel-Aty, M., Radwan, A.E.: Modeling traffic accident occurrence and involvement. Accid. Anal. and Prev. 32, 633–642 (2000)
3. Ivan, J.N., Wang, C., Bernardo, N.R.: Explaining two-lane highway crash rates using land-use and hourly exposure. Accid. Anal. and Prev. 32, 787–795 (2000)
4. Wood, G.R.: Generalized linear accident models and goodness of fit testing. Accid. Anal. and Prev. 34, 417–427 (2002)
5. Mountain, L., Fawaz, B., Jarrett, D.: Accident prediction models for roads with minor junctions. Accid. Anal. and Prev. 28, 695–707 (1996)
6. Hadayeghi, A., Shalaby, A.S., Persaud, B.N., Cheung, C.: Temporal transferability and updating of zonal level accident prediction models. Accid. Anal. and Prev. 38, 579–589 (2006)
7. Sawalha, Z., Sayed, T.: Transferability of accident prediction models. Safety Science 44, 209–219 (2006)
8. Li, X.Y., Yan, Y.S., Jiang, G.F.: Grey-Markov Model for Road Accidents Forecasting. Journal of Southwest Jiaotong University 11(2), 193–197 (2003)
9. Li, J., Shao, C.F.: Traffic Accident Forecast Model Based on BP Neural Network. Computer and Communications 24(2), 34–37 (2006)
10. Chen, P., Li, X.H., Sun, H.: Analysis of Traffic Accident Based on Fractal Theory. Journal of Highway and Transportation Research and Development 25(3), 130–133 (2008)
11. Xiao, J., Kulakowski, B.T., El-Gindy, M.: Prediction of risk of wet pavement accidents using fuzzy logic. Transportation Research Record 1717, 28–36 (1999)

Linear Array Sparsing Using the Cross-Entropy Immune Algorithm

Jian-Hua Zhang[1,2], Li Bian[3,4], and Wei-Zheng Pang[1]

[1] College of Information and Communication Engineering, Harbin Engineering University, Harbin 150001, China

[2] College of Traffic and Transport Engineering, Northeast Forestry University, Harbin,150040, China

Zhangjh811@163.com

[3] School of Electronic and Information Engineering, Harbin Institute of Technology Harbin, 150001, China

[4] College of Electronic and Information Engineering, Heilongjiang Institute of Science and Technology, Harbin, China

branran@163.com

Abstract. The main motivation to Sparsing is the reduction in cost and weight. A new approach for the synthesis of thinned uniformly spaced linear arrays is presented. The method is based on Cross Entropy and Immune theory.200 elements uniformly spaced symmetrically weighted array was thinned using the Cross Entropy Immune Algorithm to achieve a sidelobe power of less than –20dB. Thinned arrays' first null beam width is 13.5% wider than the original uniform array. The simulation results to synthesis were compared with the GA, and study of CEIA parameter choice was simply presented. It was benefit work utilizing the Cross Entropy Immune Algorithm for solving electromagnetic optimization problems.

Keywords: Linear Array, Cross-Entropy, Immune Algorithm, Parameter Choice.

1 Introduction

Thinning antenna arrays is the strategic elimination of a subset of active elements in the array in order to maintain similar radiation properties as the full array, but using a smaller number of elements in doing so. The main motivation to thinning is the reduction in cost and weight. Achievable designs by statistical array thinning of large arrays are presented by some scholar [1].In modern times, some intelligence methods [2] have all been used to thinning large arrays with great success. This paper addresses a different statistical approach for thinning linear arrays based on cross-entropy theory[3,4] .Lower sidelobes and wider first null beam width can be obtained as for the same filled array illuminated with uniform weighting.

2 Cross Entropy Immune Algorithm

Cross-Entropy (CE) is general stochastic optimization technology based on a fundamental principle of information theory called cross entropy (or Kullback-Leibler).In 1997, CE

H. Tan and M. Zhou (Eds.): CSE 2011, Part I, CCIS 201, pp. 109–114, 2011.

was first introduced by Reuven Y.Rubinstein[5] as an adaptive importance sampling for estimating probabilities of rare events and was extended soon thereafter to include both combinatorial and continuous optimization., The IA method has been widely used to solve the optimization problems by applying the same operation principle of human immune system. The capability of IA method for pattern recognition and memorization does provide a more efficient way to solve the discrete optimization problem as compared to the GA. information entropy shows its simple and effective characteristicsin solving the quantity of combinatorial optimization, and compensate for the slow speed of the immune algorithm in search of the optimal value process, A new approach for the synthesis of thinned uniformly spaced linear arrays is presented. The method is based on Cross Entropy and Immune theory.

2.1 Procedure

The computation procedure of CEIA method is executed as follows

step1: Antigens recognition
step2: Production of initial antibody population
step3: Affinity calculation
step4: Evaluation and selection
step5: Crossover and mutation
step6: Optimal strategy decision

The diversity[7] of feasible strategies in the population is measured between the antibodies and it will be increased toprevent local optimization during the searching process of optimal solution.the entropy *Ej* of the *j*th gene (*j*=1, 2,..., *M*) is defined as

$$E_j = -\sum_{i=1}^{N} P_{ij} log P_{ij} \tag{1}$$

where *N* is the number of antibodies and *Pij* is the probability of the *i*th allele coming out of the *j*th allele, the diversity of all genes is calculated as the mean value of informative entropy

$$E = \frac{1}{M} \sum_{j=1}^{M} E_j \tag{2}$$

the affinity between antibodies defined as

$$\left(AB_{ij}\right) = \frac{1}{1 + E(2)} \tag{3}$$

where *E(2)* is the information entropy of these two antibodies, *(AB)ij* is the affinity between the *i*th antibody and the *j*th antibody, so that 0<*(AB)ij*<1

2.2 Characteristic

The characteristic of immune algorithm Based on the information entropy can be summarized with the following

(1) The information entropy in evaluating the solution similarity of groups can objectively reflect its meaning

(2) The selection mechanism based on concentration can Guarantee the Algorithm convergence and the solutions group diversity
(3) Introducing threshold function can further improve the algorithm performance

3 Numerical Example

In the following, the presented array thinning synthesis results refer to a 200-element linear array for various degrees of thinning and for symmetrical positions of the turned ON element distributions. The considered array features an embedded isotropic element pattern and the inter-element distance d is equal to 0.5λ.

The score function is defined as the maximum sidelobe power of the far-field magnitude in the sidelobe region $\lambda/Nd < |u| < 1$of the original uniformly spaced array,

$$Score = \max\left|\frac{EP(u)}{FF_{\max}} 2\sum_{n=1}^{N/2} w_n \cos\left(k\cdot(n-0.5)d\cdot u\right)\right|^2 \quad (4)$$

N = Number of elements in the array = 200
w_n = Amplitude weight of element n, $w_n \in [0,1]$
d = Spacing between elements of original uniform array= 0.5λ
k = Wave number = $2\pi/\lambda$
u =cosφ, 0 <φ< 180o with 1000 equally spaced sample points between [0,1]
$EP(u)$ = Element pattern = 1 for isotropic sources
$FFmax$ = Peak value of far-field pattern $= 2\sum_n w_n$

The goal is to minimize this score function in the sidelobe region of the original uniformly spaced array. The optimized result represents the minimum peak sidelobe power for this design.

4 Results and Discussion

The design parameters for the CE method are given in Table 1. The initial values for the success probabilities of the N/2 Bernoulli distributions for the amplitude weights areset equal to 0.5. This gives each weight an equally likely chance of converging to 0 or 1.Initializing these values towards the extremes of 0 or 1 can help bias the thinning process.

Table 1. Types sizes for camera-ready papers

Symbol	Quantity	Value
α	Smoothing Parameter	0.7
ρ	Sample Selection Parameter	0.1
K	Population Size	100
w_n	Values of Array Element Weights	[0,1]
$P_m^{(0)}$	Initial Values for Success Probability	0.5

The overall best score achieved during optimization was –20.1647 dB and was located at the first sidelobe of the thinned array. The resulting radiation pattern and progression of Bernoulli success probabilities are shown in Figure 1. The resulting weight coefficients are presented in Table 2. It is apparent that the density of elements is greatest towards the center of the array and both element 1 and 100 are turned on maintaining the same aperture length as the original uniform array.

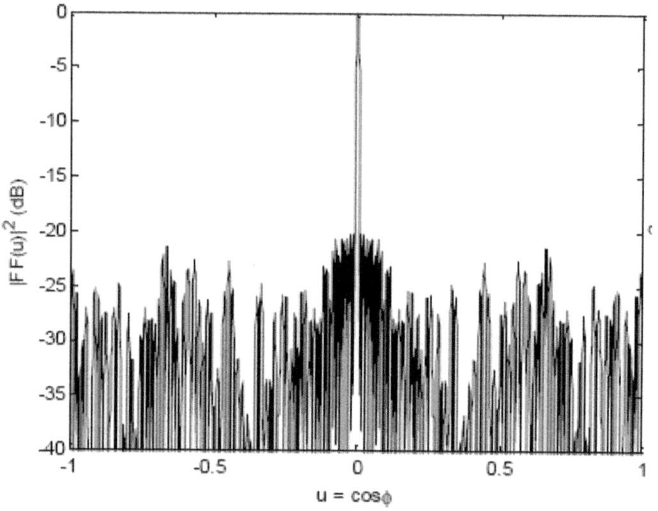

Fig. 1. Magnetization as a function of applied field

Table 2. Solution of array thinning procedure for symmetric linear array

Solution	Score (dB)	Element No.	Array Weights
			11111111111111111111
		n=1~50	11111111110111111011
			1111111011
CEIA	20.16		10110111110011101110
			11001011011010001011
		n=51~100	1111111111
			11111111111111111111
			11111111111111111111
		n=1~50	1111001111
GA	22.09		
			10011111110111110100
			00101011100100101110
		n=51~100	0010101101

The results achieved using CE are similar to those presented in [6]. The measurable for the array pattern computed using GA is given in Table 3.

Table 3. Comparison of CEIA results to literature

Solution	PSP(dB)	BW(deg)	No.Active Elements	Element Gain(dB)
CEIA	-20.1647	1.295	164/200(82%)	22.15
GA	-22.09	1.46	154/200(77%)	21.8

5 Study of CEIA Parameter Choice

Two measurable quantities were recorded:

1)The average peak sidelobe power
2)Number of iterations required for convergence

The results of the study are given in Figure 2. Overall, there are obvious tradeoffs between speed of convergence and the number of elite samples required for accurately calculating the best score.

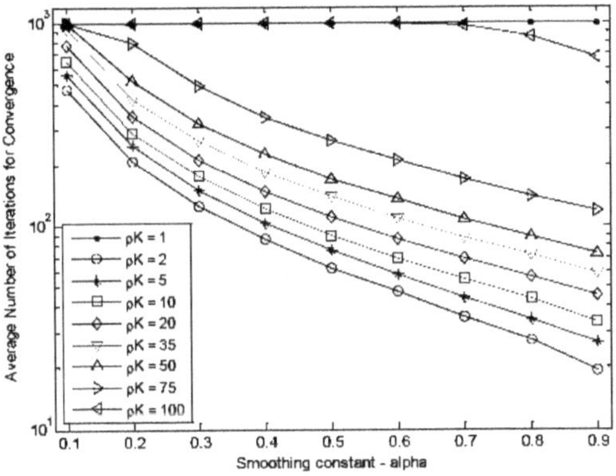

Fig. 2. Average number of iterations before convergence

6 Conclusions

This paper introduced the use of the CEIA theory for thinning periodic linear arrays to obtain the lowest possible peak sidelobe level. The presented results demonstrate that the new method is quite effective to synthesize both highly filled as well as massively thinned linear arrays. A comparison with published results for similar thinned array designs proved that the new method achieved the lower peak sidelobe and wider first null beam width results for all considered cases.

References

1. Ho, S.L., Yang, S.Y., Ni, G.Z., Wong, K.F.: An improved PSO method with application to multimodal functions of inverse problems. IEEE Trans. Magn. 43(4), 1597–1600 (2007)
2. Deligkaris, K.V.: Thinned Planar Array Design Using Boolean PSO With Velocity Mutation. IEEE Trans. Magn. 45(3), 1490–1493 (2009)
3. Ho, S.L., Yang, S.: The Cross-Entropy Method and Its Application to Inverse Problems. IEEE Trans. Magn. 46(8), 3401–3404 (2010)
4. Connor, J.D., Foo, S.Y., Weatherspoon, M.H.: Synthesizing antenna array sidelobe levels and null placements using the cross entropy method. In: Proc. 34th IEEE Annu. Conf. Industrial Electronics, IECON 2008, pp. 1937–1941 (2008)
5. Rubinstein, R.: The cross entropy method for combinatorial and continuous optimizations. Method. Comput. Appl. Probabil. 2, 127–190 (1999)
6. Haupt, R.L.: Thinned Arrays Using Genetic Algorithms. IEEE Trans. Antennas and Propagat. 42(7), 993–999 (1994)
7. Dasgupta, D.: Artificial Immune Systems and Their Applications. Springer, Heidelberg (1999)

A Study on the Difference of IT Skill between Retrained Professionals and Recent Graduates

Weixin Yao

School of Business and Administration
DongHua University
ShangHai, China 200051
yaoweixin@163.com

Abstract. In order to go back to the active workforce, many unemployed IT professionals choose to upgrade their skills by accepting retraining. Being older and often far from their college education, these workers often demonstrate poor results during the employment screening tests because most of time the employment screening and interviews are evaluated by using the same procedure as the recent college graduates. The results of the tests introduced in this paper show that if memorizing part is removed these professionals can perform at the same or even better level than recent college graduates. It proves out that the hiring companies can take into consideration those retrained IT professionals.

Keywords: comparison, professionals, graduates, retrain, IT Skill.

1 Introduction

In the last decade, the method of managing decisions in the IT companies was influenced by the multitude of financial, business and social crises starting from the notorious dot-com depression of the early 2000s [1], followed by the IT downturn connected to the events of 9.11[2] and the financial crisis which began in 2007. In order to save costs and have better control over the development efforts a large number of IT companies are considering bringing their IT functions back in-house.

In China IT sector we see that many skilled IT professionals endeavor returning back to work. A large number of them are being retrained to obtain new skills related to the new technology offerings from UFIDA, HP, Microsoft, IBM, etc. Although they are well qualified to perform general IT duties, they are lack of working experience with the skills they had recently acquired[3]. In order to make the most correct decision from human resource and business perspective, HR managers and IT managers must decide on how to classify these members of the workforce and how to approach them in the best possible way[4].

Because of the aforesaid constraints, the IT management often retreats towards the second most obvious way: hiring the latest graduates from the IT training schools, teaching them business skills required to succeed in the IT branch of the particular organization, merging them into the working environment. IT training schools today perform double tasks: they educate technical college graduates who decided to make Information Technology into their career and retrain those who are already a part of the

H. Tan and M. Zhou (Eds.): CSE 2011, Part I, CCIS 201, pp. 115–119, 2011.

IT community but lost their employment due to downsizing in the recent financial crises. Those members of the second group already have the required skills. The remaining question is whether they would be able to catch up with the new technology in the new IT environment.

Many employers today try to test their perspective employees before bringing them in-house for the face-to-face interview. Karten's[5] discussion is centered on the aptitude tests. The role of aptitude tests is very similar to the technical filtering performed today. Many of the technical skill evaluations resemble the subject exams taken at the high school and diploma levels. Former high school and even university students who recently graduated from the IT programs have acquired a mighty skill of passing these exams with relative ease. However, Spiller[6] asserts that a large number of students cannot correlate their knowledge with real life situations. On the other hand the re-trained workers often tumble over those exams because they are often much older and do not have as good a memory. Because of the fact that those skill tests are often conducted by the third party over the Internet , it is hard for the HR managers to evaluate the extent of the real skills of those re-trained workers. It is also difficult for them to decide whether bring them back for the face-to-face interview based on their test scores.

2 Experiment Preparation

The study described following in this paper is based on the data collected during the exams of the students of the Information Technology Program and the exams of the re-trained IT professionals who have a previous experience in the field but had to be reeducated on the new technology skills to be employable in Shanghai, China. The students of the IT program are the recent graduates of a three-year technical college. Most of them do not have any work experience and their study process was practically uninterrupted.

The participants of the re-training program were offered an entry exam to verify their suitability for the program and knowledge of programming. The quality of the skills in the group can be proven by the fact that by the end of the four months course six of these IT professionals found a job based on the skill set they possessed before entering the program.

The members of both control groups were trained in the subject of Java development. The regular college course "Introduction to Java" was based on three hours a week of study over 16 weeks (48 hours in total). Students were subjected to the regular midterm and final exams upon that their subject grade was determined.

Those professionals of the second group had a dense program. The course was delivered in three-hour sections four days a week over four weeks (48 hours in total). The participants had a test in each of the first three course weeks. The final exam taken at the end of the fourth week was practically identical to the final exam of the IT course.

The same college faculty taught both groups and the same professor created the tests and graded them. Both groups of students were given the same break to finish the tests. The total score was calculated by dividing the number of correctly answered questions to the overall number of questions. The partially answered questions were getting partial marks.

3 Results of Experiment

The result of the experiment was listed in the following two tables. Table 1 contains the result obtained from examining the retrained IT professionals. Table 2 contains the result obtained from examining the recent IT program graduates.

In the course of experiment, the first two tests were completed by IT professionals were based on the same principles as the ones used for the students of the IT program, i.e. all materials were to be memorized and no books/laptops were allowed. During the last two tests the IT professionals were allowed using books and computers.

Table 1. Results of Retrained IT Professionals

No	Week1	Week2	Week3	Final	No	Week1	Week2	Week3	Final
1	81	79	88	74	12	93	75	95	93
2	98	74	94	84	13	93	75	98	89
3	86	82	96	87	14	45	67	65	71
4	72	75	78	80	15	93	93	99	79
5	91	71	92	92	16	74	95	97	82
6	69	47	95	77	17	79	89	89	88
7	57	45	60	73	18	56	49	88	74
8	84	69	98	80	19	85	89	89	85
9	98	85	96	95	20	83	89	98	98
10	69	82	98	80	21	81	69	89	83
11	79	55	95	98	22	77	67	97	82

Table 2. Results of IT Program Graduates

No	Midterm	Final	No	Midterm	Final
1	84	74	11	90	53
2	76	68	12	80	73
3	87	62	13	46	57
4	78	62	14	82	48
5	79	74	15	85	63
6	91	83	16	76	55
7	79	64	17	86	80
8	79	72	18	74	68
9	90	72	19	85	58
10	83	65	20	82	71

According to the outcome of the experiment, we can conclude the following corollaries:

(1) Despite having little or no experience at all, the students who study uninterrupted can exceed the seasonal IT professionals on the tests that rely solely on the memory.

(2) The IT professionals will perform at least not worse than the students if they are given the opportunity to use any available materials (internet, books, course slides, etc.)

4 Discussion the Results

The present and recent past economic conditions lead to a large number of layoffs in the IT industry. IT professionals possess good domain knowledge and multiple years of industry experience. During the period of layoff, they are eligible to participate in the government sponsored training programs and are receiving unemployment benefits. The aim of these programs is to aid these professionals to return back to the employment. The experience in software development these candidates already possess will have helped them to fill up the new industry vacancies. The main reason for their participation in the retraining programs is the lack of knowledge of the new IT technology.

Companies employing computer programmers today hesitate between two kinds of requirements: soft (domain knowledge) skills and hard (technology) skills. It is difficult to determine whether mature professionals or college students have different levels of soft skills. However, it is obvious to notice that domain knowledge is never screened first. If they start screening from the technical skills, companies will able to automate and simplify the process. However, this approach also makes those who may succeed in doing the job into disadvantage if they are not able to memorize major computing concept and model.

When the candidates applying to a certain position, many companies usually have the unwritten requirements of the years of experience and maturity. If a company decides to hire a college graduate, HR manger will be inclined to choose straight examination style testing for the screening procedure. However, if the company is willing to consider a recently retrained mature professional, they would like to change the screening procedure from exam style testing to the technical interview. Because many tests today require straight memorizing of the software concept, the companies using these tests may end up with the candidates who were the best at passing the tests but who are not appropriate for doing the job at hand.

The results of the experiments indicate that the approach towards testing of the candidates who apply for the relatively low level technical positions should be changed in order to give a consideration to those IT professionals who have enough overall experience in the marketplace but have to apply for the positions in the areas that are new for them. The screening party may allow all candidates to use any possible source of information if changing the questions from requiring straight answers to the ones calling for the understanding of the subject. The results of the experiment show that a significant number of candidates would still fail the screening even if all information is available during the test. If employers change their approach, they may be able to successfully evaluate the members of the workforce with the large practical experience. The successful passing of the screening tests would give them the opportunity to present all of their skills and experience to the hiring company during a more meaningful next level interview.

References

1. Lewellen, J.: Discussion of The Internet downturn: Finding valuation factors in Spring 2000. Journal of accounting & economics(0165-4101) 34(1-3), 237 (2003)
2. Posner, E.A., Vermeule, A.: Crisis Governance in the Administrative State: 9/11 and the Financial Meltdown of 2008, University of Chicago Law Review 1613 (2009)
3. Hoffman, T.: EDS Pushing Massive IT Retraining Effort. Computerworld 39(10), 14 (2005)
4. Gatta, M.: Low-Skill Workers, Technology, and Education: A New Vision for Workforce Development Policy. The Economic and Labor Relations Review 19(1), 109–127 (2008)
5. Karten, H.: Pros and Cons of Standardized Aptitude Tests for Programmers. Computerworld 16(28) (1982)
6. Spiller, S.: Trend spotting. Supply Management 9(12), 37 (2004)

Construction of Distributed System for Network Public Opinion Monitor and Analysis

Xin Zha* and Liangming Li

Department of Information and Engineering, Zibo Vocational Institute, Zibo, 255314, China
lilm@nuaa.edu.cn

Abstract. The system of network public opinion monitor and analysis could detect and process the massive public opinion data in the internet automatically, thus the difficult in traditional manual processing is effective solved. In this paper, the construction of distributed system for network public opinion monitor and analysis is presented. Firstly, the importance of monitoring and analyzing network public opinion is summarized, and then the system structure and infrastructure as well as main function are introduced, after that the main solving problems are analyzed. The proposed system is an important assistant tool for decision making to deal with the emergency, which could improve the ability of public opinion management.

Keywords: network public opinion, information aggregate engine, real-time tracking to URL library.

1 Introduction

Public sentiment is the people's attitude to the society governor and policies, which is existed in certain time and social space and is about the happen, development and change of the social event. The propagated information in the internet is people's view and attitude about the social phenomenon and hot issues. It's involved in the topic of politics, economy, military, entertainment, sports, health, science and technology, personal life and so on [1]. Network public sentiment maps the social public sentiment from reality to internet and reflects it directly, in which the social public opinion and development trend are presented directly and quickly. It has become the weatherglass of important field such as politics, economy and culture and has drawled high attention of the nation and government [2].

There are also certain negative effects of network public opinion for the internet freedom, such as the rumor spread, privacy disclosure, extreme and irrational personal attack. Moreover, the hostile forces initiated the offensive "peaceful evolution" to our nation by the internet. Thus, the network public opinion has become important factor to sustainable and orderly social development as well as social harmony and stability.

How to make the best use of the circumstances and improve the analysis ability to public opinion are the serious issues and challenges to comprehend and guide the development trend of pubic opinion.

---

* This paper was supported by the Science and Technology Program of Shandong province College (No. J10LG79).

H. Tan and M. Zhou (Eds.): CSE 2011, Part I, CCIS 201, pp. 120–125, 2011.

2 Research Status

The conception of TDT (Topic Detection and Tracking, TDT) first appeared in 1996 when the DARPA (Defense Advanced Research Projects Agency DARPA) of America require a new technical to judge the news theme automatically from data flow without manual intervention. The Online event detection and tracking is one of the research subjects, and both the Carnegie Mellon University and University of Massachusetts have researched the similar project and achieved positive results.

With the development and popularization of information transformation technology the network is considered as the best platform for information communication and knowledge sharing. It is recognized as the forth media after newspaper, broadcasting and television and has became one of the important carrier to reflect the public opinion, and consequently more and more attention had paid to it.

However, the research of network public opinion lack support of the subject system in our country and need further investigation, therefore consecutive and high quality researches were rare [3]. The network public opinion monitor and analysis system is a tool that gathers, classifies, integrates and filters the various information from the network to generate the real-time reports for hot spot information and netizen's opinion and so on. Most of the system about the network public opinion monitor and analysis in market belong to software, however the system that could encapsulated in hardware is the development trend [4] [5]. In this paper we introduce the construction of network public opinion monitor and analysis system and it can be encapsulated in hardware.

3 System Design

When design the system we first clarify the methods of information publishing and receiving, and then analyze the mechanism and rules of information dissemination, after that we summarize the necessary method and condition for public opinion monitor and analysis to find a feasible way according to the information exchanging mode. The system design is introduced below.

3.1 System Architecture

Usually, most of the practical projects of software belong to the single architecture of B/S or C/S, however we combine B/S with C/S when design the system architecture. Thus, the user could visit the URL in the internet at anytime and centralize the system update and maintenance with the B/S architecture; on the other hand, the client in C/S has powerful processing ability to ensure the faster interaction and strong security [6]. The designed system could meet the demand both the central office and the changeable location.

3.2 System Structure

The design object of distributed system for network public opinion monitor and analysis including: importing the information aggregate engine and the mechanism of emotion analysis and judgment, establishing the preplan mechanism for public opinion, implementing the strategic management for URL, could be encapsulated in hardware. The system could observe, analyze, study and judge the netizen's ideological trend and then the public opinion could achieve the real-time transformation and provide support for network manager to make decision. The system structure is given in Fig. 1.

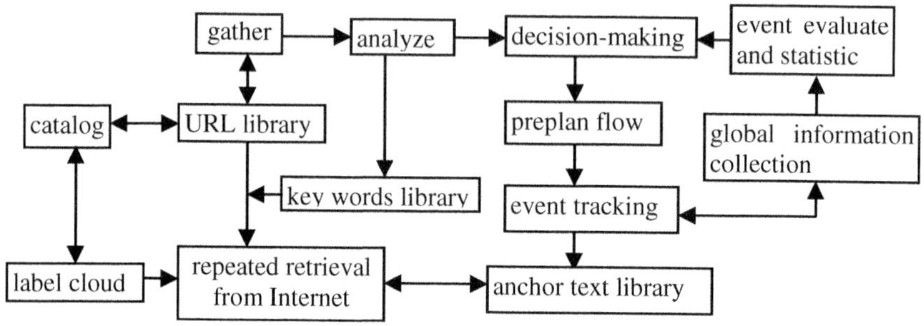

Fig. 1. System structure

3.3 Function Module of the System

1) Tendentiousness analysis module

Hot topics are identified in the given period according to the parameters, such as the authority of the source, the quantity of comments and the intensiveness of speaking time. The viewpoint expressed in the public opinion is analyzed to offer analysis reference for finding out the tendentiousness of the netizens' ideological tendency.

2) Information tracking module

The hot spot information is tracked and its tendentiousness and tendency are analyzed. The tracking contents include source, reproduced quantity, reproduced address, area distribution, information publishers and so on. All the information is tracked according to the flow in Fig. 2.

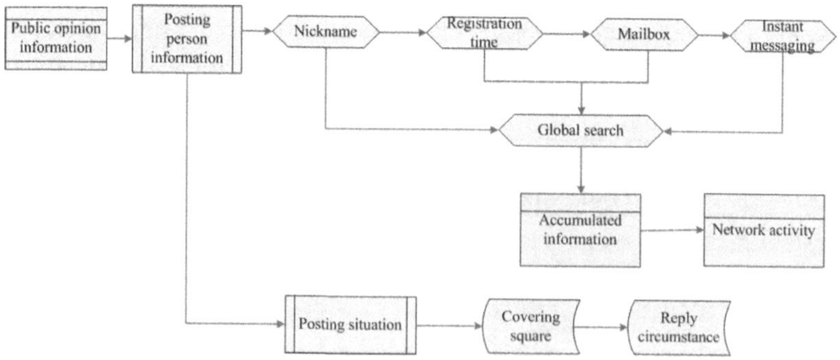

Fig. 2. Affairs flow chart

3) Emergency analysis module
Emergency information is monitored, analyzed and tracked, so it will be aware earlier. The hot spot information and emergencies from processed public opinions are matched to the corpus of the information and the rules of the alarm monitoring information, therefore, the important public opinions are sent to the public opinion manager. This module plays the role of alarm system and could prevent all kinds of vicious incidents.

4) Report generation module
The various reports that browsed at the client are generated according to the processing results from public opinion analysis engine. Information retrieval function is provided, hence the hot topics and tendentiousness could be inquired according to specified conditions and the content of the information could be browsed, therefore, it could provide support of decision-making for the internet managers.

4 Resolved Main Problem

The system overcomes the limitation of bandwidth and the control strategies of server access. It implements the strategic management for URL and real-time tracking of URL library to effectively achieve the target that “what you needed is what you get". The test environment including: Intel core2 quad processor, 32G memory, 1G network speed, 20 single-node thread pools and 1,500 nodes are allocated to each thread; the maximum of concurrent traversal in each node is 300,000 URL. Considering the persistence and stability the thread time delay is set as 2 minutes, so when the user initiates a topic the system will grasp it within 10 minutes and the minimum is 500 milliseconds. As a result, the search efficiency of engine in single node is much higher than Google’s.

The system extended nodes by established the cloud computing terminals, and realized the distributed collaborative of internet information processing for cloud computing. It could be operated at multiple platforms and could be encapsulated in hardware.

Considering the internet environment the main sources of public opinion including: news, comment, BBS, blog, Really Simple Syndication (RSS). The information aggregate engine and emotion analysis and judgment are employed to control the coverage and coordination of public opinion supervision by integrating the mechanism of information retrieval, collection, analysis and processing. Besides, the preplan mechanism for public opinion was established. If the public opinion information was emerged it will be responded and processed in the shortest time to avoid was widespread. In addition, the public opinion information is analyzed and calculated to generate statistical reports for network manager. Therefore, the management for network public opinion is improved to a new level. The solution for repeat collection of posting is shown in Fig. 3.

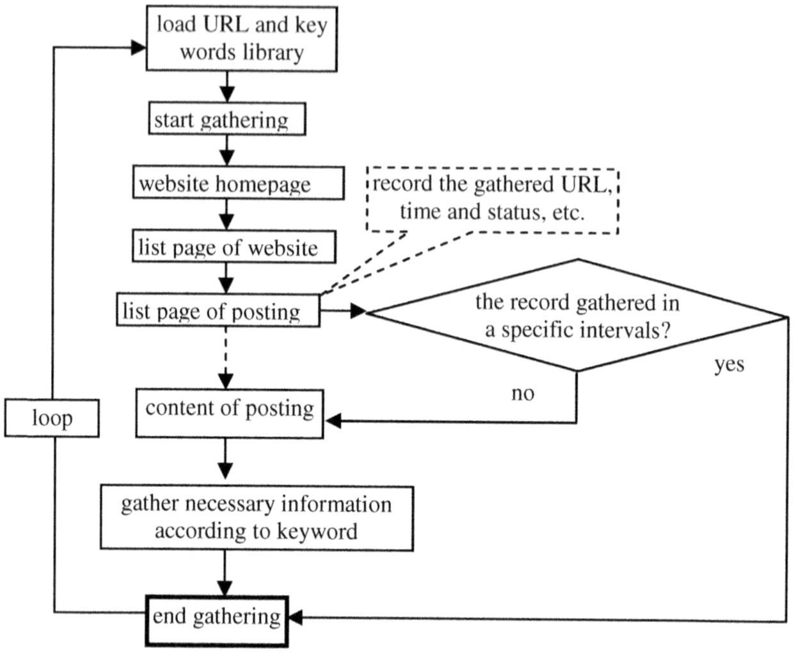

Fig. 3. The solution for repeat collection of posting

5 Conclusion

The distributed system of network public opinion monitor and analysis changes the way of information collecting by active information send instead of passive search and the keywords are filtrated by creating index table. Besides, large-scale deployment of the system could realize the management of information collection with cloud computing technique and the topic information is analyzed by traversing the available information in the internet. Therefore a digital and clustering platform is established and the report mechanism of public opinion is multilevel and multi-privilege, which will provide more effective data for decision making.

References

1. Zhang, Y.W., Qi, J.Y., Ma, J., et al.: Research on the Mechanism of Public Opinion on Internet for Abnormal Emergency Based on the System Dynamics Modeling. Journal of Intelligence 9, 2–6 (2010)
2. Xiang, J.: Analysis of Net-Mediated Public Sentiment Information Based on the Opinion Mining Technology. Journal of Modem Information 11, 46–49 (2010)
3. Cui, W., Zeng, R.X., Wang, G.H.: Bibliometric Analysis of Internet Public Opinion in China. Information Science 1, 131–135 (2011)

4. Dean, J., Ghemawat, S.: Simplified data processing on large clusters. In: OSDI 2004: Proceedings of the 6th Conference on Symposium on Operating Systems Design & Implementation, p. 10. USENIX Association, Berkeley (2004)
5. McCallum, A., Nigam, K., Ungar, L.H.: Efficient Clustering of High-Dimensional Data Sets with Application to reference Matching. In: Knowledge Discovery and Data Mining, pp. 169–178 (2000)
6. Liu, G.M., Zheng, Q.P.: Study of Web Technology and Its Solutions Based on B/S Model in Power System. Guangdong Electric Power 2, 67–70 (2008)

Application of an Expert System for Roadway Support Based on C/S

Zhao Wen-tao[1], Zhu Chang-xing[2], and Hu Rui[1]

[1] College of Computer Science Technology Henan Polytechnic University Jiaozuo, China
[2] School of Civil Engineering Henan Polytechnic University Jiaozuo, China
zwt@hpu.edu.cn

Abstract. This paper introduces the concept and principle of an expert system for roadway support, The system is designed based on C/S(Client/Serve)mode and routine, structure and function of design is discussed. Furthermore, the author has developed and realized each module of the expert system by Delphi 7.0 development kit combined with Microsoft SQL Server 2008 database management system. At present, the system has been successfully applied in Yi Ma coal mine, which achieves a good economic benefit in practice use.

Keywords: expert system for roadway support, Client/Serve, database management system.

1 Introduction

In recent years, safety situation of coal mine is generally safety in china, but roadway has occurred frequently deformation failure, for example roof collapsed, wall squeezed, bottom uplifted, rock cracked, rock burst etc. How to better solve the problem of deformation and failure of roadway, and achieve surrounding rock quality standardization of roadway and scientific support methods that becomes hot issues of common concern. To ensure the safety production and improve efficiency of production, it is necessary to develop the expert system for roadway support. At present, many people are engaged on the research of expert system in china, such as Wang Zi-jun, Wang Lin, Wang Guang-hong, etc. These expert systems of roof support in coal mine that were put forward exist some problems, namely, design of data structure is simple and the expert system does not support complex data types, and meet the engineering demands and form intelligent judgments. In order to overcome limitation of the above mentioned system, new technical methods are put forward. The author has developed a new expert system for roadway support by a development platform based on Visual C++ language and SQL Server 2008 database system. The system achieves a good economic benefit in practice use.

2 Expert System Principles

Expert system is a program system based on artificial intelligence computer. It includes much knowledge and experience of expert level in some field and utilizes expert

H. Tan and M. Zhou (Eds.): CSE 2011, Part I, CCIS 201, pp. 126–131, 2011.

knowledge to solve problems of the field. The system mainly includes six modules, man-machine interactive interface, knowledge base, global database, knowledge acquisition, inference machine and interpretation system, as shown in Fig. 1.

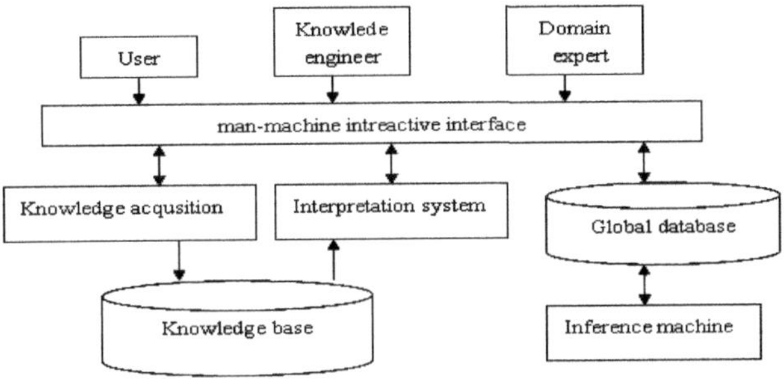

Fig. 1. The main structure of expert system

3 System Structure

3.1 Client/Server Mode

C/S structure is a system structure of computer software. Some researchers fully utilize the advantage of the two hardware environment based on C/S.

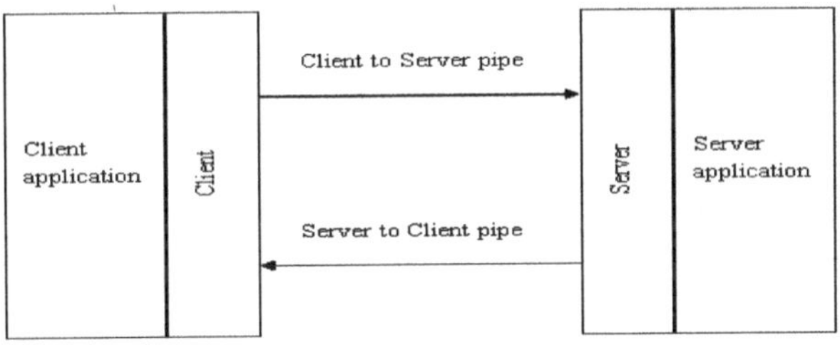

Fig. 2. The topology structure design of system

The expert system can realize the rational allocation of tasks to the Client and the Server. Some researchers can build a significant network flux, and easily realize disposal and update of multi-user and updates the management of the database server. Currently, most software systems are C/S in the form of a two-tier structure (as shown in Fig.2).

The system uses a distributed topology structure, which consists of three parts, namely, special database server (association server), two application servers and appropriate Hub for the connection. The system realizes management and maintenance by monitoring and managing system in the local area network, and establishes the connection between LAN and all levels of users, and ensures security of data management systems through the firewall. The database of application server are disposed by network .The database server is mainly used to control the overall management system and data backup copy.

3.2 Network Structure

Generally, C/S is built on a special network and small LAN. The special server supports connection and server of data exchange by LAN. This system is established based on network and developed based on application of the database technology for network.

Therefore, star network topology distributed is introduced network structure (as shown in Fig.3)

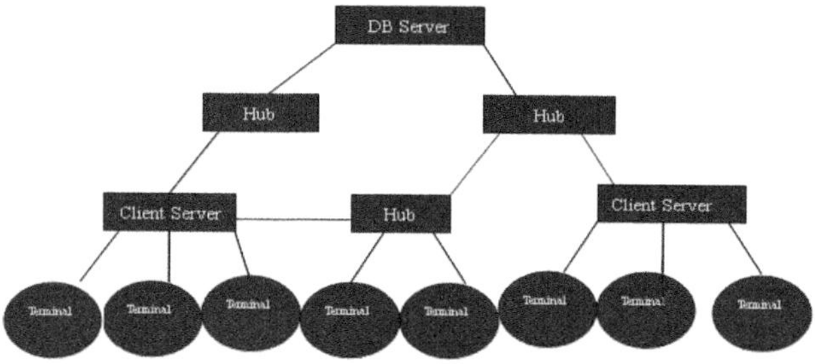

Fig. 3. Star network topology distributed

4 The Expert System for Roadway Support

According to the analysis of whole system design, the Client of the expert system for roadway support is divided into five functional modules, namely, system maintenance, analysis of underground pressure, roadway support, query and help module. The Server is divided into two functional modules, namely, data management and network management (as shown in Figure 4).

The features of expert system for roadway support are as followed:

1) System maintenance module: Different users have different permissive privileges. The general user can only use the basic right, but the privileged user can modify the knowledge base or add new knowledge base and administer the expert system for roadway support.
2) Observation and analysis of underground pressure module: According to input information of underground pressure, the user can find out the law of deformation and failure of roadway, for example, roof collapsed, wall squeezed, bottom uplifted, etc. Furthermore, the user can modify, delete and query datum mentioned above.
3) Parameters optimization of roadway support module: According to some parameters, such as surrounding rock strength of roof ,bottom , two sides, tunnel depth, pillar width ,and classification of surrounding rock quality, etc, rational support parameters are chose based on the system for roadway support, for example, space and row of bolt, type of bolt and support.

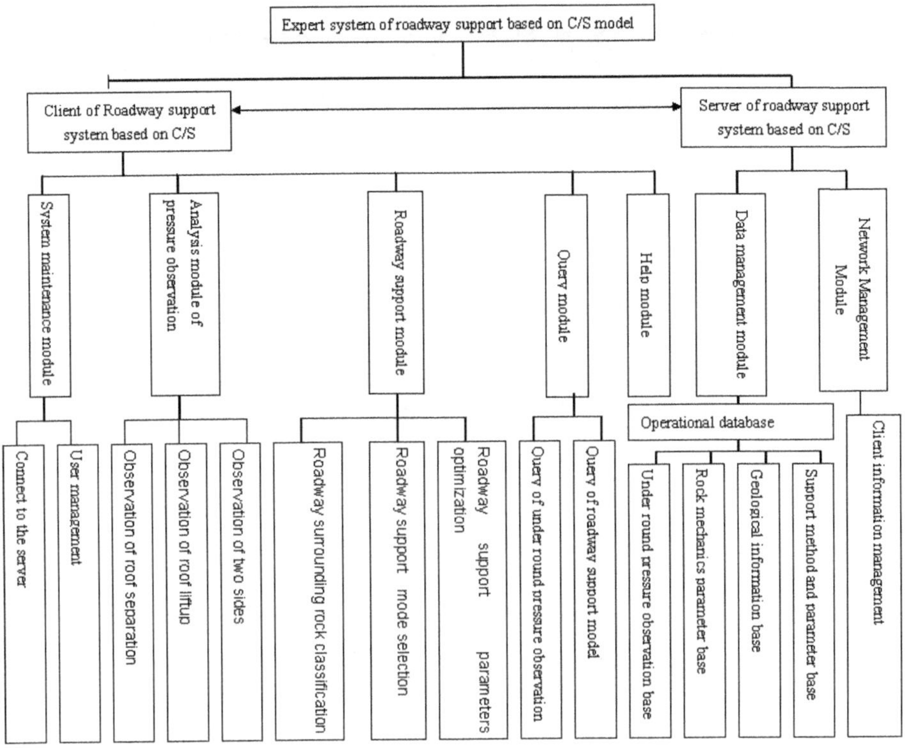

Fig. 4. The expert system for Roadway support

4) System query: The function of system query is mainly divided into two parts, that is to say, the query of underground pressure observation and roadway support modes, which provides abundance query condition and agility report forms mode, and the user can query information by different conditions of query.
5) System operation help: The part of system mainly describes system safety and operational manual which can help new user know the system.
6) Database management: It has four parts, namely the database of underground pressure observation, mechanics parameters of surrounding rock, basic geotechnical information and roadway support parameters. The user can add, modify and delete relational databases.
7) Network management: The part can manage connection information of Client.

5 Engineering Application

In order to reduce the labor strength of Yi Ma coal mine, the author has developed the expert system for roadway support. Operation interface of the system consist of two parts, namely, Client, Server interface(as shown in Fig.5,Fig.6).The expert system has realized the function of roadway support, and achieved a good result.

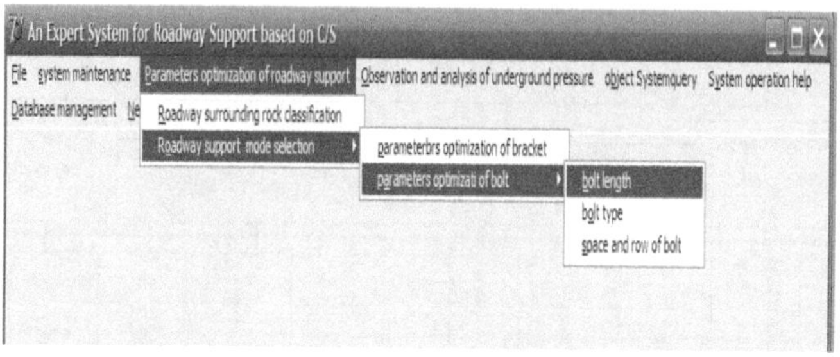

Fig. 5. Operation main interface of the system client

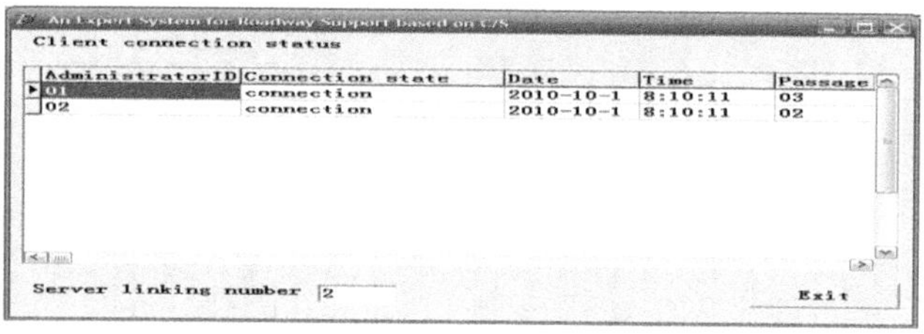

Fig. 6. Running main interface of system server

6 Conclusions

The author has developed the expert system for roadway support based on C/S. In order to complete the visual development of roadway support design in coal mine, the expert system has made use of Visual C++ development kit combined with Microsoft SQL Server 2008 database management system. The features of expert system for roadway support are as followed:

1) The establishment of the expert system for roadway support in coal mine has helped technician complete some repetition trivial routine work. Furthermore, the system has offered an highly efficient and intelligent solution method;
2) The system has a friendly interface between man-machine, which helps the user query basic information;
3) Each module of the system has relative independence, which helps the user modify information and expand the system.

References

1. Wang, G.-h., Shi, P.-f., Wang, Z.-h.: Deveopnt of Expert System of Roof Support. Shanxi Coal 26(1), 11–16 (2006)
2. Scoble, M.: Canadian mining automation evolution;The digital mine enroute to minewide. Cim Bulletin 88(990), 30–37 (1995)
3. Chadwick, J.: Mine automation. Mining Magazine, 333–343 (June 1995)
4. Charniak, E., Reisbeck, C.K., Meehan, J.R.: Artificial Intelli-gence Programming. Lawrence Erlbaum Associates, Mahwah (1996)

5. Wang, Z.-j.: The Expert System of the Roof Control Based on C/S Mode. Coal Mines (4), 45–47 (2007)
6. Zhang, W.-q., Ma, H.-t., Li, J.-b., Zhang, Y.-h.: Development of Visual Decision-Making Expert System for Supporting Design of Mine Roadways. Development of Visual Decision-Making Expert System for Supporting Design of Mine Roadways (4), 27–30 (2007)
7. Song, J.-x., Liu, Y.-f., Aen, G.-c.: Design of expert system of coal mine roof control and management based on MapInfo. Journal of Henan Polytechnic University (Natural Science) 28(6), 755–760 (2009)
8. Zixing, C., Durkin, J., Tao, G.: Advanced Expert System: Principles, Design and Applications. Science Press, Beijing (2005)
9. Shepherd, G., Kruglinski, D.: Programming with Microsoft Visual C++.Net Core Reference, translated by Pan Aimin. Tsinghua University Press, Beijing (2004)

CAGD Modeling of British Museum Great Court Roof for Exquisite Architecture*

Weishu Wei, Sanchuan Luo, Longxin Lin, and Zhanrong Chen

Colleage of Information Science and Technology, JiNan University,
Guangzhou, P.R. China, 510632
wei-ws@163.com

Abstract. In traditional architecture design, minimum energy surface and PDE methods have been widely used to design the roof and architecture of the building. This paper presents a general method to generate three-dimensional model from planar grid. In the process of British Museum Roof model construction, the paper utilizes many pairs of clockwise and anti-clockwise spiral lines and radials to construct the stable triangle grids instead of quadrilateral grids for their instability. Typical subdivision and interpolation are utilized in original grid construction. Fictitious forces are applied to relax the grids into symmetrical forms, and trinomial interpolation is used to construct the height of the roof. The resultant grids are organized; hereby the British Museum Great Court Roof is well constructed. This paper only considers and designs the "geometrical shape" modeling aspects of the British Museum Roof, and discusses the advantage of our method in constructing 3D mesh from 2D grid. It is more "general & convenient" in design and computation when compared to the William's methods.

Keywords: architecture, CAGD, nonlinear interpolation, subdivision.

1 Introduction

Geometrical shapes structure in architecture is an area of great engineering challenges and novel design ideas. Obviously the design process involves the geometry requirements and the available degrees of freedom.

Traditional shape structures are classified into shell, membrane and developable surface by Gaussian curvature. Existing literature [1,2,3] mostly aims at the realizations of shell and membrane shapes by meshes. The latter paper introduced conical meshes that have planar faces and possess offset meshes at constant face-face distance from the base mesh. They can serve as the basis of multi-layer constructions, and so for the first time the problem of multi-layered realization of a developable freeform surface by means of planar parts was solved in principle. Recently, free-form surface modeling

* This research is supported by "the Fundamental Research Funds for the Central Universities" (No.21610319) "the cooperation project for industry, Universities of Guangdong province and Ministry of Education of P.R.China"(No.2010B090400124), Jinan University Scientific Research Fund for the introduction of talents (No.50624029).

H. Tan and M. Zhou (Eds.): CSE 2011, Part I, CCIS 201, pp. 132–140, 2011.

[4~6] concept promotes the degree of freedom and artistry in model design, especially in wide span roof structures [7] designs. Multi-layer freeform surface [4] is discussed further under the consideration of the thickness. Surface is approximated [5] by various shape gird based on the fidelity of complex 3D datasets. The latter contributes on the constrained triangle meshes on the surface.

The British Museum Great Court is 73m from east to west and 97m from north to south. The center of the 44m diameters The Reading Room is offset 3m to the north of the center of the Court. In 1994, Lord Norman Foster and Partners are appointed as architects to design the Queen Elizabeth II Great Court. The work begins on March 1998, and it opens to public on December 2000. Fig 1 shows the views from top and inside.

In the Great Court Roof construction, Williams [8] brings forward a series of process. Firstly, construct the planar rectangle grids, and relax them by adding four fictitious on every node points, then generate groups of spirals by lining the diagonals in every rectangle. Moreover, three complicate surfaces are combined into a final surface. But the literature has not given the reason how they come. And the resultant Roof model has "edge-shift" problem.

Fig. 1. British Museum Court Roof photograph (a) View from top (b) View from inside

This work generates the Great Court Roof geometry surface from planar girds that is generated by mathematical functions. The grids are subdivided and relaxed into denser and smoother forms, and they are lifted through nonlinear interpolated trinomial. It provides a new way in architecture design.

2 Frame Design

Curve interpolation and surface subdivision are powerful tools in modeling and highly efficient superiority in design well-regulated mesh. The initial structural grid passes through many stages before reaching the final grid. Spiral lines and triangle mesh are applied during modeling because aesthetic perception and stability are significant in architectural design. The planar subdivision mesh is constructed before the height dimension is generated. The roof construction scheme is described as below,

- Initial flat grid construction
  - Spiral lines generation
  - Grid subdivision
  - Grid relaxation
- Roof height construction

2.1 Initial Flat Grid Construction

To construct the well-shaped spiral grids, Williams [8] uses quadrilateral and radial relaxation method to generate the initial grid. Here, the spirals are adopted directly in the initial grid construction. The initial grid passes through many stages before reaching final grid, shown in Fig 5. Primarily, the boundaries of the great court roof, the inner circle and the outside rectangle are constructed. Then the spiral and radial are generated. The arithmetical spiral equation is utilized to generate the initial grids, which is as follows,

$$
\begin{aligned}
r_i &= r_{i-1} + \Delta r \\
\rho_i &= (\sum r_i + \alpha)\theta_i + r_c
\end{aligned}
\tag{1}
$$

Where ρ, θ are the two axis in polar coordinates, $\alpha, r_c, \Delta r$ are constant.

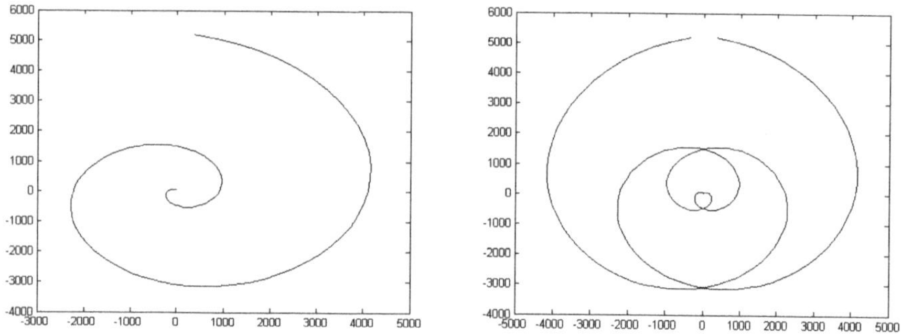

Fig 2. The spiral lines, Arithmetical spiral (b) Clockwise and anti-clockwise arithmetical spiral

The size of rectangle is 100 meters in length and 70 meters in width. The circle diameter is 44 meters and the central-point shift is 3 meters towards north. The rectangle is divided into 8 parts from east to west, and 11 parts from south to north. The inner circle is separated into 38 equivalent parts, and the corresponding points are connected respectively. The spiral formula is applied to generate the spiral lines. Shown in Fig 2.

2.2 Midpoint Subdivision

Subdivision is a widely used in modeling. To obtain a dense mesh from a coarse control mesh, subdivision algorithms like Doo-Sabin [9] or Catmull-Clark [10] can be utilized in processing the roof grid. This paper applies midpoint subdivision in plane to generate the final gird in which the edge triangles are revised, shown in Fig 3, (b) is the proper processing way.

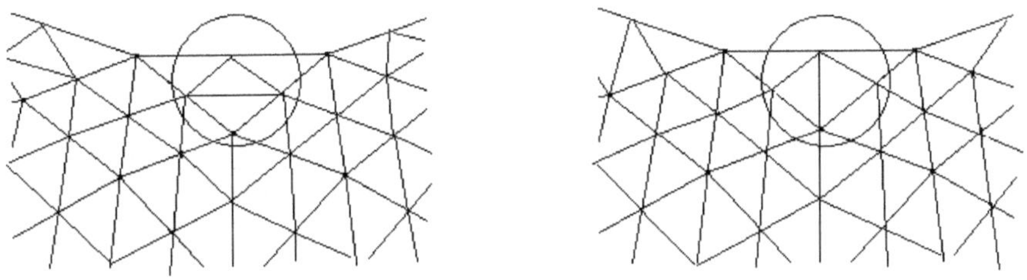

(a) (b)

Fig. 3. Edge revision of midpoint subdivision, the black lines are original grid, the blue lines are subdivided grid (a) Original process grid (b) Revised grid

2.3 Grid Relaxation

The idea of grid relaxation is great in William's [8] paper. It is very hard in constructing the grid in non-uniform way, since the shape of each cell in grid is different.

The generated flat roof grid is not smooth in appearance by only using the method above-mentioned, as the radial space distinctions are evident at the rectangle corners, shown in the Fig 5 (a) below.

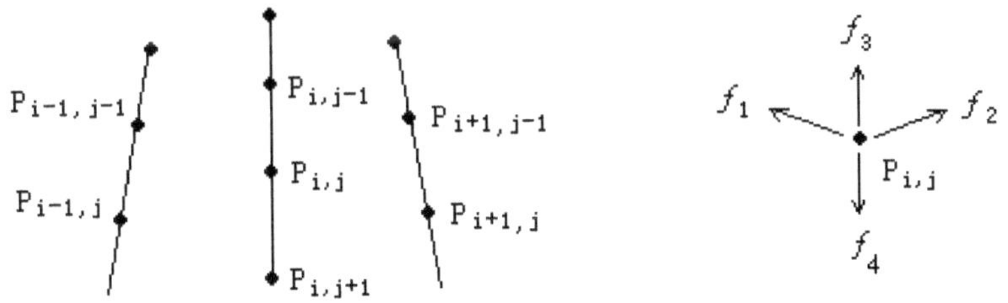

Fig. 4. Typical grid nodes and its force analysis

For the every non-edge node, which is surround by its 6 neighbors, 4 fictitious forces, f_1, f_2 point to adjacent line of its neighbor radial, f_3, f_4 point to the neighbor points of same radial's, are defined.

Let $f = -kd$, where k is constant and d is the distance between the current nodes to adjacent line or neighbor points. For instance, d1 is the distance between point $P_{i,j}$ to adjacent line $P_{i-1,j-1}P_{i-1,j}$, d3 is the distance between $P_{i,j}$ to $P_{i-1,j}$. Each non-edge point on the grid can be represented in the formal form mention above. Iterate the every P when $\sum f_i$ arrives to zero, forces attain balance.

During construction of the initial grid, a restriction is appended: angle of the arbitrary adjacent lines in spiral is close to every adjacent lines average angle of current spiral. Fig 5 (b) shows the result of relaxation.

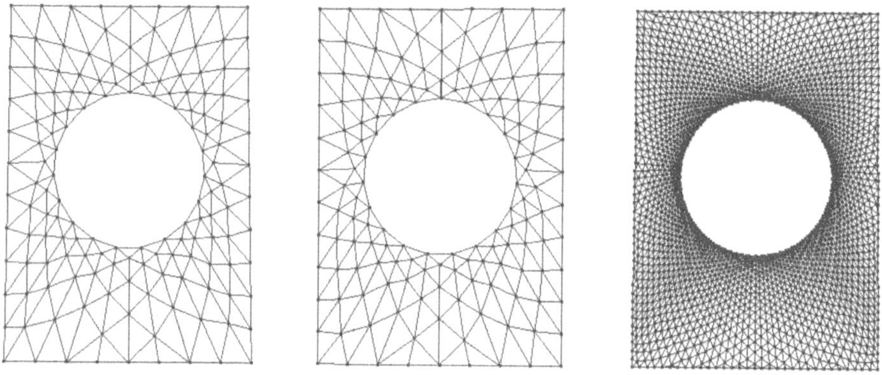

Fig. 5. (a) Grid constructed by spiral equation, (b) Effect after relaxation (3rd iteration effect), (c) Increase the radial density

3 Geometrical Height Construction

The final step is to construct the height from a planar grid. Firstly, the problem of Williams' [8] method is taken into consideration.

Williams had defined three complicate fundamental surface functions z1, z2, z3, and had combined them together to generate the height of the surface, but the research

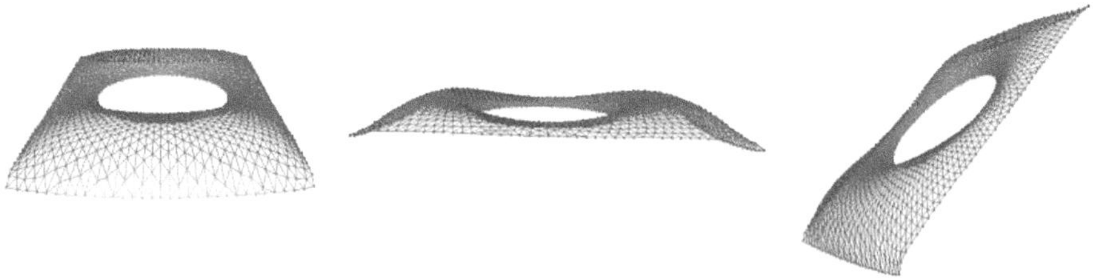

Fig. 6. The edge-shift problem: roof generated by Williams' method, (a) Frontal view (b) Side view (c) Custom view

does not indicate how to generate these 3 "magic" functions. Simulating results are shown in the Fig 6. The bottom edges of the surface are not in the same plane (result in edge-shift problem) by only combining three surfaces as one mentioned by Williams. The experimental model size and the formula parameters are accordant to the Literature [8]. Obviously, the combined complicate fundamental surface has a difficult problem at the edge-control. And it is not a general method.

In the proposed method, thrice polynomial and curve interpolation are used to generate the height dimension of the roof. As is shown in Fig 7, every point in rectangle region is described by polar coordinate.

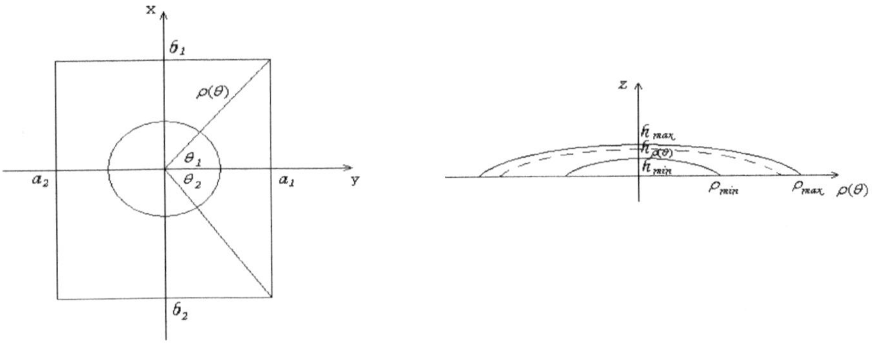

Fig. 7. (a) Initial frame of the roof, (b) Span interpolation between max and the min span

The disparity of the spans between great court boundary and the reading room boundary, defines trinomial,

$$z(\theta) = f_{span}(\rho(\theta)) = -m(\rho(\theta))\left|\rho(\theta) - k(\rho(\theta))\right|^3 + h(\rho(\theta)) . \tag{2}$$

while,

$$\rho(\theta) = \begin{cases} a_1 / \cos\theta & \theta \in [0, \theta_1) \\ b_1 / \sin\theta & \theta \in [\theta_1, \pi - \theta_1) \\ a_2 / \cos\theta & \theta \in [\pi - \theta_1, \pi + \theta_2) \\ b_2 / \sin\theta & \theta \in [\pi + \theta_2, 2\pi - \theta_2) \\ a_1 / \cos\theta & \theta \in [2\pi - \theta_2, 2\pi) \end{cases} \tag{3}$$

where $\theta_1 = \arctan(\frac{b_1}{a_1}), \theta_2 = \arctan(\frac{-b_2}{a_1})$

$$
\begin{aligned}
k(\rho(\theta)) &= \frac{1}{2}\rho(\theta) + r_c \\
m(\rho(\theta)) &= \frac{h(\rho(\theta))}{\left|\frac{1}{2}\rho(\theta)\right|^3} \\
h_1(\rho(\theta)) &= h_{\min} + \frac{\rho(\theta) - \rho_{\min}}{\rho_{\max} - \rho_{\min}}(h_{\max} - h_{\min}) \\
h_2(\rho(\theta)) &= \frac{1}{2}(h_{\max} - h_{\min})\sin(\pi \cdot \frac{\rho(\theta) - \rho_{\min}}{\rho_{\max} - \rho_{\min}} - \frac{\pi}{2}) + \frac{1}{2}(h_{\max} + h_{\min})
\end{aligned}
\tag{4}
$$

where r_c is the radius of the circle, $h_{\max}, h_{\min}$ are the maximum and minimum height of the arch, $\rho_{\max}, \rho_{\min}$ are the maximum and minimum lengths from rectangle edges to the circle center.

Scheme $h_1(\rho(\theta))$ is linear interpolation, while scheme $h_2(\rho(\theta))$ is sine function interpolation, which is smoother than scheme h1 and adopted in this paper. The thrice polynomial can be extended to n-polynomial, while it takes more expense.

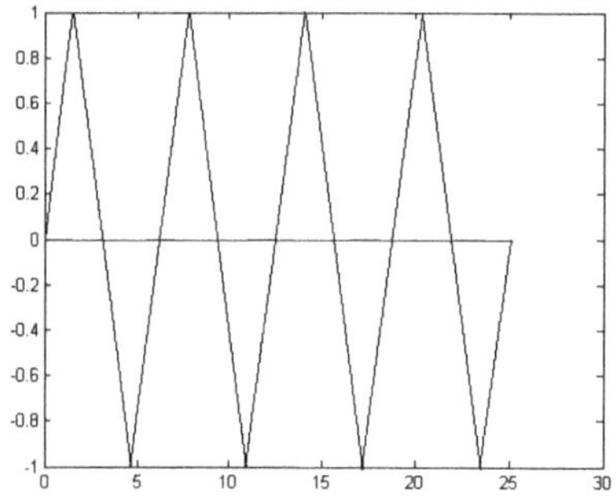

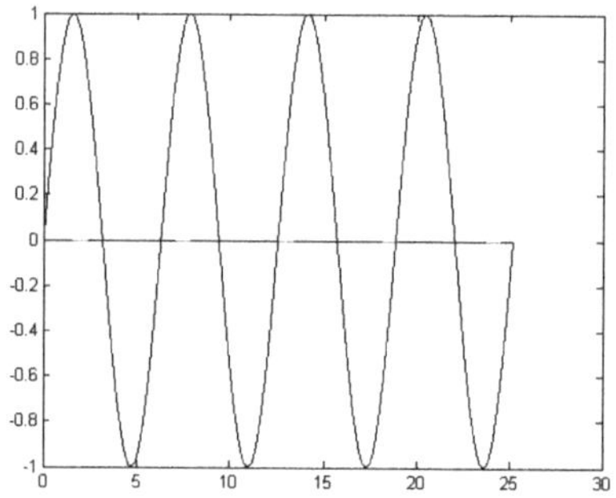

Fig. 8. The height dimension interpolation (a) Linear interpolation (b) Sine function interpolation

4 Experiment Result

In the experiment, the constants are $\alpha = 5.3$, $\Delta r = 2.9$, r_c =22, a_1 =35, a_2 =-35, b_1 =47, b_2 =-53, $h_{\max}$ =5.66, $h_{\min}$ =3.05, $\rho_{\max} = \sqrt{a_1^2 + b_2^2}$ =63.51, $\rho_{\min} = a_1$=35.

The experiment is implemented using Visual C++ and OpenGL on Pentium 2.6G Hertz, 256m Ram. The final models and their run time are presented in Table 1. Fig 5 (c) shows the effect of density 4 times, Fig 9 shows the effect of density 2 times.

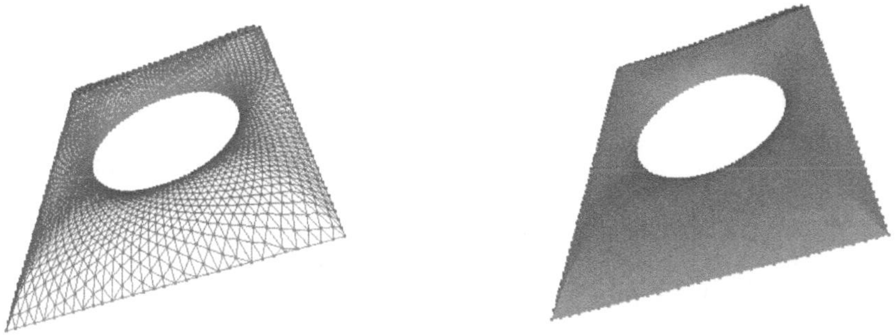

Fig. 9. The final grid & rending result

Table 1. Different density of the roof grid

Density times	Vertex	Face	Time(s) (iterate 5 times)
1	150	243	0.05
2	629	1144	0.09
4	2562	4896	0.30

5 Conclusion

This paper focuses on "geometrical shape" modeling aspects of the British Museum Great Court Roof. The classical CAGD methods, such as interpolation and subdivision are powerful tools that are used during construction, and the complicate surface functions are ignored. The paper presents a general three-dimensional model generation method from planar grids. It is effective in controlling model edge problem compare to the "magic" combined function. Spiral, reverse-spiral and radial are applied directly to generate exquisite triangle grid in planar design. It is not possible to say that the methods applied in this paper is the optimum; it provides a novel and convenient way when compared to the approach that had utilized complicate functions and a possibility in architecture design.

References

1. Heki, K.: Shells, Membranes and Space Frames. Elsevier Science Ltd., Amsterdam (1986)
2. Chilton, J.: Space Grid Structures. Architectural Press, London (1999)
3. Liu, Y., Pottmann, H., Wallner, J., Yang, Y.L., Wang, W.: Geometric modeling with conical meshes and developable surfaces. ACM Trans. Graphics 25(3), 681–689

4. Pottmann, H., Liu, Y., Wallner, J., Bobenko, A., Wang, W.: Geometry of multi-layer freeform structures for architecture. ACM SIGGRAPH, ACM Transactions on Graphics (TOG) 26(3) (2007)
5. Cohen-steiner, D., Alliez, P., Desbrun, M.: Variational shape approximation. ACM Trans. Graphics 25(3), 905–914
6. Frey, W.: Modeling buckled developable surfaces by triangulation, Computer-Aided Design 36(4), 299–313
7. Barnes, M.R., Dickson, M.G.T., Telford, T.: Widespan roof structures. Architectural Press, London (2000)
8. Williams, C.J.K.: The analytic and numerical definition of the geometry of the British Museum Great Court Roof. In: Burry, M., Datta, S., Dawson, A., Rollo, A.J. (eds.) Mathematics & Design 2001, pp. 434–440. Deakin University, Geelong (2001)
9. Doo, D., Sabin, M.: Behaviour of recursive division surfaces near extraordinary points. CAD 10(6), 356–360 (1978)
10. Catmull, E., Clark, J.: Recursively generated B-spline surfaces on arbitrary topological meshes. CAD 10(6), 350–355 (1978)

Scale and Rotation Invariant Salient Point Detection on 3D Mesh*

Weishu Wei, Sanchuan Luo, Longxin Lin, and Zhanrong Chen

College of Information Science and Technology, Jinan University,
Guangzhou, Guangdong, P.R. China
wei-ws@163.com

Abstract. This paper presents a novel salient point detection method for 3D mesh surface, and introduces a space scale-rotation invariant local feature descriptor to perform reliable matching between objects. We can find out similar geometry features by matching up the local feature descriptors in different objects by nearest neighbor principle. Furthermore, we demonstrate the effectiveness and discuss the potential application of the proposed method.

Keywords: salient point detection, 3D mesh, feature matching.

1 Introduction

Feature detection and match is a fundamental task in image analysis, computer-vision and object recognition. In traditional pattern recognition, lots of methods had developed in the past decade. Recently, many novel concepts and techniques appear, such as mesh saliency, shape-retrieval and 3D object alignment.

Our approach is motivated by salient "high curvature point" detection, since in psychology, people found that sight is fast focus on "high curvature" and moving object or part [1]. For each point, we compute discrete Gaussian curvature [2] and compare them in various scales to find stable and representative feature points on surface and generate local feature descriptor for each salient point. Finally, we search for the best match of salient point between two different objects using the nearest Euclid distance. The contributions of this paper include: (1) "high curvature" salient point detection and filtration (2) 3D scale-rotation invariant feature descriptor for feature point matching.

2 Related Works

In the past decades, most of the work has focused primarily on matching shapes in 2D images. Appearance-based object recognition methods, viewpoint and scale invariants

* This research is supported by "the Fundamental Research Funds for the Central Universities" (No.21610319) "the cooperation project for industry, Universities of Guangdong province and Ministry of Education of P.R.China"(No.2010B090400124), Jinan University Scientific Research Fund for the introduction of talents (No.50624029).

H. Tan and M. Zhou (Eds.): CSE 2011, Part I, CCIS 201, pp. 141–144, 2011.

recognition approaches, such as SIFT algorithm [3], provides robust 3D object recognition in low-dimension.

In the computer graphics (3D) field, 3D shapes matching were developed mainly for shape-retrieval and other applications. Funkhouser et al. [4] develop a new shape-based matching algorithm that uses spherical harmonics to compute discriminating similarity measures. It provides better performance than related global shape-matching methods. Gal et al. [5] define a compound saliency grade to describe subpart features on a global triangular mesh, and match features in database using index and geometric hashing.

We address the problem of salient point detection and matching on 3D mesh surface. And extract the "high-curvature" point selectively. At the same time, the constructed feature descriptor is scale and rotation invariant that related to the global or local parts of the object. Our approach processes 2-manifold surface element geometry feature and match the proximate descriptors between models.

3 Salient Point Detection and Filtration

The first stage is to detect locations that are invariant to scale change of the graphics can be accomplished by searching for stable features across all possible scales. Here, we adopt heat diffusion equation to construct scale space. Assume a continuous surface S is given. The surface diffusion equation defines a continuous set of evolving surfaces S(t) subject to

$$\frac{\partial x}{\partial t} - \lambda \Delta x = 0 \tag{1}$$

All the parameters can be referenced in do Carmo [6]. Equation (1) defines an evolving surface where each point on the surface moves in the direction defined by the surface normal with a speed given by the mean curvature. The equation itself is an approximate low-pass filter.

Gaussian curvature is the direct "meaningful" geometric magnitude of surface feature description. The Gaussian curvature discrete solution can be computed by Laplacian [2] approximately.

In order to detect the local maxima and minima, each sample point is compared to its 1-ring neighbors in the current scale mesh and neighbors in the coarse scale generated by the diffusion equation (1). Actually, the equation is a space filter to select local stable feature points.

4 Local Feature Descriptor Matching

This section defines a space local feature descriptor to perform feature point matching. These descriptors are isolated to each other and rotation invariant on 3D model surface. One obvious approach would be to sample adjacent 1-ring (or n-ring) vertices around local Gaussian curvature extrema at the original scale to construct feature descriptors, and to match these descriptors using a normalized correlation measure. The descriptor is composed of totally 5 vectors: mean curvature normal direction N_k, the principal direction e_1, e_2 and their opposite vectors. The principal curvature vectors are computed by PCA.

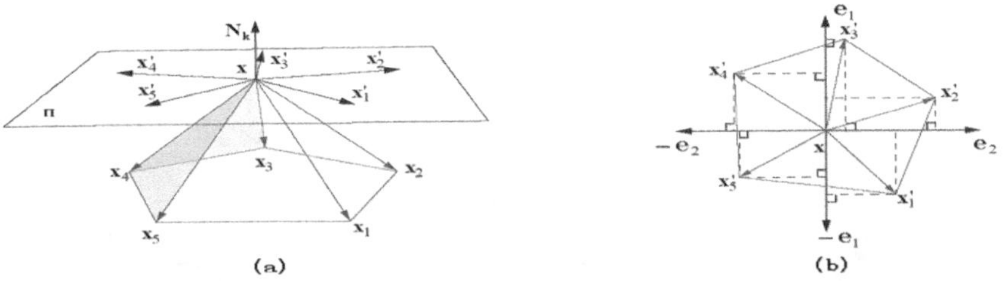

Fig. 1. Space rotation invariant local feature descriptor. (a) 1-ring neighbor points 1st projection to tangent plane, (b) 2nd projection to local feature descriptor (4 component vectors).

In order to enlarge the match capability in some complicated situations, such as distortions and deformations, we pick a local feature descriptor in object 1, and seek for the nearest distance (d_1) and 2nd nearest distance (d_2) descriptor in object 2. If the distances ratio (d_1/d_2) satisfy $d_1/d_2<\eta$ (η is the given threshold), then we accept this pair of matching points. If $\eta=0$, the pair of matching points is precise match. Reduce the threshold, the number of matching pairs would decrease, but more precise & stable. The probability that a match is correct can be determined by distances ratio.

5 Experiment Result

The experiments were implemented by MATLAB and run on a 2.4GHz PC. Fig 3 demonstrates the salient points built on large and small models' surface. Table 1 contains the statistic information corresponding to Fig.2. Fig.3. shows the feature points matching on deformation models

Fig. 2. Building salient point on models' surface. The frame contains three vectors: principal curvature vectors K1 (red), K2 (green) and mean curvature normal Nk (blue).

Table 1. The statistics of salient points for various models that corresponding to Fig.2

Models	Vertices	Faces	Salient Points	Times (s)
Hippo	23105	46202	2599	40
Dinosaur	16996	33988	1465	33
Plant	4292	4292	336	7
Hand	1023	2042	123	3
Beetle	988	1763	103	2

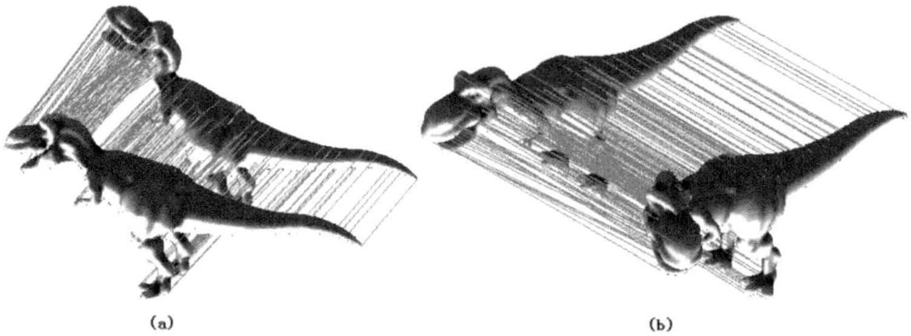

Fig. 3. Deformation model feature point matching. The original dinosaur contains 16996 vertex, 33987 faces, and 317 feature points. (a) The deformed (head turned up) model contains 312 feature points, result in 297 match points, (b) the deformed (head turned left) model contains 315 feature points, result in 267 match points.

6 Conclusion and Discussion

In this article, we present a novel 3D mesh salient point matching algorithm. It is based on an analysis of the surface to define a set of stable and representative local feature descriptors that captures elementary geometric features of original mesh. It is more precise compare to those methods only detect the scale-space extremum. The descriptors can deal with complex meshes and with large regions that have no significant details. The proposed salient point detection and matching method has the potential applications in 3D model recognition and retrieval.

References

1. Howlett, S., Hamill, J., O' Sullivan, C.: An Experimental Approach to Predicting Saliency for Simplified Polygonal Models. In: Proceedings of the 1st Symposium on Applied Perception in Graphics and Visualization (2004)
2. Meyer, M., Desbrun, M., Schroeder, P., Barr, A.: Discrete Differential Geometry Operators for Triangulated 2-Manifolds. Visualization and Mathematics (2002)
3. Lowe, D.G.: Distinctive image features from scale-invariant key-points. International Journal of Computer Vision 60(2), 91–110 (2004)
4. Funkhouser, T., Min, P., Kazhdan, M., Chen, J., Halderman, A., Dobkin, D., Jacobs, D.: A search engine for 3D models. Transactions on Graphics 22(1), 83–105 (2003)
5. Gal, R., Cohen-or, D.: Salient geometric features for partial shape matching and similarity. ACM Transaction on Graphics 25(1), 130–150 (2006)
6. Do Carmo, M.P.: Differential Geometry of Curves and Surfaces. Prentice Hall, Englewood Cliffs (1976)

Design of Test Learning Object Based on ActionScript

Liang Miao[1] and Xiang Li[2]

[1] Kaifeng Institute of Education, Kaifeng, China
[2] Software College of Kaifeng University, Kaifeng, China
cai8net@sohu.com

Abstract. The paper mainly illustrated how to develop the test resourse database in teaching software under the guidence of learning object theory and technology. By a systematic analysis to test learning object, the specific design method was found. A true/false question was listed as an example through Flash ActionScript3.0 technology and practice shows that the development efficiency has been greatly improved.

Keywords: Learning Object, test, ActionScript, Component.

Test Learning Object is one of the most important learning object types. This learning object makes the test and evaluation in education process much efficient by taking advantage of the interactivity, multimedia, and intelligence of computer. In test learning object, the students tend to have a permanent memory, active thinking, and timely feedbacks with an even chance for all those involved. The success enjoyment will stimulate them for higher development.

1 Relevant Technology and Theory

1.1 Learning Object

Integrable ware is the teaching information, teaching management databases and platforms gathered and applied by teachers and students, according to their teaching demand. In the integrable ware, the content of the whole lesson is divided into several independent coursewares, just like "building blocks", one of which can be a process of demonstration, a retrospect of history, an explanation of a problem, or a description, and so on. Teachers can, according to their actual teaching need, freely combine these small cousewares to produce the desired courseware, like building blocks.

The study of Resources for Education begins with the theory of integrable ware, which has extremely popularized the idea of the share of resources for education. But the integable ware is principally discussed in ideology, with some inherent defects and no uniform standard in its practical operation. So it cannot effectively promote the share of resources for education in the project level, and indeed cannot make it evolve to a higher stage.

In the 21th century, the technology of learning object attracts more and more attention from the international field of educational technology. Learning object, as a standard for learning technology, has been widely accepted in the present international world, and is far superior than the integrable ware in idea, technology and structure and

H. Tan and M. Zhou (Eds.): CSE 2011, Part I, CCIS 201, pp. 145–148, 2011.

generally viewed as a critical approach to the share and reusability of resources for education in the international field of educational technology.

Learning object is anything with Reusability and can be used to support digital learning resources. The outstanding features of learning object lie in its digitalization, reusability, and the support of learning process. The most obvious feature of the learning object is reusability which is the early aim of IEEE set LOM (Learning Object Meta-data) standard intention. Only to ensure maximum reuse of educational resources can achieve a wide range of high-quality educational resources network sharing. Compared with the ordinary learning content, such learning subject has the features of accessibility, adaptability, persistence, durability, interoperability, reusability and so on. By following certain polymerizing norms, the technology of learning object packages and polymerizes the learning content, making it a complete, independent Sharable Content Object, SCO, which will be packaged, according to certain Content Packaging, CP, so that resources can be shared and transferred in different learning management system (Learning Management System, LMS).

1.2 Flash and ActionScript3.0

Flash, produced by Adobe Company, is an excellent software, including the functions of animation design, game, web site development, multimedia software development and so on, supplying the developers with abundant imagination and powerful technological support. With the issue of Flash CS3, Flash's scripting, ActionScript has also been upgraded to ActionScript3.0, the milestone in the developing history of ActionScript, which, like JAVA, basing on ECMAScript (the internationally normalized programming language), has actually achieved Object Oriented Programming, OOP.

In a variety of educational software development platforms, Flash has the powerful capacity of comprehensive developments. As to the integration of multimedia materials, Flash has the perfect media-supported function, and can be imported various media formats, such as graphic images, voices, video, three-dimensional animations and so on. Besides, Flash itself is far better than other development platforms in the function of animation. On reciprocity, Actionscript3.0 provides a powerful object-oriented programming capacity. On the support of network, Flash is the program development software, applied to web. And because of the vector graphic technology, the file made by it is small enough to be suitable to develop the educational software based on web. On the standard of SCORM (Sharable Content Object Reference Model), the educational software developed by Flash can describe meta-data and pack the content according to the standard of SCORM, and can make data transmission with Learning Management System, LMS when SCORM runs.

2 Analysis on the Design of Test Learning Object

Test plays an important role in checking the result of students' learning and later enhancing. It serves as catalyzes in transferring knowledge into ability. It can test the students' learning, foster their ability and widen their horizon. Test should not be constant repetition nor deviate from the essence of teaching. In designing and developing the teaching software, by taking the learning object theory as a guide, the test as learning object, it will be very interactive, intelligent, and friendly. Besides, the reusability of test learning object makes it much more efficient.

Being one of the most powerful objects in Flash software, Component is an important technology in the design and development of teaching software. The components in ActionScript 3.0, which are objects with encapsulated code and external interfaces, can be used in fast teaching software development. Each component has a corresponding class, in which the method, category and event has been defined. All the components formed the API.

User interface component are indispensable parts in developing test learning objects. A powerful vivid test learning object can be accomplished by UI component and the excellent program ability of ActionScript 3.0. UI component mainly include the radio button, the check box, the pull down list, and the list box, of which the former two are the normal ones in developing test learning object. For example, in the one out of several situation, RadioButton is often used in forming the optional ones in the "true or false" and "multiple-choice" question.

3 Example for the Development of Test Learning Object

"true or false" question is one of the most common and easy-developing test categories. See the following example.

Open a new Flash document(ActionScript3.0), input the stem of the "true or false" question. drag the two RadioButtons to the stage and arrange them.

Choose the 1st RadioButton, set the object name is yesRb, lable is "A Right", groupName is tm, value is 0. Choose another RadioButton, and also set the object name is noRb, label is "B Wrong", groupName is tm, value is 1.

Label and groupName are two important index of RadioButton, of which groupName is compulsory. Label defines the explanation beside the radio button. In RadioButton, those who have the same groupName will become a very important index. By the only one choice, reselection can be avoided in the same group. The present two RadioButtons belong to the same group tm. Only A or B is allowed instead of both. Being a user defined one associate with RadioButton, Value is the judge of the answer. If value is 1, it is correct. Otherwise, it is wrong.

On a new layer, drag a TextArea to the stage and defined the subject as result. Add the following program code to the 1st frame of the new layer.

```
//Register MouseEvent.CLICK
noRb.addEventListener(MouseEvent.CLICK, clickHandler);
yesRb.addEventListener(MouseEvent.CLICK, clickHandler);
// Then define clickHandler function
function clickHandler(event:MouseEvent):void {
    // If the value of the chosen RadioButton is 1
    if (event.target.value==1) {
    //In TextArea there will be a "correct" feedback
          result.text="You are great! correct!";
    } else {//otherwise
    //In TextArea, there will be a "wrong" feedback
          result.text=" Wrong! Please think it over!";
    }
}
```

In the above program code, “target” fall into the same category with the Event class. It can store the memory of the event target. For example, if the 1st RadioButton is chosen, the target of the event object will be the RadioButton named noRb.

In the design of test learning object, interactivity and feedback are indispensible. Interactivity by RadioButton and feedback by TextArea here. Being encapsulated components, RadioButton are good practical program interfaces. It is easy for them to perform the interactivity function for the test learning object. In perform the feedback function, TextArea component or dynamic text object can be used. The feedback is expressed by text information. The feedback function of the test learning object can be more powerful by adding some movie clip components including animation effect, sound reminders etc.

References

1. Wiley, D.A.: Connecting learning objects to instructional design theory, `http://reusability.org`
2. Tang, J., Guo, L.: The research on M-learning of Mblog. The Knowledge and Technology of Computer 7, 5656–5658 (2009)
3. You, Z.: Basis of Multimedia Art. Higher Education Press, Beijing (2003)
4. Xie, Y.: Design of Multimedia Educational Software. Publishing House of Electronics Industry, Beijing (1999)
5. Miao, L.: Courseware policy analysis of navigation. China Information Technology Education, Beijing (2009)
6. Huang, J.: Multimedia teaching about the development of software and practice. E-education Research, Beijing (2001)
7. Li, F.: Try to discuss multimedia courseware visual messages process and its target. China Education Info, Beijing (2011)

Design of Equal Probability Store Algorithm for Flash Memory

Leqiang Bai, Cheng Cheng, and Jialin Wang

School of Information and Control Engineer, Shenyang Jianzhu University
110168 Shenyang, China
baileqiang@sjzu.edu.cn, chengcheng4524683@163.com,
wjl116090451@163.com

Abstract. To improve the overall performance and service life of the flash memory, a new type of file management algorithm for flash memory has been designed. A new linear ordering function is added to the traditional file management system. Its function is to balance the used frequency of every part in the flash memory. The new file should be stored in the space whose writing times are smaller, thus improving the overall efficiency, extending the service life of flash memory. In the same operating conditions, only the former half or even less space has been used repeatedly in the traditional file management system, while in the new system, files are stored equally in all regions, the writing times of every part are balanced basically. The capability of the management system designed in this paper is better than the traditional one, especially in the case of being operated more times.

Keywords: flash memory, equal probability, writing times, store algorithm.

1 Introduction

Flash memory is a non-volatile memory that has been widely used in various portable and embedded devices. Flash memory is divided into two types: NOR-type and NAND-type. The NAND-type flash memory, in which the density of the storage unit is very high and the speed of writing and deleting is very fast, is mainly used as large-capacity data storage [1]. The difficulty in application of NAND flash memory is how to manage flash memory. This paper focuses on NAND-type flash memory.

The main function of storage space management for flash memory is to improve the efficiency in the process of operating, to accelerate the speed of operation and to manage the using frequency of flash in each unit. In the traditional file management system, the process of writing and reading data follows the order from the front to the end [2]. The advantage of this approach is that the speed of operation is very fast. However in this case, the file operations are basically confined to the former part of the flash memory even a smaller space. Usually the former part of the space has been used many times, but the latter one has been rarely used [3]. The use of the space is extremely unreasonably, thereby the service life of flash memory is short.

To solve this problem, many algorithms have been proposed, such as the Cost-Benefit proposed by Kawaguchi, the Considering Recovery Efficiency and Loss

H. Tan and M. Zhou (Eds.): CSE 2011, Part I, CCIS 201, pp. 149–155, 2011.

of Balance proposed by Wells; the CAT (Cost Age Times) proposed by Chiang and so on [4]. These methods optimize the file management system by garbage collector. In this process, a large number of data is recorded and the calculation is very complicated [5]. So they are not very suitable for embedded systems whose resources are limited.

The new file management algorithm designed by author has been used a different concept of file management, to solve this problem in the file storage process. In the process of writing file, management system allocated memory dynamically. So it makes up for the lack of traditional management system, helps to improve the utilization of storage space, thereby extends the life of flash memory.

2 Design Ideal

In the traditional file system, the degree of storage space being used is uneven. The new type of file management is adding a new flash memory management algorithm to the basis of the traditional file management system. The purpose of designing this system is to improve the shortcoming of the traditional file management system.

Suppose the definition of the sequences of memory blocks is A= $\{X_1, X_2, X_3 \ldots X_i \ldots X_w\}$, in which w is a positive integer. The sequence of storage file is B= $\{Y_1, Y_2, Y3 \ldots Y_j \ldots Y_p\}$, in which p is a positive integer. Each piece (X_i) consists of four parts: X_{i1}, X_{i2}, X_{i3} and X_{i4}. X_{i1}=i, the first part of X_i is the number of X_i in the sequences of memory blocks. X_{i2}=n, in which n is the writing times of X_i, after a writing operation to the block, X_{i2}=n+1. If the file Y_j, in which j is the number in the sequence of storage file, is stored in the block X_i, X_{i3}=j. In many cases, as the size of a file will not be exactly equal to the size of memory block, often needs to use more than one flash memory block to store the same file. So files need to be split into several parts, each part put into one flash memory block, there will be X_{k3}=j, X_{m3}=j, in which k and m are positive integers. Details of the file are shown in Fig.1. To avoid confusion in the process of finding and deleting files, the system assigns a file numbers to each segment. It shows the name of the file and the part of the position in the file, such as $X_{i3}=j_1$, $X_{k3}=j_2 \ldots X_{m3}=j_k$. The pointer which points to the next flash block is stored in X_{i4}. Details of the storage space of file system are shown in Fig.2.

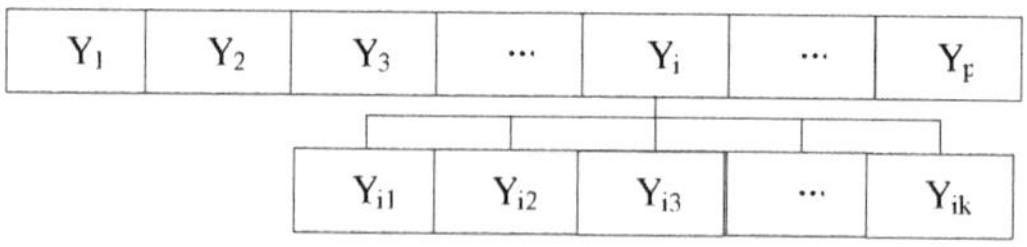

Fig. 1. The sequence of storage file

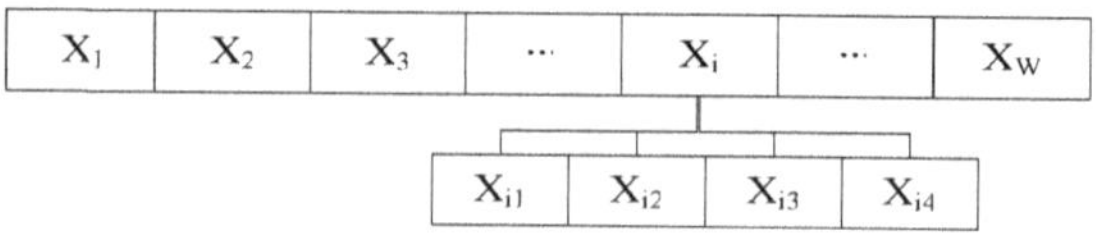

Fig. 2. The storage space of file system

2.1 Loss of Balance Algorithm

As the writing times of each flash piece are limited, some mechanisms need to be adopted, making the writing times of each flash piece achieve a balanced in the process of writing files [6]. The service life of flash memory is prolonged. This problem is called Loss of Balance [7].

Although Loss of Balance Algorithm requests the writing times achieving a balanced, literacy rate also should be taken into consideration. So the goal of the algorithm is to minimize the writing times of each block under the premise of the equilibrium condition.

Suppose the maximum times of writing is H, the maximum times of difference value of writing times is TH, E_i is the writing number of the block X_i, in which i is a random positive integer between 1 and w. The mathematical description of Loss of Balance Algorithm is as follow:

$$\max\{E_i\} \le H \tag{1}$$

$$\max\{E_i\} - \min\{E_i\} \le TH \tag{2}$$

2.2 Equal Probability Store Algorithm

The Equal Probability Store Algorithm is the improvement of Loss of Balance Algorithm. It joins a new algorithm to the process of file writing. New files are written in the flash memory blocks, whose writing times are smallest.

Description of the Equal Probability Store Algorithm is as follow: Suppose the definition of the sequence of memory blocks is A= $\{X_1, X_2, X_3 \ldots X_w\}$, in which w is a positive integer. At a certain moment, a certain part of the sequence of memory blocks which are unoccupied is $C_{org}= \{\ldots X_a, X_b, X_c, X_d, X_e, X_f \ldots\}$, in which a, b, c, d, e are positive integers. Before the new files are written to flash memory, system sorts writing times of all blocks. Select one data as key data (key). There are two variables: i and j, i=0, j=w-1.If the first data is the key, key= X_{12}. Forward search from j, like Equation (3) Backward search from i, like Equation (4), Repeated operation until i=j.

$$A[j]\begin{cases} \ge key:\ j = j-1 \\ < key:\ A[j]\ exchange\ with\ A[i] \end{cases} \tag{3}$$

$$A[i]\begin{cases} \le key:\ i = i+1 \\ > key:\ A[i]\ exchange\ with\ A[j] \end{cases} \tag{4}$$

After the operation, the order of C_{org} is changed as: $C_{new}= \{\ldots X_b, X_a, X_e, X_d, X_f, X_c \ldots\}$. So the new file is stored in the first space of C. If the file is too large to be stored in one block, it can be stored in the second, third, fourth space in turn. When new file needs be written, repeat the above steps. The writing times of each block are balanced as time passes.

In order to make understanding algorithm more convenient, establish a mathematical model of this algorithm. Suppose there are w blocks in the flash memory. The largest writing times of each block is H. Sequence E is a group of files which need store : E= {P_1, P_2, P_3...P_i...P_L}, in which L is a positive integer. It is a certain part of B. Sequence F is a group of files which have stored : F= {Q_1, Q_2, Q_3...Q_i ...Q_L}. The process of P_i mapped to Q_i is an update request. In the process of operation, all the writing times of any block should be no more than H.

$$\underset{i=1}{\overset{w}{MAX}} \ write\_time(i) \le H \tag{5}$$

If there is one block whose writing time is more than H, the process of operation is over. The writing times have been recorded.

3 Implement the Algorithm

The concrete realization method of Equal Probability Store Algorithm is as follow.

3.1 Realization Method

Designed two independent dynamic linked lists, one is called writing linked list. It is used to store physical addresses of the space which is available. The other is called deleting linked list. It is used to store physical addresses of the space which is already occupied of flash memory. Two lists have the same structure.

Every block has four areas. They are the Area of Numbers (X_{i1}); the Area of Writing times (X_{i2}), the Area of File information (X_{i3}) and the Area of Pointer (X_{i4}). The contents of every area have been shown in Fig.1. The process of file storage has been completed through the cooperation of various pieces.

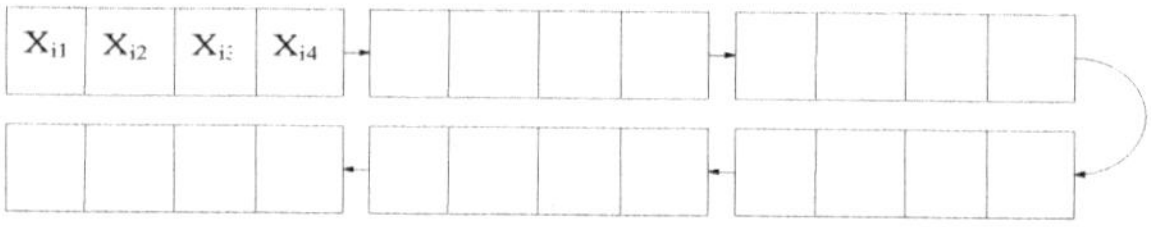

Fig. 3. The structure of the list

3.2 Working Process

When receiving a new instruction, the system of Equal Probability Store Algorithm will begin with a judgment. To find whether the instruction is writing instruction or deleting instruction. If it is a writing instruction, the system will turn to the writing subsystem. If it is a deleting instruction, the system will turn to the deleting subsystem.

Writing subsystem. After receiving instructions, the writing subsystem will start based on a judgment. Suppose the number of blocks which the file has been occupied is represented by K. The number of blocks which are unoccupied is represented by C. The parameter of writing judgment is represented by r. The process of writing judgment is shown by Equation (6).

$$r = \begin{cases} 1, & K \le C \\ 0, & K > C \end{cases} \tag{6}$$

If r=0, write nothing. If r=1, it begins to order the writing times of blocks which are in the linked list from small to large. Then put the file into blocks in order and write the information of the file into the third area. Meanwhile the number in the second area adds one. Finally transfer the pointer from the writing list to the deleting list.

Deleting subsystem. The deleting subsystem is in contrast to the writing subsystem. After receiving instructions, deleting subsystem will start based on a judgment. Check whether are there files need to be deleted. If the answer is no, system does nothing. To the contrary, find the location of the files through the number of files. Delete the information which is stored in the block. Transfer the pointer from the deleting list to the writing list.

4 Algorithm Simulation Tests

Implement the Equal Probability Store Algorithm with C++ programming.

4.1 Preconditions

Make a few preconditions before executing the program.

The initial value of the writing times of blocks (H) and the number of blocks (W) are all set by controllers.

Suppose the size of each block is X. the size of file is Y. The number of blocks which are occupied by the file is K, at this time:

$$X = 4k \ , \ k \in Z \tag{7}$$

$$K = \left\lfloor \frac{Y}{X} \right\rfloor + a \qquad \left(a = \begin{cases} 0, & \frac{Y}{X} \in Z \\ 1, & \frac{Y}{X} \notin Z \end{cases} \right) \tag{8}$$

In order to make the contrast between the traditional file management system and the new file management system more obvious, making two systems run at the same time.

4.2 Content Design

In order to get plenty of experimental data, the paper introduces a recycling program. Input an integer H by the keyboard. H is the maximum of writing times of each block. By changing the size of H, system produces a lot of data.

In order to reflect the randomness of writing and deleting operations, system generated an integer N randomly in process of program execution.

$$\left|\frac{N}{2}\right| = \begin{cases} 0, & writing \quad operation \\ 1, & deleting \quad operation \end{cases} \tag{9}$$

4.3 Simulation Results

Due to the limit of the size of window, the paper only intercepts part of experimental results, which is shown in Fig. 4.

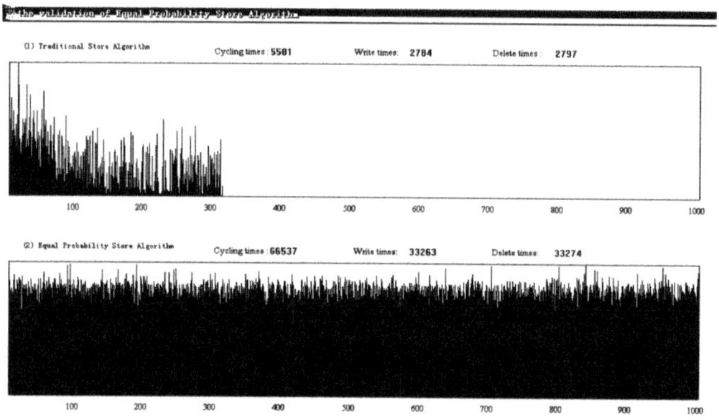

Fig. 4. Contrast of two kinds of file management algorithm when the top number of writing times is 100 million

4.4 Results Analysis

The results of two algorithms are shown in the table 1.

Table 1. The results of two algorithms

H (million) \ W (Algorithm)	Traditional Store Algorithm / Equal Probability Store Algorithm			
	262144	524288	1048576	2097152
10	54/172	96/348	218/690	628/6846
50	484/881	600/1760	1314/3418	2696/14920
100	1230/2767	1766/3522	2942/6992	3912/23966

Some illustration for the data in the table:

The data in the table is the average of the results of ten tests.

Suppose the size of the actual flash memory unit is 4k, Therefore the space whose size is 1G has 262144 units. The space whose sizes are 2G, 4G, 8G respectively have 524288, 1048576 and 2097152 units, which are the parameters of the table.

In the actual flash memory, the maximum writing times of every block is about 100 million times. So the parameters in the table of the maximum writing times are 10 million, 50 million and 100 million.

4.5 Conclusion

The result of simulation proved that the space utilization in the new file management system is higher than the traditional file management system in the same situation. The results of many experiments show that the maximum writing times of the new file management system is between 1.2 to 10 times of the traditional file management system. And the higher the maximum writing times is the more balance the writing times of each block is.

We can see through contrast diagram that the traditional file management algorithm doesn't consider of the balanced use of each piece. There are only a few blocks getting overly utilized. The blocks in the back even haven't been used in the whole process. The new file management algorithm is better than the traditional one. Using the new algorithm, every block have be fully used . The life of flash memory will certainly be lengthened.

5 Perorations

To sum up, the new file management algorithm is feasible. And it improves the traditional algorithm really. Basically it overcomes the serious defects of the traditional system. Improve the efficiency of the store. Extend the life of the flash memory.

References

1. Yue, L., Xiang, X., Jin, P.: An adaptive storage management method of flash memory. J. Small Miniature Computer System 8 (2010)
2. Su, X.: Simulation platform and applied research of flash memory storage device. China science and technology university, Anhui (2010)
3. Tang, W.: The research of large capacity NAND flash memory storage. The National Defense Science and Technology University, Hunan (2009)
4. Gal, E., Toledo, S.: Algorithms and Data Structures for Flash Memories. J. ACM Computing Surveys, 138–163 (2005)
5. Ajwani, D., Malinger, I., Meyer, U.: Characterizing the Performance of Flash Memory Storage Devices and Its Impact on Algorithm Design. In: McGeoch, C.C. (ed.) WEA 2008. LNCS, vol. 5038, pp. 208–219. Springer, Heidelberg (2008)
6. Chang, L.P.: Hybrid Solid-State Disks Combining Heterogeneous NAND Flash in Large SSDs, pp. 428–433. IEEE Computer Society Press, Los Alamitos (2008)
7. Chang, Y., Hsieh, J., Kuo, T.: Endurance enhancement of flash. In: Proceedings of the 44m Annual Conference on Design Automation, pp. 212–217. ACM Press, New York (2007)

Semantic Service in Cloud Computing

Wei Yu[1] and Junpeng Chen[2]

[1] Nanjing University, Department of Information Management, Nanjing, China
[2] Wuhan University, Computer School, Wuhan, China
yuw.nju@gmail.com, cjp.whu@gmail.com

Abstract. Cloud computing involves the provision of dynamically scalable and provides virtualized resources as a service over the Internet. In this paper, we propose a architecture to provide semantic service for document management in cloud computing. The applications of semantic service can be implemented by using techniques of web service and ontology.

Keywords: semantic service, document management, cloud computing.

1 Introduction

Cloud computing has recently emerged as an integrated infrastructure for resource sharing and computing in distributed environments. Cloud computing provides computers and other devices on demand. It typically involves the provision of dynamically scalable and often virtualized resources as a service over the Internet. The idea underlying the cloud computing is everything is service. The service model is mainly three layers [1]: Cloud Software as a Service (SaaS), Cloud Platform as a Service (PaaS), and Cloud Infrastructure as a Service (IaaS). In SaaS, the capability provided to the consumer is to use the provider's applications running on a Cloud Infrastructure. While in PaaS, the capability provided to the consumer is to deploy onto the cloud Infrastructure consumer-created or acquired application created using programming languages and tools supported by the provider. And in IaaS, the capability provided to the consumer is to provision processing, storage, networks, and other fundamental computing resources where the consumer is able to deploy and run arbitrary software, which can include operating systems and application.

Though the cloud computing has the great advantage such as on-demand self-service, broad network access, resource pooling, rapid elasticity and measured service [2], there is a shortage for cloud computing that it hasn't provided a unique semantic ground. The lack of a unique semantic ground can lead to ambiguity and ineffectiveness, especially for document management. In this paper, we proposed a architecture to provide semantic service for document management in cloud computing. The semantic service is a kind of service between PaaS and SaaS. It can provide service to users directly, like SaaS do; or programmer can create tools and software based on it, like use PaaS. The applications of semantic service can be implemented by using techniques of web service and ontology.

H. Tan and M. Zhou (Eds.): CSE 2011, Part I, CCIS 201, pp. 156–160, 2011.

2 Related Work

There are some research studied about ontology construction and management in cloud computing. An ontology is built to demonstrate a dissection of the cloud into five main layers [3]. It regards the cloud as hardware, software kernel, cloud software, infrastructure, cloud software environment and cloud application. The inter-relations and the inter-dependency between each layer are also represented in the ontology. In [4], a method about how to store and search the metadata, such as RDF is described and evaluated. It is mainly used in Yahoo! Search engine for searching and storing metadata. An ontology-based resource selection service is represented in [5]. The approach selects the ontology resource by calculating a degree of similarity function based on user's requirements. The frame work is constructed on a grid environment. However, these research on ontology have not take document management into account and can be hardly applied to document management in cloud computing. In our work, we use ontology to provide a unique semantic service for document management in cloud computing. The architecture and the procession of the semantic service are also described.

Many works have be implemented for document management in cloud computing. Google Docs [6] provides document management services such as document compliment, document searching, and document tagging to use in cloud computing. Amazon EC2 [7] and Microsoft Azure [8] can also provide document storage and searching for users. All these works can not give a unique semantic ground for document management.

3 Semantic Service for Document Management

3.1 The Architecture of Semantic Service

As shown in Fig. 1, the physical layer includes computer clusters, storage resource, network resource and data resource. These resources can be distributed and in heterogeneous types. After virtualization, these resources are unified and can be regarded as computation resource, communication resource, storage resource and data resource, on which ontology management layer can be constructed.

There are six components to compose the ontology management layer. To begin with, the ontology storage can store ontology instances and metadata using storage resource and data resource. The metadata can be directly used in semantic tagging, ontology population and other user application. While the ontology instances can be applied in ontology reasoning, ontology searching, etc. The three ontology application components based on the ontology storage are ontology search, ontology reasoning, and ontology mapping/partition. The user can search the ontology resources and perform reasoning, mapping and partition on these ontology resources through browser or using programming language. Job monitoring component can monitor the statement of the ontology resources and job execution component can monitor ontology applications and assign ontology resources to them.

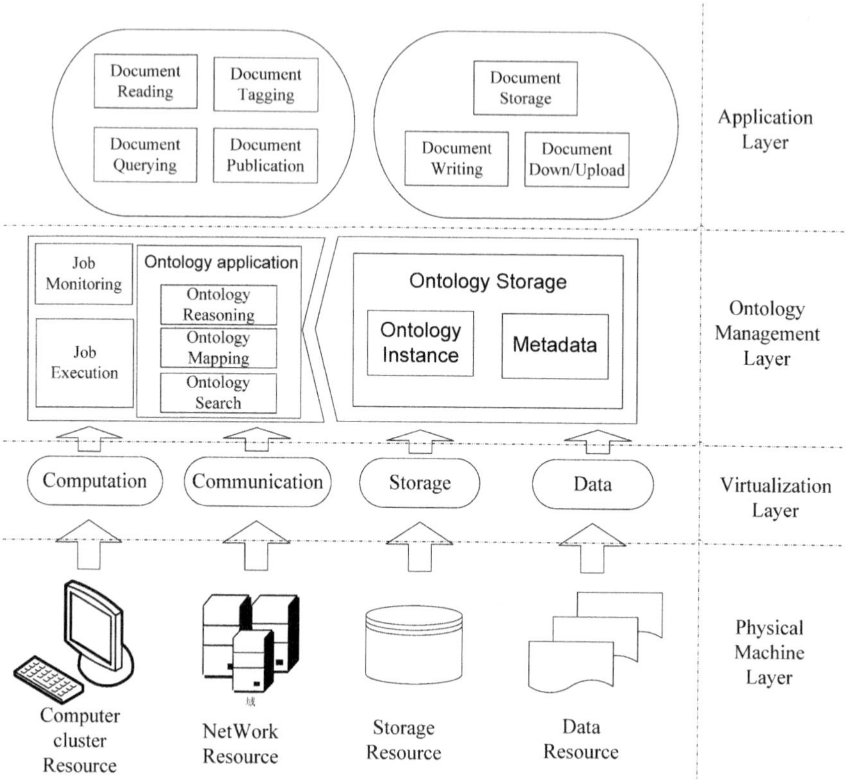

Fig. 1. The architecture of semantic service

The application layer include document storage, document down/upload, document writing, document reading, document tagging, document publication, document querying, etc. These document management services can use the ontology metadata and ontology instance from ontology management layer. On one hand, users can created personal document management by storage, tagging and searching. On the other hand, since all these document management service are based on the ontology management layer, which provided a unique semantic ground, these documents can be published and shared without any ambiguity and transformation. Hence, the efficiency can be improved and the information sharing can be easier.

3.2 The Procession of Semantic Service

From Fig.1, we can see the application layer and the ontology management layer are all based on the virtualization layer. So the semantic service for document management can be implement on different physical and software environments in cloud computing. After virtualization, the heterogeneity of different platform can be overcome.

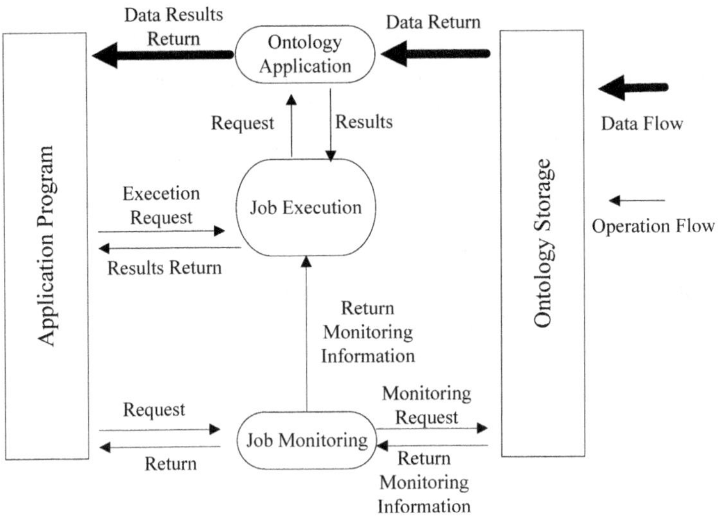

Fig. 2. The Procession of semantic service for document management

When users need semantic service in their document management applications, the application layer will send request to job monitoring component and job execution component in ontology management layer. As shown in Fig. 2, the job monitoring component will check the statement of the ontologies. If they are available, the job monitoring component will send the message of the statement to job execution component and inform the ontology storage component to send data to ontology application component. The ontology execution component will assign ontology resources to ontology application component for completing the request from the application layer.

In this procession, the operation flow is separated from the data flow. There is only operation flow between job monitoring component and ontology storage component, and the data flow will be needed only when the ontology application component require them. This separation between operation flow and data flow can improve the efficiency of the whole system.

4 Discussion

Since the application layer and ontology management layer are based on virtualization layer, the architecture can be constructed on different physical environment. It can be adopted on public cloud, private cloud, community cloud, and hybrid cloud. The virtualization technique Xen can be used to overcome the heterogeneity of the physical environments and operation systems. The application layer can be implemented using web service techniques. When the semantic services are adopted, the reasoner Kaon 2 can be used for ontology reasoning. And Falcon-AO v0.7 API can be used in ontology mapping. The whole architecture is constructed on Hadoop, which can provide the architecture for distributed computing.

5 Conclusion

Cloud computing can provide convenient to both users and programmers. In this paper, we proposed architecture to provide semantic service for document management. And the procession of semantic service is also described. The operation flow is separated from the data flow in the procession to improve the efficiency of the whole system. And our architecture can be constructed on different physical and operation environments.

Acknowledgments. This paper is supported by Humanities and Social Science Foundation of Ministry of Education of China (10YJA870014) and the project "The information communication of Internet in cloud computing" of Nanjing University.

References

1. Katzan Jr., H.: Cloud Software Service: Concepts, Technology, Economics. Service Science 1(4), 256–269 (2009)
2. Armbrust, M., Fox, A., Griffith, R., Joseph, A.D., Katz, R., Konwinski, A., Lee, G., Patterson, D., Rabkin, A., Stoica, I., Zaharia, M.: Above the Cloud: A Berkeley View of Cloud Computing. Technical Report No. UCB/EECS-2009-28 (2009)
3. Youseff, L., Butrico, M., Silva, D.D.: Toward a Unified Ontology of Cloud Computing. In: Proc. of Grid Computing Environments Workshop (2008)
4. Mika, P., Tummarello, G.: Web Semantics in the Clouds. IEEE Intelligent Systems 23(5), 82–87 (2008)
5. Yoo, H., Hur, C., Kim, S., Kim, Y.: An Ontology-based Resource Selection Service on Science Cloud. International Journal of Grid and Distributed Computing 2(4), 17–26 (2009)
6. `http://www.docs.google.com` (June 2010)
7. `http://www.aws.amazon.com/ec2/` (June 2010)
8. `http://www.microsoft.com/windowsazure/windowsazure/` (June 2010)

On Optimal Control Scheme Based on Feedforward and Inverse Models of Artificial Neural Network

Dongcai Qu [1], Guorong Zhao[1], Dong Cao[2], Jianhua Lu[1], and Binwen Lu[1]

[1] Department of Control Engineering of Naval Aeronautical and Astronautical University, Yantai, 264001, P.R. China
qdcai@21cn.com
[2] The Naval Fly Academy, Huludao Liaonin, 125000, P.R. China
qdc@yeah.net

Abstract. The mostly optimum control questions were based on precise mathematical model of the controlled object at present, and only aimed at the few parameters implementation optimization control. Because it was very difficult or imposable that established precise mathematical model of actual controlled objects.Because actual massive complex, unknown and indefinite nonlinear objects had many optimization parameters, it made conventional optimum control method no longer to be suitable to. In order to solve these problems, in the analysis optimum control principle foundation, the optimum control scheme based on the ANN's (Artificial Neural Network) feedforward / inverse model had designed. Basis on characteristics of nonlinear mapping and adaptive study of ANN's models and so on, the configuration of the ANN's feedforward and inverse models were designed. Used specialized training method of ANN models, and based on the EF(Exponential Forgetting) algorithm renewed covariance matrix, iterative training online to ANN's models were carried out, therefore obtained the ANN's models with the optimization configuration. Simulation results show that, designed optimum control structure scheme is reasonable, and ANN's controller may get good controlling effect.

Keywords: Optimum control, Neural Network(NN), Training algorithm.

1 Introduction

R.E.Bellman proposed the dynamic plan theoryin 1957 year, and Pang Terry elegant goldestablished the maximum value principle in 1958 year, these further promoted development and the application of the optimum control theory. These theories became the effective method in the solution of optimum control question. But the optimum control questions are mostly based on the precise mathematical models of controlled object, and aims to implement optimization at a few performance index. There are massive complex, unknown and the indefinite non-linear objects in fact, and are generally difficult or cannot establish its precise mathematical models. Based on ANN's (Artificial Neural Network) theories[1], by the iteration training, the threshold value parameter of the ANN's controller is obtained, hoped minimal dot of objective function is gotten.

H. Tan and M. Zhou (Eds.): CSE 2011, Part I, CCIS 201, pp. 161–167, 2011.

2 Design of Optimum Control Scheme Based on ANN's Models

2.1 Optimum Control Principle

If uses mathematics description, the optimum control questions may be described as formula functional form (1) [2-4] :

$$\begin{aligned} &\min_{u(t)\in\Omega} J = \varphi[x(t_f),t_f] + \int_0^{t_f} L[x(t),u(t),t]dt \\ &s.t. \quad \dot{x}(t) = f[x(t),u(t),t], \quad x(t_0) = x_0 \\ &\qquad \Psi[x(t_f,t_f)] = 0 \end{aligned} \tag{1}$$

From the above description, it can be obviously seen, any optimum control question included the mathematical model of controlled system, the boundary condition and the goal sets, the allowed control sets as well as the performance index function. For example, in the command signal track, model follow-up control systems of actual vehicle and spacecraft, the condition and the output track mostly use the performance index function form as formula (2) [3-4]:

$$J(u) = \frac{1}{2}e^T(t_f)Fe(t_f) + \frac{1}{2}\int_0^{t_f}[e^T(t)Q(t)e(t) + u^T(t)R(t)u(t)]dt \tag{2}$$

Among them, $e(t)=z(t)-y(t)$ is the error of tracking, $z(t)$ is the ideal output vector, $y(t)$ is the actual output vector; $F = F^T \geq 0, Q = Q^T \geq 0, R = R^T > 0$, the weighting matrix which measures important degree of various erroneous component and control component, usually takes F, Q, R as diagonal matrixes. For better adapted each kind of peculiar circumstance, $Q(t)$, $R(t)$ may use the time-variety matrix, but brings the shortcoming that causes greatly difficulty to realize the control scheme.

2.2 Design of the Optimum Control Scheme Based on ANN's Models

The direct inverse control is one inverse control method. The direct inverse control obtained a certain application in part of the robot arm and so on. Bcause the direct inverse control is one kind of open-loop control, therefore it is more sensitive to factors such as the error of inverse model recognitions, the object has time lag and some kind of disturbance, its robustness is worse [5-6]. In order to overcome the existence flaw of the direct inverse control, the designed optimum control structure scheme based on the ANN's feedforward / inverse models shows as Fig. 1 [7].

The scheme by recognizing ANN's feedforward model M_f of the controlled object P, obtains the surveillance teacher, take M_f outputs y_m as the forecast output, and produces recognizes erroneous $e(k) = y(k)-y_m(k)$ by comparison with the P output y. $e(k)$ not only uses to revise M_f, but also uses as the training signal of inverse model M_i . When training M_f , the weight and the threshold values revised M_f through recognizes error signal $e(k)$, $e(k)$ tends to 0, obtaining ANN's M_f of P, after the full training ; When training ANN's inverse model controller NC, error signal $e_u(k)= y(k)-y_r(k)$ of P outputs $y(k)$ outputs $y_r(k)$ with reference model R is possible to carry on the adjustment to the NC weight and threshold value parameter s , after the M_f reverse transmitting, and controlling P, causing $e_u(k)$ to obtain minimum, thus got optimization $u(k)$ [7]. If the transfer function of reference model R is 1, then $y(k)$ follows reference input signal $r(k)$, in ideal situation, $e_u(k)=0$, namely direct inverse control; If the R transfer function is some kind of form filter, and causes $y(k)$ to track y_r, then the system is the model reference adaptive inverse control system. When the error tends to 0, P has followed reference model R, and the performance index function of R is the performance index function of P.

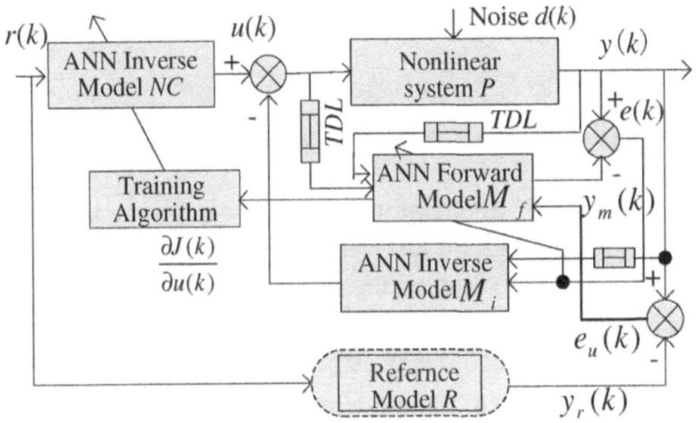

Fig. 1. Optimum control scheme based on ANN's feedforward /inverse models

The control scheme of Fig. 1 in the suppression to the disturbed noise is surpass to the tradition feedback control system. In the tradition feedback control system, the system object dynamic response and the noise jamming are mixed together to feedback to the input end. It is very difficult to eliminate the noise completely, while inverse model control system in suppression of system perturbation noise, it separately carry on control of the system dynamic response and control of eliminating the noise jamming, so mutually did not affect, which enhanced the dynamic performance and the suppression perturbation noise ability, and strengthened the system robustness. When M_f is completely precise, erroneous $e(k)$ is the system noise, if $e(k)$ is opposite feeded back to the system input port, then it can eliminate the noise. Because $e(k)$ is directly feeded back to the input then after P, the signal $e(k)$ must be able to change, therefore it connects inverse model M_i in the feedback loop, then the inverse model is approximately invariable after the entire circuit series the forward and inverse model. If the inverse model is completely precise, the loop gain is 1, then it filters out noise $e(k)$. Based on optimum control principle stated above, it takes performance index function of the controlled object as the form of formula (3):

$$J(\theta)=\sum_{p=1}^{N}\sum_{i=1}^{N_L}(r_i^{(p)}(t)-y_i^{(p)(L)}(t))^2+\rho(u^{(p)}(t))^2 \quad \rho\geq 0 \tag{3}$$

Among them, $r_i^{(p)}$、$y_i^{(p)(L)}(t)$ are respectively the expected output and the actual output of the ith outputs neuron of network output lay under the pth training pattern, N_L is the number of network output lay's nodes, u is the control signal, it allowed the control territory to take for the open set, ρ is penalty factor of control signal. Like this, through carrying on the iteration training to the network, the performance index function of formula (3) caused to obtain the minimum, and then optimum control signal u is gotten.

2.3 Training Algorithm of the ANN's Inverse Models Controller

Using the specialized learning algorithm[8] to carry on training the controller of ANN's feedforward / inverse models, its training sample set is reference signal r (either y_r) and P output signal y (or y_m), usually known the operating region, and its training sample set of ANN's inverse model is easy to obtain. When e_u approaches 0, inverse model Mi of P is obtained. For reducing e_u as far as possible, it selects the on-line training method to Mi, and renews the covariance matrix based on the algorithm EF (Exponential Forgetting) [9-10].

Regarding the optimum control scheme designed, the weight value iteration of EF algorithm renews like formula (4):

$$\begin{aligned}\hat{\theta}(t)&=\hat{\theta}(t-1)+K(t)\psi_u(t)(e_u(t)-\rho u(t-1))\\K(t)&=P(t-1)\psi(t)(\lambda I+\psi^T(t)P(t-1)\psi(t))^{-1}\\P(t)&=(P(t-1)-K(t)\psi^T(t)P(t-1))/\lambda\end{aligned} \tag{4}$$

Among them, $\psi_u(t)$, $e_u(t)$, $\psi(t)$ matrix are like formula (5)~(7) [11]:

$$\psi_u(t)=\frac{du(t-1)}{d\theta} \tag{5}$$

$$e_u(t)=\frac{\partial y(t)}{\partial u(t-1)}e(t) \tag{6}$$

$$\psi(t)=\frac{\partial\hat{y}(t)}{\partial u(t-1)}\frac{\partial u(t-1)}{\partial\theta}=\frac{\partial y(t)}{\partial u(t-1)}\psi_u(t) \tag{7}$$

θ is weight and threshold value parameters of ANN's models.

3 Simulation Researches

Supposing non-linear system is like formula (8) :

$$\begin{aligned}\dot{x}_1(t) &= x_2(t)\\ \dot{x}_2(t) &= -x_1(t) - x_2(t) - x_1(t)x_2(t) - x_1^3(t) + u(t)\\ y(t) &= x_1(t)\end{aligned} \tag{8}$$

Through the simulation experiment, obtained 1000 groups of random sample datum the first 500 groups used to the network training, the latter 500 groups used to confirm. In order to obtain the teacher's supervise signal, designs the to network model of three BP MFN (Multilayer FeedForward Network) structure, using the NNARX model structure. In order to optimize the network architecture, trained 300 times to it, thus ANN's M_f of the optimized structure is obtained; And the modelling of ANN's inverse model M_i and corresponding inverse model controller *NC*, similarly uses three BP MFN network, its network input is { $u(t\text{-}1)$, $y(t\text{-}1)$, $y(t)$, $y(t+1)$ } ($y(t+1)$ actually is $r(t+1)$), the network output is $\{u(t)\}$, similarly composes of a auto-regression structural model. The ANN's inverse model designed, its network hider layer activated function take hyperbolic tangent function, and the output layer takes the linear function. The ANN's feedforward and inverse models structure figure are like Fig. 2.

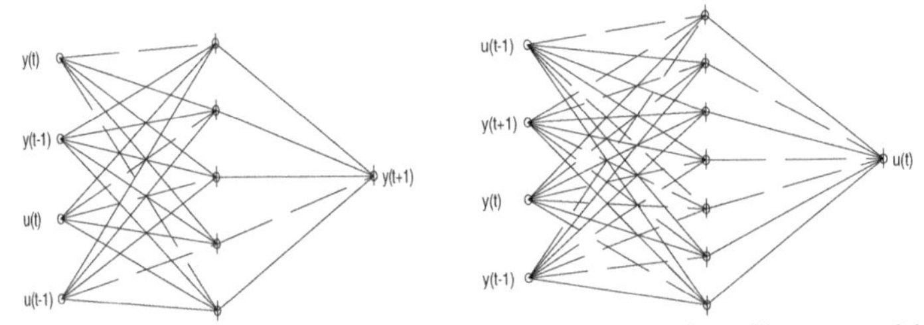

(a) Structure chart of feedforward model (b) Structure chart of inverse model

Fig. 2. Structure chart of BP MFN feedforward / inverse models

When carries on training to the network models using the EF algorithm on-line, the initial parameters of EF algorithm were set as [lamda, P_0] = [0.995 0.999], controller penalty factor ρ =1.05e-4. When each time renews the weight value matrix, the iteration operates 10 times. When did not consider reference model, its inverse model training and the control simulation result are like Fig. 3~ Fig. 4.

When has the reference model, its on-line recognized training curve of the inverse model and the control simulation curve are like Fig. 5~Fig. 6. The reference model form is $y_r(t) = \dfrac{B_r q^{-1}}{A_r q^{-1}} r(t)$, the parameter set is A_r = [1, -0.695], B_r = [0.305].

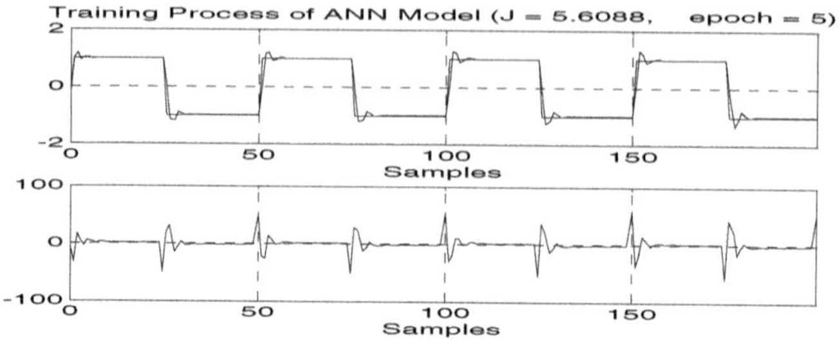

Fig. 3. Simulation curve of training of inverse model online

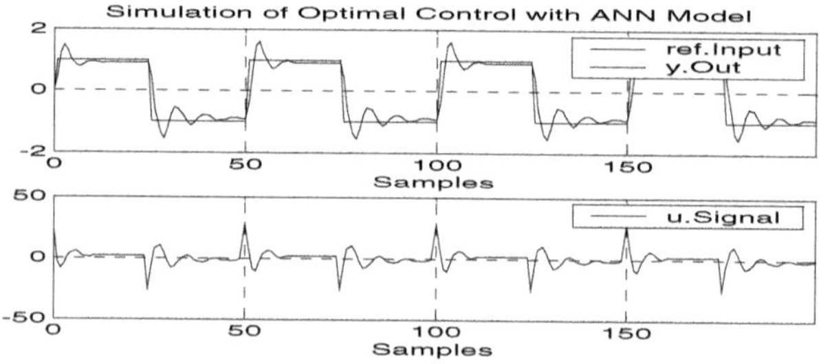

Fig. 4. Simulation curve of inverse model control based on EF algorithm

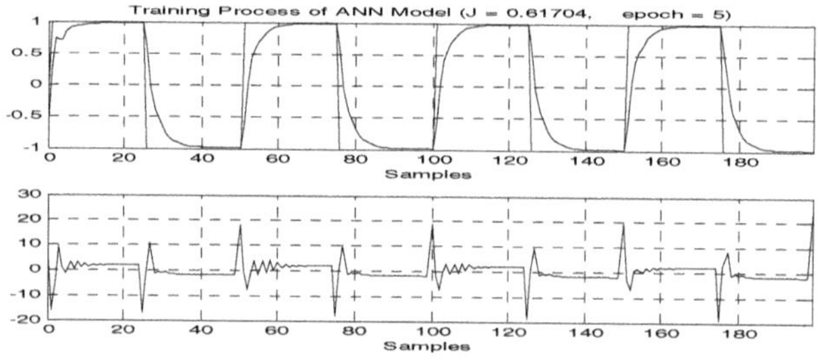

Fig. 5. Simulation curve of training of inverse model with reference model online

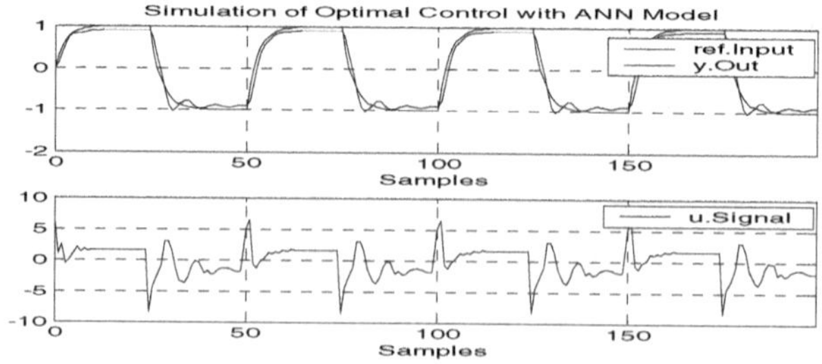

Fig. 6. Simulation curve of inverse model control based on EF algorithm with reference model

4 Conclusions

From simulation results, it can be obviously seen: the optimum control designed scheme based on the ANN's feedforward / inverse models with reasonable structure are reasonable and feasible. By full trained, ANN'models may be used to model and control for nonlinear system with good controlling effect. When the nonlinear object has inverse model, it is one kind potential method for identification and control complex and unknown nonlinear object using ANN's inverse model controller. Because designed ANN's models with simple and widespread applicable BP MFN architecture, it makes actual realization simplification, and being certain universal. The EF algorithm is generally constringency, and has good modelling effect to the complex nonlinear object. ANN's model has massive weight and threshold value parameters, and it is difficult to choose the appropriate forget factor, so EF algorithm needs further improvement.

References

1. Hopfield, J.J.: Neural networks and physical systems with emergent collective computational abilities. Proc. of the National Academy of Science (79), 2554–2558 (1982)
2. Athans, M., Falb, P.L.: Optimal Control. McGraw-Hill, New York (1966)
3. Qin, S.: Optimum control. Electronics industry publishing house, Bingjing (1984)
4. Hu, S.: Automatic control principle, 4th edn. Science press, Beijing (2004)
5. Zhang, N.-y., Yuan, P.-f.: Neural Networks and Fuzzy Control. University of Tsinghua, Beijing (1996)
6. Antsaklis, P.J.: Neural Networks in Control System: Special Section on Neural Networks for Systems and Control. IEEE Control Systems Magazine (1990)
7. Lu, Z.-g., Wu, S.-c.: Adaptive Inverse Control and Application for Nonlinear System. National Defense Industry Press, Beijing (2004)
8. Fukuda, T., Shibata, T.: Theory and application of Neural Networks for Industrial control systems. IEEE Trans. Industrial Electronics 39(6), 472–489 (1992)
9. Kosmatopoulos, E.B., Christodoulou, M.A.: Dynamical neural networks that ensure exponential identification error convergence. Neural Networks 10(2), 299–313 (1997)
10. Salgado, M.E., Goodwin, G., Middleton, R.H.: Modified Least Squares Algorithm Incorporating Exponential Forgetting and Resetting. Int. J. Control, 477–491 (1988)
11. Norgaard, M., Ravn, O., Poulsen, N.K., et al.: Neural networks for Modelling and Control of Dynamic Systems. Springer, London (2000)

Empirical Validation of Object-Oriented Metrics on NASA for Fault Prediction

Fangjun Wu

School of Information Technology
Jiangxi University of Finance and Economics
NanChang, 330013, China
wufangjun@jxufe.edu.cn

Abstract. In this study, empirical analysis is carried out to validate Chidamber and Kemerer metrics suite for predicting fault proneness when taking fault severity levels into account. The results, based on KC1 data set from the public NASA repository, indicate that 1) WMC, NOC, LCOM and CBO are reliable metrics for fault-proneness of classes across fault severity in the prediction models built by decision tree method, and 2) only CBO is reliable metrics for fault-proneness of classes across fault severity in the prediction models built by binary logistic regression method.

Keywords: Chidamber and Kemerer metrics suite, Fault proneness, Empirical analysis, Prediction.

1 Introduction

Since Morris Kenneth L. proposed object-oriented design measure in year 1989 [1], its research and applications have been developed more than two decades. Till now, researchers have got great achievements in it. For example, Chidamber S. and Kemerer C. proposed CK metrics suite [2] in year 1994, which contains WMC (Weighted Methods per Class), DIT (Depth of Inheritance), NOC (Number of Children), CBO (Coupling between Objects), RFC (Response for a Class), and LCOM (Lack of Cohesion). Bieman J. proposed TCC (Tight class cohesion) and LCC (Loose class cohesion) [3]. Lee Y. S. proposed DAC (Data abstraction coupling), MPC (Message passing coupling), ICP (Information flow-based coupling), IHICP (Information flow-based inheritance coupling) and NIHICP (Information flow-based non-inheritance coupling) [4]. Fernando Brito e Abreu proposed MOOD (Metrics for Object Oriented Design) metrics suite [5] in year 1996, which contains MHF (Method Hiding Factor), AHF (Attribute Hiding Factor), MIF (Method Inheritance Factor), AIF (Attribute Inheritance Factor), PF (Polymorphism Factor), CF (Couple Factor). Henderson B. proposed DAC(Data Abstraction Coupling), MPC(Message Passing Coupling), NOA(Number of Attributes per Class), NOM(Number of Methods per Class), NMO(Number of Methods Overridden by a subclass) and AID(Average inheritance depth of a class)[6]. Kim E. proposed CBI (coupling based on inheritance) [7]. Benlarbi S. proposed SPA (static polymorphism in ancestors), SPD (static polymorphism in descendants), SP (static polymorphism in inheritance relations), DPA

H. Tan and M. Zhou (Eds.): CSE 2011, Part I, CCIS 201, pp. 168–175, 2011.

(dynamic polymorphism in ancestors), DPD (dynamic polymorphism in descendants) and DP (dynamic polymorphism in inheritance relations) [8]. Bansiya J. and Davis C. G. proposed QMOOD (Quality Model for Object-Oriented Design) metrics suite [9] in year 2002, which contains NOH, DCC, DSC, ANA, DAM, CAM, MOA, MFA, NOP, CIS and NOM. Counsell S. proposed NHD (normalized Hamming distance based cohesion), SNHD(scaled NHD) and CAMC[10].

The rest sections are organized as follows. Section 2 summarizes related work. Section 3 describes data source, data preprocessing. Section 4 presents in detail the analytical results. Finally, Section 5 draws main conclusions of this paper.

2 Related Work

According to the ISO/IEC9126-1 software quality model [11], one of research task of software measurement is to build relationship between software internal properties (such as cohesion and couple) and external attributes (such as functional, reliability, easy usefulness, efficiency, maintainability and portability). Researchers have applied object-oriented design measure to fault prediction [12-18], change detection, reliability testing, software design style, etc. Qing Wang [12] and Yunfeng Luo [13] survey software fault prediction, and pointed out that it involved not only the number of faults, but also fault distribution, remove and legacy, etc.

Yuming Zhou and Hareton Leung [14] validated Chidamber and Kemerer metrics suite on NASA KC1 data set to predict fault proneness models with respect to high and low severity faults. Logistic regression, random forests and Bayesian network methods were adopted. They claimed that WMC, CBO and RFC were significant while DIT was not significant regardless of severity levels. Moreover, they concluded that Chidamber and Kemerer metrics suite were able to predict low severity faults in fault-prone classes better than high severity faults in fault-prone classes.

Ganesh J. Pai and Joanne Bechta Dugan [15] related Chidamber and Kemerer metrics suite to fault content and fault proneness on NASA KC1 data set. They did not categorize faults at different severity levels. Logistic regression, Poisson regression and Bayesian network methods were adopted. They concluded that WMC, CBO, LOC and RFC have significant effect on fault detection.

Jie Xu, Danny Ho and Luiz Fernando Capretz empirically [16] analyzed Chidamber and Kemerer metrics suite for defects estimation on NASA KC1 data set. Statistical analysis and neuro-fuzzy approach were adopted. They drew a conclusion that WMC, CBO and RFC are reliable metrics for defect estimation.

Cagatay Catal and Banu Diri [17] investigated the effect of dataset size, metrics set, and feature selection techniques for software fault prediction on NASA data set. They claimed that random forests provided the best prediction performance for large datasets and Naive Byes was the best prediction algorithm for small datasets in terms of the Area under Receiver Operating Characteristics Curve (AUC) evaluation parameter.

Yogesh Singh, Arvinder Kaur and Ruchika Malhotra [18] validated Chidamber and Kemerer metrics suite on NASA KC1 data set to predict fault proneness models with respect to high, medium and low severity faults. Logistic regression, decision tree and artificial neural network were adopted. They claimed that WMC, CBO, LCOM and RFC have significant effect on fault detection. They concluded that the performance of machine learning methods is better than logistic regression method with respect to all the severities of faults.

3 Empirical Data Source

This study makes use of the public data set KC1 from the NASA Metrics Data Program repository (http://mdp.ivv.nasa.org), which consists of 145 classes that are comprised of 2,107 methods. KC1 provides both class-level and method-level metrics. At the class level, there are 10 metrics, and they are PERCENT_PUB_DATA, ACCESS_TO_PUB_DATA, DEP_ON_CHILD, FAN_IN, CBO, DIT, LCOM, NOC, RFC, and WMC. At the method level, there are 21 metrics, such as LOC_BLANK, HALSTEAD_LENGTH, HALSTEAD_VOLUME, CYCLOMATIC_COMPLEXITY, NUM_OPERANDS, NUM_OPERATORS, etc. There are also some metrics about defect information, such as the number of defects and the density of defects. KC1 provides 4 files, one describing the association between classes and methods, one describing association between methods and defects, one describing association between defects and severity of faults, and one stating defect data that remains constant throughout the life cycle of each defect. The severity rating value for each defect quantifies its impact on the overall environment, with 1 being the most severe to 5 being least severe. Hence, we categorized classes into five levels: a class is said to be severity1 if it has at least one fault that its severity rating value is 1. The first severity level is named SEVERITY1. For other level is similar.

Table 1. Distributions of faulty classes

Severity rating	Number of faulty classes	Percentage of classes
1	24	16.55%
2	58	40%
3	40	27.59%
4	9	6.21%
5	2	1.38%

Table 2. Correlations between the metrics

	CBO	DIT	LCOM	NOC	DEP_ON_CHILD	FAN_IN	RFC	WMC
CBO	1	.470(**)	.257(**)	-.032	.180(*)	.460(**)	.387(**)	.245(**)
DIT	.470(**)	1	.257(**)	-.032	.000	**.746(**)**	**.654(**)**	.136
LCOM	.257(**)	.257(**)	1	-.028	.101	.233(**)	.334(**)	.318(**)
NOC	-.032	-.032	-.028	1	.133	-.081	-.050	.036
DEP_ON_CHILD	.180(*)	.000	.101	.133	1	.062	.012	-.030
FAN_IN	.460(**)	**.746(**)**	.233(**)	-.081	.062	1	**.529(**)**	.106
RFC	.387(**)	**.654(**)**	.334(**)	-.050	.012	**.529(**)**	1	**.628(**)**
WMC	.245(**)	.136	.318(**)	.036	-.030	.106	**.628(**)**	1

** Correlation is significant at the 0.01 level (2-tailed).

* Correlation is significant at the 0.05 level (2-tailed).

Correlation analysis was done among metrics by using Spearman's rank correlation coefficient method, as shown in Table 2. According to Hopkins's view, the correlated values with correlation coefficient greater than 0.5 are significant [19], shown in bold in Table 2. Partially, DIT, FAN_IN and WMC have large correlation with RFC. Similar results were found in [14, 18].

4 Experimental Results

In this study, DEP_ON_CHILD, FAN_IN, CBO, DIT, LCOM, NOC, RFC, and WMC were discussed. Decision tree and logistic regression methods were used in experiments.

4.1 Decision Tree Analyses

With well-known C5.0 algorithms in data mining software SPSS Clementine [20], prepared KC1 data set are used to classify and predict fault proneness when taking five severity levels of faults into account. In order to overcome the shortcomings of small amounts of data, 10-fold cross validation is used. Table 3 summaries the metrics used in decision tree at different severity levels. From Table 3, we can see that LCOM and WMC were significant at the first severity level; CBO, NOC, FAN_IN and WMC were significant at the second severity level; CBO, DIT, LCOM, NOC and WMC were significant at the third severity level; while RFC was not significant regardless of severity levels.

Table 3. The metrics used in decision tree at different severity levels

Metrics	SEVERITY1	SEVERITY2	SEVERITY3
CBO	×	√	√
DIT	×	×	√
LCOM	√	×	√
NOC	×	√	√
DEP_ON_CHILD	×	×	×
FAN_IN	×	√	×
RFC	×	×	×
WMC	√	√	√

The following rules are concluded at different severity level.

- if LCOM≤97 and WMC>26 then SEVERITY1=1;
- if LCOM>97 then SEVERITY1=0;
- if WMC≤26 SEVERITY1=0;
- if CBO>9 and NOC≤0 and FAN_IN>0 and WMC>18 then SEVERITY2=1;
- if CBO>2 and NOC≤0 and FAN_IN≤0 then SEVERITY2=1;
- if CBO≤2 then SEVERITY2=0;
- if CBO≤9 and WMC>18 then SEVERITY2=0;
- if NOC>0 then SEVERITY2=0;

- if NOC≤0 and FAN_IN>0 and WMC≤18 then SEVERITY2=0;
- if CBO>18 then SEVERITY3=1;
- if DIT>1 and DIT≤2 and WMC>30 then SEVERITY3=1;
- if CBO>6 and DIT≤1 and LCOM≤25 then SEVERITY3=1;
- if CBO≤6 then SEVERITY3=0;
- if CBO≤18 and DIT>1 and NOC≤0 and WMC≤30 then SEVERITY3=0;
- if CBO≤18 and LCOM>25 then SEVERITY3=0.

4.2 Logistic Regression Analyses

Table 4~8 summarize the results of the logistic regression with respect to different severity levels. Coefficient (B), standard error (S.E.), statistical significance (sig.), odds ratio (exp(B)), and Wald for each measure are described.

Table 4 presents the results of logistic regression analysis for predicting fault proneness with respect to the first severity level. From Table 4, we can see that only CBO was found to be very significant (Sig.<0.01).

Table 4. Result of Logistic regression—the first severity faults

	B	S.E.	Wald	Sig.	Exp(B)
CBO	.145	.051	8.036	**.005**	1.156
DIT	-.637	.403	2.500	.114	.529
RFC	.016	.012	1.828	.176	1.016
FAN_IN	-.538	.585	.847	.357	.584
LCOM	.004	.009	.248	.618	1.004
WMC	.007	.019	.133	.715	1.007
NOC	-17.966	5840.548	.000	.998	.000
DEP_ON_CHILD	-2.835	29014.641	.000	1.000	.059

Table 5 presents the results of logistic regression analysis for predicting fault proneness with respect to the second severity level. It can be seen from Table 5 that CBO was found to be very significant (Sig.<0.01); while DIT and LCOM were found to be significant (Sig.<0.05). Moreover, DIT and LCOM have negative coefficients.

Table 5. Result of Logistic regression—the second severity faults

	B	S.E.	Wald	Sig.	Exp(B)
CBO	.305	.059	26.555	**.000**	1.356
DIT	-.842	.330	6.498	**.011**	.431
LCOM	-.018	.007	6.296	**.012**	.982
NOC	-.498	.362	1.890	.169	.608
RFC	.015	.013	1.365	.243	1.016
WMC	.011	.022	.242	.623	1.011
FAN_IN	.086	.504	.029	.865	1.090
DEP_ON_ CHILD	19.802	28420.722	.000	.999	398188491.343

Table 6 presents the results of logistic regression analysis for predicting fault proneness with respect to the third severity level. From Table 6, we can see that CBO was found to be very significant (Sig.<0.01); while DIT was significant at 0.05 significance level. DIT has negative coefficients, which implies that classes with higher DIT value are less fault-prone.

Table 6. Result of Logistic regression—the third severity faults

	B	S.E.	Wald	Sig.	Exp(B)
CBO	.261	.057	21.242	**.000**	1.298
DIT	-.741	.350	4.483	**.034**	.477
LCOM	-.012	.007	2.679	.102	.988
FAN_IN	.457	.514	.792	.373	1.580
WMC	.013	.020	.429	.513	1.013
DEP_ON_ CHILD	-.858	1.538	.312	.577	.424
RFC	.004	.013	.123	.726	1.004
NOC	-.084	.310	.074	.786	.919

Table 7 presents the results of logistic regression analysis for predicting fault proneness with respect to the fourth severity level. It can be seen from Table 7 that CBO was found to be very significant (Sig.<0.01).

Table 7. Result of Logistic regression—the fourth severity faults

	B	S.E.	Wald	Sig.	Exp(B)
CBO	.250	.086	8.480	**.004**	1.284
RFC	.026	.014	3.323	.068	1.027
WMC	-.063	.045	1.977	.160	.939
FAN_IN	-1.141	.826	1.908	.167	.320
LCOM	.013	.019	.478	.489	1.014
DIT	-.251	.433	.336	.562	.778
NOC	-15.132	5671.041	.000	.998	.000
DEP_ON_ CHILD	-5.287	28980.996	.000	1.000	.005

Table 8 presents the results of logistic regression analysis for predicting fault proneness with respect to the fifth severity level. No metric was found to be significant.

Table 8. Result of Logistic regression—the fifth severity faults

	B	S.E.	Wald	Sig.	Exp(B)
DIT	-2.841	4.453	.407	.523	.058
FAN_IN	1.844	3.162	.340	.560	6.323
RFC	.034	.068	.249	.618	1.034
CBO	.033	.159	.044	.834	1.034
LCOM	.008	.039	.044	.834	1.008
WMC	.012	.072	.027	.869	1.012
NOC	-16.725	5521.376	.000	.998	.000
DEP_ON_ CHILD	-.276	28952.081	.000	1.000	.759

As can be seen from Table 9, the first model correctly classified 123(118+5) of the 145 classes, and its precision achieved 84.8 percent. In particular, 5 out of the 24(19+5) classes that were predicted to be fault prone actually did contain a first severity level fault. The second model correctly classified 109(73+36) of the 145 classes, and its precision achieved 75.2 percent. In particular, 36 out of the 58(22+36) classes that were predicted to be fault prone actually did contain a second severity level fault. The third model correctly classified 113(95+18) of the 145 classes, and its precision achieved 77.9 percent. In particular, 18 out of the 40(22+18) classes that were predicted to be fault prone actually did contain a third severity level fault. The fourth model correctly classified 123(136+2) of the 145 classes, and its precision achieved 95.2 percent. In particular, 2 out of the 9(7+2) classes that were predicted to be fault prone actually did contain a fourth severity level fault. The fifth model correctly classified 143(143+0) of the 145 classes, and its precision achieved 98.6 percent.

Table 9. Good-of-Fit

		Predicted			Overall Percentage
	Actual	no fault	fault	Percentage Correct	
SEVERITY1	no fault	118	3	97.5	84.8
	fault	19	5	20.8	
SEVERITY2	no fault	73	14	83.9	75.2
	fault	22	36	62.1	
SEVERITY3	no fault	95	10	90.5	77.9
	fault	22	18	45.0	
SEVERITY4	no fault	136	0	100.0	95.2
	fault	7	2	22.2	
SEVERITY5	no fault	143	0	100.0	98.6
	fault	2	0	.0	

The cut value is .500

5 Conclusions

In this study, empirical analysis was carried out to validate Chidamber and Kemerer metrics suite for predicting fault proneness when faults were categorized to five severity levels on KC1 data set from the public NASA repository. The results are concluded as follows:

- WMC, NOC, LCOM and CBO are reliable metrics for fault-proneness of classes across fault severity in the prediction models built by decision tree method.
- Only CBO is reliable metrics for fault-proneness of classes across fault severity in the prediction models built by binary logistic regression method.

Acknowledgments. This research has been supported by the Science and Technology Foundation of the Jiangxi Provincial Department of Education (Project No. GJJ10434 and GJJ11417).

References

1. Morris Kenneth, L.: Metrics for object-oriented software development environments. Massachusetts Institute of Technology, Master of Science in Management (May 1989)
2. Chidamber, S., Kemerer, C.: A metrics suite for object-oriented design. IEEE Transactions on Software Engineering 20(6), 476–493 (1994)
3. Bieman, J., Kang, B.: Cohesion and reuse in an object-oriented system. In: Proceedings CM Symposium Software Reusability (SSR 1994), Seattle, Washington, USA, pp. 259–262 (1994)
4. Lee, Y.S., Liang, B.S., Wu, S., Wang, F.: Measuring the coupling and cohesion of an object-oriented program based on information flow. In: Proceedings of International Conference on Software Quality, Maribor, Slovenia, pp.81–90 (1995)
5. Abreu, F.B., Melo, W.: Evaluating the impact of object-oriented design on software quality. In: Proceedings of the 3rd International Symposium on Software Metrics: From Measurement to Empirical Results, Berlin, Germany, March 25-26, pp. 90–99 (1996)
6. Henderson, B.: Object-oriented metrics, measures of complexity. Prentice Hall, Upper Saddle River (1996)
7. Kim, E., Kusumoto, S., Kikuno, T.: Heuristics for computing attribute values of C++ program complexity metrics. In: Proceedings of the 20th Conference Computer Software Applications, pp. 104–109 (1996)
8. Benlarbi, S., Melo, W.L.: Polymorphism measures for early risk prediction. In: Proceedings of the 21st Int'l Conference Software Engineering, pp. 334–344 (1999)
9. Bansiya, J., Davis, C.G.: A hierarchical model for object-oriented design quality assessment. IEEE Transactions on Software Engineering 28(1), 4–17 (2002)
10. Counsell, S., Swift, S., Crampton, J.: The interpretation and utility of three cohesion metrics for object-oriented design. ACM Transactions on Software Engineering and Methodology 15(2), 123–149 (2006)
11. ISO/IEC9126-1: information technology-software product quality–part 1: quality model (2001)
12. Wang, Q., Wu, S., Li, M.: Software defect prediction. Journal of Software 19(7), 1565–1580 (2008) (in Chinses)
13. Luo, Y., Ben, K.: Survey of software fault static prediction methods. Journal of Frontiers of Computer Science and Technology 3(5), 449–459 (2009) (in Chinses)
14. Zhou, Y., Leung, H.: Empirical analysis of object-oriented design metrics for predicting high and low severity faults. IEEE Transactions on Software Engineering 32(10), 771–789 (2006)
15. Pai, G.J., Dugan, J.B.: Empirical analysis of software fault content and fault proneness using Bayesian methods. IEEE Transactions on Software Engineering 33(10), 675–686 (2007)
16. Xu, J., Ho, D., Capretz, L.F.: An Empirical validation of object-oriented design metrics for fault prediction. Journal of Computer Science 4(7), 571–577 (2008)
17. Catal, C., Diria, B.: Investigating the effect of dataset size, metrics sets, and feature selection techniques on software fault prediction problem. Information Sciences 179(8), 1040–1058 (2009)
18. Singh, Y., Kaur, A., Malhotra, R.: Empirical validation of object-oriented metrics for predicting fault proneness models. Software Quality Journal 18, 3–35 (2010)
19. Hopkins, W.G.: A new view of statistics. Sport Science (2003), http://www.sportsci.org/resource/stats/
20. http://www.spss.com

Research on Current Situation of Course Construction of Webpage Design and Making

Xiaohong Wang, Li Zhou, and Yane Wang

College of Management, Beijing Union University, Beijing, China
gltxiaohong@buu.edu.cn, gltzhouli@buu.edu.cn, gltyane@buu.edu.cn

Abstract. The webpage design and making course built in 2001 in e-commerce profession of Beijing Union University is a practical and innovative course. The course reform is carried out to cultivate the abilities and greatly stimulate the interests of students. This paper studies the current situation of course construction of webpage design and making from the aspects of education standard, course content, teaching method and course assessment standard. The result of expert evaluation indicates that the construction situation of webpage design and making course is good, but there are some problems in the process of course construction. Based on the analysis, this paper puts forward with suggestions for the course construction.

Keywords: webpage design and making, course construction, teaching design, course assessment standard.

1 Introduction

Along with the rapid development of network and information technology, the Internet has become the computer information network which is the most extensive coverage, the largest scale and the most abundant of information resources in the world. As an important part of the Internet, webpage has also been very widely used. Therefore, webpage design and webpage making has temporarily become the new industry. And the ability to design and make webpage has become a popular skill, and many colleges and universities have set up the related course.

The webpage design and making course is a practical and innovative course. After learning this course, students can master the various operation techniques of webpage design and webpage making, and have the knowledge and ability to develop and maintain enterprise websites. In the teaching, some problems faced and need to be solved by university teachers are how to adopt the reasonable and reliable teaching methods and modes and make full use of multimedia teaching tools to stimulate the enthusiasm of students, and how to focus on training basic skills of webpage making staffs to achieve the teaching objectives.

2 Situation of Course Construction

To cultivate the abilities and greatly stimulate the interests of students, teachers of e-commerce profession of Beijing Union University combine with many years of

H. Tan and M. Zhou (Eds.): CSE 2011, Part I, CCIS 201, pp. 176–182, 2011.

teaching experiences to carry out course reform. This paper analyzes the current situation of webpage design and making course from the following aspects.

2.1 Course Education Standard

Based on the training objectives, theory teaching and practice teaching objectives of e-commerce profession and the business requirements of webpage designer, the course syllabus is formulated and the education standard is established. Through the teaching, the scientific thinking method and innovative ability of students are gradually cultivated, and the abilities to operate, to analyze and solve problems, to acquire new knowledge and to cooperate with others can be improved. After learning this course, students will have the following four abilities.

- The ability of website planning, construction and release.
- The ability of webpage and image creation, design and making.
- The ability of animation creation, design and making.
- The ability of acquiring certificate of Adobe webpage designer.

2.2 Course Content

In accordance with the course syllabus and education standard, the teaching content of webpage design and making course is designed by module, and the latest technique has been introduced into the teaching. The teaching content can be divided into four modules, that is, webpage basic knowledge, animation making (Flash), image processing and making (Photoshop or Fireworks), webpage making (Dreamweaver), the content of each module as shown in Table 1. Teachers can choose teaching content according to course scheduling and actual level of students.

2.3 Teaching Method

Teachers focus on combining theory with practice in the course teaching, and use project-driven teaching, case teaching, network teaching and other teaching methods, which are well received by students.

Project-Driven Teaching

Through project-driven teaching, the enterprise issues and projects are introduced in the course teaching, and it can promote the combination of theory with practice and make students apply the knowledge to practice. It can make teachers combine theoretical knowledge with practical skills of website development, and make students participate in actual project, and further understand the process of website construction and learn the specification and principles of webpage design, and master the use methods of website development tools during the process of website construction, and it can make learning process become a process of creative practice. Through the process of practice and specific inquiry, the abilities of students can be improved in knowledge, skills, team cooperation and ideological quality.

Table 1. The content modules of webpage design and making course

Content module	Specific content
Webpage basic knowledge	HTML Webpage and website design principle Web browser and server Common Internet terms
Animation making (Flash)	Basic knowledge Fundamental making technique Advanced making technique Action Script
Image processing and making (Photoshop or Fireworks)	Basic knowledge Fundamental operation Advanced application
Webpage making (Dreamweaver)	Basic knowledge Webpage layout and positioning CSS and template Database connection technique Dynamic webpage making Comprehensive application Website management

Case Teaching

The case focused on a website construction task is used to organize the teaching. As teaching, the task of website design and construction is gradually decomposed into one or more independent tasks which can take a few small cases or smaller cases for learning. Finally, these independent tasks can be combined into the case. The task of website construction will be completed when the course is end. In the process of teaching, students not only understand the process of website construction and webpage making, but also learn and master the knowledge and skills related to webpage design and webpage making.

Network Teaching

The network teaching expands the space of imparting knowledge. The website content of webpage design and making course is more abundant, as shown in Figure 1, mainly including course overview, exercise and homework, teaching courseware, practice teaching, reference materials, guidance and answering, homework submission, etc. By the network website, teachers can interact with students, answer questions and correct homework, and students can make course test online and download teaching resources for independent study.

Demo Exchange and Course Competition

In the teaching process, teachers make full use of modern educational technology and methods to vigorously carry out the teaching method of teaching-learning-doing. The methods of demo exchange and course competition are adopted to communicate with classmates after students finish their homework. It can improve the ability of creative, webpage design and webpage making, and can improve the achievement sense and stimulate the study enthusiasm of students.

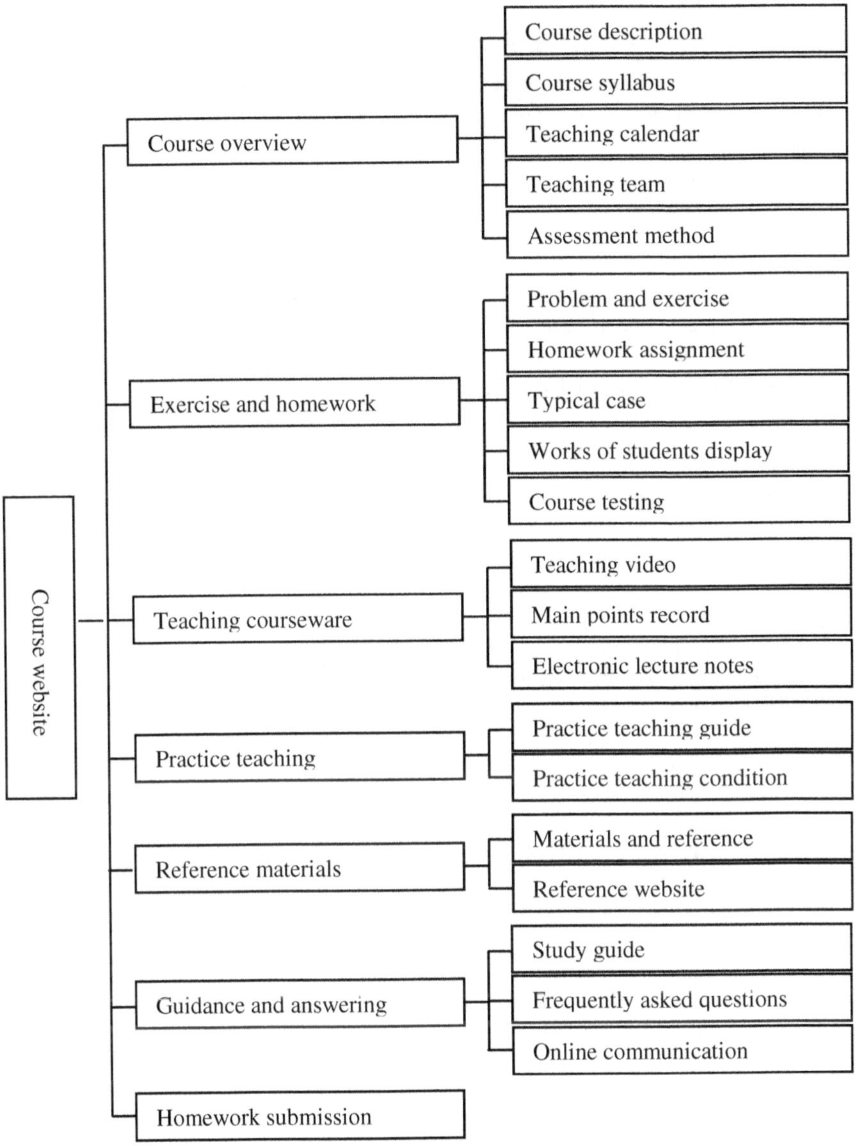

Fig. 1. The columns structure of teaching website of webpage design and making course

2.4 Assessment Standard and Method

Course Assessment Standard

The assessment standard of webpage design and making course is composed of professional quality, basic knowledge and skills, each part assessment content is as the follows:

- The part of professional quality: professional ethics, work attitude, work style, team spirit and competition consciousness.
- The part of basic knowledge: the knowledge of webpage design specifications, HTML, network image processing, animation making, website construction and maintenance.
- The part of skills: the abilities of website planning, network image editing and processing, animation making, webpage design and webpage making, website development and maintenance.

The principle of course assessment is based on basic knowledge and skills. The assessment on basic knowledge and professional quality is completed in peacetime, and the assessment on skills is completed by computer exam in the end of semester, each part weight as shown in Table 2.

Table 2. Each part weight of course assessment of webpage design and making

Focus	Professional quality	Basic knowledge	Skills
Weight	0.1	0.3	0.6

Computer Exam

Within the specified time (usually 2 hours), students use the given materials, including picture, text information, exam requirements and so on, to finish the website. By the way of simulation recruitment is to measure comprehensive abilities of creative design, understanding theme, image processing, animation making, color use, webpage layout, website management, etc.

3 Comprehensive Evaluation of Course Construction

3.1 Evaluation Index

According to the national evaluation index system of courses, we determine first-level evaluation indexes from five dimensions: teaching content, teaching condition, teaching method and mean, teaching team and teaching effect, as shown in Table 3.

The description of second-level indexes is as the follows:

- The index of course content: Teaching content can be updated, and the reform outcomes and the results of the latest developments in disciplines can be timely introduction in the teaching.
- The index of teaching content arrangement: Teaching content can integrate theory with practice, and can combine curricular with extracurricular.
- The index of materials and information: Materials construction is taken seriously and the excellent teaching materials are often used.
- The index of practice teaching condition: Practice teaching conditions can satisfy the teaching requirement and can carry out the open teaching.

Table 3. The evaluation index of webpage design and making course

First-level indexes	Second-level indexes	Score (M_i)	Rating (K_j)				
			A	B	C	D	E
			1.0	0.8	0.6	0.4	0.2
Teaching content	Course content	10	0.3	0.5	0.2		
	Teaching content arrangement	10	0.3	0.5	0.2		
Teaching condition	Materials and information	5	0.3	0.4	0.3		
	Practice teaching condition	5	0.2	0.4	0.3	0.1	
	Online teaching environment	10	0.3	0.4	0.3		
Teaching method and mean	Teaching method	10	0.3	0.4	0.2	0.1	
	Teaching mean	10	0.3	0.4	0.2	0.1	
Teaching team	Structure and quality	10	0.3	0.5	0.2		
	Teaching reform and research	10	0.3	0.4	0.3		
Teaching effect	Student assessment	10	0.5	0.3	0.2		
	Peer evaluation	10	0.4	0.4	0.2		

- The index of online teaching environment: Network teaching resources have a certain scale, and it can be updated frequently and work well and plays an important role in the teaching.
- The index of teaching method: Various advanced teaching method can be used flexibly and the study enthusiasm of students can effectively be mobilized.
- The index of teaching mean: Modern educational technology and means can be properly and fully used, and the actual effect is obtained in the aspect of stimulating interest of students and improving teaching effect.
- The index of teaching team structure and quality: Teaching team has good team spirit and the structure of team knowledge and age is reasonable, and the training plans of young teachers are reasonable.
- The index of teaching reform and research: Teaching activities are colorful, and the teaching reform is creative, and the teaching research papers with high quality have been published.
- The index of student assessment: The student evaluation is good.
- The index of peer assessment: The peer evaluation is good.

The score of comprehensive course evaluation is shown as:

$$M = \sum M_i K_i \tag{1}$$

Course Evaluation

In order to understand the situation of course construction, and to further improve the teaching effect, we have organized ten teachers and experts to evaluate webpage design and making course, the evaluation data is shown in Table 3.

Based on equation (1), we can calculate and get the evaluation score of webpage design and making course: M=80.9, which shows that the situation of course construction is good, and it reach the level of university-level courses.

4 Conclusions

4.1 Success Reasons

The webpage design and making course has been focusing on cultivating the creative ability of students, and course design is in the leading position in similar institutions. Based on the above analysis, the successful reasons of course construction can be summarized as the following aspects:

First, with advanced course design concept, the course design is based on the professional quality requirements of enterprise staffs. The teaching content and teaching method have the characteristics of applied education.

Second, with innovative materials design, the compilation of teaching materials is based on teachers' experience of teaching and practical project development.

Third, with the school-enterprise cooperation, teachers bring enterprise actual project into the teaching, and enterprise experts involve in the teaching process from the beginning of project to finishing the project acceptance.

4.2 Improvement Suggestion

Although the course construction of webpage design and making has achieved some success, there are some problems in the process of course construction, and it can be summarized as the following points.

- The work carrying out in-depth research and exploration still shows insufficient, and the teaching research activities at home and abroad are inadequate.
- The teaching resources need to accumulate continually, and the case base also needs to update timely.
- The course website is not used fully.

To solve these problems, we should improve from the following aspects:

For the teaching research activities, the teaching and research activities should be actively carried out, and should encourage teachers to participate in the meeting of teaching exchange.

For the teaching resources, various forms of learning contents, such as text material, animation, video teaching assistant learning, etc, should be provided for students.

For the course website, the course website should become the communication platform between teachers and students, and should provide interactive methods, feedback and evaluation system to promote exchange between teachers and students.

References

1. Yang, S., Liu, X.: The Research and Exploration on Educational Reform for Web Design and Production Course. Office Informatization 3 (2010) (in Chinese)
2. Wang, X., Zhou, L.: Curriculum Reform on Homepage Design and Making. Journal of Beijing Union University (Natural Sciences) 4 (2006) (in Chinese)
3. Shi, K., Gao, Y.: The Method of Teaching Designing and Making Webpage. Information Technology and Informatization. 2 (2007) (in Chinese)
4. Wu, J., Chen, Y.: Modern Education Technology Course (2003) (in Chinese)

The Relationship of House Price Rising Rate and GDP Growth Rate

Zhang Hongli

Xi'an University of Science and Technology
Shaanxi Province, China
honglizhang@sina.com

Abstract. The development of real estate industry is significant to the national economy and the people's livelihood, and the regulation of real estate is an important content of macroeconomic regulation and is controversial invariably. The key of real estate regulation is the regulation of house price, i.e. to control the rising extent of house price within a normal range. The article calculates the target range of house price regulation in 3σ Method. According to the conclusions, should control the house price rising rate/GDP growth rate of first-tier cities within [-0.31, 0.86], and that in second-tier cities within [-0.42, 1.17].The conclusions can provide a theoretical support for the stipulation of real estate regulation policies and the evaluation of the effects of real estate regulation policies.

Keywords: real estate, house price, regulation, normal range.

I Introduction

From 2003, the nation has made a series of real estate regulation policies for alleviating the economic and social contradictions resulted from the too fast rising of house price. From the second half year of 2009, the Chinese real estate market walked out the adjustment situation during the international financial crisis, with both volume and price rising, and the government is facing the difficulty of real estate regulation again. The regulation of house price is the key of real estate regulation. But the target range of house price regulation, i.e. whether the rising rate of house price is normal and requires the regulation of the government, and whether the regulation measures have achieved the predicted target, hasn't a clear definition until now. This is the purpose of the article.

2 Research Ideas

The target range of house price regulation is the reasonable range of house price fluctuation, and means the rising or declining extent of house price is coordinative with the situations of economic growth and does not need the government to intervene. When the rising extent of house price year on year is within this range, it is considered as normal and does not need to be regulated and controlled. When the

H. Tan and M. Zhou (Eds.): CSE 2011, Part I, CCIS 201, pp. 183–189, 2011.

rising extent of house price exceeds the upper limit of normal fluctuation range, it may be considered as "overheated" of the real estate market, and needs contractionary regulation; vice versa, when the declining extent of house price exceeds the upper limit of normal fluctuation range, it may be considered as "overcolded" of the real estate market, and needs expansionary regulation. According to this, the running states of real estate market can be divided into three types: normal, basically-normal, abnormal (overcolded or overheated). Currently, the main target of Chinese house price regulation is to prevent too large house price rising extent and overheated real estate market.

For convenient to study the target range of house price regulation, the article chooses two important indexes, house price rising rate and house price rising rate/urban GDP growth rate, and calculates the normal range of these two indexes in Composite Simulation Method. The Composite Simulation Method was established on the basis of Japanese experience, determined the critical values of the indexes according to the statistical law, and so to judge the running state of real estate market.

The traditional method to determine critical values is Empirical Data Method. Due to its poor accuracy, two new methods to determine critical values, Neural Network Method and 3σ Method based on normal distribution assumption, have grown up recently. Currently, the application of Neural Network Method is still at the start, not mature and perfect enough. Therefore, the article determines critical values in the modified 3σ Method.

3 Theory of 3σ

Normal distribution is the most common type of probability distribution type. 3σ Method assumes that the index variables are distributed normally, and accordingly studies the change law of indexes[ ]. The probability function of normal distribution is:

$$F(x) = \frac{1}{\sqrt{2ps}} \int_{-¥}^{p} e^{-\frac{(x-m)^2}{2s^2}} dx \tag{1}$$

Of which, is the mean value of overall samples, and is the standard deviation of overall samples.

According to the normal distribution law and formula can calculate the following probability:

$$\Phi(x) = p(\mu - \sigma < x < \mu + \sigma) = p[-\sigma < (x - \sigma) < \sigma] = p\{-1 < \frac{x-\mu}{\sigma} < 1\} \tag{2}$$

So,

$$F(x) = F(1) - F(-1) = 0.8413 - 0.1587 = 0.6826 \tag{3}$$

Similarly, can obtain:

$$p(\mu - 2\sigma < x < \mu + 2\sigma) = \Phi(2) - \Phi(-2) = 0.9546 \tag{4}$$

$$p(\mu - 3\sigma < x < \mu + 3\sigma) = \Phi(3) - \Phi(-3) = 0.9973 \tag{5}$$

$$p(\mu - 4\sigma < x < \mu + 4\sigma) = \Phi(4) - \Phi(-4) = 0.999937 \tag{6}$$

Accordingly, can obtain the following conclusion:

Firstly, assuming that all the characteristic values of indexes are subject to normal distribution, then in the total data of characteristic values near 70% are within ±σ, 95.46% within ±2σ, and only less than 5% exceed ±2σ. It shows that most of the characteristic values are distributed within ±2σ; at the same time, the indexes within ±2σcan represent the random distribution law of indexes in real estate industry.

Secondly, the principle of 3 σ is not affected by the value of σ. No matter what size the value of σ is, 68.3%characteristic values are contained within ±σ. 95.46% and 99.73% characteristic values are contained respectively within ±2σ and within ±3σ.

For more accurately defining the normal range of house price fluctuation, it is necessary to calculate those of first-tier cities and those of second-tier cities respectively. Currently, the house price in first-tier cities is on the high side, with large investment risk, weakening attraction to investment capital, and has exceeded the house purchasing ability of residents. The range of one time of standard deviation can be chosen as the upper limit of the normal range of rising extent fluctuation of house price, and the range of three times of standard deviation can be chosen as the lower limit of the normal range of declining extent fluctuation of house price. For the second-tier cities with lower house price, one time of standard deviation is too conservative, thus, two times of standard deviation is chosen as the upper limit of the normal range of house price rising extent, and the range of one to two times of standard deviation is considered as the normal range of house price fluctuation.

Taking the mean value of each index as the central value of its fluctuation, firstly calculate its central value. Then determine the normal growth range. According to the above analysis, for the first-tier cities, can regard the range of one time of standard deviation from the central value as the upper limit of normal range, and the range of three times of standard deviation as the lower limit of the normal range, i.e. [$\mu-3\sigma$, $\mu+\sigma$]. for the second-tier cities, can regard the range of one time of standard deviation from the central value as the normal range, i.e. [$\mu-\sigma$, $\mu+\sigma$]. regard the range of one to two times of standard deviation from the central value as the basic normal range, i.e. [$\mu-\sigma$, $\mu-2\sigma$] and [$\mu+\sigma$, $\mu+2\sigma$]. Regard the range of over two times of standard deviation from the central value as the abnormal (overcolded or overheated) range, i.e. [-∞, $\mu-2\sigma$] and [$\mu+2\sigma$, +∞]. In this way, the normal range of indexes in the second-tier cities is [$\mu-2\sigma$, $\mu+2\sigma$], and its boundary is the critical value for judging whether regulation is needed.

Obviously, the analysis on the regulation standards of real estate market is taking a specific economic development situation as premise. The above calculation is obtained from the statistical data of 2003~2008, therefore, its analysis conclusion is suitable for the similar macroeconomic situations. In this period, the yearly average growth rate of GDP in Chinese cities reached 10.68%, the financial institutions' loan rate of five years above was 6.12~7.20%, yearly average inflation rate was 3.2%, and the cities were in the fast urbanization development stage with yearly average growth rate of urban population of about one percent.

According to the above principles, we can calculate the normal range of house price rising rate and house price rising rate/urban GDP growth rate.

4 The Relationship of House Price Rising Rate and GDP

The indexes of house price are the most important indicators for reflecting the trend of house price variation and the situation of real estate market. According to the China Statistical Yearbook, can calculated the house price rising rate in these 35 cities in 2003～2008 (table 1).

Table 1. House Price Rising Rate in 35 Large and Middle Cities（%）

	2000	2003	2004	2005	2006	2007	2008		2000	2003	2004	2005	2006	2007	2008
Total	1.1	4.8	9.7	7.60	5.51	7.60	6.46	Qingdao	2.3	14.6	15.3	10.93	6.92	6.50	5.09
Beijing	-0.5	0.3	3.7	6.68	8.75	11.40	9.45	Zhengzhou	-0.5	2.0	4.0	6.97	5.69	6.30	3.32
Tianjin	0.0	4.1	13.5	5.97	6.70	6.90	5.84	Wuhan	1.5	3.8	8.4	6.83	3.03	5.20	4.91
Shijiazh	1.8	0.3	3.6	5.55	4.34	7.60	5.75	Changsha	-0.4	0.5	3.3	2.83	5.30	8.40	6.66
Taiyuan	1.1	2.8	6.4	5.60	3.90	4.40	5.70	Guangzhou	-2.7	-0.7	2.7	4.65	6.22	6.60	-0.16
Huhehaote	2.0	0.7	5.2	11.78	9.46	4.40	1.23	Shenzhen	-0.8	2.2	4.6	7.22	12.3	16.3	-1.86
Shenyang	3.0	7.6	15.9	7.50	6.58	6.10	4.57	Nanjing	-0.7	2.1	5.7	4.93	4.12	7.60	8.16
Dalian	0.2	0.7	4.6	9.15	10.87	7.20	4.82	Haikou	-0.6	2.7	5.9	2.53	2.80	6.60	10.4
Changchun	6.6	0.2	0.2	1.93	1.60	6.40	6.97	Chengdu	1.3	2.9	7.9	7.20	3.00	6.90	6.29
Ha'erbin	1.8	0.2	4.7	4.60	3.27	6.80	6.36	Guiyang	3.9	1.3	2.6	9.78	7.12	7.60	3.39
Shanghai	-1.4	20.1	15.9	9.72	-1.33	3.40	5.91	Kunming	0.2	-0.9	2.3	2.60	4.41	6.90	6.60
Nanjing	1.6	9.8	15.3	8.05	4.33	6.60	2.75	Chongqing	1.8	6.1	13.9	2.90	1.33	3.50	3.22
Hangzhou	4.9	6.1	11.7	9.72	2.63	7.30	8.58	Xi'an	1.3	1.4	5.0	4.28	3.59	6.40	8.06
Ningbo	5.5	16.6	13.9	6.35	2.16	8.60	9.16	Lanzhou	0.5	1.8	8.7	5.55	4.72	6.00	9.77
Hefei	0.0	4.1	5.6	6.15	1.25	1.80	8.35	Xining	1.1	1.9	4.0	3.35	2.79	3.80	7.51
Fuzhou	0.3	1.1	3.6	4.40	6.67	6.80	3.85	Yinchuan	2.2	2.1	4.4	2.65	2.33	3.90	11.7
Xiamen	0.1	2.8	7.3	8.00	6.95	7.00	2.71	Wulumuqi	2.4	-0.1	0.7	0.92	1.19	9.00	15.5
Nanchang	3.2	4.8	7.3	8.30	6.23	6.80	4.15	Qingdao	2.3	14.6	15.3	10.9	6.92	6.50	5.09
Jinan	2.8	3.1	10.3	7.55	4.27	5.20	7.22	Zhengzhou	-0.5	2.0	4.0	6.97	5.69	6.30	3.32
Wuhan	1.5	3.8	8.4	6.83	3.03	5.20	4.91	Changsha	-0.4	0.5	3.3	2.83	5.30	8.40	6.66

Then calculate the mean value and mean square deviation in these 35 cities, and determine the critical value of house price rising rate when the real estate market is under normal state in the method of 3σ.

According to this can obtain the critical value of these 35 large and middle cities under abnormal state (overcolded or overheated). When the house price rising rate exceeds the critical value in a city, it can be considered that the real estate market is overcolded or overheated in the city.

Finally, the 35 cities can be divided into first- and second-tier cities by experience. Generally, first-tier cities mean Beijing, Shanghai, Hangzhou, Shenzhen, and Guangzhou, and all the others are second-tier cities. Here taking eight typical cities, Nanjing, Tianjin, Shenyang, Wuhan, Chengdu, Chongqing, Xian, and Urumchi, to calculate their critical values of house price rising rate (table 3-6).

Table 2. Critical Value of House Price Rising Rate in 35 Large and Middle Cities （%）

	σ	$\mu+\sigma$	$\mu-\sigma$	$\mu-2\sigma$	$\mu+2\sigma$	$\mu+3\sigma$	$\mu-3\sigma$		σ	$\mu+\sigma$	$\mu-\sigma$	$\mu-2\sigma$	$\mu+2\sigma$	$\mu+3\sigma$	$\mu-3\sigma$
Total	2.53	8.6	3.59	3.59	11.16	13.69	-1.46	Zhengzhou	2.44	6.4	1.53	1.53	8.85	11.29	-3.35
Beijing	4.28	10.0	1.40	1.40	14.25	18.53	-7.17	Wuhan	2.15	7.0	2.66	2.66	9.10	11.25	-1.63
Tianjin	3.72	9.9	2.42	2.42	13.59	17.31	-5.03	Changsha	2.96	6.8	0.84	0.84	9.72	12.68	-5.08
Shijiazh	2.30	6.4	1.83	1.83	8.74	11.04	-2.77	Guangzhou	3.37	5.7	1.00	-1.00	9.11	12.49	-7.74
Taiyuan	1.72	6.0	2.55	2.55	7.71	9.43	-0.89	Shenzhen	6.22	11.9	-0.51	-0.51	18.15	24.37	-12.96
Huhehaote	3.93	8.9	1.04	1.04	12.82	16.74	-6.81	Nanjing	2.87	7.4	1.69	1.69	10.29	13.16	-4.05
Shenyang	3.82	11.1	3.51	3.51	14.96	18.77	-4.13	Haikou	3.33	7.7	1.01	1.01	10.99	14.31	-5.64
Dalian	3.73	9.1	1.63	1.63	12.82	16.55	-5.82	Chengdu	2.41	7.5	2.66	2.66	9.88	12.29	-2.15
Changchun	2.88	6.3	0.54	0.54	9.16	12.04	-5.21	Guiyang	2.86	8.0	2.24	2.24	10.82	13.67	-3.48
Ha'erbin	2.21	6.2	1.75	1.75	8.37	10.58	-2.66	Kunming	2.77	5.9	0.39	0.39	8.70	11.47	-5.15
Shanghai	7.66	15.1	-0.19	-0.19	22.79	30.45	-15.51	Chongqing	4.02	8.7	0.65	0.65	12.72	16.75	-7.39
Nanjing	4.35	11.3	2.57	2.57	15.61	19.96	-6.12	Xi'an	2.30	6.6	1.99	1.99	8.88	11.18	-2.60
Hangzhou	2.83	10.1	4.45	4.45	12.93	15.75	-1.20	Lanzhou	3.11	8.4	2.18	2.18	11.51	14.62	-4.04
Ningbo	4.60	13.5	4.30	4.30	18.09	22.69	-4.90	Xining	1.90	5.4	1.59	1.59	7.29	9.19	-2.21
Hefei	2.79	6.7	1.10	1.10	9.47	12.26	-4.47	Yinchuan	3.20	7.4	0.99	0.99	10.59	13.79	-5.40
Fuzhou	2.30	6.1	1.51	1.51	8.42	10.73	-3.09	Wulumuqi	5.40	9.6	1.17	-1.17	15.04	20.44	-11.98
Xiamen	2.83	7.8	2.15	2.15	10.65	13.48	-3.52	Zhengzhou	2.44	6.4	1.53	1.53	8.85	11.29	-3.35
Nanchang	1.70	7.5	4.13	4.13	9.22	10.92	0.73	Wuhan	2.15	7.0	2.66	2.66	9.10	11.25	-1.63
Jinan	2.52	8.3	3.26	3.26	10.81	13.33	-1.77	Changsha	2.96	6.8	0.84	0.84	9.72	12.68	-5.08
Shenzhen	6.22	119	0.51	-0.51	18.15	24.37	-12.96	Guangzhou	3.37	5.7	1.00	-1.00	9.11	12.49	-7.74

Table 3. Upper Limit of House Price Rising Rate in First-tier Cities (%)

City	Beijing	Shanghai	Hangzhou	Shenzhen	Guangzhou	Average
Critical Value for Overheated	10.0	15.1	10.1	11.9	5.7	10.56

Table 4. Upper Limit Of House Price Rising Rate in Second-Tier Cities(%)

City	shenyang	chengdu	Xi'an	nanjing	wuhan	chongqing	average
Critical Value for Overheated	14.96	14.99	8.88	15.61	9.10	12.72	14.47

Table 5. Lower Limit of House Price Rising Rate in First-tier Cities(%)

city	beijing	shanghai	wuhan	gunagzhou	average
Critical Value for Overcold	-7.17	-15.51	-12.96	-7.74	-10.84

Table 6. Lower Limit of House Price Rising Rate in Second-tier Cities(%)

City	shenyang	chengdu	Xi'an	nanjing	wuhan	Chongqing	average
Critical Value for Overcolded	-4.13	-2.15	-2.60	-5.03	-1.63	-7.39	-5.13

It can be seen from the calculated results that, the upper limit of normal rising rate is 10.56%, lower limit is -10.84%, and the target range of regulation is [-10.84%, 10.56%] in first-tier cities; the upper limit of normal rising rate is 12.47%, lower limit is -5.13%, and the target range of regulation is [-5.13%, 12.47%] in second-tier cities.

Then, calculate the house price rising rate/GDP growth rate in first-tier cities. According to the China Statistical Yearbook and the statistical yearbook in all cities over the years, can sort out the house price rising rate/GDP growth rate in first-tier cities in 2004～2008.

According to the above table calculate the mean value of house price rising rate/GDP growth rate in first-tier cities. Considered the practical situations of high-speed development of urban real estate industry in recent years, taking ±2σ as normal range is too conservative, therefore, taking [$\mu-3\sigma$, $\mu+3\sigma$] as the normal range of the index.

Then calculate the house price rising rate/GDP growth rate in second-tier cities. Considered the integrality of statistical data, selecting Xian, Nanjing, Shenyang, Wuhan, and Chongqing as the typical representatives of second-tier cities to calculate the normal range of house price rising rate/GDP growth rate.Via calculation, can obtain the mean value of house price rising rate/GDP growth rate in second-tier cities.

It can be seen from the calculated results that, the mean value 0.86 of house price rising rate/GDP growth rate in first-tier cities is the upper limit when the real estate market is under normal state, the mean value -0.31 is the lower limit, and the target range of regulation is [-0.31, 0.86]; the mean value 1.17 of house price rising rate/GDP growth rate in second-tier cities is the upper limit when the real estate market is under normal state, the mean value -0.42 is the lower limit, and the target range of regulation is [-0.42, 1.17].

5 Conclusion

The real estate market is a typical regional market. Due to the unbalanced economic development in Chinese regions and the large difference of running states of real estate market in cities, therefore, should select the regulation target and corresponding policies and tools via classification.

House price regulation is the most important content of real estate regulation. For the comparison of house price fluctuation range, should inspect whether the growth rate of house price in the same period is within the normal range by monthly data. That is to say, comparing the mean values of commercial residential building of all months to those in the same period of last year, if the growth rate in the same period exceeds the normal range determined in this article, the central and local governments should consider publishing regulation measures for the city or region. According to the practical situations in China, currently the main target of house price regulation is to prevent fast rising of house price, i.e. prevent overheating of real estate market.

According to the calculations, should control house price rising rate/GDP growth rate in first-tier cities within [-0.31, 0.86], and that in second-tier cities within [-0.42, 1.17]. Looking from the practical situations of real estate market in recent years, the normal range of house price fluctuation determined in the article is reliable. In some years real estate market was overheated, looking from the monthly comparative indexes, the house price rising extent exceeded the upper limit of normal range and needed the government to regulate and control in Beijing, Shenzhen, shanghai, Hangzhou, and Haikou, etc.

References

1. Huang, Z.: Several Theoretical Problems on Bubble Economy and Its Measurement, Financial Research (June 2002)
2. Duan Y., Tian P., Zhang X.: Relative efficiency control fuzzy system. In: Proceeding of the 46'th ISSS Annual Conference, Shanghai, China (2002)
3. Yan, H., Bin, Z.: Research on influence of macro-regulation on real estate industry in China. Price Theory and Practice (12), 45–46 (2006) (in Chinses)
4. Yin, H., Tan, S.: Policy orientation of macroeconomic regulation on Chinese Real estate market. Statistics and Decision (10), 100–102 (2006) (in Chinses)

Research and Application of Monitoring Memory by Page Fault in Linux Task Manager

Haijun Zhang[1], Bo Zhang[2], and Changchang Zhang[3]

[1,2] School of Information, Beijing WuZi University, Beijing, China
[3] Institute of Information and Engineer, North China University of Technology, China
Haijun_cumtb@yahoo.com.cn, zyjt@163bj.com, zcc0379@163.com

Abstract. Entering the command to see system information is rather inconvenient in Linux. Hence, this paper developed the graphical task manager based on monitoring page fault. Firstly, it introduced the implementation principle of task manager based on gtk programming style, Secondly, it analyzed that page fault is crucial to fulfill monitoring memory. Finally, it discussed the defect of the traditional method of obtaining page fault and presented a new method of getting page fault information by modifying the Linux kernel, compiling after reconfiguration and adding new system calls. The results show that the new method can improve the accuracy and performance a lot in monitoring memory.

Keywords: memory shortage page, Linux kernel, task manager, page fault monitor, memory allocation.

1 Introduction

By developing Linux task manager software, by simply clicking a button users can get the desired information and needs, at the same time they can also experience a good service. The traditional Linux task manager concerns most about resource information, process information, disk information, file system, I/O ports and etc., which has met the needs of users to a large extent. However, real-time dynamic monitoring of page default is not yet available. Majority method of monitoring page default is reading file saving system information by file pointer. This method is relatively simple and inefficient to be achieved. Page default monitoring was introduced in this paper. Draw the continuous real-time dynamic monitoring curve by GNOME-gtk style graphics API in Linux, allowing users to have not only static data but also dynamic and intuitive visual effects. The traditional method of obtaining page default is reading figure corresponding page default interrupt, this paper tried another new method to get page default by analyzing kernel code concerned with page default, making appropriate changes and recording the number of page default handling.

2 The Framework for Linux Task Manger

KDE and Gnome are two graphical user interface style in Linux. Given Gnome's consistent view of the development structure, ease of use and mutual maneuverability,

H. Tan and M. Zhou (Eds.): CSE 2011, Part I, CCIS 201, pp. 190–201, 2011.

the task manager's interface is implemented by making use of Gnome's graphics library —gtk +. According to the different nature, system information can be divided into two types: one is static and real time low, such as system version information, I/O ports and etc.; the other is dynamic and real-time high, such as memory information, process information and so on. In order to efficiently access the information, according to the concept of load balancing [1], the internal structure is completed by two mechanism of comprise—core state and user state. The first category of information can be obtained through the external application; the second kind of information is obtained directly by running the kernel code. Fig.1 shows the framework of the task manager.

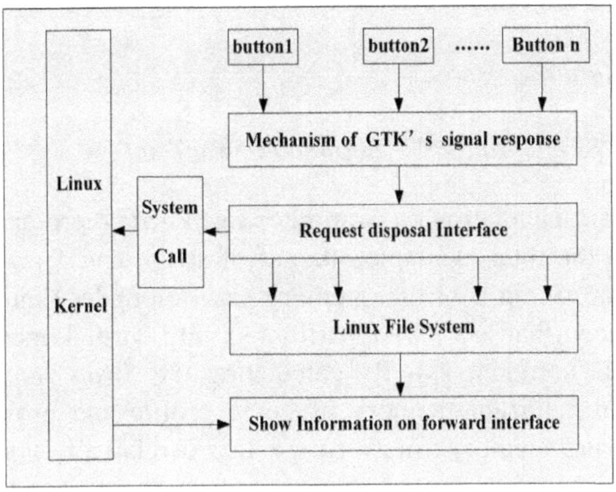

Fig. 1. The structure of the task manager design

Gtk layout manager adds buttons to the container by establishing the task manager's main window. Each button represents a kind of system information, such as button 1 for resource information, button 2 for process information. After clicking the button, Gtk signal response mechanism will transfer the corresponding signal to request processing interface and the event action is triggered. The user interface functions do different treatments by instructions: one way is the traditional practice of binding through the Linux file system to read file system information by I/O; The other way is to use system calls to access the kernel, directly getting system information. Eventually, return system information to the task manager main window for user.

3 Monitor Memory by Use of Page Default

3.1 Analysis of Page Default Monitoring

Memory, the most important system resource, is a major cornerstone of the OS. Memory usage plays a vital role in efficiency of the system. Finding effective ways to monitor memory can provide a strong assurance of system's efficient and stable operation [2].

3.1.1 Comparison of Monitoring Memory

1) Memory usage calculation

$$Mem\_rate = \left(Memtotal - MemFree\right) / Memtotal \tag{1}$$

Formula (1) gives the calculation of memory usage, *Mem_rate* presents memory usage rate, *Memtotal* presents the total amount of memory, *MemFree* presents the amount of memory free, Memory usage rate reflects use of memory to a certain extent and can tell user the current busy status of the memory, playing a good guide for user to turn off the corresponding process to release memory space. *Mem_rate* value and the memory usage were positively correlated, the greater the value is, and the more memory is used.

2) Swap rate calculation

$$Swap\_rate = 1 - SwapFree / SwapTotal \tag{2}$$

Formula (2) gives the calculation of swap rate, *Swap_rate* represents swap usage rate, *SwapFree* presents the total available amount of swap, and *SwapTotal* presents the total amount of swap. Swap is virtual memory partition under Linux, which works by changing disk space (that is, Swap partitions) into virtual memory to use after physical memory is used out [3]. By calculating the *Swap_rate*, the use of swap reflects indirectly the current memory usage in profile and provides the basis for the user to understand memory. *Swap_rate* = 0 is a relatively good sign, indicating the current physical memory is not exhausted. Once *Swap_rate*>0 indicates that the system overload, physical memory has been completely occupied. Although the above two methods give the user feedback on memory information, but only to monitor the surface of the memory in microscopy and not to reflect memory in essence.

3.1.2 The Advantages of Using a Page Fault Monitoring

Page default can make up for the lack of the above methods very well, directly revealing the true memory change in essence. Linux uses virtual memory management model that views segment and page as a unit and employs three levels of page table structure: Page Directory (PGD), Page Middle Directory (PMD) and Page Table (PTE) [4]. Memory management units (MMU) convert logical address to linear address by the hardware segment mechanism, and then convert linear address to physical address through the hardware page mechanism. Physical page is carried out as a unit in physical memory management, which is divided into three levels, namely storage, the management area and the page [5]. When a process is executed, if page requested by the process is not in memory, CPU will transfer free pages out of memory and the requested page into memory following a certain strategy [6], page's swapping out and in reflects fundamental changes in memory, so real-time grasping of memory page fault is the most direct and effective control.

3.2 The Implementation of Page Fault Monitoring

3.2.1 Page Fault Mechanism

In order to quickly analyze pages default exception types, particularly define Decision Support Matrix $A_{m\times n}$. In this matrix, row dimension presents the exception code, and the column dimension presents bit (No. 1, No. 2, No. 3 ... .), so the element a_{ij} presents the value of exception code i on bit j. The specific form was shown in Table1.

According to the value of error code, scan decision support matrix $A_{m\times n}$ and get values on different position. Then obtain exception type by scanning error information shown in Table 2, For example: error code is 7; obtain bit 0=1, bit 1=1, and bit 2=1 by scanning $A_{m\times n}$. A conclusion that the exception is caused by implementation of the general user code page writing operation can be drawn by searching Table 2 according to bit 0=1, bit 1=1, and bit 2=1.

After analysis of the exception, if it can not be handled, then call function handle_mm_fault () and exit; If it can be handled and is caused by abnormal write-protected page, call do_wp_page () to write copy; If page default is normal, then call do_no_page (), which check the virtual memory area descriptor "nopage", if nopage field is not empty, indicating that maps a disk file, nopage domain points to the function performing reading operations from disk; if nopage field is empty, indicating that virtual memory area is not mapped disk file. Therefore, do_no_ page () call do_anonymous_page () to apply for a page frame from memory block [7].

Table 1. Decision Support Matrix A

	0	1	2
0	0	0	0
1	1	0	0
2	0	1	0
3	1	1	0
4	0	0	1
5	1	0	1
6	0	1	1
7	1	1	1

Table 2. Error Code Information

	bit 2 (U/S)	*bit 1 (W/R)*	*bit 0 (P)*
0	run super user code	read	page not exist
1	run general user code	write	page exist

3.2.2 The Lack of Traditional Access to Pages Default

In the Linux file system, /proc/stat file maintains a variety of intrs' occurrence number so far from boot, in which intr 14 is a page fault. The traditional method is to use the file pointer to the file, through I/O to read intr14's number to get page default information, but this method has flaws. First of all, the occurrence of intr 14 is not only during the process of address transformation when the present bit (P) in page directory item or page table item is equal to 0 (that page is not in memory), intr 14 can also be triggered when either of parent and child processes do writing operations to the shared physical page, but the latter is not a "true page default", replication with writing is precisely illustrates this point. The parent process call fork () to create a child process, parent and child share a set of physical pages to save memory space, while access purview is set to read-only. Until there is only one side for writing, copy that piece of real physical pages to be accessible to it, and this copy of the physical page is marked as write access [8]. Such cases also produce intr14, however does not put pages into the memory but simply copy the page. Secondly, intr14 page mechanism can be used by the condition of (PG = 1) state. Or else, the value is always 0, even if the memory load multiple, bringing great inconvenience to the reader. Moreover, through the file I/O operations to read page fault, read() will be called which calls corresponding system call function to read data from disk to kernel, and copy to user space variable from the kernel again. The process is very time-consuming and inefficient.

3.2.3 New Method for Getting Page Default

In order to get the real number of page default efficiently, a new method that page default information can be fetched directly by modifying the kernel, reconfiguring, recompiling , and adding new system call is introduced based on understanding the page default mechanism. To do the following:

1) Modify the kernel code:

/usr/src/linux-2.4.20-8/include/linux/mm.h

Add "extern int pfcount" statement;

/usr/src/linux-2.4.20-8/arch/i386/mm/fault.c

add the definition of int pfcount = 0 before do_page_fault ();Then find good_area: followed by the pfcount++[9] ;

Linux kernel function do_page_fault() is designed to handle page fault, it first parses the exception addresses of the page default, if the exception address falls in the linear region (this address is legal), turn to good_area. At this circumstance, stack is gridlocked in user mode. If there are still things to the stack at this time, the exception occurred is a real page fault exception. It is not caused by a bug [10]. So page fault information can be obtained by recording the number of good_area.

2) Add a system call

- in /usr/src/linux-2.4.20-8/kernel/sys.c

```
asmlinkage int sys_get_page_fault()
 {
          return pfcount;
}
```

- /usr/src/linux-2.4.20-8/include/asm-i386/unistd.h

```
#define __NR_get_page_fault     259
```

- /usr/src/linux-2.4.20-8/arch/i386/kernel/entry.S

(add the following sentence 259 lines below entry (sys_call_table))

```
.long SYMBOL_NAME(sys_get_page_fault)
```

Application can not directly access the kernel, there are two ways to do it: (1) application access kernel under the help of Glib C liberary; (2) application access kernel directly by adding a special statement in it [11]. The kernel communicates with CPU, disks, peripherals, etc through device driver interface and with modules through modules interface. This step is mainly in the second layer shown in Fig.2. That is, add a new system call-level interface function sys_get_page_fault () to read the number of page default. The external application to obtain page default information through newly-added interface.

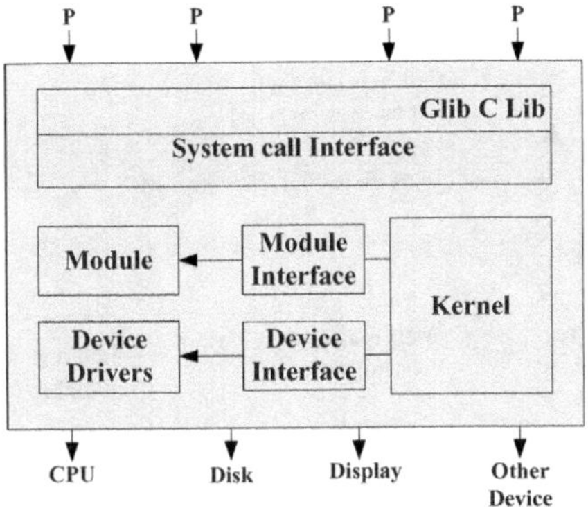

Fig. 2. Linux kernel-level framework

3) # cd /usr/include/

```
# rm -r asm linux scsi
# ln -s /usr/src/linux-2.4/include/asm-i386 asm
# ln -s /usr/src/linux-2.4/include/linux linux
# ln -s /usr/src/linux-2.4/include/scsi scsi
```

4) After cd /usr/src/linux-2.4

```
#make menuconfig
#make dep
#make clean
#make bzImage
#make modules
#make modules_install
#make install
```

After the above steps, you have built an application development platform of monitoring page fault.

3.2.4 Draw Page Default Graphic

Although the above methods can obtain page default information, but lack of statistical analysis on it. To allow users to experience more intuitive page-default, draw dynamic page default graph with correlation functions provided by gtk+. Fig.3 shows the process of drawing dynamic curve to monitor page default, in which sec variable used to record the number of second is initiated to 0, cur_persecond_count variable used to record the current number of page-default is initated to 0 and prior_persecond_count variable used to record the page-default number during prior 1s is initated to 0.

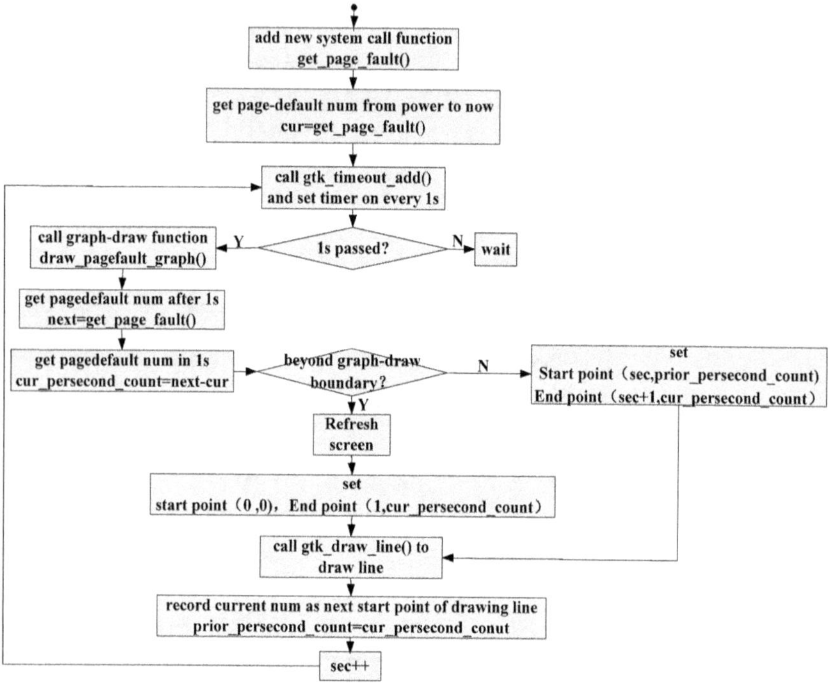

Fig. 3. Page fault monitoring algorithm flow

After modifying the kernel source code and recompiling the kernel, you can use the newly-added system call function get_page_fault () to capture the page-default number from system boot to the current. In order to obtain page-default number during 1 second, gtk_timeout_add () provided by gtk+ is triggered on every 1s and looped. The difference between cur_persecond_count and prior_persecond_count is the page default number occurred during 1s. Page default chart need to call gtk_draw_line () provided by gtk, which is called once every second and done loop(timer's internal mechanism) on purpose of achieving to monitor page fault real-time and dynamically. In order to let this curve show a continuous and smooth state, add a new variable used to record page default number in the current 1s ,shown in Fig.4. While in the drawing process, detect whether the curve has been beyond the drawing area, if so, refresh the screen and set starting point (0, 0) to draw the curve again.

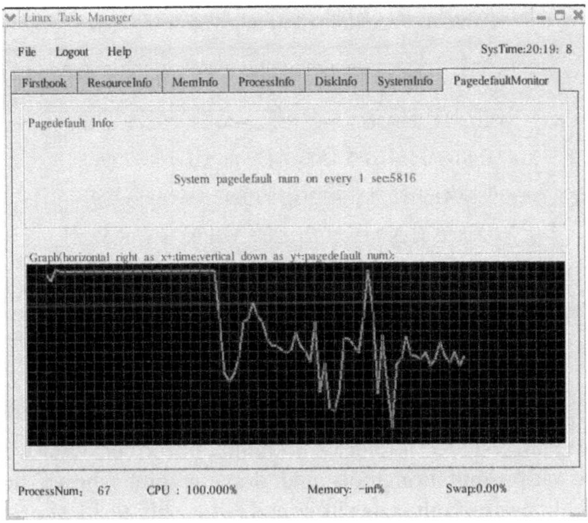

Fig. 4. Page fault monitoring under the task manager

4 Experimental Verification

4.1 Performance Analysis and Validation of New Methods

The page default can be divided into several categories according to Linux different initialization and treatment ways. One is called main page default which needs I/O operation and consumes quite a long time. However, it takes very small time to handle others [12].

Fig.4 shows page default graphic during 1 min and 26 seconds (horizontal right expresses time's positive, unit: second; vertical down expresses page default number's positive).

Collect a data every second, application shows page default number per second on terminal by printf(), and the data corresponding to the graph shown in Table 3, Table 4 below:

Table 3. Page default number before big task

	1s	2s	3s	4s	5s	6s	7s	8s	9s	10s
1	703	1212	499	499	503	499	500	500	501	500
2	502	500	500	503	502	500	500	499	501	500
3	499	502	499	499	499	499	503	501	499	500
4	499	499	500	500	500					

Table 4. Page default number after big task

	1s	2s	3s	4s	5s	6s	7s	8s	9s	10s
1	3456	6834	7269	6833	5795	3655	3454	2402	3273	3685
2	4731	5145	5144	5355	4300	5142	5482	6069	3669	7922
3	6198	8941	9150	7885	4721	4720	5142	5564	3453	499
4	3032	8095	4508	7673	10205	6246	5938	4576	5709	5774
5	5986	5563	6408	5985	4932	5775	6196	5564	6407	5816
6	6408									

Do quantitative analysis for a total of 86 numbers further, data were collected the first 20 seconds into simulation tools and draw graphic shown in Fig.5. Fig. 5 illustrates different page default states after and before big task occurred.

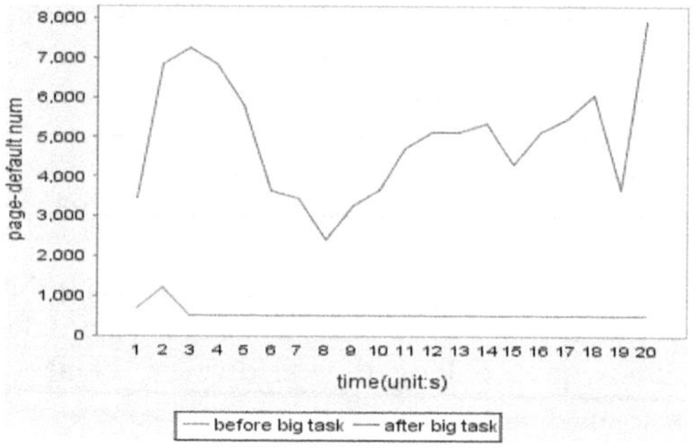

Fig. 5. Comparison before and after big task execution

From a macro point of view, when system is not busy, the curve tends to smooth and fluctuation is smaller. The range of the top 20 numbers is very small, mostly in the vicinity of 499 and 500. After inputting cat /proc/kcore, the system quickly becomes busy, curve jitters immediately, increases up and down, and jumps forward like wavy. After the implementation of big task, the number becomes larger and the difference between numbers is widened very much.

From the microscopic analysis, the size of heap and memory allocated has an influence on page default [13]. Formula (3) reflects the relationship between page default number and heap.

$$n = (1/2)\left(H + \sqrt{H^2 - 4}\right)\left(n^* + n_0\right) - n_o$$
$$H = 1 + \left(M^* - M_0\right)/\left(M - M_0\right) \quad M \le M^* \tag{3}$$

In formula (3), Parameter n^*, n_0, M^* and M_0 are the constant relevant to M , but they also depend on the application, its input data, operating system version and the page conversion strategies. M represents the size of RMB(MB), M_0 represents the number of page that can't be replaced, M^* represents the ratio of average time between a page from the first time to the last to leave the RAM and reading two new pages into memory. $M= M_0+ M^*$. Where, n represents page default number, n^* represents number of pages read for a workload recently; n_0 represents fitness between the average number of reading a page from disk and n [14]. Heap and mmap are two kinds of memory allocation in Linux. But heap allocation's priority is higher than mmap. Applying for memory is firstly from heap, once allocated, system can't release space until the heap space of process reaches maxmium or there is no continuous memory to use [15]. When the big task is executed, it will frequently use the memory, thus dramatically increasing the size of the heap. The number of page default will be larger with the increase of the heap according to Formula (3), so curve fluctuates largely. When workload is quite small, the heap size is relatively fixed, so page default number is relatively stable, drawing the flat curve. From the above, the new method can accurately and objectively reflects the situation of page default.

4.2 Comparison between New Method and Traditional Method

Set the start time and end time before and after page default, put the difference between the two values into simulation tools to draw graphic, as shown in Fig 6. Fig 6 shows time consumed to get page default information by two different methods respectively.

From Fig.6, it is clear that the new method by calling newly-added system call interface to directly access the kernel is almost no time-consuming, its performance is much better than traditional methods through I/O operations which need read the file.

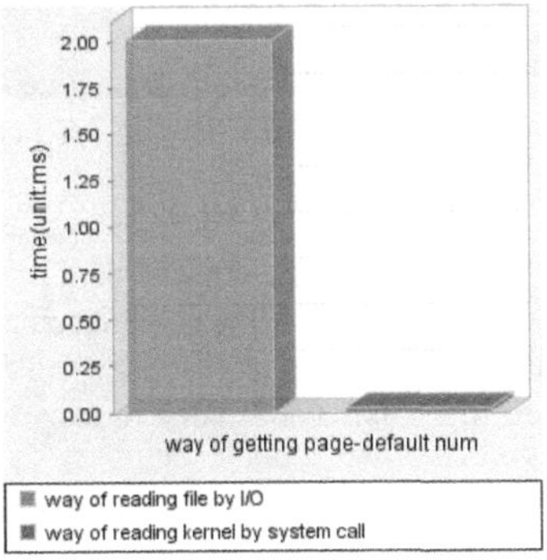

Fig. 6. Old and new methods performance comparison

5 Conclusion

This paper, based on Linux 2.4.20-8, developed the task manager. Page default can more directly reflect the memory. A new method was proposed by modifying the kernel source code and adding new system calls to monitor page fault. Experiments show than task manager's performance was improved further by integrating page default monitor into it. New method could not only reflect page default objectively and accurately, but also had a higher efficiency than traditional methods.

Acknowledgment

This paper is based on work supported by Funding Project for Academic Human Resources Development in Institutions of Higher Learning under the Jurisdiction of Beijing Municipality under Grant No. PHR200906210, Funding Project for Base Construction of Scientific Research of Beijing Municipal Commission of Education under Grant No. WYJD200902, Funding Project for Science and Technology Program of Beijing Municipal Commission of Education Under grant number KM201010037002 and National Science and Technology Supported Project between Eleventh Five-Year: Regional International Logistics Service System and Application Model under Grant No. 2009BAH46B06. This paper is also funded by Logistics Technology Engineering Research Center of Beijing Universities and Characteristic Specialty Construction Project of Beijing.

References

1. Guo, H., Wang, Z., Zhou, J.: Load balancing based process scheduling with fault tolerance in heterogeneous distributed System. Chinese Journal of Computers 28, 1812–1813 (2005)
2. Xiao, J., Chen, L.: Analysis and Research of Realization for Linux Memory Management. Computer Technology and Development 17, 187–189 (2007)
3. Ko, S., Junl, S., Ryu, Y., et al.: A new Linux swap system for flash memory storage devices. In: International Conference on Computational Sciences and Its Applications, ICCSA 2008, pp. 151–152 (2008)
4. Cheng, X., Gong, Y., Wang, X.: Study of Embedded Operating System Memory Management. Education Technology and Computer Science (ETCS), 962–965 (March 7, 2009)
5. Alkassar, E., Schirmer, N., Starostin, A.: Formal pervasive verification of a paging mechanism, pp. 110–112. Springer, Heidelberg (2008)
6. Li, Z., Zhou, M., Wan, M.: An Improved Page Replacement Algorithm Supporting Real Time Processes Based on Objrmap. Computer Engineering & Science 29, 42 (2007)
7. Xie, C., Liu, Z.: Research of Linux2.6 Memory Management. Application Research of Computers, 60 (March 2005)
8. Zhao, J.: Complete Analysis of Linux Kernel Based on the Kernel on 0.12, pp. 745–746. Machinery Industry Press, Beijing (2009)
9. Li, S., Ji, J., Yin, K.: Learning by Doing: Linux Kernel Guide, Version 2. Zhejiang University Press (2008)
10. Chen, Y., Luo, Y.: Analyzing the New Features of Linux 2.6 Management Subsystem. Computer Engineering and Applications 22, 92 (2005)
11. Ma, F., Wang, X.: Analysis and Research of System-call Mechanism in Embedded Linux System. Computer Engineering and Design, 271–273 (January 2, 2008)

12. Belogolov, S.A., Park, J., Park, J., et al.: Scheduler-assisted prefetching: efficient demand paging for embedded systems. In: The 14 IEEE International Conference on Embedded and Real-Time Computing Systems and Applications, RTCSA, pp. 111–119 (2008)
13. Tay, Y.C., Zong, X.R.: A Page Fault Equation for Dynamic Heap Sizing, pp. 201–206. ACM, New York (January 2010)
14. Tay, Y.C., Zou, M.: A page fault equation for modeling the effect of memory size. Performance Evaluation 63, 100–106 (2006)
15. Yang, F.: Implementation of Dynamic Memory Management Mechanism Based on Linux Kernel. Computer Engineering 36, 85 (2010)

Numerical Study on Critical Speed Modeling of Ultra-High Speed Grinder Spindle

C.H. Li, Z.L. Han, C. Du, and Y.C. Ding

School of Mechanical Engineering, Qingdao Technological University, 266033 China

Abstract. Based on the transfer-matrix method and taking into consideration the gyroscopic couple, the shear, the variable cross-section and other influential factors, a critical speed model was established for the multi-disk rotor of the rotor-bearing system of the grinder spindle. The critical speeds of first three orders, the modes of variation and other dynamic characteristic parameters of the grinder spindle were numerical investigated and calculated. The influences of the axial pre-tightening force of the bearing, the span of the fulcrum bearing as well as the changes in the front and rear overhangs on the critical speed of the rotor-bearing system on the grinder spindle and their pattern of changes were analyzed. The results showed that the working speed of the spindle system is much lower than the primary critical speed and can therefore stay away the resonance range effectively. Furthermore, the span of the fulcrum bearing and the overhang had significant influences on the critical speed within a certain range, and the study provided the basis and guidance for the structural design and performance optimization of the grinder spindle.

Keywords: Grinder, Spindle system, Critical speed, Ultra-high speed grinding.

1 Introduction

Generally, ultra-high speed grinding refers to the grinding with grinding wheel speed greater than 150m/s. Ultra-high speed grinding develops very rapidly in the developed countries, namely Europe, Japan and the United States, and is considered to have reached the highest peak of modern grinding technology. The spindle of Ultra-high speed grinding machine tool is a typical ultra-high speed bearings-rotor dynamics system, and its rotating speed far surpasses the critical speed of the low order system. The realization of dynamic balance is associated with the performance and stability of the whole equipment. With the increase of the rotating speed and the flexibility of, the research on the method of flexible rotor's dynamic balance appeared. The early stage method of flexible rotor's dynamic balance was put forward by Federn, which was later called vibration balance method or modal balance method. The number of times of start-up of high-speed balance was relatively less, and is of high sensitivity. The low order mode would not be affected when the balancing of high order mode was conducted, but identification was not balanced. The influence of bearing characteristics was especially great under large damping. It was not easy to achieve single mode when used near critical speed in shafting balance. Later the American Goodman formally presented influence coefficient method based on least square

H. Tan and M. Zhou (Eds.): CSE 2011, Part I, CCIS 201, pp. 202–209, 2011.

method, and its advantages were as follows: electronic computer could be used to assist dynamic balance; the identification of unbalance factors was not affected by bearing characteristics; it could balance several vibration models simutaneously, which was more convenient especially for the balance of the shafts. However, the number of times of start-up in high speed balance was more, and the susceptibility of high order modes was reduced. Based on the basic theories of rotor dynamics and structural system dynamics, dynamics theory model of the spindle system of ultra-high speed grinder was established using the transfer matrix method and the overall transfer matrix method in this study, and the simulation study was conducted on the influence of critical speed, vibration mode on the dynamic characteristics of main shaft systems of super-high speed grinder.

2 Mathematical Model of Critical Speed

2.1 Model Simplification

Ultra-high speed spindle system is a continuous elastomer. Based on the concentration mass dynamic modeling theory of the transfer matrix method, it was necessary to simplify the quality-continuous actual rotor into the rotor with a series of concentrated mass and rigid disks, which were connected by massless and flexible shaft sections in between. Threads and chamfers, as well as the influence of local non-circular section were ignored during the simplifying process of the spindle system before dispersing. Ultra-high speed grinding spindle system mainly consisted of bearings, spindle, motor rotor, and additional parts (locking nut, bearing retainer ring, encoder, sealing rings, etc.). The bearing spindle system was generally divided into sliding bearing and rolling bearing. For sliding bearing, the oil film's dynamic coefficient matrix was as follows:

$$[C]=\begin{bmatrix} c_{xx} & c_{xy} \\ c_{yx} & c_{yy} \end{bmatrix};[K]=\begin{bmatrix} k_{xx} & k_{xy} \\ k_{yx} & k_{yy} \end{bmatrix} \tag{1}$$

The coefficient matrix of the dynamic performance of bearing block was as follows:

$$[C_b]=\begin{bmatrix} c_{bxx} & c_{bxy} \\ c_{byx} & c_{byy} \end{bmatrix};[K_b]=\begin{bmatrix} k_{bxx} & k_{bxy} \\ k_{byx} & k_{byy} \end{bmatrix} \tag{2}$$

When there was not too much difference in the stiffness and the equivalent mass of the bearing block in the direction of x, y, and coupling was relatively weak, the damping effect was negligible and the bearing was considered as isotropic:

$$\begin{aligned} &k_{xx}=k_{yy};k_{bxx}=k_{byy};M_{bx}=M_{by} \\ &k_{xy}=k_{yx}=k_{bxy}=k_{byx}=0 \end{aligned} \tag{3}$$

The model was converted to a fixed in-plane, and the rigidity coefficient of elastic bearing K could be calculated according to the formula below:

$$K = \frac{k_p(k_b - M_b\omega^2)}{k_p + k_b - M_b\omega^2} \tag{4}$$

K was the total bearing rigidity coefficient of the sliding bearing, which reflected the dynamic characteristics of the oil film, the bearing block and the foundation in a comprehensive way. The total bearing rigidity coefficient of the bearing was not constant, which was different from that of the common elastic bearing of equivalent stiffness, which was related to the whirling angular velocity of the rotor. For rolling bearing, the radial stiffness of the two bearings could form a larger angular stiffness K_θ, which was calculated according to the formula below:

$$K_\theta = K_r(\frac{l^2}{4}) \tag{5}$$

Where K_r was the radial stiffness, l was the center distance between series bearings. At this time, the bearing point was selected as of the midpoint of the line connected the centers of series bearings. When the mass of the bearing itself was taken into account, it could be treated as a concentrated mass point. Q_i, M_i, θ_i, X_i represented shear, bending, angle, deflection of the right end of the i unit, respectively. The state vector could be expressed as $[Z]_i = [Q \quad M \quad \theta \quad X]_i^T$, and the relation between the state vectors of any two ends is shown below:

$$[Z]_{i+1} = [U]_i [Z]_i \tag{6}$$

Where $[U]_i$ was a transfer matrix, which satisfied mechanic equilibrium and connected the state vectors of the two sections of i and $i+1$.

2.2 Transfer Matrix for the Typical Unit

Fig. 1 shows a typical transfer matrix unit which consisted of a massless shaft of uniform section, a disk and an elastic bearing.

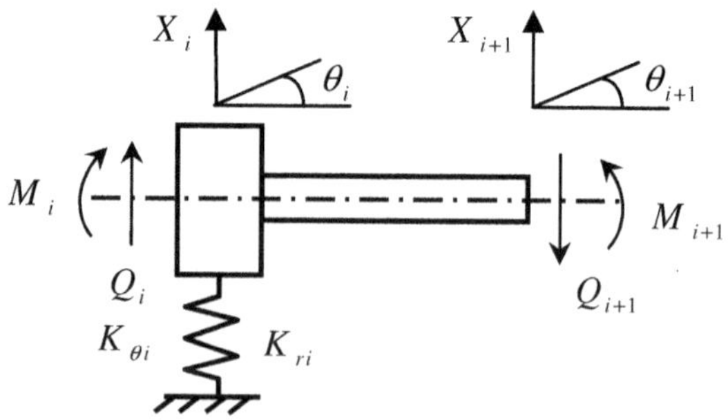

Fig. 1. The typical transfer matrix unit

$$[U]_i = \begin{bmatrix} 1 & 0 & 0 & m_i\Omega^2 - K_{ri} \\ l_i & 1 & (J_{pi}\frac{\omega}{\Omega} - J_{di})\Omega^2 + K_{\theta i} & (m_i\Omega^2 - K_{ri})l_i \\ \frac{l_i^2}{2EI_i} & \frac{l_i}{EI_i} & 1 + \frac{l_i}{EI_i}[(J_{pi}\frac{\omega}{\Omega} - J_{di})\Omega^2 + K_{\theta i}] & \frac{l_i^2}{2EI_i}(m_i\Omega^2 - K_{ri}) \\ \frac{l_i^3}{6EI_i}(1-v_i) & \frac{l_i^2}{2EI_i} & l_i + \frac{l_i^2}{2EI_i}[(J_{pi}\frac{\omega}{\Omega} - J_{di})\Omega^2 + K_{\theta i}] & 1 + \frac{l_i^3}{6EI_i}(1-v_i)(m_i\Omega^2 - K_{ri}) \end{bmatrix} \tag{7}$$

Where L was the length of unit shaft; m was the total mass of the nodes (except the mass of shaft section, the roulette mass should be added.); Ω was angular velocity of precession of the rotor; ω was angular velocity of rotation of the rotor; J_d was the diameter moment of inertia of the rotor; J_P was the polar moment of inertia of the rotor; EI was the bending rigidity of the cross section of the shaft; $v = \frac{6EI}{k_t GAl^2}$, G was the shear elastic modulus; A was the area of the cross section of the shaft; k_t was the coefficient of the shape of cross section, which was chosen as 2/3 when it was hollow circular cross section, and 0.9 when it was a solid one.

2.3 Modeling of Critical Speeds

The state vector of section of the spindle terminal was as follows:

$$[Z]_n = [U]_i [U]_{i-1} \cdots [U]_1 [Z]_0 = [U][Z]_0 \tag{8}$$

Where $[U]$ was 4×4 order matrix. The critical rotational speed during the synchronized process when $\Omega = \omega$ was usually calculated. Therefore, the element in matrix $[U]$ was the function of Ω. The boundary conditions that both sides were free ends were substituted, then:

$$[Z]_n = \begin{bmatrix} 0 \\ 0 \\ \theta \\ X \end{bmatrix}_n = \begin{bmatrix} U_{11} & U_{12} & U_{13} & U_{14} \\ U_{21} & U_{22} & U_{23} & U_{24} \\ U_{31} & U_{32} & U_{33} & U_{34} \\ U_{41} & U_{42} & U_{43} & U_{44} \end{bmatrix} \begin{bmatrix} 0 \\ 0 \\ \theta \\ X \end{bmatrix}_0 \tag{9}$$

The following result could be obtained:

$$\begin{bmatrix} U_{13} & U_{14} \\ U_{23} & U_{24} \end{bmatrix} \begin{bmatrix} \theta \\ X \end{bmatrix}_0 = 0 \tag{10}$$

For the homogeneous equation to have non-trivial solutions, the following requirement must be satisfied:

$$f(\Omega) = \begin{vmatrix} U_{13} & U_{14} \\ U_{23} & U_{24} \end{vmatrix} = 0 \tag{11}$$

$f(\Omega)$ was residual formula, and the solutions of equation $f(\Omega) = 0$ were the desired critical rotational speeds. The rope root law was applied to seek solutions in this paper. The corresponding vibration mode could be calculated after the critical rotational speeds were obtained. A proportion solution could be obtained according to the homogeneous linear equation (10). For example, if $\theta_0 = 1$, then X_0 could be calculated, and the initial state vector was thus obtained. According to Formula (8), the state vector of each computing website could be obtained. As a result, all the vibration modes in every order were known.

3 Numerical Calculation of Critical Speeds

The span of the front and the rear fulcrum bearings on the grinder spindle was 215mm, the overhang at the front end was 85mm, and the overhang at the rear end was 60mm. Bearings are HCB71909-E angular-contact ceramic ball bearings from FAG (Germany), with the actual preload of F being 216N. Matlab was used to write the computation program which was solved iteratively with the Prower method. The major modes of vibration are shown in Fig. 2. It could be seen from the Fig.2 that the deformations at the middle and front end of the spindle were relatively large, as well as the back-end deformation. The main vibration mode was the first order bending. The main vibration mode at the second order critical speed that the deformation of spindle at the front end was relatively great, while the deformation at middle and back end was slight, with almost no deformation at the back bearing.

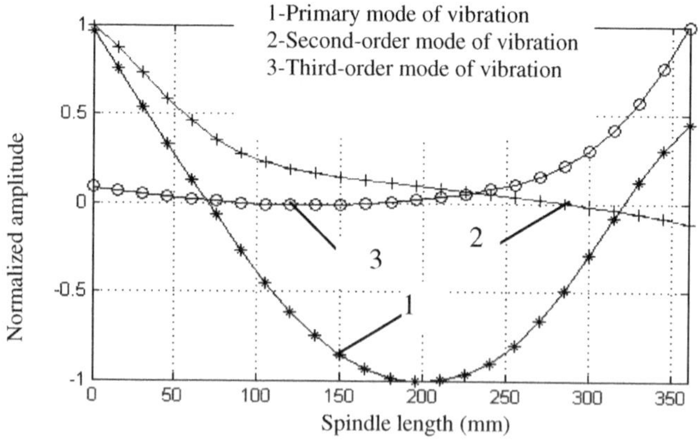

Fig. 2. Modes of vibration of different orders

The main vibration mode was swing vibration mode of the front overhang. Moreover, it could be seen from the Fig.2 that the deformation at the back end of spindle was relatively great, while the deformation at the middle and front end was slight, with almost no deformation at front bearing. The main vibration mode was the swing vibration mode of back overhang. To ensure safe and reliable operation of the rotating machinery, it was usually required, that if the rotor's rotational speed n was below the first order critical speed n_{c1}, then $n < 0.75 n_{c1}$; if the rotor's rotational speed n was above the first order critical speed, then $1.4 n_{c_k} < n < 0.7 n_{c_{k+1}}$. The maximum rotational speed of spindle of this type was 15000r/min, which was far less than that of the first order critical speed of the spindle system. Therefore, during the operation of the spindle system, resonance problem wouldn't appear. In this study, structural factors which influenced critical speed of the spindle system were mainly discussed, and the analysis is shown as follows:

3.1 Axial Pre-tightening Force

The pre-tightening degree of a bearing directly determines the bearing rigidity which concerns the inherent frequencies of the first several orders of the whole electric spindle and their dynamic response. The changes in the pre-tightening force (50-550N) and critical speeds of the first three orders of the electric spindle were calculated, as shown in Fig. 3.

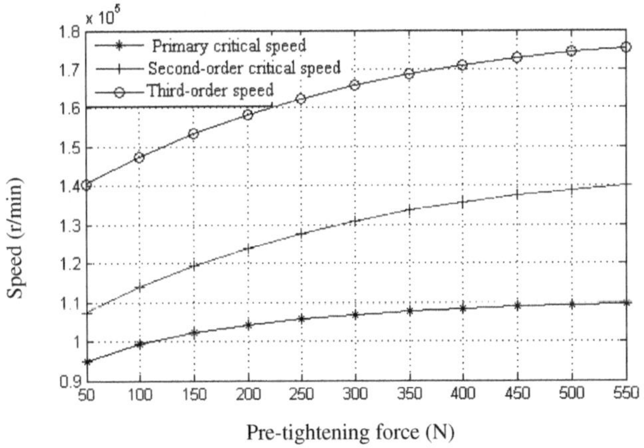

Fig. 3. Curves of influences of axial pre-tightening forces of bearings on critical speeds of spindle system

3.2 Jib Length

Fig.4 shows the curves of the influences of the front overhang on critical speeds when the axial pre-tightening force and the span of fulcrum bearings were fixed and the spindle diameter at the overhang section remained unchanged. The Fig.4 indicates that the critical speeds of different orders were reduced by the rear overhang, but within a certain range.

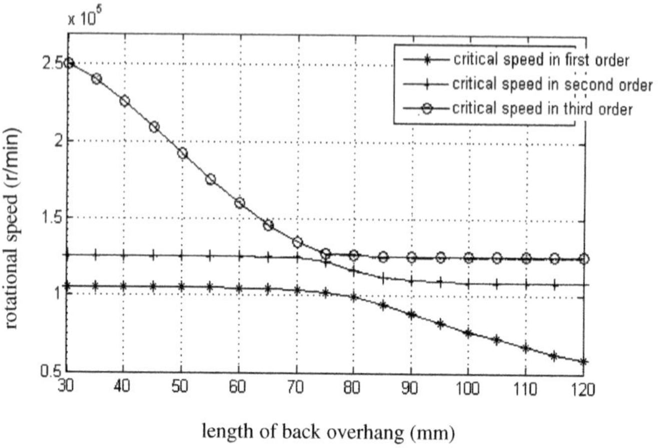

Fig. 4. Curves of influences of rear overhang on critical speeds of spindle system

3.3 Span of Bearing

By changing the length of shaft shoulder of front bearing and back bearing, the investigation of the bearing span of the spindle on the critical speed was conducted with the other structural parameters unchanged, and the influence curve is shown in Fig. 5. It could be seen from Fig. 5 that at the first order critical rotational speed, a bump appeared at the bearing span of 180mm, and this was where the optimal bearing span at the first order critical rotational speed.

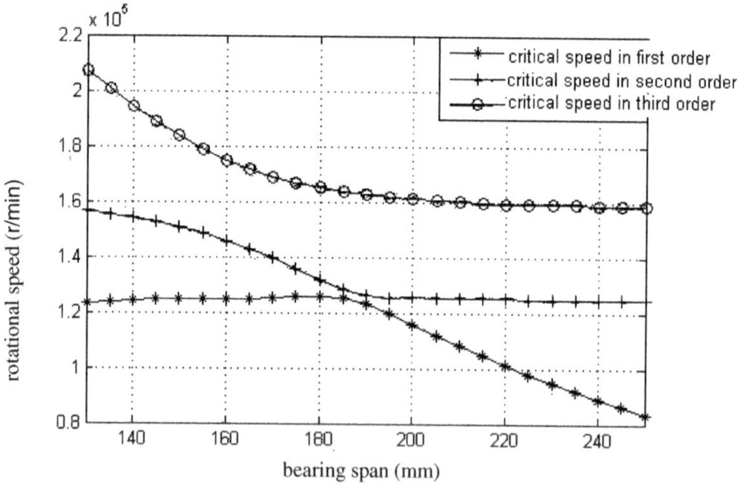

Fig. 5. Influence curve of bearing span on the critical rotational speed of spindle system

4 Conclusions

On the basis of the calculation results, the following conclusions are drawn:

(1) Increasing the pre-tightening force of bearings can improve the critical speeds of different orders of the spindle and is also highly sensitive to the influence on high orders. The comparison of the variation rates of the pre-tightening forces and corresponding critical speeds reveals that the increase in pre-tightening force can only improve the critical speeds to a limited extent.
(2) Increasing the span of fulcrum bearings has different influencing ranges for critical speeds of different orders. Within the range, the critical speed falls significantly; beyond the range, it changes steadily.
(3) Increasing the front and rear overhangs has similar influences on critical speeds of different orders to increasing the span of fulcrum bearings, the reason of which is that increasing the span of fulcrum bearings equates decreasing the front and rear overhangs.

Acknowledgments

This research was financially supported by the National Natural Science Foundation of China (50875138); the Shandong Provincial Natural Science Foundation of China (Z2008F11; ZR2009FZ007) and the Specialized Construct Fund for Taishan Scholars.

References

1. Chen, J.-S., Chen, K.-W.: Bearing Load Analysis and Control of a Motorized High Speed Spindle. International Journal of Machine Tools & Manufacture 45, 1487–1493 (2005)
2. Lee, D.S., Choi, D.H.: Reduced weight design of a flexible rotor with ball bearing stiffness characteristics varying with rotational speed and load. Journal of Vibration and Acoustics-transactions of the ASME 122, 203–208 (2000)
3. Li, C.H., Hou, Y.L., Ding, Y.C., Cai, G.Q.: Feasibility investigations on compound process: a novel fabrication method for finishing with grinding wheel as restraint. International Journal of Computational Materials Science and Surface Engineering 4, 55–68 (2011)
4. Morgan, M.N., Jackson, A.R., Wu, H.: Optimisation of fluid application in grinding. CIRP Annals-Manufacturing Technology 57, 363–366 (2008)
5. Moulik, P.N., Yang, H.T.Y., Chandrasekar, S.: Simulation of thermal stresses due to grinding. International Journal of Mechanical Sciences 43, 831–851 (2001)
6. Stephenson, D.J., Jin, T., Corbett, J.: High efficiency deep grinding of a low alloy steel with plated CBN wheels. Annals of the CIRP 51, 241–244 (2002)
7. Li, C.H., Hou, Y.L., Liu, Z.R., Ding, Y.C.: Investigation into temperature field of nano-zirconia ceramics precision grinding. International Journal of Abrasive Technology 4(2), 77–89 (2011)
8. Li, C.H., Hou, Y.L., Fang, Z., Ding, Y.C.: Analytical and Experimental Investigation of Grinding Fluid Hydrodynamic Pressure at Wedge-shaped Zone. International Journal of Abrasive Technology 4(2), 163–179 (2011)

Research on Teaching of College Programming Courses in Network Environment*

Jun Liu, Hui Li, and Lei Chen

College of Mathematical and Information, Zhejiang Ocean University, Zhoushan 316000, China
Lj19681004@163.com, 18822632@qq.com, 372261157@qq.com

Abstract. The program design course is abstract and relatively difficult to learn. The combination of network resources with classroom teaching was developed, so that the students can better understand programming courses. Learning in the network environment will train the student to utilize effectively the network resources, promoting the ability of information acquisition from network as well as the ability of information processing and utilization. The learner's capacity for question analyzing, problem solving and collaborative learning will be greatly increased.

Keywords: network environment, program design course, learner autonomy, classroom-teaching organization.

1 Introduction

In colleges or universities, the network have been covering almost all the teaching and learning environment, teaching under the network environment has become a hot researching topic. Teaching in the network environment can make originally enclosed classroom into an open environment. The teaching model under network environment is becoming important support for lifelong learning system [1]. Program design is a required course for undergraduate students, because it is a useful tool for many major courses thereafter. Achievements have been carried out on study on teaching of program design course in network environment.

2 The Teaching Objectives under the Network Environment

When teaching under the network environment, the teaching resources are provided by teacher and the learners actively participate in teaching process. In the process, the teaching goal to achieve is to improve the learners' comprehensive capacity for discipline knowledge obtaining, skills developing, information controlling. The students will have the ability of searching, processing and using education information effectively. Protect students' individual character will be protected and

* This paper was funded by Zhejiang education technology planning issues (JB101).

H. Tan and M. Zhou (Eds.): CSE 2011, Part I, CCIS 201, pp. 210–215, 2011.

the students' specialty will be fully developed. The final McDevitt (1997) have stated that "the end-product of all education should be an independent learner [2]''. The teaching under the network environment makes it possible for expanding the students' self-study space, developing the student's various abilities, especially the innovation ability.

3 The Features of Program Design Course and Its Current Teaching Situation

3.1 The Features of Program Design Course

Programming courses is characterized by the abstract concept, intense practicality, and strong correlation with mathematics. Students to learn program design course are demanded with the logical thinking ability, and also they are required to have computer practical ability. In university, most programming courses are given to is undergraduate students who don't major in computer sciences, these learners include liberal arts and science students, this course is difficult to them, especially for liberal arts students.

3.2 Current Teaching Situation

(1) The teacher-centered instruction paradigms is the mainly adopted one in current course teaching. This traditional teaching mode has its prominent advantages, the teacher in the whole teaching process as the main body, plays a leading role, organize the whole teaching process, can monitor students' classroom learning process, teaching is systematic. But this kind of mode with the teacher as the main body, ignore students' role in the teaching process, Students are little involved, not to lean actively, students completely passive receive information according to the arrangement of the teachers.

(2) To use a single means of teaching. In general, the application of multimedia technology in class is actually an electronic lecture note, it only makes the handwritten lesson plan into the electronic text on the screen, it is just a teachers' means of teaching which don't play a role of multimedia teaching. Although the education information input is great, the teaching practice and the resources of education information have not been integrated into one system.

(3) Network education resources and course teaching are separated. The project of the online course are thoroughly reviewed and discussed in reference [3] [4]. Online course is equally teacher and student centered mode, it is designed on constructivism learning theory combined with education technology and multimedia technology. In the network environment, students can learn autonomously, and discuss questions on the online BBS. But in actual teaching process, the online course had no connection with the classroom teaching, many network curriculum resources idled, didn't get effective utilization.

4 Teaching Research on Program Design Course in the Network Environment

According to current teaching status of programming courses, the classroom instruction in the teaching process is still dominant in full-time universities in China. The authors suggest that network environment should be fully applied to the classroom teaching as a supplementary means to the lectures. The openness, flexibility of online course should be fully displayed in the programming courses teaching work. The whole teaching process includes following aspects:

(1) Strengthen the intuitive teaching process in classroom. Programming courses are delivered in two parts, theory lecture and experiment, in theory class teachers must organize the whole lecture process, including of the selection of teaching materials and the plan of classroom organization. Most teachers giving program design course graduated from engineering college. They had no systematic training of teaching skills in their college time. They are lack of study on pedagogy so that many of them either repeat what the book says, or speak themselves without communication with students. Due to the lack of effective teaching organization they often talk all the time in a class, and plus the course itself is abstractness, so as to students have no interest in studying. Teaching in net environment, on the other hand, requests the teacher cannot completely repeat textbook, but should arrange course content according to the level of students, their major area and other circumstances. For example, the section of data type in the program design course is very close related to computer principle, it is difficult to understand for students who don't major in computer sciences or just begin to learn computer technology. So in such course teachers should arrange the knowledge according to the level of learners, simplify the content appropriately, aim at letting the students just can apply in programming, so that the learner in the first stage don't feel too difficult. In the classroom, teachers and students should interact increasingly, it isn't monologue but dialogue. Many college teachers viewed asking questions and doing exercises during class as a teaching method in primary school education, they thought that in higher education it is just pouring information into students' brain. Such teaching method deprives the student's participation in classroom, and no interaction between teacher and student, so that the teacher cannot know the level of knowledge that the students received and the class atmosphere are depressing. According to the current status of learners in college, the question and exercise in classroom, which often used in elementary education, also can be used in the college course of program design, and meantime organize the students in class discussion on some problems, turn the teacher's monologue classroom into teacher and students leaning together, organize classroom teaching in a variety of forms, and improve the effect of classroom teaching finally.

(2) In the experimental work, students should practice as much as possible in limited lab time. In the experiment coaching, except directly answer the questions students asked, the software fit in the laboratory should be fully used to improve efficiency of practical operation. When in experimental courses, the work of students can be monitored in real-time mode, the mistakes student easy to make can be corrected using screen broadcasting on-site. After students finishing the experiment, the exercises topic can be submitted to teacher's computer directly through student

terminal, e.g. electronic experiment report, the role of network will be felt by the student in the whole experiment course.

(3) To make full use of network education resources existing in university. For example, the course of "C Language Programming" in the university where the authors work in. Students are asked to study on the network curriculum platform after classroom teaching. On the platform, students can read the basic requirements of this course, teachers involved in, and curriculum teaching requirements. In the part of learning resources, there are basic resources such as teaching courseware, exercise help information and answer. Students can review the course sections that did not catch up with in classroom, and in addition to the homework needed to hand in, they can check the answer for other exercise themselves. When learning online, students' ability of autonomous learning is trained.

After having covered with some related content in network curriculum, students and teachers should communicate in time. Although there is an interactive area on network course platform, students and teachers can't operate simultaneously. Instead, we can use commonly used chat software to contact each other directly in the form of words, sound, and video. Example for communication in real time between an author and a student shows in fig.1. Student and teacher chat in a relaxed atmosphere, and meanwhile the problem is solved. Communication in this kind of environment, students will not be nervous. The atmosphere is lively and the learners love to join in. The learning enthusiasm will be higher, and the result of study will be better.

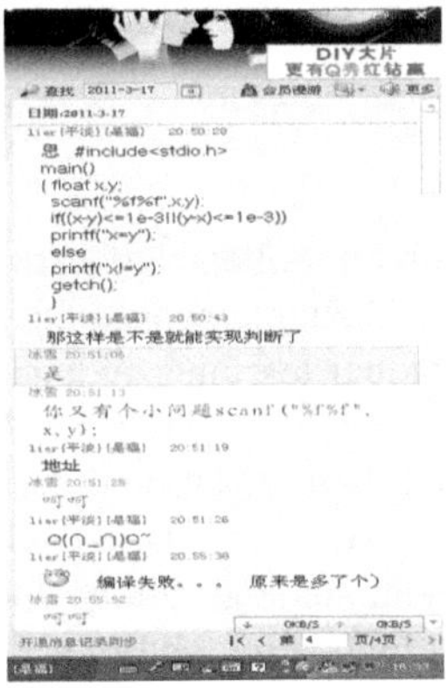

Fig. 1. Teacher-student network chat scene

(4) The main body of learning is student, how to attract the students and stimulate their interest of study requires teacher with high level of skill. In addition to the traditional classroom teaching, it is particularly important to organize learning material provided for students in the network environment. Whether learners are interested in the learning materials; whether they are interested in organization pattern of teaching activities, these will influence the learner's emotions and learning result [6]. This requires teachers to work well on organizing the activities in classroom and out classroom, and direct the students to participate in the network learning. Teachers play a leading role in the education under the network environment. They are

designers and directors for teaching process. The teacher should be a teaching researcher, not only to teach students how to learn, but also to study how to let the student to learn autonomously [3]. To achieve this goal, the teacher must have ability for design and development, ability to organize the learning resource effectively, and to develop attractive web-course learning system. In learning process, teachers should guide students to participate in the study and cooperate actively. Assessment is used to promote and diagnose learning process. The teacher should develop good network learning environment, so that broaden the study ways that students can choose a fit leaning style to participate in according to their own leaning habit. Only when students involved in learning in the network course designed by teachers, this new teaching mode can play a role and obtain a good teaching result [7]. Both in classroom teaching and network courses the learning objective and content must be given first. It is a very effective teaching way to introduce the teaching contents to the class from a living example. When translate the abstract content of programming course into a vivid example, it would be best if the example is related to the livelihood or majoring area the students familiar with, that will be better to stimulate students' interest in study and can make the difficult content to be accepted easily. A kind of relaxed learning circumstances can be established using the internet chat software, students can be guided to participate in communication, discussion in groups, and consolidate the learned knowledge under the help of the teachers. By discussion thoroughly, students can expand the scope of knowledge, with broader teaching resources, so as to bring about the significance construction of knowledge.

5 Conclusion

According to present situation of college education in China, network teaching methods should be fully used as a supplement to the classroom teaching that must be organized well. Through individual learning, inquiry-based learning, and interactive learning on the opening net class, the course of Program Design may be not as difficult as what the students felt before. Through teaching practice, a good result has been carried out in the students who went in our university in 2009 and 2010. After teaching in network environment, students' ability for autonomous learning, problem analysis, problem solving, and innovation ability are all greatly increase, these laid a solid foundation for students to apply computer technology into their major study.

References

1. Zhao, H., Sun, B.: Construction of Emotional Teaching Environment Based on Virtual Reality. China Educational Technology 4, 101–104 (2009)
2. McDevitt, B.: Learner Autonomy and the Need for Learner Training. Language Learning Journal (16), 34–39 (1997)
3. Li, J.: Research on Net Class Teaching Model of College Program Design. In: CDMD (2005)

4. Chen, Y.: Instruction Study on Java Programming Language in the Network Environment. In: CDMD (2007)
5. Lu, L.: Discussion on the Way of Cooperative Learning Based on the Internet. Science and Technology Information 5, 79 (2009)
6. Yu, L.: Strategy on Broaden the Students' Participation in Learning Using the Network Environment. China Educational Technology 10, 79–82 (2009)

Decoding the Binary (71, 36, 11) Quadratic Residue Code

Hung-Peng Lee* and Hsin-Chiu Chang

Department of Computer Science and Information Engineering
Fortune Institute of Technology, Kaohsiung City 831, Taiwan
hpl@center.fotech.edu.tw, p01244@center.fotech.edu.tw

Abstract. In this paper, an efficient algebraic decoding algorithm (ADA) is proposed to correct all patterns of five errors or less in the binary systematic (71, 36, 11) quadratic residue (QR) code. The method is based on the modification of the ADAs developed by Reed *et al* and Lin *et al*. The proposed conditions and the error-locator polynomials for decoding this code will be derived. Simulation result shows that the average decoding time of the proposed ADA is faster than the ADA proposed by Chang *et al*.

Keywords: syndrome, QR code, error pattern, algebraic decoding algorithm.

1 Introduction

The well-known QR codes, introduced by Prange [1], are cyclic BCH codes with a code rate close to 1/2 and generally have large minimum distances. If an overall parity check bit is used, the rate is exactly 1/2, so that most of the known QR codes are the best-known codes. For example, the (24, 12, 8) QR code, also named extended Golay code, has been used for numerous communication applications, including the Voyager I imaging system link of NASA [2].

In the past few decades, several decoding techniques have been developed to decode some QR codes. The ADAs given in [3-13] exploit different techniques to find the unknown syndromes in order to use the error-locator polynomials to correct different error positions in the received word. The ADA of the binary (71, 36, 11) QR code given in [8] is inefficient because it does not use the conditions to distinguish the number of errors in the received word. In each decoding procedure, the inverse-free Berlekamp-Massey algorithm [8] is used to determine the error-locator polynomial of the received words. However, if the received words have many errors, then the decoding time will be pessimistic. Besides, the simulation results of the decoding time were absent in [8].

In this paper, an efficient ADA is proposed to decode the binary systematic (71, 36, 11) QR code. This ADA consists of four steps: First, we use $S(I, J)$ matrix to obtain the unknown syndrome, say S_7. Next, we use the Newton identities to determine the error-locator polynomial. Third, we derive the conditions for different number of errors. Finally, a Chien search method [14] is used to find the roots of the error-locator polynomial and the error locations are given by the roots of error-locator

* Corresponding author.

H. Tan and M. Zhou (Eds.): CSE 2011, Part I, CCIS 201, pp. 216–223, 2011.

polynomial. The decoding times for different number of errors have been verified by a C++ program and compared with the ADA proposed by Chang *et al.* [8].

The remainder of this paper is organized as follows: The background of the (71, 36, 11) QR code is briefly introduced in Section 2. The proposed ADA is described in Section 3. Computer simulation results are shown in Section 4. Finally, this paper concludes with a brief summary in Section 5.

2 Background of the Binary (71, 36, 11) QR Code

A binary QR code (n, k, d) is defined algebraically as a multiple of its generator polynomial $g(x)$ over $GF(2^m)$, where n is the code length, $k = (n + 1)/2$ is the message length, and d be the minimum Hamming distance of the code. Let the length of this code be a prime number of the form $n = 8l \pm 1$ where l is a positive integer, and let m be the smallest positive integer such that n divides $2^m - 1$. The set Q_n of quadratic residues modulo n is the set of nonzero squares modulo n; that is, $Q_n = \{j \mid j \equiv x^2 \bmod n, 1 \leq x \leq (n\text{-}1)/2\}$. For the binary (71, 36, 11) QR code, the components of codeword are in $GF(2^{35})$, its quadratic residue set is

$$Q_{71} = \{1,2,3,4,5,6,8,9,10,12,15,16,18,19,20,24,25,27,29,\\ 30,32,36,37,38,40,43,45,48,49,50,54,57,58,60,64\}. \quad (1)$$

Let α be a root of primitive polynomial $p(x) = x^{35} + x^2 + 1$. Let the element $\beta = \alpha^u$, where $u = (2^m - 1)/n = (2^{35} - 1)/71 = 483{,}939{,}977$, is a primitive 71th root of unity in $GF(2^{35})$. The generator polynomial of the binary (71, 36, 11) QR code is defined by

$$g(x) = \prod_{i \in Q_{71}} (x - \beta^i) = x^{35} + x^{33} + x^{28} + x^{27} + x^{26} +\\ x^{25} + x^{24} + x^{17} + x^{13} + x^8 + x^7 + x^5 + x^4 + x + 1. \quad (2)$$

The degree of $g(x)$ is 35 which is the multiplicative order of integer 2 modulo the code length 71; that is, $2^{71} \equiv 1 \bmod 71$. Since $d = 11$, the inequality $2v + 1 \leq 11$ is valid, where v is the actual number of errors to be corrected. Hence, the binary (71, 36, 11) QR code allows for the correction of up to $t = \lfloor (d-1)/2 \rfloor = 5$, where t denotes the error-correcting capability and $\lfloor x \rfloor$ denotes the greatest integer less than or equal to x.

The codewords of the binary systematic (71, 36, 11) QR code, which is a multiple of the $g(x)$, can be expressed as the coefficients of a codeword polynomial; that is, $c(x) = \sum_{i=0}^{70} c_i x^i = m(x)g(x)$, where $c_i \in GF(2)$ for $0 \leq i \leq 70$, and $m(x) = \sum_{i=0}^{35} m_i x^i$ denotes the information polynomial, where $m_i \in GF(2)$ for $0 \leq i \leq 35$. Let polynomial $p(x) = p_{34}x^{34} + \cdots + p_1 x + p_0$ be the parity-check polynomial of $c(x)$, where $p_i \in GF(2)$ for $0 \leq i \leq 34$. Also, let $m(x)x^{n\text{-}k}$ divide by $g(x)$, then we have

$$m(x)x^{n\text{-}k} = q(x)g(x) + d(x). \quad (3)$$

Multiplying both sides of (3) by x^k and using $x^n = 1$, we yield

$$d(x)x^k + m(x) = (q(x)x^k)g(x). \quad (4)$$

In (4), the term $(d(x)x^k + m(x))$, which is a multiple of $g(x)$, is a codeword given by

$$c(x) = d(x)x^k + m(x) = p(x) + m(x) \,. \tag{5}$$

The codeword polynomial has $m(x)$ in its lower k bits; therefore, this type of codewords is called the systematic code. Let $r(x)$ be the form $r(x) = c(x) + e(x)$, where $e(x)$ is the error-pattern polynomial defined by $e(x) = e_{70}x^{70} + \cdots + e_1x + e_0$, where $e_i \in GF(2)$ for $0 \le i \le 70$. The syndromes of the code are defined by

$$S_i = r(\beta^i) = c(\beta^i) + e(\beta^i) = e(\beta^i)\text{, for all } i \in Q_{71} \,. \tag{6}$$

If we cannot use (6) to obtain syndromes directly, then these syndromes are called unknown syndromes. For the binary (71, 36, 11) QR code, S_7 is an unknown syndrome. If there are v errors in $r(x)$, then the error polynomial has v nonzero terms over $GF(2)$; that is, $e(x) = x^{r_1} + x^{r_2} + \cdots + x^{r_v}$, where $0 \le r_1 < r_2 <¼< r_v \le 70$. For i Î Q_{71}, the syndrome can be written as $S_i = X_1^i + X_2^i + \cdots + X_v^i$, where $X_j = \beta^{r_j}$ for $1 \le j \le v$ are called the error locators. Assuming that v errors occur, the error-locator polynomial $L(z)$ of degree v is defined by

$$L(z) = \prod_{j=1}^{v}(z - X_j) = \sigma_v z^v + \cdots + \sigma_1 z + \sigma_0 \,, \tag{7}$$

where $\sigma_v = 1$. The roots of $L(z)$ are X_j. If $\sigma_0, \sigma_1, \ldots, \sigma_v$ are known, then the roots of $L(z)$ and the error locators X_j can be obtained by applying Chien search method. The error locators X_j and the coefficients σ_i are related by the following equations:

$$\begin{aligned} &\sigma_v = 1 \\ &\sigma_{v-1} = -(X_1 + X_2 + \ldots + X_v) \\ &\sigma_{v-2} = X_1X_2 + X_1X_3 + \ldots + X_{v-1}X_v) \,. \\ &\cdots \\ &\sigma_0 = (-1)X_1X_2 \cdots X_v \end{aligned} \tag{8}$$

If there are enough consecutive known syndromes, then we can directly solve σ_j, where $1 \le j \le v$, from the Newton's identities [19]. However, if there are not enough consecutive syndromes, we first have to find the unknown syndrome, and then to obtain $L(z)$ from the Newton identities. Once $L(z)$ is obtained, then the roots of $L(z)$ can be found. In order to evaluate the unknown syndrome, a technique developed by He *et al.* [7] is summarized as below. Now, let $I = \{i_1, i_2, ..., i_{v+1}\}$ and $J = \{j_1, j_2, ..., j_{v+1}\}$ be two subsets of Q, where $i_1 \ne i_2 \ne ... \ne i_{v+1}$ and $j_1 \ne j_2 \ne ... \ne j_{v+1}$. Define a $(v+1) \times (v+1)$ matrix $S(I, J)$ as follows:

$$S(I,J) = \begin{bmatrix} S_{i_1+j_1} & S_{i_1+j_2} & \cdots & S_{i_1+j_{v+1}} \\ S_{i_2+j_1} & S_{i_2+j_2} & \cdots & S_{i_2+j_{v+1}} \\ \vdots & \vdots & \ddots & \vdots \\ S_{i_v+j_1} & S_{i_v+j_2} & \cdots & S_{i_v+j_{v+1}} \\ S_{i_{v+1}+j_1} & S_{i_{v+1}+j_2} & \cdots & S_{i_{v+1}+j_{v+1}} \end{bmatrix}, \tag{9}$$

where the summation of the indexes is modulo n. Apparently, we have rank $(S(I, J)) \le v$, which, yields the following equation:

$$\det(S(I, J)) = 0\ , \tag{10}$$

where $\det(\cdot)$ is the determinate function.

3 ADA of the Binary (71, 36, 11) QR Code

This section consists of two subsections. Subsection 3.1 introduces how to compute the unknown syndrome, say S_7. Subsection 3.2 shows how to exploit the algebraic method to derive the proposed error-locator polynomials and conditions for $1 \le v \le 5$.

3.1 Evaluation of the Unknown Syndrome

From one error to three errors, namely $1 \le v \le 3$, we do not need any unknown syndrome since there are enough consecutive syndromes to decode the code. For $v = 4$ and $v = 5$, there is only an unknown syndrome S_7. Thus, we first have to solve the unknown syndrome S_7 and then obtain the error-locator polynomial.

Case 1 to *Case* 3: Not need any unknown syndrome.

Case 4: We choose $I_4 = \{0, 1, 3, 4, 5\}$ and $J_4 = \{0, 1, 4, 5, 15\}$, where the index of I and J denotes that they are valid only for this case. Then, we get, by (9), the matrix

$$S(I_4, J_4) = \begin{bmatrix} S_0 & S_1 & S_3 & S_4 & S_5 \\ S_1 & S_2 & S_4 & S_5 & S_6 \\ S_4 & S_5 & \underline{S_7} & S_8 & S_9 \\ S_5 & S_6 & S_8 & S_9 & S_{10} \\ S_{15} & S_{16} & S_{18} & S_{19} & S_{20} \end{bmatrix} . \tag{11}$$

In (11), all entries are known syndromes except S_7. Next, by (11), we can obtain an polynomial $f(S_7)$ of degree 1 given by $f(S_7) = \sum_{i=0}^{1} c_i S_7{}^i = c_1 S_7 + c_0$, where c_0 is a constant term and c_1 is the leading coefficient of $f(S_7)$. Thus, the value of S_7 can be computed by

$$S_{7(4)} = \det(c_0)/\det(c_1)\ , \tag{12}$$

where the index to S_7 to obtain the notation $S_{7(4)}$ indicates that it is valid only for this case and the coefficients are

$$c_1 = \begin{bmatrix} S_0 & S_1 & S_4 & S_5 \\ S_1 & S_2 & S_5 & S_6 \\ S_5 & S_6 & S_9 & S_{10} \\ S_{15} & S_{16} & S_{19} & S_{20} \end{bmatrix} \text{ and } c_0 = \begin{bmatrix} S_0 & S_1 & S_3 & S_4 & S_5 \\ S_1 & S_2 & S_4 & S_5 & S_6 \\ S_4 & S_5 & 0 & S_8 & S_9 \\ S_5 & S_6 & S_8 & S_9 & S_{10} \\ S_{15} & S_{16} & S_{18} & S_{19} & S_{20} \end{bmatrix} . \tag{13}$$

Case 5: In this case, we choose two pairs of subsets: $I_5^1 = \{0, 1, 2, 4, 7, 24\}$, $J_5^1 = \{0, 1, 3, 5, 8, 36\}$, $I_5^2 = \{3, 4, 5, 12, 15, 45\}$, and $J_5^2 = \{0, 3, 4, 15, 33, 45\}$. Then, we obtain the following matrices:

$$S(I_5^1, J_5^1) = \begin{bmatrix} S_0 & S_1 & S_2 & S_4 & \underline{S_7} & S_{24} \\ S_1 & S_2 & S_3 & S_5 & S_8 & S_{25} \\ S_3 & S_4 & S_5 & \underline{S_7} & S_{10} & S_{27} \\ S_5 & S_6 & \underline{S_7} & S_9 & S_{12} & S_{29} \\ S_8 & S_9 & S_{10} & S_{12} & S_{15} & S_{32} \\ S_{36} & S_{37} & S_{38} & S_{40} & S_{43} & S_{60} \end{bmatrix} \text{ and}$$
$$S(I_5^2, J_5^2) = \begin{bmatrix} S_3 & S_4 & S_5 & S_{12} & S_{15} & S_{45} \\ S_6 & \underline{S_7} & S_8 & S_{15} & S_{18} & S_{48} \\ \underline{S_7} & S_8 & S_9 & S_{16} & S_{19} & S_{49} \\ S_{18} & S_{19} & S_{20} & S_{27} & S_{30} & S_{60} \\ S_{36} & S_{37} & S_{38} & S_{45} & S_{48} & \underline{S_7} \\ S_{48} & S_{49} & S_{50} & S_{57} & S_{60} & S_{19} \end{bmatrix}. \tag{14}$$

According to (1), the underlined syndromes given in (14) are unknown syndromes S_7. They yield polynomials $f(S_7)$ and $g(S_7)$ of degree 3 shown as follows:

$$f(S_7) = \sum_{i=0}^{3} c_i S_7^{\,i} \text{ and } g(S_7) = \sum_{i=0}^{3} c_i S_7^{\,i} . \tag{15}$$

A greatest common divisor of $f(S_7)$ and $g(S_7)$ denoted by $F(S_7) = \gcd(f(S_7), g(S_7))$ is a polynomial of maximal degree that is a factor of both $f(S_7)$ and $g(S_7)$. It comprised exactly the common roots of $f(S_7)$ and $g(S_7)$. We use Euclid's algorithm to obtain the $F(S_7)$. Obviously S_7 must be the root of $F(S_7)$. The $F(S_7)$ is always a polynomial of degree 1 in five-errors case. Therefore, $F(S_7)$ is given by $F(S_7) = d_1 S_7 + d_0$, where d_1, $d_0 \in GF(2^{35})$. Therefore, the unknown syndrome S_7 can be computed by

$$S_{7(5)} = d_0 / d_1 , \tag{16}$$

where the index to S_7 to obtain the notation $S_{7(5)}$ indicates that it is valid only for this case.

3.2 Determination of the Error-Locator Polynomials and the Conditions

The following Newton identities are used to define the coefficients of the error-locator polynomial $L(z)$:

$$S_1 + \sigma_1 = 0 \tag{17a}$$

$$S_3 + \sigma_1 S_1^2 + \sigma_2 S_1 + \sigma_3 = 0 \tag{17b}$$

$$S_5 + \sigma_1 S_4 + \sigma_2 S_3 + \sigma_3 S_2 + \sigma_4 S_1 + \sigma_5 = 0 \tag{17c}$$

$$S_7 + \sigma_1 S_6 + \sigma_2 S_5 + \sigma_3 S_4 + \sigma_4 S_3 + \sigma_5 S_2 = 0 \tag{17d}$$

$$S_9 + \sigma_1 S_8 + \sigma_2 S_7 + \sigma_3 S_6 + \sigma_4 S_5 + \sigma_5 S_4 = 0 \tag{17e}$$

Thus, from (17a) to (17e), the coefficients $\sigma_1, \ldots, \sigma_5$ are nonzero. For computing the syndromes and the coefficients, the following theorems and a corollary are necessary, for a detailed proof see [8].

Theorem 1. Let (n, k, d) be a binary QR code with Q_n, the set of quadratic residues modulo n, and the base set S. Then the error pattern has a weight of at most one, if and only if the following two conditions hold:

1) $S_i = S_1^i$, for all $i \in S$. 2) $S_1^{n+1} = S_1$.

Corollary 1. If $S = \{1\}$, i.e., if $Q_n = Q_1$, then the error pattern has a weight of at most one, if and only if $S_1^{n+1} = S_1$.

Theorem 2. Let the error pattern of a QR code has a weight $j \geq 2$, then we have $S_{n-1}\sigma_j = \sigma_{j\text{-}1}$.

The error-locator polynomial $L_v(z)$ for $0 \leq v \leq 5$ can be obtained as follows:

Case 0: No error. By (17a), the condition is $S_1 = 0$. By (7), $\sigma_1 = \sigma_2 = \sigma_3 = \sigma_4 = \sigma_5 = 0$ and $L_0(z) = 0$.

Case 1: One error. By Corollary 1, the condition is $S_1^{71} = 1$. By (7), $\sigma_2 = \sigma_3 = \sigma_4 = \sigma_5 = 0$. By (17a), we obtain $\sigma_1 = 1$, and $\sigma_0 = S_1$. The $L_1(z)$ is obtained as follows:

$$L_1(z) = z + S_1 = 0 \ . \tag{18}$$

Case 2: Two errors. By (22) shown below, let the numerator of σ_0 be equal to zero, then we obtain the following condition:

$$X_3^2 + S_1 Y_5 = 0 \, . \tag{19}$$

In the case of exactly two errors, a computer search shows that (19) is always zero; in the case of $v \geq 3$, (19) is always nonzero.

By (7), $\sigma_3 = \sigma_4 = \sigma_5 = 0$. By (17a) and (17b), we obtain $\sigma_2 = 1$, $\sigma_1 = S_1$ and $\sigma_0 = (S_3 + S_1^3)/S_1$. Thus, the $L_2(z)$ is obtained as follows:

$$L_2(z) = z^2 + S_1 z + X_3/S_1 = 0 \, , \text{ where } X_3 = S_1^3 + S_3 \, . \tag{20}$$

Case 3: Three errors. A computer search shows that, in the case of exactly three errors, the determinant of c_1 in (12) is always zero; in the cases of over three errors, the determinant of c_1 is always nonzero. Therefore, we obtain the following condition:

$$\det(c_1) = 0 \, . \tag{21}$$

By (7), $\sigma_4 = \sigma_5 = 0$. By (17a) to (17c), we obtain $\sigma_3 = 1$, $\sigma_2 = S_1, \sigma_1 = Y_5/X_3$, and $\sigma_0 = (X_3^2 + S_1 Y_5)/X_3$, where $Y_5 = S_1^2 S_3 + S_5$. Thus, $L_3(z)$ is obtained as follows:

$$L_3(z) = \sigma_3 z^3 + \sigma_2 z^2 + \sigma_1 z + \sigma_0 = 0. \tag{22}$$

Case 4: Four errors. Again, in the case of exactly four errors, a computer search shows that the d_1 in (16) is always zero. Therefore, we obtain the following condition for the case of four or five errors:

$$d_1 = 0. \tag{23}$$

By (7), $\sigma_5 = 0$. By (17a) to (17d), we obtain $\sigma_4 = 1$, $\sigma_3 = S_1$, $\sigma_2 = (S_1 X_7 + S_3 X_5)/(S_1 X_5 + S_3 X_3)$, $\sigma_1 = X_3 + S_1 \sigma_2$, and $\sigma_0 = (Y_5 + X_3 \sigma_2)/S_1$, where $X_5 = S_1^5 + S_5$ and $X_7 = S_1^7 + S_7$. Thus, $L_4(z)$ is obtained as follows:

$$L_4(z) = \sigma_4 z^4 + \sigma_3 z^3 + \sigma_2 z^2 + \sigma_1 z + \sigma_0 = 0. \tag{24}$$

Case 5: Five errors. The d_1 in (16) is always nonzero. Besides, $S_0 = 1$ by (8). Thus, we have the condition given by

$$d_1 \neq 0 \text{ and } S_0 = 1. \tag{25}$$

By (17a) to (17e), we obtain $\sigma_5 = 1$, $\sigma_4 = S_1$, $\sigma_3 = \dfrac{X_3 Y_9 + X_5 (X_7 + S_1 Y_3)}{X_3 Y_7 + Y_5 X_5}$, $\sigma 2 = X_3 + S_1 \sigma_2$, $\sigma_1 = \dfrac{Y_9 + Y_7 \sigma_2}{X_5}$, and $\sigma_0 = Y_5 + S_1 \sigma_4 + X_3 \sigma_2$, where $Y_3 = S_3^2 + S_1 S_5$, $Y_7 = X_7 + S_1 S_3 X_3$, $X_9 = S_1^9 + S_9$, and $Y_9 = X_9 + S_1^4 Y_5 + S_3^2 X_3$. Thus, $L_5(z)$ is given by:

$$L_5(z) = \sigma_5 z^5 + \sigma_4 z^4 + \sigma_3 z^3 + \sigma_2 z^2 + \sigma_1 z + \sigma_0 = 0. \tag{26}$$

4 Simulation Results

The proposed ADA has been written in a C++ program. On an Intel Q6600 PC with Window XP operating system, all 14,051,255 error patterns were created and input to the proposed ADA. This ADA is perfectly with an average decoding time of 2.711ms per error pattern and is about 10% faster than the decoding algorithm given in [8]. The CPU execution time is given in detail in Table 1. From Case 2 to Case 5, the proposed ADA directly uses the new conditions to obtain their corresponding error-locator polynomials. Obviously, the proposed ADA yields a faster and more efficient decoding algorithm compared with the decoding algorithm given in [8].

Table 1. CPU Execution Time to Decode the Binary (71, 36, 11) QR Code (in mili second)

Algorithms	Number of errors					
	1	2	3	4	5	Average
Proposed ADA	0.008	0.169	0.315	2.207	2.858	2.711
ADA given in [8]	0.008	0.198	0.391	2.483	3.165	3.009

5 Conclusions

The proposed ADA for decoding the binary systematic (71, 36, 11) QR code is able to decode this code completely and efficiently. The proposed conditions for different number of errors are derived and the proposed ADA can directly decode the received word according to these new conditions. Simulation results show that the average decoding time of the proposed ADA is about 10% faster than Chang's ADA.

References

1. Prange, E.: Cyclic error-correcting codes in two symbols. AFCRC-TN-57-103, Air Force Cambridge Research Center, Cambridge, Mass (1957)
2. Wicker, S.B.: Error Control Systems for Digital Communication and Storage. Prentice Hall, Englewood Cliffs (1995)
3. Elia, M.: Algebraic decoding of the (23, 12, 7) Golay codes. IEEE Trans. Inf. Theory 33(1), 150–151 (1987)
4. Reed, I.S., Yin, X., Truong, T.K., Holmes, J.K.: Decoding the (24, 12, 8) Golay code. Proc. IEE 137(3), 202–206 (1990)
5. Reed, I.S., Yin, X., Truong, T.K.: Algebraic decoding of the (32, 16, 8) quadratic residue code. IEEE Trans. Inf. Theory 36(4), 876–880 (1990)
6. Reed, I.S., Truong, T.K., Chen, X., Yin, X.: The algebraic decoding of the (41, 21, 9) quadratic residue code. IEEE Trans. Inf. Theory 38(3), 974–986 (1992)
7. He, R., Reed, I.S., Truong, T.K., Chen, X.: Decoding the (47, 24, 11) quadratic residue code. IEEE Trans. Inf. Theory 47(3), 1181–1186 (2001)
8. Chang, Y., Truong, T.K., Reed, I.S., Cheng, H.Y., Lee, C.D.: Algebraic decoding of (71, 36, 11) (79, 40, 15), and (97, 49, 15) quadratic residue codes. IEEE Trans. on Comm. 51(9), 1463–1473 (2003)
9. Truong, T.K., Chang, Y., Chen, Y.-H., Lee, C.D.: Algebraic decoding of (103, 52, 19) and (113, 57, 15) quadratic residue code. IEEE Trans. on Comm. 53(5), 749–754 (2005)
10. Truong, T.K., Shih, P.Y., Su, W.K., Lee, C.D., Chang, Y.: Algebraic decoding of the (89, 45, 17) quadratic residue code. IEEE Trans. Inf. Theory 54(11), 5005–5011 (2008)
11. Lin, T.C., Truong, T.K., Lee, H.P., Chang, H.C.: Algebraic decoding of the (41, 21, 9) quadratic residue code. Inf. Sci. 179(19), 3451–3459 (2009)
12. Lin, T.C., Chang, H.C., Lee, H.P., Chu, S.I., Truong, T.K.: Decoding of the (31, 16, 7) quadratic residue code. J. Chin. Inst. Eng. 33(4), 573–580 (2010)
13. Lin, T.C., Lee, H.P., Chang, H.C., Chu, S.I., Truong, T.K.: High speed decoding of the binary (47, 24, 11) quadratic residue code. Inf. Sci. 180(20), 4060–4068 (2010)
14. Chien, R.T.: Cyclic decoding procedure for the Bose-Chaudhuri-Hocquenghem codes. IEEE Trans. Inf. Theory 10(4), 357–363 (1964)
15. MacWilliams, F.J., Sloane, N.J.A.: The Theory of Error Correcting Codes. North Holland, Amsterdam (1977)

An Efficient Decoding Algorithm for the (73, 37, 13) Quadratic Residue Code

Hung-Peng Lee* and Hsin-Chiu Chang

Department of Computer Science and Information Engineering
Fortune Institute of Technology, Kaohsiung City 831, Taiwan
hpl@center.fotech.edu.tw, p01244@center.fotech.edu.tw

Abstract. An efficient table lookup decoding algorithm (TLDA), called the syndrome and syndrome difference decoding algorithm (SSDDA), is presented to decode the binary systematic (73, 37, 13) quadratic residue (QR) code, which has the error-correcting capability to correct up to six-bit errors. The essential concept of this algorithm is based on the property of the weight of syndrome and the weight of syndrome difference to greatly reduce the memory size of the lookup table. The proposed algorithm only requires a small lookup table, called the compact lookup table (CLT), which only consists of 8,473 syndromes and their corresponding error patterns. The memory size of the CLT is only about 2.55% of the lookup table proposed by Lin *et al.* A C++ program has been executed to check all error patterns of this QR code.

Keywords: quadratic residue code, lookup table, error pattern, syndrome.

1 Introduction

The well-known QR codes, introduced by Prange [1] in 1957, are cyclic BCH codes with code rates greater than or equal to one-half. In addition, the codes generally have large minimum distances so that most of the known QR codes are the best-known codes. The code augmented by a parity bit, for example, the (24, 12, 8) QR code was utilized to provide error control on the Voyager deep-space mission [2].

In the past decades, several decoding techniques have been developed to decode the QR codes. The algebraic decoding algorithms (ADAs) given in [3-12] used the error-locator polynomial to find the different error positions. Recently, some TLDAs given in [13-16] play an important role in error-correcting decoding and they have faster decoding speed than the ADAs. However, the TLDAs require a memory space in the decoder chip and they increase the decoding cost rapidly when the code length is large. Although, the ADAs does not need any lookup table; however, it requires a large number of operations in finite field. These complicated computations will lead to a decoding delay when the code length is large.

For the binary (n, k, d) QR code, the error-correcting capability t is defined by $t = \lfloor (d-1)/2 \rfloor$, where the symbol $\lfloor x \rfloor$ denotes the greatest integer less than or equal

* Corresponding author.

H. Tan and M. Zhou (Eds.): CSE 2011, Part I, CCIS 201, pp. 224–231, 2011.

to x, n is the length of the code, k is the message length of the code, and d is the minimum Hamming distance of the code. For example, the binary (73, 37, 13) QR code can correct up to $t = \lfloor (d-1)/2 \rfloor = \lfloor (13-1)/2 \rfloor = 6$ errors. The decoding of the binary (73, 37, 13) QR code was first proposed by Chen *et al.* [6]; however, the algebraic decoding algorithm is very complicated and it has to compute the syndromes and the error-locator polynomials in finite field. In this paper, we will propose a novel memory-efficient SSDDA to decode the binary systematic (73, 37, 13) QR code; the memory size of the CLT needed in the SSDDA is only about 2.55% of the lookup table proposed by Lin *et al.* [16]. Moreover, the proposed decoder is verified with checking all the correctable error patterns by a computer simulation.

The remainder of this paper is organized as follows. In section 2, the background of binary systematic (73, 37, 13) QR codes is briefly introduced. The generation of the CLT is exhibited in section 3. Section 4 describes in detail the proposed SSDDA. Simulation results are shown in section 5. Finally, some concluding remarks of this paper are given in section 6.

2 Background of the Binary Systematic (73, 37, 13) QR Code

A QR code is a type of cyclic code [2]. A binary (n, k, d) QR code is defined algebraically as a multiple of its generator polynomial $g(x)$ over $GF(2^m)$. Let the length of this code n be a prime number of the form $n = 8l \pm 1$ where l is a positive integer, and m be the smallest positive integer such that n divides $2^m - 1$. Also, let $k = (n + 1)/2$ be the message length and d be the minimum distance of the code. Its generator polynomial as a cyclic code is given by

$$g(x) = \prod_{i \in Q_n} (x - \beta^i) \ , \tag{1}$$

where β is a primitive nth root of unity in $GF(2^m)$ and Q_n denotes the set of quadratic residues given by

$$Q_n = \{j \mid j \equiv x^2 \bmod n,\ 1 \leq x \leq (n\text{-}1)/2\}. \tag{2}$$

Since $2 \in Q_n$, the set Q_n is closed under multiplication by 2. Thus Q_n can be represented as a disjoint union of cyclotomic cosets, modulo n. These cyclotomic cosets are given by

$$Q_r = \{r2^j \mid j=0, 1,\ldots, n_r\text{-}1\} \ , \tag{3}$$

where n_r is the smallest positive integer such that $r2^{n_r} \equiv r \bmod n$, n_r divides $(n\text{-}1)/2$ and r is the smallest element in Q_r. The r is called the representative element of the cyclotomic cosets Q_r. The set S, consisting of all representatives of the QR code, is called the base set of the QR code. These definitions and properties cause the identity

$$Q_n = \bigcup_{r \in S} Q_r \tag{4}$$

relating Q to the cyclotomic cosets, modulo n. For the binary (73, 37, 13) QR code, the components of codeword are over in $GF(2^9)$. The base set of this QR code is S = {1, 3, 5, 9, 11, 13, 17, 25}; therefore, the all cyclotomic cosets are given by

$$\begin{array}{ll} Q_1=\{1,2,4,8,16,32,64,55,37\} & Q_{11}=\{11,22,44,15,30,60,47,21,42\} \\ Q_3=\{3,6,12,24,48,23,46,19,38\} & Q_{13}=\{13,26,52,31,62,51,29,58,43\} \\ Q_5=\{5,10,20,40,7,14,28,56,39\} & Q_{17}=\{17,34,68,63,53,33,66,59,45\} \\ Q_9=\{9,18,36,72,71,69,65,57,41\} & Q_{25}=\{25,50,27,54,35,70,67,61,49\}. \end{array} \quad (5)$$

We choose 4 cyclotomc cosets, such as r = 1, 3, 9, 25, to form Q_{73}. Therefore, by (4), the quadratic residue set of this code is obtained by

$$\begin{aligned} Q_{73} = Q_1 \cup Q_3 \cup Q_9 \cup Q_{25} = \{&1,2,3,4,6,8,9,12,16,18,19,23,24,25,27,32, \\ &35,37,38,41,46,48,49,50,54,55,57,61,64,65,67,69,70,71,72\}. \end{aligned} \quad (6)$$

Let α be a root of primitive polynomial. Then, α generates the multiplicative group of nonzero element in $GF(2^9)$. Let the element $\beta = \alpha^u$, where $u = (2^m - 1)/n = (2^9 - 1)/73 = 7$, is a primitive 73th root of unity in $GF(2^9)$. The generator polynomial $g(x)$ shown below is composed of four binary irreducible polynomials:

$$\begin{aligned} g(x) &= \prod_{i \in Q_{73}} (x - \beta^i) = g_1(x) g_3(x) g_9(x) g_{25}(x) \\ &= x^{36} + x^{34} + x^{32} + x^{31} + x^{30} + x^{28} + x^{25} + x^{24} + x^{22} + x^{21} + x^{20} + x^{19} + , \\ &\quad x^{18} + x^{17} + x^{16} + x^{15} + x^{14} + x^{12} + x^{11} + x^{8} + x^{6} + x^{5} + x^{4} + x^{2} + 1. \end{aligned} \quad (7)$$

where $g_1(x)$, $g_3(x)$, $g_9(x)$, and $g_{25}(x)$ are the minimal polynomials of β^1, β^3, β^9, and β^{25} with coefficients in $GF(2)$, respectively; that is, $g_r(x) = (x - \beta^r)(x - \beta^{2r}) \cdots (x - \beta^{2^8 r})$ and $\beta^{2^i r} \in GF(2^9)$ for $0 \le i \le 8$. The degree of $g(x)$ is 36, which is the multiplicative order of the integer 2 modulo the code length 73; that is, $2^{36} \equiv 1 \bmod 73$.

A codeword of the binary systematic (73, 37, 13) QR code is a polynomial $c(x) = c_{70}x^{72} + \cdots + c_1 x + c_0$ such that it is a multiple of $g(x)$. If the codeword $c(x)$ is transmitted through a noisy channel, then the received polynomial $r(x) = r_{72}x^{72} + \cdots + r_1 x + r_0$ can be expressed as the sum of the codeword polynomial $c(x)$ and the error polynomial $e(x) = e_{72}x^{72} + \cdots + e_1 x + e_0$. For simplicity, let the message or information, codeword, error pattern, received word, and syndrome be expressed as the binary vector forms $\mathbf{m} = (m_{k-1}, \ldots, m_1, m_0)$, $\mathbf{c} = (c_{n-1}, \ldots, c_1, c_0)$, $\mathbf{e} = (e_{n-1}, \ldots, e_1, e_0)$, $\mathbf{r} = (r_{n-1}, \ldots, r_1, r_0)$, and $\mathbf{s} = (s_{n-k-1}, \ldots, s_1, s_0)$, respectively. For the binary systematic (73, 37, 13) QR code, it follows from [2, p85] that the systematic $k \times n = 37 \times 73$ generator matrix $\mathbf{G}$ can be expressed as follows:

$$\mathbf{G} = \left[\mathbf{P}_{k\times(n-k)} \mid \mathbf{I}_k\right]_{k\times n} = \begin{bmatrix} p_{0,0} & p_{0,1} & \cdots & p_{0,35} & 1 & 0 & \cdots & 0 \\ p_{1,0} & p_{1,1} & \cdots & p_{1,35} & 0 & 1 & \cdots & 0 \\ \vdots & \vdots & \ddots & \vdots & \vdots & \vdots & \ddots & \vdots \\ p_{36,0} & p_{36,1} & \cdots & p_{36,35} & 0 & 0 & \cdots & 1 \end{bmatrix}_{37\times 73}, \quad (8)$$

where $\mathbf{I}_k$ is the $k \times k = 37 \times 37$ identity matrix and $\mathbf{P}_{k\times(n-k)}$ is the matrix of size $k \times (n - k) = 37 \times 36$.

The codeword of systematic form can be obtained in matrix form by

$$\begin{aligned}\mathbf{c} = \mathbf{mG} &= (m_{36} \ \ldots m_1 \ m_0)\mathbf{G} \\ &= (p_{35} \cdots p_1 \ p_0 | m_{36} \ \ldots m_1 \ m_0)\end{aligned}, \tag{9}$$

where the $(p_{35},\ldots, p_1, p_0)$ is the parity-check part of **c** and the $(m_{36},\ldots, m_1, m_0)$ is the message part of **c**. The systematic parity check matrix **H** of size $(n - k) \times n = 36 \times 73$ can be expressed as follows:

$$\mathbf{H} = \left[\mathbf{I}_{n-k} \mid \mathbf{P}^T_{k\times(n-k)}\right]_{(n-k)\times n} = \begin{bmatrix} 1 & 0 & \cdots & 0 & p_{0,0} & p_{1,0} & \cdots & p_{36,0} \\ 0 & 1 & \cdots & 0 & p_{0,1} & p_{1,1} & \cdots & p_{36,1} \\ \vdots & \vdots & \ddots & \vdots & \vdots & \vdots & \ddots & \vdots \\ 0 & 0 & \cdots & 1 & p_{0,35} & p_{1,35} & \cdots & p_{36,35} \end{bmatrix}_{36\times 73}, \tag{10}$$

where $\mathbf{P}^T_{k\times(n-k)}$ is the transpose matrix of $\mathbf{P}_{k\times(n-k)}$ and $\mathbf{I}_{n-k}$ is the $(n - k) \times (n - k) = 36 \times 36$ identity matrix. The vector form of the syndrome can be defined by

$$\mathbf{s} = \mathbf{rH}^T, \tag{11}$$

where $\mathbf{H}^T$ denotes the $n \times (n - k) = 73 \times 36$ transpose matrix of **H**; that is, $\mathbf{H}^T = \begin{bmatrix} \mathbf{I}_{36} \\ \hline \mathbf{P}_{37\times 36} \end{bmatrix}_{73\times 36}$.

The proposed algorithm only needs to compute the syndrome of **r** for every received word and the complicated computation of the error-locator polynomial can be completely avoided. This is the reason why the proposed algorithm significantly reduces the computational complexity. If **r** occurs with no error, then the syndrome $\mathbf{s} = \mathbf{rH}^T = (\mathbf{c} + \mathbf{0})\mathbf{H}^T = \mathbf{cH}^T = \mathbf{0}$, where **0** denotes a zero vector. Otherwise, $\mathbf{s} = \mathbf{rH}^T = (\mathbf{c} + \mathbf{e})\mathbf{H}^T = \mathbf{0} + \mathbf{eH}^T = \mathbf{eH}^T$.

3 Formation of the Compact Lookup Table

The full size of the syndromes and their corresponding error patterns in a lookup table is $\sum_{i=1}^{t} C_i^n$. Therefore, for the (73, 37, 13) QR code, the full size of the lookup table is $\sum_{i=1}^{6} C_i^{73} = 186{,}404{,}113$, and thus this table is what is called the full lookup table (FLT). One syndrome needs 5 bytes to store in memory and its corresponding error pattern needs 10 bytes to store in memory. In other words, the total memory size of the FLT needs 186,404,113 × (5 bytes + 10 bytes) = 2,796,061,695 bytes ≈ 2.6 Gbytes. Thus, searching a syndrome in such a huge table is impracticable.

The lookup table decoding algorithm (LTDA) developed in [13], a type of shift-search method [4], needs $\sum_{i=1}^{6} C_i^{73} - \sum_{i=1}^{6} C_i^{36} = 184{,}012{,}618$ syndromes and their corresponding error patterns; that is, this lookup table needs 184,012,618 × (5 bytes +

10 bytes) ≈ 2.546 Gbytes memory size to store such a huge lookup table. The shift-search method deletes all $v = t$, where $v \le t$ is the actual number of errors occurred, patterns and keeps $1 \le v \le t - 1$ patterns in lookup table.

The syndrome decoder with a reduce-size lookup table (RSLT) [2,p119] is a very efficient method of decoding linear cyclic codes over a noisy channel for moderate code lengths. In essence, the syndrome decoder is a minimum distance decoding using the syndromes corresponding to their error patterns in the lookup table. Due to the property of cyclic code, the size of the RSLT can be greatly reduced up to $1/n$ of the size of the FLT. In this case, it uses a coset leader to represent a coset with the same syndrome. So the size of the RSLT only needs 186,404,113/73 = 2,553,481 syndromes and their corresponding error patterns; that is, the RSLT needs 2,553,481 × (5 bytes + 10 bytes) ≈ 36.53 Mbytes memory size to store in the memory. However, this memory size of the RSLT is still too large that we need to further reduce the memory size of the RSLT.

Lin *et al.* [15] proposed the TLDA combined with the condensed lookup table (COLT), a type of shift-search method [4], to further reduce the memory size of the RSLT. The COLT requires $(\sum_{i=1}^{5} C_i^{73})/73$ = 16,173,661/73 = 221,557 syndromes and their corresponding error patterns; that is, it only needs 221,557 × (5 bytes + 10 bytes) ≈ 3.17 Mbytes memory size. However, the size of the COLT is still large for DSP or embedded system software implementation. Thus, we further develop a novel SSDDA with CLT to reduce the size of the COLT. Now, we give the definition for the proposed CLT.

Definition. The compact lookup table (CLT) is a table of all the error patterns of weight v occurred only in the message part together with their corresponding syndromes, where $1 \le v \le \lceil t/2 \rceil$ and $\lceil x \rceil$ denotes the smallest integer greater than or equal to x.

Therefore, for the binary (73, 37, 13) QR code, the SSDDA only needs generating the error patterns with weight $1 \le v \le \lceil t/2 \rceil = 3$. For the binary systematic (73, 37, 13) QR code, the number of the syndromes and their corresponding error patterns in the CLT is $\sum_{i=1}^{3} C_i^{37} = 8{,}473$. So the total memory size of the CLT is only 8,473 × (5 bytes + 5 bytes) = 84,730 bytes / 1,024 ≈ 85.4 Kbytes, and the size is the least memory size of the lookup table in the literature. By using such a small table, the proposed SSDDA can decode the total 186,404,113 error patterns of the binary (73, 37, 13) QR code. The relationship of the syndromes and their corresponding error patterns in the proposed CLT is shown in Table 1(a).

In order to reduce the searching time in the CLT, it is well-known that the famous binary search algorithm is utilized instead of performing an exhaustive search. However, the syndromes need to be arranged in ascending order. The relationship of the syndromes in ascending order and their corresponding error patterns in the CLT is shown in Table 1(b). Let $N = 8473$ be the number of all syndromes in the CLT. Then, the time complexity of finding a syndrome in the CLT is at most $O(\log_2 N)$ = $O(\log_2(8{,}473)) \approx 13.05$ times. If a full search algorithm is used to find the syndrome in the CLT, then the time complexity is at most O(8,473) = 8,473 times. By using the

Table 1. Syndromes and Their Corresponding Error Patterns in the CLT (in Hexdecimal)

(a) Ascending order by error patterns

Errors	Syndromes	Error patterns
	$\mathbf{s}_1$ = (5D37FD975)	$\mathbf{e}_1$ = (0000000001)
	$\mathbf{s}_2$ = (BA6FFB2EA)	$\mathbf{e}_2$ = (0000000002)
1	⋮	⋮
	$\mathbf{s}_{36}$ = (574DFF65D)	$\mathbf{e}_{36}$ = (0800000000)
	$\mathbf{s}_{37}$ = (AE9BFECBA)	$\mathbf{e}_{37}$ = (1000000000)
	$\mathbf{s}_{38}$ = (E75806B9F)	$\mathbf{e}_{38}$ = (0000000003)
	$\mathbf{s}_{39}$ = (74DFF65D4)	$\mathbf{e}_{39}$ = (0000000005)
2	⋮	⋮
	$\mathbf{s}_{702}$ = (2BA6FFB2E)	$\mathbf{e}_{702}$ = (1400000000)
	$\mathbf{s}_{703}$ = (F9D601AE7)	$\mathbf{e}_{703}$ = (1800000000)
	$\mathbf{s}_{704}$ = (CEB00D73E)	$\mathbf{e}_{704}$ = (0000000007)
	$\mathbf{s}_{705}$ = (B488112DD)	$\mathbf{e}_{705}$ = (000000000B)
3	⋮	⋮
	$\mathbf{s}_{8472}$ = (BB488112D)	$\mathbf{e}_{8472}$ = (1A00000000)
	$\mathbf{s}_{8473}$ = (7CEB00D73)	$\mathbf{e}_{8473}$ = (1C00000000)

(b) Ascending order by syndrome values

Syndromes	Error patterns
$\mathbf{s}_1$ = (000E188C3)	$\mathbf{e}_1$ = (1000004200)
$\mathbf{s}_2$ = (0001C31187)	$\mathbf{e}_2$ = (0000008400)
$\mathbf{s}_3$ = (00316DDD7)	$\mathbf{e}_3$ = (0003040000)
$\mathbf{s}_4$ = (0034F12E1)	$\mathbf{e}_4$ = (0040022000)
$\mathbf{s}_5$ = (00386230E)	$\mathbf{e}_5$ = (0000010800)
$\mathbf{s}_6$ = (003AEEDA3)	$\mathbf{e}_6$ = (0000000106)
$\mathbf{s}_7$ = (0044354FD)	$\mathbf{e}_7$ = (0040003000)
⋮	⋮
$\mathbf{s}_{8467}$ = (FFC7BD6F3)	$\mathbf{e}_{8467}$ = (0200008080)
$\mathbf{s}_{8468}$ = (FFCF4CB26)	$\mathbf{e}_{8468}$ = (0001400004)
$\mathbf{s}_{8469}$ = (FFDB8C774)	$\mathbf{e}_{8469}$ = (0200000480)
$\mathbf{s}_{8470}$ = (FFDE4013E)	$\mathbf{e}_{8470}$ = (0002002020)
$\mathbf{s}_{8471}$ = (FFE7E2FA5)	$\mathbf{e}_{8471}$ = (0020008040)
$\mathbf{s}_{8472}$ = (FFFA4345C)	$\mathbf{e}_{8472}$ = (0100050000)
$\mathbf{s}_{8473}$ = (FFFBD3E22)	$\mathbf{e}_{8473}$ = (0020000440)

binary search algorithm compared to the full search algorithm, the average searching time can be saved up to 649.3 times. Therefore, the SSDDA is naturally suitable for both software and hardware implementation.

4 Proposed Decoding Algorithm

A memory-efficient SSDDA with the CLT for decoding the binary systematic (73, 37, 13) QR code is presented to further reduce the size of the lookup table given in [15].

Given a received word $\mathbf{r}$. First, the syndrome $\mathbf{s}$ is computed and the weight of this syndrome $w(\mathbf{s})$ is then computed. If $w(\mathbf{s}) = 0$, it denotes that there are no errors in $\mathbf{r}$, namely $\mathbf{r} = \mathbf{c}$. If $w(\mathbf{s}) \leq 6$, then the all errors are in the parity check part of $\mathbf{r}$. Then we shift the syndrome left 37 bits to form a 73-bit length word, and the corrected codeword can be obtained by subtracting (modulo 2) this 73-bit length word from the received word $\mathbf{r}$. If $w(\mathbf{s}) > 6$, it denotes that at least one error is in the message part of $\mathbf{r}$. Next, using the well-known binary search algorithm, we search the CLT whether the syndrome is in the CLT or not. If the syndrome is found in the CLT, namely, $\mathbf{s} = \mathbf{s}_j$ for some $1 \leq j \leq 8{,}473$, at most $\lceil t/2 \rceil = 3$ errors are in the message part of $\mathbf{r}$, and then subtract the error pattern of the syndrome from the received word $\mathbf{r}$ to obtain the corrected codeword. Otherwise, set the counter j to be zero. Subtract the syndrome $\mathbf{s}_j$ in the CLT to obtain the syndrome difference $\mathbf{s}_{dj}$, and compute the weight of this syndrome difference $w(\mathbf{s}_{dj})$. If $3 \leq w(\mathbf{s}_{dj}) \leq 5$, then we shift this syndrome difference left by 37 bits to form a 73-bit length word. Finally, the vector $\mathbf{r}$ subtracts this 73-bit length word and subtracts the corresponding error pattern to correct the $\mathbf{r}$. If $w(\mathbf{s}_{dj}) \geq 6$ and $j \leq 8{,}473$ then set $j = j + 1$ and continue this step. If $w(\mathbf{s}_{dj}) \geq 6$ and $j > 8{,}473$, then go to next step. Let the vector $\mathbf{r}$ is cyclically shifted left by 36 bits and compute its weight $w(\mathbf{s})$. If $4 \leq w(\mathbf{s}) \leq 6$, then $\mathbf{r} = \mathbf{r} - (\mathbf{s} << 37)$ and cyclically shift $\mathbf{r}$ left by 37 bits to obtain the corrected $\mathbf{c}$. Next, Compute the syndrome difference $\mathbf{s}_{dj} = \mathbf{s} - \mathbf{s}_j$ for $1 \leq j \leq 8{,}473$ and its weight $w(\mathbf{s}_{dj})$. If $3 \leq w(\mathbf{s}_{dj}) \leq 5$, then $\mathbf{r} = \mathbf{r} - (\mathbf{s}_{dj} << 37) - \mathbf{e}_j$ and cyclically shift **r** left by 36 bits to obtain the corrected **c**. Otherwise, the received word is over 6 errors and we declare a decoding failure. The decoding steps of the SSDDA are stated explicitly as below:

The decoding steps of the SSDDA are stated explicitly as below:

1. Given a received word $\mathbf{r} = \mathbf{c} + \mathbf{e}$.
2. By (11), compute the syndrome of **r** and its weight $w(\mathbf{s})$.
3. If $w(\mathbf{s}) = 0$, then no error has occurred. Go to step 14.
4. If $w(\mathbf{s}) \le 6$, then $\mathbf{c} = \mathbf{r} - (\mathbf{s} << 37)$. Go to step 14.
5. Search whether **s** is in the CLT. If **s** is in the CLT, that is $\mathbf{s} = \mathbf{s}_j$ for some $1 \le j \le 8{,}473$ corresponding to some error pattern $\mathbf{e}_j$, then $\mathbf{c} = \mathbf{r} - \mathbf{e}_j$. Go to step 14.
6. Compute the syndrome difference $\mathbf{s}_{dj} = \mathbf{s} - \mathbf{s}_j$ for $1 \le j \le 8{,}473$ and its weight $w(\mathbf{s}_{dj})$.
7. If $3 \le w(\mathbf{s}_{dj}) \le 5$, then $\mathbf{c} = \mathbf{r} - (\mathbf{s}_{dj} << 37) - \mathbf{e}_j$. Go to step 14. Otherwise, go to step 8.
8. Set $j = j + 1$. If $j \le 8{,}473$, then go to step 6, else go to step 9.
9. Cyclically shift **r** left by 36bits. By (11), compute the syndrome of this new **r** and its weight $w(\mathbf{s})$.
10. If $4 \le w(\mathbf{s}) \le 6$, then $\mathbf{r} = \mathbf{r} - (\mathbf{s} << 37)$ and cyclically shift **r** left by 37 bits to obtain the corrected **c**. Go to step 14.
11. Compute the syndrome difference $\mathbf{s}_{dj} = \mathbf{s} - \mathbf{s}_j$ for $1 \le j \le 8{,}473$ and its weight $w(\mathbf{s}_{dj})$.
12. If $3 \le w(\mathbf{s}_{dj}) \le 5$, then $\mathbf{r} = \mathbf{r} - (\mathbf{s}_{dj} << 37) - \mathbf{e}_j$ and cyclically shift **r** left by 37 bits to obtain the corrected **c**. Go to step 14.
13. $w(\mathbf{e}) > t = 6$. Declare a decoding failure.
14. Stop or go to step 1 to correct next received word.

5 Simulation Results

The proposed decoder written in C++ program is implemented on an Intel Q6600 PC with Windows XP operating system. All 186,404,113 error patterns are generated and are executed by the proposed SSDDA. The SSDDA can perfectly correct all error patterns with an average decoding time of 678.56μs per error pattern. The simulation results of different errors are shown in Table 2.

Table 2. The CPU Execution Time of Decoding the (73, 37, 13) QR Code (in μs)

Number of errors	1	2	3	4	5	6	Average
Decoding time	1.7002	2.5378	22.863	286.47	482.94	701.54	678.56

6 Conclusions

In this paper, a memory-efficient SSDDA with CLT is developed to correct the binary systematic (73, 37, 13) QR code up to six errors. The key idea of the SSDDA is based on the fact that it exploits the weight of syndrome and the weight of syndrome difference to reduce the memory size of the lookup table. The SSDDA only requires 85.4 Kbytes memory space to store the CLT and it can decode the total 186,404,113 error patterns of the binary (73, 37, 13) QR code. Up to now, the memory size of the proposed CLT is the least in the literature and the average decoding time only needs 678.56μs. However, it is expected that the memory size of the CLT can be further reduced and the SSDDA can be used in the soft-decision decoder in the future.

References

1. Prange, E.: Cyclic error-correcting codes in two symbols. AFCRC-TN-57-103, Air Force Cambridge Research Center, Cambridge, Mass (1957)
2. Wicker, S.B.: Error Control Systems for Digital Communication and Storage. Prentice Hall, Englewood Cliffs (1995)
3. Elia, M.: Algebraic decoding of the (23, 12, 7) Golay codes. IEEE Trans. Inf. Theory 33(1), 150–151 (1987)
4. Reed, I.S., Yin, X., Truong, T.K., Holmes, J.K.: Decoding the (24, 12, 8) Golay code. Proc. IEE 137(3), 202–206 (1990)
5. Reed, I.S., Truong, T.K., Chen, X., Yin, X.: The algebraic decoding of the (41, 21, 9) quadratic residue code. IEEE Trans. Inf. Theory 38(3), 974–986 (1992)
6. Chen, X., Reed, I.S., Truong, T.K.: Decoding the (73, 37, 13) quadratic residue code. IEE Proceedings on Computer Digital Techniques 141(5), 253–258 (1994)
7. He, R., Reed, I.S., Truong, T.K., Chen, X.: Decoding the (47, 24, 11) quadratic residue code. IEEE Trans. Inf. Theory 47(3), 1181–1186 (2001)
8. Chang, Y., Truong, T.K., Reed, I.S., Cheng, H.Y., Lee, C.D.: Algebraic decoding of (71, 36, 11) (79, 40, 15), and (97, 49, 15) quadratic residue codes. IEEE Trans. on Comm. 51(9), 1463–1473 (2003)
9. Truong, T.K., Chang, Y., Chen, Y.-H., Lee, C.D.: Algebraic decoding of (103, 52, 19) and (113, 57, 15) quadratic residue code. IEEE Trans. on Comm. 53(5), 749–754 (2005)
10. Chen, Y.H., Truong, T.K., Chang, Y., Lee, C.D., Chen, S.H.: Algebraic decoding of quadratic residue codes using Berlekamp-Massey algorithm. J. Inf. Sci. Eng. 23(1), 127–145 (2007)
11. Truong, T.K., Shih, P.Y., Su, W.K., Lee, C.D., Chang, Y.: Algebraic decoding of the (89, 45, 17) quadratic residue code. IEEE Trans. Inf. Theory 54(11), 5005–5011 (2008)
12. Lin, T.C., Chang, H.C., Lee, H.P., Chu, S.I., Truong, T.K.: Decoding of the (31, 16, 7) quadratic residue code. J. Chin. Inst. Eng. 33(4), 573–580 (2010)
13. Chen, Y.H., Truong, T.K., Huang, C.H., Chien, C.H.: A lookup table decoding of systematic (47, 24, 11) quadratic residue code. Inf. Sci. 179(14), 2470–2477 (2009)
14. Chen, Y.H., Chien, C.H., Huang, C.H., Truong, T.K., Jing, M.H.: Efficient decoding of systematic (23, 12, 7) and (41, 21, 9) quadratic residue codes. J. Inf. Sci. Eng. 26(5), 1831–1843 (2010)
15. Lin, T.C., Lee, H.P., Chang, H.C., Chu, S.I., Truong, T.K.: High speed decoding of the binary (47, 24, 11) quadratic residue code. Inf. Sci. 180(20), 4060–4068 (2010)
16. Lin, T.C., Chang, H.C., Lee, H.P., Truong, T.K.: On the decoding of the (24, 12, 8) Golay code. Inf. Sci. 180(23), 4729–4736 (2010)

A New Genetic Algorithm Using Gap Matrixes for Multiple Sequence Alignment

Jin Zhang[1] and Zhen Wang[2]

[1] School of Information Science and Engineering, University of Jinan, 250022 Jinan, China
[2] College of Information Science and Engineering, Shandong University of Science and Technology 266510 Qingdao, China

Abstract. As is well known, multiple sequence alignment (MSA) is a widely used technique in molecular sequence analysis, and the object of MSA is to find optimal alignment for several sequences. By using gap matrixes, this paper devised a new genetic algorithm to solve MSA problem, and the approach is examined by using a set of standard instances taken from the benchmark alignment database BAliBASE. Numerical simulations are performed to verify the significance of the proposed algorithm.

Keywords: Bioinformatics, Multiple sequence alignment, Gap matrixes, Genetic operators.

1 Introduction

MSA is an essential tool for analyzing biological sequences. In recent years, numerous techniques have been used to align multiple sequences. The progressive approach is the most commonly used heuristic method by gradually aligning the closest pair to build MSA [1]. Its main disadvantage is the found alignments that may by trapped in local optima. In other words, if mistakes are made in intermediate alignments, they cannot be corrected later when more sequences are added into the alignment process. Furthermore, there is no objective function to evaluate the performance for multiple sequence alignment. Another approach is to use an extension of dynamic programming for simultaneously aligning multiple sequences, such as MSA [2] and DCA [3], etc. In general, these algorithms often have higher quality solutions than that of progressive approach. However, the drawbacks of these algorithms are the complexity in running time and memory requirements. Thus, they can only be applied to problems with limited number of sequences.

In addition, there are stochastic optimization methods which are used to solve multiple sequence alignment such as simulated annealing (SA) [4], Gibbs sampling [5] and genetic algorithm (GA) [6,7]. Genetic algorithm is based on the concept of biological evolution and biological genetics. Genetic algorithms operate on chromosome-like data structures that encode possible solutions of the problems, and apply crossover and mutation operators to generate new chromosomes in a search

H. Tan and M. Zhou (Eds.): CSE 2011, Part I, CCIS 201, pp. 232–240, 2011.

space. Then, based on the principle of survival-of-the-fittest, chromosomes with good performance are selected though selection operator. Recently, genetic algorithms with local search have been considered as good alternatives for solving optimization problems [8, 9].

In this paper, we present the genetic algorithm using gap matrixes to explore and exploit search spaces for multiple sequence alignment. It has both the advantage of GA, the ability to find feasible solutions and to avoid premature convergence, and the ability to search over the subspace and then to move out of local optima.

2 Multiple Sequence Alignment

MSA is an extension of pair-wise sequence alignment (PSA). Nowadays, MSA has become an important tool in molecular biology, and especially, it can provide key information for sequence analysis. Now we describe MSA as follows.

Let $S=(s_1, s_2, \ldots\ldots, s_n)$ be a set of sequences defined over an alphabet Σ, $s_i = s_{i1}s_{i2}\ldots\ldots s_{il_i}, (1 \le i \le n), s_{ij} \in \Sigma, (1 \le j \le l_i)$, l_i is the length of the $i-th$ sequence. Σ include A, C, G and T which represent four different types of nucleotides for DNA sequences. In addition to protein sequences, Σ includes A, R, N, D, C, Q, E, G, H, I, L, K, M, F, P, S, T, W, Y and V which represent twenty amino acids. For sequences group S, we try to find an optimal alignment $S' = (s'_1, s'_2, \ldots\ldots, s'_n)$ such that:

(1) s'_i is an extension of s_i by inserting some gaps,

(2) $\forall i, j$, the length of s'_i is equal to that of s'_j,

(3) $\sum_i \sum_j sim(s'_i, s'_j)$ is maximized or $\sum_i \sum_j \cos t(s'_i, s'_j)$ is minimized where $sim(X,Y)$ and $\cos t(X,Y)$ are some sequence similarity and alignment cost functions defined for sequences X and Y.

3 Algorithm

3.1 Population Initialization and Fitness function

Under the condition that the value of $L (L \ge L_{\max})$ is fixed, some gaps is inserted randomly in $s_1, s_2, \cdots, s_n$, then $(s_1, s_2, \cdots, s_n)$ is turned into $(s'_1, s'_2, \cdots, s'_n)$ which can be denoted by a $n \times L$ symbol matrix A_1 (gaps denoted by "_"). By the same way, $A_2, A_3, \cdots, A_K$ is generated and then we get the initial population of size K.

By using of SP (sum-of-pairs) function, we evaluate the fitness of chromosomes. When computing the fitness, a chromosome must be converted into the alignment form. The fitness function can be described as follows:

$$SP\_Score(S') = SP\_Score(s_1', s_2', \cdots, s_n')$$
$$= \sum_{i=1}^{L} Column\_Score(X^*_{1,i}, X^*_{2,i}, \cdots, X^*_{n,i})$$
$$Column\_Score(X^*_{1,i}, X^*_{2,i}, \cdots, X^*_{n,i}) = \sum_{1 \le p \le q \le n} Pair\_Score(X^*_{p,i}, X^*_{q,i})$$

The SP_Score function is represented for the sum-of-pairs score of alignment S' whose length is L. The score of the $i-th$ column is denoted by $Column\_Score(X^*_{1,i}, X^*_{2,i}, \ldots\ldots, X^*_{n,i})$, where $X^*_{u,i} (1 \le u \le n)$ indicates that the symbol in the $u-th$ row and $i-th$ column. $Pair\_Score(X^*_{p,i}, X^*_{q,i})$ is the score of the two symbols $X^*_{p,i}, X^*_{q,i}$ in column i. The value of the $Pair\_Score$ function based on weight matrixes of DNA or protein.

3.3 Building Gap Matrixes

Recently, genetic algorithms to MSA were presented, and also many crossover or mutation operators were designed based on alignment symbol matrixes above. However, But these algorithms have many drawbacks. For example, one point crossover can be very disruptive, especially at the junction point. By the way of other crossover method (such as multiple point crossover, uniform crossover, block crossover and so on), rationality about two parents applying these method must be considered. Sometimes, one alignment (the child) outputted need to insert or delete gaps to ensure that the length of all sequences are equal. Moreover, the massive memory space will be allocated in order to store the whole population.

In order to prevent these things from happening, we build gap matrixes which are assembled by using symbol matrixes. Some simple cases are taken for examples. Fig.1 shows an alignment composed of four DNA sequences which are ATCATGCCG, CGGTTG, ATTCGTCG, and ACGTG. Some gaps are inserted randomly in these sequences so that the length of every sequence is turned into a fixed value (such as 10).Given population size 6, Fig.2 shows the initial population after inserting gaps randomly.

ATCATGCCG
CGCTTG
ATTCGTCG
ACGTG

Fig. 1. Four DNA sequences

```
A_TCATGCCG      ATCA_TGCCG      ATCATGC_CG
C_G_C_T_TG      C__GCT_T_G      C_GCT_T_G_
ATT_CG_TCG      AT_TCG_TCG      ATTCG_TC_G
_A_C_G_T_G      A_CG__T_G_      A___CGT_G_

   (a)             (b)             (c)

_ATCATGCCG      ATCATGCC_G      ATCATG_CCG
CGCT_T_G__      __CG_CTT_G      _C_G_C_TTG
A_T_TCGTCG      AT_TCGTCG_      ATTC__GTCG
_A__C__GTG      AC__G__T_G      A_C_GT___G

   (d)             (e)             (f)
```

Fig. 2. The initial population after inserting gaps randomly

We can get four decimal number vectors (1), (1,2,3,4), (3,5) and (0,1,2,3,4) from (a), while every decimal number in vectors indicates a space position in a sequences of an alignment (the first position is zero). Similarly, it is not difficult to known that (4), (1,1,4,5), (2,5) and (1,3,3,4,5) from (b), (7), (1,4,5,6), (5,7) and (1,1,1,4,5) from (c) , (0), (4,5,6,6), (1,2) and (0,1,1,2,2) from (d), (8), (0,0,2,5), (2,8) and (2,2,3,3,4) from (e), (6), (0,1,2,3), (4,4) and (1,2,4,4,4) from (f). The vectors with equal length can be assembled a new matrix. So four decimal number matrixes (called gap matrixes)

$$\begin{pmatrix} 1 \\ 4 \\ 7 \\ 0 \\ 8 \\ 6 \end{pmatrix}, \begin{pmatrix} 1 & 2 & 3 & 4 \\ 1 & 1 & 4 & 5 \\ 1 & 4 & 5 & 6 \\ 4 & 5 & 6 & 6 \\ 0 & 0 & 2 & 5 \\ 0 & 1 & 2 & 3 \end{pmatrix}, \begin{pmatrix} 3 & 5 \\ 2 & 5 \\ 5 & 7 \\ 1 & 2 \\ 2 & 8 \\ 4 & 4 \end{pmatrix}, \begin{pmatrix} 0 & 1 & 2 & 3 & 4 \\ 1 & 3 & 3 & 4 & 5 \\ 1 & 1 & 1 & 4 & 5 \\ 0 & 1 & 1 & 2 & 2 \\ 2 & 2 & 3 & 3 & 4 \\ 1 & 2 & 4 & 4 & 4 \end{pmatrix}$$

are constructed.

Without loss of generality, by inserting some gaps, N sequences can be turned into a random population with size K . Every individual of the population is an alignment whose length is kept constant L . In the following algorithm pseudo code, the value of L range from all integers in $[L_{\max}, 1.2 \times L_{\max}]$ and every integer is tested exhaustively in order to find the optimal solution. We find all gap position vectors in all alignment matrixes and the dimensions of these vectors are denoted by $L_1, L_2, \cdots, L_N$. According to the method above, N gap matrixes, whose dimensions are denoted by $K \times L_1, K \times L_2, \cdots, K \times L_N$ respectively, can be assembled by using gap position vectors. Experience shows that gaps inserted in an alignment are certainly in the minority and massive memory space is saved.

3.4 The Genetic Operators

(1) The gap crossover

In our approach, all genetic operators act inside every gap matrix. We consider a $K \times L$ gap matrix assembled as follows:

$$\begin{pmatrix} a_{11} & \cdots & a_{1L} \\ \vdots & \ddots & \vdots \\ a_{K1} & \cdots & a_{KL} \end{pmatrix}$$

Two types of gap crossover operators called one-point crossover and two-point crossover are deigned. In one-point crossover process, two parent chromosomes(row vectors in the gap matrixes) are randomly selected and used to produce two child chromosomes given one crossover position randomly. An example of one-point crossover is depicted in Fig.3 .Two stochastic row vectors (the $i-th$ vector and the $j-th$ vector)are chosen in a gap matrix and cutting point is randomly selected, and then one new gap matrix is generated after crossover. We set the length of substring exchanged to 2. Similarly, two-point crossover is depicted in Fig.4.We set the length of substring exchanged to 3.

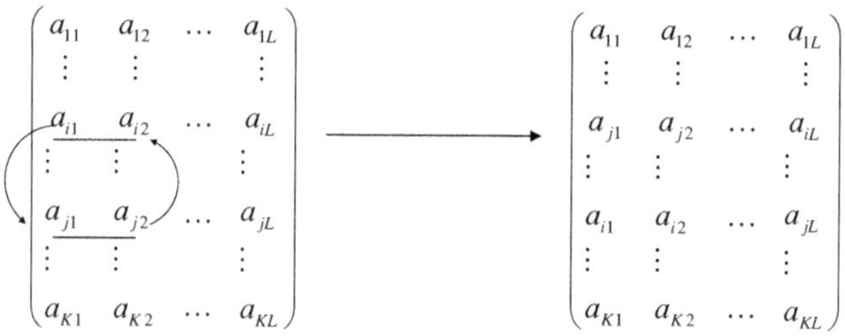

Fig. 3. One-point crossover

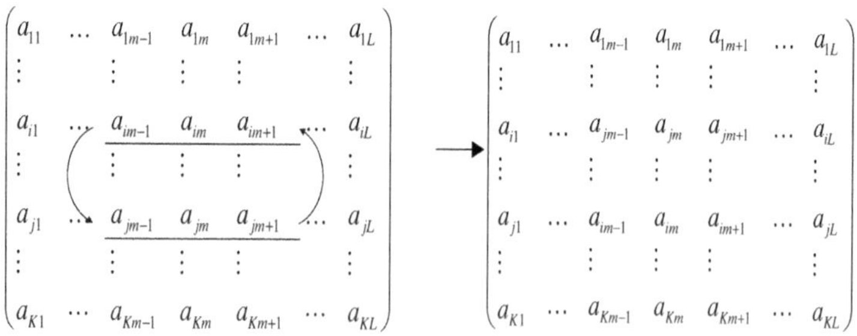

Fig. 4. Two-point crossover

(2) The gap mutation

Three types of gap mutation operators are designed: move operator, union operator and dividing operator, which also act inside every gap matrix. The corresponding transformation of DNA sequence is shown in Fig.5. Any one operator is chosen randomly for keeping randomicity. The length of gap positions for moving, uniting and dividing are set randomly, too.

A_ A_CGACC_TTA_CGTT_CAG_GT_T

↓

Move operator: **A AC_G_ACC_TTA_CGTT_CAG_GT_T**
Union operator: **A_ A_CGACC_TTACGTT___CAGGT_T**

Fig. 5. The transformation of DNA sequence corresponding gap mutation

Move operator : some elements in a gap vector can be shifted from original positions to other positions, such as shifting the first two elements of (1,2,7,10,14,17,19) and getting (3,4,7,10,14,17,19).

Union operator : some elements in a gap vector can be merged. For example, three elements 10,14,17 of (1,2,7,10,14,17,19) can be merged into 14,14,14 of (1,2,7,14,14,14,19) in order to achieve consecutive spaces in one position.

Dividing operator : inverse operation of union operator.

(3) Discuss

There are many advantages using the proposed algorithm to solve MSA problem.

1) The gap crossover and mutation operators designed above give expression to the randomicity so that they have strong ability of global random search. Maintaining diversity of population can overcome early convergency.
2) Massive memory space is saved in that only gap matrixes need to store.
3) Don't worry about whether the child of crossover or mutation is reasonable in that the length of every row vector in every gap matrix won't be changed after genetic operating.
4) The method can be applied to some specific MSA problems in the biological context, for example, one sequence in the group can't be changed in GA.

3.5 The Pseudo Codes

Procedure of the genetic algorithm using gap matrixes (called GapM algorithm) for MSA is as follows:

begin
$L := L_{max}$; // L_{max} is the length of the longest sequence in N sequences ;
The best individual← any alignment whose length is L

```
While L≤⌈1.2×L_max⌉ do
begin
population P whose size is set to K is generated and
the length of every individual is fixed as L;
working out  fitness values of every individual in P ;
the optimal individual under L ←the optimal individual
which is chosen based on all fitness values in P ;
gen:=0;
while gen<EG do //EG is the number of
evolutionary generations
begin
   choosing K multiple sequence alignment matrixes by
   roulette wheel selection in P ;
   turning K multiple sequence alignment matrixes into
   N (the number of sequences) gap matrixes ;
   the gap crossover process described in 3.4(1)  ;
   the gap mutation process described in 3.4(2)  ;
   turning N gap matrixes into K multiple sequence
   alignment matrixes ;
   P := K multiple sequence alignment matrixes ;
   working out fitness values of every individual
   in P ;
   If  the optimal individual in P is better than the
  optimal individual under L
  the optimal individual under L :=the optimal individual
 in P ;
  gen:=gen+1 ;
end
If the optimal individual under L is better than the
 best individual
the best individual:=the optimal individual under L ;
L:=L+1 ;
end
Output the best individual ;
end
```

4 Test Cases

In order to compare this MSA method with other algorithms , we can refer to the benchmark alignment database BAliBASE which contains 142 protein reference alignments that belong to five categories (we select 10, 10, 5, 5 and 5 reference alignments respectively averaging). By BaliScore Procedure [10], we can get SPS score and CS Score. Table 1 indicates that our algorithm generally performs better than other common algorithms.

Table 1. Comparisons of the SPS and CS of the three algorithms

	The average of SPS			The average of CS		
	GapM	Muscle	ClustalW	GapM	Muscle	ClustalW
Ref1(10)	0.873	0.796	0.748	0.818	0.735	0.704
Ref2(10)	0.807	0.754	0.712	0.465	0.421	0.398
Ref3(5)	0.783	0.725	0.699	0.485	0.433	0.414
Ref4(5)	0.761	0.733	0.689	0.498	0.442	0.429
Ref5(5)	0.842	0.792	0.761	0.698	0.623	0.592

Acknowledgments

This work was supported by the Natural Science Foundation of China under Grant 60573065, and the Scientific Research Foundation of the University of Jinan under grant XKY0821.

References

1. Thompson, J.D., Higgins, D.G., Gibson, T.J.: CLUSTAL W: improving the sensitivity of progressive multiple sequence alignment through sequence weighting, position-specific gap penalties and weight matrix choice. Nucl. Acids Res. 22, 4673–4680 (1994)
2. Lipman, D.J., Altschul, S.F., Kececioglu, J.D.: A tool for multiple sequence alignment. Proc. Natl. Acad. Sci. USA 86, 4412–4415 (1998)
3. Stoye, J., Moulton, V., Dress, A.W.: DCA: an efficient implementation of the divide-and-conquer approach to simultaneous multiple sequence alignment. Comput. Applic. Biosci. 13(6), 625–626 (1997)
4. Myers, E.W., Miller, W.: Multiple sequence alignment using simulated annealing. Comput. Appl. Biosci. 4(1), 11–17 (1988)
5. Lawrence, C., Altschul, S.F., Boguski, M., Liu, J., Neuwald, A., Wooton, J.: Detecting subtle sequence signals: a Gibbs sampling strategy for multiple alignment. Science 262, 208–214 (1993)
6. Isokawa, M., Wayama, M., Shimizu, T.: Multiple sequence alignment using a genetic algorithm. Genome Inform. 7, 176–177 (1996)
7. Notredame, C., Higgins, D.G.: SAGA: sequence alignment by genetic algorithm. Nucl. Acids Res. 24(8), 1515–1524 (1996)

8. Goldberg, D.E.: Genetic Algorithm in Search, Optimization, and Machine Learning. Addison-Wesley, New York (1989)
9. Kolen, A., Pesch, E.: Genetic local search in combinatorial optimization. Discr. Appl. Math. Combin. Oper. Res. Comput. Sci. 48, 273–284 (1994)
10. Plate-Forme Bio-Informatique de Strasbourg, http://bips.u-strasbg.fr/fr/Products/Databases/BAliBASE/bali_score.c

An Analysis on the Park-and-Ride Travel Selection from the Perspective of Bottleneck Theory

Chunping Hu[1], Jianfeng Liu[2], Yilin Ma[2], and Jing Wang[2]

[1] Traffic and Transportation School of Beijing Jiaotong University
liujf78@sohu.com
[2] Beijing Transportation Research Center, Fengtai Liu li qiao nan lu jia 9, Shou Fa Da Sha A 506, Beijing China
ljf@bjtrc.org.cn, ma.191@osu.edu, wangj@bjtrc.org.cn

Abstract. This paper is about Beijing's rail transit network, which, as a connector between urban center and peripheral areas, has attracted many residents to travel by subway feeder buses. In addition, the terminals of this network have been furnished with Park-and-Ride (P&R) lots, which have formed a P&R system of a feeder-car organization for rail transit. The paper summarizes P&R experiences from around the world, as well as the characteristics and scale of the rail transit network in Beijing. Next, a model of P&R travel mode selection based on road bottlenecks is created. In addition, the P&R demand at Tiantongyuan, a terminal station of Beijing Subway 5, is predicted. The paper is a useful reference for P&R construction and the analysis of public-transit attraction.

Keywords: bottleneck theory; P&R (Park-and-Ride); subway terminal.

1 Foreword

The feeder mode optimization study of Beijing's rail transit is intended to enhance the connection between rail transit travel and car travel in the areas peripheral to the urban center. This is to create a P&R system and induce commuters to take public transit to and from their work. In this paper, we analyze how to enhance the P&R planning, construction, and utilization at large stations in the subway network based on the experiences from around the world, as well as the characteristics and scale of Beijing city.

P&R facilities are mainly classified by their location and function.

(1) Location-based classification of P&R facilities: Beijing's P&R facilities are geographically classified into satellite facilities, near-distance facilities, mid-distance facilities, and remote facilities based on the zoning of parking policies. Refer to Table 1 for details.
(2) Function-based classification of P&R facilities: P&R facilities are generally classified based on their functions to determine the criteria of site selection and analyze their suitability on the construction phase. P&R facilities with different

H. Tan and M. Zhou (Eds.): CSE 2011, Part I, CCIS 201, pp. 241–249, 2011.

functions can be used to meet the varied land-using characteristics and parking policies in different regions. In Beijing, the P&R facilities may be classified into four types by their functions, namely, informal P&R lots, joint use P&R lots, park-and-pool lots, and public transit center P&R lots.

Table 1. Location-based classification of P&R facilities

Type of facilities	Geographic scope
Satellite P&R facilities	An area of 62km2 at the perimeter of old urban area and CBD (Central Business District)
Near-distance P&R facilities	An area that is 6-9km away from the old urban area
Mid-distance P&R facilities	An area that is 9-20km away from the old urban area
Remote P&R facilities	An area out of the fifth ring road and 20km away from the old urban area

In this paper, our focus of study is to analyze the P&R demand created by the attraction of urban express public transit, which is mainly composed of rail transit, at the congested road bottlenecks in urban peripheral areas. It also analyzes the demand-supply relationship of near-distance P&R facilities by illustrating the P&R facilities in an urban peripheral area surrounding Tiantongyuan subway terminal.

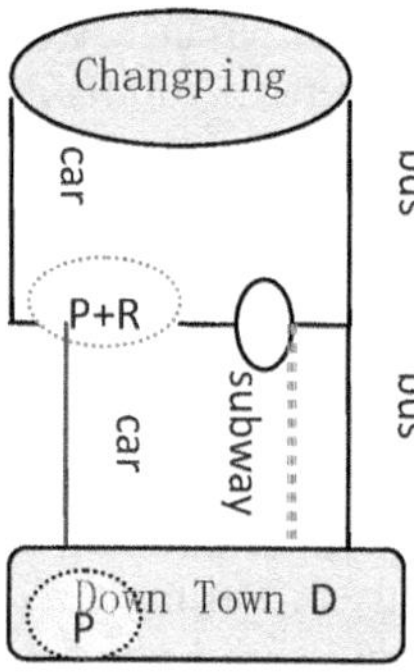

Fig. 1. Traffic model choice

2 Theoretical P&R Analysis at Bottlenecks

From the perspective of bottleneck theory, parking lots are furnished at road bottlenecks, where car travelers may choose either to wait in a queue or park their cars and ride by subways or other public transit vehicles. We use a Logit stochastic equilibrium selection model to study how people would choose between private vehicles and subways at peak periods under the rigid demand by examining the Tiantongyuan North Station on Beijing Subway 5. Specifically, we assume that a road is connected to the subway line to form multiple combinations to enter the urban center from Changping District of Beijing. Every morning, travelers depart from their living area 0 in Changping District, and go to work at their work place D in the urban center. The Li - Tang (Lishuiqiao – Xiaotangshan) Road in parallel to the subway station is a bottleneck and a P&R lot is available near the subway. There is also a lot at D. The travelers may choose from one of the three transport modes: 1. They may drive their cars all the way to the work place; 2. They may directly arrive at the work place by the subway; and 3. They may first drive their cars to the bottleneck, park the cars, and ride the subway to the work place. Refer to Table 1 for details.

2.1 Basic Assumptions and Definition of Symbols

Suppose a simple transport network consisting of the residence place O and work place D, which are connected to each other by a road. The network is served by three transport modes, namely private cars (Mode 1), buses (Mode 2), and rail transit (Mode 3). Every morning, there are N travelers departing from O to go to work at work place D. These travelers include N1 travelers choosing private cars, N2 choosing buses, and N3 choosing to first drive cars and then ride the rail transit. Suppose the road ingress is a bottleneck.

To facilitate our description, the following symbols are introduced:

α- Expense of unit time of travel
β- Expense of unit time of early arrival
γ - Expense of unit time of late arrival
λ-Influence coefficient of buses to cars
P - Parking charge at work place
D - Passengers carried by each bus
H -Departure interval of buses
F_{bus}-Bus fare
F_{sub}-Rail transit fare
π -Un it congestion cost
g(N)-Congestion function related to the number of persons N
s_1 -Traffic capacity through the bottleneck
s_2 -Conveying capacity of buses
t^* -Ideal instant of arrival
t_0 -Departure instant of traveler who will arrive at the destination at instant t^*
T_f-Free riding time on road
t_i^q -Earliest departure instant of mode i
t_i^{q*}-Latest departure instant of mode i
$t_w(t)$-Road queuing time of travelers departing at instant i
C_1 -Variable cost of bus operation
C_2 -Variable cost of rail transit operation
F_1 -Fixed cost of bus operation
F_2 -Fixed cost of rail transit operation

2.2 Cost Analysis of Travel Modes Based on Bottleneck Theory

(1) Car travel

Congestion can only occur at road bottlenecks, where queue appears if vehicles arrive at a rate of s1. In such a case, the O-D riding duration T(t) = Free riding duration on road + Road queuing time of travelers departing at instant t, i.e.:

$$T(t) = T_f + T_W(t) \tag{1}$$

Assume a peak period of $[t_1{}^q, t_1{}^{q^*}]$. The traveling expense of each car traveler consists of the time consumption, the delay expense of early or late arrival for job, the fuel expense, and the daily parking charge at the work place.

$$C_1(t) = \begin{cases} \alpha T(t) + \beta(t^* - T(t) - t) + F_{car} + P) & t \in [t_1^q, t_0] \\ \alpha T(t) + \gamma\big(t - t^* + T(t)\big) + F_{car} + P) & t \in [t_0, t_1^q] \end{cases} \tag{2}$$

t* is the ideal instant of arrival, $t + T(t)$ is the departure instant + riding duration. Therefore, $t - t^* - T(t)$ is the time of early arrival; and $t + T(t) - t^*$ is the time of late arrival.

Because travelers always expect to minimize their traveling expense, they will choose the travel time by weighing between the riding duration and delay expense. If no traveler can reduce his/her traveling expense by changing the departure time, the traffic flow on the road is balanced. All travelers departing during the peak period will have the same traveling expense as one another.

The first and last travelers will not queue, while the travelers departing during the peak period will certainly queue. The road bottleneck will run in full load throughout the peak period, which will last:

$$t_1{}^{q^*} - t_1{}^q = N_1 + \lambda(t_1{}^{q^*} - t_1{}^q) / H)$$

$t_1{}^{q^*} - t_1{}^q * s_1$ is the total passing persons during the peak period and $t_1{}^{q^*} - t_1{}^q / H$ is the number of departing buses, which is multiplied by λ the influence coefficient of buses to cars, to obtain the total number of passengers carried by buses. If these passengers are added to the demand quantity of cars, we get the total passing persons. Therefore,

$$t_1{}^{q^*} - t_1{}^q = N_1 / (s_1 - \lambda / H) \tag{3}$$

The first traveler only bears the delay expense of early arrival as a result of advance departure, as well as the expense of free riding. His/her travel expense should be:

$$C_1{}^q = c_1(t_1{}^q) = \alpha T_f + \beta(t^* - T_f - t_1{}^q) + \pi g(N_2) + F_{car} + P \tag{4}$$

The last traveler only bears the delay expense of late arrival as a result of postponed departure, as well as the expense of free riding. His/her travel expense should be

$$C_1{}^{q^*} = c_1(t_1{}^{q^*}) = \alpha T_f + \gamma(t_1{}^q + T_f - t^*) + F_{car} + P \tag{5}$$

Because all travelers will have the same travel expense when the traffic flow reaches a balance, we can get the following results from formula (3) ~ (5):

$$t_1^q = t^* - \gamma/(\beta+\gamma)\ [\ N_1/(s_1-\lambda/H)]-Tf \tag{6}$$

$$t_1^{q^*} = t^* + \beta/(\beta+\gamma)[\ N_1/(s_1-\lambda/H)]-T_f \tag{7}$$

Therefore, the car travel expense is:

$$C_1 = \alpha(t_1^{q^*}) = \alpha T_f + \beta\gamma/(\beta+\gamma)[N1/(s_1-\lambda/H)] + F_{car} + P \tag{8}$$

(2)Bus travel

The total travel expense of each bus traveler includes the underway time expense, delay expense, expense of waiting time and fare. This paper assumes that the travel expense of bus travelers consist of time consumption (including the riding time, walking time, and bus-waiting time), fare, delay expense, and the expense caused by body-contact congestion.

Because buses and private cars share the same roads, they have to consume the same queuing time as one another at road bottlenecks. In addition, because travelers will travel during the peak period in the morning, the traveling buses are fully loaded. The congestion expense caused by congestion is expressed with $g(N_2)$.

Therefore, the bus travel expense may be expressed as:

$$C_2(t) = \begin{cases} \alpha T(t) + \beta(t^* - T(t) - t) + \pi g(N_2 + F_{bus} & t\epsilon[t_2^q, t_0] \\ \alpha T(t) + \gamma(t - t^* + T(t)) + \pi g(N_2 + F_{bus} & t\epsilon[t_{0,} t_2^{q^*}] \end{cases} \tag{9}$$

Bus travelers, again, have to select their travel time. If they choose to depart in advance, they can easily take buses and arrive at their work places because there are fewer persons waiting for buses and fewer vehicles on the road. However, delay expense of early arrival will be caused. Traveling at the mid-period may create no delay expense, but congestion expense caused by congestion has to be born. Some travelers choose to depart at a later time to avoid congestion and queuing on the road. This creates the delay expense of late arrival. As travelers weigh between the congestion expense and delay expense by selecting the departure time, the traffic flow will gradually be balanced.

If a bus departs at instant t_2^q, travelers only incur the delay expense of early arrival, the time expense of free bus riding, and the fare. Therefore, their travel expense is:

$$C_2^q = \alpha T_f + \beta(t^* - T_f - t_2^q) + \pi g(N_2) + F_{bus} \tag{10}$$

If a bus departs at instant t_2^q ,travelers only incur the delay expense of late arrival, the time expense of free bus riding, and the fare. Therefore, their travel expense is:

$$C_2^{q^*} = \alpha T_f + \gamma(t_2^{q^*} + T_f - t^*) + \pi g(N_2) + F_{bus} \tag{11}$$

Now we are studying the bus travel during a peak period $[t_2^q, t_2^{q^*}]$,and all buses departing during such a period are fully loaded, therefore:

$$t_2^{q^*}-t_2^q=N_2H/d \qquad (12)$$

Because $(t_2^{q^*}-t_2^q)/H$ is the number of running buses, N_2 is equal to the number of running buses. Because all bus travelers will have the same travel expense at a balanced state, we can obtain the following results from formula (10) ~ (12):

$$t_2^q=t^*-\gamma/(\beta+\gamma)(N_2/s_2)-T_f \qquad (13)$$

$$t_2^{q^*}=t^*+\beta/(\beta+\gamma)(N_2/s_2)-T_f \qquad (14)$$

The travel expense by ground public transit is obtained as follows:

$$C_2 =\alpha T_f +\beta\gamma/(\beta+\gamma)(N_2H/d)+ \pi g(N_2)+F_{cbus} \qquad (15)$$

(3)Rail transit travel

Because the rail transit mode features large capacity, high speed, high punctuality rate, and no restriction by the road bottlenecks, the penalty expense of early (late) arrival can be ignored. Therefore, the time consumption only includes the free riding time. The time that takes to arrive at and leave stations and to wait for trains is assumed to be a constant included in the free riding time. As a result, if a traveler chooses the rail transit mode, the expense that he/she incurs should be composed of the time consumption, fare, and the expense created by body-contact congestion. The expense of all travelers taking rail transit is expressed as:

$$C_3=\alpha TF+\pi g(N_3)+F_{sub} \qquad (16)$$

3 Predicting P&R Demand Based on Logit Stochastic Equilibrium Model

3.1 Background of Tiantongyuan P&R

A P&R lot is available at Tiantongyuan North Station, the terminal station of Subway 5. The lot serves the Tiantongyuan zone, as well as the Changping zone to the north. According to its network of backbone roads, Changping District can be divided into four traffic sub-areas as shown in Figure 2.

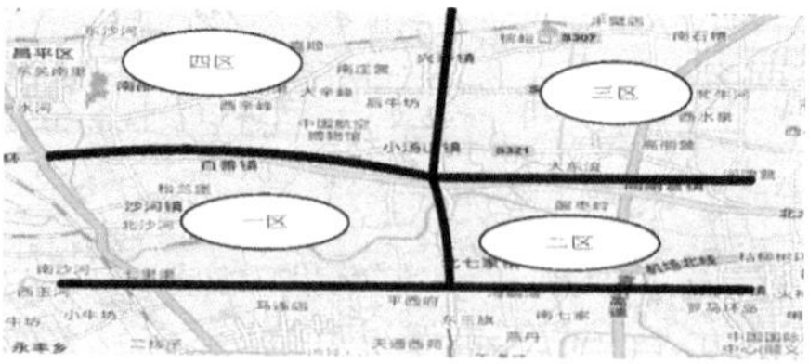

Fig. 2. Traffic sub-zoning in Changping District

The commuting passenger flow by cars from the traffic sub-zones in Changping District to the traffic sub-zones in the urban center composes the OD distribution of passenger flow through the P&R facilities at Tiantongyuan subway terminal station. The generated traffic volume N0 of the OD distribution can be obtained by investigation. Next, the generated traffic volume N in future years can be predicted based on the annual growth rate of cars in Changping District. This should be the total demand of car travel within the attracting range of the P&R facilities at Tiantongyuan terminal in future years. Given several value ranges of N, the P&R demand is analyzed using the Logit stochastic equilibrium selection model of P&R at the bottleneck under fixed demand.

A general utility function is used to depict the utility of each travel mode, i.e.

$$U_i=U-C_i+\varepsilon_i,\quad i=1,2,3 \tag{17}$$

where, U is a constant that represents the utility that the traveler can get from one travel, such as his/her daily average income; and random item ε_i represents the estimation error resulting from incorrect information or other factors. Assume that ε_i are independent and identically distributed Gumbel variables with a mean value of zero. It can be proven that the selection of traffic mode follows the following Logit stochastic equilibrium model: $N_i = N\, e^{-\theta C_i} \Big/ \sum_{j=1,2,3} e^{-\theta C_j}$ (18)

where, θ is a positive parameter about the variance of the stochastic variable. Larger θ means a lower error of traveler's understanding on the travel utility and a more tendency to select the travel mode with the lowest cost. Set $\delta=\beta\gamma/(\beta+\gamma)$. The costs of the three modes from the residence place to the work place are :

$$\begin{aligned} C_1 &=\alpha T_f +\delta N_1/(s_1-\lambda/H)+ F_{car}+P \\ C_2 &=\alpha T_f +\delta N_2\, H/d+\pi g(N_2)+ F_{bus} \\ C_3 &=\alpha T_f +\delta N_2\, H/d+\pi g(N_3) +F_{sub} \end{aligned} \tag{19}$$

If N is given and all cost parameters are known, the number of persons of each travel mode can be obtained using the above model formula and the cost function of the previous section.

3.2 Parameter Assignment of Bottleneck Model

α=20RMB/h, β=15 RMB /h, γ=30 RMB /h, λ=30, d=50ps/veh, H=[1/12,1/6]h, F_{bus}=RMB[0,2.6], F_{sub}=RMB2, S_2=50ps/vehicle, T_f=2/3=0.67, F_{car}=RMB5. As such, $\delta=\beta\gamma/(\beta+\gamma)=10$, and $\theta=0.5$. As seen from the current situation, car travelers will seldom get rid of their cars and take buses. Therefore, we set the bus congestion expense as $\pi g(N_2)$= 50000; $\pi g(N_3)$= 30; P=0

$$C_1 =\alpha T_f +\delta N_1/(s_1-\lambda/H)+ F_{car}+P=18.4+10^* N_1/(s_1-180)$$
$$C_2 =\alpha T_f +\delta N_2\, H/d+ F_{bus}=50010+N_2 /30$$
$$C_3=\alpha T_f +\delta N_2\, H/d+\pi g(N_2)\, F_{bus}$$

$$X = \frac{N \times e^{\frac{-5N_1}{s_1-180}-9.2}}{e^{\frac{-5N_1}{s_1-180}-9.2} + e^{\frac{-N_2}{60}-25005} + e^{-21}} \qquad Y = \frac{N \times e^{\frac{-N_2}{60}-25005}}{e^{\frac{-5N_1}{s_1-180}-9.2} + e^{\frac{-N_2}{60}-25005} + e^{-21}}$$

3.3 Solution of Logit Stochastic Equilibrium Selection Model of P&R at Bottlenecks under Fixed Demand

By simplifying the known parameters, the three equations of Formula (19) can be simplified to:

$$C_1=A+BN_1+C \tag{20}$$

$$C_2=D+EN_2+F \tag{21}$$

$$C_3=G \tag{22}$$

Set θ=Q. The following results can be obtained from formulas (18) and (20)-(22):

$$N_1 = \frac{N \times e^{-Q\times BN_1 - Q(A+C)}}{e^{-Q\times BN_1 - Q(A+C)} + e^{-Q\times EN_2 - Q(D+F)} + e^{-QG}} \tag{23}$$

$$N_2 = \frac{N \times e^{-Q\times EN_2 - Q(D+F)}}{e^{-Q\times BN_1 - Q(A+C)} + e^{-Q\times EN_2 - Q(D+F)} + e^{-QG}} \tag{24}$$

$$N_3=N-N_1-N_2 \tag{25}$$

Solving steps:

(1) Define parameters N1, N2, and m.
(2) Conduct iteration, with the N1 and N2 values ranging from 1 to N.
(3) Continue iteration until | (N1-X)| + | (N2-Y)| <m.

Table 2 illustrates the calculation result at N=3000.

Table 2. P&R demand of different S_1 at N=3000

N_1, cars (Capita)	1856	2611	2929	2984	2993
Buses	0	0	0	0	0
N_3, P&R (capita)	1144	389	71	16	7
S_1	1000	1500	2000	2500	3000

4 Analyzing the Conclusion of P&R Demand

Li-Tang Road has one lane in each direction in Tiantongyuan area. The distance between vehicles is about 1m during peak periods. The length of a car is about2m, and its speed is about 5km/s. As such, the traffic capacity is about 5,000/(1+2)=1666≈1500. See Figure 3 for the P&R demand.

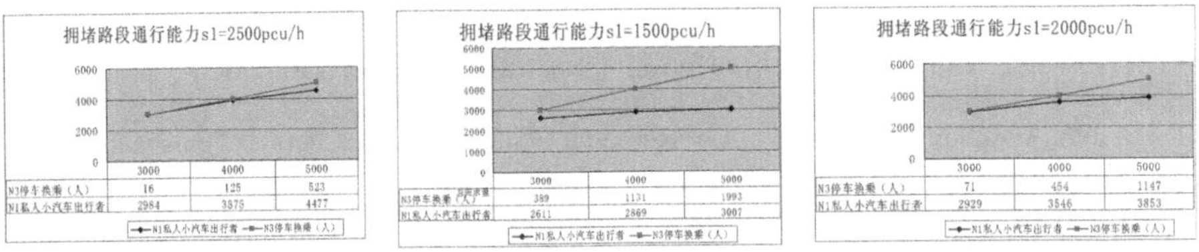

Fig. 3. P&R demand with different demand scale N and traffic capacity S1

Furthermore, given a total demand of 3,000 at P=10, the P&R demand should be 389 lots. If the total demand N increases to 4,000 persons while the traffic capacity remains 1,500, the P&R demand will increase to 1,131 lots; that is, 742 lots should be additionally provided. P&R demand will more significantly increase as parameters P, S1, and N change. Therefore, the government should make scientific and logical decisions to coordinate between the expansion of congested road bottlenecks and the scale of P&R demand.

References

1. Kuan, S.N., Ong, H.L., Ng, K.M.: Solving the feeder bus network design problem by genetic algorithms and ant colony optimization. Advances in Engineering Software (7), 35–359 (2006)
2. Shoaib Chowdhury, Md., Chien, S.I.-J.: Optimization of Transfer Coordination for Intermodal Transit Network. J. Transport Research Board 80th Annual Meeting (January 7-11, 2001)
3. Demetsky, M.J., Hoel, L.A. Virkler, M.R.: A Transit Station Design Process. J. TRR 662 (1978)
4. Korf, J.L., Demetsky, M.J.: Analysis of Rapid Transit access Mode Choice. J. TRR 817 (1981)
5. Yao, X.: A Study on the Coordination of Lines and Networks between Rapid Rail Transit and Conventional Public Transit in Cities. Chang'an University, Xi'an (2005)
6. Wang, Y., Zhang, X.: Analyzing the Selection of Commuting Transfer Mode in Urban Areas Neighboring Subway Terminals. J. World Railw. (6), 39–42 (2008)
7. Zhang, X.: Urban Parking Planning and Management, pp. 122–123. China Architecture & Building Press, Beijing (2006)

Simulation Analysis of Traction Control System for Four-Wheel-Drive Vehicle Using Fuzzy-PID Control Method

Zhixin Liu, Renjun Wan, Yongwan Shi, and Hong Chen

China Automotive Technology and Research Center, P.O. Box No. 10 Tianshannanlu, Chenglindao, Hedong District, 300162 Tianjin, China
{Liuzhixin,Wanrenjun,Shiyongwan,Chenhong}@catarc.ac.cn

Abstract. A dynamic model of four-wheel-drive vehicle was established and the Traction Control System (TCS) algorithm based on fuzzy-PID control was realized through rectifying the output torque of engine in real time and then switching parameter of fuzzy-PID controller was studied. The fuzzy logic controller was designed with MATLAB fuzzy control toolbox. Contrastive simulation has been carried out with SIMULINK, which has the better results than those based on common fuzzy control in controlling effect.

Keywords: Fuzzy-PID Control, Traction Control System, Slip Ratio, Four wheel drive.

1 Introduction

Traction Control System (TCS) is a new kind of active safety control system, which can improve a driver's ability to control a vehicle under adverse conditions, such as in wet or icy road, and control the slip ratios of driving wheels work in the optimum traction performance conditions in the real-time so as to maximize the traction force between the vehicle's tires and the road. At present, logic threshold method based on tests is widely used in TCS, but its control algorithm is too complicated, furthermore, it needs lots of tests to acquire the thresholds. Therefore, lots of scholars began to use different control methods to research on TCS[1～4], such as PID control, fuzzy control, and optimal control and so on.

Because of the strong nonlinearity of vehicle system, the controllers based on mathematic models are very difficult to design with traditional control theory. Though fuzzy control method has lots of advantage to be suit for TCS design compared with other methods, common fuzzy control cannot eliminate the steady state error efficiently and its control effects are inferior to those with little error by PID control. In this paper, a TCS algorithm based on Fuzzy-PID control method was presented and with two kinds of control methods contrastive simulation analyses were investigated on the accelerative process of a given four-wheel-driven vehicle.

2 Four-Wheel-Drive Vehicle Dynamic Model

The four-wheel-drive vehicle dynamics used for simulation included an engine model, a transmission system model, a one-wheel rotational model and a simple linear vehicle model. Only longitudinal dynamics are considered in this paper.

H. Tan and M. Zhou (Eds.): CSE 2011, Part I, CCIS 201, pp. 250–257, 2011.

2.1 Model of the Engine

The output torque of the engine is:

$$M_e = \frac{M_s e^{-sT_1}}{1+sT_2} \tag{1}$$

Where M_s is the steady torque under this throttle opening, T1 and T2 are time constants, s is the operator of Laplace transform.

2.2 Model of the Transmission System

Kinetically analysis on rotational masses including of engine, gearbox, power transfer, front and rear transmission shafts, front and rear main retarder, front and rear differential, we can obtain the angular acceleration of the differential shell:

$$\dot{\omega}_0 = (M_e i_g i_{fd} i_0 \eta - \sum_{i=1}^{4} F_{xi} R_i - \sum_{i=1}^{4} F_{zi} f_i R_i) / I_{eq} \tag{2}$$

Where F_{xi} are driving forces provided from ground (i=1,2,3,4 corresponding to the wheels in front and left, front and right, rear and left, rear and right, respectively); i_g, i_{fd}, i_0 are the transmission ratios of gearbox, power transfer, and main retarder; R_i are radius of tires, F_{zi} are loads of wheels; f_i are rolling resistance coefficients; I_{eq} is the equivalent moment of inertia of the transmission system

$$I_{eq} = I_e \cdot i_g^2 \cdot i_{fd}^2 \cdot i_0^2 + I_g \cdot i_{fd}^2 \cdot i_0^2 + (I_{fd} + I_c) \cdot i_0^2 + 2I_0 \tag{3}$$

Where $I_e, I_g, I_{fd}, I_c, I_0$ are the moments of inertia of engine, gearbox, power transfer, transmission shaft, main retarder respectively, From kinetic analysis of each driving wheel, we can obtain angular accelerations of each driving wheel.

$$\begin{cases} \dot{\omega}_1 = \dot{\omega}_0 + [(F_{x2}R_2 + F_{z2}f_2R_2) - (F_{x1}R_1 + F_{z1}f_1R_1)]/(2I_{w1}) \\ \dot{\omega}_2 = \dot{\omega}_0 + [(F_{x1}R_1 + F_{z1}f_1R_1) - (F_{x2}R_2 + F_{z2}f_2R_2)]/(2I_{w2}) \\ \dot{\omega}_3 = \dot{\omega}_0 + [(F_{x4}R_4 + F_{z4}f_4R_4) - (F_{x3}R_3 + F_{z3}f_3R_3)]/(2I_{w3}) \\ \dot{\omega}_4 = \dot{\omega}_0 + [(F_{x3}R_3 + F_{z3}f_3R_3) - (F_{x4}R_4 + F_{z4}f_4R_4)]/(2I_{w4}) \end{cases} \tag{4}$$

2.3 Tire Model

The dual-line tire model was adopted in this paper. The adhesion coefficient of the ground could be computed as follows:

$$\mu = \begin{cases} \mu_h S / S_T & S \le S_T \\ (\mu_h - \mu_g S_T)/(1 - S_T) - (\mu_h - \mu_g)/(1 - S_T)\, S & S > S_T \end{cases} \tag{5}$$

Where μ_h the maximum adhesion coefficient, μ_g is the adhesion coefficient when wheel is skidded, $S_i = 1 - V_{xi} / (\omega_i \cdot R_i)$ is the slip of drive wheel, S_T is the optimum slip value, V_{xi} is the velocity of each driving wheel.

2.4 Model of Full Vehicle

When the resistance of air, rolling resistances of tires , the effect of turning system and the effects of side motion and lateral swing motion were ignored, assuming that the model was just in longitudinal linear motion . The dynamic equation for a vehicle model was set up as follows:

$$m\dot{V}_x = \sum_{i=1}^{4} F_{xi} \tag{6}$$

3 Design of Fuzzy-PID Control Algorithm

As we know, Excessive slip of vehicle drive wheel resulted from the output torque of engine exceeded the adhesion limit between the tire and the ground. So TCS could be realized by properly reducing the output torque of vehicle engine reasonably. In this paper, we regulated the output torque of engine by controlling the throttle opening so that the driving slip could be controlled to round the expected value. The design of the Fuzzy-PID controller was when the values of the error of the slip ratio and the derivation of the error of the slip ratio were large, TCS system adopted fuzzy control so as to take advantage of the quick response and strong anti-jamming ability of fuzzy controller, conversely, TCS system adopted PID control so as to give play to the strong points of PID control, such as its good stead-state behavior and high precision.

3.1 Design of the Fuzzy Controller

A fuzzy controller with single variable and two dimensions was designed and we defined the error of the system as $E = S - S_T$ and the derivative of the error as $\dot{E} = dE / dt$. Where S is the actual slip, S_T is the target slip, here we set S_T = 0.2. In the fuzzy inference process both E and $\dot{E}$ were selected as the input linguist variables and $\triangle\theta$, the variable of throttle opening was selected as the output linguist variable. The defuzzification was performed with Mamdani maximum-minimum method and 42 control rules were designed. The all membership functions of the input language variable were taken as triangle format.

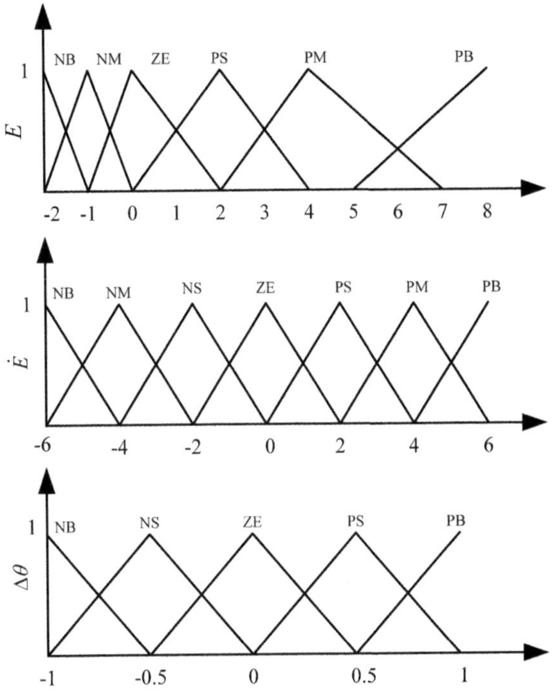

Fig. 1. Membership functions of E, $\dot{E}$ and $\Delta\theta$

Because the changing range of slip ratio is [0, 1], thus the changing range of E is [-0.2, 0.8], its universe was set as [-2, +8], and the universe of $\dot{E}$ was set as [-6, +6]. Six sub-items of E and Seven sub-items of $\dot{E}$ were chosen, that were "NB, NM, ZE, PS, PM, PB" and "NB, NM, NS, ZE, PS, PM, PB". The universe of the control variable of throttle opening $\triangle\theta$ was taken as [-1, 1], its sub-items were "NB, NS, ZE, PS, PB". The membership functions were all taken as triangular distribution, as shown in Fig. 1. According to the relationships among the slip error ,derivative of slip error and output torque of vehicle engine, together with the properties of TCS and the experience of manual control, aggregate of fuzzy logic control rules of variance of throttle opening were described for the TCS controller based on optimal target slip ratio shown in Table 1.

3.2 Design of the PID Controller

The error between actual slip and target slip was set as PID control object, and the throttle opening was set as output variable. According to the error of system, PID controller would calculate the output variable by regulating the output torque of the engine so as to keep the slip ratio at the round of the target slip ratio. Its calculation as follows:

Table 1. Table of fuzzy control rules

E	$\dot{E}$						
	NB	NM	NS	ZE	PS	PM	PB
NB	PB	PB	PB	PS	PS	PS	PS
NM	PB	PB	PB	PS	PS	ZE	ZE
ZE	PS	PS	PS	ZE	NS	NS	NS
PS	PS	ZE	ZE	ZE	NS	NS	NS
PM	NS	NB	NB	NB	NB	NB	NB
PB	NB	NB	NB	NB	NB	NB	NB

$$\begin{cases} u(t) = u(t-1) + \Delta u(t) \\ \Delta u(t) = k_p(E(t) - E(t-1)) + k_i E(t) + k_d(E(t) - 2E(t-1) + E(t-2)) \end{cases} \tag{7}$$

Where k_p 、 k_i 、 k_d were the proportional coefficient, integral coefficient and differential coefficient of PID controller, $E(t)$ was the error of slip ratio at t moment, $\Delta u(t)$ was the throttle opening at t moment.

3.3 Switching Index of Fuzzy-PID Controller

It was not only necessary to take into account the effect of the error, but also the derivative of the error when we determined the switch parameter, which would avoid overshoot of PID controller. Therefore, switching index was set as follows:

$$X = \frac{|E|}{E_m} + \frac{|\dot{E}|}{\dot{E}_m} < X_m \tag{8}$$

Where E_m and $\dot{E}_m$ were thresholds of the error and its derivative, X_m was the switching threshold, combining the simulations, we set $E_m = 0.02$, $\dot{E}_m = 0.75$, $X_m = 1.5$

4 Simulation Results and Analysis

The block diagram of the simulation model was shown in Fig. 2, and its principle was as follow: The initial throttle opening was given by accelerator pedal and the slip of driving wheels were calculated according to the model of vehicle; then the slip of driving wheel and its changing ratio were put into fuzzy-PID controller; the variance of throttle opening was obtained by the calculation of fuzzy-PID controller so that actual position of throttle could be obtained by summing it with the initial input of throttle; the adjusted engine torque was fed back to the vehicle system module, consequently the slip of driving wheels were regulated so as to make it towards its optimum value. The major parameters in the simulation were: m=4400kg; h=0.8m; R=0.42m; I_e=0.29kg.m^2; i_g=3.894; i_{fd}=0.19; I_w=2.86 kg.m^2, k1=10, k2=1and k3=100.

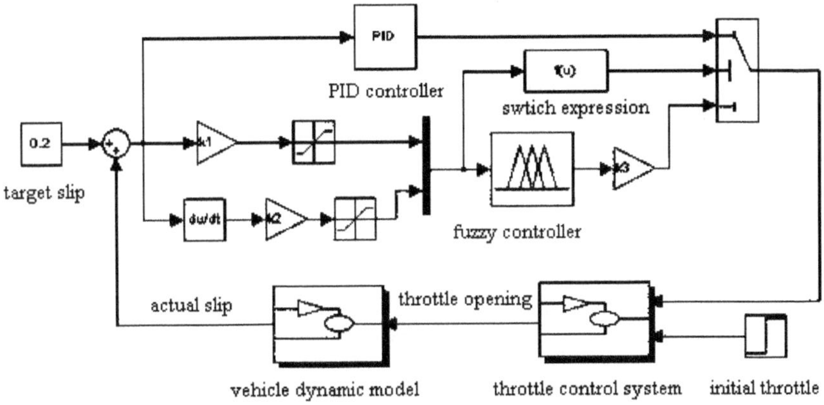

Fig. 2. Simulation model of TCS system

Two kinds of simulation conditions were: frozen road with adhesion coefficient 0.2 and split adhesion coefficient road (0.2/0.5); full load; the throttle was fully opened; the vehicle run straightly 5s by acceleration from startup; neglected the dynamic gear process of clutch. The simulation results were shown in Fig. 3~Fig.4. It showed that with the Fuzzy-PID controller, the control effect on the slip of driving wheel is superior to that with common fuzzy controller. The reason was the former could make full use of the advantages of these two kinds of control methods, which meant when in the phrase of big error, the slip could be controlled in the near of optimal value quickly with the robust of fuzzy control, then with PID control to diminish overshot. From Table 2, we easily found that the vehicle velocity at 5 second was 5.663m/s with Fuzzy common fuzzy control while it was 5.197m/s at 5s without TCS control, it increased about 8.2%, and traction forces of front driving wheel and rear driving wheel were all increased, approximately by 12% and 13.5% respectively, at the same time, the speed of the vehicle was 5.712m/s at 5s when with Fuzzy-PID control. The speed has been increased by 9.0%, and traction forces of front driving wheel and rear driving wheel were all increased, approximately by 13.2% and 14.5% respectively. As dissertated above, Fuzzy-PID control was superior to common fuzzy control in improving the kinetic property and traction property of vehicle.

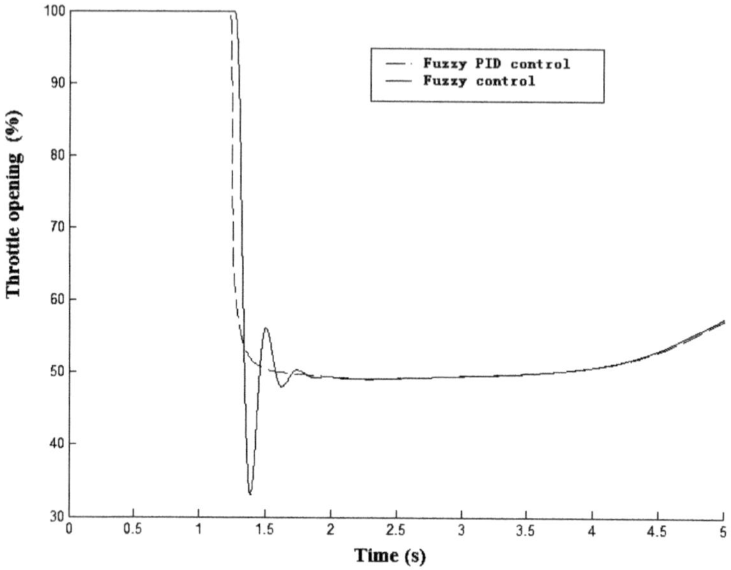

Fig. 3. Curves of throttle opening of engine with two control methods

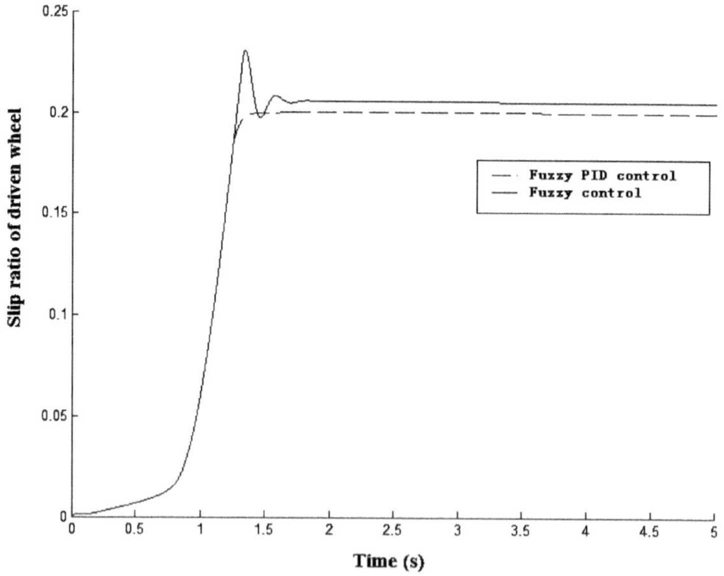

Fig. 4. Curves of slips of drive wheel with two control methods

Table 2. Vehicle dynamic characteristics at 5 s

working condition	Control methods	Vehicle speed(m/s)	Front wheel traction force (N)	Rear wheel traction force (N)
uniformity road (0.2)	Fuzzy control	5.663	906.3/906.3	1249.7/1249.7
	Fuzzy-PID	5.712	916.6/916.6	1261.3/1261.3
	No control	5.197	809.3/809.3	1101.1/1101.1
Split road (0.2/0.5)	Fuzzy control	5.425	898.7/895.5	1241.8/1238.7
	Fuzzy-PID	5.551	909.2/906.1	1253.6/1250.5
	No control	4.939	728.1/747.1	987.9/1006.9

5 Conclusions

In this paper, we built a model of the accelerative process of a four-wheel-drive vehicle, and a Traction Control System (TCS) based on fuzzy-PID control method was realized, which took the driving slip ratio as the control object. And dynamic simulation has been carried out with SIMULINK. Some of conclusions could be got from the simulation results as follows:

1) The simulation results shows that TCS based on fuzzy-PID control could quickly control the slip of driving wheel to its expected value so that the excessive spinning of driving wheels could be prevented effectively.
2) Fuzzy-PID control was superior to common fuzzy control in improving the kinetic property and traction property of vehicle.

References

1. Shin, M., Han, J.: Formalized Design Procedure for Networked Control Systems. SAE2007-01-1625
2. Si, L.: Anti skid system of vehicle—ABS and ASR. China Communications Press, Beijing (July 1996)
3. Liu, Z.: The control methods research of traction control system on NJ2045 off road vehicle and the exploitation of simulation software: (dissertation of master degree). Jilin University, Changchun (2003)
4. Cheok, K.C., Hoogterp, F.B.: Fuzzy Logic Approach to Traction Control Design. SAE960957

Neuron with Sliding-Mode Control for Nonlinear Systems

Yeong-Chin Chen[1], Lon-Chen Hung[2], and Shuh-Han Chao[2]

[1] Department of Computer Science and Information Engineering, Asia University, Taiwan
[2] Department of Computer Science and Multimedia Design, Taiwan Shoufu University, Taiwan
ycchenster@gmail.com

Abstract. In this paper, we present a sliding-mode control scheme for nonlinear systems which integrates an auto-tuning single neuron. The single neuron with an adaptive SMC controller is used to achieve adaptation. It is verified that this controller has few adjustable parameters, excellent robust performance and is adaptive.

Keywords: Neuron, Sliding-Mode, Nonlinear System.

1 Introduction

Generally, physical systems have certain non-linear and time-varying behaviours and various uncertainties and thus it is difficult to establish an appropriate model for controller design. In control applications, compensation for friction is the paradigm to achieve high-precision performance.The sliding-mode control theory has been developed and applied to closed-loop control systems for the last three decades [1-3]; it is commonly known as the sliding-mode control (SMC) and is a nonlinear control strategy that is well known for its robust characteristics. The essential characteristic of SMC is that the feedback signal is discontinuous, switching on one or more manifolds in state space. When the state crosses each discontinuity surface, the structure of the feedback system is altered. All motion in the neighborhood of the manifold is directed toward the manifold. Note that a sliding motion occurs in which the system state repeatedly crosses the switching surface. When the system states stay in the sliding surface, the equivalent control is capable of making the system stay in the surface.

The main feature of SMC is that it uses a high-speed switching control law to drive the system states from any initial state onto a user-specified surface in the state space, or switching surface, and keeps the state on the surface for all time. In the design of the sliding mode control law it is assumed that the control can be switched from one value to another infinitely fast [4]. However, this is impossible to achieve in practical systems because finite time delays are present for control computation, and limitations exist in the physical actuators. This chattering behavior is especially unacceptable in process control and thus has received considerable notice from the research community [7-11]. The Chattering phenomenon is a major shortcoming of SMC, which makes the control force unnecessarily large, leading to low control accuracy. There are two causes of chattering. Similarly to the systems in canonical

H. Tan and M. Zhou (Eds.): CSE 2011, Part I, CCIS 201, pp. 258–265, 2011.

form, chattering can be caused by fast dynamics which were ignored in the ideal model.

Improved generalization performance for error-based neural network learning can be obtained with techniques such as validation, pruning or constructive algorithms [12-13]. The methods are based on the principle that generalization is associated with the number of network weights. This study presents a hybrid auto-tuning neuron with a sliding-mode system for the tracking control of a nonlinear system. The aim of this study is to overcome some of the shortcomings of conventional robust controllers such as a model-based adaptive controller which requires the system dynamics in detail.

The proposed single neuron with a SMC scheme possesses two eminent advantages: (1) it guarantees the stability of the controlled system, and (2) no constrained conditions and prior knowledge of the controlled plant is required in the design process. Efforts have been made in developing control schemes to achieve the control object. As a result, it is shown that the proposed method is feasible and effective.

2 System Description

In this paper, we consider a class of SISO n-th order nonlinear systems in the following form,

$$x^{(n)} = f(x,...,x^{(n-1)}) + g(x,...,x^{(n-1)})u + d(t)$$

$$y = x \tag{1}$$

where f and g are unknown real continuous nonlinear functions of states, $g \neq 0$, d is disturbance, u is control input and y is the system output [1-3]. Let the control objective be the force of state vector **x**. The PID control tunes the controller parameters for any control system in order to attain the optimum results for its output [8,9]. To overcome this time problem, the techniques provide perfect approximation to the actual plant due to the usage of simpler plant, added to other computation methods [11-15].

$$u(t) = k_p e(t) + k_i \int_0^t e(\tau)d\tau + k_d \frac{d}{dt}e(t) \tag{2}$$

where $u(t)$ denotes the plant input gains, e is system error, k_p , k_i , k_d are proportional, integral, respectively.

3 The Neuro-PID Control Design

The single neuron adaptive manner produces the functions of adaptation and self-adjustment by tuning the weights. The method of modulating the parameter is the center of single neuron and the structure of the single neuron controller is as shown in Fig. 1 [8-11]:

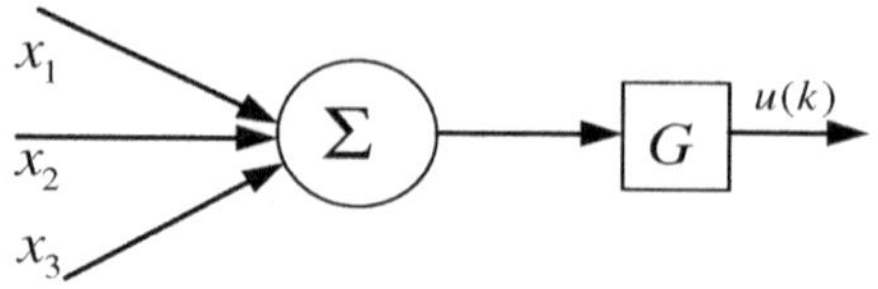

Fig. 1. The single neuron structure

The structure of single neuron PID control force is:

$$u(k) = G\sum_{i=1}^{3} w_i(k)x_1(k) \tag{3}$$

In order to derive the self-tuning neuron control algorithm, we will define the mathematical notations of the neuron model, as shown in Fig. 2.

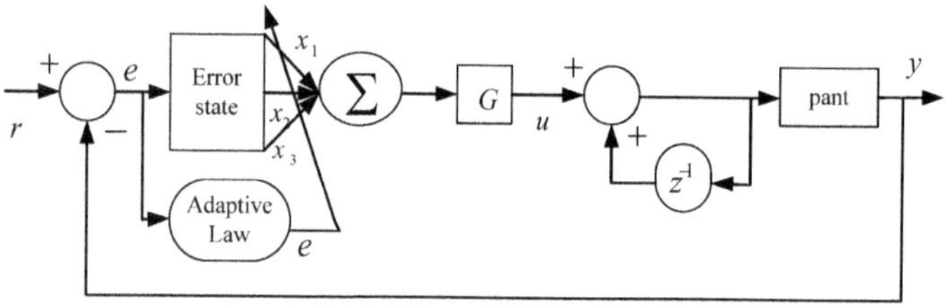

Fig. 2. The neuron with PID control

The quadratic performance index of input error in (4) and the gradient descent method is then applied to find the updated algorithms for output weight w_i, node center and radius parameter stated as follows [12]:

$$e(k) = \frac{1}{2}[y_r(k) - y(k)]^2 \tag{4}$$

By (4) lead to the weighting w_i of update law

$$\begin{aligned}\Delta w_i(k+1) &= w_i(k+1) - w_i(k)\\ &= \eta_i e(k+1)\frac{\partial y(k+1)\partial u(k)}{\partial u(k)\partial w_i(k)}\end{aligned} \tag{5}$$

where η_i is learning rate. By (4) substitution (5) to obtain

$$\Delta w_i(k+1) = \eta_P G e(k+1) e(k)\frac{\partial y(k+1)}{\partial u(k)} \tag{6}$$

$$\Delta w_2(k+1)=\eta_I Ge(k+1)\Delta e(k)\frac{\partial y(k+1)}{\partial u(k)} \tag{7}$$

$$\Delta w_3(k+1)=\eta_D Ge(k+1)\Delta^2 e(k)\frac{\partial y(k+1)}{\partial u(k)} \tag{8}$$

where η_p , η_i , η_d are proportional, integral, and derivative gains, respectively, $\partial y(k+1)/\partial u(k)$ is an unknown function, G is a positive value and $sign[\partial y(k+1)/\partial u(k)]$ to replace [12-15]

$$sign(x)=\begin{cases}+1 & x\ \geq 0\\ -1 & x\ <0\end{cases} \tag{9}$$

then

$$x_1(k)=e(k) \tag{10}$$

$$x_2(k)=\Delta e(k)=e(k)-e(k-1) \tag{11}$$

$$x_3(k)=\Delta^2 e(k)=e(k)-2e(k-1)+e(k-2) \tag{12}$$

The structure of single neuron PID controller is shown in Fig. 2, where $y_r(k)$ is the reference signal, $x_1(k)$ is the input, G is a proportion coefficient, $e(k)$ is the error, and $y(k)$ is the output feedback [8-11]. The single neuron has a strong self tuning and adjustment capacity. The coefficient tuning in the PID method is combined with a single neuron, which can solve the problem of the PID coefficient tuning and can improve dynamic performance of PID algorithm by the weight adjustment of the single neural to adapt the variation of network traffic on-line. The control output of the neuron is [13,14]

$$u(k)=u(k-1)+k\sum_{i=1}^{3} w_i'(k)x_i(k) \tag{13}$$

The single neuron with PID controller has the capability of self-adaptation and self-learning and the weighting update law is [12,13]:

$$w_1(k)=w_1(k-1)+\eta_p z(k)u(k)x_1(k) \tag{14}$$

$$w_2(k)=w_2(k-1)+\eta_i z(k)u(k)x_2(k) \tag{15}$$

$$w_3(k)=w_3(k-1)+\eta_d z(k)u(k)x_3(k) \tag{16}$$

Compared with a traditional PID controller, the weights $w_1(k)$, $w_2(k)$, $w_3(k)$ correspond to the integral factor, proportional and differential coefficient of PID controller separately.

The proposed control based on SMC to adjust weighting of the neuron. According to the certainty equivalent controller (14), (15) and (16) can only be rewritten as:

$$w_1(k) = w_1(k-1) + k_p z(k)u(k)\sigma_1(k) \tag{17}$$

$$w_2(k) = w_2(k-1) + k_i z(k)u(k)\sigma_2(k) \tag{18}$$

$$w_3(k) = w_3(k-1) + k_d z(k)u(k)\sigma_3(k) \tag{19}$$

where

$$\sigma_1(k) = s(k) = \lambda e(k) + e(k-1) \tag{20}$$

$$\sigma_2(k) = s(k) - s(k-1) \tag{21}$$

$$\sigma_3(k) = s(k) - 2s(k-1) + s(k-2) \tag{22}$$

A switching surface in the error space is defined as $s(k)$. The problem of tracking error being equal to system states reach sliding surface $s=0$, and then move along the sliding surface when $t>0$. In order to prove the stability and robustness of the proposed controller, the following stability theorem is considered by the quadratic performance index (4) base on SMC, and the final formula of single neuron weights adjusted is (17)-(22).

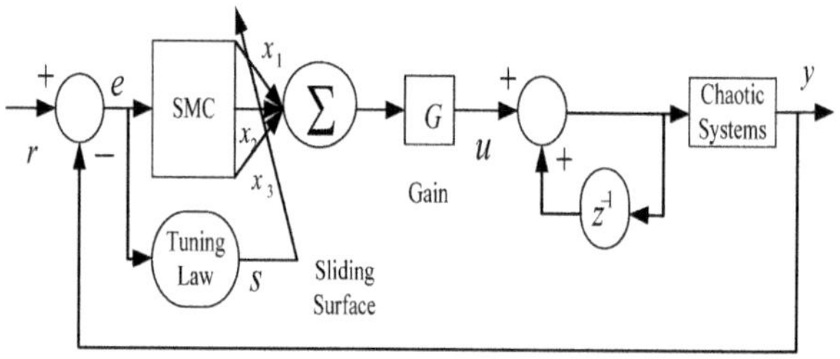

Fig. 3. The neuron with SMC Control

The whole on-line training algorithm only needs to adjust the connect weights between the hidden unit and output unit. It is easy to reduce the computation and dynamic response time.

4 The Computer Simulation and Result

Consider the following a nonlinear system, as follows:

$$y(k) = 0.368y(k-1) + 0.26y(k-2) + 0.10u(k-1) + 0.632u(k-2) \tag{23}$$

The input signal of a nonlinear system is a square wave $r_{in}(k) = 0.5\,\mathrm{sgn}(\sin(4\pi t))$, the sampling time is 1ms. Simulation results are shown in Figs. 4-9. The simulated neuron with PID control, the tracking for square function is shown in Fig.4, the error signal of sate trajectory is shown in Fig. 5, the trend of the control force is shown in Fig. 6. The proposed control system simulates the result, the tracking for square function is shown in Fig.7, the error signal of sate trajectory is shown in Fig.8, the trend of the control force is shown in Fig. 9.

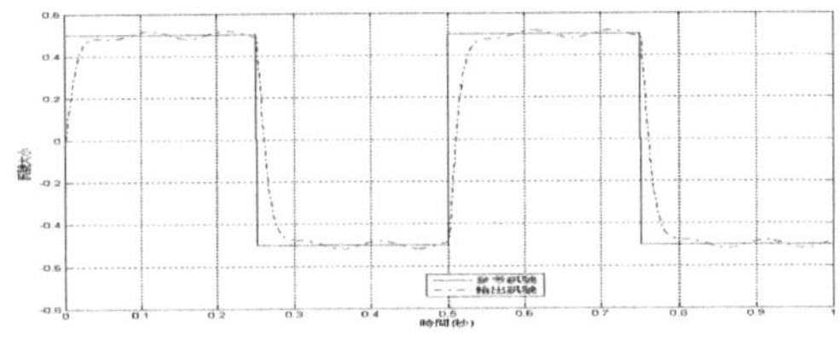

Fig. 4. The state signal trajectory for the neuron with PID control

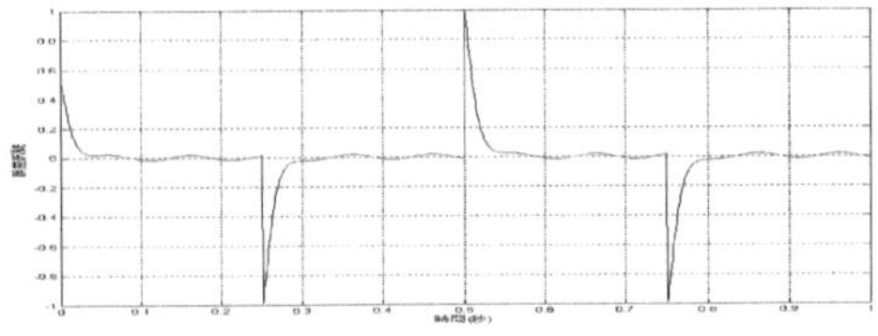

Fig. 5. The error signal of sate trajectory for the neuron with PID control

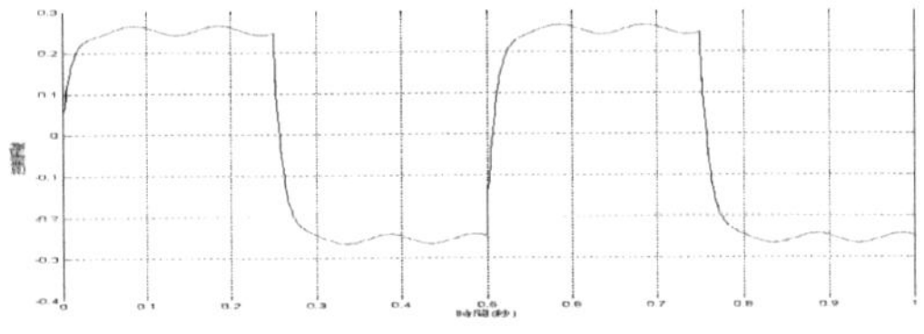

Fig. 6. The control signal for the neuron with PID control

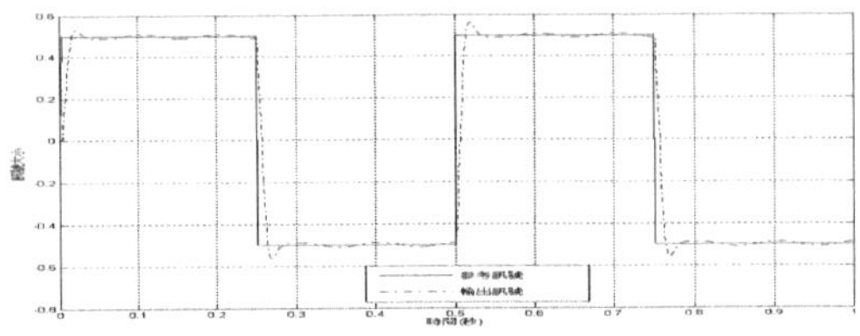

Fig. 7. The state signal trajectory for the neuron with SMC control

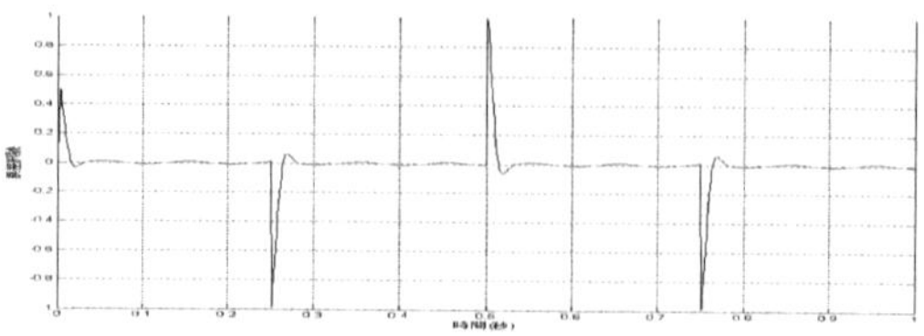

Fig. 8. The error signal of sate trajectory for the neuron with SMC control

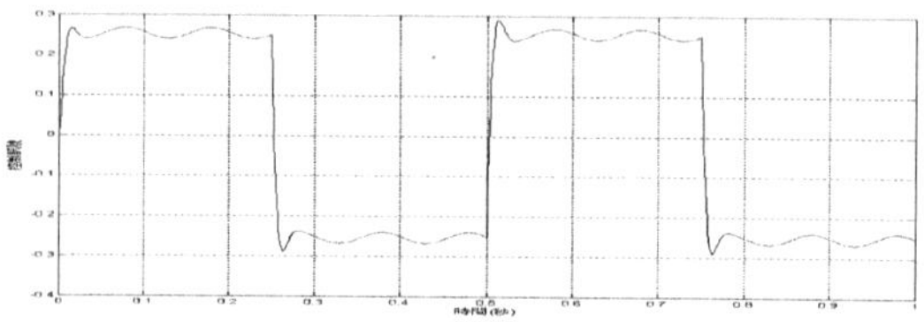

Fig. 9. The control signal for the neuron with SMC control

5 Conclusions

A single neuron self-adaptive with SMC controller, which is self-learning and self-adaptive is designed, and the results of the simulation test indicate that the proposed system has strong robustness, simple structure and good adaptability. Compared with traditional methods, this method improves the searching speed and can obtain a global optimal value. The simulation result shows that the influence caused by the load disturbance and model parameters varieties are restrained, the system robustness is improved.

References

1. Hung, J.Y., Gao, W., Hung, J.C.: Variable structure control: A survey. IEEE Trans. on Ind. Electron 40(1), 2–22 (1993)
2. Saaj, C.M., Bandyopadhyay, B., Unbehauen, H.: A new algorithm for discrete-time sliding-mode control using fast output sampling feedback. IEEE Trans. Ind. Electron. 49(3), 518–523 (2002)
3. Wai, R.J.: Adaptive sliding-mode control for induction servomotor drive: Electric Power Applications. IEE Proceedings 147(6), 553–562 (2000)
4. Wang, W.J., Zhao, Y.D., Liu, D.: Design of a stable sliding-mode controller for a class of second-order underactuated systems. IEE Proc. Control Theory Appl. 151(6), 683–690 (2004)
5. Bennett, S.: Development of the PID controllers. IEEE Control Systems Magazine 13(2), 58–66 (1993)
6. Shi, C.X.M., Wang, Z.Q.: Single neural PID Control for sensorless switched reluctance motor based on RBF neural network. Intelligent Control and Automation, 8069–8073 (2006)

7. Su, H.T., Samad, T.: Neuro-Control Design: Optimization Aspects. Neural Systems for Control 2, 259–288 (1997)
8. Wu, W., Bai, Z.M.: Performance Analysis of an Improved Single Neuron Adaptive PID Control. Intelligent Information Technology and Security Informatics, 22–25 (2010)
9. Omatu, S., Fujinaka, T., Yoshioka, M.: Neuro-PID control for inverted single and double pendulums. In: IEEE International Conference on Systems, Man, and Cybernetics, vol. 4, pp. 2685–2690 (2000)
10. Omatu, S., Yoshioka, M.: Self-tuning neuro-PID control and applications. In: IEEE International Conference on Systems, Man, and Cybernetics, vol. 3, pp. 1985–1989 (1997)
11. Izadi, H., Pakmehr, M., Moghaddam, M.M.: Designing Autolanding Neuro-Controller using PID and optimal strategies. In: IEEE Aerospace Conference, pp. 1–10 (2005)
12. Xu, Z., Ruan, J., Min, J.: Adaptive neuro sliding mode control of uncertain nonlinear system with dead zone input. Intelligent Control and Automation, 4723–4726 (2008)
13. Jing, C., Wu, W., Lin, M.: Performance Analysis for neuro sliding mode control with gain adjustment. Computer Engineering and Applications 1, 56–59 (2010)
14. Wu, W.: Adaptive neuro sliding mode control for inverted pendulum. Computer Engineering and Technology 1, 135–138 (2010)
15. Xu, Z., Min, J., Jian, R.: Adaptive Neuro sliding mode control of nonlinear system. Intelligent Computation Technology and Automation, 284–288 (2008)

RBF Network with Sliding-Mode Control for Chaos Systems

Yeong-Chin Chen[1], Lon-Chen Hung[2], and Shuh-Han Chao[2]

[1] Department of Computer Science and Information Engineering, Asia University, Taiwan
[2] Department of Computer Science and Multimedia Design, Taiwan Shoufu University, Taiwan
ycchenster@gmail.com

Abstract. In this paper a robust intelligent RBF neural network tracking control system combined with a distance-based sliding-mode control technique is proposed for a class of chaos systems. The proposed adaptive control scheme is developed for a class of chaotic systems with unknown bounded uncertainties. The adaptation laws are derived using a Lyapunov stability analysis, so that both system tracking stability and error convergence can be guaranteed in the closed-loop system. It is used to demonstrate the effectiveness and performance of the proposed robust control technique.

Keywords: Neuron, Sliding-Mode, Nonlinear System.

1 Introduction

Over the past few years many chaotic systems have been developed and analyzed [1-8]. Chaotic systems are essentially nonlinear systems having the properties of being broadband, noise-like and difficult to predict [22]. A fundamental characteristic of a chaotic system is its extreme sensitivity to the initial conditions; this means that small differences in the initial state can lead to extraordinary differences in the system state. Some effective methods have been developed for chaos control during the past decade since the well known OGY control method [16], which stabilizes unstable periodic orbits embedded in chaotic attractors using small control input signals. Many researchers have managed to control chaotic systems based on exact chaotic models [7,8,19-24]. On the other hand, intelligent modeling with control methodologies based on fuzzy logic and neural networks [3-6] have also been used. An RBF network [25,26] with sliding-mode control (SMC) for a second order nonlinear system has also been developed.

In the proposed RBF network with distance-based sliding-mode control system (DSMC) the main tracking controllers is a RBF network which is used to mimic an ideal controller. It has an on-line learning ability to deal with parametric uncertainty and disturbances by adjusting the control parameters. A distance-based sliding-mode controller is designed via the Lyapunov stability theory in order to guarantee the high quality of the controlled system. A Duffing-Holmes system is used as an illustration of the effectiveness of the proposed control design method.

H. Tan and M. Zhou (Eds.): CSE 2011, Part I, CCIS 201, pp. 266–273, 2011.

2 Problem Formulation

For simplification, we only consider two-order uncertain non-linear chaotic systems, but the approach can be generalized to high-order systems. The uncertain non-linear chaotic system is described as [2-6]:

$$\dot{x}_i(t) = x_{i+1}(t)$$

$$\dot{x}_n(t) = f(\mathbf{x},t) + \Delta f(\mathbf{x},t) + u(t) + d(t) \tag{1}$$

wher $\mathbf{x}(t) = [x_1(t), x_2(t), ..., x_n(t)] = [x(t), \dot{x}(t), ..., x^{(n-1)}(t)] \in R^n$ despite states vector $i = 1,2,...,n-1$, $f(\mathbf{x},t) \in R$ the non-linear system and assuming all system dynamics, $u(t) \in R$ is control input, $\Delta f(\mathbf{x},t)$ is the non-linear system dynamics which can be unknown, and $d(t)$ denotes the unknown external disturbance. In general, the parameter uncertainty and the noise perturbation are assumed bounded, i.e.

$$|\Delta f(\mathbf{x},t)| < k_1 \|\mathbf{x}\| \text{ and } |d(t)| < k_2 \tag{2}$$

where k_1 and k_2 are positive values. The tracking error is defined as $e_i(t) = x_i(t) - x_{di}(t)$, and the derivative of tracking error can be represented as:

$$\dot{e}_i(t) = e_{i+1}(t), \ i = 1,2,...,n-1,$$

$$\dot{e}_n(t) = f(\mathbf{x},t) + \Delta f(\mathbf{x},t) + u(t) + d(t) - \dot{x}_{di} \tag{3}$$

The control goal considered in this paper is that for any given target orbit $x_{di}(t)$, the proposed control $u(t)$ which such that the resulting tracking error vector satisfies.

$$\lim_{t\to\infty} \|e_i(t)\| = \lim_{t\to\infty} \|x_i(t) - x_{di}(t)\| \to 0 \tag{4}$$

3 Design of the Proposed Controller

In this paper, the RBF network with DSMC is used as the nonlinear approximator. Fig. 1 shows the general structure of the RBFNN with n inputs and m outputs. A RBFNN is a three-layered NN which has a universal approximation property for continuous real-valued functions [20, 21].

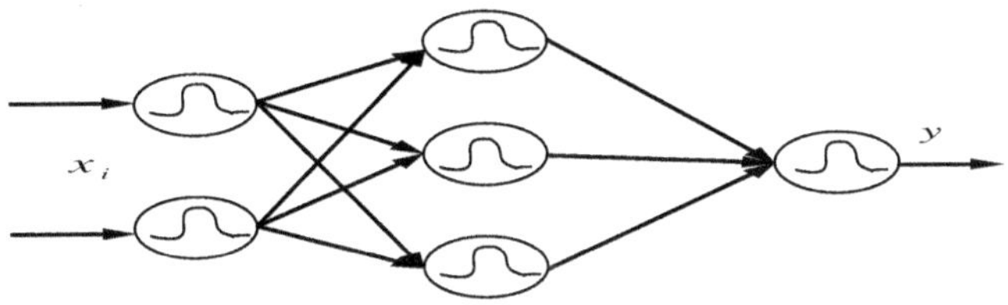

Fig. 1. The Radial basis function neural network structure

Define a performance function

$$E(k)=\frac{1}{2}e^2(k)=\frac{1}{2}(x_d(k)-x_i(k))^2 \tag{5}$$

In the network layer of an RBF network the parameter's formulation are tuning, then according to the gradient descent method, the learning algorithm of weights, node center and variance are derived as follows:

$$w_j(k+1)=w_j(k)+\eta e(k)h_j(k) \tag{6}$$

$$c_{ji}(k+1)=c_{ji}(k)+\eta e(k)h_j(k)w_j(k)h_j\frac{x_i(k)-c_{ji}(k)}{b_j^2(k)} \tag{7}$$

$$b_j(k+1)=b_j(k)+\eta e(k)h_j(k)w_j(k)h_j\frac{\| x_i(k)-c_j(k)\|^2}{b_j^3(k)} \tag{8}$$

where $j=1,2,3$ and η is learning rate, $\|\cdot\|$ is the Euclidean norm, x_i is input vector, c_{ji} is the central position of the neuron of the Gaussian function. The weightings w_j, between hidden layer neurons and output layer neurons are adjusted based on an adaptive rule[22,23]. The output layer is essentially a set of linear combiners. Let $s(t)$ input value of the proposed control

$$s(t)=ce(t)+\dot{e}(t) \tag{9}$$

where c is the coefficients of a Hurwitz polynomial. The proposed control scheme

$$u=\sum_{j=1}^{m}w_j\exp(-\frac{\| s-c_j\|^2}{b_j}) \tag{10}$$

where $s(t)$ is the parameter of a sliding-mode plane, m is the number of neurons. The control object such that $s(t)\dot{s}(t)$ tend to zero. The control objective is to design a robust RBF-based with DSMC controller so that the chaotic system follows the desired trajectory even in the presence of disturbances. Now, consider the RBF network update law

$$F=s(t)\dot{s}(t) \tag{11}$$

then

$$dw_j=-\eta\frac{\partial F}{\partial w_j(t)}=-\eta\frac{\partial s(t)\dot{s}(t)}{\partial w_j(t)}=-\eta\frac{\partial s(t)\dot{s}(t)}{\partial u(t)}\frac{\partial u(t)}{\partial w_j(t)} \tag{12}$$

where $\eta>0$. By (12) the weights between input neurons and hidden neurons are updated by the following:

$$\frac{\partial s(t)\dot{s}(t)}{\partial u(t)} = s(t)\frac{\partial \dot{s}(t)}{\partial u(t)} = -bs(t) \tag{13}$$

$$\frac{\partial u(t)}{\partial w_j(t)} = \exp(-\frac{\| s - c_j \|^2}{b_j}) \tag{14}$$

and the update of RBF network weighting

$$dw_j = \gamma s(t)\exp(-\frac{\| s - c_j \|^2}{b_j}) = \gamma s(t) h_j(s) \tag{15}$$

where w_j are weighting values and h_j is the output of the RBF network. Hence, the result of (15) can not be achieved. Choi, et al. [18] suggest a distance-based sliding-mode control design method with a sole input variable instead of the error and the change-of-error (or all process state variables) to represent the contents of the input variables. This paper proposes a method by DSMC with an RBF network which could generate the absolute value of the switching magnitude in the sliding-mode control law using the error and the change-of-error. In Fig. 2, let $M(e,\dot{e})$ be the point of intersection of the switching line and the line perpendicular to the switching line from an operating point $N(e_1,\dot{e}_1)$ and d_1 can be expressed as [17, 18].

$$d_1 = [(e - e_1)^2 + (\dot{e} - \dot{e}_1)^2]^{1/2} = \frac{|\dot{e}_1 + \lambda e_1|}{\sqrt{1+\lambda^2}} \tag{16}$$

$$d_s = \mathrm{sgn}(s)\frac{|\dot{e} + \lambda e|}{\sqrt{1+\lambda^2}} = \frac{\dot{e} + \lambda e}{\sqrt{1+\lambda^2}} = \frac{s}{\sqrt{1+\lambda^2}} \tag{17}$$

where

$$\mathrm{sgn}(s) = \begin{cases} 1 & \text{for } s > 0, \\ -1 & \text{for } s < 0. \end{cases} \tag{18}$$

The Lyapunov function is chosen as:

$$V = \frac{1}{2} d_s^2 \tag{19}$$

then

$$\dot{V} = d_s \dot{d}_s = \frac{s}{\sqrt{1+\lambda^2}} \cdot \frac{\dot{s}}{\sqrt{1+\lambda^2}} = \frac{s\dot{s}}{1+\lambda^2} \tag{20}$$

By (20) to conduct the RBF network with distance-based SMC update law

$$dw_j = \gamma d_s(t)\exp\left(-\frac{\| d_s - c_j \|^2}{b_j}\right) = \gamma d_s(t) h_j(s) - \alpha | d_s(t) | w_j \tag{21}$$

where λ , γ and α are positive symmetric constant matrices determining the adaptation rate. Here a RBF network with DSMC controller is proposed and a stability theorem is presented for the tuning algorithm eqns.

4 The Computer Simulation and Result

The system of interest here is an uncertain Duffing-Holmes system, which can be described by [6,7,23]

$$\dot{x}_1(t) = x_2(t)$$

$$\dot{x}_2(t) = -p_1 x_1(t) - p_2 x_2(t) - x_1^3(t) + q\cos(\omega t) + d(t) + u(t) \tag{22}$$

where $p_1 = -1$, $p_2 = 0.25$, $q = 7$, $u(t)$ is the control input, the disturbance is $d(t) = 0.1\sin(0.1t)$. The control objective is to drive the uncertain chaotic system to the following trajectory $x_d(t) = \sin(1.1t)$. The Gauss parameters of the initial weight vector are $\mathbf{c}=[-3\ -1.5\ 0\ 1.5\ 3]$, $\mathbf{b} = [1\ \ 1\ 1\ 1\ 1]^T$. Here the objective is to propose a control to let the system output track the desired $\sin(1.1t)$ input.

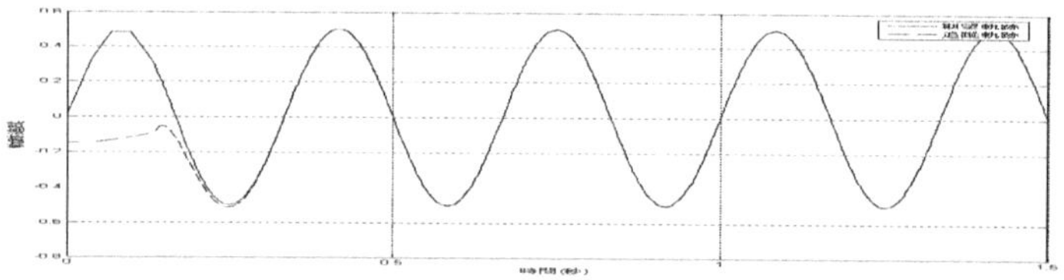

Fig. 3. The state $x_1(t)$ response of RBF system

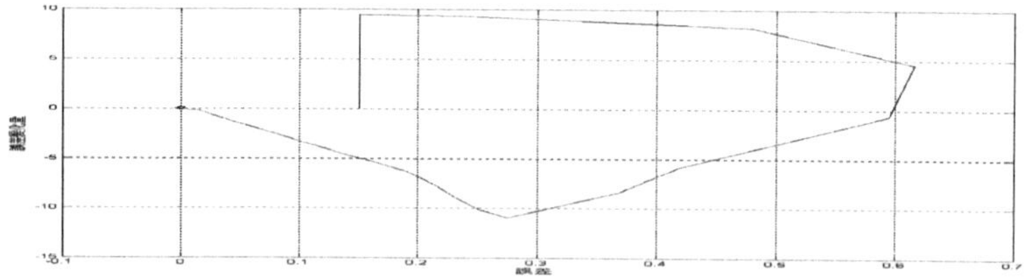

Fig. 4. The state $x_1 - x_2$ phase plane of RBF system

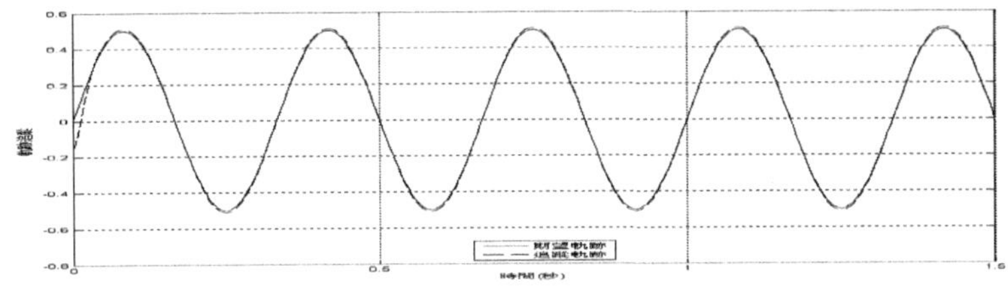

Fig. 5. The state $x_1(t)$ response of RBF with DSMC system

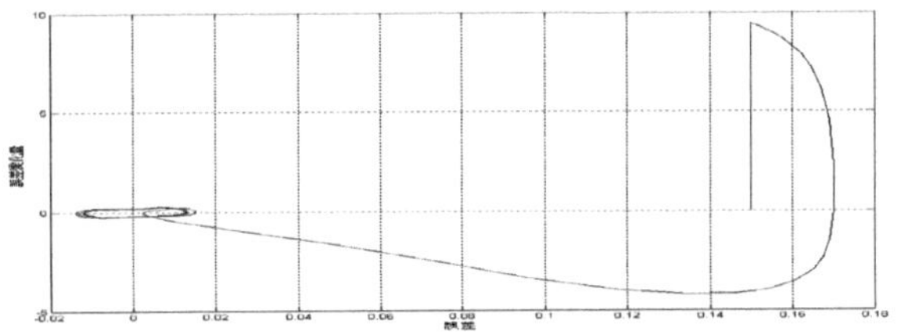

Fig. 6. The state $x_1 - x_2$ phase plane of RBF with DSMC system

Simulation results are shown in Figs. 3-6. The phase plane trajectory is plotted in Fig. 4 and Fig. 6. These simulations reveal the chaotic responses. The DSMC with RBF network simulation results are shown in Fig. 5 and Fig. 6. The simulation results show that with the proposed DSMC with RBF system we can achieve favorable tracking performance without control chattering for the Duffing-Holmes chaotic system.

5 Conclusions

We have proposed a method of DSMC for nonlinear systems using RBF networks. A distance-based adaptive sliding-mode controller for Duffing-Holmes system is proposed. Its performance was better than that of either the SMC or RBF network. The simulation results show the applicability and the effectiveness of the proposed approach.

References

1. Li, Z., Han, C., Shi, S.: Modification for synchronization of Rossler and Chen chaotic systems. Physics Letters A 301(3-4), 224–230 (2002)
2. Cao, J., Li, H.X., Ho, W.C.: Synchronization criteria of Lur'e systems with time-delay feedback control. Chaos, Solitons & Fractals 23(4), 1285–1298 (2005)

3. Kakmeni, F.M.M., Bowong, S., Tchawoua, C.: Reduced-order synchronization of uncertain chaotic systems via adaptive control. Communications in Nonlinear Science and Numerical Simulation 11(7), 810–830 (2006)
4. Wang, C.C., Su, J.P.: A novel variable structure control scheme for chaotic synchronization. Chaos, Solitons & Fractals 18(2), 275–287 (2003)
5. Huang, L., Wang, M., Feng, R.: Synchronization of generalized Henon map via backstepping design. Chaos, Solitons & Fractals 23(2), 617–620 (2005)
6. Cao, J., Li, H.X., Ho, W.C.: Synchronization criteria of Luynchronization of Rossler and Chen chaotic dynamical systems using active control. Physics Letters A 278(4), 191–197 (2001)
7. Wang, Y., Guan, Z.H., Wen, X.: Adaptive synchronization for Chen chaotic system with fully unknown parameters. Chaos, Solitons & Fractals 19(4), 899–903 (2004)
8. Zhang, H., Ma, X.K.: Synchronization of uncertain chaotic systems with parameters perturbation via active control. Chaos, Solitons & Fractals 21(1), 39–47 (2004)
9. Pecora, L.M., Carroll, T.L.: Synchronization in chaotic systems. Physical Review Letters 64(8), 821–825 (1990)
10. Behera, L., Gopal, M., Chaudhury, S.: Inversion of RBF networks and applications to adaptive control of nonlinear systems. IEE Proceedings of Control Theory and Applications 142(6), 617–624 (1995)
11. Li, Y., Qiang, S., Zhuang, X., Kaynak, O.: Robust and adaptive backstepping control for nonlinear systems using RBF neural networks. IEEE Trans. on Neural Networks 15(3) (2006)
12. Peng, H.T., Ozaki, H., Ozaki, V.T.: A parameter optimization method for radial basis function type models. IEEE Trans. on Neural Networks 14(2), 432–438 (2003)
13. Lian, J., Lee, Y., Zak, S.H.: Variable neural direct adaptive robust control of uncertain systems. IEEE Trans. on Automatic Control 53(11), 2658–2664 (2008)
14. Feng, J., Ng, K.T.: An adaptive demodulator for the chaotic modulation communication system with RBF neural network: Chow, Circuits and Systems I. IEEE Trans. on Fundamental Theory and Applications 47(6), 902–909 (2000)
15. Leung, H., Hennessey, G., Drosopoulos, A.: Signal detection using the radial basis function coupled map lattice. IEEE Trans. on Neural Networks 11(5), 1133–1151 (2000)
16. Muller, A., Elmirghani, J.M.H.: Novel approaches to signal transmission based on chaotic signals and artificial neural networks. IEEE Trans. on Communications 50(3), 384–390 (2002)
17. Choi, B.J., Kwak, S.W., Kim, B.K.: Design of a single-input fuzzy logic controller and its properties. Fuzzy Sets and Syst. 106(3), 299–308 (1999)
18. Choi, B.J., Kwak, S.W., Kim, B.K.: Design and stability analysis of single-input fuzzy logic controller. IEEE Trans. on Systems, Man and Cyber., Part B 30(2), 303–309 (2000)
19. Jamal, M.N., Ammar, N.N.: Chaos control using sliding-mode theory. Chaos, Solitons & Fractals 33(2), 695–702 (2007)
20. Ablay, G.: Sliding mode control of uncertain unified chaotic systems: nonlinear analysis. Hybrid Systems 3(4), 531–535 (2009)
21. Yau, H.T.: Design of adaptive sliding mode controller for chaos synchronization with uncertainties. Chaos, Solitons & Fractals 22(2), 341–347 (2004)
22. Konishi, K., Hirai, M., Kokame, H.: Sliding mode control for a class of chaotic systems. Physics Letters A 245(6), 511–517 (1998)
23. Lu, Z., Shieh, L., Chen, S.G., Coleman, N.P.: Simplex sliding mode control for nonlinear uncertain systems via chaos optimization. Chaos, Solitons & Fractals 23(3), 747–755 (2005)

24. Chang, J.F., Hung, M.L., Yang, Y.S., Liao, T.L., Yan, J.J.: Controlling chaos of the family of Rössler systems using sliding mode control. Chaos, Solitons & Fractals 37(2), 609–622 (2008)
25. Guo, H., Lin, S., Liu, J.: A radial basis function sliding mode controller for chaotic Lorenz system. Physics Letters A 351(4-5), 257–261 (2006)
26. Jianjun, N., Yongling, F., Xiaoye, Q.: Design and application of discrete sliding mode control with RBF network-based switching Law. Chinese Journal of Aeronautics 22(3), 279–284 (2009)
27. Selami, B., Musa, A.: Stable modeling based control methods using a new RBF network. ISA Transactions 49(4), 510–518 (2010)

Test Case Generation Based on Program Invariant and Adaptive Random Algorithm

Yuan Yuan[1], Zeng Fanping[1, 2], Zhu Guanmiao[1], Deng Chaoqiang[1], and Xiong Neng[1]

[1] Department of Computer University of Science and Technology of China
[2] Anhui Province Key Lab of Software in Computing and Communication, Hefei, Anhui, PR China
yuan0523@mail.ustc.edu.cn, billzeng@ustc.edu.cn, zgmzgm@mail.ustc.edu.cn, dengcq@mail.ustc.edu.cn, exn1016@mail.ustc.edu.cn

Abstract. Testing is a critical activity to find software errors. And choosing an effective test suite is the key problem in software testing area. Program invariant, as an attribute of program, can record the implementation state of test case very well and reveal the coverage of program data. In this paper, we integrate adaptive random testing and invariant technology, and present a new method which makes full use of the feedback information of program invariant and invalid case suite to generate the next case. Experiment results show that, compared with other similar methods, running for the same time, our method can achieve higher coverage and faster convergence speed.

Keywords: Random testing, Program invariant, Adaptive random algorithm, Test case generation.

1 Introduction

Software problems are as old as the computer itself. Huge data losses have been caused by software errors. It is a wake up call to the software industry, and also gets us to start to re-recognize the importance of software testing. Test case generation is a very important aspect in software testing. The quantity and quality of test cases significantly determine the quality of software testing.

Recently, the automated test case generation method attracts more and more attention. It can avoid the drawbacks of manual method, and effectively improve the efficiency. The simplest and most common automatic test case generation method is Random Testing (RT) [1]. It selects data randomly from the program domain as test case. It is easy to implement and automate, but the weaknesses hinder its application. In some situation it can not cover code paths well, and it is prone to generate redundant data. Adaptive Random Testing (ART) [2] [3] is an enhanced form of RT. It not only retains the advantages of RT, overcomes its shortcomings, but also effectively increases the efficiency. ART distributes test cases evenly within the input space, making it explore program failure with few test cases than RT. It has been observed that

H. Tan and M. Zhou (Eds.): CSE 2011, Part I, CCIS 201, pp. 274–282, 2011.

the adjacent test cases often reveal the same program fault[4], therefore uniformly distributed test cases can find the first fault-revealing case (the case that reveal program's fault) more effectively, which is the main idea of ART. Experiments show [2] that with the judgment criteria of detecting the first fault of a program, ART does outperform pure Random Testing significantly (up to 50%).

A program invariant [5] is an attribute which keeps true at one or some points of a program, and also a logical statement describing the immovability property of a running program. It can help software developer understand data structure, algorithms, and some other operations of the program effectively. As an attribute of program, invariant is well suited for recording the implementation state of test case, and effective guide for adding new cases and help to discard the invalid test cases. In addition, there is now a mature automatic extraction tool Daikon [5] [6] [7] available. Daikon, developed by MIT, is an open source dynamic invariant extraction tool, which is also the most mature and the most widely used invariant extraction tool currently.

In this paper, we propose a new method to select test case randomly. We use the dynamic invariant which is automatic extracted by Daikon during the execution of the program as the criteria to determine whether the test case is effective. Our method makes full use of the feedback information of invalid test cases and likely invariant to guide the selection of the next test case.

The rest of this paper is organized as follows. Section 2 introduces the related work. Section 3 explains in detail the test case automatic generation method. Section 4 shows the verification experiment, and finally summarizes this paper and discusses further work.

2 Related Work

Harder et al. [8] proposed a method that is checking whether the Operational Abstraction (that is what we call program invariant) has changed as standard, to filter test cases, but this method requires a test case library existing in advance, and then retains the test cases that make the program dynamic invariant change.

Randoop [9] [10] developed by the Program Analysis Group of MIT is an open source tool for Java and .NET to generate test cases automatically. Its main idea is "oriented random test cases generation", that is "random generation, systematic pruning". Its ability of finding software faults and the testing efficiency has been verified by the software testing team of Microsoft, and it has been adopted by Microsoft .NET development team in 2008.

In literature [11], Fanping Zeng, Qing Cao combine the invariant technology and random testing, and present a monotonic increasing feedback method with the evaluating criteria being whether the result of the invariant changes. With the core of this, they realize a complete test case generation and filtration technology.

Eclat [12] developed by the Program Analysis Group of MIT is a test case generation tool for Java. It also uses Daikon to extract invariant, but it requires users to provide a test case running correctly to extract the program invariant, and it uses .class files as input.

3 Test Case Generation

3.1 The Local Continuity Principle of the Failure Space

Research has found that [4], the inputs that reveal the same failure of a program tend to distribute in one or more contiguous areas. Chan et al. [13] have observed the distribution of the fault-revealing inputs and roughly classified the failure space to the following three categories: point pattern, strip pattern and block pattern.

Fig. 1. In the figures, the shaded areas represent the fault-revealing regions. The left figure is the point pattern, in which the fault-revealing inputs are stand alone points or small separate continuous intervals; The middle is the strip pattern, the fault-revealing inputs are usually zonal distributed; And the right is the block pattern, the main feature is that the fault-revealing inputs are always concentrated in either one or a few single block regions.

The research on the failure-causing inputs found that, the failure-causing input has local continuity in the program domain. That means in the contiguous regions the inputs often reveal the same error. And the inputs that can not reveal program errors are also distributed in one or more contiguous areas. Thus, we can draw the conclusion that the failure space also has local continuity.

3.2 Test Case Generation Based on Invariant and ART

We always get some feedback information about program invariants from the input cases, and the effective cases will change the program likely invariant suite and make it closer to the complete invariant suite, while the invalid cases will not change it.

According to the local continuity principle of the failure space and FCSC ART (Fixed Size Candidate Set of Adaptive Random Testing) [2] we can get the inspiration that when select the next test case, we could choose the case that is as far as possible from the invalid test case suite. That is to say, if the invalid case suite is empty we could generate the next case randomly; Otherwise random generated N cases stored in a candidate case suite temporarily, and choose the furthest case from the invalid case suite as the next case (here N is a definite number, and the experiments in section 4.1 verify how the N affects the results). To do this can increase the probability that the selected case skip the continuous failure regions, thereby increase the probability that the selected case is an effective case, and make the likely invariant suite approach to the complete invariant suite faster, and generate superior test case suite with faster convergence speed.

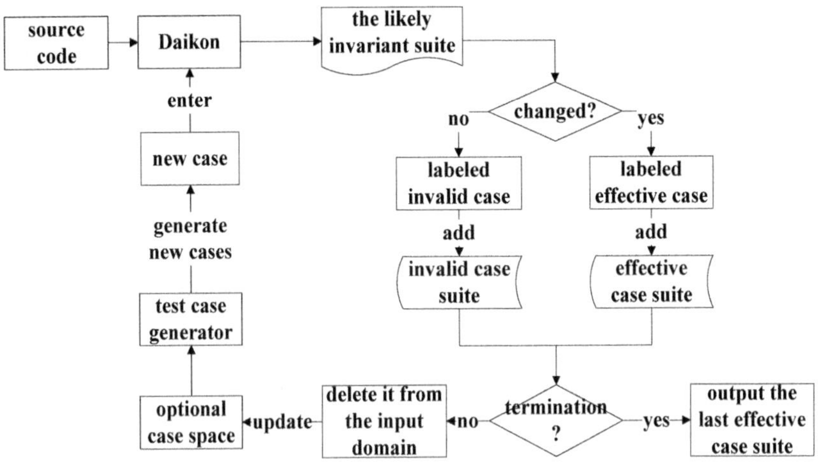

Fig. 2. The general frame of the test case generation is shown above. We use the program likely invariant as criterion to judge the selected case is effective or not, and use the feedback information of the invariant and the invalid case suite as guidance to choose the next case.

In the paper, we name the method that based on this selection algorithm ARTINV. Correspondingly, we name the algorithm that adopted the pure random method to select test case RANDINV.

3.3 The Convergence Speed of Test Case Suite

Here we define a concept: *the convergence speed of test case suite.* Just as the name implies, test case suite's convergence speed, is the generated speed of the effective test case suite.

During the execution of a program, effective cases change the program likely invariant suite and are added to the effective case suite, while the invalid cases are added to the invalid case suite. Along with the increase of the program's run time, the likely invariant suite gets close to the complete invariant suite until they match. Subsequently the generated test cases will no longer change the likely invariant suite. It means that all the new cases are invalid, and the effective case suite will not change.

The convergence speed is a criterion used to measure the automatic test case generation algorithm. Assuming the total time the program runs is R, and in the Nth time, the likely invariant suite become equal to the complete invariant suite, then this case is the last element added to the effective case suite, that is to say after the Nth time, the generated cases are invalid. So with the same R, N smaller, the case suite's convergence speed faster, and corresponding the case generation algorithm would have better performance. Another situation, that after program runs R times, the likely invariant suite is still not equal to the complete invariant suite, and the program at least still needs to run M times to make the suite no longer change. In this scenario, M smaller, the case suite's convergence speed would be faster.

It should be noted that, in the paper, we use the program complete invariant suite as the compared standard, only to verify the effectiveness of the algorithm. In practical application, it is not needed to extract the program complete invariant suite earlier.

3.4 The Similar Coefficient of the Likely Invariant Suite

In order to quantitatively describe the convergence speed, we here define *the similarity coefficient of the likely invariant suite*. We record it as SIMI. If it is failed to extract the complete invariant suite, the SIMI is defined as the times that the program at least still need to run to make the likely invariant suite equal to the program complete invariant suite, and to facilitate the distinction, we record the parameter negative here. If the complete invariant suite has been extracted, then the SIMI is defined as the program total run times the two suites matched, and here denoted it as positive.

In conclusion, using different algorithm to generate case suite, and with the same run times, if the SIMI are all positive or negative, that they are all extract the complete invariant suite or all do not, then the closer the coefficient is to 0, the better is the performance of the algorithm. Reflected in the two-dimensional coordinates, that means, the closer the coefficient is to the X-axis, the better is the performance of the algorithm. And if one SIMI is negative and another is positive, that is a method extracted the complete invariant suite and the other didn't, then the former method is more superior.

4 Experiment and Verification

There are two testing programs, and the program description is shown in Table1. In order to count and compare coverage easily, the two test programs both use branch-structure.

Table 1. The test program description

Program	Description	Code lines	Public functions
Mulriple	Return the absolute value, reciprocal or multiple of the input data	48	4
MyMath	The most value of the input data or the simple arithmetic	90	7

4.1 Experiment of the Candidate Case Suite Size

In our method, the candidate case suite is used to temporarily store the candidate cases in the process of test case selection. Intuitively, the bigger the candidate test case suite, the greater the candidate cases, so the probability that the selected case is the effective will increase. The following use the program Mulriple as test program to observe how the size impact on the SIMI coefficient and the coverage.

In the experiment, we assume the candidate case suite size is 5, 10, 20, 50, 80, and 100 respectively. The result shown in Figure3 and Figure4 (in order to observe clearly we ignore the result of the size is 20 and 80, because their curves are very similar).

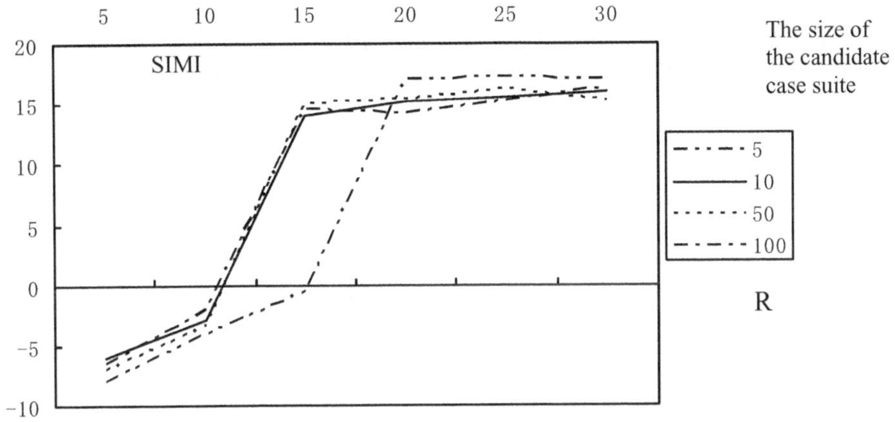

Fig. 3. The horizontal axis represents the run time of the program, and vertical axis is the SIMI coefficient. And from the figure we can see that when the size of candidate suite size is greater than 10, the SIMI coefficient is similar, and obviously better than the size is 5.

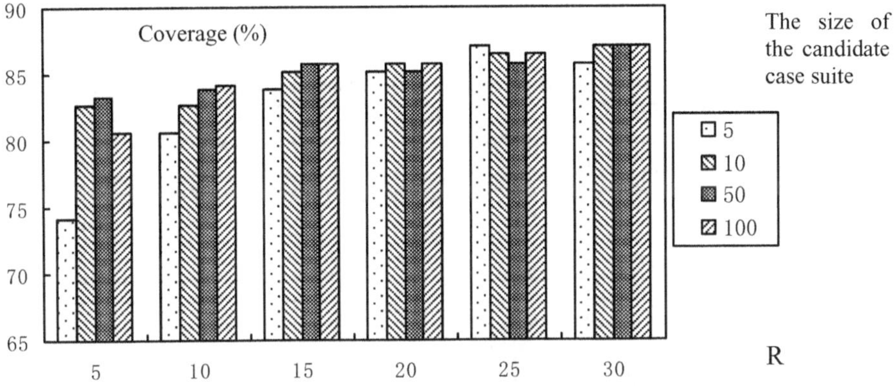

Fig. 4. The horizontal axis also represents the program run time, and the vertical axis refers to the coverage. It shows that when the candidate case suite size is greater or equal to 10, the coverage is close, and obviously better than if the size is 5.

From Fig.3 and Fig.4, We can get conclusion that, when the candidate case suite size is greater or equal to 10, the performance of the algorithm is similar, and obviously better than the situation that the size is 5. Besides the bigger the candidate suite size, the higher the computational cost for test case selection. So we set the size of the candidate case suite to 10 in the following experiments.

4.2 Test Case Generation Algorithm

Literature [10] has verified the superiority of the test case generation method based on random testing and invariant technology (that we called RANDINV algorithm), here we mainly compare the ARTINV algorithm and the RANDINV algorithm. In the experiment, the size of the candidate case suite is 10, and the meaning of the coordinate axis is the same with Fig.3 and Fig.4 in Section 4.1. The following use the program Mulriple and MyMath as test program to observe the performance of the method. The result is shown in Fig.5 and Fig.6.

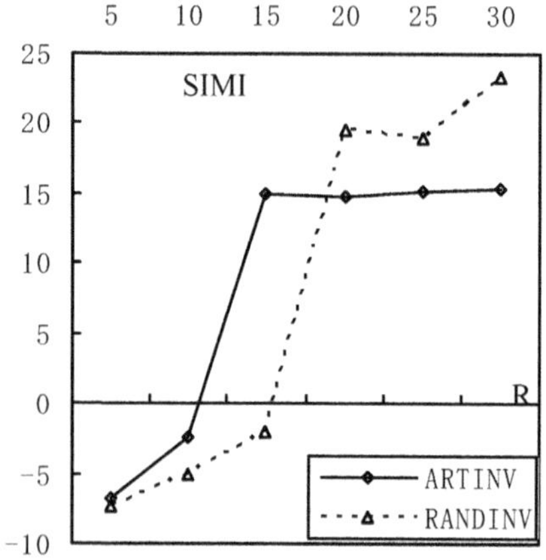

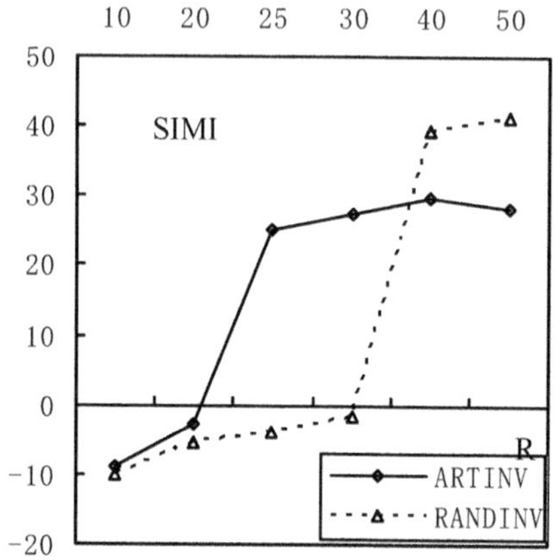

Fig. 5. The left figure is show the SIMI coefficient of program Mulriple, and the right is about program MyMath. In the figures, the solid line is the SIMI coefficient of the test program using the ARTINV method, and the dotted line records the result with the RANINV method. From the trend of the curve in the graph, we can see that, compared with RANDINV algorithm, the ARTINV algorithm has faster convergence speed when the programs run for the same amount of time.

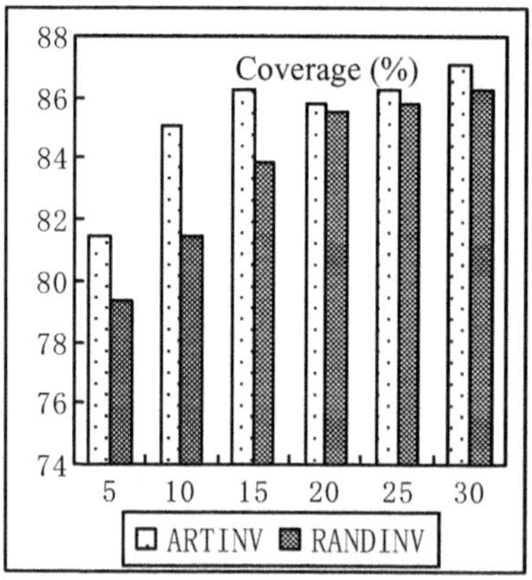

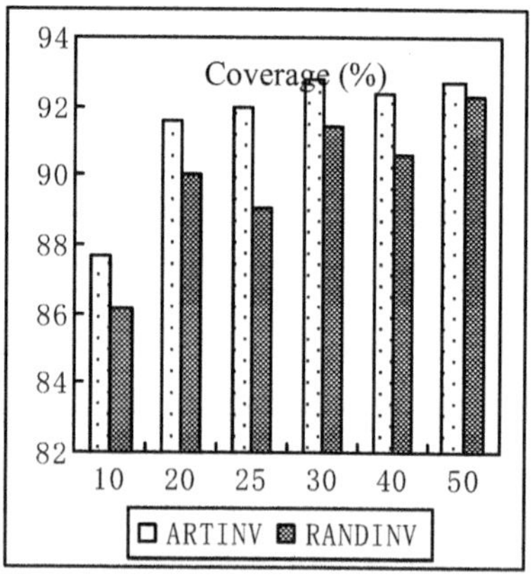

Fig. 6. The left figure is the coverage information of program Mulriple, and the right is about program MyMath. And in each the figure, the left column represents the coverage information with the ARTINV algorithm. From the figure, we can see that when the programs run for the same amount of times, the program coverage with ARTINV algorithm is higher than for the RANDINV algorithm. And the advantage is obviously if the programs are run only a few times.

In conclusion, we demonstrated that ARTIINV is a more effective test case selection algorithm. Compared with RANDINV algorithm, it has higher coverage and faster convergence speed. Thus, we come to the conclusion that the ARTINV algorithm is better than the RANDINV algorithm.

5 Summarize and Further Work

In the paper, we proposed a new method for automatic test case generation, which mainly draws on the idea of an improved algorithm compared to the pure random algorithm, named Adaptive Random algorithm. It is combined with the local continuity principle of the failure space, jumping choose test case in the input domain. This method not only overcomes the shortcomings (low coverage and high redundancy) of Random Testing, but also increases the convergence speed of the effective case suite and improves the efficiency of software testing. Through experiments we verified the rationality and effectiveness of the method.

In the further, we will continue to work on the following two aspects. First, we play to constrain the random space through the invariant to reduce the invalid case space and increase the probability of hitting the effective case, thus improving the tests efficiency. Second, we also play to avoid extract the program likely invariant suite repeatedly. To do this can reduce the needed time, and enhance its application value.

Acknowledgements

This work was supported by Natural Science Foundation of Anhui Province (Grant No. 11040606M131).

References

1. Hamlet, R.: Random Testing. In: Encyclopedia of Software Engineering, pp. 970–978 (1994)
2. Chen, T.Y., Leung, H., Mak, I.K.: Adaptive Random Testing. In: Maher, M.J. (ed.) Proceedings of the 9th Asian Computing (2004)
3. Liu, H., Xie, X.D., Yang, J., Lu, Y.S., Chen, T.Y.: Adaptive Random Testing by Exclusion through Test Profile (2010)
4. Ammann, P.E., Knight, J.C.: Data Diversity: An Approach to Software Fault Tolerance. IEEE Transactions on Computers 37(4), 418–425 (1988)
5. DAIKON version 4.6.2., `http://groups.csail.mit.edu/pag/DAIKON/`
6. Michael, D. E.: Dynamically Discovering Likely Program Invariants, PhD thesis, Dept. of Computer Science and Eng., Univ. of Washington, Seattle, Wash. (August 2010)
7. Michael, D.E., Jeff, H.P., Philip, J.G., McCamant, S., Pacheco, C., Matthew, S.T., Chen, X.: The DAIKON System for Dynamic Detection of Likely Invariants. Science of Computer Programming 69(1-3), 35–45 (2007)
8. Harder, M., Mellen, J., Ernst, M.D.: Improving Test Suites via Operational Abstraction. In: ICSE 2003, Proceedings of the 25th International Conference on Software Engineering, Portland, Oregon, May 6-8, pp. 60–71 (2003)

9. Pacheco, C., Shuvendu, K.L., Ball, T.: Finding Errors in .NET with Feedback-directed Random Testing. In: ISSTA 2008: International Symposium on Software Testing and Analysis, Seattle, Washington, July 20-24 (2008)
10. Pacheco, C., Lahiri, S.K., Ernst, M.D., Ball, T.: Feedback-directed Random Test Generation. In: ICSE 2007: Proceedings of the 29th International Conference on Software Engineering, Minneapolis, MN, USA (2007)
11. Zeng, F.P., Cao, Q., Mao, L.L., Chen, Z.D.: Test Case Generation Based on Invariant Extraction. In: WiCom 2009: 5th International Conference on Wireless Communications, Networking and Mobile Computing, pp. 1–4 (2009)
12. Pacheco, C., Michael, D.E.: Eclat: Automatic Generation and Classification of test inputs. In: Gao, X.-X. (ed.) ECOOP 2005. LNCS, vol. 3586, pp. 504–527. Springer, Heidelberg (2005)
13. Chan, F.T., Chen, T.Y., Mak, I.K., Yu, Y.T.: Proportional Sampling Strategy: Guidelines for Software Testing Practitioners. Information and Software Technology 38, 775–782 (1996)

Employing the E-Learning Platform to Monitor and Control the Teaching and Learning Process

Juan Li[1] and Xue-rong Cui[1,2]

[1] Department of Computer and Communication Engineering, China University of Petroleum (East China), 266555 QingDao, China
[2] Department of Information Science and Engineering, Ocean University of China, 266100 QingDao, China
lijuanlijuan@sina.com, cuixuerong@163.com

Abstract. In order to monitor and control the teaching and learning process in real-time, the e-learning platform is developed via computer network, programming language and database. This article describes the implementation of the platform and introduces the modules in the e-learning platform by which teachers may monitor the effect of teaching, students may know the effect of learning and teachers may know the feedback real-time evaluation of teaching by students. As a result, teachers and students may adjust their teaching-learning methods, contents and schedules and then teaching-learning quality would be improved.

Keywords: E-learning platform, teaching and learning process, teaching-learning quality, computer network, evaluation of teaching.

1 Introduction

As a flourishing field, e-learning at large (including distance learning, Web-based learning, and digital game-based learning) has attracted increasing attention from both industry and academic sectors. Meanwhile, the dramatic increase in the number of students brings difficulties for teachers to teach and for students to learn. Therefore, there is some studies to solve the problem vie e-learning platform.

In [1], an e-learning Platform based on .Net is built and students are able to use this platform to attend lessons and to practice as part of their learning experience with a certain set of tools. The interaction and interface of the platform are very good, but there is lack of monitoring of the teaching and learning process.

In [2], an educational platform is presented which offers to students the possibilities to connect remotely via Internet to Programmable Logic Controllers (PLCs). But this article just focuses on the PLCs while not the process of teaching and learning.

In [3], monitoring students' activities is accomplished through various techniques like creating log files or adding records into a table which just talks about the techniques of programming but other monitoring methods are not mentioned.

The remainder of the paper is organized as following. In section 2 we described how we implement the platform which focuses on the programming techniques. Section 3 introduces the modules of the e-learning platform. Section 4 presents our conclusions.

H. Tan and M. Zhou (Eds.): CSE 2011, Part I, CCIS 201, pp. 283–287, 2011.

2 Implementation of the Platform

The implementation of the platform employed the following techniques: Browser/Server (B/S) architecture, Microsoft Active Server Pages (ASP) programming language and Microsoft Access database.

2.1 Browser/Server Architecture

With the development of software architecture, different kinds of software architectures are widely used, among which, Client/Server (C/S) architecture and B/S architecture are the most common two architectures.

Under B/S architecture, the whole system is divided into three relatively independent layers: presentation layer, business logic layer and data service layer, which are called three-tier B/S architecture. This architecture makes the client so thin that the user can operate all the modules in the platform with just a browser, such as IE (Internet Explore). At the same time, software installation, modification and maintenance are all carried out at server side, so the cost of development and maintenance is reduced largely.

With the development of internet, most students accept the Internet and e-mail as a tool enhancing the teaching and learning process. Only 1% of respondents did not use the Internet at all, which means that it is a commonly accepted as a source of information [4].

2.2 ASP Programming Language

ASP programming language is the most common server-side scripting languages. One common use of ASP is to gather data at one time and display them at another time. For example, you can use ASP to save the results of each test into database and then display them during the students' and the teachers' querying. Operating database isn't the only thing that can be done using ASP. You can also design web forms that allow users to upload files to your site. For example, students can upload their homework to website, and then teachers can download the homework and check it.

2.3 Microsoft Access Database

Microsoft Access is an application which is bundled as part of the Microsoft Office suite. It can not only be used to create small and midsize database for the Microsoft Windows family of operating systems but also can be used as a database server for a web-based application. On the other hand, it is also supported by ADO, ODBC, and the .NET Framework, etc.

For example, in this platform, we created more than 10 tables in the Access database to store data, such as students (Student_ID, Student_Name, Class, Password, etc.) and homework (Student_ID, Filename, Upload_Date, Homework_ID).

2.4 AJAX

One of the most important challenges for web application developers is the requirement for a fast and responsive user interface. AJAX was primary designed and developed with the intent to solve these problems.

AJAX is short for Asynchronous JavaScript and XML, which allows web pages to be updated asynchronously by exchanging small amounts of data with the server side. This means that it is possible to update parts of a web page, without reloading the whole page. AJAX makes web-based applications more like desktop-based applications.

3 Modules of the E-Learning Platform

3.1 Teachers Monitor and Control the Learning Process in Real-Time

The monitoring of learning process should be considered from the micro level. Good scores come from the monitoring and controlling of the whole teaching process, not come from the final examination. In the learning process, teachers should always monitor the learning process and then discover, support, assist and guide the students who have problems. Teachers can find out the students who learned well and the students who learned badly and then take effective measures to enable the teaching is timely, accurate and remedial. At the same time, teachers may find out the grasping situation of each knowledge point, so teachers can adjust the teaching methods, contents and schedules. Moreover, the scores are usually opening, transparent and automatically generated, so teacher's interference may be reduced and avoided.

In this e-learning platform, the following measures are taken to strengthen the monitoring and controlling of learning process.

1) Network Registration
In large classes, for example, more than 100 people, it will waste a lot of class time to call the roll. In this platform, when "Network Registration" module is used, hundreds of students' registrations can be completed in seconds. At the same time, the IP address and registration time can be stored in the database. This module can not only improve the speed of calling the roll but also can eliminate the "registering for other people" phenomenon.

2) Login Frequency
The platform can automatically record the times that students log in and the duration time that students use the platform. In this way, teachers may find out how active of students to learn the course.

3) Homework Submission
Interface to submit homework is provided by the platform and the time that the homework is submitted is automatically recorded. According to the order of submission time and the quality of homework teachers may find out how active for students to finish their homework.

4) Excellent Articles Collection
In this module, students and teachers can publish excellent articles on the platform for other students to read and learn. According to number of reading times and publishing times, teachers may find out how active of students to read these articles.

5) Online Question and Answer
In this module, students can ask questions, both teachers and students can answer. These questions are often common questions among students, so that it is easy for teachers to grasp the overall situation of the students' learning. Meanwhile, according to the times of student's answering and the quality of the answer, teachers may find out the learning quality of students.

6) Homework Plagiarism Detection
This module can compare and detect plagiarism among large-scale documents. After homework is submitted, teachers can use this module to detect whether two documents might be similar. So in this way, students dare not copy homework. It can also reduce teachers' workload and improve the teaching quality.

3.2 Students Get Early Warning and Monitor Themselves in Real-Time

According to the scores statistics, students can find out their learning situation and their ranking among students so that it can conduct self-evaluation and achieve the purpose of self-education which is also a process of encouragement.

In the platform, the following two steps are used to warn students in Real-time.

1) Homework Score
After Students submit their homework, the platform can automatically store the scores into database. Students and teachers can query and rank the scores.

2) Quiz Score
The platform offers online quiz. After the key chapter is finished, the teacher will control a specified time to give an exam.

3.3 Teachers Get Real-Time Feedback on the Evaluation of Teaching

In most school, the teaching evaluation is carried out in the end of the semester, which lacks of real-time guidance for the present semester. Through this platform, a very smooth channel is provided for students to put forward their requirements and their evaluations of the teacher's teaching, especially for some students who are timid. In this way, teachers can earn more objective evaluation of teaching.

1) Anonymous Recommends
By this module, students can give real-time anonymous comments and suggestions to teachers.

2) Evaluation of Teachers
By the evaluation of teachers at any time, teachers may know of the result of students' evaluations.

3) Survey
Teachers can publish survey topics at any time, survey results are displayed in the form of charts.

Table 1. Comparison between the four classes that used and did not used this e-learning platform

Used or Not	Class	Excellent	Good	Medium	Pass	Fail	Average Score
Not Used	MBA0903	13.33	36.67	33.33	13.33	3.33	78.9
Not Used	MBA0904	23.33	30	30	13.33	3.33	79.7
Not Used	Average	18.33	33.335	31.665	13.33	3.33	79.3
Used	MBA0905	23.33	43.33	30	3.33	0	83.2
Used	MBA0906	33.33	23.33	26.67	13.33	3.33	81
Used	Average	28.33	33.33	28.335	8.33	1.665	82.1

4 Conclusions

We have used this platform in China University of Petroleum (East China) in tens of classes for many years. Table 1 shows the contrast of students' score of *Programming Language (VF)* in the second semester of the 2009-2010. Class MBA 0904, MBA 0903 and class MBA 0905, MBA 0906 are the same major and used the same examination paper at the same time, but class MBA 0904 and MBA 0903 did not use this platform and class MBA 0905 and MBA 0906 used this platform.

Contrast (as shown in Table 1) finds that when using the platform, the average score is higher by 2.8%, the excellent rate is higher by 10%, and both the pass and failure rates are lower than not using the platform.

References

1. Llopis, M., Llopis, C.: Net e-Learning Platform. In: Eighth IEEE International Conference on Advanced Learning Technologies, pp. 664–665. IEEE Press, New York (2008)
2. Alaba, O.B., Nicolae, M., Dobrescu, R., Abass, O.A., Popescu, C.: Educational platform for process controlling via Internet. In: 2nd International Conference on Adaptive Science & Technology, pp. 361–365. IEEE Press, New York (2009)
3. Mihaescu, C.: E-Learning Platform Used for Monitoring and Analyzing User Traffic. In: The International Conference on Computer as a Tool, pp. 815–818. IEEE Press, New York (2005)
4. Suchanska, M., Keczkowska, C.: Some Aspects of Employing the Moodle Platform as a Tool for Enhancing the Teaching and Learning Process. In: The International Conference on Computer as a Tool, pp. 2465–2467. IEEE Press, New York (2007)

Multi-Agent System in Land-Use Change Modeling

Rong Fu, Lijie Pu, Min Qian, and Ming Zhu

School of Geographic and Oceanographic Sciences, Nanjing University, Nanjing, China
haorenfurong@gmail.com, ljpu@nju.edu.cn,
moneyminn@gmail.com, zhumingnju@126.com

Abstract. This article examined the recent work on land-use change using the modeling of multi-agent system (MAS). As a typical model of artificial intelligence, MAS has become an area of considerable interest within geographical research to explain complex, uncertain and fuzzy courses, such as simulation and analysis of land-use change. This article demonstrated the framework of MAS model, emphasizes on the empirical applications in the context of land use, identifies the limitations of them, and suggests possible future study trends.

Keywords: Multi-agent system, land use change, artificial intelligence.

1 Introduction

Land-use change is a complicated phenomena and process at both spatial and temporal scale, and is constrained by biophysical factors and anthropogenic influences. At regional level, the socioeconomic impacts highlight [1-3]. Various models have been brought forward to explain the rules of land-use change process, and of them, multi-agent system(MAS) model has been proven to be a helpful and creative approach with the development of GIS tools[4,5].

Before its applications into the study of land-use, agent-based model has been widely applied in the area of social sciences [6-8]. MAS has its advantages in simulating and interpreting the cumulative decision-making of heterogeneous, autonomous and decentralized agents. In land-use of the real world, different stakeholders take their own positions; likewise, agents achieve their goals in system-level according to their rules. Besides, the coordination among agents, between the agents and the environment are considered to have contributed highly to the whole complex system [9, 10].

The paper is organized as follows. The next section presents the theoretical underpinning of MAS, including basic concepts, methods and mechanism, and gives a brief description of MAS applications. In section 3, recent applications of MAS to land-use change modeling are divided into three parts: simulation for land use change, land use planning and spatial evolution of urban land. Some limitations and problems the research mentioned above is faced are discussed in the section 4, and they are rooted from the structure and mechanism of MAS and revealed during modeling process. Besides pointing out the challenges, this paper also offers some promising ways to improve MAS modeling to be more suitable for land-use change study.

H. Tan and M. Zhou (Eds.): CSE 2011, Part I, CCIS 201, pp. 288–295, 2011.

2 Multi-Agent System: An Effective Spatial Modeling Tool

Across the relevant literature, there is a lack of the basic introduction to MAS in most cases. The concept of MAS is derived from Distributed Artificial Intelligence (DAI) in computer science and it is one of the most important DAI systems. It has been widely used in Virtual Reality, E-business, intelligent user interface and industrial intelligent controlling [9, 11].

Before jumping to the introduction of MAS, the concept of agent is presented as follows. Taking a mainstream opinion, agent is an autonomous entity which observes and acts upon an environment and directs its activity towards achieving goals. It can be used to describe various entities [12, 13].

A group of agents, a specified environment, interaction or communication and corresponding behavior complete a typical MAS model. Generally, MAS is a system composed of multiple interacting intelligent agents, which have several important characteristics: autonomous, decentralized, social and interactive with the environment [13, 14]. Reactive agent, cognitive agent and hybrid agent are three kinds of common agents in experimental design. The environment is perceived by the agent living in it, and it affects the behavior of agents; in return, the behavior of agents impacts the environment [4]. No agent has a full global view of the entire system, or the system is too complex for an individual agent to make practical use of knowledge, that can explain why the interaction makes a crucial part [15, 16].

When benefits or goals of different agents conflict with each other, the system would carry on spontaneous coordination itself, which is called the basic internal management mode of MAS. There are three main ways for the coordination for potential application use: coordination based on partial integral planning; coordination based on united intention; coordination based on social norm.

3 Applications to Land-Use Change Modeling

Unlike previous models (equation-based model, system model, statistical model, etc.) applied in land-use research, MAS model, to some extent, overcomes their disabilities in deciphering the interactive and dynamic process of a decentralized-nested hierarchy in a spatially-explicit way [4]. This model can directly react to the environment based on the knowledge, belief and intention sealed in the rules of individual agents. In most cases, it is a spatial reasoning with anthropogenic factors taken into consideration.

In this part of the paper, we have chosen to focus our review on three key areas where the greatest volume of work has been conducted. Though the content of the respective areas may overlap strictly speaking, each kind of application stresses their own particular concerns and employs suitable model structures. It is also worth noting that, recent research on MAS modeling in land-use is mostly combined with Cellular Automata (CA) grounded on GIS data to represent spatial features.

3.1 Applications in Land-Use Dynamic Simulation

In early studies, there have been a string of studies on the patterns and speed of urban expansion. A typical work by Ligtenberg[21] on the multi-actor-based land-use modeling, describes a typical MAS modeling approach combining cellular automata. In this model, CA is used to infer the knowledge needed by agents to make decisions about the future spatial organization of a certain area. After conceptual construction, he implements SWARM library to design agents at the edge of urban area.

In later research, the associated model of MAS and CA was being improved by elaboration and refinement of rule sets (beliefs, intentions, preference, etc.). Some Chinese scholars employed the MAS-CA model to analyze the rapid urban sprawl of China in recent years [22-24].

There has been a string of studies on farmers' decision-making on land-use in household level. Work by Tom P. Evans [25] has extended the scope of MAS modeling, his research calibrated the MAS model when attempting to examine and measure scale dependency of this model. Besides, in response to the doubts about the definition and framework of MAS before modeling, as well as the verification and validation after it, Diego Valbuena [26] tried to stress the typology of this model.

3.2 Applications in Land-Use Planning

When it comes to the land-use planning in urban regions, the government plays a decisive role, and public interests should be the basic premise and concern f. Nevertheless, the conflicts among the interests of the communities, residents and environment always inevitably exist, and MAS here provides with a potential tool to reconcile contradictions to a compromise.

Steve M. Manson [27] gave a good example in this area. His agent-based model constructs the "Actor-Institution-Environment" structure to fit the interactive mechanism of MAS model, and makes analysis of different planning scenarios with the interaction of agents.

However, there is still a long way for the real practice of MAS in the land-use planning process. Debates and doubts about the utility and credibility of MAS remain. Yet, this tool did allow effective examination of the impacts of policy alternatives. As a result, it would firmly present feasible suggestion for the revising of the general plan of land use [28, 29].

3.3 Applications in Spatial Evolution

In fact, this part, to some extent, overlaps with the other two kinds of application above. The reason we bring it forward is that, the literature in this part involves various entities to be agents and enriches the content of MAS modeling. As Xue L [30] suggests, socioeconomic behavior and individual choices are highly correlated with land use and land cover change through time and space, he creates agents in a more specific sense. Families, companies, the government, banks, and real estate developers etc. could be drawn into the nonlinear simulation of spatial evolution of urban regions during the process of rapid and intense urbanization. Rather than focusing on the common evolution patterns derived from classical theories, his research enhanced the UrbanSwarm software platform to compare the results of simulation under different patterns. Furthermore, for policy-making and public management of the real world, he offers a practical assessment system using MAS tools. As another exploration in depth and extent, Tao HY [22] integrated multi-agent model with GIS to measure current residential pressure by estimating agent's pressure caused by both basic house price and housing environment value.

4 Modeling Improvement

The MAS modeling is becoming an outstanding tool that bridges theoretical and empirical conceptions in computational geography. From the existing MAS design and operation, we can recognize some problems and limitations, which will be presented in the following part in a step-by-step order.

4.1 Definition and Parameterization of Agents

Agents are defined and parameterized in many different ways depending on the objectives of the research, mostly decided by the respective function of actors playing in the system, or out of consideration for spatial explicit expression. The main types of agents and their characters will be listed in the following table.

Table 1. The Typical Agent Types and their Characters

agent type	characters and decision rules
government	authority of decision-making, achieving for benefits in regional or national scale, coordinator of the conflicts and compromises, have dominant concerns in different scenarios
household	farmers: adhere to natural and social rules in agricultural production, but also esthetic needs; urban residents: locate differentially depending on the balance of income and housing price
NGO	environment-oriented, avoiding wild development, highlighting sustainable land-use planning
corporation	especially for manufacturing industries, considering land prices and infrastructure
developer	market-oriented, coordinating with the government and consumers
bank	organizer of the financing chain, supporting other agents

Recent research are basically at micro or meso-level, even taking homogeneous and ideal region for pilot test to escape from the complexity and redundancy for large amount of computing at large scale. Another obstacle comes from the resolution and completeness of input data and information materials. We suggest some possible solutions to the problem. One is to employ the hierarchical placement controller in large-scale simulation. In terms of time scale for simulation, the choice for proper step size in MAS modeling depends on, not only the capacity to achieve equilibrium for the simulation software, but also the quality and quantity of the input data.

4.2 Selection and Formulation of Rule Sets

Before simplifying the diversified agent behavior by designing rule sets, it's vital for researchers to determine the objectives of the simulation. Besides, the selection of rule sets is related to the scale of modeling as well as the features of agents. In a word, we need to concern about both quantitative analyses and social reality during the criteria selection.

According to tab.1, different agents have their corresponding strategies in land-use decision. A typology of behavior can be defined and concluded for a specific identity. A variety of methods have been applied in rule sets construction. Classified by different ways, they are qualitative and quantitative analyses, socio-economic approaches and artificial intelligence approaches (like expert knowledge system, machine learning method, neural networks and other participatory process). How to choose a proper method during the selection and formulation of rule sets depends on the agent character and data accessibility. When necessary, a detailed sample survey for information and data should be carried out to increase the accuracy of formulation.

4.3 Communication and Coordination among Agents

In the theory of artificial intelligence, agents in these MAS models undertake their activities according to the original rule sets in the beginning. And affected by the environment and other agents, the rule sets will be adapted gradually during the evolution of the system, which makes communication and coordination among agents crucial to the results of the modeling. As most MAS we discuss in land-use issues are distributed systems where individual agents have a sealed database about beliefs and knowledge about the environment, agents are able to communicate and coordinate with each other to achieve information-sharing. This part of the model derives from the experience of human behavior. Equally, the behavior of agents is also contagious in the community.

Due to different social regimes, the land-use policies derived, and different developing periods set for the environment of the modeling, these coordinating ways were applied in light of local conditions. Norms in the MAS system are defined as uniform and coercive social rules for agents to obey, not necessary to be consistent with the rules in the real world. Instead, they are a persistent and desiring mode for group behavior. For MAS designers, norms are generated by offline-design or dynamic design, the later one will be updated in pace with the changes of the system.

In the recent research, however, the application of communication of agents is limited and elementary. For instance, the blackboard model fits the information exposure in land-use decision in a relatively mature land market. Yet, the quantitative research of the agent communication and coordination has seldom discussed.

4.4 Verification and Validation

Not only to assess the uncertainty and accuracy of the typology and parameterization of MAS, but also to modify and improve the modeling, scholars repeated attempts to verify the steps and validate the results of MAS simulation. Some approaches have been put into effect in the verification and validation. Depending on the concrete circumstances, there are methods like Kappa Index of Agreement coefficients, Multi-resolution Goodness of Fit, Monte Carlo Uncertainty Measurement and so on.

In addition, as the result of the limitation in scale issues, incompleteness of input data, and the complexity of computation during the modeling process, researchers also employ on-the-spot investigations and comparison with the results of other models to verify the accuracy of MAS modeling. On one hand, the modeling basis (survey samples, census, and GIS data) is not fully accessible for researchers and rely on scale levels; on the other hand, the research object (human decision) is observed as random and uncertain behavior. Hence the efforts to improve the accuracy and perfection of MAS modeling have to be sustained.

4.5 Software Platform for Modeling

For researchers without software programming skills, the appearance of MAS simulation software actually equip them with a direct and relatively easy access to develop modeling platform in their special fields of study. Most MAS software platforms can support visual observation and parameter adjustment for comparative studies across teaching and research of various disciplines.

Since 1990s Santa Fe Institute developed Swarm [31], which is essentially a collection of software libraries, written in Objective C for constructing discrete event simulations of complex systems with heterogeneous elements, more and more universities and institutions have started to dedicate to the popularization and utilization of MAS modeling. Until recently a lot of MAS software has been implemented for practical uses, such as Ascape、RePast、TNG-Lab、AgentSheets and etc. Releasing open source in C or Java language is the trend for developing relevant software. The way of implementation evokes ideas from many other disciplines. As a result, the versions update constantly. At the same time, the diversity of software platforms causes difficulties for researchers during the selection for appropriate framework. Another obstacle in carrying out MAS modeling is how to input spatial data and information about land-use conditions effectively. To solve these problems, it's necessary to design interface for MAS software to GIS tools. Only the CORMAS platform prepares the interface to MapInfo for integrating information from different sources. Some researchers also build new software platform integrated with GIS modules to solve the problems.

5 Conclusions

This article synthesizes Multi-Agent System solutions to land-use change by reviewing the applications of various MAS approaches in land-use issue studies from the literature. These applications are labeled into three categories by the objectives of them. From these applications, we can conclude that the MAS has become a useful and promising approach when explaining the complex, uncertain and fuzzy courses in land-use change.

Admittedly, besides its advantages, recent MAS modeling still have some limitations. From the fourth part of this article, the modeling improvement organized by the steps of designing the system, we can conclude that the accuracy and completeness of this model are generally limited by data accessibility and scale issues (spatial and temporal), as well as the complexity of human behavior. Quantitative and comprehensive simulations are still rare in this field. To tap the potential of this model, interdisciplinary cooperation is encouraged as MAS model construction involves a variety of subjects, such as computer science, urban studies, engineering, geography, system dynamic theory, economics, psychology and so on; any obstacle initiated by the subjects will restrict the development of modeling.

However, the trend of MAS approach as an effective solution for land-use change research is obvious in the reviewed publications. Although the number of applications presented in this article is not complete, but we have tried to be as comprehensive as possible to give typical samples of applications in demonstrating the possible applications. As a tool from bottom to top, MAS avoids some drawbacks of conventional analysis method in land-use studies and takes into account human factors as a complement for physical factors, whereas it is still limited in its ability to simulate all the complexities involved in the operation of land-use systems. Future effort is needed in improving the model, especially in the integration with spatial tools and extensive applications in a more accurate and reliable way.

References

1. Verburg, P.H., Chen, Y.Q.: Multi-scale characterization of land use patterns in China. Ecosystems 3, 369–385 (2000)
2. Rindfuss, S.J., Walsh, B.L., et al.: Developing a science of land change: challenges and methodological issues. Proceedings of National Academy of Sciences 101 (2004)
3. Veldkamp, A., Verburg, P.: Modeling land use change and environmental impact. Journal of Environmental Management 72, 1–3 (2004)
4. Parker, D.C., Manson, S.M., et al.: Multi-Agent Systems for the Simulation of LUCC: A Review. Annals of the Association of American Geographers 93(2), 314–337 (2002)
5. Nie, Y., Chen, H., et al.: Simulation of urban land use change based on multi-agent and GIS. Application Research of Computers 26(7) (2009) (in Chinese)
6. Arthur, W.B.: Designing economic agents that act like human agents: A behavioral approach to bounded rationality. American Economic Review, Papers and Proceedings 81(2), 353–359 (1991)
7. Durlauf, S.: Statistical Mechanics Approahces to Socioeconomic Behavior. In: Arthw, W.B., Durlauf, S., Lane, D. (eds.) The Economy As an Evolving Complex System II. Santa Fe Institute Studies in the Sciences of Complexity, pp. 81–104. Addison-Wesley, Reading (1997)
8. Bousquet, F., Le Page, C.: Multi-agent simulations and ecosystem management: a review. Ecological Modelling 176(3), 313–332 (2004)
9. Jennings, N.R., Sycara, K., Wooldridge, M.J.: A roadmap of agent research and development. Journal of Autonomous Agents and Multi-Agent Systems 1(1), 275–306 (2008)
10. Fu, W.: A Trial Research on the Design and Decision Expert System of Land Rational Use. Journal of Applied Sciences 19(1), 4–19 (2001) (in Chinese)
11. Wu, N., Silva, E.A.: Artificial intelligence solutions for urban land dynamics: a review 24(3), 246–265 (2010)

12. Rouchier, J., Bousquet, F.: A multi-agent model for describing transhumance in North Cameroon: Comparison of different rationality to develop a routine. Journal of Economic Dynamics and Control 25, 527–559 (2001)
13. Sawyer, R.K.: Artificial societies: multi agent systems and the micro-macro linking sociological theory. Sociological Methods Research 31, 325–363 (2003)
14. Turner, B.L.: Vulnerability as a human-environmental interaction: Example from Southern Yucatan. In: Abstracts of Global Change Open Science Conference. Congrex Holland BV, Amsterdam (2001)
15. Matthews, R., Gilbert, N., Roach, A., Polhill, J., Gotts, N.: Agent-based land-use models: a review of applications. Landscape Ecology 22, 1447–1459 (2007)
16. van Oel, P.R., et al.: Feedback mechanisms between water availability and water use in a semi-arid river basin: A spatially explicit multi-agent simulation approach. Environmental Modelling and Software 25, 433–443 (2010)
17. Zhang, X., Cui, W.: Integrating GIS with Cellular Automaton Model to Establish a New Approach for Spatio-temporal Process Simulation and Predictio. Acta Geodaetica et Cartographica Sinica 30(2), 148–155 (2001)
18. Yang, Q., Li, X., Liu, X.: Urban Land Use Change Research Based on Agent and Cellular Automata. Acta Geographica Sinica 7(2), 78–83 (2005) (in Chinese)
19. Yang, Q.-S., Xia, L.: Integration of Multi-agent Systems with CA for Simulating Urban Land Expansion. Scientia Geographica Sinica 27(4), 542–548 (2007) (in Chinese)
20. Yang, Q.-S., Li, X.: Agent-based micro-simulation of urban industrial spatial evolution. Scientia Geographica Sinica 29(4), 515–522 (2009) (in Chinese)
21. Ligtenberg, A., Bregt, A.K., van Lammeren, R.: Multi-actor-based land use modelling: spatial planning using agents. Landscape and Urban Planning 56(1), 21–33 (2001)
22. Tao, H., et al.: Method Exploration of Geographical Spatial Differentiation Based on Multi-agent: A Case Study of Urban Residential Simulations. Acta Geographica Sinica 62(6), 579–588 (2007) (in Chinese)
23. Peng, C., Du, N., Liu, Y.: Understanding Residential Expansion in Big Cities Using MAS/RE. Geomatics and Information Science of Wuhan University 32(6), 548–551 (2007) (in Chinese)
24. Zhang, H., Zeng, Y., et al.: Urban Land Expansion Model Based on Multi-agent System and Application. Acta Geographica Sinica 63(8), 869–881 (2008) (in Chinese)
25. Evans, T., Kelley, H.: Multi-scale analysis of a household level agent-based model of landcover change. Journal of Environmental Management 72(1), 57–72 (2004)
26. Valbuena, D., Verburg, P., Bregt, A.: A method to define a typology for agent-based analysis in regional land-use research. Agriculture, Ecosystems & Environment, 27–36 (2008)
27. Manson, S.M.: Agent-based dynamic spatial simulation of land-use/cover change in the Yucatan peninsula, Mexico. In: 4th International Conference on Integrating GIS and Environmental Modeling (GIS/EM4), Banff, Alberta, Canada, September 2-8 (2000)
28. Le, Q.B., et al.: Land use dynamic simulator (LUDAS): a multi-agent system model for simulating spatio-temporal dynamics of coupled human–landscape system. 1. Ecological Informatics 3(2), 135–153 (2008)
29. Le, Q.B., et al.: LUDAS 2. Scenario-based application for impact assessment of land-use policy. Ecological Informatics 3(2), 135–153 (2010)
30. Xue, L., Yang, K.: Research on Urban Evolution Using Agent-Based Simulation. Systems Engineering- Theory and Practice 12(12), 1–9 (2003) (in Chinese)
31. Francesco, L., Benedikt, S.: Economic Simulation in Swarm: Agent-based Modeling and Object Oriented Programming. Social Science Academic Press (2004)

The Design and Implementation of Network Video Surveillance System Based on Davinci Chips

Peicen Han, Zhaohui Ye, and Shiyuan Yang

Department of Automation,Tsinghua University,
Beijing 100084, China
hanpeicen@163.com

Abstract. This paper realizes a network video surveillance system based on DM6446 and OMAP3530. DM6446 works as the IP camera and OMAP3530 as the client-end. Both DM6446 and OMAP3530 are Davinci Digital Media System-on-Chips which contain an ARM core and a DSP core. IP camera is developed in the framework of ENCODE. In the Writer thread of ENCODE, network functions are added to send data stream. The client-end is based on a media player DECODE. DECODE is transplanted onto OMAP3530MINI board. DECODE is based on DMAI (Davinci Multimedia Application Interface) which is designed for rapid development of multimedia applications, and DMAI is modified to let DECODE receive data from IP camera rather than read from a file. The remnant area is used in the client-end to ensure that data speeds of the client-end and IP camera are matched.

Keywords: video surveillance system, SoC, DM6446, DMAI, OMAP3530.

1 Introduction

The development of video surveillance system has gone through three stages [1][2]. The first stage is the analog video surveillance system that uses analog closed circuit television (CCTV) signal to transmit images. The technology is mature, but the scope of monitoring is small. It is also inflexible and inconvenient to collect and store data. Meanwhile, bandwidth of analog signal is limited.

The second stage is the "analog - digital" monitoring systems where digital video recorder (DVR) works as the core. The front-end of the system is from the camera to the DVR and it also uses analog signal to transmit image, the same as video surveillance systems of the first stage. The back-end is DVR implementing recording, playback, objects detection, behavior recognition and support for limited IP network access, etc.

The third stage is network video surveillance system, which is based on the Internet to achieve large-scale monitoring. IP Camera is growing up with the development of embedded technology. Embedded processors of the camera such as DSPs collect and compress data according to MPEG4 or H.264. Then the data are sent to the remote operation terminal via TCP/IP, UDP, or RTP/RTCP and other network protocols.

H. Tan and M. Zhou (Eds.): CSE 2011, Part I, CCIS 201, pp. 296–302, 2011.

Network video surveillance system is becoming more and more intelligent, involving data transmission security, data encoding and decoding, motion detection, tracking, behavior analysis, warning and so on. There are a lot of literature works on this research. The paper [3] pointed out that the video analysis plays a key role in the video surveillance system. The procedure is first to identify the object, then track, and analyze abnormal behavior. The paper [4] also describes the structure of intelligent network video surveillance system based on video analysis.

The Davinci chip integrates ARM core, DSP core and accelerators on one chip. ARM processor is good at handling complicated tasks, such as communications and peripherals control, while DSP processor works as a co-processor to ARM to implement complex signal processing algorithms so that the burden of ARM processor is reduced. Both ARM and DSP complement each other for very rich multimedia applications. Compared to "Microprocessor chip+en/decode chip" in the market, Davinci chips simplify the design of system and it's convenient to upgrade the system, especially the algorithm running on the DSP.

This paper uses two Davinci chips, that is, DM6446 Dual-Core (ARM+DSP) chip, and OMAP3530 (ARM+DSP+2D/3D Accelerator) chip, to design a network video surveillance system. OMAP3530 is a processor for mobile applications, such as mobile phones, GPS systems, laptop computers and some other low-power portable applications. OMAP3530 in a single chip integrates ARM Cortex-A8 processor, TMS320C64x + DSP core, 2D/3D accelerators and a wealth of audio and video interfaces. OMAP3530 can also be used for 2D/3D gaming, video conferencing, 3G multimedia mobile phone, PDA and some other high-performance devices and applications.

2 Hardware Design

In this network video surveillance system, DM6446 works as the IP camera and OMAP3530 as the client-end. In order to develop DM6446, TDSEVM6446 evaluation board is chosen. As to OMAP3530, ICETEK MINI board is chosen.

2.1 Hardware Architecture of IP Camera

Hardware design of IP Camera is shown in Figure1. ARM core communicates with DSP through DSPLink and controls LCD, camera and Ethernet. DSP core compresses data. The standard of compression is H.264.

Operating system running on the ARM core is Linux. ARM core is responsible for control of peripherals, task management and scheduling of each module.

ARM and DSP communicate through DSPLink. DSP core is responsible for the implementation and acceleration of signal processing algorithms, but can not control peripherals. All the tasks of peripherals are handled by ARM core.

Video Processing Front End (VPFE) is responsible for data capture, Video Processing Back End (VPBE) is responsible for data display. VPFE converts the original image of RGB format into YUV format in order that data can be processed by DSP. VPBE converts the YUV image into NTSC or PAL format so that the LCD can display the video.

DM6446 also integrates Ethernet Media Access Controller (EMAC). There is a PHY chip on the board connecting EMAC, so that the board can log onto the Internet via Ethernet interface. TCP/IP protocol is used to transmit data.

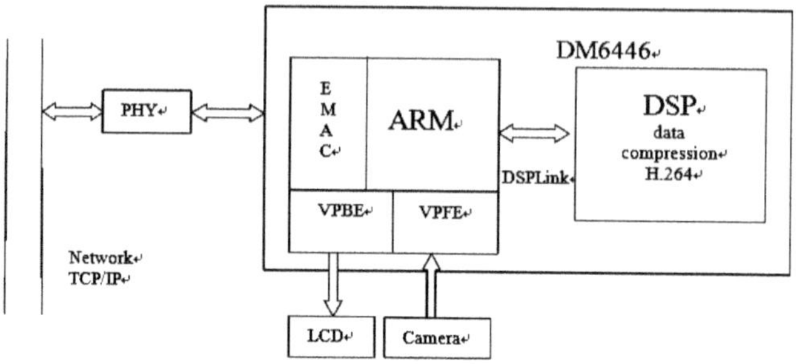

Fig. 1. Hardware design of IP Camera. ARM core communicates with DSP through DSPLink and controls LCD, camera and Ethernet. DSP core compresses data.

2.2 Hardware Architecture of Client-End

Hardware design of Client-end is shown in Figure2. There is no PHY chip or Ethernet interface on the MINI board, so a USB-to-Ethernet converter is used to log onto the Internet. ARM core integrates USB controller, so a USB hub is connected in order to use more USB-based devices.ARM core also integrates DVI-D interface, so video can be displayed on DVI-based LCD.

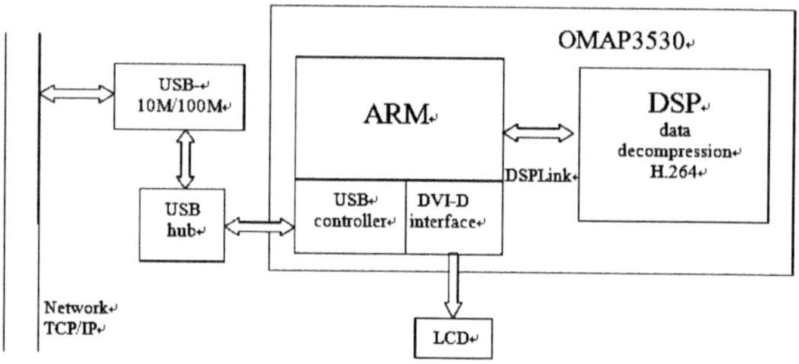

Fig. 2. Hardware design of Client-end. USB-to-Ethernet is used to log onto the Internet and a USB hub is used to expand more devices.

3 Software Design

TDSEVM6446 board first initializes the camera, LCD, and other local devices. Then it waits for video requests from the client. When receiving the client request, the board captures the video, compresses data and transmits data to the client. Client-end receives the data, decompresses the data, and displays them on the LCD. The flow chart of the system is shown in Figure3.

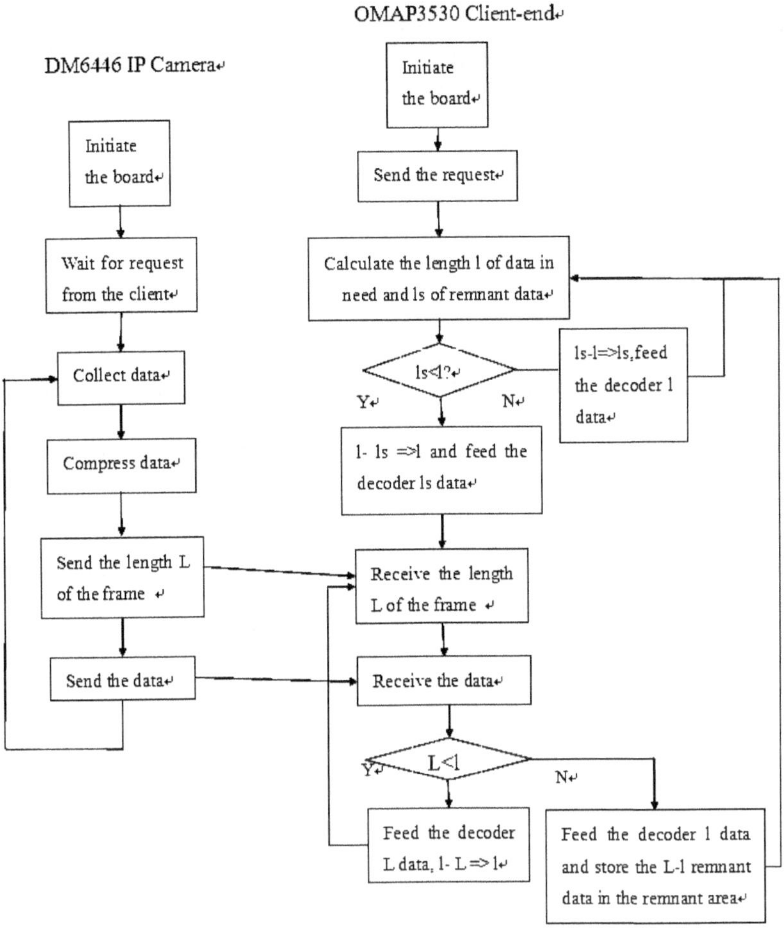

Fig. 3. The flow chart of the system. The DM6446 board initializes devices, waits for video requests, captures the video, compresses data and transmits data to the client. Client-end receives the data, decompresses the data, and displays them on the LCD. Remnant area is used to make sure that speeds of IP Camera and Client-end are matched.

3.1 Software Architecture of IP Camera

TDSEVM6446 board first initializes the camera, LCD, and other local devices. Then it waits for video requests from the client. When receiving the client request, the board captures the video, compresses data and transmits data to the client.

ENCODE is one of demos along with TDSEVM6446 board [5]. It captures video, displays the video on the local LCD and stores the video as a file in a local disk. ENCODE is modified so that IP Camera can realize the function drawn in the Figure3.

ENCODE is based on thread technology. There are four threads in ENCODE: capture thread, video thread, display thread and writer thread. Capture thread controls the camera and captures original data. Video thread gets data from Capture thread and compresses data. Display thread also gets data from Capture thread and displays data on the local LCD. Writer thread gets compressed data from Video thread and stores them in a file. Data are passed through the threads by using FIFO.

In order to send data onto the internet, the procedure main.c and the procedure writer.c are modified to wait for request and send the stream. As to the protocol, TCP/IP is chosen and sockets are used to transmit data.

3.2 Transplantation of Decode

DECODE is a media player designed for EVM board along with DVSDK (Digital Video Software Development Kit). DECODE can play video with formats of .wma, .264, .mpeg4, etc. But it cannot run on MINI board because MINI board is quite different from EVM board. DECODE is transplanted onto MINI board and Figure4 shows that DECODE plays a file of format h.264 on MINI board.

DECODE is also based on thread technology. There are three threads in DECODE: loader thread, video thread and display thread. Loader thread loads data from a file and sends data to video thread. Video thread receives data and decompresses them, then sends the decompressed data to display thread. Display thread converts data from YUV to RGB and displays them on LCD. DECODE is transplanted onto MINI board and it is shown in Figure 4.

Fig. 4. DECODE plays a file of format h.264 on MINI board. DECODE is modified and transplanted onto MINI board.

3.3 Software Design of Client-End

Client-end receives the data, decompresses the data, and displays them on the LCD. DECODE is used as the software of Client-end. It is known from above that DECODE is based on DMAI. DMAI is a thin utility layer on top of the operating system (Linux or DSP/BIOS) and the Codec Engine (CE) to assist in quickly writing portable applications on a DaVinci platform [6]. DMAI is modified but DECODE need not.

DMAI is defined by a set of C files and functions. In the procedure Loader.c, there're several functions defining how to read data from a file. And DECODE implements these functions to read data, decode them and display them. These functions are modified so that data are received by TCP/IP rather than read from a file.

Because data are from IP Camera, the length of the data may not equal to what the decoder needs. An array is used as a remnant area. Figure3 shows how the data are processed. The decoder firstly calculates the length of data it needs, then looks up the remnant area to find out whether the data are enough. If there are enough data, the decoder just uses the data in the remnant area; if not, the decoder consumes the data and receives a new frame from IP Camera. When the new frame arrives, the decoder is firstly fed up, then remnant data are put into the remnant area. Then the decoder decompresses the data.

4 Implementation of the Whole System

The video surveillance system is shown in Figure 5. Resolution is PAL, which is 720x576. Frame rate is 25fps. The system has 3-second delay, because DMAI is designed to play video files, and the decoder is required to pre-read 1500000 data. It takes about 3 seconds for pre-reading. The quality of video will decline if the object moves more quickly.

Fig. 5. The video surveillance system. Resolution is PAL, which is 720x576. Frame rate is 25fps.

5 Summary

The video surveillance system takes the advantage of SoC and simplifies the development of circuit. Resolution is PAL, which is 720x576. Frame rate is 25fps. This system can be used in home safety, public security, traffic monitoring, manufacturing monitoring and so on. Since OMAP3530 is designed for portable device, the client-end can also become mobile by use of 3G, GPRS, WLAN, etc.

This system has 3-second delay, so future work is to transplant our own decoder, meanwhile, the system should be more intelligent including tracking and behavior analysis.

References

1. Raty, T.D.: Survey on Contemporary Remote Surveillance Systems for Public Safety. IEEE Transactions On Systems, Man, And Cybernetics—Part C: Applications And Reviews 40(5) (2010)
2. Valera, M., Velastin, S.A.: Intelligent distributed surveillance systems: a review. IEE Proc.-Vis. Image Signal Process. 152(2) (2005)
3. Regazzoni, C.S., Cavallaro, A., Wu, Y., Konrad, J., Hampapur, A.: Video Analytics for Surveillance: Theory and Practice. IEEE Signal Processing Magazine (2010)
4. Liu, L., Li, Z., Delp, E.J.: Efficient and Low-Complexity Surveillance Video Compression Using Backward-Channel Aware Wyner–Ziv Video Coding. IEEE Transactions on Circuits And Systems For Video Technology 19(4) (2009)
5. Texas Instruments: Encode Demo for the DVEVM/DVSDK 1.2. spraa96a (2007)
6. Texas Instruments: Davinci Multimedia Application Interface, `http://www.processors.wiki.ti.com/index.php/DMAI`

A New Control Scheme Based on Computer for Automatic PMD Compensation in Optical Fiber Communication Systems

Junyi Zhang[1,*], Jinnan Zhang[2], Rongguo Zhang[2], and Huiping Gao[1]

[1] School of Electronic Engineering
[2] Country Key Laboratory of Information Photonics and Optical Communications,
Beijing University of Posts and Telecommunications,
Beijing 100876, China
Gaohp2011@gmail.com

Abstract. This paper demonstrates a universal digital signal processing (computer) application for adaptive polarization mode compensation (PMD) compensation utilizing GTPSO algorithm in optical transmission systems. It is significant and challenging to establish an effective logic control compensator due to the time-varying and statistical properties of PMD, especially in high-speed optical fiber communication systems. We designed a low power-consume computer-based integrated control system to complete first-order PMD and second-order PMD compensation. The searching process and the tracking process for automatic PMD compensation could be completed in less than 10ms and 1ms.

Keywords: computer, PMD compensator, GTPSO.

1 Introduction

Polarization mode dispersion causes time and channel dependent pulse distortions in high-speed optical communication systems, potentially limiting their transmission capacity [1, 2]. Dynamic variation in optical fiber makes dispersion compensation difficult to implement, because PMD changes stochastically over time. So some kind of adaptive PMD compensation is often indispensable. PMD compensation mainly consists of three parts in the experiments: the PMD monitoring unit, the compensation unit, and the logic control unit [3]. To compensate PMD in the shortest time, control unit plays an important role. Using high-speed AD chip, DA chip and digital signal processing can reduce the compensation time. We introduce the computer system as an improved logic control unit used in PMD adaptive compensation system. 1-order PMD and 2-order PMD compensation were implemented with this scheme.

* Junyi Zhang was born in Hebei, China, in November 1975. He received the Ph.D Degree in electromagnetic and microwave technology from Beijing University of Posts and Telecommunications, BUPT. His research interests include PMD compensation, computer science and access networks.

H. Tan and M. Zhou (Eds.): CSE 2011, Part I, CCIS 201, pp. 303–310, 2011.

2 The Theory of PMD and PMD Compensation

2.1 Polarization Mode Dispersion

Polarization mode dispersion has its origins in optical birefringence [1]. In a single mode fiber, an optical wave traveling in the fiber can be represented as the linear superposition of two orthogonal polarized HE11 modes. The two modes and in the ideal fiber, which has a perfect circular symmetric cross-section, are indistinguishable (degenerate) with the same time group delay. However, real fiber has large amounts of asymmetry due to imperfections in manufacturing process or mechanical stress on the fiber after the manufacture as shown in Fig. 1. The degeneracy of and modes are broken by the asymmetry, resulting in birefringence with a difference in the phase and group velocities of the two modes.

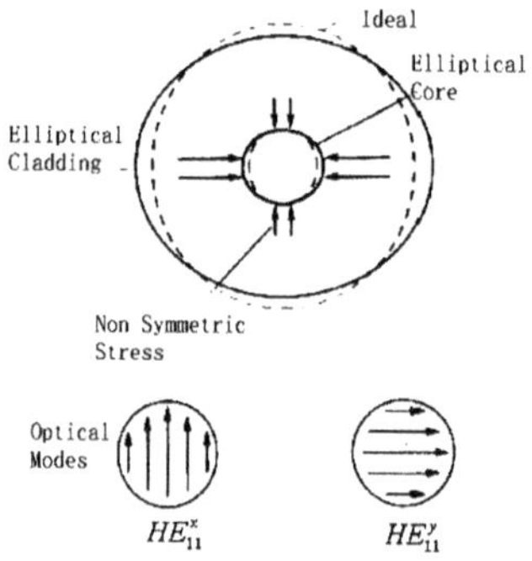

Fig. 1. Asymmetry of a real fiber and degeneracy of two orthogonal HE11 modes

If a pulsed optical wave linearly polarized at 45°to the birefringence axis is launched into a birefringent fiber, the pulse will be split at output end of the fiber due to the different group velocities between two HE11 modes. As shown in Fig.2, this resulting in a signal distortion in optical transmission system. The time separation between two modes is defined as differential group delay (DGD). This phenomenon is called polarization mode dispersion. Roughly speaking, the fast axis and the slow axis are called principal states of polarization (PSP).

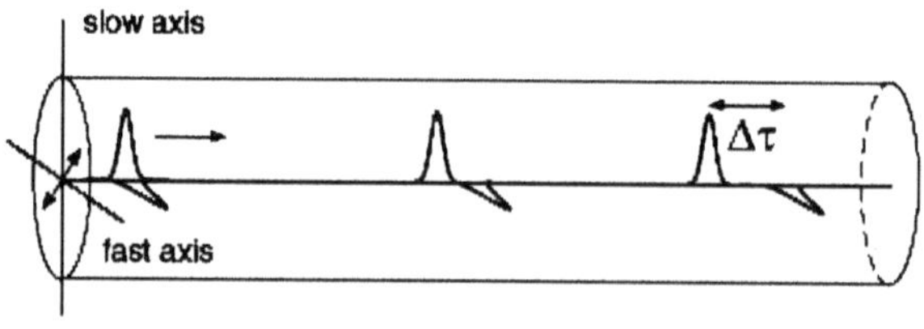

Fig. 2. Pulse splitting due to birefringence

2.2 The Configuration of Adaptive PMD Compensation

As mentioned in the introduction, PMD compensation mainly consists of three parts in the experiments: the PMD monitoring unit, the compensation unit, and the logic control unit. A logic control unit based on computer has been proposed here. It is widely believed that the one-stage compensator is able to compensate the first-order PMD. For the one-stage compensator, the compensation unit is composed of a polarization controller whose function is to transform the state of polarization (SOP) of input optical wave into output state, and a differential group delay line with the purpose of eliminating the DGD of the input optical signals. One-stage compensator has 3 or 4 control parameters (or degrees of freedom (DOF)), three for PC and one for DGD line, to be controlled depending on whether the differential group delay line (DGD) is fixed or varied. Since degree of polarization (DOP) of the distorted optical signals can indicate the variation of PMD in a fiber [4], we used DOP as the feedback signal in the PMD monitoring unit. In the logic control unit we adopt gradient particle swarm optimization (GTPSO) algorithm as the control algorithm. Figure 3 shows the configurations of one-stage compensators.

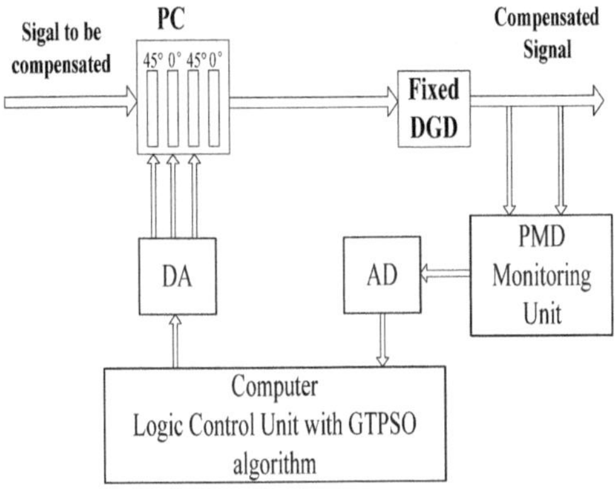

Fig. 3. The configurations of one stage PMD compensator

3 The Computer Control System

3.1 The Computer System Design

For a PMD compensation system, computer control unit should be able to complete the control task of first-order PMD and second-order PMD compensation. Sampling the feedback signal needs the data-acquisition systems (DAS) implement four simultaneous-sampling from an in-line polarimeter in the PMD monitoring unit. The realization of first-order PMD compensation needs to control a polarization controller (PC). A PC and a subsequent birefringent element is the simplest optical PMD compensator (PMDC) which possesses the adjustment of three degrees of freedom. This requires the DA chip can output three voltage signals in the same time. To achieve second-order

PMD compensation, the DA chip should simultaneously output at least six channels of voltage signals for two PCs. If the group delay line is varied, an additional DA chip was required to output simultaneously the seventh voltage signal. For a computer-based PMDC, the computer should complete three tasks, AD conversion for the feedback signals, DA conversion for the control voltages to the PCs, running the control algorithm which is most important among the three tasks.

3.2 Experiment Setup

The experiment setup is shown in Fig.4. 80Ghit/s 223-1 of DQPSK formats are produced at the wavelength 1551nm. The PMD emulator consists of two-section units of two manually adjusted polarization controllers (PC1 and PC2) and two polarization maintaining fibers pieces (PMF1 and PMF2) of 60ps and 30ps DGD. An optical band-pass filter with 3dB bandwidth of 0.8nm is used to suppress ASE noise form EDFA. For three-stage PMD compensator, each stage has an electrically controlled polarization controller and a delay line. For the electrically polarization controllers, each of them has four fiber-squeezer cells to be adjusted with 0-10V voltage, out of which only three cells are used for PC3 and PC4, one cell for PC5 in the experiment. Therefore there are seven voltages to he controlled, which is 7 degrees of freedom (DOF) problem. The delay lines PMF3 and PMF4 are with DGDs of 30ps and 35ps respectively. As the PMD monitor, an in-line polarimeter is used to measure instantaneously the Stokes parameters S0, S1, S2, S3 and DOP in fiber link. The logic control unit adjusts the voltages of seven cells of PC3, PC4, and PC5 to searching the optimum of the whole fiber link by using GTPSO algorithm according to the DOP feedback signals, as shown in Fig.4. The effectiveness of PMD compensation is observed by eye diagram on the oscilloscope.

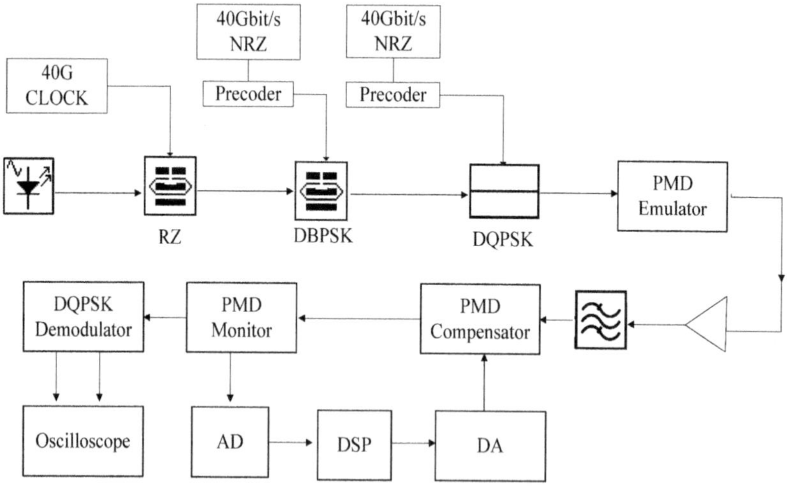

Fig. 4. Experiment setup for adaptive three-stage PMD Compensation

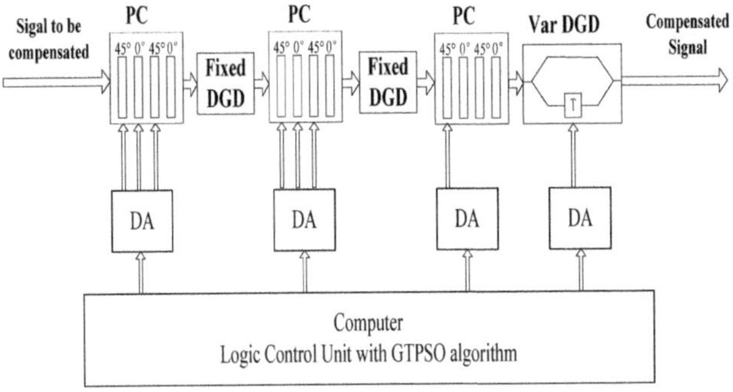

Fig. 5. The configurations of three-stage compensators

4 GTPSO Algorithm

In order to improve the convergent speed of the particle swarm optimization (PSO) algorithm in the control of real-time polarization mode dispersion (PMD) compensation, we apply a new gradient method to PSO algorithm in this paper. We call this new algorithm GTPSO. The particle swarm optimization (PSO) algorithm is a new community intelligence optimization method firstly proposed by Kennedy and Eberhart in 1995 [3]. To be exactly similar with other global optimization algorithm, the PSO algorithm tends to suffer from premature convergence.

Many improvements have been suggested [4, 5, 6] to overcome the problem of premature convergence. GTPSO method proposed in this paper is also one of them. The main principle of this method is adding a new gradient method to PSO to improve the performance of it.

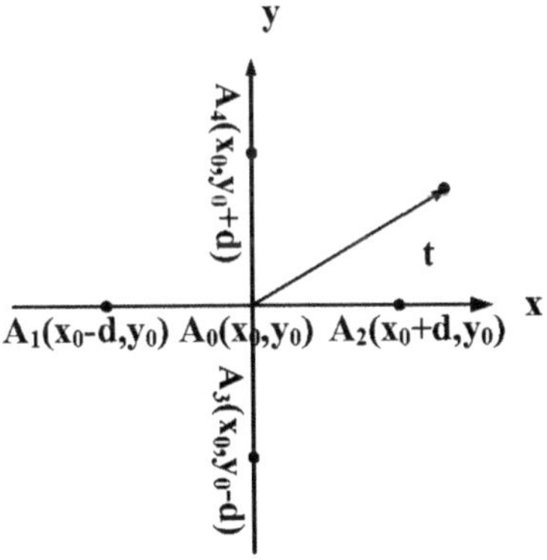

Fig. 6. The principle of the gradient method

We take a two-dimensional problem for example. The principle of the gradient method is depicted in Fig 6. For the x-dimension we choose one position on the left and right of the former global best position (A0(X0, Y0)) respectively. So the two positions are A1(X0-d, Y0) and A2(X0+d, Y0). Then compare the fitness of the two positions. Suppose the fitness of A2 is better than that of A1, so we choose the positive direction to move along. Using the same means we can find out which direction to move along in y-dimension. We also suppose it is the positive direction. Then we can get a vector A= [|f(A2)-f(A0)|, |f(A4)-f(A0)|], where f is the fitness. The direction of vector A is the moving direction in the two-dimensional hyperspace. We make the moving length be equal to t (t is a constant), and we achieve a new position. If only the latter position is better than the former one, the moving will be continued. At last, we can find a best position and the gradient method is finished.

Then the PSO algorithm begins. We update the particles' positions using PSO algorithm, and compare the fitness of the new present best positions with the fitness of the former global best position and choose a best position as the present global best position. Next, choose a better position between this present global best position and the best position achieved from the gradient method as the final present global best position. Then, carry on the procedures for several times until the criterion is met.

5 Experiment Results

We got a data table achieved from the adaptive PMD compensation experiment depicting the relationship between DOP and variable voltages of the polarization controller. Then, we tested GTPSO and PSO algorithm using this data table by simulation. We regarded DOP as the fitness, and variable voltages as arguments. Our aim was to find the best DOP in the data table. We conducted 50 times of the simulation, and the max iteration for each time was 50. Fig.7 shows the relationship between the best DOP we find and the iteration.

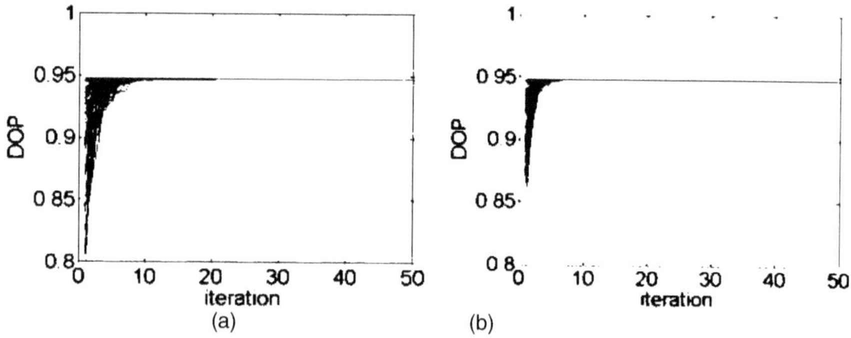

Fig. 7. The best DOP vs. iteration (a) PSO; (b) GTPSO

The simulation shows both two methods have found approximately the same DOP and position. Also, from Fig 8 we can get some conclusions: particles from both of the two methods have not been locked into the local sub-optima; both of the two methods get the precise results in 50 times; the speed of GTPSO method is higher than that of PSO algorithm.

Then we set a threshold and conduct the program for 50 times. For each time, when the threshold is met, the search will be ended and the final iteration number will be recorded. Fig.8 shows the relationship between the number of the corresponding iteration records and the iteration. From Fig.9 we can get the mean convergence iteration number. The mean convergence iteration number of PSO algorithm is 3.12, and that of GTPSO method is 2.18. So the speed of GTPSO method is higher than that of PSO algorithm.

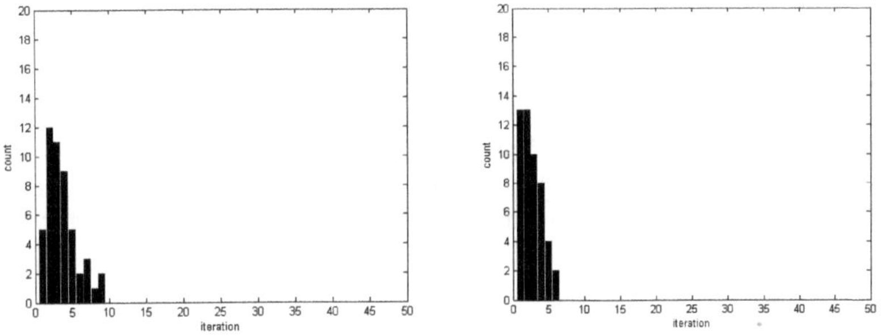

(a) (b)

Fig. 8. The number of the corresponding iteration records vs. Iteration (a) PSO; (b) GTPSO

The compensation performance of the PMD adaptive compensator using both algorithm was tested through experiment. The time of one particle for each iteration was measured. 20 particles were used and the iteration was 5 in each searching process. Running the searching function for 10000 times cost 15s, so the time of one particle for one iteration was 15us. The searching process and the tracking process for automatic PMD compensation using GTPSO algorithm could be completed in less than 10ms and 1ms respectively while the searching process and the tracking process using PSO algorithm need about 14ms and 1.2ms. Experiment results are shown in Fig.10.

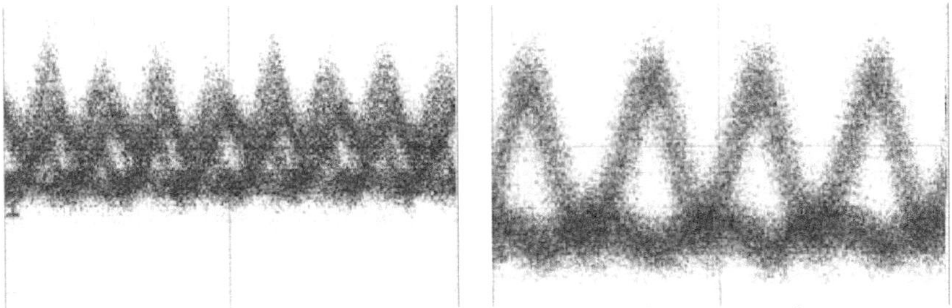

(a) Without compensation (b) With compensation

Fig. 9. The eye diagram in 80G/s DQPSK system

6 Conclusions

Using the computer-based control unit, we have realized an experiment for first-order PMD and second-order PMD compensation. A new PSO algorithm, the GTPSO method, combined with a new gradient method algorithm, was introduced as control algorithm, which was very suitable for multi-dimensional problem in PMD compensation. The result shows GTPSO method is better than PSO algorithm in the convergent speed. As a result, we get the conclusion that GTPSO method is a better method for real-time PMD compensation.

Acknowledgments

This research is supported by the Fundamental Research Funds for the Central Universities (2009RC0401, 2009RC0405), the China Postdoctoral Science Foundation funded project (20100470259), Specialized Research Fund for the Doctoral Program of Higher Education, the Fundamental Research Funds for the Central Universities and Youth Innovation Project of BUPT.

References

1. Kogelnik, H., Jopson, R.M., Nelson, L.: Polarization-mode dispersion in Optical Fiber Telecommunications IV B. In: Kaminow, I., Li, T. (eds.) Academic, New York (2002)
2. Shtaif, M., Boroditsky, M.: The effect of the frequency dependence of PMD on the performance of optical communications systems. IEEE Photon. Technol. Lett. 15(10), 1369–1371 (2003)
3. Zhang, X., Zheng, Y., Shen, Y., Zhang, J., Yang, B.: Particle swarm optimization used as a control algorithm for adaptive PMD compensation. IEEE Photon. Technol. Lett. 17(1), 85–87 (2005)
4. Noé, R., Sandel, D., Mirvoda, V.: PMD in high-bit-rate transmission and means for its mitigation. IEEE J. of Select. Topics in Quantum Electron. 10(2), 341–355 (2004)
5. Burr-Brown Corporation, 12-bit quad voltage output digital-to-analog converter (April 2000)
6. Zhang, J., Yuan, X., Fang, G., Zhang, X., Huang, Y.: A New Control Scheme based on computer for Automatic PMD Compensation in Optical Fiber Communication Systems. NEWCAS-TAISA (2009)
7. Francia, C., Bruyère, F., Thiery, J.–P., Penninckx, D.: Simple dynamic polarization mode dispersion compensator. Electron. Lett. 35, 414–415 (1999)
8. Noé, R., Sandel, D., Yoshida-Dierolf, M., Hinz, S., Mirvoda, V., Schöpflin, A., Glingener, C., Gottwald, E., Scheerer, C., Fischer, G., Weyrauch, T., Haase, W.: Polarization mode dispersion compensation at 10, 20, and 40Gb/s with various optical equaliziers. J. Lightwave Technol. 17, 1602–1616 (1999)
9. Buchali, E., Baumert, W., Bulow, H., Poirrier, J.: A 40Gb/s eye monitor and its application to adaptive PMD compensation. OFC 2002, WE6 (2002)
10. Zhang, X., Yu, L., Zhang, Y., Shen, Y., Zhou, G., Chen, L., Xi, L., Yuan, T., Zhang, J., Yang, B.: Two-stage adaptive PMD compensation experiment for 10-Gb/s optical communication system. Chin. Opt. Lett. 1(11), 630–633 (2003)
11. Zhang, X., Xi, L., Yu, L., Zhou, G., Zhang, J., Zhang, N., Wu, B., Yuan, T., Chen, L., Zhang, H., Chen, S., Yao, M., Yang, B.: Two-stage adaptive PMD compensation in 40-Gb/s OTDM optical communication system. Chin. Opt. Lett. 2(6), 316–319 (2004)

A New Algorithm for the Calculation of Spatial Derivatives in Computer Simulation of Seismic Waves

Baotong Liu

School of Physics and Information Science,
Tianshui Normal University, China
liubt@citiz.net

Abstract. In numerical simulation of seismic waves, the accuracy and efficiency depend on the method used for calculating the spatial derivatives in the wave equation and on the method for the time integration. Errors in the numerical calculation are mainly from the approximation of spatial derivatives. This study presented a new algorithm for the calculation of spatial derivatives. It enables us to extend simulations to shorter wavelengths. An example of reverse-time migration of a synthetic data set showed that the numerical dispersion could be significantly reduced with respect to schemes that are based on finite differences.

Keywords: Wave equation, Numerical simulation, Derivative, Finite-difference method.

1 Introduction

Numerical solution of wave equation is routinely used for generating synthetic seismic surveys. These simulations are also the basis of reverse-time migration. An effective numerical simulator must be both accurate and computationally efficient. The generation of effective numerical simulators has been the topic of active research in recent years. The accuracy and efficiency of the numerical simulation depend on the method used for calculating the spatial derivatives in the wave equation and on the method for the time integration. For the time integration, second-order differencing in time is the simplest method; however, with this approach, numerical dispersion is always present unless extremely small time steps are used, which in turn make the numerical simulation very costly. Dablain presented a high-order time-integration scheme that reduces numerical dispersion and, for a given accuracy, improves computational efficiency [1]. More accurate and efficient time-integration schemes that allow an arbitrary time-step size were introduced [2]; thus, the time-integration error can be made arbitrarily small without compromising numerical efficiency. The main source of errors in the numerical calculation is therefore in the approximation of spatial derivatives.

For the spatial derivative approximation, the fastest and least accurate method is second-order finite difference, whereas the pseudospectral method is the most accurate but considerably slower. In general, there is a trade-off: For a specified accuracy,

H. Tan and M. Zhou (Eds.): CSE 2011, Part I, CCIS 201, pp. 311–314, 2011.

a lower order method will require a large number of grid points with a small number of calculations per point, whereas a higher order method will require fewer grid points but more calculations per point. Examination of the numerical phase velocity dispersion curves for explicit finite difference schemes shows that although higher order schemes improve the accuracy, there is a saturation effect whereby the rate of improvement per order of the difference operator decreases for higher orders. Experience indicates that the most economical order is somewhere between fourth order and eighth order. Another method to design explicit derivative operators is by spectral matching of the response in the wavenumber domain. This approach presents an improvement over the finite-difference method in the ability to propagate correctly short-wavelength components; however, the approach suffers from the same drawback of finite differences in that long-derivative operators fail to bring significant improvement in accuracy. An alternative approach for spatial derivative calculation is to use implicit or recursive derivative operators that are based on a Pade approximation [3]. The idea behind this approach is that rational expansions often converge faster than power series expansions, and, indeed, for a specified accuracy, this approach is more efficient than explicit finite differences; however, as with ordinary difference approximations, the method is very accurate for the longer wavelengths but less accurate for the shorter wavelengths.

This study presented a novel algorithm for the calculation of spatial derivatives. I described the design of spatial derivative operators and compared their accuracy with the accuracy of explicit derivative operators. Then, a numerical example was presented, in which simulations that have recursive operators were compared with fourth-order finite-difference simulations and pseudospectral numerical simulations for the 2D constant density acoustic wave equation.

2 The Calculation of Spatial Derivatives

2.1 Recursive Second-Derivative Operators

Given a function $f(x)$, we denote its sampled values by $f[j]=f(x=jdx)$. The recursive second-derivative approximation can be written as

$$\frac{d^2 f}{dx^2}[j]=\frac{a_0+a_1\boldsymbol{\Delta}_1+a_2\boldsymbol{\Delta}_2+\cdots+a_N\boldsymbol{\Delta}_N}{1+b_1\boldsymbol{\Delta}_1+b_2\boldsymbol{\Delta}_2+\cdots+b_M\boldsymbol{\Delta}_M}f[j], \tag{1}$$

Where $\boldsymbol{\Delta}_k f[j]=f[j+k]+f[j-k]$.

We consider operators for which $M\leq N$. In this case, equation 1 can be recast in an equivalent form:

$$\frac{d^2 f}{dx^2}[j]=\left(c_0+\cdots+c_{N-M}\boldsymbol{\Delta}_{N-M}+\frac{d_0}{1+\beta_0\boldsymbol{\Delta}_1}+\cdots+\frac{d_{M-1}}{1+\beta_{M-1}\boldsymbol{\Delta}_1}\right)f[j]. \tag{2}$$

Equation 2 is more convenient for calculations, whereas equation 1 is more suitable for the design of the coefficients. The first terms in equation 2, $c_0+\cdots+c_{N-M}\boldsymbol{\Delta}_{N-M}$, form an explicit operator. Each of the implicit terms $[d_j/(1+\beta_j\Delta_1)]f(j)$ forms a tridiagonal equation system. In terms of cost, each explicit term in equation 2 requires one multiplication, whereas each implicit term requires two multiplications.

2.2 Operator Design

The coefficients a_1 and b_1 in equation 1 are calculated by an L_∞ norm fit in the spectral domain [2]. A substitution of $f[j]=e^{ikx}$ in equation 1 for $x=jdx$ yields the fitting equation

$$a_0+\sum_{j=1}^{N}2a_j\cos(jkdx)+\sum_{j=1}^{M}2b_jk^2\cos(jkdx)=-k^2. \tag{3}$$

In the Remes algorithm, the fitting equation is applied to N+M+2 value of k, where an error term of alternating sign is added to each equation. The resulting (N+M+2)×(N+M+2) system of linear equations writes

$$a_0+\sum_{j=1}^{N}2a_j\cos(jk_Ldx)+\sum_{j=1}^{M}2b_jk_L^2\cos(jk_Ldx)+(-1)^Le=-k^2,$$

$$L=1,\cdots,N+M+2. \tag{4}$$

The unknowns are $a_0,a_1,\cdots,a_N,b_1,\cdots,b_M$, and the error is e. The N+M+2 wavenumber components k_L are within the range $0\le k_L<k_{\max}$, where $k_{\max}$ is specified by the user. The value of $k_{\max}$ should be set to give the best compromise between a small value of the error e and the largest wavenumber component that can be propagated with little numerical dispersion.

2.3 Staggered Recursive First-Derivative Operators

Given a sampled function $f[j]=f(x=jdx), j=0,\cdots,N_x-1$, the staggered first-derivative operator can be written as

$$\frac{df}{dx}\left[j+\frac{1}{2}\right]=\frac{a_0\nabla_0+a_1\nabla_1+a_2\nabla_2+\cdots+a_N\nabla_N}{1+b_1\Delta_1+b_2\Delta_2+\cdots+b_M\Delta_M}f[j], \tag{5}$$

where $\Delta_k f[j+1/2]=f[j+k+1]+f[j-k]$ and $\nabla_k f[j+1/2]=f[j+k+1]-f[j-k],k=0,1,\cdots$. This form of the operator maintains the required oddness of the first derivative.

3 An Example of Simulation

The algorithm was tested in a 2D example of zero-offset reverse-time migration with the constant density acoustic wave equation. The model has a constant velocity of

4500m/s (Figure 1). The maximum frequency in this example was 80 Hz, the horizontal and vertical grid spacing was 27m, and the time step was 2ms. Figure 2a-d, respectively, show migrated images that were obtained with the fourth-order finite-difference method, the 2-1 operator method, the 3-1 operator method, and the pseudospectral method. The numerical dispersion is most prominent in Figure 2a of the fourth-order finite-difference method. Figure 2b of the 2-1 recursive method is somewhat improved, whereas the improvement in Figure 2c of the 3-1 recursive method is very obvious. In fact, the result in Figure 2c is almost as good as the result of the pseudospectral method in Figure 2d.

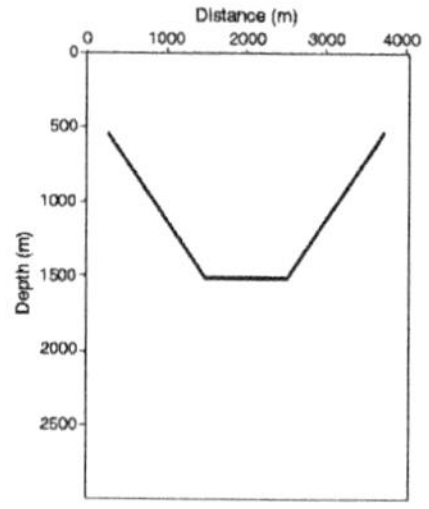

Fig. 1. Depth model: Constant velocity

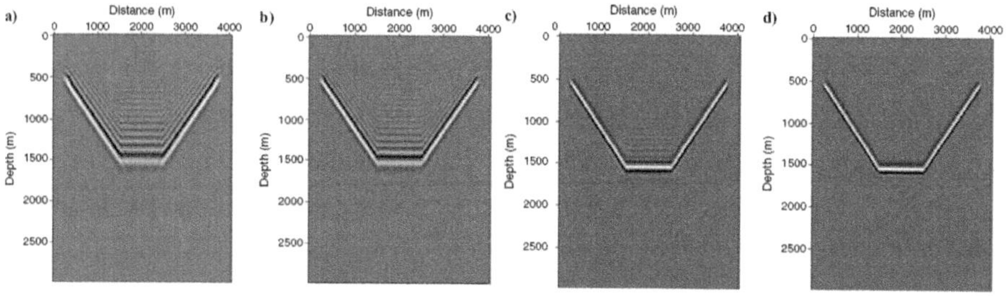

Fig. 2. Reverse-time migration results. (a) Fourth-order finite-difference operator(4-0); (b) implicit operator(2-1); (c) implicit operator(3-1), and (d) pseudospectral method.

References

1. Dablain, M.A.: The Application of High-order Differencing to the Scalar Wave Equation. Geophysics 51, 54–56 (1986)
2. Stoffa, P.L., Pestana, R.C.: Numerical Solution of the Acoustic Equation by the Rapid Expansion Method-A One Step Approach. In: 79th Annual International Meeting, pp. 2672–2675. SEG Press, Houston (2009)
3. Zhou, H., Liao, Q., Ortigosa, F.: Construction and Analysis of an Optimized Compact Finite Difference Scheme for RTM. In: 70th Annual International Meeting of EAGE (2009)

Sentiment Feature Identification from Chinese Online Reviews

Jiani Yao, Hongwei Wang*, and Pei Yin

School of Economics and Management, Tongji University, Shanghai, China
Tel.: 86-21-65983943
yuki_nini@hotmail.com, hwwang@tongji.edu.cn,
evawater@163.com

Abstract. Using statistical machine learning methods to select features and reduce dimensionality for sentiment classification of Chinese online reviews based on hotels. The results showed that: sentiment classification of Chinese online reviews will obtain the highest accuracy when taking adjectives, adverbs and verbs together as the feature. The best reduction method is Document Frequency, followed by Chi-square Statistic, and Information Gain is the worst. Mutual Information is not suitable for the sentiment classification of Chinese online reviews while Factor Analysis can be a potential method though merely used.

Keywords: Text feature; Sentiment analysis; Customer reviews; Natural language statistics.

1 Introduction

In recent years, there is an ever-increasingly strong involvement of online users with the development of the Internet. They make reviews on products (or services) as well as current events via the Internet. The initiative and the level of online reviews boost. It is said that the Internet has become not only an information warehouse, but also the emotional communication garden for online users.

Online reviews reflect the writer's opinions or views on things, characters or events. Nowadays, the size of Chinese online reviews is exploding. However, most e-commerce websites neglect the value management of online reviews. Although some have been aware of the importance of reviews management, they are unable to identify the emotional information from reviews automatically because of the weak analytical tools.

The so-called sentiment analysis of online reviews is to analyze the unstructured online reviews so as to identify the users' emotional tend -- whether be "happy " or "sad", or to determine their views of agreement, or even mining the emotional evolution with the time. Because of the difference in language structures and cultural background between English and Chinese, the research results focused on sentiment analysis in English are unable to be applied to Chinese reviews directly. In particular, the sentiment feature identification and extraction of Chinese online reviews has restricted the effect of Chinese sentiment classification.

* Corresponding author.

H. Tan and M. Zhou (Eds.): CSE 2011, Part I, CCIS 201, pp. 315–322, 2011.

2 Related Studies

2.1 The Basic Process of Sentiment Classification

In essence, the sentiment classification of Chinese online reviews is a kind of text classification. The basic process is shown in Fig. 1. Similar process is followed by sentiment classification.

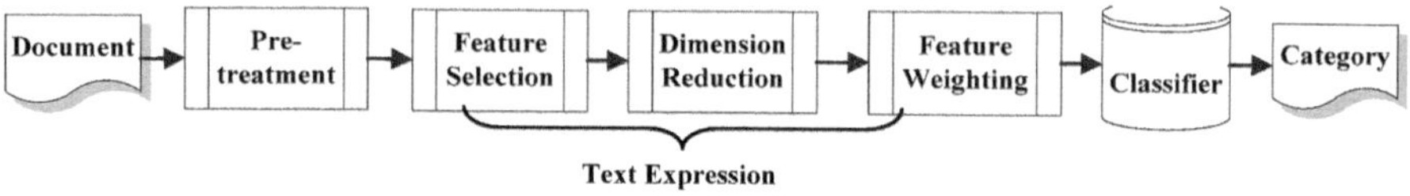

Fig. 1. The process of text classification

2.2 The Choice of Classifier

The Classifier commonly used in text classification including Support Vector Machines (SVM), Maximum Entropy (ME), Naïve Bayes (NB) and so on.

Research on text classification shows that SVM classification usually performance well, especially in the case of limited training samples, the effect is better than the other classifiers. For this reason, SVM has become the preferred sentiment analysis classifier. Xia HS [1], Li J [2], Pang [3], Ye Qiang [4], [5] all have shown the excellent performance of SVM over the other Classifiers. Based on the above analysis, we select SVM as the emotional classifier of Chinese online Reviews.

2.3 Method of Text Representation

Vector Space Model, referred to as VSM, is an effective method for text representation. VSM model addresses three issues: feature selection [6] [7] [8], feature dimension reduction [9] [10] [11], and feature weight calculation [3].

2.4 Research and Commentary

Overall, the existing researches mostly focus on subject-oriented text classification while few studies were conducted in sentiment classification. Online Reviews sentiment classification in Chinese mainly use statistical machine learning methods, with relatively mature classification algorithm, but emotional feature identification and dimension reduction methods are still insufficient. Part of speech and a combination of part of speech are likely to become potential emotional features. Furthermore, feature dimension reduction (methods such as DF, IG, CHI, MI, FA, etc.) and the weight set, will also affect the emotion classification.

3 Experimental Design of Feature Identification

3.1 The Experiment of Feature Identification

The basic process is shown in Fig. 2. In this paper, there are four typical feature selection methods: DF (document frequency), IG (information gain), CHI ($\chi 2$ statistic), MI (mutual information) and one method of feature extraction as FA (Factor Analysis). The training corpus collected is coped with these five algorithms and various eigenvectors are obtained for experiments under different thresholds.

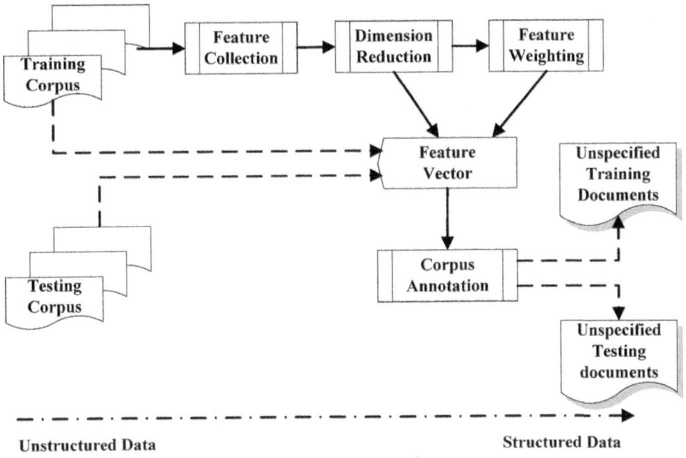

Fig. 2. Feature identification process

3.2 Test Set Selection

We choose the Chinese emotional mining-ChnSentiVorp as the corpus (http://www.searchforum.org.cn/tansongbo/corpus-senti.htm). The corpus taken from comments on the hotel in Ctrip (http://www.ctrip.com) organized by Tan Songbo, etc., last updated on December 19th, 2008. The size of the corpus is 10,000. 2000 classified comments have been selected as the training corpus, including 1000 positive and negative each apart. Another 1000 comments have also been selected as a test corpus.

3.3 Collection of Features

The features are collected from all texts in the training corpus in order to form a feature set. Feature must be perfectibility and differentiated. We take words and expressions as feature, choose the ICTCLAS System developed by the Institute of Computing Technology of Chinese Academy (http://ictclas.org/) to do the word segmentation and POS tagging. Extract adjectives, adverbs and verbs from the corpus with slightly manual adjusting. The extractive process is shown in Fig. 3.

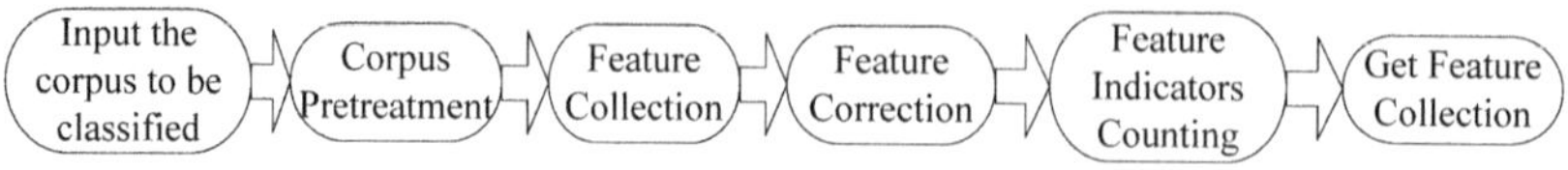

Fig. 3. Feature selection process

3.4 Dimension Reduction of Features

After feature collection, we obtain a high-dimensional feature eigenvector. There are two dimension reduction methods: one is called feature selection which is based on a certain criteria to select some most distinguished parts from the original Feature Sets, such as document frequency, information gain, CHI statistics and mutual information.

The other is based on a principle, constructing a transformation from the original feature space to the low-dimensional one, which will transform the classification information contained in the original feature space to the new low-dimensional one [13]. Such as principal component analysis, linear case analysis, factor analysis, etc.

Relatively speaking, the complexity of the former one is low, thus it is widely used. The features obtained by the latter one are more close to the semantic description of the text. In this paper, we take four of the former dimension reduction method (DF, IG, CHI and MI) and one of the later one (FA).

3.5 Feature Weight Sets

For sentiment classification, the emotion types are basically determined when some key emotional features occur. That is to say, it is not important how many times a feature with emotional information occurs, but whether or not it appears and in which categories it appears. Based on above considerations, we take the Boolean method to calculate feature weights.

4 Experimental Results

4.1 The Poor Performance of Mutual Information

Through our experiment, it is obviously showed that the top 59.27% features' MI values are equal. These features appear only in negative categories. Among them, the low-frequency words (appear no more than 3 times) take up 91.28%. It will inevitably lead to a huge overhead cost in time and space if we use MI method. Therefore, the paper argues that mutual information method is not suitable for sentiment analysis oriented text feature selection, so we abandon it in the next experiments.

4.2 The Comparison of Feature Performance under Different Parts of Speech

Though experiments, we have obtained a total of 3560 valid features. In the emotional text, adjectives take a relatively larger proportion than adverbs do. We set the dimension of 100 and take different feature reduction algorithm experiments on these three parts of speech, adverbs combined with verbs and adjectives, adverbs combined with verbs respectively. The accuracy of classification is shown in Table 1:

Table 1. The performance comparison of feature vectors under different parts of speech and various algorithms

POS	DF	IG	CHI
Adjective	78.4%	78.7%	80.4%
Adverb	74.6%	71.3%	71.2%
Verb	74.5%	72.4%	73.3%
Adverb and Verb	79.2%	76.3%	75.0%
Adjective, Adverb and Verb	81.3%	80.8%	81.4%

It can be seen from the data in Table 1:

① The feature vectors have the best classification performance if we take the three parts of speech (adjectives, adverbs and verbs) together as the feature set.
② In the three parts of speech, the adjective make the greatest contribution to the classification.
③ Combination of adverbs and verbs can also improve the classification accuracy.

4.3 The Comparison of Eigenvectors Performance under Different Thresholds and Algorithm

According to the conclusions of Table 1, we take the combination of adjective, adverbs and verbs to select the feature, minimize the negative impact on the classification by part of speech.

Table 2. The performance comparison of different feature reduction algorithm

Number of feature	DF Accuracy (%)	IG Accuracy (%)	CHI Accuracy (%)
50	77.8	78.9	79.7
100	81.3	80.8	81.4
200	84.5	81.2	82.7
300	85.3	83.9	84.3
400	85.5	84.2	84.4
500	85.9	82.0	85.1

Table 2, Fig. 4 show the different classification results when the number of feature is 50,100,200,300,400,500 under the algorithm of DF, IG and CHI.

Previous studies show that the effect of text classification usually is: CHI> IG> DF, while in this paper, the results show that: DF> CHI> IG. Hence, it can be concluded that DF algorithm is dominant in the emotion-based text classification. The reasons leading to this result are as follows:

① Most words in the emotional text are rich in sentiment. The more intense a mood is, the more words with biased feelings will be used. Especially, reviews are generally direct. The words used for comments are generally vernacular and alike, rarely presented in a fancy or uncommon way. Thus, resulting in high-frequency words has greater impact on classification.

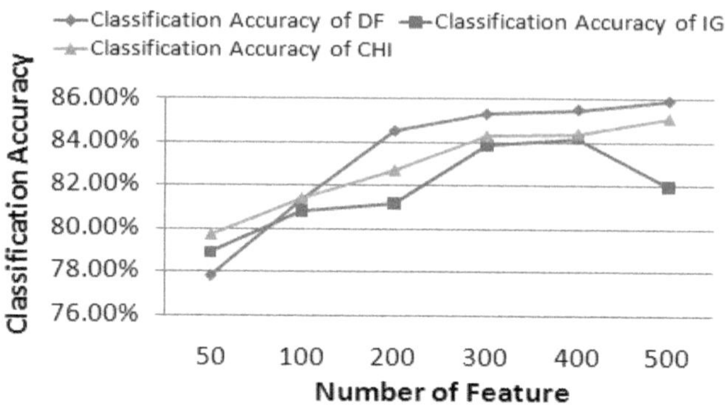

Fig. 4. The classification accuracy of different feature reduction algorithm (%)

② Adjectives, adverbs and verbs with emotional characteristics have been chosen as features in the experiment at first, unconsciously removing a large part of high-frequency words without emotional discrimination. In addition, the human factors may more or less influence the manual feature identification. Therefore, it also leads the results of DF to a certain degree of amplification.

4.4 The Comparison of Eigenvectors Performance under Three Feature Selection Method Integrated with Factor Analysis

Based on the study above, we take the combination of adjective, adverbs and verbs to select the feature. Respectively, using DF, IG, and CHI method reduce the dimension to 100. Next, using factor analysis as a further feature extraction, drop the dimension to 50. Compare these Eigenvectors obtained by FA with former ones by feature selection. As the restrictions of SPSS version, this experiment part uses 800 corpuses to establish the model, 400 for each class. 400 other corpuses are used for test and 200 for each class.

From the data in Table 3 and Fig. 5, Eigenvectors abstracted by FA based on FD and IG have better performances than those selected merely by feature selection methods. However, the case on CHI showed unusual advantage. With the experimental data in Table 2, it can conclude that 83% is abnormal data as a model structured by 800 corpuses should be less accurate than that by 2000 ones. But it is undeniable that, eigenvector obtained by CHI do better in the case of low dimension.

Table 3. The classification accuracy Comparison between FA and Feature Selection Methods

Dimension Reduction Method	DF	IG	CHI
	Accuracy (%}	Accuracy (%)	Accuracy (%)
Factor Analysis	76.0	75.3	75.3
Feature Selection	74.5	75.0	83.0

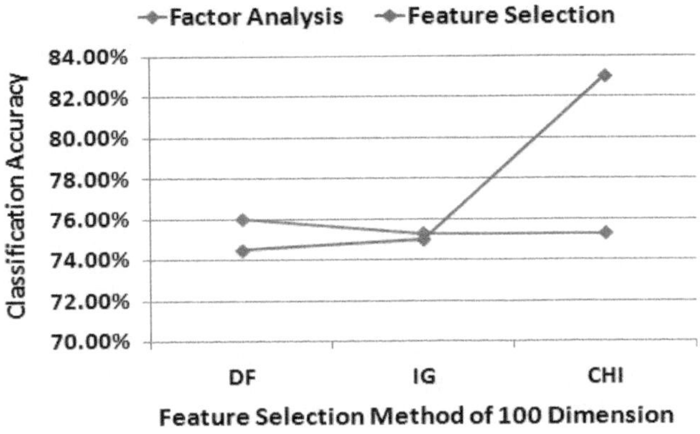

Fig. 5. The classification accuracy comparison between FA and feature selection methods

5 Conclusions

In sentiment classification of online reviews, the best performance will be obtained when the adjectives, adverbs and nouns selected together as the feature, for the adjective has a better classification effect and make a greater contribution to the emotional text than the other two.

The classification accuracy rate rise with the increasing feature number of each feature selection algorithm (DF, IG and CHI), then in some particular part of the values, it began to stabilize or even decline, which confirm the assumption that it is not true that the more the feature number is the better result will be.

It was discovered that MI method does not apply to feature selection of sentiment text classification. It was also found that, in the remaining three feature selection methods except MI, DF has the best classification effect, followed by CHI method, and IG method is the worst.

Feature selection method integrate with factor analysis can have a better effect on interpretation of the original features. The new features are more representative. But because of the limited corpus size, this advantage is not well performed.

Acknowledgments. This work is partially supported by both the National Natural Science Foundation of China under Grant No. 70971099 and Shanghai Leading Academic Discipline Project (B310).

References

1. Xia, H., Peng, L.: SVM-Based Comments Classification and Mining of Virtual Community: For Case of Sentiment Classification of Hotel Reviews. In: the International Symposium on Intelligent Information Systems and Applications (IISA 2009), Qingdao, pp. 507–511 (2009)

2. Li, J.: An Approach of Sentiment Classification Using SVM for Chinese Texts. In: International Conference on Artificial Intelligence - 50 years' achievements, future directions and social impacts, Las Vegas, pp. 759–761 (2006)
3. Pang, B., Lee, L., Vaithyanathan S.: Thumbs up? Sentiment classification using machine learning techniques. In: Conference on Empirical Methods in Natural Language Processing, Philadelphia, pp. 79–86 (2002)
4. Ye, Q., Zhang, Z., Law, R.: Sentiment classification of online reviews to travel destinations by supervised machine learning approaches. J. Expert Systems with Applications 36, 6527–6535 (2009)
5. Ye, Q., Lin, B., Li, Y.-j.: Sentiment Classification for Chinese Reviews: A comparison between SVM and semantic approaches. In: International Conference on Machine Learning and Cybernetics, Guangzhou, pp. 2341–2346 (2005)
6. Turney, P.: Thumbs up or Thumbs down? Semantic orientation applied to unsupervised classification of reviews. In: The 40th Annual Meeting of the Association for Computational Linguistics (ACL), Philadelphia, pp. 417–424 (2002)
7. Mullen T, Collier N.: Sentiment analysis using support vector machines with diverse information sources. In: EMNLP 2004, Barcelona, pp. 412–418 (2004)
8. Xu, J., Ding, Y.-x., Wang, X.-l.: Sentiment Classification for Chinese News Using Machine Learning Methods. J. Chinese Information Processing 21, 95–100 (2007)
9. Ng, H.T., Goh, W.B., Low, K.L.: Feature selection, perceptron learning and a usability case study for text categorization. In: the 20th Annual International ACM SIGIR Conference on Research and Development in Information Retrieval, Philadelphia, pp. 67–73 (1997)
10. Mladenic, D., Grobelnik, M.: Feature selection for unbalanced class distribution and naive Bayes. In: The 16th International Conference on Machine Learning (ICML), Bled, pp. 258–267 (1999)
11. Yang, Y., Pedersen, J.O.: A Comparative Study on Feature Selection in Text Categorization. In: The 14th International Conference on Machine Learning (ICML), Nashville, pp. 412–420 (1997)
12. Tang, H.-f., Tan, S.-b., Cheng, X.-q.: Research on Sentiment Classification of Chinese Reviews Based on Supervised Machine Learning Techniques. J. Chinese Information Processing 21, 88–108 (2007)

Q&A System Based on Personalized Service

Yibo Chen[1], Chanle Wu[1,2], Jiyan Wu[1], Ming Xie[1], Xiaojun Guo[1], Lian He[1], Xianbin Xu[1], and Zhaohui Cai[1]

[1] Computer School of Wuhan University, Wuhan, 430072, China
[2] National Engineering Research Center for Multimedia Software, Wuhan, 430072, China
{wuchl,ybchen}@whu.edu.cn

Abstract. It tremendously impacts the degree of satisfaction of users whether E-learning system can promptly and effectively solve the user's problems. In e-Learning, the users become thinkers from audience. To a puzzling question, they often seek help through the search, consulting friends or posting on BBS. However these methods guarantee neither progress of learning nor validity of the selected way. In this paper, Q&A System Based on Personalized Service (QASBPS) is proposed. The service based on semantic web technology, using semantic information extraction and multi-document summarization technology to generate answers. Otherwise, the most direct and effective way is to consult the peoples, who have mastered the knowledge point about explaining and illation. So the system use the user's social relationship map and interest map to recommend helpers.

Keywords: personalized recommendation, e-Learning, Q&A system.

1 Introduction

Today's technology in information systems changes also the state of the art in education [1]. With the development of Internet, the demand of e-Learning has greatly increased [2]. In order to make best use of these e-Learning systems, adaptivity and personalization of the e-Learning systems are a must. To enhance the teaching quality in e-Learning environments, numerous research works have been done. It has been indicated that adaptive learning is a critical requirement for promoting the learning effect of students [3]. Adaptive learning provides the adaptive learning materials, learning strategies and/or courses according to a student's learning style [4]. In e-Learning, the users become thinkers from audience, and to puzzling questions, there is no teacher to explain. So it is very important to provide instant Q&A service.

Q&A systems, such as Yahoo! Answer, the user build a problem with natural language, waiting for other users to help. But the time cost is uncertain, and impacting by human factors, it is difficult to ensure the effectiveness. In addition, how to find the high-quality answer from a large number answers is a great challenge. Therefore, there are some of issues, such as timely, accuracy, efficiency, human factors and so on.

In this paper, QASBPS is proposed, which applies semantic web technology, takes advantage of the friendship and the group membership to recommend answers and personalized helper based on the user's preferences, learning styles and. The paper

H. Tan and M. Zhou (Eds.): CSE 2011, Part I, CCIS 201, pp. 323–330, 2011.

there are several innovations are as follows: 1) Using semantic information extraction and multi-document summarization technology to generate answers. 2)Focused on human itself, solving the user's questions by recommending the most suitable helper; 3) To provide personalized helper for users through collaborative recommendation technology; 4) Improving the performance of personalized recommendations based on on-line friends, community users, the system user's three layer recommendation model.

2 Related Works

To the best of our knowledge, the work is one of the first attempts to utilize social relations among people, combine with personalized recommendation technology, and help user to solve practical problems in e-Learning. So far, related research in this area mostly focused on how to collect and automatically generate the corresponding answer from the Internet and how to find high-quality answer from a large number of answers in Q&A system.

2.1 Q&A System

The different between traditional Q&A and community Q&A is the traditional Q&A focus on how to automatically generate answers, but the community Q&A focus on how to find the high-quality answers out. A retrieval model was proposed based on language modeling, which extracts non-textual features to predict the quality of answers [5]. In [6], the author tries to find the obvious features out, it include structure, text and community. A framework is proposed to composite these heterogeneous features. Otherwise, there are some of researchers use machine learning to solve such problems, such as [7], [8]. Our research is different with the above, we focus on how to use semantic web technology to find the suitable answers from learning resources and helpers to help the user solving the problem based on the user's social relationship, interest, learning style and so on.

2.2 Recommendation System

There are large of research about the application of recommender system in e-Learning. Such as AVS(Altered Vista System), RACOFI (Rule Applying Collaborative Filter), QSIA(The Questions Sharing and Interactive Assignments), CYCLADES. In [9], the author developed a recommender system for learning objects that is based on sequencing rules that help users be guided through the concepts of ontology of topics. In [10], the author proposed a learning resource recommender system based on the hybrid recommendation approach, which combines social-based with information-based recommendation techniques. [11] focused on e-learner's emotion category, emphasizing on e-learner's emotional interaction, analyzing interactive Chinese texts, building emotion category database and strategies of database of sentiment adjustment, realizing the real-time emotion analysis and recommendation algorithm. The above studies focus on the personalized recommendation of learning resources, but each person's learning ability is different, just only to recommend the appropriate resources cannot assure the effectiveness and real-time of resolution the problem of users. Otherwise, these studies only used the interest map, ignored the social relationship map. So we focus on recommend appropriate helper to solve the problem according to the interest map and social relationship map.

2.3 Personalized Learning Service

In [12], we proposed a personalized learning service framework based on Semantic Web Technologies. The framework made full use of ontology to construct the semantic metadata model and user profile, mining and utilizing the friendship and membership to provide personalized navigation, recommendation, Q&A and customizing services. By providing personalized navigation service to satisfy the user needs of browse; providing personalized recommendation service to satisfy the user requirements of search; providing personalized Q&A service to satisfy the user needs of questions; providing the personalized customizing services to meet the user demands of learning by self. Personalized Q&A system is an important part of personalized learning service, influence the user experience. In this paper, Q&A system is proposed which adopts 3 levels Q&A system architecture.

The core of personalized learning services is user ontology which is the key point of personalized service; the concept hierarchy of user ontology are as follows: root node={node name, pre-condition, Learning style, reputation}, sub-node={node name, pre-condition, parent node, child node, visit number}, leaf node={node name, pre-condition, parent node, difficulty, Completion status}.

Pre-condition is the prerequisite to learn the knowledge, and reputation is computed based on the participation in the discussion, post, Email, etc., whose value ranges from 1 to 5. Duff [13] states that learning style is composite of characteristic cognitive, affective, and psychological factors that serve as relatively stable indicators of how a learner perceives, interacts with, and responds to the learning environment. The estimate approach mainly base on probability and classification, such as Bayes-based [14], [15], KNN and GA based [16], NBTree and Binary Relevance classifier[1], and so on. We estimate the learning style through using the KNN and GA based method, and the learning style is divided into 32 types, the value from 1 to 32.

3 Q&A System workflow

Q&A system workflow is as show in Figure 1.

Step 1: users describe the questions through input box using natural language;
Step 2: the system analyzes the user' input and semantic extent based on domain knowledge ontology;
Step 3: matching the user's input with answers and case database, if matching, return the result sets to user and into step 5, else into the step 4;
Step 4: matching the expanded questions with learning object database, if matching, return the result sets to user;
Step 5: users give the results of feedback, if feedback is "good", then add or update semantic Q&A answers and case database, Q&A semantic answer and case database mainly storage the semantic information of the user operation. It including two sections, one is the process of solving problem; two is the answers of question. On the other hand, the system will automatically match the

user's input with learning object database when couldn't find the right answers in the Q&A answer and case databases, retrieval and extract the answers from learning resources through semantic information extraction and Multi-document summarization technologies; if feedback is "bad", then recommend helper to solve problems.

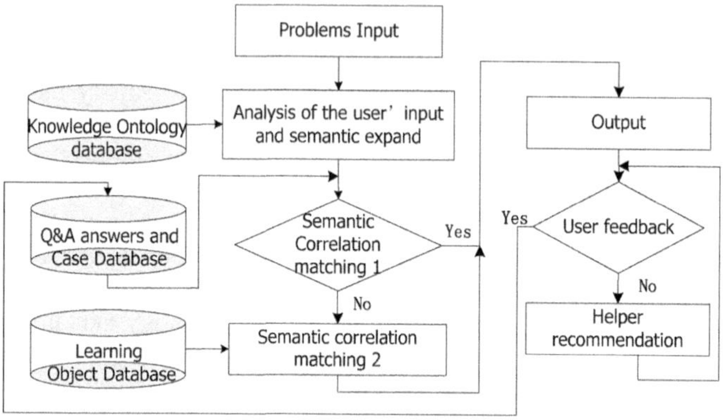

Fig. 1. Workflow of Q&A system

4 Q&A Answers Recommendation

Answers recommendation based on semantic web technology, using the base-content recommendation method to provide personalized knowledge answers for users.

On the one hand, the system analyzes the user's inputs, extract relevant semantic information, and match it with the Q&A semantic information database. If matched, then return a sorted list to learner through the personalized recommendation algorithm based on content, according to the degree of correlation between the user input and matching content.

5 Q&A Helper Recommendation

Helper recommendation uses the collaborative recommendation method according to the user's knowledge background, friendship and membership. The process to generate the list of recommendations includes three layers. The selection of helper depends on three indicators: 1) the similarity of user interest; 2) learning styles; 3) reputation.

Online friends: The system determines the friends that can help the user to solve the problem, and calculates the similarity of interest and learning style between the friend and the user. The user similarity is the product between the similarity of interest and that of learning style. The top-6 friends form the recommendation list. If the number of friends is less than 6, the vacancies will be filled from the community.

Community Online User: If either the user has no friends or online friends or the number of the recommended helper is less than 6, the system will determine the community users that can help the user to solve the problem, and then calculates the similarity of interest and learning style between the community user and the problem user. The reputation need to be taken into account when computing user similarity.

Online users: Searching system online user need to satisfy one of the three conditions, 1) new user; 2) neither is the community user nor have friends; 3) the number of the recommendation helper less than 6. The computing method is the same as Community Online User.

6 Experiment System Design

6.1 Mainly Function Module

Experimental system mainly includes semantic information extraction, multi-document summarization, and annotation, personalized recommendation and semantic retrieval 4 modules. It is as show in 2,3 and 4.

The main function of semantic information extraction, multi-document summarization, and annotation is extracting the description sentences which related with the user's input. To compute the similarity and relationship between sentences and selecting the highest correlation sentences to generate the answers.

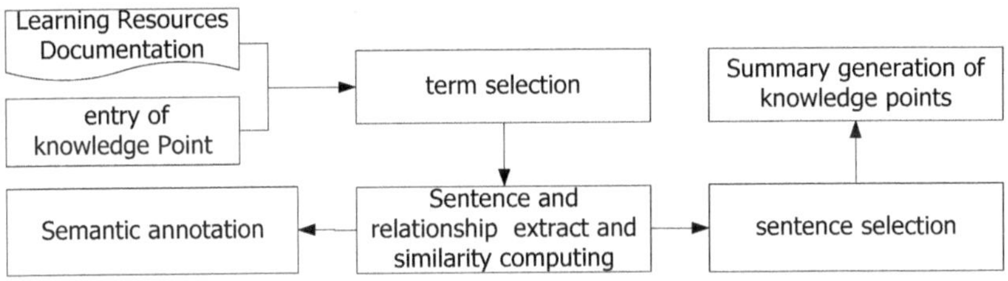

Fig. 2. Workflow of semantic information extraction, summarization, and annotation

Semantic retrieval module is as show in figure 3. Firstly, system segment the user's input to words set through NLP module; Express generation module expand the words set semantic and generate the query expression; and then calling reasoning engine to analyze and reason the RDF, RDFs or OWL files to generate a outcomes set according to certain rules; at last, system generate automatically the list of search results.

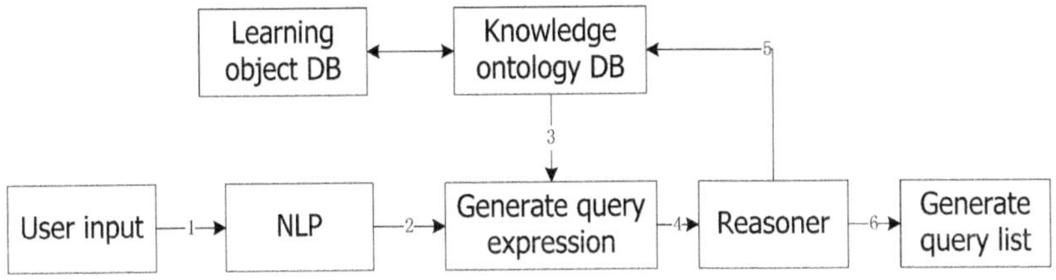

Fig. 3. Workflow of retrieval

Personalized recommendation module is as show in figure4, this module needs to use different workflow to process answers and helpers recommendation respectively.

The workflow of answers recommendation is 1-2-4-6. Firstly, system gain the answers set through the semantic retrieving; and then extract the knowledge background and interests from users ontology; Calling based-content recommendation algorithm to filter the answers which does not conform to the needs of the user, finally generating answer list.

The workflow of helper recommendation is 2-3-4-5-6. Firstly, system extract the knowledge background and interests from users ontology; And then calling the collaborative filtering recommendation algorithm to generate helpers list to solve the problem according to user similarity and three-level recommended architecture.

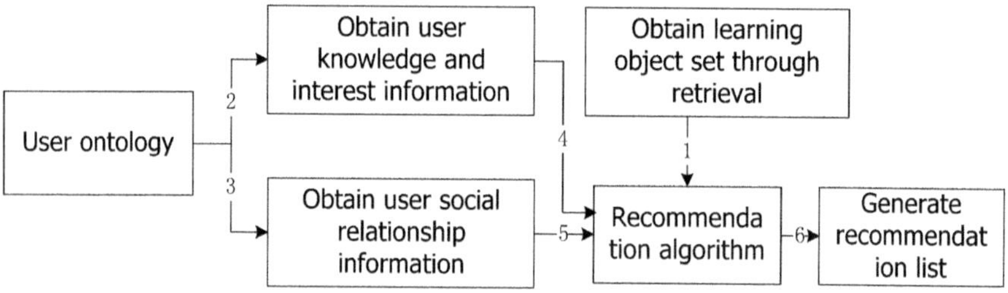

Fig. 4. Workflow of recommendation

6.2 User Interface

The user interaction interfaces are as show in the figure 5 to 6. Figure 5 is the learning interface; the user can select the recommendation interface to gain the helpers when they encounter problems. Figure 6 is the recommendation interface, the user can know that where the helpers come from.

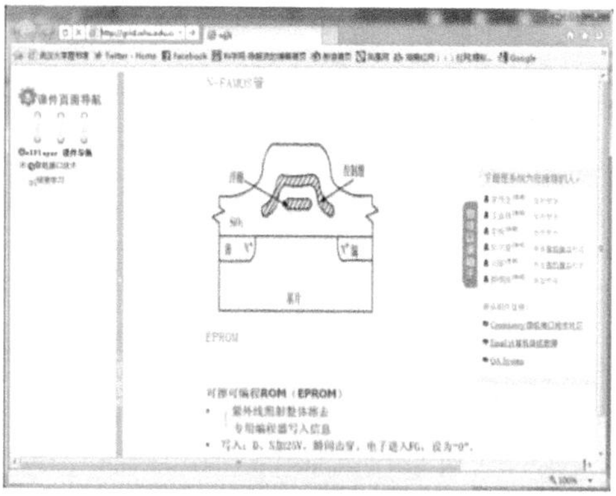

Fig. 5. Learning interface

Fig. 6. Recommendation interface

7 Conclusion and Future work

E-Learning is a very challenging research field; appropriate and personalized learning supporting approach can help the user to get knowledge quickly and effectively. This paper use semantic information extraction and multi-document summarization technology to generate answers. Focused on human itself, solving the user's questions by recommending the most suitable helper; to provide personalized helper for users through collaborative recommendation technology; Improving the performance of personalized recommendations based on on-line friends, community users, the system user's three layer recommendation model. At the same time, there are also some problems, such as how the system will handle if there is no helper found, how to assure the precise of recommendation. Future work will focus on the improving of the recommendation precise and provide some of interface, such as QQ, MSN, Facebook, Twitter, Renren and so on, and test the possibility of to get a better online support services through these interface to notify the helper.

Acknowledgments

This work was supported by the Fundamental Research Funds for the Central Universities (3105005), and Wuhan science and technology plan project (201010621209), the National Program for Elaborate Courses "Computer System and Interface" construction project, Hubei teaching reform project "network education resource sharing architecture and application model research".

References

1. Özpolat, E., Akar, G.B.: Automatic detection of learning styles for an e-learning system. Computers & Education, 355–367 (2009)
2. Wirt, J., et al.: The condition of education 2004. National Center for Education Statistics. National Center for Education Statistics, Washington (2004)
3. Graf, S., Kinshuk, P.: An approach for detecting learning styles in Learning Management Systems. In: Proceedings of the Sixth International Conference on Advanced Learning Technologies, ICALT 2006 (2006)
4. Trantafillou, E., Poportsis, A., Demetriadis, S.: The design and the formative evaluation of an adaptive educational system based on cognitive. Computer and Education 41(1), 87–103 (2003)
5. Jeon, J., et al.: A framework to predict the quality of answers with non-textual features. In: Proceedings of the 29th Annual International ACM SIGIR Conference (2006)
6. Liu, Y., Bian, J., Agichtein, E.: Predicting information seeker satisfaction in community question answering. In: Proceedings of the 31st Annual International ACM SIGIR Conference (2008)
7. Bian, J., et al.: Finding the right facts in the crowd: factoid question answering over social media. In: Proceeding of the 17th International Conference on World Wide Web (2008)
8. Ko, J., Nyberg, E., Si, L.: A probabilistic graphical model for joint answer ranking in question answering. In: Proceedings of the 30th Annual International ACM SIGIR (2007)

9. Avancini, H., Straccia, U.: User recommendation for collaborative and personalised digital archives. International Journal of Web Based Communities 1(2), 163–175 (2005)
10. Tian, F., et al.: Can e-Learner's emotion be recognized from interactive Chinese texts? In: Proceedings of the 2009 13th International Conference on Computer Supported Cooperative Work in Design, CSCWD (2009)
11. Zhuhadar, L., Nasraoui, O.: Semantic Information Retrieval for Personalized E-learning. In: 2008 20th IEEE International Conference on Tools with Artificial Intelligence (2008)
12. Chanle, W., Jiyian, W., Yibo, C., Ming, X., Xiaojun, G., Weichen, X.: Personalized Learning Service Framwork Based on Semantic Web Technologies. In: Proceedings of IEEE CSSS 2011 (June 2011)
13. Duff, A.: Approaches to learning: The revised approaches to studying inventory. Active Learning in Higher Education 5(1), 56–72 (2004)
14. García, P., Schiaffino, S., Amandi, A.: An enhanced Bayesian model to detect students' learning styles in Web-based courses. Journal of Computer Assisted Learning 24(4), 305–315 (2007)
15. García, P., et al.: Evaluating Bayesian networks' precision for detecting students' learning styles. Computers & Education 49(3), 794–808 (2007)
16. Chang, Y., et al.: A learning style classification mechanism for e-learning. Computers & Education 53, 273–285 (2009)

Internship Company in Campus: A New Way to Cultivating Practical Ability of Economics and Management Majors students

Jing Chen

School of Economics and Management of Shenyang Aerospace University, Shenyang 110136, China

Abstract. As well as the college graduates were surplus in recent years, the employing units have put forward higher requirements for the practice ability to the students of economics and management specialty, and the tranditional cultivating methods of practice ability can't adapt to the needs of the development of the society. The practice company was put forward to establish in order to cultivate the students' practice ability of economics and management majors based on the analysis on the advantages and disadvantages of traditional ways. The basic function of internships firms was summarized, and the governance structure and operation mode was designed based on the analysis on the development status of domestic and overseas practice companies. The conclusion was drawn that internships companies is an effective way of cultivating the students' practice ability.

Keywords: economics and management specialty; practice ability; internship firm.

1 Introduction

Graduates in colleges and universities have been superfluous for few years, under the background, the employing units have put forward higher and higher requirements for the practice ability of the graduates so that they were expected to work as soon as they were employed. But the old syllabuses have been used in many colleges and universities at present. Or the syllabuses have been revised although, but it is still out of line with the social needs, which make the graduates can't conform to the employers' requirements.

Many companies unwilling to provide internships opportunity for the student of economics and management majors, because they worried about affecting the enterprise's normal production or giving away enterprise's commercial secrets for accepting students practice. But most of the application of the economics and management theory must be combined with the enterprise management practice. Therefore, colleges and universities should pay more attention to practical ability training mode innovation, and strengthen to cultivate the economics and management major students' practice ability, in order to adapt to the new requirements of times and employing units. To organize economics and management majors students to found an internships company and

H. Tan and M. Zhou (Eds.): CSE 2011, Part I, CCIS 201, pp. 331–336, 2011.

manage it independently in accordance with market rules under teacher's guidance not only can cultivate students' practice ability, but also can make full use of the resources of colleges and universities.

2 Overview of the Practical Ability Cultivation Mode of Economics and Management Students

The traditional practical ability cultivation modes of economics and management majors students were mainly as the following types combining the author's practice experience of guiding students for many years:

2.1 Internships

Internship is the most direct method of teaching practice, such as metalworking practice, cognition practice (professional internship), production internship (Working Practice [1]) and so on. The students can obtain direct and profound perceptual knowledge through personally participate in operation or attendants. Also internship is easy to organize and carry out. But no matter what kind of practice cannot combine the theory with practice, which led to snatch a transient glance of a landscape because the practice was carried out after studying the theory for a long time.

2.2 Simulated Training

Simulated training includes artificial simulated training and computer simulation training. Artificial simulated training is mainly applied to simple program, stronger skills operational course, such as accounting simulated training, etc. While the computer simulation training is mainly applied to complicated program but stronger operational business courses, such as securities trading simulated training, etc. Simulated training can enable students to obtain strong perceptual knowledge, exercise their operational skills, and easy to be organize and carried out. But simulated training is easy to be limited by some factors such as training venues, facilities, equipment and computer hardware and software.

2.3 Role Imitating Teaching

The role of simulation teaching is that the students are divided into different groups and an actual case was given to each group, team members play different roles of the case, and then based on the conditions, environment and background material provided in the case, each actor makes corresponding decision to solve problems of the case. The role of simulation teaching can carry out immediately after the theoretical teaching of corresponding chapter was completed, which can deepen the grasping of theory, and exercise the student theory's practice ability. But too theoretical decisions may be made because the actual company management operations can't be contacted during the whole process.

Each kind of cultivating mode above has its own characteristics but lack authenticity, and the effect of cultivation of students' practical ability is not adequate.

3 The Development Situation of Internship Firms in China and Foreign Countries

Business simulation company is a very important way among the ways of cultivating the students' practice ability in foreign countries. Business simulation company is simulated the actual companies management in which the students play the company employees to trade with the other Business simulation companies.

Business simulation company in foreign countries had nearly 40 years of history, At present, more than 2,700 business simulation companies have been set up in nearly 30 countries in Europe and Australia, the United States, Canada which formed a network in the world [2]. These business simulation companies traded with each other according to the international general trading rules and laws. A coordination agency - the center office has been set in each country. The business activities of the business simulation companies among the countries were coordinated by the headquarters of the European simulating (internship) enterprises network set in Essen Germany [3]. The special teaching method of Business simulation company has been proved to be a very successful practice ability cultivation mode.

In China there are few colleges and universities to cultivate students' practice ability by establishing internship or business simulation company at present. Most of them are higher vocational schools, and most of them are still in discussion or research. There's only guang dong depiction of vocational and technical college really established internship supermarket in 2001.

4 The Basic Idea of Establishing Internship Firm

To found internship firm according to the modern enterprise system relying on the economics and management school of colleges and universities and manage it independently in accordance with market rules under teacher's guidance not only can cultivate students' practice ability, but also can make full use of the resources of colleges and universities.

4.1 The Function of Internship Firm

The basic function of internship firm should meet the requirements of social demand, training objectives and characteristics of school according to the syllabus and the units' request of students' practical ability, which not only cultivate students' practice ability but also promote the development of the school. The basic function of internship firm should be as following:

(1) To carry out professional practice according to the syllabus and the units' request of students' practical ability. Colleges and universities should always pays attention to the social and economic situation and variation tendency, master the requirements variation of unit to economics and management students' practical ability, adjust the syllabus and training plan dynamically so that the students can satisfy the employing units' demands. Several professional businesses are involved in the actual management of internship firm. So the practice ability of students of

interrelated majors of economics and management school can be cultivated by carrying out professional internship.

(2) To rich the speciality teachers' practice experience and train "multiple quality" teachers [3]. Most of the teachers have the experience of enterprise management position and have rich practical experience in universities abroad. But in domestic universities, many economics and management teachers became professional teachers directly as soon as they graduated from school which made them lack of management enterprise. In the process of teaching, it's difficult to put theory and practice corresponding, and can not cultivate the students' practical ability. Professional teachers as a tutor while manage the internship firm with students can Enrich their practice experience and became a "multiple quality" teacher.

(3) To provide work-study opportunities for students

Internship firms can also develop various promotion activities according to the fact except for providing professional practice. During activities, students can be organized to attend after school time or holiday, which not only can provide them more professional practice opportunities but also can provide some income for them by work-study [4].

(4) To deepen the contact with external enterprises

Internship firms can contact with external enterprises extensively through the businesses of product procurement, sales and distribution and so on. On one hand, the students can contact with and understand the enterprise extensively; On the other hand the students can get comprehensive, system, persistent and real exercise through the business of negotiation with external enterprises and market survey, shopping business [5]. In addition, the students can show their various talents through during contacting with external enterprises which made they could be realized deeply by them so that to improve their employment probability after graduating.

(5) To raise internship funds. Internship must consume certain outlay while insufficient outlay is the important factor that affects the effect of training students' practical ability. Part of the earnings of internship firm can be as practice outlay.

4.2 The Governance Structure of Internship Firm

(1) The organizational structure of internship firm

Internship firms should be led by economics and management school of college or university directly in accordance with the requirements of modern enterprise system and company law, and enact all kinds of management systems and departments responsibilities(be shown as fig 1). The colleges or universities can be as one shareholders of the internship firm to keep the benefit of the internship firm be fit for theirs so that they can support to set up internship firms.

(2) The working capital sources and exit mode of internship firm

The working place of internship firm can be provided gratis or as shares by colleges or universities. The working capital has two types: start-up outlay and daily operational outlay. Start-up outlay can be obtained by appropriating at one time from internship outlay, capital injection of colleges or universities, and capital injection of economics and management school, The start-up outlay is mainly used for setting up internship firm and buy the necessary operating equipment. The daily operational outlay can be raised from the internships: all the internships should buy some corresponding shares according to their positions and the equivalence principle of responsibility, right and interest, in order to enhance their sense of responsibility and the authenticity of management process [6].

The Equity funds of the internships can't withdraw after their expiration but can be transferred to the next round of internship students. If they made loss for firm, their equity funds should be deducted until to all. If there is profit in firm, their equity funds should be returned entirely and give a certain amount of disposable cash incentives according to the actual earnings and the evaluation results. The input of college or university and economics and management school can't withdraw when the internship firm exists, but can participate in the distribution of the company's profits.

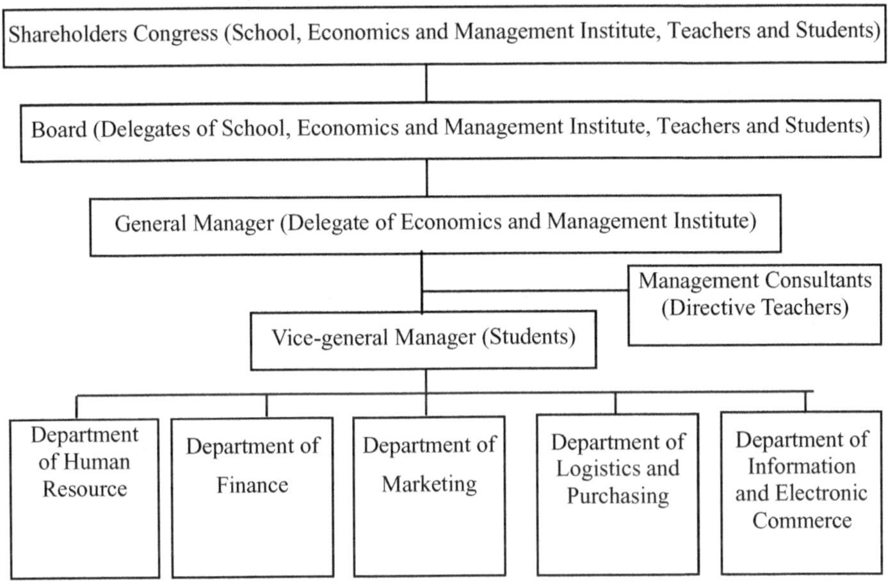

Fig. 1. The Organizational Structure of Internship Firm

4.3 The operations of internship firm

1) The definition of the target market

The target market of internship firm should be strictly restricted in the campus because its purpose is mainly to provide practice opportunities for students. The reasons are as the following: the first, running in campus don't need registration through department of industrial and commercial and tax, thus can reduce a lot of the probable obstacles and accelerate the progress of setting up internship firm. The second is convenient for managing the internships and controlling the management process. The third is convenient for coordination the time contradiction between lessons and firm management. The fourth, customers are college students, which is a stable market and benefit for firm management continuously and stably.

2) The determination of managers
According to the teaching plan of various majors, students of corresponding majors are arranged to practice in internship firm. Because the company business will involve different professional business, so students of different majors are arranged to practice in internship firm at the same time according to company business management fact. Each student's internship position should be determined through competition which was finished by students of human resource management major under the guidance of the teachers, in accordance with the recruitment process and hiring standard of off-campus enterprises.

3) The selection of operation mode
Once the internship firm was set up in accordance with modern enterprise system, it should be managed independently and been financial self-sufficiency by the students under teacher's guidance. The operational model can be chosen as supermarket because what the students purchased are mainly daily consumptive goods. Two management teams should be installed because the practice was mainly carried out after school time, and arranged the two management teams' work shift well according to their class time.

5 Conclusion

Internship firms have been proved an effective way to cultivate college students' practice ability. Certainly, there will be some contradictions and conflicts when internship firm was set up in campus such as the contradiction between school's economic interests and running characteristics, the time conflict between firm management and their lessons, the interest conflict between internship firm and other operators in the same campus and so on. These contradictions and conflicts need to be coordinated by school, and must be solved during college internship was founded and operated.

References

1. Yao, H.-f.: To explore the Mode of Working Practice and Build the System of Open Education. China Higher Education 6, 48–49 (2009)
2. Jin, L.-q.: The Teaching Idea and Practice of Business Simulation Company. World Education Information 9, 24–25 (2004)
3. Chen, Y.-h.: Draw in Spiration from Germany Vocational Education. Journal of Haidian University 4, 44–48 (2001)
4. Wang, N.-l.: Discussion on Internship firm pattern of Marketing Major. Vocational & Technical Education Forum 2, 44–47 (2007)
5. Yang, Q.-x.: The Innovation of Teaching Mode of Higher Vocational Colleges to Cultivate Students' Vocational Ability. Higher Education Exploration 5, 68–71 (2006)
6. Zhao, J.-m.: Practice Company: A Probe into the Practical Training Model for Students Majoring in Marketing. Journal of Guangdong Aib Management College 2, 16–20 (2005)

A New Symmetry of De Bruijn Sequences

Wei Zheng, Tongyu Xu, Chunling Chen, and Na Li

College of Information and Electric Engineering,
Shenyang Agricultural University, Shenyang, China
Zzww1210@163.com

Abstract. In this paper a new symmetry called AND/OR symmetry of de Bruijn sequences is presented. The theoretical results are proved on the necessary and sufficient condition for de Bruijn sequences having AND/OR symmetry. The de Bruijn sequences can be categorized into five classes by AND/OR symmetry. Using AND/OR symmetry, a large class of de Bruijn sequences can be derived easily. Data of five classes of de Bruijn sequences is provided for orders $4 \le n \le 6$.

Keywords: Feedback Shift Registers; de Bruijn Sequences; AND/OR Symmetry.

1 Introduction

In recent years, the growth of applications of nonlinear PN sequences has led to PN sequences such as de Bruijn sequences playing an important role in spread spectrum communications, coding theory, cryptography and multimedia services. Due to their good randomness properties and a large linear complexity, much effort has been devoted to various aspects of de Bruijn sequences [4, 5, 6].

In section 2, we state some knowing de Bruijn sequence facts. In sections 3, we present the AND/OR symmetry of de Bruijn sequences. By this symmetry, all order n de Bruijn sequences are divided into five classes, and detailed data is provided for orders $4 \le n \le 6$.

2 Properties of De Bruijn sequence

As well known, the order n de Bruijn sequences are the $2^{2^{n-1}-n}$ period 2^n binary sequences in which each n–tuple appears exactly once [2]. They are usually generated recursively using an n stage feedback shift register (nFSR for short) [3]. The structure of an nFSR can be depicted in figure 1.

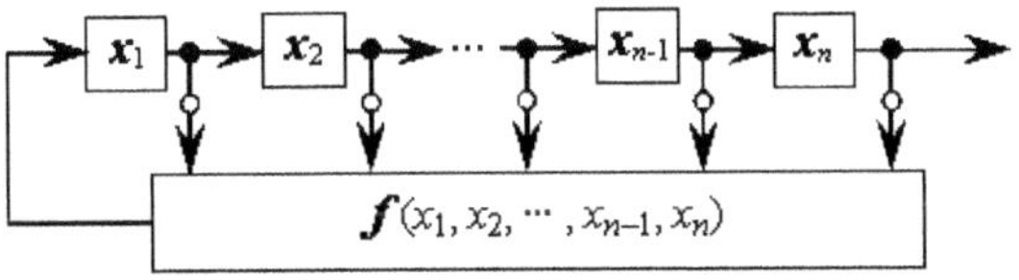

Fig. 1. An n–stage shift register with feedback function f

H. Tan and M. Zhou (Eds.): CSE 2011, Part I, CCIS 201, pp. 337–342, 2011.

Let $s = (s_0, s_1, s_2, ..., s_k, ..., s_{2^n-1})$ denote the output sequence. The sequence bits can be calculated from lower index to higher index with the recurrence

$$s_k = f(s_{k-1}, s_{k-2}, \cdots, s_{k-n+1}, s_{k-n}), \qquad k \geq n$$

where f is the feedback function of sequence s. In what follows, we assume that all functions to be considered are Boolean functions. Next we need to introduce some definitions and notation.

The set of all order n de Bruijn sequences will be denoted by $DS(n)$. The complement cs and the reverse rs of a de Bruijn sequence $s = (s_0, s_1, \cdots, s_{2^n-1})$ are defined by $cs = (\bar{s}_0, \bar{s}_1, \cdots, \bar{s}_{k-1})$ and $rs = (s_{k-1}, \cdots, s_1, s_0)$, where $\bar{s}_i$ denotes the binary complement of s_i.

For later reference, we summarize the following well–known facts about de Bruijn sequences [1, 3].

Fact 1: If $s \in DS(n)$, then $cs, rs \in DS(n)$.

Fact 2: For $s \in DS(n)$ with feedback function $f = f(x_1, x_2, \cdots, x_{n-1}, x_n)$, the functions $cf = f(\bar{x}_1, \bar{x}_2, \cdots, \bar{x}_{n-1}, x_n)$ and $rf = f(x_{n-1}, \cdots, x_2, x_1, x_n)$ are feedback functions of cs and rs respectively.

Fact 3: The feedback function $f(x_1, x_2, \cdots, x_n)$ of each order n de Bruijn sequence has the following properties:

(1) $f(x_1, x_2, \cdots, x_n) = f'(x_1, x_2, \cdots, x_{n-1}) + x_n$, that is, the function $f(x_1, x_2, \cdots, x_n)$ is nonsingular.

(2) The term 1 always appears.

(3) Either term $x_1 x_2 \cdots x_{n-1}$ or term $x_1 \vee x_2 \vee \cdots \vee x_{n-1}$ appears, where $x_i x_j$ denotes logical AND operation, $x_i \vee x_j$ denotes logical OR operation.

3 AND/OR Symmetry of De Bruijn Sequences

As well known, each nFSR sequence has two symmetries as follows:

(1) Two sequences s_1 and s_2 are said to be 0/1 symmetric, $s_1 = cs_2$ and $s_2 = cs_1$, if one is the sequence obtained from the other, by interchanging 0 and 1 in the other.

(2) Two sequences s_1 and s_2 are said to be forward/reverse symmetric, $s_1 = rs_2$ and $s_2 = rs_1$, if one is the sequence obtained from the other, by interchanging s_i and s_{k-1-i} in the other, where k is the length of the sequence.

Similarly, we define a new symmetry called as the AND/OR (logic) symmetry, and is denoted by l.

Definition 1. Two Boolean functions f_1 and f_2 containing $x_1x_2\cdots x_{n-1}$ or $x_1 \vee x_2 \vee \cdots \vee x_{n-1}$ are said to be AND/OR (logic) symmetric, $f_1 = lf_2$ and $f_2 = lf_1$, if one is the Boolean function obtained from the other, by interchanging $x_1x_2\cdots x_{n-1}$ and $x_1 \vee x_2 \vee \cdots \vee x_{n-1}$ in the other. Two sequences s_1 and s_2 are said to be AND/OR (logic) symmetric, $s_1 = ls_2$ and $s_2 = ls_1$, if s_1 and s_2 are the sequences generated by AND/OR symmetric f_1 and f_2, respectively.

From fact 2 and definition 1 above, for the nFSR sequences, one has three symmetries as follows:

- 0/1 symmetry —

  $s = (s_0, s_1, \cdots, s_{k-1}) \Leftrightarrow cs = (\bar{s}_0, \bar{s}_1, \cdots, \bar{s}_{k-1})$

  $f = f(x_1, x_2, \cdots, x_{n-1}, x_n) \Leftrightarrow cf = f(\bar{x}_1, \bar{x}_2, \cdots, \bar{x}_{n-1}, x_n)$
- forward/reverse symmetry —

  $s = (s_0, s_1, \cdots, s_{k-1}) \Leftrightarrow rs = (s_{k-1}, \cdots, s_1, s_0)$

  $f = f(x_1, x_2, \cdots, x_{n-1}, x_n) \Leftrightarrow rf = f(x_{n-1}, \cdots, x_2, x_1, x_n)$
- AND/OR symmetry —

  $s = (s_0, s_1, \cdots, s_{k-1}) \Leftrightarrow ls = (t_0, t_1, \cdots, t_{k-1})$

  $f = f(x_1, x_2, \cdots, x_{n-1}, x_n) \Leftrightarrow lf = f + x_1x_2\cdots x_{n-1} + x_1 \vee x_2 \vee \cdots \vee x_{n-1}$

Example 1. Consider two feedback functions

$$f_1(x_1, \cdots, x_{17}) = x_6 + x_1\bar{x}_2\bar{x}_3x_4x_8\bar{x}_{12} + x_1x_2\cdots x_{16} + \bar{x}_{17},$$
$$f_2(x_1, \cdots, x_{17}) = x_6 + x_1\bar{x}_2\bar{x}_3x_4x_8\bar{x}_{12} + x_1 \vee x_2 \vee \cdots \vee x_{16} + \bar{x}_{17}.$$

Let s_1 and s_2 denote the sequences generated by the feedback functions f_1 and f_2, respectively, so that $s_1 = ls_2$ and $s_2 = ls_1$. It is easy to verify that s_1 and s_2 are both order 17 de Bruijn sequences.

The following corollary is immediate consequence of fact 3.

Corollary 1. Let $s \in DS(n)$ with AND/OR symmetry, then the feedback functions of s, cs, rs and ls can be expressed in following forms

$$f = f_0(x_1, x_2, \cdots, x_{n-1}) + x_1 \vee x_2 \vee x_{n-1} + \bar{x}_n = f_1(x_1, x_2, \cdots, x_{n-1}) + x_1x_2\cdots x_{n-1} + \bar{x}_n$$
$$cf = \bar{f}_0(\bar{x}_1, \bar{x}_2, \cdots, \bar{x}_{n-1}) + x_1x_2\cdots x_{n-1} + \bar{x}_n = \bar{f}_1(\bar{x}_1, \bar{x}_2, \cdots, \bar{x}_{n-1}) + x_1 \vee x_2 \vee \cdots \vee x_{n-1} + \bar{x}_n$$
$$rf = f_0(x_{n-1}, \cdots, x_2, x_1) + x_1 \vee x_2 \vee x_{n-1} + \bar{x}_n = f_1(x_{n-1}, \cdots, x_2, x_1) + x_1x_2\cdots x_{n-1} + \bar{x}_n$$
$$lf = f_0(x_1, x_2, \cdots, x_{n-1}) + x_1x_2\cdots x_{n-1} + \bar{x}_n = f_1(x_1, x_2, \cdots, x_{n-1}) + x_1 \vee x_2 \vee x_{n-1} + \bar{x}_n,$$

where f_0 and f_1 are $n-1$ variables Boolean functions, and terms 1, $x_1x_2\cdots x_{n-1}$, and $x_1 \vee x_2 \vee \cdots \vee x_{n-1}$ do not appear in f_0 and f_1.

For any de Bruijn sequence, there are 0/1 symmetry and forward/reverse symmetry. But not all de Bruijn sequences have AND/OR symmetry. If we know the feedback function f of a de Bruijn sequence with AND/OR symmetry, we can directly write the feedback functions of eight de Bruijn sequences as follows.

$$f = x_6 + \bar{x}_1 x_3 x_4 x_6 x_7 \bar{x}_{12} + x_1 x_2 \cdots x_{16} + \bar{x}_{17},$$

$$lf = x_6 + \bar{x}_1 x_3 x_4 x_6 x_7 \bar{x}_{12} + x_1 \vee x_2 \vee \cdots \vee x_{16} + \bar{x}_{17},$$

$$cf = x_6 + x_1 \bar{x}_3 \bar{x}_4 \bar{x}_6 \bar{x}_7 x_{12} + x_1 \vee x_2 \vee \cdots \vee x_{16} + \bar{x}_{17},$$

$$clf = x_6 + x_1 \bar{x}_3 \bar{x}_4 \bar{x}_6 \bar{x}_7 x_{12} + x_1 x_2 \cdots x_{16} + \bar{x}_{17},$$

$$rf = x_{11} + \bar{x}_5 x_{10} x_{11} x_{13} x_{14} \bar{x}_{16} + x_1 x_2 \cdots x_{16} + \bar{x}_{17},$$

$$rlf = x_{11} + \bar{x}_5 x_{10} x_{11} x_{13} x_{14} \bar{x}_{16} + x_1 \vee x_2 \vee \cdots \vee x_{16} + \bar{x}_{17},$$

$$crf = x_{11} + x_5 \bar{x}_{10} \bar{x}_{11} \bar{x}_{13} \bar{x}_{14} x_{16} + x_1 \vee x_2 \vee \cdots \vee x_{16} + \bar{x}_{17},$$

$$crlf = x_{11} + x_5 \bar{x}_{10} \bar{x}_{11} \bar{x}_{13} \bar{x}_{14} x_{16} + x_1 x_2 \cdots x_{16} + \bar{x}_{17}.$$

Lemma 1. [3]. For $n > 1$ and $s \in DS(2n)$, $cs \neq rs$.

Each de Bruijn sequence s has 0/1 symmetry and forward/reverse symmetry, it follows that, if $ls \in DS(n)$, we can at most derive eight de Bruijn sequences: $s, cs, rs, crs, ls, cls, rls, crls$. For some s, $ls = cs$ or $ls = crs$. This is illustrated next.

Example 2

(1) For $s \in DS(10)$ with feedback function $f = x_2 \vee x_7 + x_3(x_2 + x_7) + x_1 x_2 \cdots x_9 + \bar{x}_{10}$. We can see that $lf = cf = x_2 \vee x_7 + x_3(x_2 + x_7) + x_1 \vee x_2 \vee \cdots \vee x_9 + \bar{x}_{10}$.

(2) For $s \in DS(12)$ with feedback function $f = x_6 + \bar{x}_1 x_6 x_7 + \bar{x}_5 \bar{x}_6 x_{11} + x_1 \cdots x_{11} + \bar{x}_{12}$. One can verify that $lf = crf = x_6 + \bar{x}_1 x_6 x_7 + \bar{x}_5 \bar{x}_6 x_{11} + x_1 \vee \cdots \vee x_{11} + x_{12}$.

As described above, all order n de Bruijn sequences can be divided into five classes, and the number of de Bruijn sequences in each class for orders 4 through 6 is presented in Table 1.

Table 1. The distribution of five classes of de Bruijn sequences for orders $4 \leq n \leq 6$

Classes	I	II	III	IV	V	Total
$ls \in DS(n)$?	no	no	yes	yes	yes	
Properties	$cs \neq rs$	$cs = rs$	$ls \neq cs$ & $ls \neq crs$	$ls = cs$	$ls = crs$	
$n = 4$	8	0	0	4	4	16
$n = 5$	1248	64	672	64	0	2048
$n = 6$	59467584	0	7631008	5024	5248	67108864

In the sequel, $DS_j(n)$ will be denoted the set of all de Bruijn sequences in class *j*, where *j* = I, II, III, IV, and V.

4 Theoretical Results

In this section, we analyze the feedback functions of de Bruijn sequences with AND/OR symmetry, and some theoretical results are presented.

The set of all order *n* de Bruijn sequences with AND/OR symmetry will be denoted by $LDS(n)$. Let $DS_0(n)$ (resp. $DS_1(n)$) denote the set of all sequences obtained from de Bruijn sequences, by removing a single zero (resp. one) from the longest run of zeros (resp. ones), and $DS_{0/1}(n)$ is the union of $DS_0(n)$ and $DS_1(n)$. Let $DS_{01}(n)$ denote the set of all sequences obtained from de Bruijn sequences, by removing a single zero from the longest run of zeros and a single one from the longest run of ones.

Theory 1. For $s \in LDS(n)$, $cs, rs \in LDS(n)$.

Proof. It can be easily seen that $lcf = clf$ and $lrf = rlf$, it follows that $lcs, lrs \in DS(n)$, and hence, $cs, rs \in LDS(n)$. □

Theory 2. Let *f* be any nonsingular Boolean function, and let *ls* and s' be the sequences generated by lf and $\overline{f}$. Then $ls \in DS(n)$ if and only if $s' \in DS_{01}(n)$.

Proof. Note that $f = lf + x_1x_2\cdots x_{n-1} + x_1 \vee x_2 \vee \cdots \vee x_{n-1}$, thus $\overline{f} = lf + x_1x_2\cdots x_{n-1}$ $+ \overline{x_1}\,\overline{x_2}\cdots\overline{x_{n-1}}$.

Since $ls \in DS(n)$, therefore, $\overline{f}$ splits the de Bruijn cycle into a cycle of length $2^n - 2$ and two cycles of length one. Note that the longest cycle corresponds to the longest sequence s' generated by $\overline{f}$, hence, $s' \in DS_{01}(n)$.

Conversely, since $\overline{f}$ is a feedback function of $s' \in DS_{01}(n)$, $\overline{f}$ generates a cycle of length $2^n - 2$ and two cycles of length one. Note that $lf = \overline{f} + x_1x_2\cdots x_{n-1} + \overline{x_1}\,\overline{x_2}\cdots\overline{x_{n-1}}$, thus lf is a feedback function which joins these three cycles to form a de Bruijn cycle, and hence, $ls \in DS(n)$. □

References

1. Fredricksen, H.: A survey of full length nonlinear shift register cycle algorithms. SIAM Rev. 24, 195–229 (1982)
2. de Bruijn, N.G.: A combinatorial problem. Proc. Nederlanske Akademie van Wetenschappen 49, 758–764 (1946)
3. Golomb, S.W.: Shift Register Sequences, 2nd edn. Aegena Park Press, Laguna Hills (1982)

4. Etzion, T.: Linear complexity of de Bruijn sequences–old and new results. IEEE Trans. Inform. Theory 45(2), 693–698 (1999)
5. Seberry, J., Zhang, X.-M., Zheng, Y.: Nonlinearly balanced boolean functions and their propagation characteristics. In: Stinson, D.R. (ed.) CRYPTO 1993. LNCS, vol. 773, pp. 49–60. Springer, Heidelberg (1994)
6. Goresky, M., Klapper, A.M.: Pseudo–noise Sequences Based on Algebraic Feedback Shift Registers. IEEE Trans. Inform. Theory 52(4), 1649–1662 (2006)

The Weighted Generalized Solution Tikhonov Regularization Method for Cauchy Problem for the Modified Helmholtz Equation

Lei You*

College of Science, Guangdong Ocean University, Zhanjiang, China, 524088
leiyoux@gmail.com

Abstract. In this paper, the Cauchy problem associated with the modified Helmholtz equation is discussed. The weighted generalized solution Tikhonov regularization method has been used to deal with the illposedness of the problem. Error estimates are obtained with a priori strategy and a posteriori choice rule to find the regularization parameter. We also show that the method can be realized by Fast Fourier Transform(FFT). Numerical examples show that the proposed method is effective and stable.

Keywords: Cauchy problem; Ill posed problem, Discrepancy principle, Regularization.

1 Introduction

In this paper, the following Cauchy problem for the modified Helmholtz equation will be considered:

$$\Delta u(x,y) - k^2 u(x,y) = 0, \quad 0 < x < \pi, \quad 0 < y < 1, \tag{1}$$

$$u(x,0) = g(x), \quad 0 \le x \le \pi, \tag{2}$$

$$u_y(x,0) = 0, \quad 0 \le x \le \pi, \tag{3}$$

$$u(0,y) = u(\pi,y) = 0, \quad 0 \le y \le 1, \tag{4}$$

where $k > 0$ is a real number. In practice, the data at $g(x)$ is often obtained on the basis of reading of physical instrument. So only the perturbed data $g^\delta(x)$ can be obtained. We assume that the exact and measured data satisfy

$$\|g - g^\delta\| \le \delta. \tag{5}$$

where $\delta > 0$ denotes the noisy level, $\|\cdot\|$ denotes the L^2- norm. This equation arises naturally in many physical applications[1], for example, in implicit marching schemes for the heat equation, in Debye-Huckel theory, in the linearization of the Poisson-Boltzmann equation [5,6,12] and so on. It is well known that

* Corresponding author.

H. Tan and M. Zhou (Eds.): CSE 2011, Part I, CCIS 201, pp. 343–350, 2011.

the problem (1)–(4) is severely ill posed, i.e., the solution does not depend continuously on the given Cauchy data and any small change in the given data may cause large change to the solution[4,13]. Thus it is impossible to solve the problem using classical numerical methods and requires special techniques to be employed. In recent years, several techniques have been developed for it, such as the Landweber method with boundary element method (BEM) [8], the conjugate gradient method [7], the method of fundamental solutions(MFS) [3,9,14], the quasi-reversibility method and truncated method[10,11] and so on.

In this paper, the weighted generalized solution Tikhonov regularization method is presented to deal with the illposedness of the problem. First, we introduce an auxiliary equation, which will build a bridge between the weighted generalized solution Tikhonov regularization method and the problem. We also show that the regularization parameters can be chosen by the discrepancy principle.

This paper is organized as follows. In section 2, we will give the method to construct approximate function. The convergence results will be found in section 3. Some numerical results are given in section 4 to show the efficiency of the new method.

2 Preliminaries

In this section, we present some preliminary materials which will be used throughout the paper. Let $\phi_l(x) = \sin(lx)$, it can be verified that $\{\phi_l(x)\}_{l=1}^{\infty}$ is the solution of Sturm-Liouville problem:

$$\begin{cases} \phi'' + \lambda\phi = 0, & 0 \le x \le \pi, \\ \phi(0) = \phi(\pi) = 0. \end{cases} \tag{6}$$

Clearly, $\{\phi_l(x)\}_{l=1}^{\infty}$ is an orthogonal system in $L^2(0,\pi)$, i.e.,

$$\int_0^{\pi} \phi_l(x)\phi_n(x)dx = \frac{\pi}{2}\delta_{l,n}. \tag{7}$$

So if we let $g \in L^2(0,\pi)$, then we can write $g(x) = \sum_{l=0}^{\infty} \hat{g}_l \phi_l(x)$, where

$$\hat{g}_l = \frac{2}{\pi}\int_0^{\pi} g(x)\phi_l(x)dx, \quad l = 0, 1, 2\ldots, \tag{8}$$

In this case, it is easy to verify that the exact solution of problem (??) can be given as

$$u(x,y) = \sum_{l=1}^{\infty} \hat{g}_l\phi_l(x)\cosh\left(\sqrt{l^2+k^2}y\right) \tag{9}$$

Denote an operator T_y as following

$$T_y\phi(x) =: \sum_{l=1}^{\infty} \hat{g}_l\phi_l(x)\cosh\left(\sqrt{l^2+k^2}y\right). \tag{10}$$

We have the following lemmas,

Lemma 1. *For* $0 \le y \le 1$,

$$\cosh\left(\sqrt{l^2+k^2}y\right)^{1/y} \le \cosh\left(\sqrt{l^2+k^2}\right), \quad \forall l \in \mathbb{N}, k \in \mathbb{R}. \tag{11}$$

Lemma 2. *If* $\|T_1 g\| \in L^2(0,\pi)$, *then for* $0 \le y \le 1$,

$$\|T_y g\| \le \|g\|^{1-y}\|T_1 g\|^y \tag{12}$$

Proof. By the Hölder inequality and Lemma 1, for any fixed y

$$\begin{aligned} \|T_y g\|^2 &= \|\textstyle\sum_{l=1}^{\infty} \hat{g}_l \phi_l(x) \cosh\left(\sqrt{l^2+k^2}y\right)\|^2 = \sum_{l=1}^{\infty} \frac{2}{\pi}\hat{g}_l^2 \cosh^2\left(\sqrt{l^2+k^2}y\right) \\ &= \textstyle\sum_{l=1}^{\infty} (\sqrt{\frac{2}{\pi}}\hat{g}_l)^{2(1-y)} (\sqrt{\frac{2}{\pi}}\hat{g}_l)^{2y} \cosh^2\left(\sqrt{l^2+k^2}y\right) \\ &\le \left(\textstyle\sum_{l=1}^{\infty}\left((\sqrt{\frac{2}{\pi}}\hat{g}_l)^{2(1-y)}\right)^{\frac{1}{1-y}}\right)^{1-y} \left(\sum_{l=1}^{\infty}\left((\sqrt{\frac{2}{\pi}}\hat{g}_l)^{2y}\cosh^2\left(\sqrt{l^2+k^2}y\right)\right)^{\frac{1}{y}}\right)^{y} \\ &\le (\textstyle\sum_{l=1}^{\infty} \frac{2}{\pi}\hat{g}_l^2)^{1-y} \left(\sum_{l=1}^{\infty} \frac{2}{\pi}\hat{g}_l^2 \cosh^2\left(\sqrt{l^2+k^2}\right)\right)^{y} \\ &= \|g\|^{2(1-y)}\|T_1 g\|^{2y} \end{aligned} \tag{13}$$

3 The Weighted Generalized Solution Tikhonov Regularization Method

For any ill posed problem some a priori assumption on the exact solution is needed and necessary, otherwise, the convergence of the regularization approximate solution will not be obtained or the convergence rate can be arbitrary slow[2]. In this paper, we will assume there hold the following a priori bounds

$$\|u(x,1)\| \le E. \tag{14}$$

The idea of the method in this paper is to deal with the problem consists of two stages:

- Reconstruct a new function f^δ from the perturbed data g^δ, which is a better approximation of the exact function g in some sense.
- Take $u^\delta(x,y) = T_y f^\delta(x)$ as a approximation of $u(x,y)$,

In the following, we give a method to reconstruct ϱ^δ from the perturbed data ρ^δ based on the weight generalized Tikhonov regularization method.

First, we introduce the auxiliary equation

$$If = g \tag{15}$$

where $I : X = L^2(0,\pi) \to L^2(0,\pi) = Y$ is an identity operator. Suppose L is a linear closed operator, $\mathcal{D}(L) \subset X, \overline{\mathcal{D}(L)} = X$ and the operator pairs (I, L) satisfies the complementation condition:

$$\|If\|^2 + \|Lf\|^2 \ge C\|f\|^2, \forall f \in \mathcal{D}(L), \tag{16}$$

where the constant $C > 0$. We introduce a new inner product

$$\langle f_1 , f_2 \rangle_* = \langle If_1 , If_2 \rangle + \langle Lf_1 , Lf_2 \rangle \tag{17}$$

and the space X equipped with the inner product $\langle \cdot , \cdot \rangle_*$ is notated as X_*, then we have the space X_* is a Hilbert space [2]. We know the Moore-Penrose generalized solution $\mathcal{I}^{\dagger} f$ of equation

$$\mathcal{I} f = g \tag{18}$$

is the weighted generalized solution of equation (15) and the adjoint operator $\mathcal{I}$ is [2]

$$\mathcal{I}^* = (I^* I + L^* L)^{-1} I^* \tag{19}$$

If the condition (14) is hold, the operator L can be given as

$$L = T_1. \tag{20}$$

The perturbed form of (15) is

$$\mathcal{I} f = g^{\delta} \tag{21}$$

The weighted generalized Tikhonov regularization solution ϱ_L^{α} of equation (21) can be obtain by solving the following equation[2]

$$(I + \alpha L^* L) f = g^{\delta}, \tag{22}$$

where $\alpha > 0$ is the regularization parameter. It well known that f_L^{α} is the minimizer of the Tikhonov functional[2]

$$\Phi(f) = \|f - g^{\delta}\|^2 + \alpha \|Lf\|^2 \tag{23}$$

In the following, we give an explicit expression of ϱ_L^{α} . Suppose that $g^{\delta}(x) = \sum_{l=1}^{\infty} \hat{g}_l^{\delta} \phi_l(x)$ and $f_L^{\alpha}(x) = \sum_{l=1}^{\infty} \hat{f}_l^{\delta} \phi_l(x)$, then by (10) and (20)

$$L^* L \varrho = \sum_{l=1}^{\infty} \hat{f}_l^{\delta} \cosh\left(\sqrt{l^2 + k^2}\right) \phi_l(x) \tag{24}$$

So we can get

$$\hat{f}_l^{\delta} = \frac{1}{1 + \alpha \cosh\left(\sqrt{l^2 + k^2}\right)} \hat{g}_l^{\delta} \tag{25}$$

That is to say

$$f_L^{\alpha}(x) = \sum_{l=1}^{\infty} \frac{1}{1 + \alpha \cosh\left(\sqrt{l^2 + k^2}\right)} \hat{g}_l^{\delta} \phi_l(x) \tag{26}$$

Then the approximation solution can be given as

$$u_L^{\delta,\alpha}(x, y) = T_y f_L^{\alpha} = \sum_{l=1}^{\infty} \frac{1}{1 + \alpha \cosh\left(\sqrt{l^2 + k^2}\right)} \hat{g}_l^{\delta} \phi_l(x) \cosh\left(\sqrt{l^2 + k^2} y\right) \tag{27}$$

4 The Choices of Regularization Parameter α and Convergence Results

The Morozov's discrepancy principle is used as a posteriori rule in this paper, i.e., choosing α from the following equation

$$\|f_L^{\alpha_2} - g^\delta\| = \delta. \tag{28}$$

From the theories of Tikhonov regularization, the following lemma is hold[2].

Lemma 3. *Let g^δ satisfies (5), $u_L^{\delta,\alpha_2}(x,y)$ is defined by (27) and (28), $\mathcal{I}^\dagger g \in \mathcal{R}((\mathcal{I}_n^*\mathcal{I}_n)^\nu)$, $0 \le \nu \le \frac{1}{2}$, then*

$$\|f_L^{\alpha_2} - \mathcal{I}^\dagger g\|_* \le C_\nu \|\mathcal{I}^\dagger g\|_\nu^{\frac{1}{2\nu+1}} \delta^{\frac{2\nu}{2\nu+1}} \tag{29}$$

Theorem 4. *Let g^δ satisfies (5), $u_L^{\delta,\alpha_2}(x,y)$ is defined by (27) and (28). If the condition (5) and (14) are hold, then for $0 \le y \le 1$*

$$\|u_L^{\delta,\alpha_2}(x,y) - u(x,y)\| = O\left(\delta^{1-y}\right). \tag{30}$$

Proof. Owing to $g \in \mathcal{D}(T_1)$, so

$$g = \mathcal{I}_n^\dagger g \in \mathcal{R}((\mathcal{I}_n^*\mathcal{I}_n)^0).$$

From Lemma 3,

$$\|T_1(g - f_L^{\alpha_2})\|^2 = \|L(g - f_L^{\alpha_2})\|^2 \le \|f_L^{\alpha_2} - g\|_*^2 \le C_0^2\|g\|_*^2 \le C_0^2(\|g\|^2 + E^2). \tag{31}$$

From (5) and (28),

$$\|f_L^{\alpha_2} - g\| \le \|f_L^{\alpha_2} - g^\delta\| + \|g - g^\delta\| \le 2\delta. \tag{32}$$

The assertion of theorem will be obtained by (31), (32) and Lemma2.

5 Numerical Implementation

In practical problem, the perturbed data of functions is usually given at nodes. In this case, our approach can be realized by a discrete sine transform of the data.

Give $N-1$ knots

$$x_i = i\pi/N, i = 1, \ldots, N-1$$

The noisy vector $\mathbf{g}^\delta = (\mathbf{g}_1^\delta, \ldots, \mathbf{g}_{N-1}^\delta)$ of the vector $\mathbf{g} = (\mathbf{g}_1, \ldots, \mathbf{g}_{N-1}) = (\rho(x_1), \ldots, \rho(x_{N-1}))$ are given and the condition

$$\|\mathbf{g}^\delta - \mathbf{g}\|_{l^2} \le \delta$$

is assumed.

Then the expansion

$$\mathbf{g}_i^\delta = \sum_{l=1}^{N-1} \hat{\mathbf{g}}_l^\delta \sin(lx_i), \quad i = 1, \ldots, N-1$$

can be obtained, where the coefficients

$$\hat{\mathbf{g}}_l^\delta = \frac{2}{N} \sum_{i=1}^{N-1} \mathbf{g}_i^\delta \sin(lx_i), \quad l = 1, 2, \ldots, N-1.$$

then we can give the approximate function as follows

$$u_L^{\delta,\alpha}(x,y) = \sum_{l=1}^{N-1} \frac{1}{1 + \alpha \cosh^2(l)} \hat{\mathbf{g}}_l^\delta \sin(lx) \cosh(ly) \tag{33}$$

We cannot find an explicit analytical solution to (1)-(4), we set forth the examples as follows: take a $g(x) \in L^2(\Omega)$ and solve the well-posed problem:

$$\Delta u(x,y) - k^2 u(x,y) = 0, \quad 0 < x < \pi, 0 < y < 1, \tag{34}$$

$$u(x,1) = g(x), \quad 0 \le x \le \pi, \tag{35}$$

$$u_y(x,0) = 0, \quad 0 \le x \le \pi, \tag{36}$$

$$u(0,y) = u(\pi,y) = 0, 0 \le y \le 1 \tag{37}$$

to get an approximation to $u(x,0)$. Then put a random noise to $u(x,0)$ to get f_δ. The last will be solved by the above-mentioned approaches and compared with the solution of (34)-(37) to show the efficiency and stability of the method.

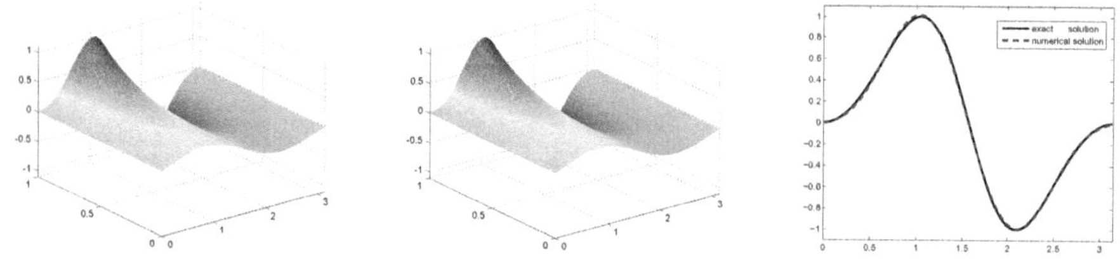

(a) $u(x,y)$ (b) $u_m^\delta(x,y)$ (c) $u(x,1)$ and $u_m^\delta(x,1)$

Fig. 1. Results of Example 1, $\delta = 0.001$

As g we take the following functions:
Example 1: $g(x) = x(\pi - x)$
Example 2: $g(x) = \sin(\pi \cos(x))$
Example 3: $g(x) = \begin{cases} x & , 0 \le x \le \frac{\pi}{2}, \\ \pi - x & , \frac{\pi}{2} < x \le \pi \end{cases}$

The perturbed discrete data are given by

$$\mathbf{f}_i^\delta = \mathbf{f}_i + \epsilon_i$$

where $\{\epsilon_i\}_{i=0}^{N-1}$ are generated by Function randn$(N,1)\times\delta$ in Matlab. All examples are computed by using Matlab with parameters $\tau = 1.01, k = 2$.

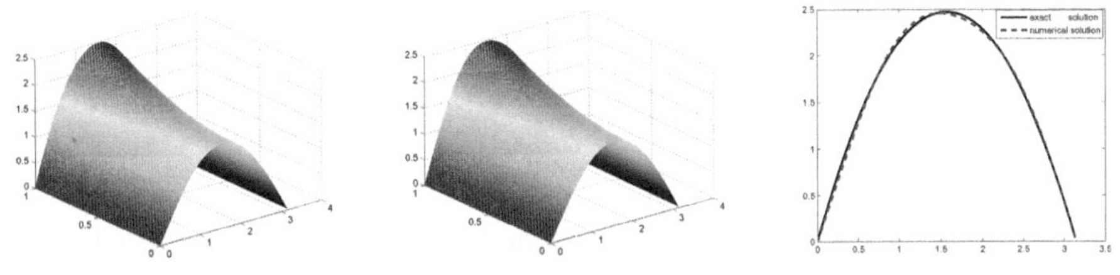

(a) $u(x,y)$ (b) $u_m^\delta(x,y)$ (c) $u(x,1)$ and $u_m^\delta(x,1)$

Fig. 2. Results of Example 2, $\delta = 0.001$

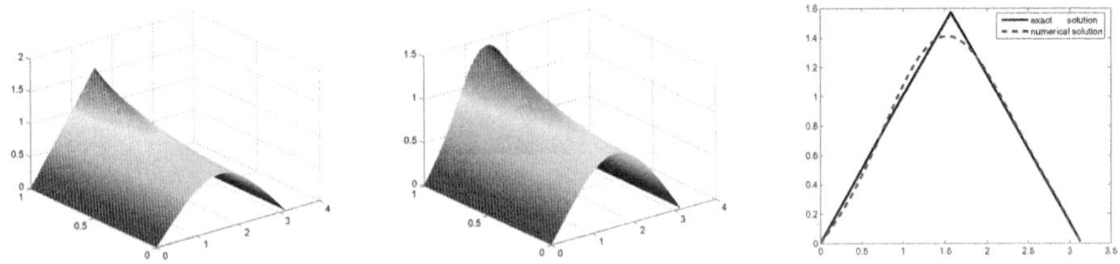

(a) $u(x,y)$ (b) $u_m^\delta(x,y)$ (c) $u(x,1)$ and $u_m^\delta(x,1)$

Fig. 3. Results of Example 3, $\delta = 0.001$

The numerical results are shown in Fig. 1-3, it can be seen that the proposed numerical solutions are accurate and stable.

6 Conclusion

We have proposed a new method to solve a Cauchy problem for the modified Helmholtz equation in a rectangular domain and obtained stable convergence estimates. The numerical results show that the proposed method is effective and stable. Compare with the method in [11], our method does not need the priori information.

References

1. Cheng, H., Huang, J., Leiterman, T.J.: An adaptive fast solver for the modified Helmholtz equation in two dimensions. Journal of Computational Physics 211(2), 616–637 (2006)

2. Engl, H.W., Hanke, M., Neubauer, A.: Regularization of inverse problems. Springer, Netherlands (1996)
3. Hon, Y.C., Wei, T.: Solving Cauchy problems of elliptic equations by the method of fundamental solutions. Boundary Elements XXVII, WIT Trans. Model. Simul 39, 57–65 (2005)
4. Isakov, V.: Inverse problems for partial differential equations. Springer, Heidelberg (2006)
5. Juffer, A.È.H., Botta, E.F.F., van Keulen, B.A.M., van der Ploeg, A., Berendsen, H.J.C.: The electric potential of a macromolecule in a solvent: A fundamental approach. Journal of Computational Physics 97(1), 144–171 (1991)
6. Liang, J., Subramaniam, S.: Computation of molecular electrostatics with boundary element methods. Biophysical Journal 73(4), 1830–1841 (1997)
7. Marin, L., Elliott, L., Heggs, P.J., Ingham, D.B., Lesnic, D., Wen, X.: Conjugate gradient-boundary element solution to the Cauchy problem for Helmholtz-type equations. Computational Mechanics 31(3), 367–377 (2003)
8. Marin, L., Elliott, L., Heggs, P.J., Ingham, D.B., Lesnic, D., Wen, X.: BEM solution for the Cauchy problem associated with Helmholtz-type equations by the Landweber method. Engineering Analysis with Boundary Elements 28(9), 1025–1034 (2004)
9. Marin, L., Lesnic, D.: The method of fundamental solutions for the Cauchy problem associated with two-dimensional Helmholtz-type equations. Computers & Structures 83(4-5), 267–278 (2005)
10. Qian, Z., Fu, C.L., Li, Z.P.: Two regularization methods for a Cauchy problem for the Laplace equation. Journal of Mathematical Analysis and Applications 338(1), 479–489 (2008)
11. Qin, H.H., Wei, T.: Quasi-reversibility and truncation methods to solve a Cauchy problem for the modified Helmholtz equation. Mathematics and Computers in Simulation (2009)
12. Russel, W.B., Russel, W.B., Saville, D.A., Schowalter, W.R.: Colloidal dispersions. Cambridge University Press, Cambridge (1992)
13. Tikhonov, A.N., Arsenin, V.Y., John, F.: Solutions of ill-posed problems. Vh Winston, Washington, DC (1977)
14. Wei, T., Hon, Y.C., Ling, L.: Method of fundamental solutions with regularization techniques for Cauchy problems of elliptic operators. Engineering Analysis with Boundary Elements 31(4), 373–385 (2007)

RBF Neural Network Case Teaching Research

JingBing Li*, HuaiQiang Zhang, YouLing Zhou, and Yong Bai

School of Information Science and Technology, Hainan University, Haikou 570228, China
Jingbingli2008@hotmail.com, zhq0319@163.com

Abstract. In this paper, the RBF neural network case teaching has been studied. In the actual teaching process, we find it more difficult for student to learn the course, duing to the RBF neural network curriculum theory is more stronger. Many students do not know how to use the theory to solve practical problems.Therefore, we equip students with basic knowledge of RBF neural network through case teaching. In this paper , a RBF neural network example has been analysised and applied to enable the students to learn RBF neural network. Teaching practice shows that case teaching can achieve better teaching effectiveness.

Keywords: Case teaching; RBF neural network; Tourists quantity.

1 Introductions

Many universities have set "artificial neural network " course to their undergraduate and graduate students. This course has many features[1]: much mathematical deduction, stronger curriculum theory, less effective of conventional teaching ,much difficult to master. For this reason, we have adopted a case teaching in the teaching of RBF neural network. Through an example of RBF neural network prediction in tourists quantity, we enable students to understand the RBF neural network's basic principle, using method and how to solve practical problems.

2 RBF Neural Network Course Design Case

With the development of Hainan international tourism island strategy, Hainan Province travel services will have a new period of development. During this period, the number of tourism will continue to increase in Hainan which will cause some damages to the Hainan Provincial Tourism landscape resources and the environment. Therefore, in the Hainan international tourism island development planning and feasibility study process, Hainan tourism scale is the scientific basis for forecasting tourism development, establishing tourism management decisions, reasonable controlling visitors scale, realizing the sustainable development of Hainan tourism. Tourists quantity is decided by many objective factors. The forecast of tourist quantity has not good ways now. As the number of visitors has a good nonlinear characteristic and the RBF neural network is better used to handle nonlinear problems, the RBF neural network can apply to forecast

* Corresponding author.

H. Tan and M. Zhou (Eds.): CSE 2011, Part I, CCIS 201, pp. 351–355, 2011.

the tourists quantity[2] . The article establishs prediction model and predictes the tourists quantity .In this way we achieve the purpose of forecasting tourism quantity and demonstrate the basic principles, learning steps and how to use of RBF neural network to students.

2.1 The Construction and Forecast of RBF Model on Forecasting Tourist Quantity

2.1.1 RBF Neural Network Input Variables and Output Variables

Input variable selection is an important task before the RBF neural network modeling, whether to choose a set of input variables which can best reflect the reason for desired output changes is directly relating to the performance of neural network prediction. The number of tourist is restricted by many factors, for example, geography, environment, culture, government policy, etc. If all these factors are considered, it will bring a lot of inconvenience to predict. Tourists quantity every five years as the neural network input variables is the innovation of the article, so input samples can be determined by the input variable. We can select the sixth year number of tourists after every five years as the neural network output variable[3].

Table 1. The actual tourist quantity of Hainan Province in 1990 to 2 009

Year	1990	1991	1992	1993	1994	1995	1996
Tourists quantity	113.46	140.61	247.37	274.41	289.60	361.01	485.82
Year	1997	1998	1999	2000	2001	2002	2003
Tourists quantity	791.00	855.97	929.07	1000.76	1124.76	1254.54	1234.11
Year	2004	2005	2006	2007	2008	2009	
Tourists quantity	1402.88	1516.47	1605.02	1873.78	2060.00	2250.33	

Note: Table 1 Data from the Hainan Provincial Bureau of Statistics

2.1.2 Determining Training Samples and Test Samples

From the above we can determine the number of input neuron of RBF neural network is 5, and the number of output neurons is 1. Treating the samples as follows [6]: Input neuron P=[p(t-5),p(t-4),p(t-3),p(t-2),p(t-1)]; Output neurons T=[p'(t)]. Where, t=1993, 1994 ... ... 2008, P (t) denote the normalized number of tourism at t year. In this method, we can obtain the training samples and test samples.

2.2 RBF Neural Network Training and Prediction

Creating a precise neural network by Newbe function, this function creates RBF network, automatically select the number of hidden layer and make the error to 0. MATLAB codes are as follows[4] [5]:

```
p=mapminmax(p,0,1);
[t,ts]=mapminmax(t,0,1);
spread=1.5;
net=newrbe(p,t,spread);
```

Where p is the input vector, t is the target vector. spread is the density of basis functions, spread is larger the function is smoother, where selecting spread=1.5.Mapminmax is normalized function.

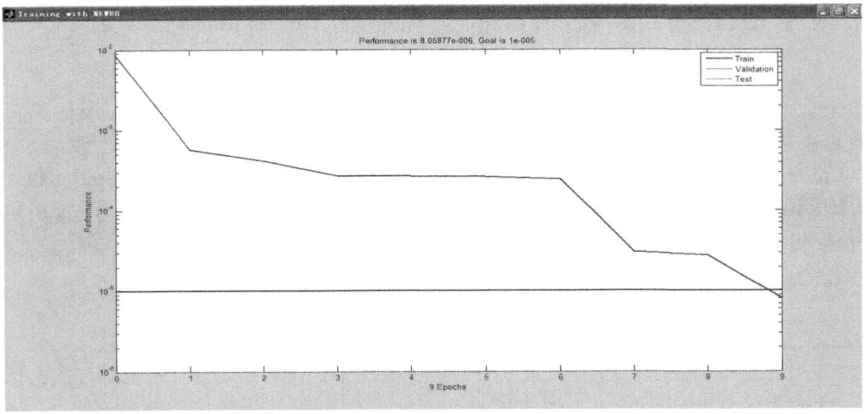

Fig. 1. RBF neural network trainning result

Then we can get the RBF neural network learning and training curve, shown in figure 2.

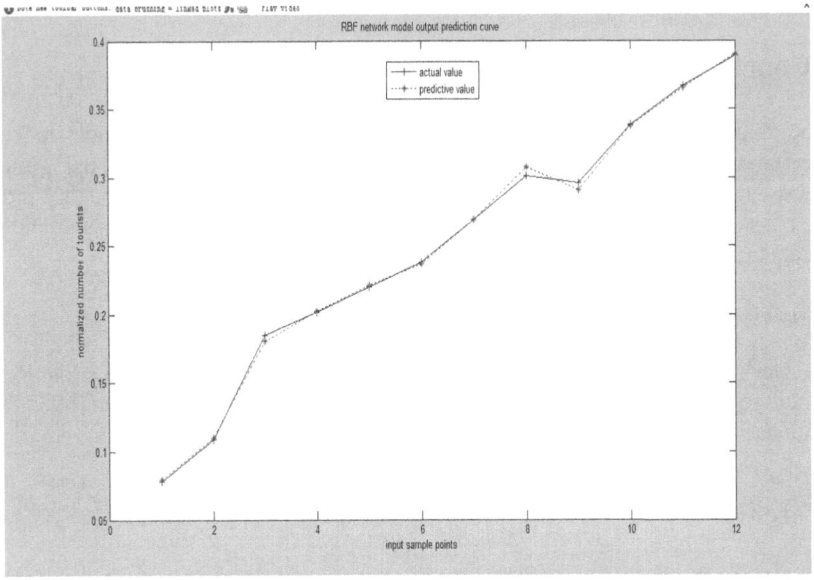

Fig. 2. RBF neural network learning and training curve

Then testing the neural network and verifying the prediction performance. MATLAB codes are as follows:

```
p_test=mapminmax(p_test,0,1);
y=sim(net,p_test);
y=mapminmax('reverse',y,ts);
```

Where, P_test is the network test samples. The results are as follows.

```
y= 1650.32  1811.25  2105.63   2210.35
```

We compare the actual value to the perdictive value, get the of the RBF neural network's accuracy which can reach more than 90%.

Enter the actual value from 2006 to 2009, we can obtain the predicted value in 2010.Similarly, after a multi-step iterative, we can get the predicted value from 2011 to 2019, shown in table 2.

Table 2. Predictive value of tourist quantity from2010 to 2019

Year	2010	2011	2012	2013	2014
Predictive value(millior	2486.35	2663.28	2845.64	3021.28	3259.4
Year	2015	2016	2017	2018	2019
Predictive value(millior	3387.65	3467.83	3532.56	3606.33	3650.5

As can be seen from Table 2, after a slow growth phase from 2010 to 2015, tourist quantity in Hainan Province will be gradually stabilized, reach to 36~37 million.

3 Conclusion

Through analysis of the RBF neural network case teaching, we have made students to understand the RBF neural network's basic principle, training process, using method and how to solve practical problems by neural network modeling. Teaching practice have proved that case teaching could achieve better teaching effectiveness on the more abstract artificial neural network program.

Acknowledgements

This work is partly supported by Hainan University Graduate Education Reform Project (yjg0117), and by Natural Science Foundation of Hainan Province (60894), and by Education Department of Hainan Province project (Hjkj2009-03).

References

1. Wei, H.-k.: Neural network structure design theory and method. National Defence Industry Press, Beijing (February 2005)
2. Sun, Y.-p., Zhang, L., Lv, R.-y.: Tourist quantity forecast by using neural network. Human Geography 17(6), 50–52 (2002)

3. Li, J.-b., Zhang, H.-q.: Application of BP neural network model on forecasting the number of tourists in Hainan province. In: 2010 International Conference on Computer and Communication Technologies in Agriculture Engineering (CCTAE) (2010)
4. Zhang, D.-f.: MATLAB Neural Network Application Design. Mechanical Industry Press, Beijing (January 2009)
5. Zhang, D.-f.: MATLAB Neural Network Simulation and Application. Electronic Industry Press, Beijing (June 2009)

Teaching Methodological Research on Computer-Related Course for Liberal Art Undergraduates

Xin Chen, Xiu-fang Wang, and Yong-hua Zhang

College of Information Science and Engineering,
Shandong University of Science and Technology,
Qingdao, Shandong Province, China
xxwar@163.com

Abstract. In China, a number of the liberal art undergraduates enter into tech universities. Liberal art undergraduates have opportunities to make good use of educational resources such as teachers, labs in tech universities. Computer teachers teach liberal art undergraduates computer-related courses. Teaching methodological research is important at the interdisciplinary situation. The teaching methods, task-driven, cased-based, teamwork, are applied in classes, which help liberal art undergraduates master advanced, practical computer technology efficiently.

Keywords: Liberal Art Undergraduates, Task-driven, Computer-related courses, Case-based.

1 Introduction

For the reason of expand enrollment of higher education in China, the number of the liberal art undergraduates has increased gradually in a number of tech universities. In the background of industrialization in China, the employment opportunities for the liberal art undergraduates are relatively few [1]. How the liberal art undergraduates in tech universities take the science and technology advantages to train them all kinds of skills available and increase job opportunities in the world nowadays is a problem worthy of study [2][3]. National Teaching Guiding Committee for Liberal Art Majors under the Ministry of Education has laid down the basic teaching requirement of College Computer Courses for liberal art undergraduates [4]. We teach the liberal art undergraduates the computer-related courses for many years, and we all have graduated from Computer Science, while we are not very familiar with each Liberal Art major. In the long process of computer technology education, we summarize some ways and means on teaching methodology as below, especially for the liberal art undergraduates. The end of education is to direct them apply information technologies in order to afford job opportunities on a more extensive scale for them.

2 The Education Series of Computer-Related Courses for Liberal Art Majors

Liberal art majors mainly are Legal, Administrative, Chinese Language and Literature, Foreign language, Music, Art and design etc. The liberal art undergraduates have the

H. Tan and M. Zhou (Eds.): CSE 2011, Part I, CCIS 201, pp. 356–361, 2011.

demand for computer-related courses. They usually have two or three computer-related courses during the university. We have set up different computer courses targeted to different liberal art majors based on national basic requirement of college computer teaching for liberal art majors [4]. Though extensive research, the liberal art majors are divided into three series based on educational feasibility in our university. The three series are series of literature and laws, series of non-music art and series of music. Tab1 lists the teaching contents of each series and which the majors are included in each series.

We have set up two computer-related courses required for each series. The content of Computer Course 1 is different for each series. Computer Course 1 and Computer Course 2 are similar of each series for the importance of Internet technology. The course of basic DBMS technology is focus on the basic knowledge of database management system, the concept of relational database, the database design and application for DBMS. Basic multimedia technology, which is for the series of Non-music art, focus on the basic technology of graphics and images, which contains the concept of graphics and images, the application of graphics and images processing software. Basic multimedia technology, which is for the series of Music, focus on the basic technology of audio, which contains the concept of audio and the application of audio processing software. Meanwhile, the classification of three series is considered teacher resources.

The new technology of computer has developed rapidly. Updating teaching material is very necessary. Deleting the outmoded contents or technology and adding advanced technology is as same as important. An acknowledged advanced technology must be selected. Liberal Art undergraduates have fewer opportunities than tech undergraduates to touch the new technology. So they look forward to learning some of them. For example, in VF course, the structure of the web DBMS is introduced, and difference between Web DBMS and VF DBMS is interpreted. In basic Internet technology course, many interesting Internet services are introduced into the classes, such as Google Map, Blog, Internet disk, Twitter and so on.

Table 1. Teaching contents of computer-related course in each series

Series	Majors	Computer Course 1	Computer Course 2
Series of Literature and Law	Law, Administrative, Advertising theory, Chinese Language and Literature, English language, Japanese language, Secretarial professionals.	Basic DBMS technology	Basic Internet technology
Non-music art	Fine Art, Art design, Advertising design, Industry design.	Basic multimedia technology (focus on technology of graphics and images)	Basic Internet technology
Music	Music	Basic multimedia technology (focus on technology of audio)	Basic Internet technology

3 The Teaching Methods in Practice

The thinking way is quite different between the liberal art undergraduates and the science and engineering undergraduates. Therefore, teaching the same computer course, teacher must use the varied means. The training of the ability of computer application replace with explaining the blunt formula, principle and theory. The goal of teaching them how to program is the training of computational thinking ability. The goal of teaching them how to use general software is improving the practical ability and creativity, which they can solve some computer-related problems after graduation. Task-driven, case-based and teamwork-study is well applied in teaching practice.

3.1 Task-Driven

The liberal art undergraduates' attitude towards computer-related courses is complicated. On one hand, they are interested in computer technology; on the other hand, they are afraid of the difficulties of the courses and are afraid of not passing the exam. Therefore, how to keep them interesting throughout the whole course period become very important.

Task-driven [5] is one of the teaching means based on the educational theory of constructivism [6]. Task, teacher and students interacts each other. During the classes, task is the main line, and teacher is the leader, and students are the subject. The feature of computer-related course lies in its powerful practicality. Liberal art undergraduates' knowledge structure and thinking ways are carefully considered. In the class preparation, the design of tasks is the key. A good task design can play a multiplier effect.

In course of basic DBMS technology, Visual FoxPro (ab. VF) is taught to the liberal art undergraduates. Though VF is not a common development tools nowadays, it is useful to help undergraduates to study the knowledge of relational database and the thinking of object-oriented programming, because of its concise interface. Another important reason is VF is one of the subjects in National Computer Rank Examination (ab. NCRE) Level 2. It is not necessary for all liberal art undergraduates to pass the NCRE Level 2. Many liberal art undergraduates look forward to pass the NCRE. The NCRE certification increases the weight of their employment. The target of teaching plan for VF is clear. However, it is not required all undergraduates to pass the NCRE. The teaching contents are easy to decide, which the knowledge points is included. But the difficulty of the knowledge points is not easy considered all liberal Art undergraduates. Task-driven play an important role in solving the problem. Tasks are designed on many knowledge points, which are the testing points in NCRE Level 2 VF, and each task set different difficulty degrees. Undergraduates in classes complete tasks based on their own different situations. Undergraduates who look forward to getting the certification of NCRE desire to complete the tasks well and teachers instruct them a lot. While, other undergraduates just complete tasks in order to pass the course exam. It is strategy in the design of comprehensive tasks. A task designed contains of knowledge points as many as possible. Meanwhile, completing task is easy but doing well is difficult. The task gives undergraduates full scope to creativity.

For example, in VF course, a comprehensive task is designed, which contains many knowledge points such as new database, new data table, input data records, the relation between two or more tables, set reference integrity. Fig 1 shows the task contents in detail and the change of requirement and difficulty.

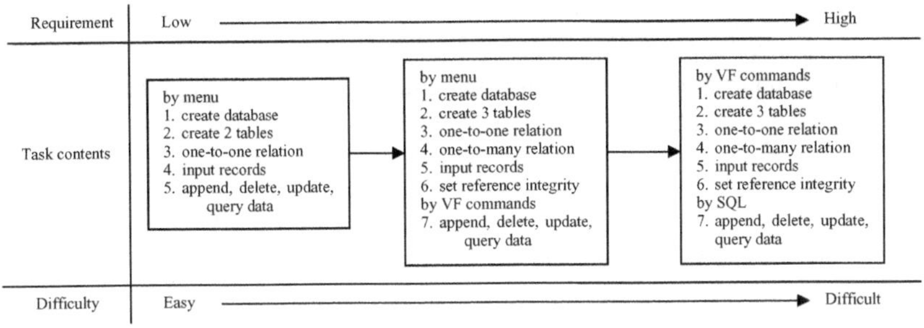

Fig. 1. The task design in VF course

The task requirement is different with the different level of the undergraduates. The minimum requirements of the task is creating a database, which contains the VF operations of new a database and two table, input 10 records at least to every table, table data meet reference integrity. Undergraduates, with low level, only create a simple database and tables, and the relation of the two tables is one-to-one, which is met to the lowest requirement of the course. Undergraduates, with high level, create a complicated database, which contains 3 or more tables. Two of them are one-to-one relation or one-to-many relation. Student with high level is guided to complete a small library DBMS. A library DBMS contains of 3 tables at least, which is reader-table, book-table, and lend-table. If undergraduates complete 3 tables, and the task becomes more difficult than before, which is required to set primary key and foreign key in tables. The relations between 3 tables should be analyzed. If a reader can lend only one book and each book is only one, the relations between 3 tables are simple. When undergraduates complete the simple database, they realize immediately that the simple situation is impossible in real world. And then, the one-to-many relations of reader-table and lend-table, book-table and lend table are defined. All the records are met to be reference integrity. If undergraduates complete the task above, the task becomes more complicated than they have done. They are demanded to construct SQL to query, append, delete and so on.

For the beginner of the database design, the task above is not such easy. When they complete the basic part of the task, teachers encourage them to do more difficult part than before step by step. Task is from easy to difficult, and the knowledge points are contained more and more.

Computer-related courses for liberal art undergraduates, with the feature of strong practical, are taught by progressive approach. The theory of relational database, such as relational paradigm is not mentioned, but how to operate VF DBMS is deeply interpreted.

3.2 Case-Based Teaching

One of the educational means, case-based teaching [7], is used in the course. Case-based teaching is a special method, and cases are from real events and real situations. The method of case-based teaching plays an important role on Management. We try it on computer-related courses for liberal Art undergraduates and achieve a good result.

Undergraduates pay more interesting in discussion these real cases than hypothetical problems and help them participating in classes voluntarily.

Many liberal art undergraduates become clerks after graduation. It is not enough to be only familiar with Office Software. Querying, statistics, indexing is common in most companies, and basic Internet technology is used in daily office work, Undergraduates want to know how to adapt the office situation as soon as possible. Computer course 2, which is list on Tab 1, focuses on how to use such Internet technology as FTP, WWW, Email, and so on. What cases are used in Computer course 2 is the key. Simulating a real office situation is one of the cases. In classes from the beginning, basic knowledge has been explained, such as IP address, types of cables, principle of router, making network plug, which is by the traditional teaching mean. After that, undergraduates are demanded to prepare connecting to Internet before setting up a small company, which the main business is trade or an online store, which like a task but this task is a team-work group of 4 or 5 undergraduates, which comes from real situation. At real situation, only one Internet line is paid in order to cut costs and team undergraduates share it. The problems of constructing network crop up. Cabling, choosing router, configuring computer and setting IP address have to be done one by one. They search information to solve all problems by all means after class. If all of their computers connect Internet, the teaching target arrives successfully. In a common company, there usually is a server. Sharing files is one of the server roles. Setting up a FTP server is contained in the course. The operations of FTP server, uploading, downloading and file management, is practiced in the case.

3.3 Teamwork-Study

Learning computer technology is mastering to be proficient in some software. However, the function of some software is very large. It is difficult for a student alone to grasp the trivial operations. Meanwhile, teacher is impossible to teach the technology in detail. If undergraduates cooperate and share what they have learned and practiced with each other, they could get a satisfactory effect on it. The contents are so much that the teaching hours are limited. Teamwork-study is one of an effect method. Teamwork [8] is a process, which team members support and help each other to pursue a same target. Teamwork-study is two practical ways in class. One is that teamwork is during the whole studying process, which is applicable to completing a relative large task and members of the team usually organize voluntarily. The way is called teamwork-process-study. The other one is that single student's exam result is the team result. Members of the team are organized at random. Members have to cooperate with others whatever they like. The way is called teamwork-result-study.

In our teaching practice, constructing a Web site is a teamwork task, achieving by teamwork-process-study. It contains many knowledge points and it requires many kinds of software especially for the dynamic web pages. One member is in charge of web site art design making some elements by Firework and Flash, one is in charge of gathering material and hyperlinks, one is in charge of making web by Dreamweaver, and one is in charge of data source by Access DBMS. They assign the task as they like. Another assignment is that each member complete some associated pages, and then these pages are hyperlinked together at last. One member is in charge of data source. This means all team members learn all software. It takes more time than the former assignment. Liberal art undergraduates are few of course hours, so the first assignment is suitable.

Associating all members' exam results in a team is the feature of teamwork-result-study. Associating exam results mean a team member's quiz result influence others'. Computer courses' hours usually divided into 2 same parts. One is in traditional classes and the other is in computer Lab. All quizzes are in computer Lab. The strategy is that every team member tests different knowledge point and gains one result, which is not the final result. The team member's final result is the average of all team members' quiz results. The advantage of the strategy is pushing the slower student.

Team-work-study is not only adaptive to the liberal art student but also tech undergraduates in computer-related courses. Especially, liberal art undergraduates spend a little time on computer. They are trained team spirit, which is a bonus.

4 Conclusion

Research on teaching methodology of computer courses is deeply in Computer Science. Liberal art undergraduates have less computational thinking than tech and science undergraduates. In teaching practice, it took us many years to summarize the methods, which apply in undergraduates grade by grade. Sometimes, teachers have taught them hand by hand to operate computer. Some undergraduates didn't understand the teaching requirement, and teachers explained over and over again. The design of tasks and cases need rich experience and they are refined in classes for years.

Acknowledgment. This Work is supported by Educational Research Project of "SUST Stars".

References

1. Song, H.-s.: Research in the Reasons of Liberal Arts Undergraduates' Difficulty in Seeking Jobs and its Countermeasures. Journal of Anhui University of Technology (Social Sciences) 27(3) (May 2010) (In Chinese)
2. Liang, X.-m.: Research on the Teaching Methods of Basic Computer Science of Liberal Arts in the University. Journal of Hengyang Normal University 29(6) (December 2008) (In Chinese)
3. Tang, G.-h.: Research on computer education for liberal arts undergraduates in universities for nationalities. Jounal of Southwest University for Nationalities-Natural Science Edition (November 2005) (In Chinese)
4. Teaching Guiding Committee for College Liberal Art Majors under the Ministry of Education. The Basic Teaching Requirement for College Computer Courses (2006) (In Chinese)
5. Gao, Y.-x.: Application of "task-driven" method in computer basic teaching. Journal of University of Science and Technology Liaoning 33(2) (April 2010) (In Chinese)
6. Duffy, T.M., Cunningham, D.J.: Constructivism: Implications for the Design and Delivery of Instruction. In: Handbook of Research on Educational Communications and Technology, USA (1996)
7. Wilson, B.G.: Constructivist learning environments: case studies in instructional design,USA, pp. 49–56 (1996)
8. Buller, J.L.: The Essential College Professor: A Practical Guide to an Academic Career,USA, pp. 124–130 (2010)

Intelligent and Collaborative Q&A Mechanism Based on Learning Communities

Tongzhen Zhang* and Ruimin Shen

E-Learning Lab, Shanghai Jiao Tong University, China
{tzzhang,rmshen}@sjtu.edu.cn

Abstract. Q&A is a very important step of a process of learning. This paper analyses some problems in Q&A which both teachers and learners are facing in e-learning, and proposes a novel Q&A mechanism combining automatic Q&A and collaborative Q&A technologies. In detail, this paper proposes an intelligent answer machine using Semantic Words, Keywords and their respective weights to describe the feature of a question, a keywords reverse abstracting policy, and a question matching algorithm; this paper also proposes a personalized question deliver policy to other learners with high enough login frequence, low question load and in the same learning community where all learners have similar interests, and a promoting mechanism for collaborative Q&A. By this novel Q&A mechanism, this paper hopes to offer a timely response to a learner's question, and reduce the load on teachers.

Keywords: Q&A, intelligent answer machine, personalized learning, collaborative learning, learning community.

1 Introduction

Due to the geographical dispersion and time limitation, lots of learners choose to study at e-learning platforms [1]. But e-learning faces many new challenges, and one of them is that when learners are puzzled and are eager to get help from a teacher, then a problem occurs: the teachers can not be always online, and even when they are online, they could not resolve so many questions from hundreds of online learners. So an efficient Q&A mechanism is an eager application requirement in e-learning. In fact, except for e-learning, Q&A technology itself has now attracted more attention of researchers. The well accepted methods can be divided into two types: automatic and collaborative Q&A. Automatic Q&A makes use of the universality and commonness of questions, stores and indexes vast pairs of questions and answers in a question bank, then when a people poses a question to Q&A, the system will parse, reason and provide related questions and their answers in the question bank automatically [2], [3]. While interactive inquiry technology organizes all users into an efficiently cooperative network. When a user poses a question in an interactive inquire platform, it's

* Corresponding author, Tongzhen Zhang, 200240, E-learning Lab, Dept. of Computer Science and Engineering, Shanghai Jiao Tong University, Shanghai, China, tzzhang@sjtu.edu.cn

H. Tan and M. Zhou (Eds.): CSE 2011, Part I, CCIS 201, pp. 362–368, 2011.

other users, but not the system itself, analyse and understand the abstract semantic of the question, and then give the answer to the question. It has been a hot point and used as an aids of research in Search Engine, such as, sina iask [4], Yahoo knowledge hall [5]. Following, we call interactive inquiry in e-learning as collaborative Q&A, because this method shows an efficient cooperation and collaborative activity among learners. In this paper, we will discuss some challenges whiich they are facing respectively, and propose some novel solutions and combine them to give an efficient and effective Q&A mechanism to meet the application requirment in e-learning.

2 Intelligent Answer Machine

The automatic Q&A mainly solves three issues[6], [7]: parsing and understanding the semantic of the posed question automatically, matching and gaining the questions with the same or similar semantic from the question bank, and giving a more reasonable and competitive ranking list to the questioner. In semantic analysis, extracting keywords is usually an efficient and effective way, but it still remains a big challenge in chinese due to the different character of language itself (without any space between words in a sentence). The majority of these systems make use of natural language understanding technology to complete word segmentation, part-of-speech tagging and syntactic analysis on a chinese sentence, the performance is not efficient due to the time-comsuming, low accuracy, and complex of this method itself. In matching and gaining the similar questions, the similarity degree of two questions is measured by the proportion of the common keywords in both of them while it implies that the relation between different keywords was ignored, such as fruit and apple, in fact, they have a very closed relation in semantic. On the other hand, actually even when all keywords are same, the emphasis points in both questions can still be a little different, these factors also should be taken into acount in matching process.

2.1 Question Description Based on Keywords and Their Weights

We divide keywords in general sense into two types: Semantic Words and Keywords. Semantic Words here are some sepcial keywords with clear-cut semantic information, such as "difference","concept",etc. All these words mark the type of a question without involving any knowledge point it refers. On the contrary, Keywords show the knowledge points it covers. The former is interdisciplinary while the later is about a certain topic, such as a special course. These two types can have different influences in matching questions and should be considered separately. Even different keywords possess different intensities in semantic, that is they occupy different semantic proportions in a question, these factors also should be consided. A question usually have a Semantic Word and several Keywords with their weights to identify the semantic proportions. Fig.1 shows the relation between Keywords and questions, it forms a semantic network.

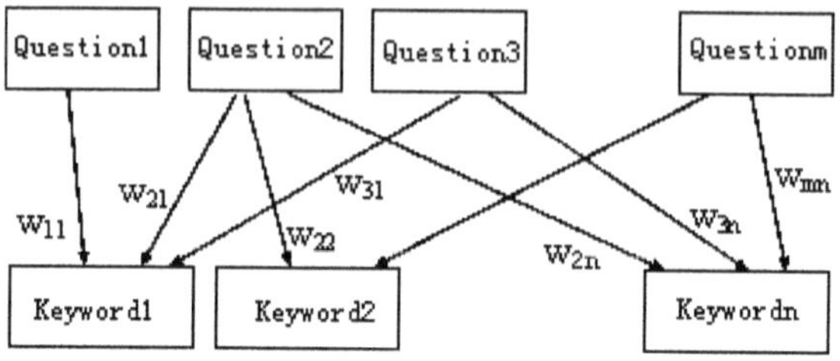

Fig. 1. Keywords semantic network of questions

2.2 Keywords Abstracting Reversely from a Question

For predetermined questions offered by teachers, the semantic labels can be finished by asking the teachers. For question posed by a learner, the system has to parse and label the question automatically. As what has been discussed ahead, natural language processing technology usually brings a complex, time-consuming, and even sometimes a lowly accurate result. Now we will consider the matter in the reverse direction by organizing beforehand a Semantic Words bank including most common ones, a Keywords bank including all the knowledge points a special course covers. Then detect each Semantic Word to see if it exists in this question. To reduce the detecting time, we can detect the high-frequency Semantic Word first, and if one has been found in the question then stop immediately. We can do that in the same way during detecting the Keywords, but the stop condition is only when the number of Keywords detected being in the question reaches the total of words in it, then stop, otherwise, scan all ones in the bank. Certainly, we should eliminate the effect of the number of the function words while counting. At this stage, we assign the same value as the weight to each Keywords in label, such as, 0.20, if there are five Keywords existing in the label, then with the feedback of learners, the weight will be changed seperately and automatically.

2.3 Question Matching Algorithm

In view of the Semantic Word, Keywords, weights and visited frequency of a question, we give a matching algorithm below: Assume for the question Q_N, posed at the moment, its Semantic Word is sw_N, the pairs of Keywords and their weights are $SK_N=\{(sk_{N1},w_{N1}),(sk_{N2},w_{N2}),\cdots,(sk_{Nt},w_{Nt})\}$; for each question Q_O, stored in the bank, the Semantic Word is sw_O, the pairs of Keywords and their weights are $SK_O=\{(sk_{O1},w_{O1}),(sk_{O2},w_{O2}),\cdots,(sk_{Or},w_{Or})\}$, the visited freqence of Q_O is f_O. Then the similarity degree $Sim\,(Q_N,Q_O)$ can be obtained by the following policies:

If Q_N、Q_O are the same from the viewpoint of word string, Q_O is regarded as the same question as Q_N, and $Sim\,(Q_N,Q_O)=1$.

If $SK_N \cap SK_O=\phi$, then Q_O is regarded as an irrelevant question, and $Sim\,(Q_N,Q_O)=0$.

If $SK_N \cap SK_O \neq \phi$, then Q_O is regarded as a relevant question. Now we assume:

$SK = SK_N \cap SK_O = \{(sk_{O1}, w_{O1}), (sk_{O2}, w_{O2}), \cdots, (sk_{Op}, w_{Op})\}$, here $p = |SK|$, then:

$$Sim\,(Q_N, Q_O) = \alpha K_p + \beta (n_{NO} / n_N) \sum_{i=1}^{p} w_{Oi} + \gamma \log f_O,\ \ \alpha > \beta >> \gamma. \tag{1}$$

Especially, α, β, γ are constant factors valued from 0 to 1, and $\alpha + \beta + \gamma = 1$, If $sw_N = sw_O$, then $K_p = 1$, else $K_p = 0$, then normalize $Sim\,(Q_N, Q_O)$ to make sure $Sim\,(Q_N, Q_O) <= 1$ by:

$$Sim\,(Q_N, Q_O) = Sim\,(Q_N, Q_O) / \max\,(Sim\,(Q_N, Q_{Oi})). \tag{2}$$

Using an exp Sim_T, each Q_O satisifing the condition $Sim\,(Q_N, Q_O) > Sim_T$, is added to the ranking list presented to the questioner according to the similarity degree in descending order.

2.4 Dynamically Changing of Keyword Weight Based on Learners' Feedback

For each question in ranking list, the questioner need to give three types of feedback: satisfied, unsatisfied, and ignore (the default value). The system will modifies the weight of a Keyword according to satisfied and unsatisfied feedback:

Satisfied: If the similarity is 1, all the weights remain unchanged, while if the similarity is less than 1, the weights in Q_O will be modified, Assume:

$SK = SK_N \cap SK_O = \{(sk_{O1}, w_{O1}), (sk_{O2}, w_{O2}), \cdots, (sk_{Op}, w_{Op})\}$, $\overline{SK} = SK_O - SK = \{(sk_{O1}, w_{O1}), (sk_{O2}, w_{O2}), \cdots, (sk_{Oq}, w_{Oq})\}$,

For any Keywords in set SK:

$$w_{Oi} = w_{Oi}(1 + \mu), i = 1, \cdots, p, \mu \in R^+. \tag{3}$$

For any Keywords in set $\overline{SK}$:

$$w_{Oi} = w_{Oi}\left(1 - \frac{w_{SK}\mu}{q}\right), i = 1, \cdots, q. \tag{4}$$

Unsatisified:

For any Keywords in set SK:

$$w_{Oi} = w_{Oi}(1 - \theta), i = 1, \cdots, p, \theta \in R^+. \tag{5}$$

For any Keywords in set $\overline{SK}$:

$$w_{Oi} = w_{Oi}\left(1 + \frac{w_{SK}\theta}{q}\right), i = 1, \cdots, q. \tag{6}$$

3 Personalized and Collaborative Q&A

Personalized and Collaborative learning technologies are two hot points in e-learning research area. The first provides different learners with different learning services according to their assorted features [8]. While the second emphasizes a learning policy that is some learners should groupe together, and each of them benefits from their collaborative hehavior and aims to reach better learning outcome[9]. We combine these two technologies to propose a personalized collaboratice Q&A scheme. We can image, facing numerous questions delivered by other learners, the learners will feel a ponderous burden, how can they find a suitable question they can answer, and avoid to be boring? The search engine now just catchs the focus by the question the user posed just now, and list all the related questions and their answers [12], while this benefits the questioners but has no use for the responsers. We propose a policy of delivering the questions only to the learners who are interested in the same topic of the question, and limit the quantity of questons they are facing under their load.

3.1 Self-organized Learning Communities

By analysing the learning activities, we can cluster learners by AI technology into communities. In our early work [10], [11], we cluster learners according to their interests reflecting from knowledge points involved in learning acitivities, and construct learning communities. The interest feature of a community is described by a vector of knowledge points and their weights. All the learners in the same community have similar interests, each learner belongs to several communities due to his or her multiple interests. The communities and the apportionment of learners are dynamic and adjustable followed along with the learning activities automatically.

3.2 Personalized Question Delivering

For each question delivered, we have labeled it automatically by the system, then compare the Keywords of this question with the interest feature of each community, If they are similar enough, then all the learners in this community are the candidates we can deliver. Other factors here we consider are the time limit of the question, login frequency and question capability of each candidate. For a candidate, organizing a ranking list of related questions according to these factors. Usually, an overdue question will disappear automatically, and questions about to expire are placed first. Few questions are delivered to the candidates with low login frequency, and we always count the questions unresolved in his ranking list before delivering a new question to someone, if the count has reached the candidate's capacity, then stop to do so. By this way, we provide a personalized question delivering policy.

3.3 Promoting Mechanism of Collaborative Q&A

How to encourage the learers to help other ones is still a challenge in a collaborative learning enviroment [9]. We give the responsers some rewards, such as Ad Points, according to the feedback. More Ad Points, more learning materials for free. When the teacher grades the learners, we add collaborative proportion in a learner's grade according to the quantity and quality of the responses he or she has made to promote the learners more active in the collaborative Q&A system.

4 A Novel Uniform Framework of Q&A Mechanism

Combining the solutions decribed above, we give a novel uniform framework of Q&A Mechanism in an e-learing environment as showing in Fig.2.

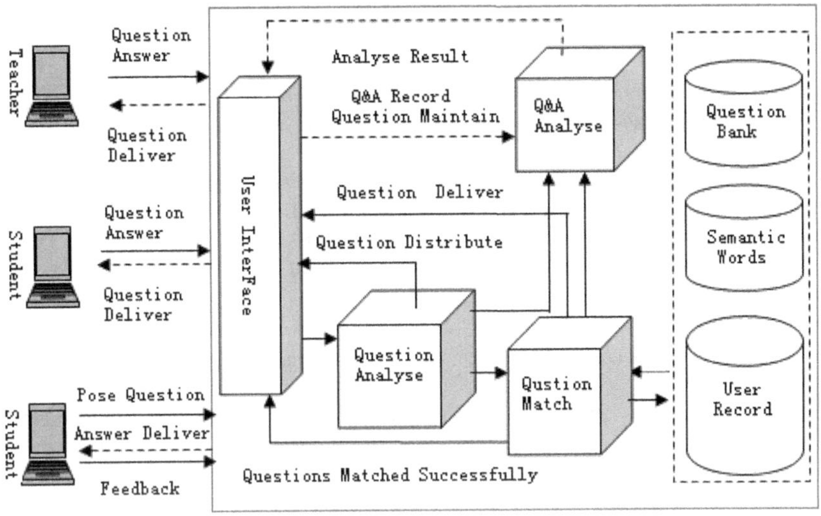

Under this framework, when a learner poses a question to the system, the system analyses and labels the question with features (Semantic Words, Keywards and their respective weights), matches the questions in the question bank, and present a ranking list of pairs of question and answer matched sucessfully. Once one of the answers satisfies the questioner, the Q&A proccess is over now; on the opposite, the question is delivered to the teacher and other learners in the same community waiting for their responses, If some other learner responses this question and his answer gets a good feedback or just the teacher himself gives the answer, then the answer with its question will be stored again in the question bank, this will rich the bank and make it more efficient later, and the learner responser will win different awarded scores for his collaborative activity according to the feedback from the questioner.

5 Conclusions

This paper analyses some problems in Q&A both teachers and learners are facing in e-learning. To offer a timely response to a learner's question, and reduce the load on teachers, we propose a novel Q&A mechanism combining automatic Q&A and collaborative Q&A technologies. In detail, on automatic Q&A, we propose an intelligent answer machine using Semantic Words, Keywords and their respective weights to describe the feature of a question, a keywords reverse abstracting policy, and question matching algorithm; on collaborative Q&A, to increase the possibility of getting responses to the question and release the unrelated learners from disturbing, we propose a personalized deliver policy for the question to other learners belonging to the same learning community in which learners have similar interests, To encourage other learners to be active and give a timely response to a question, all the learners whoes answer gaining good feedbacks win a collaborative reward of score.

References

1. Analysis of Educational Resource Database, Wed Site Market, http://research.cnnic.cn
2. Shen, R.M., Li, X.J.: Multi-Media Automatic Answer Machine by Support Question Scene. Computer Engineering and Applications 12, 101–103 (1999)
3. Liu, Q.B., Huang, R.H., He, K.K.: Intelligent Question and Answer System Design and Implementation. Distance Education in China 83, 43–48 (2000)
4. Sina Iask Website, http://www.iask.com
5. Liu, W.: BuyAns-An Incentive & Collaborative Platform For Knowledge Acquisition. In: 2nd International Conference on Semantics, Knowledge and Grid, Guilin, China, pp. 632–637 (2006)
6. Zhang, T.Z., Shen, R.M.: Question Matching Algorithm Research and Implementation in Answer Web. Computer Engineering and Applications 39, 103–105 (2003)
7. Jinwei, C., Robles-Flores, J.A., Roussinov, D., Nunamaker, J.F.: Automated Question Answering From Lecture Videos: NLP vs. Pattern Matching. System Sciences, In: 38th Annual Hawaii International Conference, Hawaii, pp. 55–61 (2005)
8. Lu, J.: A Personalized E-Learning Material Recommender System. In: 2nd International Conference on Information Technology for Application, Harbin, China, pp. 374–379 (2004)
9. Hadwin, A.F., Gress, C.L., Page, J.: Toward Standards For Reporting Research: A Review of The Literature on Computer-Supported Collaborative Learning. IEEE Computer Society, Washington DC (2006)
10. Zhang, T.Z., Shen, R.M.: Multi-Interest Self-Organizing Learner Community Model And Constructing Algorithm. Chinese Journal of Electronics 19(1), 18–22 (2010)
11. Zhang, T.Z., Shen, R.M., Lu, H.T.: Using Non-Negative Matrix Factorization to Cluster Learners and Construct Learning Communities. Chinese Journal of Electronics 24(2), 207–211 (2011)
12. Li, H., Hu, D., Hao, T., et al.: Adaptation Rule Learning For Case-Based Reasoning. In: 3rd International Conference on Semantics, Knowledge and Grid, Xi'An, China, pp. 44–49 (2007)

Reform of Base Computer Teaching Based on a Set of Papers Analysis

Jun-Ling Li[1,2] and Yun-Tao Ni[1,2]

[1] College of Computer Science and Information Engineering, Harbin Normal University, Harbin150025, China
[2] Heilongjiang Provincial Key Laboratory of Intelligence Education and Information Engineering, Harbin 150025, China

Abstract. For improving teaching quality of basic computer teaching, the random samples of 190 students of 2008 in the final exam papers were taken and analyzed in detail, we find drawbacks in basic computer teaching; so we explored the teaching mode and method for different professional by research and referencing successful experiments of other college and university. The mode and method was applied to students of 2009 and 2010, it is proved to be effective.

Keywords: Paper Analysis, Basic Computer Teaching, Teaching Mode, Measures.

1 Introduction

How to explore the mode and method for base computer teaching is hot topics in teaching reform of universities. At present, universities assume responsible for training applied talent with enough theory bases, strong innovation ability and a solid practical ability, so successes of base computer teaching or not depends on whether more popular talents are trained for the society. Examination is a very important part of the teaching. We not only obtain proper evaluation of examinations by scientific and rational analysis on papers, but also help us to get feedback information about the teaching and know students degree of mastering knowledge, teachers should find out problems for student to improve teaching quality, and then solve it. [1]

2 The Structural Characteristics of Paper and Analysis

It was written examination, structure and characteristics of papers maintained the stability of the previous years, and there were some changes and innovations. The total score of examination paper was 100 points. The kinds of Questions are explanation of terms, calculating, false or true, single choice, fill in the blank, short answer and practical error correction. In which explanation of terms, short answer and practical error correction question were subjective questions, and the rest were objective questions. Their respective score was 10, 10, 10, 20, 20, 20 and 10 points; the time of exam was 120 minutes. The course content was distributed into the exam according to syllabus;

H. Tan and M. Zhou (Eds.): CSE 2011, Part I, CCIS 201, pp. 369–376, 2011.

the difficulty of examination paper was medium, distribution of difficulty and ease was balanced. According to psychology theory, the arrangement order of questions was presented from easy to difficult.

The random samples of 190 students of 2008 in the final examination were taken. The highest score is 99 points, the lowest score is 39 points, and the average score is 74.38 points. In which the number above 90 points is 18; the number of 80-89 points is 59; the number of 70-79 points is 57; the number of 60-69 points is 45; the number of exam failed is 20.

Students' scores of various kinds of questions were shown in Fig.1. -- Fig.7.

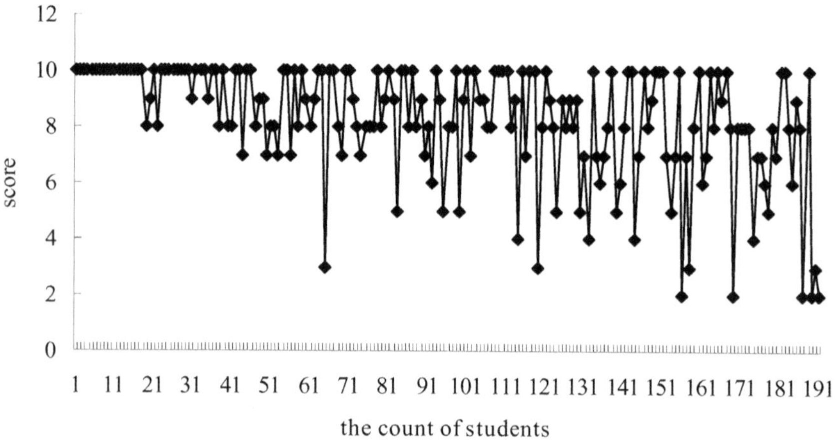

Fig. 1. Students' scores on explanation of terms

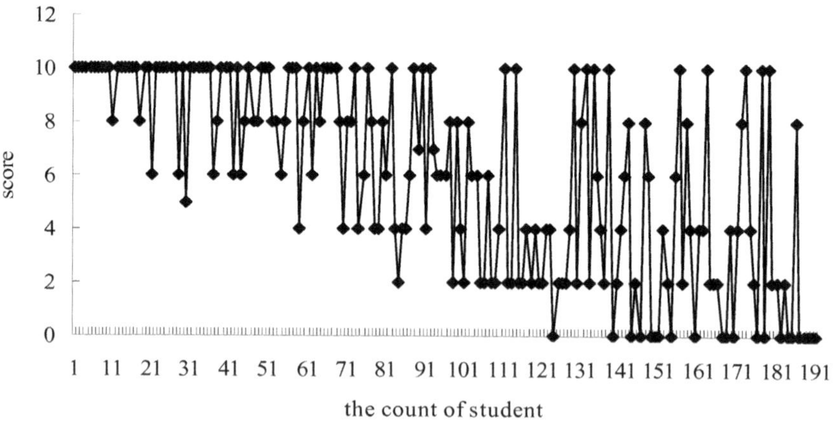

Fig. 2. Students' scores on calculation

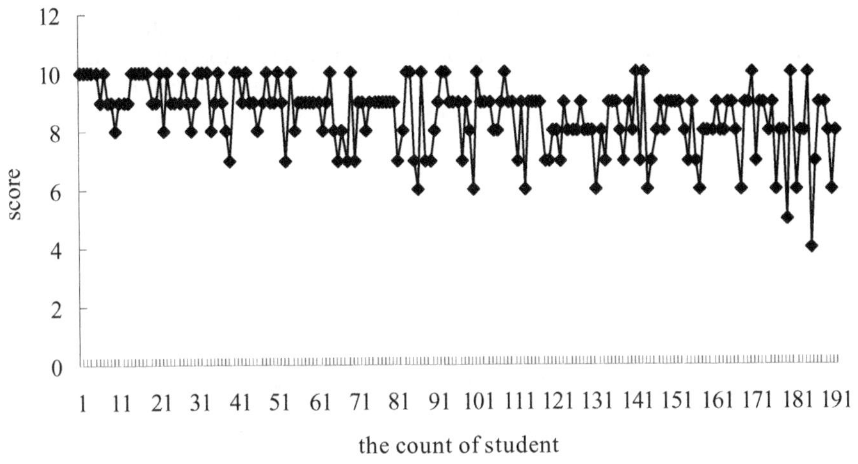

Fig. 3. Students' scores on false or true

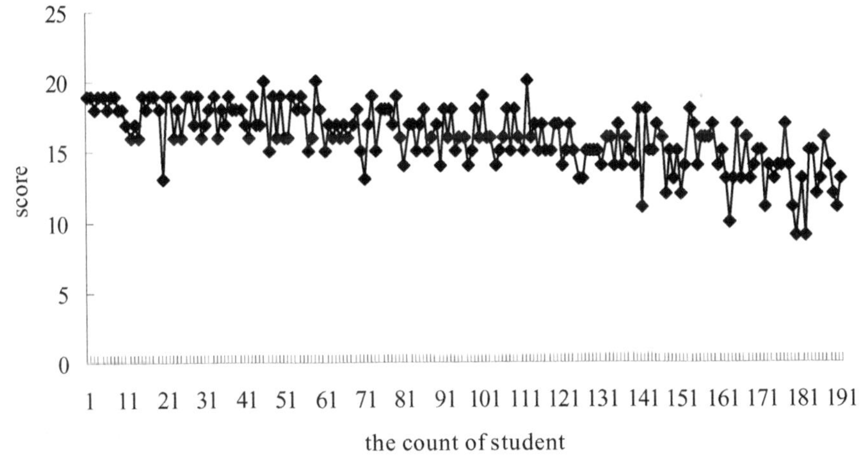

Fig. 4. Students' scores on single choice

We calculated the average score of various kinds of paper from Fig. 1.--Fig. 7, they are 8.31937 points, 6.02618 points, 8.53927 points, 16.0366 points, 13.9581 points, 16.3927 points and 5.10471 points. We also can calculate their average scoring rate shown in Fig.8.

According the above data we can see that the scoring rate of some kind of paper is much lower, such as Calculating, fill in the blank and practical error correction. From which we can draw the conclusion that first students are still lack of the skilled practical ability on computer. For the same operation, there are many ways, not all students can master these, some actual operation can not be applied flexibly, so the scoring rate is lower in practical error correction. Second, computer term was not expressed accurately for students, and a thorough understanding of some basic knowledge don't master well, so it exists many problems in basic knowledge.

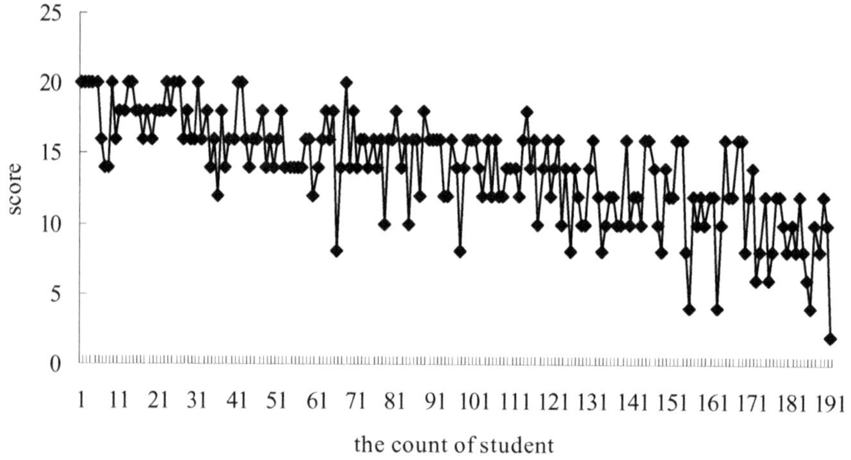

Fig. 5. Students' scores on fill in the blank

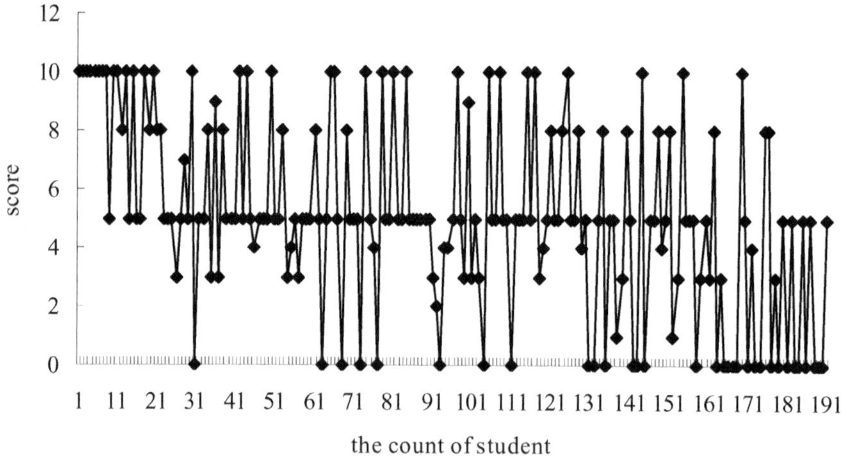

Fig. 6. Students' scores on short answer

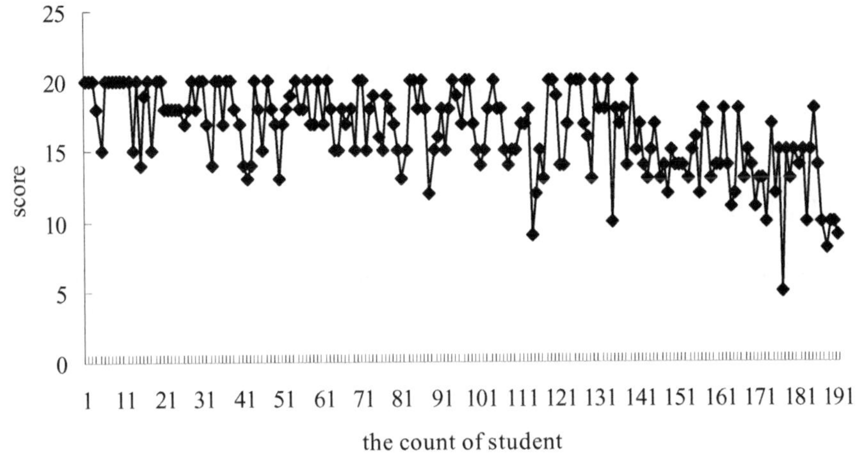

Fig.7. Students' scores on practical error correction

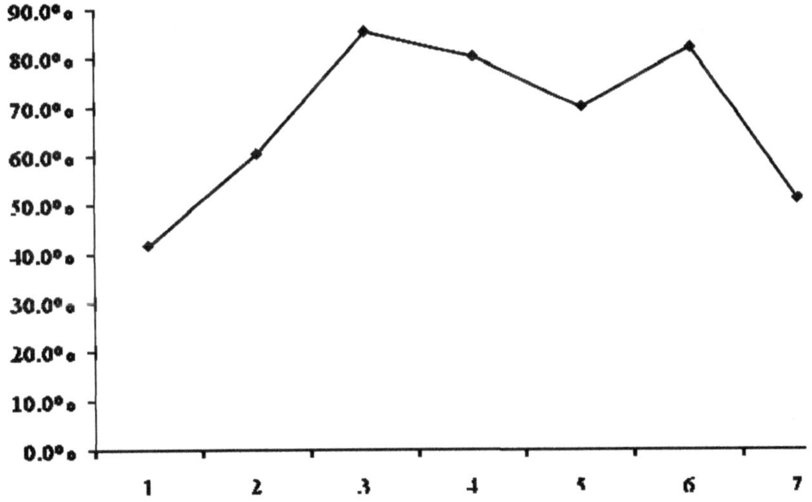

Fig. 8. Students' average scoring rate of various types of paper

With the popularity of computer, practical skills on computer for students compared to freshman before have been increasing significantly, but their computer knowledge is not systematic. Their practical skills on computer are very different because they are from different area. at the same time, because junior high school and high school don't attach importance to computer education, the students in the university isn't still enough emphasis on the subject, they are not interested in teaching content and lack of motivation of learning.

For teacher, teachers in the teaching process not fully played their dominant position, course content was confined within the material, there is no better knowledge of extension; modern, innovative teaching ideas were not formed and so on.

It is more important that computer technology update so fast that it gives teachers, supporting laboratories, teaching facilities and teaching resources put forward higher requirements.

3 Measures on Teaching Reform

We found many problems in teaching by paper analysis, so teachers in the Institute of Public Department had a careful investigation and research, and referenced successful experience of basic computer teaching from other colleges and universities, the reform measures are below:

3.1 The Interest of the Students in Learning Should Be Trained

How to train and maintain the interest in learning for students is very important. In the teaching process, a sense of accomplishment is very important. After their confidence is built gradually, the interest in learning can be gradually cultivated and be sustainable. Therefore, in order to achieve Integration of the knowledge and interest, teachers should play the leading role in the student-centered teaching and take full account of the various teaching. In the learning process, teachers should gradually develop their ability of independent learning, for a student's progress and a bright spot, encouragement and praise should be given by teachers. For example, according to the discipline of teaching content, our department organized some contest and rewarded outstanding students.

3.2 Construct More Appropriate Model for Basic Computer Teaching

Teaching should focus on the training of ability, we discard the single teaching mode before, for different teaching contents, we should select more appropriate teaching mode. For example, the case-driven teaching mode [2], it has the three steps of "ask problem-solve the problem-inductive analysis ", in the teaching typical tasks around analyzing and solving problems is selected carefully in order to help student learn how to solve practical problem. Finally students learn knowledge by inductive analysis. It proved to be an effective teaching mode; it is the process from the "knowledge" to "ability ", from "know" to "do". Students are rescued from the boring "menu" type of teaching, instead the lively, practical case learning mode.

3.3 Select the Different Computer Teaching Content According to Different Professional

According to the employment situation of students for many years, the feedback information of graduates and teaching practice, we realize that basic computer teaching should focus on the practical skills of using computer; students can use their acquired computer knowledge to analyze and solve practical problems in their professional field. Computer teaching content should be closely related to their different professional, in the teaching processing teachers should introduce selective those effective, systematic, comprehensive and strong software for students, students will learn new knowledge in order to solve actual problems by using these software.

3.4 Strengthen the Practice of Computer Operating

In the computer teaching, in order to develop practical skills of students, we attach great importance to the experimental course of students. Each speaker teachers are directly involved in the guidance on the computer in order to know situation of student , and help students to solve questions on time in the experimental course. In each course there are clear content and practical tasks, before experiment, student have rehearsal and preparation, and teachers explain in detail purposes, tasks, content, process and requirements of experiments. Do so, it can avoid the blindness of practice on the computer, but also greatly improve the utilization of the computer to ensure quality of teaching. We use the "Limbo" multimedia teaching software to monitor the situation of students on the computer at any time. Teacher will explain in detail the common issues of students. We provide for students rich teaching resources on the network teaching platform and the services of submit online, resources to download, online, discussion etc.

3.5 Various Forms of Evaluation Method

Various forms of teaching methods and evaluation methods should be combined to develop effectively the practical skills of students, for example, for a strong theoretical course, we can have written examination, for certain practical course, we can have a written examination and examination on the computer, for more practical course, we can have an examination on the computer., except for written examination and examination on the computer ,we can examine and evaluate the comprehensive ability of mastering the knowledge through a complete system design. Such as project design, teachers will help students to choose topic according to situation of students. Through such an approach, it will help students to promote their comprehensive ability of computer practice, and it will better reflect the employment-oriented.

3.6 The Cultivation of High-Quality Teachers

It will be the key to build an elite team of computer teachers. Teachers have been training by a variety of ways to improve the professional skills in our institute.

4 Conclusions

Reforms of Computer-based education in college and university is a long-term and arduous task, we will continue to explore and seek the teaching methods and models, it will be more suitable for basic computer courses to train more popular computer applied talent for the community.

References

1. Feng, X.M., Li, K.J., Yan, S., Liu, X., Wang, W.: Paper analysis and its guiding role of teaching. Northwest Medical Education 4, 698–700 (2009)
2. Yu, F., Ding, Y.H.: Basic Computer Course for Reform and Practice. Teaching Resources and Platform 2, 118–119 (2009)
3. Li, F.R., Liu, Y.F., Li, H.Y.: Computer Basic Education Teaching Reform Experiment. Gansu University 2, 115–117 (2009)

The Research of Attitude toward Computers and Books of Chinese College Student

Hongting Li[1], Xiaobo Ma[1], Yangli Wang[1], and Weidan Xu[2]

[1] Department of Psychology, Zhejiang Sci-Tech University, Hangzhou 310018, PR China
lihongting@zstu.edu.cn
[2] College of Business Administration, Zhejiang Gongshang University, Hangzhou 310018, PR China
xuweidan2002@mail.zjgsu.edu.cn

Abstract. In order to find out the students' attitudes difference toward books and computers and compare the difference between the Westerns and Chinese, this study investigated the attitudes toward books and computers of Chinese college students through questionnaire revised from CAM questionnaire scale. The results showed: firstly, similar to Westerns results, the college students in China preferred books than computers, and took books as the first learning tools; Secondly, gender and Major background had no significant effect on the attitudes toward books and computers; Thirdly, the comparison results showed that there were significant culture difference in attitudes toward books and computers between the Westerns and Chinese students.

Keywords: Attitude; Books and Computers; CAM scale.

1 Introduction

With the increasing and ubiquitous use of computer technologies, the importance and use of computers has increased dramatically over the last two decades all over the world (Popovich, et al., 2008). At the same time, it will maybe reduce the need to have physical access to material such as books. For example, more and more people prefer using electronic books to paper books in some environment such as on the subway or in the bed.

Plenty of researches have compared the difference between computer and book. For example a study have ever compared how academics write using hard copy and computers found that the former facilitated greater ease in viewing (as simultaneous cross comparisons among multiple pages could be made), provided better portability, and reduced visual strain(Wood, et al., 2002). Chalmers proposed that the current problem to be solved was making computers easier to use, so there would be more learners to use (Chalmers, 2000). However, hard copy books tended to be thought of as more permanent, they could be accessed without the use of technology, and they were easily transportable (Oborne & Holton, 1988).

The difference between paper and electronic books, such as physical characteristics maybe result in the different attitudes or preference. Based on the four components of

H. Tan and M. Zhou (Eds.): CSE 2011, Part I, CCIS 201, pp. 377–384, 2011.

the attitude which included cognitive, emotional, behavioral, and perceptive control, Noyes have conducted an investigation about the attitudes toward computers and book of young people in UK. The results showed that people have a strong affection for books, prefer them to computers for learning purposes, and expect to learn more from them(Noyes and Garland, 2004). In the follow-up study, their finding that the students preferred to learn from books was replicated. Furthermore, with some open questions, they also investigated the reasons why there was such preference for books amongst the undergraduate population. The results showed that the reasons for these preferences included practical usability issues, media-related usability, experience and aesthetic values (Noyes and Garland, 2006).

Some researchers have investigated the factors that affect attitude toward computers and books. Studies of gender differences in attitudes toward computer technology tend to focus on several areas including men's and women's interests in computers, their perceptions of computers, their level of confidence and self-efficacy when working with computers, stereotypical views about computer users, the effect of experience and access to computers, and whether math anxiety transcends computer anxiety among male and female students (Shashaani, 2001). For example, Shashaani (1994) found that there were significant differences in the computer interest between different genders. Boys were more interested in computer than girls, while girls were more afraid, nervous and uncomfortable to use the computer. Maurer (1994) found that compared with men, women were lack of a positive attitude and experience. The researchers also found that, on the contrary, women obviously like computers than men.

In addition, others have compared attitude differences to using computer in different majoring backgrounds people and the results showed a significant difference. For example, Liu found that the students major in mathematical and scientific education majors have a lower anxious level than the students of major in English, natural and social education when facing computer (Liu, 1992). Liao (1996) found that in normal colleges, students of different major were different in computers confidence and interest, and students major in engineering feel more comfortable than other majors. Chen (1986) also found that the attitude toward computer were significant different between information major students and non-information major students in business school. However, one research which used adults as subjects showed that the attitudes of students of different major were not different. Additionally, Akbulut (2008) assessed the attitudes of Turkish university students with a high level of proficiency in English toward computers and found that learners had positive attitudes toward CALL(Computer Assisted Language Learning) due to computers' potential to sustain independence learning, collaboration, instrumental benefits, empowerment, comfort and communication. The findings also showed that gender and age did not have an effect on CALL attitudes, whereas PC ownership, PC time, and experience with the internet were found to be related to students' attitudes toward CALL.

From this review of the literature, there were still seldom researches aiming to investigate the attitude differences toward computers and books and its influencing factors in Eastern culture. The researches about different gender effect to the attitude toward computer obtained incongruent conclusions as well as major factors. Hence, in this study, we will study Chinese university students' attitude toward computers and books and compare the difference of different gender and major backgrounds.

2 Methods

2.1 Participants

A total of 210 college students participated in the questionnaire survey. The samples were selected according to convenient sampling. Their ages ranged from 17 to 25, with a median of 20. The students were majoring in various fields. Among the 210 participants, 110 students (50 males and 60 females) major in liberal arts (including language science, law, and social science etc.) and 100 students (50 males and 50 females) major in science (including engineering, mathematics, and chemistry). All responses were anonymous.

2.2 Materials

The questionnaire was revised according to the CAM devised by Kay (1989). It contained three sections. The first section included questions on demographics. The second section included affective scales with 10 dimensions (likeable/unlikeable, good/bad, happy/unhappy, comfortable/uncomfortable, calm/tense, full/empty, natural/artificial, exciting/dull, fresh/suffocating and pleasant / unpleasant). The scale was Likert scale with 7 points of agreement between the positive and negative dimensions. The third section included two emotional and preference questions (1. Which do you prefer to use when learning, computer or book? 2. Please briefly describe why do you favor computer or book?).

2.3 Procedure

Participants were asked to complete the questionnaire by making their chosen response on each scale for both computers and books, and then to answer the three preference questions. The response formats were explained and participants were asked to work through the questions in their own time.

3 Results

3.1 Attitudes toward Books and Computers Line Version

The internal consistency reliability analyses as measured by the Cronbach alpha coefficient showed that the alpha value of attitude toward computers Scale was 0.90 and value of the attitude toward books scale was 0.91. The overall reliability coefficient value was 0.89.

The Wilcoxon Signed Ranked test was used to determine whether significant differences existed between the ratings for books and computers on each dimension. The results in Table 1 showed there were significant differences only on five dimensions including the good/bad ($p<0.05$) comfortable/ uncomfortable ($p<0.05$), calm/tense ($p<0.05$), full/ empty ($p<0.05$), natural / unnatural ($p<0.05$).

Table 1. 10 dimensions result of affective scales

	Dimensions	Computers		Books		Z
		M	SD	M	SD	
1	Likeable/Unlikeable	5.52	1.23	5.38	1.35	1.31
2	Good/Bad	4.42	1.14	5.17	1.33	-2.69
3	Happy/Unhappy	5.38	1.19	5.20	1.21	1.63
4	Comfortable/Uncomfortable	5.06	1.27	5.45	1.22	-3.33
5	Clam/Tense	4.77	1.41	5.59	1.26	-6.53
6	Full/Empty	4.34	1.50	5.63	1.28	-9.31
7	Natural/Unnatural	4.76	1.37	5.68	1.20	-8.01
8	Exciting/ Dull	4.85	1.39	4.73	1.34	0.87
9	Fresh/ Suffocating	4.76	1.34	4.67	1.34	0.70
10	Pleasant/Unpleasant	5.00	1.19	5.05	1.25	-0.42

3.2 Gender Comparison

The Wilcoxon Signed Ranked test was used to compare the attitudes toward computers and books on different gender. To computer, the results showed that there were significant difference on only three dimensions of happy/unhappy ($p<0.05$), comfortable/uncomfortable ($p<0.05$), pleasant/unpleasant ($p <0.05$).

To book, the results showed no significant gender difference on all the dimensions except happy/unhappy ($p>0.05$).

Totally, it showed that the attitudes toward books of male and female students were more agree with. However, to the attitudes toward computers, male students were more positive compared to female students.

Table 2. 10 dimensions result of different gender of affective scales

	Dimensions	Male		Female	
		Computer	Book	Computer	Book
1	Likeable/Unlikeable	5.66(1.27)	5.23(1.38)	5.39(1.18)	5.50(1.31)
2	Good/Bad	5.56(1.12)	5.77(1.01)	5.47(1.06)	5.74(1.11)
3	Happy/Unhappy	5.57(1.23)	5.03(1.23)	5.19(1.14)	5.35(1.18)
4	Comfortable/Uncomfortable	5.29(1.11)	5.30(1.18)	4.84(1.36)	5.58(1.25)
5	Clam/Tense	4.88(1.46)	5.59(1.23)	4.66(1.36)	5.58(1.29)
6	Full/Empty	4.44(1.55)	5.60(1.26)	4.25(1.47)	5.66(1.29)
7	Natural/Unnatural	4.80(1.47)	5.56(1.19)	4.73(1.27)	5.78(1.21)
8	Exciting/ Dull	4.95(1.46)	4.62(1.28)	4.76(1.32)	4.84(1.39)
9	Fresh/ Suffocating	4.71(1.37)	4.55(1.35)	4.80(1.32)	4.78(1.33)
10	Pleasant/Unpleasant	5.22(1.12)	5.00(1.19)	4.80(1.22)	5.09(1.30)

3.3 Majoring Comparison

Both to computers and to books, the Wilcoxon Signed Ranked test yielded no significant majoring differences on ten dimensions (p>0.05). Both Liberal Arts and Science students had the same attitudes toward computers and books.

Table 3. 10 dimensions result of different majoring of affective scales

	Dimensions	Liberal Arts		Science	
		Computer	Book	Computer	Book
1	Likeable/Unlikeable	5.61(1.21)	5.40(1.44)	5.42(1.25)	5.34(1.25)
2	Good/Bad	5.45(1.07)	5.77(1.08)	5.59(1.10)	5.73(1.04)
3	Happy/Unhappy	5.41(1.18)	5.32(1.30)	5.33(1.21)	5.06(1.10)
4	Comfortable/Uncomfortable	5.03(1.25)	5.50(1.25)	5.08(1.29)	5.39(1.20)
5	Clam/Tense	4.74(1.39)	5.76(1.18)	4.80(1.44)	5.40(1.32)
6	Full/Empty	4.35(1.49)	5.77(1.26)	4.33(1.53)	5.48(1.28)
7	Natural/Unnatural	4.86(1.39)	5.73(1.26)	4.66(1.34)	5.62(1.14)
8	Exciting/ Dull	4.95(1.31)	4.74(1.39)	4.74(1.47)	4.73(1.28)
9	Fresh/ Suffocating	4.89(1.32)	4.70(1.42)	4.61(1.36)	4.64(1.26)
10	Pleasant/Unpleasant	5.05(1.12)	5.11(1.31)	4.95(1.26)	4.98(1.18)

3.4 Majoring Comparison

To the question "Which do you prefer to use when learning, computer or book?", as shown in Figure1, overall 12.4% of respondents stated a preference to learn by the computers to 43.3% for books. In addition, 37.6% responded that they would prefer to use both and only 1% would prefer to use neither books nor computers. 5.7% of the respondents expressed no opinion. Chi-squared analyses indicated that there was a significant difference between the responses, χ^2=155.381, p<0.05. The further

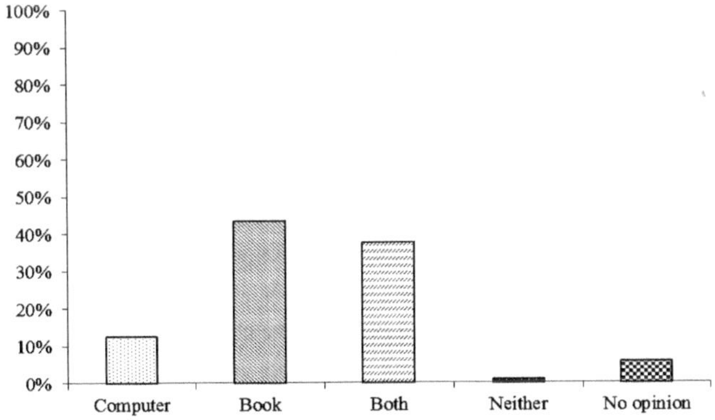

Fig. 1. "Which do you prefer to use when learning, computer or book?"

Chi-squared analyses compared the response of students of different gender and majoring. The results indicated that there was no significant difference on gender (χ^2=1.371, p>0.05) or on majoring (χ^2=3.592, p>0.05).

4 Discussions

Totally this study wanted to answer four questions: Whether there was any difference between college students' attitudes toward computers and books? Whether was the major background a factor that maybe influences the attitude toward computers and books? Whether was the gender a factor that maybe influences the attitude toward computers and books? Whether there was any difference in different culture? The results showed that attitude of college students toward computers and books existed differences and attitudes toward books were more active than computer. As a whole, there were no significant differences between different gender and majoring students in attitudes toward computers and books.

Noyes and Garland (2004) results showed that college students held a more positive attitude toward books. People preferred to learn through books and also expected learn more from books. In addition, on the dimensions of calm/tense and natural/unnatural, students are particularly negative on computers. The researchers believed that the computer's interactive and dynamic may be used to interpret in the dimension of calm/tense and the reason why people used books more naturally mainly was because people were more familiar with books.

In this study, among the total 10 dimensions, on five dimensions (Likeable/Unlikeable, Good/Bad, Happy/Unhappy, Exciting/Dull, Fresh/ Suffocating) it was found a significant difference in the attitude toward books and computers and the average score of the computers were higher than the books although the difference was not significant. Via interviewed, the reason why students gave a more positive score to computer mainly was because of the aesthetic and appearance of the computer.

But on other five dimensions: Comfortable/Uncomfortable, Calm/Tense, Full/Empty, Natural/Unnatural, Pleasant/Unpleasant, the average scores of the books were significant higher than the score of computers. It showed that when people used the book, they felt more calm, natural and fulfillment, which coming from their habits and their familiarity of books.

The findings of the comparison of the gender in the present study showed some similarities as well as differences in several aspects of computer attitudes, as compared with the findings of recent studies conducted in the Western culture. Shashaani (1997) found that female students in the United States were less interested in computing than were male students and Zhao (2007) study of the attitudes toward the computers showed that men's attitude toward the computer are better than women's. In this study, the attitudes toward books of male and female students were more coincident. To the attitudes toward computers, male students were more positive compared to female students on three dimensions. However, from the answer of the question "Which do you prefer to use when learning, computer or book?" it showed that there was no significant difference between different genders. That was to say the desire for computer learning was not gender-specific. Maybe the reason was for the growing number of women entering science subjects and computer has been a more general tool for all the undergraduate students.

Comparison of the attitudes toward computers and books of the different majoring backgrounds proved that there was no significant difference. The reason maybe also was owing to the extensive application of computer technology, which has gone deep into every profession.

In this study, every respondent were asked to answer an open question "Please briefly describe why do you favor computer or book". After summed all the answers, the reasons for preference of computers and books were summarized as below:

Computers Preferred:

1) Computer is more convenient, quickly and efficient.
2) Computer information is more comprehensive, intuitive and easy to find.
3) Computer is more freedom, fun and attractive.
4) Book is boring, and to find information is not convenient.

Book Preferred:

1) Book is easy to carry, record, direct and easy to watch.
2) Reading book is calm, and the reader can be more relax, focused and ease of in-depth thinking.
3) The knowledge of books is systematic and be trusted.
4) Computer has radiation and visual stress that do harm to the health.

5 Conclusion

Firstly, similar to Westerns results, the college students in China preferred books than computers, and took books as the first learning tools; Secondly, gender and Major background had no significant effect on the attitudes toward books and computers; Thirdly, the comparison results showed that there were significant culture difference in attitudes toward books and computers between the Westerns and Chinese students.

Acknowledgments. This research was supported by 2010 Zhejiang QianJiang Talent Foundation 1013371-M and humanities and social sciences Youth Foundation of National ministry of education 10YJCZH036.

References

1. Popovich, P.M., Gullekson, N., Morris, S., Morse, B.: Comparing attitudes towards computer usage by undergraduates from 1986 to 2005. Computers in Human Behavior 24(3), 986–992 (2008)
2. Wood, E., Willoughby, T., Sprecht, J., Porter, L.: An examination of how a cross-section of academics uses computer technology when writing academic papers. Computers and Education 38(1), 287–301 (2002)
3. Chalmers, P.: User interface improvements in computer-assisted instruction the challenge. Computers in Human Behavior 16(5), 507–517 (2000)
4. Oborne, D.J., Holton, D.: Reading from screen versus paper: There is no difference. International Journal of Man-Machine Studies 28(1), 1–9 (1998)

5. Noyes, J.M., Garland, K.J.: Students' attitudes toward books and computers. Computers in Human Behavior 21(1), 233–241 (2004)
6. Noyes, J.M., Garland, K.J.: Explaining students' attitudes toward books and computers. Computers in Human Behavior 22(2), 351–363 (2006)
7. Shashaani, L.: Gender difference in computer experience and its influence on computer attitudes. Journal of Educational Computing Research 11(4), 347–367 (1994)
8. Shashaani, L.: Gender differences in computer attitudes and use among college students. Journal of Educational Computing Research 16(1), 37–51 (1997)
9. Shashaani, L., Khalili, A.: Gender and computers: similarities and differences in Iranian college students' attitudes toward computers. Computers & Education 37(3-4), 41–51 (2001)
10. Maurer, M.M.: Computer anxiety correlates and what they tell us: A literature review. Computers in Human Behavior 10(3), 369–376 (1994)
11. Akbulut, Y.: Exploration of the attitudes of freshman foreign language students toward using computers at a Turkish state university. The Turkish Online Journal of Educational Technology 7(1), 18–31 (2008)
12. Liao, Y.C.: Teachers' attitudes toward educational computing in Tai wan. Technology and Teacher Education Annual 5, 75–79 (1996)
13. Liu, M., Reed, M.W., Philips, P.: Teacher education students and computers: Gender, major, prior computer experience, occurrence, and anxiety. Journal of Research on Computing in Education 24, 457–467 (1992)
14. Chen, M.: Gender and computers: The beneficial effects of experience on attitudes. Journal of Educational Computing Research 2, 265–282 (1986)
15. Zhao, F.M.: The correlation research of Master's attitude toward computer Master's thesis of Capital Normal University, Beijing, China (2007)

The Calculation Method of Road Travel Time Based on License Plate Recognition Technology

Guixiang Liu[1], Zhongyou Ma[2], Zhongguo Du[1], and Can Wen[1]

[1] School of Computer Engineering, Qingdao Technological University, 266033, Qingdao, China
[2] Hisense Trans-Tech Co., LTD, 266071, Qingdao, China
lgx_9133@163.com

Abstract. Travel time is a very important indicator which reflects the situation of road traffic. This article designed a method for computing the road travel time by the driving path which was obtained based on license plate recognition technology. With analysis of the on-site verification results, this paper showed that the algorithm can satisfy the accuracy and timeliness in the complex road conditions.

Keywords: Travel time, License plate recognition, Data correction, Event-driven.

1 Introduction

Travel time of vehicles is the time when the vehicle travels between two points in the road sections, including all delays and road time-consuming [1]. Road travel time is the average time of all vehicles on the road during a time. However, it is impossible to measure the travel time of all vehicles in the real environment. As the sample have the same expectations with the overall. Then, the average travel time of the effective sample vehicles is usually used as the road travel time [2]. When the proportion of the samples is high, the conformity degree of the calculation results and true circumstance is also high.

Road travel time is a very intuitive and effective indicator to reflect the road traffic situation. It can be seen as basis for the state of road congestion and travel time prediction. However, by the existing method which collects the traffic flow, it is difficult to get the travel time indicators accurately. Presently, there are mainly two methods for computing the travel time. One is through the coil, microwave, video and other fixed monitoring equipments to collect the vehicle's instantaneous speed passing test point and reckon road travel time. This method is greatly influenced by road conditions, so the accuracy is very difficult to guarantee. The other way is based on floating cars, electronic tags and other mobile detection technologies. By the vehicle's driving path, we can compute the road travel time. Because it is needed to pre-install collecting devices on the sample vehicles, so it is difficult to ensure the effective number of samples [3].

H. Tan and M. Zhou (Eds.): CSE 2011, Part I, CCIS 201, pp. 385–389, 2011.

In this paper, we presented a road travel time calculation method based on license plate recognition technology. It collected vehicle traffic information and calculated travel time in regional sections by monitoring equipments such as bayonet socket, electronic police and so on.

2 Calculation of Travel Time

At present, the road monitoring equipments such as card port, multi-functional electronic police and so on are basically laid on the main road in domestic large and medium-sized cities. Many of these devices have the function of license plate recognition which is usually used for single security or illegal capture. As the license plate recognition technology based on the images or videos is very mature, the recognition rate can reach 90%. Therefore, the article aims to use these monitoring equipments to collect the traffic flow information. By the collected data such as the vehicle license plate, travel time and place, we can compute the road travel time.

By searching the traffic data which are collected by equipments, we can get a vehicle's traveling path in a particular time. By computing the passing time from the starting point to the end point in the traveling path, we can get the vehicle travel time T. The average travel time in a time period is:

$$T = \frac{\sum_{k=1}^{n} T_k}{n}$$

Specially, T_k is an effective sample, which indicates vehicles that drive straight along the road and whose licenses can be effectively recognized. Sample covers far more than the usual sampling plan of floating car or electronic tag. Therefore, the calculated travel time is more in line with road sections in actual situation.

The algorithm which computes the average travel time in road sections is not complicated, but the algorithm's performance, exception handling and smoothing processing are very difficult.

2.1 Performance Handling

The algorithm aims to address the travel time calculation of the city-level road network. It needs to deal with millions level vehicle data per day and calculate for the thousands of road sections. Therefore, the algorithm needs to address the computing performance and stability problems for the massive data. So the system is designed with event-driven mechanism to process in real-time. When the external collecting devices capture the event that a car passed away, it will send the message to the hub and the process and the progress of computing the travel time is triggered. The travel time is computed in real-time. Compared with the method which checks the data of all cars in a regular time and computes the results on the uniform, the algorithm proposed in this article avoids time delay effectively caused by a large number of queries and computation in a computing period.

To solve the path retrieval speed for cars and storage problems, a thread-safe memory storage scheme is adopted. Take vehicle plate license as index and save vehicular traffic information in memory. When vehicle information is collected, the vehicle travel path can also be obtained quickly by vehicle license.

2.2 Exception Handling

The data collected from the front-end may include license recognition errors, decks, temporary parking and other abnormal data. These factors will cause errors in travel time calculation. Additionally, transmission fault can cause data loss, so the algorithm needs exception handling to get rid of the interference. Exception handling includes the screening of abnormal data, correction and compensation for missing data. Abnormal data can be determined by the threshold method. For example, it requires elimination and correction if the data exceeds the threshold range. Correction and compensation are used to choose the time-related historical data and replace. Relevant historical data is extracted in accordance with the weekend, working days, holidays, rush hour and other rules. It is also weighted according to the correlation relationship.

2.3 Smoothing Processing

Smoothing process aims to avoid too much calculation volatility and tries to eliminate the interference of emergent events for the results. Since the traffic status have continuity characteristics and the two adjacent travel time periods are relevant, so the algorithm utilizes the exponential smoothing for the processing of the calculation result. It selects interval data associated with time to revise the calculation result which aims to reduce the data fluctuation and ensure a relatively stable state for the result.

3 Experiments

In order to verify the actual effect of the algorithm, we do field testing in the city of WeiFang. It adopts a contrastive validating solution which utilizes manual sampling data and calculation data. We selected several road sections with obvious representation which covers the trunk road, business street, schools, etc. These road sections are fixed capture devices with the function of license plate recognition. Sampling person adopted timing sampling, vehicle sampling and video sampling through artificial crossing. The time of sampling is in the morning and evening peak period, holidays, night, etc. After all kinds of sample data were gathered, it was compared and analyzed with the calculated travel time.

Through data analysis for 34 road sections from November 8th to November 29th, the fitting degree of the average artificial sample data and the data from system computation is 86.34%. After correction and smoothing, the fitting degree is 91.31%. The calculation and publish of the data are in one second.

From the results, it can be seen that the results obtained from this travel time algorithm is basically consistent with the actual road conditions. The calculation accuracy and performance indicators are able to meet the practical application. At present, the algorithm this article designed is applied in an intelligent transportation design scheme in a city. The accuracy of the induced information in area was obviously improved. It played an important role in active shunt, alleviated congestion and road utilization ratio. The application effect was very obvious.

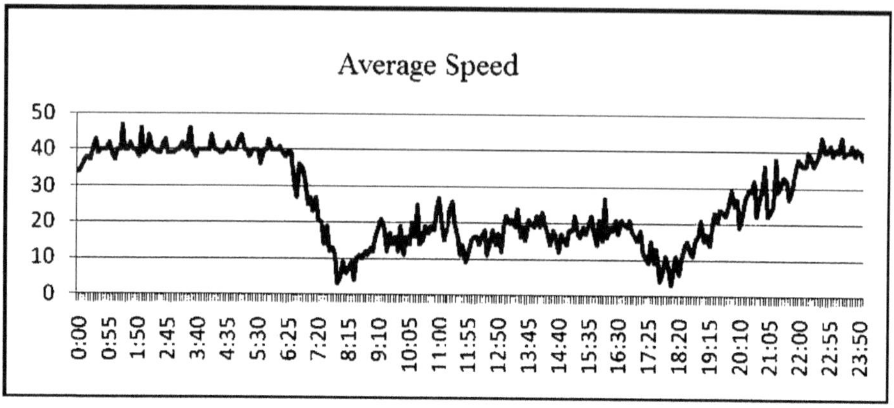

Fig. 1. Average speed in road sections by calculation

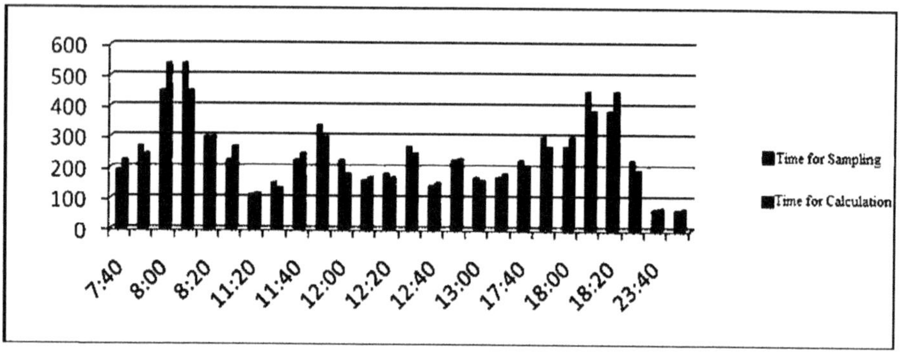

Fig. 2. Comparison of sample data and calculation results

4 Conclusion

The calculation method of travel time proposed in this article can make full use of the existing road surveillance equipments and the technical achievements of license plate recognition technology. Acquisition equipment investment is reduced. Compared with the traditional method of speed estimation of monitoring points, it is more consistent with the actual road conditions. Besides, with the event-driven method and calculation in real time, it can meet the requirements of the timeliness for complex road conditions in large city. It has important practical significance in changing traffic congestion in cities.

References

1. Peng, S.: Research of Traffic Application Based on Travel Time Detection System. JCA (November 2007)
2. Aihua, Z.: Research of Road Travel Time Prediction Based on Floating Car Data. Beijing Jiaotong University, Beijing (2007)
3. Li, J.: Research of Key Technologies for State Recognition of Urban Traffic Congestion. Southwest Jiaotong University, Chengdu (2009)

Modeling and Analysis for Reconfigurable Cell Based on Stochastic Petri Net*

Chunling Ding[1], Guosun Zeng[2], and Fuhuan Wang[2]

[1] Department of Chemistry, Tongji University, Shanghai 200092, China
[2] Department of Computer Science and Technology, Tongji University, Shanghai 200092, China
{dingcl,gszeng}@tongji.edu.cn

Abstract. Reconfigurable architecture is an important trend of current high-performance parallel computing. Reconfigurable cell is the critical part of a prototype system of the new-concept, high-efficiency and new-type computer. Currently, such prototype system is at the stage of feasibility analysis and experimental research. This paper proposes a method to model the reconfigurable cell based on stochastic Petri net. For its structural properties, such as accessibility, boundedness and safety, we present the logical correctness verification. As to its performance properties, such as stable state probability, transition rate and throughput, we present the quantification analysis. Especially, this paper discusses the effects between dynamic reconfiguration time and task response time under three different conditions. The work of this paper may offer some reference value for the research and analysis of the coming new-type computer architecture.

Keywords: reconfigurable computing, reconfigurable cell, stochastic Petri net, structure analysis, performance evaluation.

1 Introduction

ASIC and general-purpose processors are two methods to implement traditional computation. ASIC uses special integrated circuit to complete the task. This method can achieve high speed and efficiency, but it is hardly flexible and adaptable, or not programmable. When the task has been changed we must change relevant circuits. Contrary to ASIC, general-purpose processors do not need to be changed when system functions are changed. It is flexible, or programmable, but its performance is worse. Reconfigurable technology based on FPGA has excellent performance like ASIC, and has flexibility like general-purpose processors. Its logic function modules or communication links among modules can be kept to programming, meaning that the hardware circuits may be changed at any time with the change of application

* Supported by the 863 program under grant of 2009AA012201, the joint of NSFC and Microsoft Asia Research under grant of 60970155, the Ph.D. Programs Foundation of Ministry of Education under grant of 20090072110035, the State Key Laboratory of High-end Server & Storage Technology under grant of 2009HSSA06.

H. Tan and M. Zhou (Eds.): CSE 2011, Part I, CCIS 201, pp. 390–400, 2011.

requirements[1]. As a result, FPGA is becoming hot research in the area of high-performance computing architecture [2,3,4,5].

Our national 863 Program, the development of new-concept, high-efficiency computer architecture and system (No.2009AA012201), was approved in 2009. Complying with the trends of high-efficiency computer, this program is devoted to further study on new concept, new theory and new technology of high-efficiency computer architecture. The concrete tasks are analyzing requirements for various application areas, studying the high-efficiency computer architecture, especially various hybrids/heterogeneous architecture. Then we should propose a new-concept reconfigurable architecture, HRCA (hybrid reconfigurable computing array), which is based on various accelerated processors and very fit for different applications. At the same time, we also need computing model, programming method, compile optimization technology and resources management to support HRCA.

The rest of this paper is organized as follows. Section 2 introduces the background and relative technology. Section 3 models the reconfigurable cell based on stochastic Petri net. In section 4, we present the detailed analysis of structure correctness for reconfigurable cell. In section 5, we present the performance evaluation for reconfigurable cell. Finally, we conclude the paper in section 6.

2 Reconfigurable Cell of New-Concept, High-Efficiency Computer Architecture

2.1 HRCA

With the development of hardware manufacturing and computation processing, application requirements become more diverse, complicated and unpredictable. Traditional computer architecture based on Von Neumann faces many impenetrable barriers. For example, "Computing wall", "Memory wall" and "I/O wall" lead to actual running performance is only 5%-10% of perk performance. Therefore, we put forward the idea of hybrid reconfigurable computing array, as shown in figure 1, in order to achieve strong adaptability and high performance for computer system.

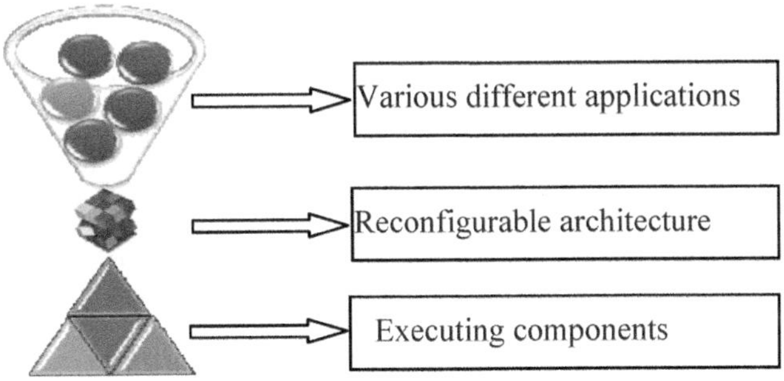

Fig. 1. The principle of HRCA

HRCA consists of many single reconfigurable cells, reconfigurable interconnection and I/O units. The most important component of HRCA is the reconfigurable cell, which supports different computational requirements by reconfiguring hardware. Reconfigurable interconnection builds asynchronous communication network, realizing the data exchange between cells and I/Os. Reconfigurable I/O units are responsible for communication with external devices. The basic idea of HRCA is to dynamically reconfigure these single cells, interconnection, and I/O in term of application requirement. Specifically, at first, according to various application programs, some basic algorithms, such as sort, vector multiplication, FFT, and so on, are picked out and directly mapped to relevant computer architecture. Basic algorithm is executed as a whole so that it can eliminate the overhead of fetching and decoding instruction on traditional processors. In a word, these basic algorithms are processed by high scalable reconfigurable cells. Thus HRCA can achieve high efficiency and high hardware utilization for a wide range of applications.

2.2 Reconfigurable Cell

Because HRCA is now in the stage of feasibility study, we expect to develop a small-scale prototype system, named reconfigurable cell, to check the correctness and feasibility of design method for the whole project. We have designed the prototype system depicted in figure 2.

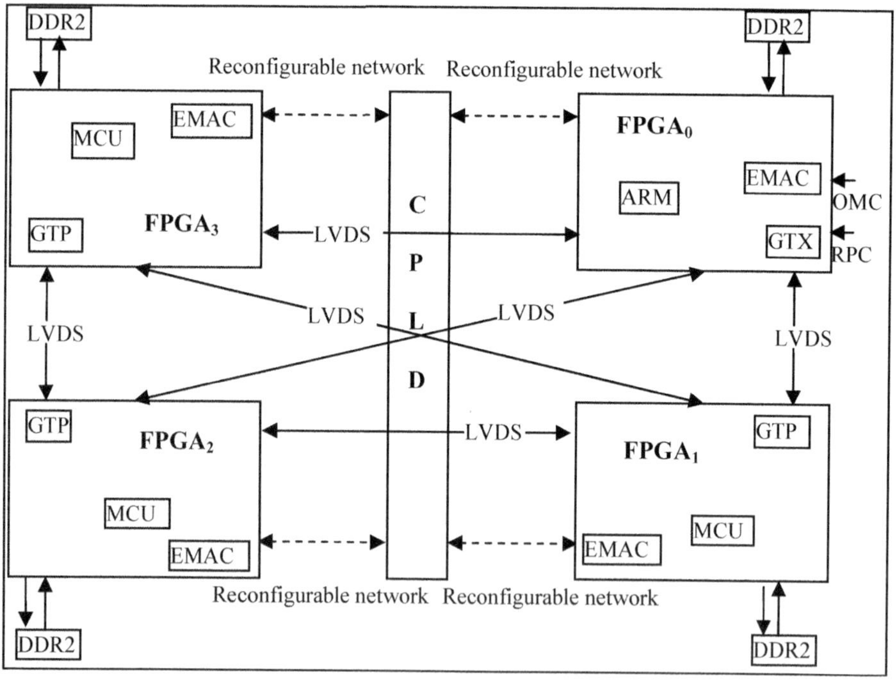

Fig. 2. The architecture of reconfigurable cell

The components in figure 2 are explained as follows: (1) DDR2 (Double Data Rate 2) is used as memory. It can access data at the 4 times speed of internal control bus. (2) CPLD (Complex Programmable Logic Device) can receive and transmit reconfigurable instructions to processing nodes with the changing requirements. (3) LVDS (Low-Voltage Differential signaling) are used for data transmission and memory sharing among FPGAs with low noise and low power consumption. (4) RPC network is used for users to transmit data without knowing bottom network protocol. (5) OMC network transmits logic function information to reconfigurable cell. (6) EMAC (E-Motion Multi Axis Controller) is the interface of transmitting reconfigurable information. (7)MCU (Micro Control Unit) is embodied in each FPGA, and do initialization and control for FPGA. (8) ARM (Advanced RISC Machines) is processing unit in each FPGA. (9)GTX/GTP is data transmission platform for distributed applications to interconnect among FPGAs.

The main functions of reconfigurable cell are processor reconfiguration and task computation. When the computational task has arrived, the reconfigurable cell begins to work. Static reconfigurable information is transmitted to $FPGA_0$ from OMC network. Then reconfigurable information is forwarded to CPLD through the interface EMAC of $FPGA_0$, further transmitted to other collaborative FPGAs. Each FPGA carries out static reconfiguration by own control unit. However, the application requirements may be changed in the course of task computation, reconfigurable cell need be reconfigured. In this situation, OMC network transmit the dynamic reconfigurable information to $FPGA_0$, other FPGAs also get this information like static reconfiguration process. Similarly, FPGAs carry out dynamic reconfiguration. After two reconfigurations, data from PRC network can be processed. Meanwhile $FPGA_0$ get the data and assigns some data to other FPGAs by LVDS channels. Each FPGA executes its computation and return relevant result. Finally RPC collects all results and return them to the superior unit or system.

3 Model of Stochastic Petri Net for Reconfigurable Cell

3.1 The Concept of Stochastic Petri Net

Definition 1. A Petri net (PN) is a 5-tuple PN=(S, T; F, W, M_0), where S is a finite set of places, T is a finite set of transitions, F is a mapping function between places and transitions, W is a weight function, M_0 is an initial mark[7,8,9].

Definition 2. A stochastic Petri net (SPN) is a 6-tuple SPN=(S, T; F, W, M_0, λ) comprised of S, T, W, F, M_0 defined like PN. Besides, $\lambda = \{\lambda_1, \lambda_2 \ldots \lambda_m\}$ is a finite set of average firing rate. λ_i represents mean firing rate of transition per time unit, and $1/\lambda_i$ represents mean service time.

SPN is homogenous with Markov chain. We can construct Markov chain by reachable graph of SPN and get the stable probability of each state. Then correctness verification and performance evaluation can be carried on.

3.2 The Proposed Model

Generally speaking, processors or interfaces can be considered as places in Petri net, operations among processors and interfaces can be considered as flows in Petri net, an executed task on processor can be regarded as a transition, and data can be regarded as token. So it is possible to descript and analyze the architecture of reconfigurable cell based on Petri net. For simplicity, we give some assumptions as follows:

(1) In figure 2, four FPGAs have same functions and operations.
(2) $FPGA_1$, $FPGA_2$, $FPGA_3$ all provides memory for $FPGA_0$, and their access speeds are identical.
(3) The speed of initializing and processing of four FPGAs are same.
(4) In order to describe FPGA change hard circuits and logic functions before and during computational task executed, we suppose there are only two reconfigurations in the course of task executed, one is static reconfiguration, the other is dynamic reconfiguration.
(5) Each time, a task which is executed is represented as a token.

After the above assumptions, we can build the mapping relationship between reconfigurable cell and SPN as shown in table1 and table 2.

Table 1. Mapping between resources and places

Resource	Place	Initial Token
Starter	s_1	1
OMC Network	s_2	0
EMAC of $FPGA_0$	s_3, s_5	0
ARM of $FPGA_0$	s_4	0
CPLD	s_6	0
EMAC of $FPGA_i$	s_i, $1 \le i \le 3$	0
MCU of $FPGA_i$	s_{i+9}, $1 \le i \le 3$	0
RPC Network	s_{13}, s_{29}	0
GTX of $FPGA_0$	s_{15}, s_{16}, s_{21}, s_{28}	0
GTP of $FPGA_i$	s_{i+16}, s_{i+21}, s_{i+24}, $1 \le i \le 3$	0
Controller	s_{14}, s_{20}	0

Table 2. Mapping between operations and transitions

Operation	Transition	Rate	Firing Rate
Start	t_1	λ_1	α_1
Transmit information	t_2, t_4, t_5	λ_2	α_2,α_4, α_5
Start ARM	t_3	λ_3	α_3
Start MCU	t_7	λ_4	α_7
Reconfigure $FPGA_i$	t_6	λ_5	α_6
Transmit information	t_{10}	λ_6	α_{10}
Input data	t_8	λ_7	α_8
Transmit data by LVDS	t_9, t_{16}	λ_8	α_9, α_{16}
control diversion	t_{11}	λ_9	α_{11}
$FPGA_i$ process data	t_{i+12}, $1 \le i \le 3$	λ_{10}	α_{i+12}
sum results and transmit	t_{17}	λ_{11}	α_{17}

Moreover, it is the most important to model the static reconfiguration and dynamic reconfiguration. Before a computational task is executed, static reconfiguration in a FPGA is necessary. Under trigger of transition t_1, static reconfigurable information is first transmitted to $FPGA_0$ from OMC network s_2. $FPGA_0$ continue to forward reconfigurable information to other FPGAs s_{10}, s_{11}, s_{12}. Then each FPGA carry out static reconfiguration operation at transition t_6. Once static reconfiguration finished, reconfigurable cell begin to process data at transition t_8. $FPGA_0$ collect data and assign data by LVDS to other three FPGAs s_{17}, s_{18}, s_{19} at transition t_9. When data assignments and computational operations done, we suppose application requirement is changed at this moment, which means that FPGAs must update their logic functions. So FPGAs should carry out dynamic reconfiguration to adapt the changing requirement at transition t_{10}. The process of dynamic reconfiguration is similar to the static one. After dynamic reconfiguration, FPGAs renew their functions and begin a new round of data assignments and computational operations at transition t_{12}, t_{13}, t_{14}, t_{15}. The final results are gathered to RPC network s_{29}. The whole model for reconfigurable cell based on SPN is depicted in figure 3.

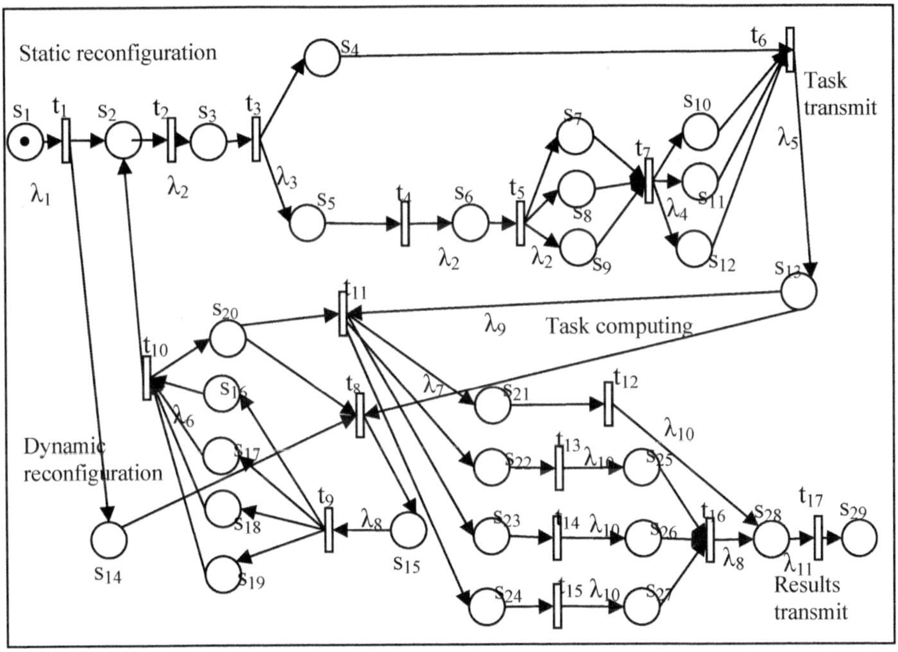

Fig. 3. Model for reconfigurable cell base on SPN

4 The Analysis of Structure Correctness

Logical structure correctness is the basic requirement for reconfigurable cell. For this purpose, we employ the following analysis method based on SPN. The relationship among states of reconfigurable cell corresponds to reachability graph of SPN.

The boundness of parameters, such as processors, interfaces in reconfigurable cell is verified by the boundness theory of SPN. Similarly, safety and liveness of reconfigurable cell correspond to deadlock, liveness and trap of SPN.

During computational tasks are executed, the number of tokens possessed by processors and interfaces describe the running states of reconfigurable cell. For example, at the stage of initialization only the Starter s_1 has one token, so the initial state can be denoted as M_0 (s_1 (1)). Because the number of tokens is changed with different transition t_i is fired, then the running states M_i is changed with it. Under trigger of transitions, all running states of reconfigurable cell form a reachability graph as shown in figure 4.

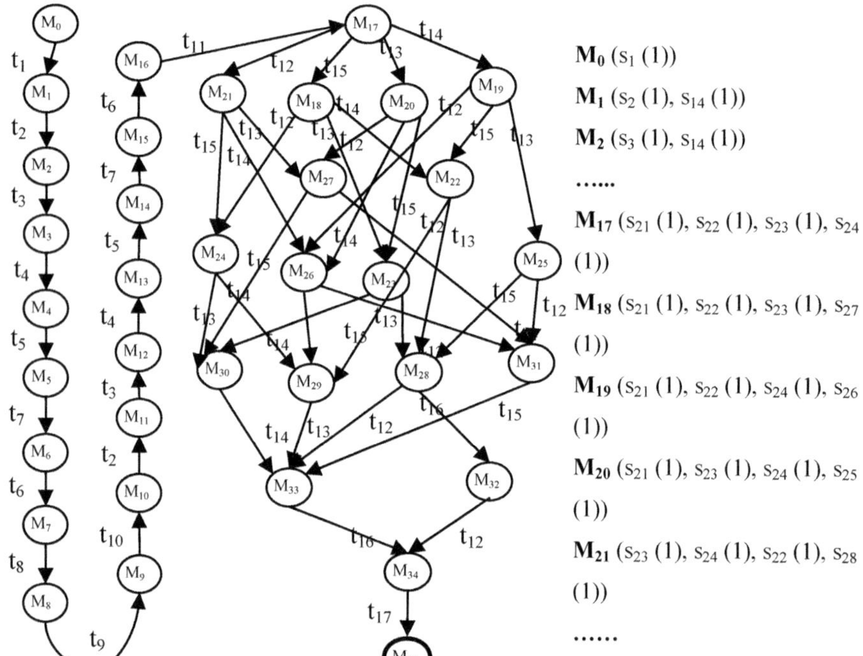

Fig. 4. Reachability graph of reconfigurable cell

In figure4, M_0 denotes initial state, M_{35} denotes terminal state. M_i (s_j (m)) represents that place s_j has m tokens. M_0 can get to M_7 by transition sequence of t_1 t_2 t_3 t_4 t_5 t_7 t_6, which represents the process of static reconfiguration. M_7 can get to M_9 by transition sequence of t_8 t_9, which represents the process of data transmission and task assignment. M_9 can get to M_{17} by transition sequence of t_{10} t_2 t_3 t_4 t_5 t_7 t_6, which represents the process of dynamic reconfiguration. M_{17} to M_{35} represent computational tasks are being executed. By means of reachability graph, we can get the following conclusions.

Proposition 1. Reconfigurable cell is reachable, namely, it can get to terminal state from initial state by a series of operations.

Proof: Omitted due to space limitation.

Proposition 2. Suppose processors and interfaces in reconfigurable cell have limited capabilities, they will not overflow during computational tasks are executed.

Proposition 3. if a system can not occur this situation that other transitions will not fired after one transition is just fired, the system is called deadlock-free and the system is safe. Thus reconfigurable cell is safe.

Similarly, reconfigurable cell also holds other structural properties, such as liveness, fairness, repeatability, conservation.

5 Performance Evaluation

Time characteristic is another important aspect of reconfigurable cell. To evaluate performance, we construct Markov chain by reachability graph of reconfigurable cell, and then we can calculate the stable probability, firing rate, throughput and the task response time.

5.1 Stable State Probability in Three Cases

Stable state probability is the key to performance evaluation. In reconfigurable cell, FPGAs realize high speed interconnection by GTX/GTP, and the bandwidth is about 100Mbps~6.5Gbps. FPGAs realize data transmission by LVDS where the transmission rate is 1Gbps on single channel, and 1.25Gbps on multi-channel. Each FPGA processes data at speed of 1Gbps. Thus in figure 3, λ_1, λ_2, λ_3, λ_4, λ_5, λ_6, λ_7, λ_{11}denote the transition rate of t_1, t_2, t_3, t_4, t_5, t_6, t_7, t_8, t_{10}, respectively, they are in the range of 0.1~6.5Gbps. λ_8 denotes the transition rate of t_9, t_{16}, it is in the range of 1~1.25Gbps. λ_{11} denotes the transition rate of t_{12}, t_{13}, t_{14}, t_{15}, it is 1Gbps. We will evaluate performance under the following assumptions.

Case 1: suppose the transition rates are very slow, λ_1, λ_2, λ_3, λ_4, λ_5, λ_6, λ_7, λ_{11} is 0.1, λ_8 is 1, λ_{10} is 1.

Case 2: suppose the transition rates is medium, λ_1, λ_2, λ_3, λ_4, λ_5, λ_6, λ_7, λ_{11} is 2, λ_8 is 1, λ_{10} is 1.

Case 3: suppose the transitions rate is very high, λ_1, λ_2, λ_3, λ_4, λ_5, λ_6, λ_7, λ_{11} is 6.5, λ_8 is 1.25, λ_{10} is 1.

To construct Markov chain, the transitions in figure 4 are replaced by relevant firing rate. Let x_i be the stable state probability at M_i, $1\le i \le 21$. According to the equilibrium equations of Markov chain: $(\sum\lambda_j)x_i=\sum(\lambda_k x_k)$, thus we can get each x_i as follows.

In the case 1, the stable state probability x_i=0.0594, $0\le i \le 7$ and $9\le i \le 16$, x_8=0.00594, x_i=0.0004, $18\le i \le 27$, x_{28}=0.0007, x_{17}= x_{29}= x_{30}= x_{31}=0.0015, x_{32}=0.0007, x_{33}=0.0022, x_{34}=0.0297.

In the case 2, the stable state probability x_i=0.04, $0\le i \le 7$ and $8\le i \le 16$, x_8=0.08, x_i=0.0067, $18\le i \le 27$, x_{28}=0.01, x_{17}= x_{29}= x_{30}= x_{31}=0.02, x_{32}=0.01, x_{33}=0.0468, x_{34}=0.04.

In the case 3, the stable state probability x_i=0.026, 0≤ i ≤7 and 9≤ i ≤16, x_8=0.1356, x_i=0.0141, 18≤ i ≤27, x_{28}=0.0057, x_{17}= x_{29}= x_{30}= x_{31}=0.0424, x_{32}=0.007, x_{33}=0.1063, x_{34}=0.0175.

5.2 Firing Probability and Throughput

Firing probability and throughput are another performance metrics. Firing probability α_i of transition t_i reflects the frequency of operations in reconfigurable cell. The throughput of reconfigurable cell reflects the number of finished task per time unit [9]. While the throughput of each transition t_i, TH(t_i), equals $\alpha_i \times \lambda_i$, where α_i is firing probability α_i and λ_i is firing rate of t_i. Using the above stable state probability in three cases, we can get firing probability of transitions as given in table 3, and throughput as given in table 4.

Table 3. Firing probability of transition

Transition t_i	Firing probability αi Case 1	Case 2	Case 3
t_1, t_3, t_8, t_9, t_{10}, t_{11}	0.0594	0.0400	0.2880
t_2, t_4, t_5, t_6, t_7	0.1188	0.0800	0.5760
t_{12}	0.0529	0.0802	0.1440
t_{13}, t_{14}, t_{15}	0.00538	0.0802	0.1440
t_{16}	0.0029	0.0568	0.1152
t_{17}	0.0297	0.0400	0.0239

Table 4. Throughput of transition

Transition t_i	Throughput TH Case 1	Case 2	Case 3
t_1, t_3, t_8, t_{10}, t_{11}	0.00594	0.0800	0.1690
t_2, t_4, t_5, t_6, t_7	0.01188	0.1600	0.3380
t_9	0.05940	0.0400	0.0325
t_{12}	0.00530	0.0802	0.1397
t_{13}, t_{14}, t_{15}	0.00540	0.0802	0.1694
t_{16}	0.00290	0.0568	0.1400
t_{17}	0.00297	0.0800	0.1138

5.3 Reconfigurable Time and Task Response Time

For reconfigurable cell, reconfigurable time is the time that is spent on reconfiguring operations including static reconfigurable time and dynamic reconfigurable time. Static reconfigurable time equals the ratio of average mark to throughput during static reconfiguring operations, while dynamic reconfigurable time equals the ratio of average mark to throughput during dynamic reconfiguring operations. Task response time is the time that is spent on the entire computational task executed including task transmitting time, task waiting time and task computing time. Specifically, task transmitting time equals the ratio of average mark to throughput during task transmission. Task waiting time equals dynamic configurable time, because FPGAs need to carry out dynamic reconfiguration after logic functions changed. Task computing time equals the ratio of average mark to throughput during the task is been computing.

In the model of reconfigurable cell based on SPN, let $D(s_i)$ be the average mark of place s_i, then $D(s_i)=\sum P(M_{M(si)})$, where $M(s_i)$ represents the tokens that place s_i can get. $P(M_{M(si)})$ represents the sum of stable state probability of s_i, whose token equals $M(s_i)$. The process of static reconfiguration includes place s_i, $1\leq i \leq 12$, transition t_i, $1\leq i \leq 7$, so the average mark of static reconfiguration, $D_s=\sum D(s_i)$, $1\leq i \leq 12$. The throughput of static reconfiguration, $TH_s=\sum TH(t_i)$, $1\leq i \leq 7$. The process of dynamic reconfiguration includes place s_i, $2\leq i \leq 12$, transition t_i, $2\leq i \leq 7$, $i=10$, thus the average mark of dynamic reconfiguration, $D_d=\sum D(s_i)$, $2\leq i \leq 12$. The throughput of dynamic reconfiguration, $TH_d=\sum TH(t_i)$, $2\leq i \leq 7$, $i=10$. Similarly, the average mark of task computation, $D_c=\sum D(s_i)$, $21\leq i \leq 28$. The throughput of task computation, $TH_c=\sum TH(t_i)$, $11\leq i \leq 17$. Therefore, static reconfigurable time $RT_s=D_s/TH_s$, dynamic reconfigurable time $RT_d=D_d/TH_d$, reconfigurable time $RT_r=RT_s+RT_d$, task transmitting time $RT_t=D_t/TH_t$, task computation time $RT_c=D_c/TH_c$, and task response time $RT_{task}=RT_t+ RT_d+ RT_c$. The concrete time data are given in table 5.

Table 5. Time performance of reconfigurable cell (time unit is second)

Conditions / Time	Reconfigurable cell		
	Case 1	Case 2	Case 3
Static reconfigurable time of FPGA	24.17	1.21	0.37
Dynamic reconfigurable time of FPGA	23.33	1.17	0.36
Task transmitting time	13.10	8.00	5.17
Task computation time	4.03	1.93	1.91
Task response time	40.46	11.10	7.44

6 Conclusions and Future Work

This paper addresses the architecture and work principle of reconfigurable cell, and launches its structure and performance analysis based on stochastic Petri net. We have constructed a reachability graph of SPN for reconfigurable cell. It has proved that reconfigurable cell can successfully arrive at terminal state from initial state and the processors or interfaces will not overflow, thus it has verified the logical structure correctness of reconfigurable cell. Meanwhile, this paper also constructs a Markov chain, in which stable state probability, throughput, and task response time can be calculated in three different conditions. Therefore, we have realized performance evaluation for reconfigurable cell. The resulting data show that reconfigurable cell can adapt various application requirements, and task response time will become shorter if dynamic reconfigurable time is very shorter.

At present, our research goal is to model and analyze the reconfigurable cell, which is the critical part of hybrid reconfigurable computing array (HRCA). The conclusions in this paper need to be checked and improved in the real architecture of HRCA, which is our future research.

References

1. Duan, R., Fan, X., Gao, D.Y., Shen, G.: Reconfigurable computing technology and developing trends. Computer Applications Research 8, 14–17 (2004)
2. Estrin, G., Bussellt, B., Turn, R., Bibb, J.: Parallel processing in a restructurable computer system. IEEE Transactions on Electronic Computers 12(5), 747–755 (1963)
3. Kartashev, S.I., Kartashev, S.P.: A multicomputer system with dynamic architecture. IEEE Transactions on Computers 28(10), 704–721 (1979)
4. Hauser, J.R., Wawrzynek, J.: GARP: a MIPS processor with a reconfigurable coprocessor. In: Proceedings of IEEE Workshop on FPGAs Custom Computing Machines, Napa Valley, California, pp. 12–21 (1997)
5. Kiran, B., Viktor, K.: Reconfigurable computing: architectures, models and algorithms. Current Science: Special Section on Computational Science 78(7), 828–837 (2000)
6. Zeng, G.S., Chen, H.Z.: Inquiring the description of heterogeneity among computational systems. Computer Science 30(12), 16–22 (2003)
7. Wu, Z.H.: Introduction of Petri net. China Machine Press, Beijing (2006)
8. Lin, C.: Stochastic Petri Net and System Performance Evaluation. Tsinghua University Press, Beijing (2009)
9. Zhang, P., Liu, C.Y.: A tool of system performance analysis: stochastic Petri nets. Military Communications 24(2), 31–34 (2003)
10. Shan, Z.G., Lin, C.: Modeling and analysis of task scheduling in computational grids using stochastic high-level Petri nets. Journal of System Simulation 19(1), 199–202 (2007)

A Dynamic Construction Method for Web Service Combination

Yajun Liu[1], Lisha Gao[2], and Weifeng Wang[1]

[1] School of Computer Science & Engineering, Southeast University,
Nanjing 210096, China
yjliu@seu.edu.cn
[2] Nanjing Power Supply Company
Nanjing, China
gaolisha@js.sgcc.com.cn

Abstract. Aim at the optimization Web service combination issues, this paper presents a dynamic construction method for Web service composition based on the executed complexity, this method focuses on the structure of Web service combination, analyzes the structural parameters of Web service combination, and the relationship between the executed time of algorithm and the structural parameters. Experiments and studies have shown that the method for Web service combination based on the executed complexity is correct and more efficient.

Keywords: Web service combination, Integer programming algorithm, Genetic algorithm, the executed complexity.

1 Introduction

As a new distributed computing model, Web service possesses self-contained, modular, loosely coupled, standards-based, highly integration, etc. It has become a common focus in industrial and academic. Atomic services offer usually some simple functions; they can not meet the needs of complex applications. In order to achieve a complete business function, these distributed atomic services need to be combined according to certain business logic to form a new, more powerful combination service, which meets the needs of different complex applications. In the Web environment, there are usually more than one Web services which meet the users functional needs, therefore, it is a key issue in this field that select the appropriate Web services to build a Web service composition meeting requirements.

Many researchers have done a lot of researches about the optimization of Web service combination issues, and some progresses have been made. Currently, efficient methods to solve Web service combination problem are: integer programming [1] and genetic algorithm [2] [3]. But with the rapid development of Web services applications, the structure of composite service has become more diverse and dynamic [4] and each method can not efficiently handle all types of service combination structure. This thesis proposes a Web service combination method based on the executed complexity,

H. Tan and M. Zhou (Eds.): CSE 2011, Part I, CCIS 201, pp. 401–406, 2011.

it focuses on the structure of Web service combination, analyzes the structural parameters of Web service combination, and the relationship between the executed time of algorithm and the structural parameters.

2 Structure of Web Service Composition

In process-oriented Web service composition, the executed path have sequential structure, parallel structure, selection structure and repeat structure [5]. The repeat structure can be reduced to a sequential structure by supposition and the num of repeat. Therefore, executed of all Web service combination can be regarded as a directed graph. Let us suppose that every W_i is a service, Fig.1 shows different structures of Web service combination.

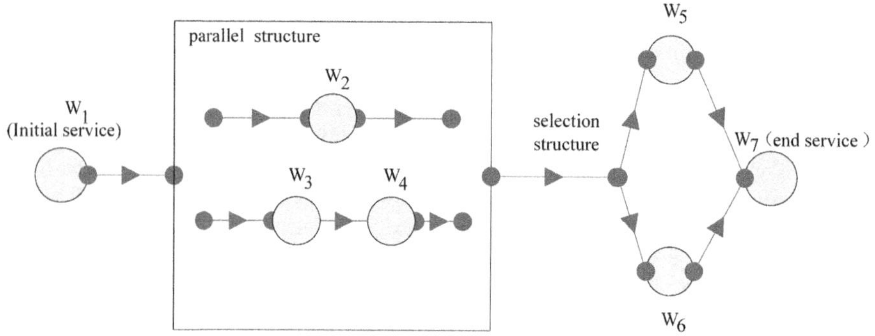

Fig. 1. Web service composition

Algorithm efficiency is different for different structures of Web service combination. If the number of executed path and the number of service are a few, then integer programming is more effective than genetic algorithm; if the number of executed path and the number of service are more, then executed efficiency of genetic algorithm is more steady than integer programming.

3 Structural Parameters of Web Service Composition

a. The number of executed path (p)

Definition 1. A executed path is defined as a service sequence of Web service combination $\{W_1, W_2, \ldots, W_i, \ldots, W_n\}$, W_1 is a initial service, W_n is a end service.

The number of executed path shows the number of called algorithm in integer programming and genetic algorithm. Thus, the number of executed path is one factor that influences the executed time of Web service combination. Fig.2 shows the executed path of Web service combination in Fig.1.

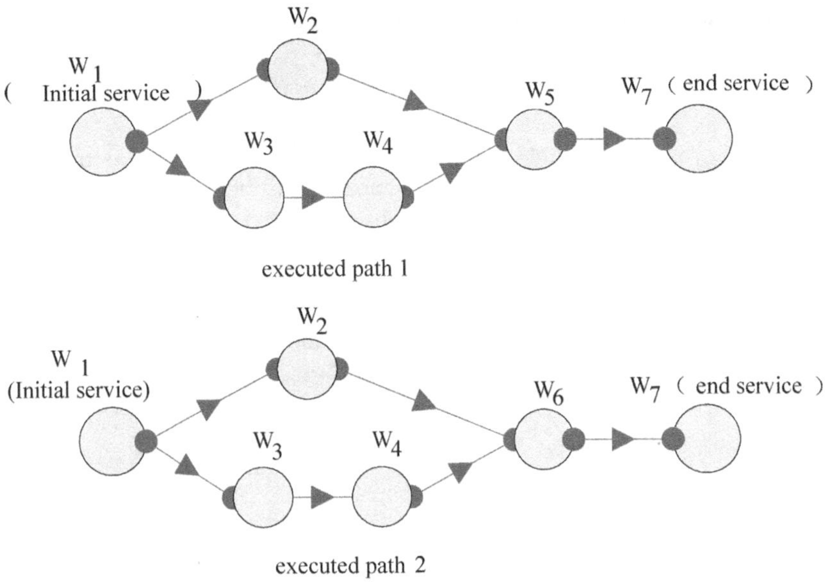

Fig. 2. The executed path of Web service composition

b. The number of abstract service in executed path (a)

Definition 2. The number of abstract service in executed paths is defined as the executed length of Web service combination.

The number of abstract service in executed path is also one factor that influences the executed time of Web service combination. But, this factor only influences integer programming algorithm.

c. The number of specific service (b)

Definition 3. The number of specific service is defined as practical services that are dynamic bind to abstract service.

It will reflected the choice multiplicity of Web service combination, also increased the complexity of service combination construction.

d. The total quantity about abstract service (A)

Because the executed time of two algorithms increases along with the increase of abstract service, in which the executed time of genetic algorithm is the linearity increases, but the executed time of integer programming is multinomial. Therefore, the total quantity of abstract service is also considered as a structural parameter of Web service combination.

4 The Executed Complexity Function of Algorithm

Definition 4. The executed complexity of algorithm $= F_{algorithm}(p, a, b, A)$

Here, $F_{algorithm}$ is an executed complexity function of algorithm, p is the number of abstract service in executed path, a is the number of abstract service in executed path, b is the number of specific service to bind to abstract service, A is the total quantity about abstract service.

Through experiment, we have found a fact that structural parameters of Web service combination affect the executed efficiency of algorithm. Let us suppose that F_{IP} is executed complexity function of integer programming algorithm and F_{GA} is executed complexity function of genetic algorithm, then:

$$F_{IP} = C_1 * a^{2.532} * b^{0.943} * p + C_2 . \tag{1}$$

$$F_{GA} = C_1 * A + C_2 . \tag{2}$$

There, C_1 and C_2 are constants that are valued d by system configuration. C_1 and C_2 will be smaller for great and power computing capacity system.

5 A Dynamic Construction Method for Web Service Combination Based on the Executed Complexity

According to structural parameters of Web service combination and the executed complexity function of algorithm for two kinds of Web service combination construction algorithm, this article proposes a dynamic construction method of Web service combination based on the executed complexity function of algorithm. These steps are listed as follows:

1. Getting every structural parameter;
2. Reading system configuration in order to define the executed complexity function of algorithm;
3. Taking structural parameter (p,a,b,A) into formula(1) and formula(2), calculating executed complexity functions of algorithm;
4. Selecting a smaller executed complexity function of algorithm in step 3, constructing Web service combination;
5. Handling result and saving, getting ready for the executed of Web service combination.

6 Experimental Result and Analysis

In experiment, we generate randomly fifty group structures of Web service combination and QoS values of specific service corresponding to abstract services in every Web service combination. Experimental steps are listed as follows:

1. Using the method to calculate all states of Web service combination, we obtain the absolute optimal solution of Web service combination;
2. Using separately integer programming algorithm and genetic algorithm to construct Web service combination and calculate whole reliability of Web service combination;
3. Executing repeatedly step 1 and step 2, recording the error of absolute optimal solution after executing construction algorithm, and calculating average error.

According to above-mentioned steps, average error is 0.22%. The experiment result proves enough that algorithm in this paper is correct.

Then we are separately use of integer programming algorithm, genetic algorithm and construction algorithm based on the executed complexity to construct Web service combination (every group executes 100 times). Finally, we contrast to total time of executed and correction of selection algorithm for three kinds of algorithm. Table 1 shows executed result.

Table 1. Experiment result

The total executed time of integer programming algorithm	459.2 sec
The total executed time of genetic algorithm	364.0 sec
The total executed time of construction algorithm based on the executed complexity function of algorithm	215.7 sec
Correction of selecting algorithm	95%
Error time / the total time	3%

The experiment result shows that construction algorithm based on the executed complexity function of algorithm is better than integer programming algorithm and genetic algorithm.

7 Conclusion

Because of the limitation of sole algorithm, this paper presents a dynamic construction method based on the executed complexity function of algorithm. This method analyzes the structural parameters of Web service combination, the relationship between the executed time of algorithm and the structural parameters, and proposes an executed complexity function of algorithm, on the basis of executed complexity function of integer programming algorithm and genetic algorithm, it can dynamically select construction algorithm of Web service combination. Experiment result shows that construction algorithm based on the executed complexity function of algorithm is correct and effective.

Acknowledgments

This paper is supported by national Key science and technology projects of China (2008AA01Z113), national natural fund science (6526000000) and key laboratory of computer network and information integration (southeast university) of ministry of education, P. R. China.

References

1. Zeng, L., Benatallah, B., Ngu, A.H.H., Dumas, M., Kalagnanam, J., Chang, H.: QoS-aware middleware for Web services composition. IEEE Transactions on Software Engineering 30(5) (2004)
2. Zo, H., Nazareth, D.L., Jain, H.K.: Measuring Reliability of Applications Composed of Web Services. hicss. In: 40th Annual Hawaii International Conference on System Sciences (HICSS 2007), p. 278c (2007)
3. Canfora, G., Penta, M.D., Esposito, R., Villani, M.L.: An approach for qos-aware service composition based on genetic algorithms. In: GECCO 2005: Proceedings of the 2005 Conference on Genetic and Evolutionary Computation, pp. 1069–1075. ACM, New York (2005)
4. Hwang, S., Lim, E., Lee, C., Chen, C.: Dynamic Web Service Selection for Reliable Web Service Composition. IEEE Trans. Serv. Comput. 1(2), 104–116 (2008), http://dx.doi.org/10.1109/TSC.2008.2
5. Li, B., Su, Z., Zhou, Y., Gong, X.: A User-Oriented Web Service Reliability Model, Systems, Man and Cybernetics. SMC (2008)

Personalized Design on Bilingual Teaching of Computer Science in Chinese Universities

Yi Yang and Li Yan

College of Computer Science and Information Engineering
Chongqing Technology & Business University
Chongqing, China
ycy88lj@sina.com, jsjyl@ctbu.edu.cn

Abstract. With the ever increasing international exchange in IT industry, there is an urgent need for IT talented persons who not only have expertise but also are proficient in foreign languages to provide and promote bilingual teaching in Chinese universities, a practice which can both share excellent teaching resources and experience from abroad and cultivate high-quality international talent. However, there have been some problems. This paper analyzes the current problems in bilingual teaching in computer science and proposes a reform idea about personalized design in some aspects of bilingual teaching such as teaching, learning, evaluation, and assessment. The paper also describes various design points in the process. Furthermore, a bilingual teaching course in "Information Security" is provided as an example to give a detailed analysis of the specific implementation.

Keywords: bilingual teaching; computer science; teaching reform; personalized design.

In the 21st century, higher education in China is undergoing major adjustments and change, and the decision to carry out bilingual teaching in computer science courses is an attempt to train more international talents and allow them access to more normalized expression of domain knowledge, more cutting edge technology, and broader horizons of subject knowledge. Furthermore, it helps to bring education in computer science and technology in line with international standards [1]. Over the years, there have been continuous efforts to explore the appropriate bilingual teaching methods. In this context, a reform idea about personalized design in some aspects of bilingual teaching such as teaching, learning, evaluation, and assessment was proposed.

1 Several Important Issues on Bilingual Teaching

Even though bilingual teaching of computer courses has been in existence nearly a decade in Chinese universities, a number of key issues still remain unclear. Therefore, it is necessary to clarify the following issues.

H. Tan and M. Zhou (Eds.): CSE 2011, Part I, CCIS 201, pp. 407–412, 2011.

1.1 Goal of Bilingual Teaching

Bilingual teaching means the use of mother tongue and a second language (such as English) in school for teaching of curriculum subjects. With two languages as the medium of instruction, it can improve students' professional competence and foreign language proficiency during the teaching process. The former is the primary objective and the latter is the secondary.

1.2 Teaching Materials Selection

Teaching material selection directly affects bilingual teaching. There are two reasons for selection of excellent original foreign textbooks. First, most of the foreign textbooks were written by experts in the field, who have unique logical structure and innovative ways of thinking. Second, information science was developed earlier in Europe and the US, which have accumulated a lot of good ideas and experience in professional education, and, compared with Chinese textbooks, have designed relatively more systematic, rational, and comprehensive teaching materials.

1.3 Cultivation of Foreign Language Ability

During the bilingual teaching process, language ability requirements should be gradual, starting from the most basic reading and gradually extended to writing and speaking. Advanced international computer technology papers and technical documents are mostly written in English, and cultivation of undergraduates' English reading habits and abilities will allow them easier access to the cutting-edge academic knowledge and enhance their learning confidence.

1.4 Bilingual Teaching Quality Evaluation

On the "individuality-enhanced harmony" principle, teaching quality evaluation and student assessment should be based on the course features and the individual differences of students. Aiming at lifelong learning objectives and student development, evaluations at different levels should be designed to avoid the shortcomings of arbitrary single assessments and to achieve the purpose of assessment and evaluation [2]- [4].

2 Hierarchical Objectives and Requirements of Teaching and Learning

In addition to allowing students to master the professional knowledge and skills and apply them to solve practical problems, bilingual teaching is also an effective way to improve their foreign language ability and apply it to search information written in English. However, differences between individual students cannot be ignored. With unrealistic teaching objectives, the teaching process would become a "joke," let alone the teaching effect. Based on the idea of personalized training, bilingual teaching in computer course can utilize hierarchical positioning [5]- [6].

As students' foreign language ability varies, teaching objectives and requirements will be set to three levels of advanced, intermediate and beginner according to the frequency of foreign language use in classroom. The advanced level has high requirements for instructors and students, with instructors being proficient in teaching expertise in English, and foreign instructors and domestic instructors who have teaching experience in foreign universities are generally selected. Accordingly, students must be strictly tested in English reading and listening. The requirements for intermediate level are relatively lower. Some outstanding professional instructors who are proficient in foreign language can deliver the lecture, with one or two teaching assistants helping students with reading and exercises. For student enrollment status, it is partly determined based on foreign language reading and listening tests. The beginner level is the bottom line of bilingual teaching, with the same teaching staff as the intermediate level. Those students who are not eligible for the first two levels will be placed in this level. Specific course requirements for these three levels are shown in Table 1.

Table 1. Hierarchical bilingual teaching objectives and requirements

Level	Textbook	Lecture & discussion	Courseware	Exercises	Examination
Advanced	Original foreign textbook	English	English	English	Examination paper in English, answer in English
Intermediate	Original foreign textbook	Mainly in English, partly in Chinese	English	English +Chinese	Examination paper in English, answer in Chinese
Beginner	Original foreign textbook + Chinese translation	Chinese	English + Chinese	Chinese	Examination paper in English, answer in Chinese

Hierarchical objectives and requirements are beneficial to personalized instruction implementation for students. The next step is to develop a teaching quality evaluation and student assessment system.

3 Design Diversified Bilingual Teaching Evaluation and Assessment System

There has been debate on traditional single-subject evaluation and mid-term/final examination methods. In order to improve its reliability and validity, it is necessary to establish a scientific evaluation and assessment system during the bilingual teaching reform process.

The new evaluation system should be characterized with diversity in index and methods. To solve the problem of single-subject evaluation, multiple-subject evaluation must be implemented. Besides students, supervisors, colleagues, and even instructors can also participate in evaluation. For evaluation items, process should be given preference over result. Accordingly, comprehensive expert measurement can be used to determine the weight of evaluation subjects and evaluation items respectively, which will be then normalized to facilitate easier comparison of evaluation results.

The current study effect is generally evaluated by mid-term and final exams. This assessment is relatively simple and arbitrary, with its single focus on results over process, a practice which ultimately leads to plagiarism, cheating and other fraudulent acts and man-made injustice. To better assess bilingual courses, self-evaluation can be combined with mutual-evaluation, and both process and result will have equal weight. It can also be implemented by other assessments such as oral tests, academic discussions, project practices, etc. The reform aims to focus on students' experience in classroom learning, experiments and other professional practices.

4 Personalized Reform and Implementation of Bilingual Teaching Course "Information Security"

4.1 Teaching Objectives and Methods

"Information Security" has been taught as a bilingual course for more than 5 years. Based on students' actual English proficiency in our school, it is appropriate to set teaching objective at intermediate and beginner levels. English textbooks and courseware PPT were used in classroom teaching. Key terms and conceptual knowledge were consistently explained in English, while difficult knowledge was taught first in Chinese followed by English. Students were encouraged to use English to obtain professional knowledge, and opportunities were created to increase their use of English. For example, some students were selected to read chapters from textbooks and translate, and simple oral tests and class discussion should be done in English to enhance their English reading comprehension, retrieval and translation capabilities [7].

In order to help students integrate theory with practice, labs were set up to let them understand and grasp the applied technology and implementation process of information security. Students were divided in groups and they should help each other to complete the group project, which helps them to understand the importance of teamwork. Meanwhile, students were required to do experiments by using English experiment software and instructions and write lab reports or project documents in English, which can help them to improve their English proficiency [8].

4.2 Textbook Selection

Good textbooks benefit bilingual teaching, so the outstanding original textbook Cryptography and Network Security (Second Edition) published by McGraw-Hill Education Publishing House was selected. The textbook includes simple language, clear structure, and innovative ideas. It systematically introduces various kinds of encryption technology, network security protocols and implementation techniques, and offers specific case studies. In addition, it is well designed in the content, such as italicized major content sections, key issues explained with graphics, key terms and exercises listed in each chapter. That design brings convenience not only to instructors, but also to students for preview and review.

4.3 Teaching Quality Evaluation

A good teaching quality evaluation system must be scientific and objective. We have designed 5 first-level indexes, namely leadership, supervision, colleague, student and instructor, 7 secondary-level indexes, namely organization, attitude, method, technology, content, basic skill, and effect and 25 third-level indexes. On this basis, the weights of all levels of index were determined respectively, and the end evaluation result was calculated by means of fuzzy comprehensive evaluation [9].

4.4 Assessment Methods

Assessment is the means to check the learning result. In order to promote student enthusiasm, a variety of assessment tools were employed, which both attach importance to the end result and the process. For the theoretical part, the test score was composed of a number of items, including classroom discussion, oral quizzes, exercises, mid-term and final exam. For the practical part, the score was based on lab participation, the quality of lab report, and lab contribution. In order to avoid laziness, plagiarism, and fraud, self-evaluation was combined with mutual-evaluation. For example, students first self-evaluated their own exercises and lab reports, which were then randomly assigned to other students for evaluation. Specific exam methods and grading scales are shown in Table 2.

Table 2. Exam methods and grading scale

Exam content	Exam stage	Grading method	Exam type	Grading scale
Specialized terminology + Basic theory	Tests	Instructor evaluation +Student mutual-evaluation + Student self-evaluation	Classroom discussion + Oral quizzes + Exercises	10%
Comprehensive expertise	Mid-term exam	Instructor evaluation	Closed exam in English	20%
Comprehensive expertise	Final exam	Instructor evaluation	Closed exam in English	50%
Professional experiment skills	Practice exam	Instructor evaluation + Student mutual-evaluation + Student self-evaluation	Lab attendance + Lab report + Lab contribution	20%

4.5 Effect of Bilingual Teaching

The survey conducted at the end of the "Information Security" course among 95 students shows that 75.3% of the students have made great progress in the professional application of theoretical knowledge and their ability to learn and use English, 52.8% of the students can use the methods and skills learned from the bilingual course to search English documents on the Internet on their own, and 36.2% of the students can complete the innovation topics and write English abstracts of research reports or technical papers under the guidance of instructors. What is most exciting is that 82.1% of the students show increased interest and initiative in learning and affirm the reform of bilingual teaching.

5 Conclusion

Bilingual teaching in computer course is the inevitable trend of teaching reform in Chinese universities. Practice shows that bilingual teaching will allow students not only to master the theory of computer-related knowledge, and to apply the knowledge to analyze and solve practical engineering problems, but also offer them an opportunity to become familiar with specialized terminology and the English expression, and to improve their spoken and written English. With the help of personalized design on teaching reform, it can help students overcome fear and weariness of bilingual courses and greatly improve the quality of bilingual teaching. How to develop and reform bilingual teaching is currently still a problem that demands further study in Chinese universities.

References

1. Li, Z.: The Practice and Research on the "Bilingual Teaching" of Computer Speciality. Journal of Human Institute of Humanities Science and Technology 4, 118–120 (2007)
2. Duan, W., Jin, Z.: Experience and Discussing on Computer Network's Bilingual Teaching. Journal of east China institute of Technology 3, 274–277 (2009)
3. Xiao, Y.: Considerations on Bilingual Education. Journal of Higher Education Management 3, 86–89 (2007)
4. Li, C., Wu, Y., Liu, Y.: Research of Bilingual Teaching Progress in China's Universities. Journal of Higher Education Management 5, 76–77 (2007)
5. Li, Y., Wang, L.: A Survey on Bilingual Teaching in Higher Education Institute in the Northeast of China. Journal of Language Teaching and Research 4, 353–357 (2010)
6. Li, H.: Development Tendency of Bilingual Education in Colleges and Universities—— Based on the Survey of Seven Colleges and Universities in Beijing. J. Higher Education (Research & Evaluation) 12, 71–75 (2008)
7. Zhou, Y., Jin, W.: Discussion of Bilingual Teaching for Information Courses in Local University. J. Higher Education Forum 12, 53–55 (2010)
8. Lei, L.: Practices and Thoughts of Bilingual Teaching for Operating System. Journal of Computer Education 8, 95–97 (2010)
9. Xiang, X., Yi, Z., Xu, Y., Luo, J., Hou, H.: Design and Implementation of Teaching Quality Evaluation System in Colleges and Universities: Based on Fuzzy Comprehensive Evaluation Method and Browser/Server Structure. Journal of Hunan Agricultural University (Social Sciences) 2, 77–79 (2010)

Multiprocessor System-Level Modeling and Analysis on Platform FPGA

Zhang Lei[1,2], Shang You[1], and Feng YongQing[3]

[1] Xinxiang University, P.R. China
[2] Wuhan University of Technology, P.R. China
[3] Government Information Centre, Xinxiang, P.R. China
{zhang.xxu,shangyou68}@gmail.com, xiaoqing701@sohu.com

Abstract. MPSoC are being developed to support a large number of applications running on the modern embedded systems. Designing such complex systems proves to be a challenge. Most of current design methodologies rely on creating the design by hand, and are less investigated, so the design is error-prone and time-consuming. And some design tools have been used for the design flow, but they are still limited to single-processor systems. In this paper we present a design methodology to setup the MPSoC designs in a systematic model and assign the multiple applications for the MPSoC architecture. The design architecture is inferred from the application specifications, and customized by the allocation policies. This design flow is useful for fast design exploration in MPSoC systems. And we present results of a case study to illustrate these usages.

Keywords: MPSoC System, High Level Petri net, Embedded System design, Modeling and Analysis.

1 Introduction

With the rapid improvement of microprocessor technology, MPSoC system, featured as high in performance, extensible, small in size and low in power consumption is able to meet requirements of complex embedded systems for computing performance, power consumption and cost, thus having become one of the mainstream development trends of embedded systems [1]. Currently, MPSoC is widely used in computer communication, digital media, auto electronics, medical electronics, aviation and aerospace, industrial control and many other fields, and the relevance of research topics on MPSoC has engaged many enterprises and institutes in research on MPSoC, such as programming model, task scheduling, system development, debugging environment and system safety[2].

Recently, there has been a growing interest in design and modeling methods targeted towards the co-design of complex MPSoC system [3], [4]. Recent years Model Checking has been extensively used in the verification of hardware and software of the embedded systems. Predicate Abstraction [5] is modified by many scientists and used in the hardware and software verification of the embedded systems. The PISH

H. Tan and M. Zhou (Eds.): CSE 2011, Part I, CCIS 201, pp. 413–417, 2011.

co-design system, partitions the hardware and software of the embedded systems with Petri Net. In this paper, we design and analyze the parallel processing of an MPSoC (multiprocessor system on chip) system architecture, and establish an Event Count Model to capture the timing characters of system, for generally evaluation on the system performances of CPU utilization and processing speed up. We illustrate the function of high level colored time Petri net and CPN Tools in the system design. We also can analyze the Petri net graph using CPN Tools which will give great help to the designers.

2 MPSoC System Design Method

2.1 Architecture Overview

A high performance FPGA was used to implement an h.264 encoder, and the primary MPSoC video system is built on the XUPV5-LX110T Development Board from Xilinx In figure 1, a simplified block diagram of the FPGA board architecture is shown.

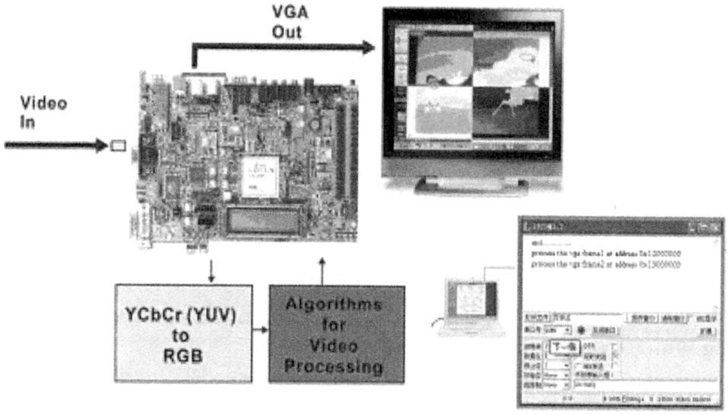

Fig. 1. Video Processing of MPSoC System

Our experiments are built on the FPGA, with setting the MPSoC system on FPGA, the heterogeneous multi-core processor architecture has been designed for the special use of mass data computation. The MPSoC has five MBs (Macro Blaze), which is a software IP core of 32bit general CPU. These MBs are connected by the on chip high speed bus directly. The Main Processor is in charge of the system controller and initialization, and other Synergistic Processors execute parallel video data computation separately. So there is potential competition to the occupation of bus data transmission. There should be some methods to be evaluated for scheduling and communication of system.

2.2 Architecture Abstract

And for the system Petri net model, system components should be abstract, there are only two kinds of CPU cores integrated on the chip, one is the main processor (MP), which is used to run most of the system instructions such as scheduling instructions, logical instructions; another is synergistic processors (SP), which is generally used to execute the customized special instructions, such as vector instructions, multimedia instructions. This can bring accelerations for parallel executions of independent video data computation. Practically, SPs can be same or different designed for more efficiency and expansion according to different requests.

In the abstract multiprocessor architecture "Reg" and "Buf" are the places where the interaction instructions and temporary data of executions are stored and judged separately. The execution results will be written back to "Buf".

3 Event Count Model

An Event Count Model captures the timing characteristics by counting the number of data items in a unit interval time. This count is used to update the relative count variables with the system Petri net. Several guard values can be used to decide at which time the timing characteristics will fire a transition. In this paper, the guard values are denoted as $t \Diamond p$ a function of conjunctions of atomic presents of set $\{<,>,=,\leq,\geq\}$ t is a count variable, p may be a constant or parameter of other variable. Furthermore, in a high level timed Petri net model, a token will be denoted as $1'x@t$ meaning a colored token x with time label t. An Example ECM is shown in Figure 2. The tasks are executed on three modules(A,B,C), In the initialization on A module, the system will execute i items in a unit of time, ($i \in [1,3]$), and when the total number of tasks on A exceeds 9 then tasks will be transferred onto B if the task count is 10 or onto C if the task count exceeds 10. B module execute 1 to 2 tasks and C execute 2 to 4 tasks in a unit of time, and tasks will return to run on A while the task count exceeds 5. Once C is entered it never moves to others again. Further system scheduling and communication between A and B costs 5 unit of time, and that between A and C costs 4 unit of time. Thus we can simulate the automaton and get a possible run A(0@0) → A(3@1) →A(5@2) →A(7@3) →A(10@4) →B(0@9) →B(1@10) → B(2@11) →B(4@12) B(5@13) →B(6@14) →A(6@19) →A(7@20) →A(8@21) →A(11@22) →C(11@26) →A(13@27) , that executes tasks as: (3@1, 2@2, 2@3, 3@4, 1@20, 1@21, 3@22) on A, (1@10, 1@11, 2@12, 1@13, 1@14) on B, and (2@27) on C.

With this diagram, the running process of a simple MPSoC architecture can be simulated and each step of the execution is mapped with different state. Some useful CPN Tools can also be used to make some further analysis.

We have run the MPSoC system under 100MHz system clock. In this example the baseline case allocates the tasks with the invariable blocks onto these processors, and the improved case use the fuzzy dynamic scheduling to allocate the blocks onto the appropriate processor. The improved case can achieve better performance, because it minimizes the difference of processor's executing time so that there are less communications and higher utilization.

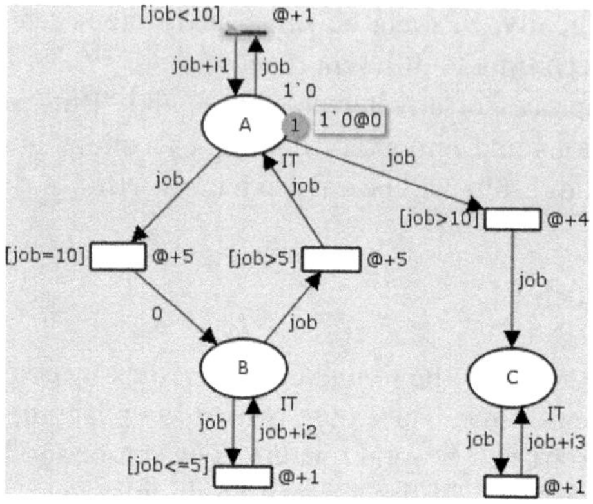

Fig. 2. Example of Event Count Model

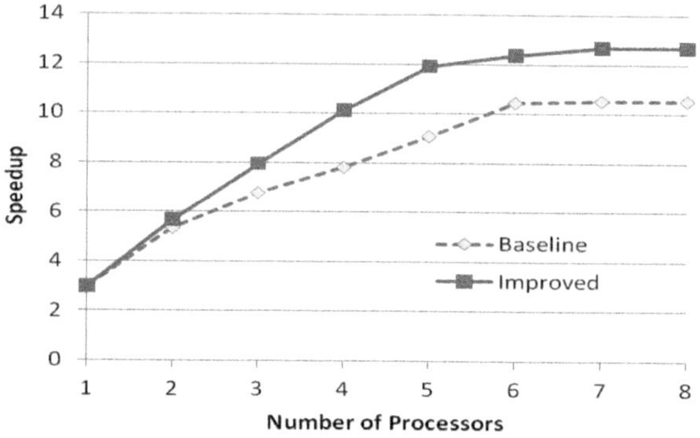

Fig. 3. Speedup ratio of CTPN model and real FPGA system

4 Conclusion

Through the above case, which design and analyze a multiple video processing on the MPSoC system, we illustrate the framework of design the system with a high level colored time Petri net and functions of CPN Tools in the design and simulation. And the future design work is to establish the accurate timing model of detail, and research the methods of description with less Petri net nodes, which will be better for perform formal co-design and co-verification of complex SoC design.

References

1. Wolf, W.: The future of multiprocessor systems-on-chips. In: Proc. 41st Annual Conference on Design Automation, pp. 681–684 (2004)
2. Baruah, S., Nathan, F.: The feasibility analysis of multiprocessor real-time systems. In: Proc. EuroMicro Conference on Real-Time Systems, pp. 85–94 (2006)
3. Kapasi, U.J., et al.: Programmable stream processors. IEEE Computer 36(8) (2003)
4. Maxiaguine, A., Kunzli, S., Chakraborty, S., Thiele, L.: Rate analysis for streaming applications with on-chip buffer constraints. In: ASP-DAC (2004)
5. Benini, L., De Micheli, G.: Networks on Chips: A New SoC Paradigm. Computer 35(1), 70–78 (2002)
6. Maciel, P., Barros, E., Silva, M., et al.: Resource Sharing Estimation by Petri Nets in PISH Hardware/Software Co-Design System. In: 2000 IEEE International Conference on Systems, Man, and Cybernetics, October 8-11, vol. 5, pp. 3165–3170 (2000)

Multiple Applications Design and Synthesis for Multiprocessor System

Feng BingCan[1], Zhao PeiZhang[1], and Feng YongQing [2]

[1] Xinxiang University, P.R. China
[2] Government Information Centre, Xinxiang, P.R. China
blueSCC@soho.com, xxzpz@tom.com, xiaoqing701@sohu.com

Abstract. This paper studies the methodologies of system design and analysis, and derives ideas for designing the system on multiprocessor architecture performing parallel video stream processing. Aiming to the limitation of current design tools, we model the Multiple Applications design models by a proposed high level colored time Petri nets. To present the timing constraints of video processing, a concept of ECM (Event Count Model) is proposed for describing the timing character. The whole system is established in a multiple hierarchy Petri net model for simulating the asynchronous and concurrent interactions of system. And the multiple applications are investigated for design the MPSoC architecture and the applications synthesis. A formal co-verification approach with CPN Tools is proposed, and also a multiple applications case is studied for illustration these usages.

Keywords: Multiprocessor System, Petri net, Embedded System design, Design and Synthesis.

1 Introduction

MPSoC system, featured as high in performance, extensible, small in size and low in power consumption, is able to meet requirements of complex embedded systems for computing performance, power consumption and cost, thus having become one of the mainstream development trends of embedded systems [1]. Currently, MPSoC is widely used in computer communication, digital media, auto electronics, medical electronics, aviation and aerospace, industrial control and many other fields, and the relevance of research topics on MPSoC has engaged many enterprises and institutes in research on MPSoC, such as programming model, task scheduling, system development, debugging environment and system safety[2]. Recently, there has been a growing interest in design and modeling methods targeted towards the co-design of complex MPSoC system [3], [4].

The use of stable formal methods to design and analysis the MPSoC system is a difficult problem. The best way to tackle such a problem is to design the system by communication driven method [5]. So formal verification research becomes more and more popular and using Petri net is a distinct feature of common design methodology, an example of this overall methodology based on formal specification of SoC system design is shown in [6]. Petri net is used as a formal executable method for

H. Tan and M. Zhou (Eds.): CSE 2011, Part I, CCIS 201, pp. 418–421, 2011.

design and analysis of concurrent, discrete-event dynamic systems [7]. Our design methodology is based on recent advances on asynchronous design with Petri net.

In this paper, we design and analyze the parallel processing of a MPSoC (multi-processor system on chip) system architecture, and establish an Event Count Model to capture the timing characters of system, for generally evaluation on the system performances of CPU utilization and processing speed up. We illustrate the function of high level colored time Petri net and CPN Tools in the system design. Petri nets show more advantages to make the complex design and analysis more simple and clear about the process of the video system active figure. We also can analyze the Petri net graph using CPN Tools which will give great help to the designers.

2 MPSoC System Architecture

2.1 Architecture Overview

Our experiments are built on the FPGA, with setting the MPSoC system on FPGA as shown in Figure 1, the heterogeneous multi-core processor architecture has been designed for the special use of mass data computation. The MPSoC has five MBs (Macro Blaze), which is a software IP core of 32bit general CPU. Each processor has a local L1 cache to load and store data used by executing unit. So there is potential competition to the occupation of bus data transmission. There should be some methods to be evaluated for scheduling and communication of system.

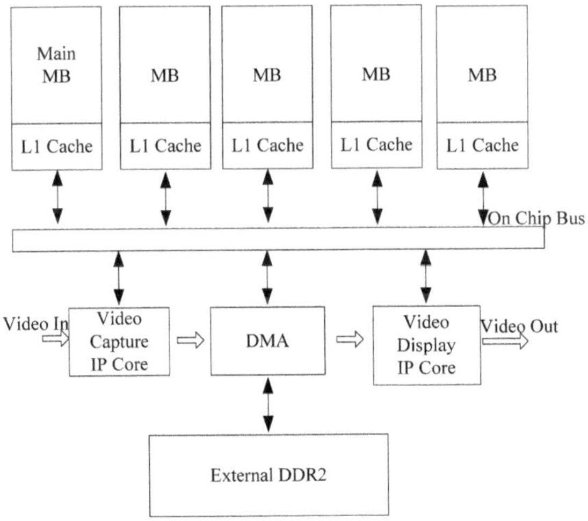

Fig. 1. Architecture of MPSoC System for Video Processing

2.2 Architecture Abstract

The system interface process will be designed as two modules. One of these modules is the control set, used for transfer various system instructions on registers; and another is data buffer set, which is a non-burst buffer allows data be transferred.

The system timing information is described by an Event Count model, and the timing characteristics is translated into a high level timed Petri net description to be transferred with system interactions.

In the abstract multiprocessor architecture "Reg" and "Buf" are the places where the interaction instructions and temporary data of executions are stored and judged separately. The execution results will be written back to "Buf".

3 MPSoC Modeling

The MP and SP cores in MPSoC system architecture run synchronously, so Petri net is just a useful tool to describe this asynchronous and concurrent system. The process of the modeling is generally the following.

(1) Each execution step can be inserted into a hierarchy subpage of transition of component, where the core logic design is described as a subnet in detail. The places "Reg" and "Buf" are the input/output the core, they are displayed in several pages vertically;
(2) The timing characteristics are using in the subpage architecture design, the tasks tokens are described with a product color set, <Data, Func, Time>.
(3) For the data must be processed in the right order, that need a ID sequence control inserted into the Petri net. "Dataload" represents loading correct data from buffer into the executing cores.
(4) The MP core sets the data parsing parameters, and initializes other SP cores data ID, so the each of the cores has its own video data.

With this diagram, the running process of a simple MPSoC architecture can be simulated and each step of the execution is mapped with different state. Some useful CPN Tools can also be used to make some further analysis.

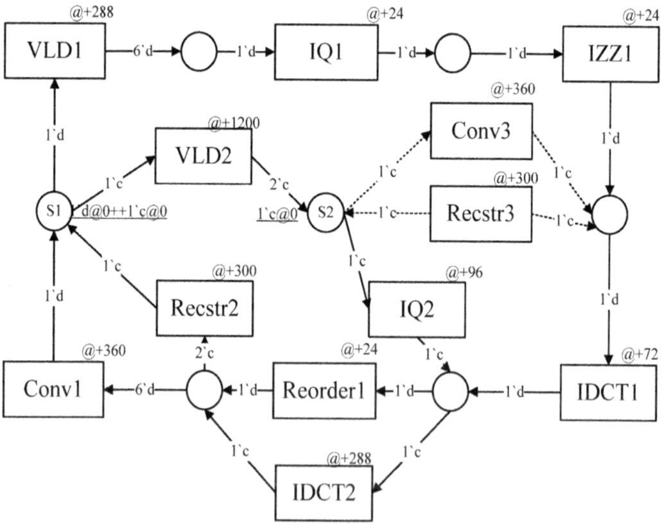

Fig. 2. Petri Net Diagram of Multiple Video Processing Applications Modeling

Table 1. Simulation Results

Policy	*Init token*	*A1*	*A2*	*A3*	*Cpu executions(ms)*			
					Cpu0	Cpu1	Cpu2	Cpu3
Parallel execution	S1:3` d++1`c S2:1`c	248	350	743	7753	4312	2442	2113
	S1:1`d ++1`c S2:3`c	144	617	1289	12553	6696	2933	2463
Load balance	S1:3`d ++1`c S2:1`c	248	350	743	2254	4917	5054	4342
	S1:1`d ++1`c S2:3`c	144	617	1289	2930	7816	7571	6323

4 Simulation and Analysis

The CPN Tools has a powerful simulation and analysis tool. It can calculate state space of the net, and also calculate a strongly connected components (SCC) graph. We run the simulation the CTPN model with CPN Tools, with different CPU numbers. Comparing to the results of real MPSoC system on FPGA, Figure 6 shows the CTPN model of Multiple Video Processing Applications, and the table shows the CPN simulation results with two application allocation policies.

5 Conclusion

Through the above case, which design and analyze a video coding process on the MPSoC system, we illustrate the framework of design the system with a high level colored time Petri net and functions of CPN Tools in the design and simulation. In the more complex design in detail, using Petri net makes the complex design and analysis more simple and clear. And the model can be further extended.

The simulation result shows that this design idea of CTPN model is effective to the system design. And the future design work is to establish the accurate timing model of detail, and research the methods of description with less Petri net nodes, which will be better for perform formal co-design and co-verification of complex SoC design.

References

1. Wolf, W.: The future of multiprocessor systems-on-chips. In: Proc. 41st Annual Conference on Design Automation, pp. 681–684 (2004)
2. Baruah, S., Nathan, F.: The feasibility analysis of multiprocessor real-time systems. In: Proc. EuroMicro Conference on Real-Time Systems, pp. 85–94 (2006)
3. Kapasi, U.J., et al.: Programmable stream processors. IEEE Computer 36(8) (2003)
4. Maxiaguine, A., Kunzli, S., Chakraborty, S., Thiele, L.: Rate analysis for streaming applications with on-chip buffer constraints. In: ASP-DAC (2004)
5. Benini, L., De Micheli, G.: Networks on Chips: A New SoC Paradigm. Computer 35(1), 70–78 (2002)
6. Yakovlev, A., Furber, S., Krenz, R., Bystrov, A.: Design and Analysis of aSelf-Timed Duplex Communication System. IEEE Transactions on Computers 53(7) (July 2004)
7. Cortadella, J., Kishinevsky, M., Kondratyev, A., Lavagno, L., Yakovlev, A.: Logic Synthesis of Asynchronous ontrollers and Interfaces. Springer, Heidelberg (2002)

Research of Access Authorization Model Based on Trust Negotiation in the P2P Network

Junyao Ye[1], Yanhong Wang[1], and Yinglian Wang[2]

[1] College of Information Engineering, Jingdezhen Ceramic Institute, Jingdezhen, China
{sdyejunyao,jdzwyh2008}@126.com
[2] College of Mechanical and Electronic Engineering,
Jingdezhen Ceramic Institute, Jingdezhen, China
sdwyl@126.com

Abstract. This article constructs the access authorization model under the P2P network, which solves the resource access authorization problem under high security environment. Firstly, it designs the access control strategy of the model, then analyzes the four role logical operators and designs the grammar rules of the access control strategy. Lastly, construct a high security trust negotiation based on security function, which makes the security of the model has been greatly improved.

Keywords: P2P, Access Authorization, Trust Negotiation, Security Function.

1 Introduction

P2P network is an open distributed network, do not have a centralized access control center. Entities are equal and loose in the P2P network. Peer entity shares information and resources through direct interconnection, without depending on the central server. When the user selects the trading partners, they aren't knowing the status of the entire network, which is because the network exists anonymity. Further, there are several risk in the network, such as malicious attacks, fraud and pretender,etc.

When the services the user provided need high security, the existing mode of resource access which takes the trust as the basis for the final access authorization decision has significant risk. Trust negotiation is an effective expansion of the objective trust management, which provides an access authorization mode on objective resources based on voucher. The mode does not depend on the identity of an entity as a basis for authorization, but depend on the attribute of an entity as a basis for final authorization. It is an efficient mode on resource access authorization under cross-domain environment[1], which can solve the issues on resource access authorization of high security requirements.

2 Access Authorization Model Based on Trust Negotiation

Access authorization model based on trust negotiation is in Figure 1. The model consists of three parts, which are service provider selection , trust voucher collection and

H. Tan and M. Zhou (Eds.): CSE 2011, Part I, CCIS 201, pp. 422–427, 2011.

access authorization decision. Service provider selection is responsible for the discovery of service provider, and assess the quality of service through the trust evaluation mechanism. Trust voucher collection controlles the disclosure process of voucher through trust negotiation,finally obtain the disclosure voucher set between the two sides. Access authorization decision uses the disclosure voucher and access controll strategy as the input of consistency validator to final decision.

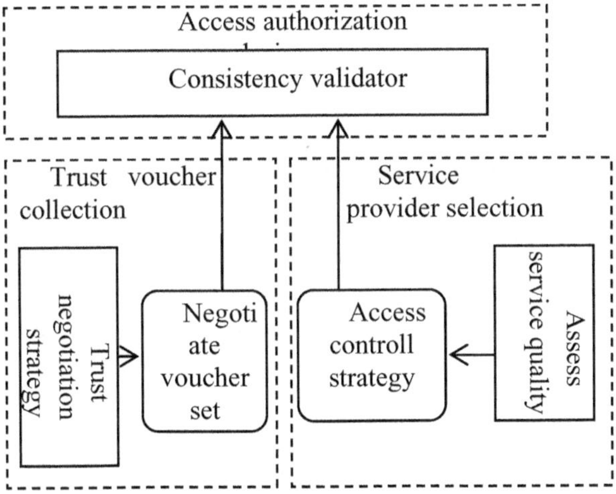

Fig. 1. Access authorization model based on trust negotiation

We can extract six elements from Figure 1, they are R, P, Q, AC, NS and MD. Specific meaning of each element is as follows.

(1) Service requester(R): Service requester has some attribute voucher, through the inner attribute field to indicate the attribute an entity owns. It certify to own someone's attribute voucher by its private key.
(2) Service provider(P): Service provider provides servicces to service requester. Requester finds provider who can provide satisfactory service by service discovery mechanisms.
(3) Assess service quality(Q): Service ability among service providers is different because they cope with different affair. Therefore we need to assess the service ability by some corresponding mechanism.
(4) Access controll strategy(AC): Service provider sets the appropriate access control rules according to what service security level it has owned. Access control rules mainly reflect in the specific attribute of service requester.
(5) Trust negotiation strategy(NS): It's an important component of the model. It can be used to negotiate the resource disclosure process, and provides appropriate security protection to sensitive resource.
(6) Access make decision(MD): It makes decision to determine what operating authority service requester owns, mainly according to the attribute voucher requester submitted and service protection strategy.

3 Access Control Strategy Based on Trust Negotiation

Access control strategy based on trust negotiation is an important part of the model, which is the description tool for service provider to service security protection requirements. At present, RT language[2] has great impact on access control strategy description language in objective trust management. Trust negotiation has more demanding on the access control strategy language. If we would like to use RT language as access control strategy description language in the trust negotiation, we need corresponding expansion of the RT in protection of sensitive resources and voucher restrict[3]. This article designs the access control strategy inner rules base on RT_1^T role logic.

3.1 Design on Access Control Strategy

Access control strategy uses the role as the core in the model. Role can be divided into a single role and the logic role. Both negotiation can define different roles according to the resources of its own. Every resource can map a single role or logic role. If entity has a role, that means the attribute of the entity satisfyed the set of rules of the role.

There are two cases of submitting voucher in the negotiation process. (1) Submit role voucher: When the role voucher of the service requester satisfied the access control strategy of the sevice provider, provider can access the entity according to the pre-established access control strategy. (2) Submit attribute voucher: When service requester doesn't have any role voucher, or what role voucher it has can satisfy access control strategy, service provider find corresponding role on service and obtain the corresponding attribute voucher. Service requester can get service after it provided the voucher to service provider in the negotiation process.

3.2 Analysis on Role Logic Operator

There are four role logic operators in the RT_1^T. They are link operator, intersection operator, integration operator and exclusive operator.

(1) link operator $(\cdot)$

The logic role linked by link operator expressed a delegation of authority relations. For example, $A{\bullet}R \leftarrow A{\bullet}Role_1{\bullet}Role_2{\bullet}Role_3$ have the following meanings: $A \xrightarrow[C_1]{Role_1} B \xrightarrow[C_2]{Role_2} C \xrightarrow[C_3]{Role_3} X, so A \xrightarrow[C_1C_2C_3]{R} X$

The above equation shows A consider B has Rolel, B consider C has Role2, C consider X has Role3, so A consider X has Role R. From above, we know link operator can express delegation of authority relations.

(2) intersection operator $(\cap)$

Intersection operator can express logic and relation between roles. For example, $A{\bullet}R \leftarrow B_1{\bullet}Role_1 \cap B_2{\bullet}Role_2 \cap B3{\bullet}Role_3$ have the following meanings:

$$A \xrightarrow[B_1]{Role_1} X, A \xrightarrow[B_2]{Role_2} X, A \xrightarrow[B_3]{Role_3} X, so A \xrightarrow[B_1B_2B_3]{R} X$$

The above equation shows that entity A consider entity X has role R on condition that X has Role1,Role2,Role3.

(3) integration operator （⊙）

Integration operator can express not appearing repeat role. For example, $A \bullet R \leftarrow B_1 \bullet Role_1 \odot B_2 \bullet Role_2 \odot B_3 \bullet Role_3$ have the following meanings:

$$B_1 \xrightarrow[C_1]{Permission} X, B_2 \xrightarrow[C_2]{Permission} X, B_3 \xrightarrow[C_3]{Permission} X; so A \xrightarrow[C_1C_2C_3]{R} X$$

$$B_1 \in members(Role_1), B_2 \in members(Role_2), B_3 \in members(Role_3)$$

The above equation shows that if entity X obtain the authority of entity Bl, B2, B3 from different role, Role1, Role2, Role3. So entity X has own role R.

(4) exclusive operator （⊗）

Exclusive operator can express not appearing repeat entity. For example, $A \bullet R \leftarrow B_1 \bullet Role_1 \otimes B_2 \bullet Role_2 \otimes B_3 \bullet Role_3$ have the following meanings:

$$B_1 \xrightarrow[C_1C_1^{'}]{Permission} X, B_2 \xrightarrow[C_2C_2^{'}]{Permission} X, B_3 \xrightarrow[C_3C_3^{'}]{Permission} X; 则 A \xrightarrow[C_1C_2C_3C_1^{'}C_2^{'}C_3^{'}]{R} X$$

$$B_1 \in members(Role_1), B_2 \in members(Role_2), B_3 \in members(Role_3)$$

The above equation shows that if entity X obtain the authority of entity Bl, B2, B3 from different role, Role1, Role2, Role3. So entity X has own role R.

4 Construction of Trust Negotiation Protocol and Security Analysis

4.1 Construction of Trust Negotiation Protocol

We construct a high security trust negotiation based on security function. They negotiate between two sides through chaotic circuit[4][5] and memoryless transfer protocol[6]. It implements secure access authorization between requester and provider by establishing trust negotiation protocol-SFEBTN, without trusted third party. It also can provide high secure protection to resource protection strategy and voucher between the two sides. The negotiation process is in Figure 2.

The protocol guarantee that service requester can get chaotic value which service provider sets according to the attribute which it held. In the whole protocol process, Bob can't know the attribute of Alice, and Alice doesn't know the meaning of the value it has gotten. In short, when Alice has owned the attribute what Bob needs, it would get correct detection results. The steps of the protocol are as follows.

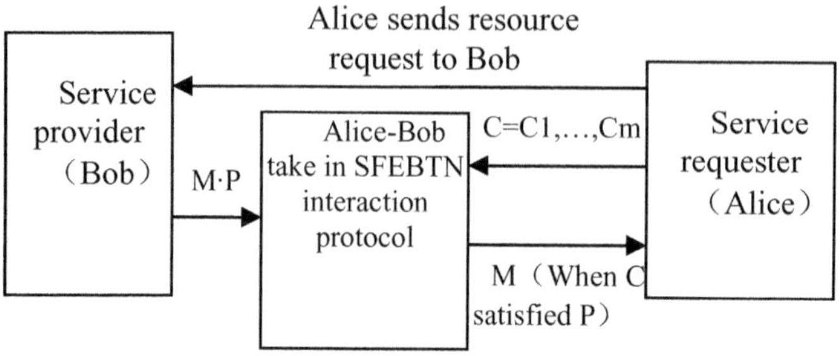

Fig. 2. Trust negotiation protocol process

(1) $Alice \rightarrow Bob: E(a_1), E(a_2), ..., E(a_n)$

Alice selects semantically secure homomorphic encryption scheme E[7], and defines m polynomial P(k), $P(k)=(B_1-k)\ (B_2-k)...(B_n-k)=a_0+a_1k+...+a_nk^n$, whose roots are $B_1, B_2, \ldots, B_n$. It also uses homomorphic encryption scheme E to encrypt polynomial coefficients, and gets $E(a_0)$, $E(a_1)$, $E(a_2)$, …, $E(a_n)$, then send to Bob.

(2) $Bob \rightarrow Alice: E[s \bullet P(y)+t]$

Bob randomly selects s,t $\in Z_M^*$ and $(m_0^0, m_0^1), \cdots, (m_{l-1}^0, m_{l-1}^1)$ 、 $(n_0^0, n_0^1), \cdots, (n_{l-1}^0, n_{l-1}^1)$, and according to the each bit of t to get $m_0^{x_0}, ..., m_{l-1}^{x_{l-1}}$, uses homomorphism attribute to calculate $E[s \bullet P(y)+t]$, then sends the results to Alice[8].

(3) $Alice \leftrightarrow Bob: n_0^{x_0^{'}}, ..., n_{l-1}^{x_{l-1}^{'}}$

Alice uses homomorphic encryption scheme E to decrypt $E[s \bullet P(y)+t]$, and gets $t^{'} = s \bullet P(y)+t$, then acquires the corresponding bit $n_0^{x_0^{'}}, ..., n_{l-1}^{x_{l-1}^{'}}$ of t' by executing memoryless transfer protocol.

4.2 Security Analysis to Trust Negotiation Protocol

SFEBTN protocol guarantee that Alice can acquire what service it requests under this prerequisite, which is that service requester Alice owns voucher set to satisfy service protection strategy. It also provides secure protection to sevice protection strategy of provider and voucher of requester. We now analyze the security of the protocol as follows.

(1) In the first two steps of the trust negotiation protocol, provider selects random number ki, and uses Ci to encrypt which in the voucher set who can satisfy service protection strategy. Just because the encrypted information is a random

number, whether service requester has owned voucher Ci or not, the decrypted information B1, ..., Bn are random numbers. From above, We know that it can't conjecture whether the voucher is satisfied for service protection strategy from the decrypted information, therefore service protection strategy is protected by the protocol in the first two steps.

(2) In the third step of the protocol, service provider Bob and service requester Alice execute attribute equivalence test protocol. According to the protection attribute, Bob doesn't know what Alice has input, so it assures the information security of Alice's voucher. Alice doesn't know the specific Bi equal to k, so it assures the security of Bob's resource protection strategy.

5 Conclusion

In the P2P network, the access authorization model based on trust negotiation can solve the resource access authorization problem. The model constructs a high security trust negotiation based on security function, which makes the security of the model has been greatly improved. Trust negotiation protocol-SFEBTN guarantee that Alice can acquire what service it requests under this prerequisite, which is that service requester Alice owns voucher set to satisfy service protection strategy. It also provides secure protection to sevice protection strategy of provider and voucher of requester.

Acknowledgments

This work is supported in part by The Youth Science Foundation of Jiangxi Province,China grant # GJJ10222.

References

1. Li, J., Huai, J.: Research of auto trust negotiatio. Journal of Software 17(1), 24–133 (2006)
2. Li, N., John, C.: Design of a role-based trust management framework. In: Proceedings of the 2002 IEEE Symposium on Security and Privacy, pp. 114–130. IEEE Computer Society Press, Los Alamitos (May 2002)
3. Seamons, K., Winslett, M., Yu, T.: Requirements for Policy Language for Trust Negotiation. In: Proeeedings of the Third IEEE International Workshop on Policies for Distributed Systems and Networks, pp. 68–79 (2002)
4. Malkhi, D., Nisan, N.: Fairplay: A Secure two-Party computation system. In: Proceedings of the 13th USENIX Security Symposium, USENIX, pp. 287–302 (2004)
5. Li, J., Li, N.: Policy-hiding access control in open environment. In: Proceedings of ACM Symposium on Principles of Distributed Computing (PODC), pp. 29–38 (2005)
6. Garay, J., MacKenzie, P., Yang, K.: Efficient and universally composable committed oblivious transfer and applications. In: Naor, M. (ed.) TCC 2004. LNCS, vol. 2951, pp. 297–316. Springer, Heidelberg (2004)
7. ElGamal, T.: A Public-Key Cryptosystem an a Signature Scheme Based on Discrete Logarithms. IEEE Trans. on Information Theory IT-31, 469–472 (1985)
8. Malkhi, D., Nisan, N.: Fairplay: A Secure two-party computation system. In: Proceedings of the 13th USENIX Security SymPosium, USENIX, pp. 287–302 (2004)

Reconstructing 3D Model of Carotid Artery with Mimics and Magics

Huiyan Shao[1], Haiqiang Qin[2], Yuanyuan Hou[1], Hong Xia[1], and Ping Zhou[1]

[1] School of Biomedical Engineering, Capital Medical University, Beijing, China, 100069
[2] Department of Neurology, Tiantan Hospital, Beijing, China, 100050
merina.xia@gmail.com, yanword@163.com

Abstract. The technology of Three-Dimension (3D) reconstruction of medical images has been playing an increasingly important role in modern clinical medicine. With application softwares' advent, physicians can explore the method of 3D entity reconstruction more conveniently and easily. This paper aims to provide physicians with a feasible method for 3D entity reconstruction of carotid artery. The raw carotid artery images derived from patients undergoing the test of high resolution carotid artery MRI. Then with the aid of the Mimics toolkit, raw images were used to generate the 3D model of carotid blood. Finally, Magics carried out the step of 3D extension and Boolean Operation to produce the 3D model of carotid wall.

Keywords: 3D entity reconstruction, carotid artery, MR imaging, Mimics, Magics.

1 Introduction

Nowadays the carotid artery disease has become a common disease threatening the health of old people[1]. Because of the increase of work pressure and lack of exercise, patients suffering this disease tend to be younger in age. Carotid artery stenosis, arteriosclerosis, along with the existence of plaque may obstruct the blood flowing to the brain and heart, a trend that easily induce cerebral stroke and coronary heart disease[1,2].

Clinically, ultrasonic test, MR and CT are used to diagnose pathological changes of the carotid artery[2]. However, the acquirable data is so multi-dimensional[3] that it is difficult to synthesize and analyze the information in terms of one certain sequence of 2D images. This is why the 3D reconstruction technique[4,5,6] is put forward. With the 3D model of the carotid artery, researchers can step further to the calculation of hemodynamic parameters, the analysis of plaque and even the study of solid-fluid coupling affect. The conventional 3D reconstruction method relies on the complicated computer programs written by the professional programmers, which can be hardly mastered by doctors. To help doctors accomplish this reconstruction task more easily, we propose and employ two softwares: Mimics and Magics, and discuss the steps and methods of reconstructing the 3D model of carotid artery with them.

H. Tan and M. Zhou (Eds.): CSE 2011, Part I, CCIS 201, pp. 428–433, 2011.

2 Methods and Steps

2.1 Acquisition of the Raw Images

The following operations were accomplished in department of neurology, Tiantan Hospital. High resolution carotid artery MR was performed in patients[7]. With the patient prone, the surface coil was put in his/her neck with the 3.0T MR scanner(Trio-Tim, Siemens, Germany) applied there. The first step lied in the scanning of the sagittal and the coronal plane to identify the carotid artery bifurcation. Secondly, the 3D-TOF sequence scanning was employed within the scope of 2cm above and below the carotid artery bifurcation. After the selection of 4 to 6 planes from the areas with a high plaque incidence, the high resolution MR scanning was undertaken. In this final step, the ECG-gated technique and black blood technology were used and T1-weighted images (T1WI), T2-weighted images (T2WI) and proton density weighted images(PDWI) were eventually obtained.

2.2 3D Reconstruction of the Carotid Blood

Mimics software (Materialise's interactive medical image control system[8], by Materialise Company in Belgium) is a widely-used software in the field of 3D reconstruction. Its advantages are obvious. Taking possession of a friendly interface and demanding easy operations, Mimics is quite helpful for the beginners. The greatest benefit is that it can read the DICOM image automatically and convert the output data into the required format.

After Mimics reads the raw images of carotid artery; it chooses the 3D TOF image sequence spontaneously. Then the operators take the responsibility for the next steps.

* To determine the direction of the three planes: the sagittal plane, the coronal plane and the transverse plane;
* Drawing a line passing though the region of interest(ROI), that is, the region which is intended to be reconstructed;
* To adjust the threshold value so that it can distinguish the ROI from its surroundings;
* To mark the ROI with another color.

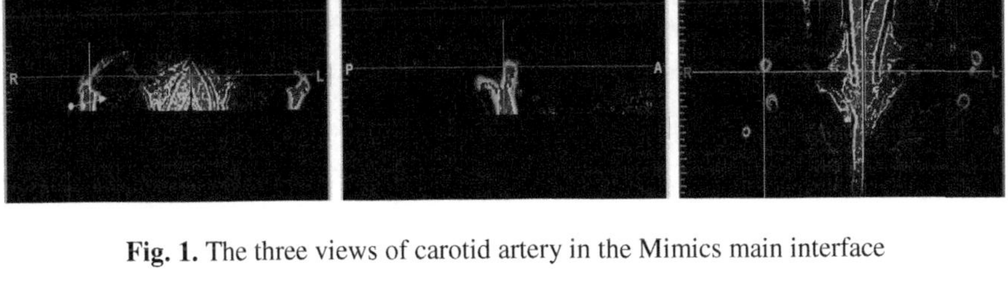

Fig. 1. The three views of carotid artery in the Mimics main interface

With the steps above finished, Mimics can realize the operation of reconstruction with its interior program[9,10,11]. Figure1 shows the three views of carotid artery in the Mimics main interface and figure2 presents the output 3D model generated from the 3D TOF images by Mimics.

Fig. 2. The 3D model generated from the 3D TOF image

The picture of the transverse plane in figure2 reveals that the 3D model is of solid structure. Actually, this model is the right model of the carotid blood. To illustrate this point, we offer the four typical image sequences obtained from the MR imaging, shown in figure3. We have to point out that the 3D TOF image (3-A) is different from the other three images (3-B/C/D) in the following two aspects.

* In the 3D TOF image, the carotid wall is of hypo intensity (pointed by the arrow in 3-A) compared to the blood. While in the other three images, the carotid wall turns out to be of high intensity because of the application of black blood technology[12,13].
* In the 3D TOF image, the gray level of carotid blood can be remarkably distinguished from that of the surrounding area with a proper threshold, while in the other three images the gray level of the ROI and the surrounding area is close, thus Mimics cannot select out the carotid artery automatically.

With the analysis above, we can get the reason why Mimics have chosen the 3D TOF image sequence spontaneously and also deduce that the 3D model obtained is the real model of blood, which is of high intensity.

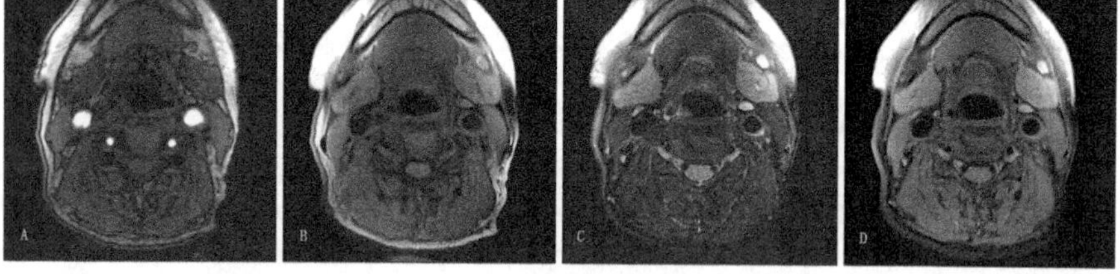

Fig. 3. The four typical image sequence of the MR images of carotid artery. A. 3D TOF image; B. T1-weighted image (T1WI); C. T2-weighted image (T2WI); D. Proton density weighted image (PDWI).

The 3D model of blood can be transformed into the smoothing 3D finite element model to perform the hemodynamic analysis in the future. However, when it comes to the fluid-solid coupling[14], this model is not sufficient due to lack of the carotid wall part. To make up for this weakness, we introduce a feasible solution below.

2.3 3D Reconstruction of the Carotid Wall

2.3.1 Determining the Thickness of Carotid Wall

Our solution is to extend the radius of the blood model with the thickness of carotid wall and then get the 3D model of wall by the Boolean Operation. Before the 3D extension, we need to determine the thickness of the wall.

The carotid wall, like other main artery wall, consists of three membranes---intma, media and adventitia, whose structures and functions vary. As the adventitia takes the least role, in clinical research the thickness of the carotid wall is always replaced by the carotid intima-media wall thickness(IMT). Currently, tremendous numbers of researchers are working on the relationship between carotid artery disease and IMT[15,16]. IMT , defined as the maximum distance between the tubal antrum-intima interface and the media-adventitia interface, can be directly detected with the non-invasive high resolution ultrasound in three locations---the remote end of carotid artery, the carotid artery bifurcation, the proximal end of internal carotid artery[17,18].We get that IMT of the patient we study (Cheng Lanying) equals to 0.82mm and plan to use this value as the extent of the 3D extension.

2.3.2 3D Extension and Boolean Operation

The output images exported by Mimics can be of STL format, which stores the information of the triangular patches on the surface of the 3D model. Magics software can read and process this model.

Taking the advantage of IMT and Magics, we can accomplish the 3D extension and Boolean Operation. Figure4 presents the schematic diagram of 3D extension and Boolean operation.

In the Boolean Operation, more than two objects can be transformed into a new shape by the set calculation of union, intersection or subtraction. In most cases, these three calculations can be realized upon the enclosed 3D model[19]. Here what we use is the calculation of subtraction. The steps are offered below[20]:

* To define two objects A and B. A represents the model of the carotid blood while B is implied the meaning of the artery model after extended which contains both the wall and the blood;
* Magics read A and B, and establish the information of the enclosed surface;
* To test whether or not there remains the intersection (our result is that A and B have no part of intersection);
* To judge the containing relationship between A and B(our conclusion is that B contains A);
* To go on with the calculation of subtraction(B-A), and finally get the 3D model of the carotid wall.

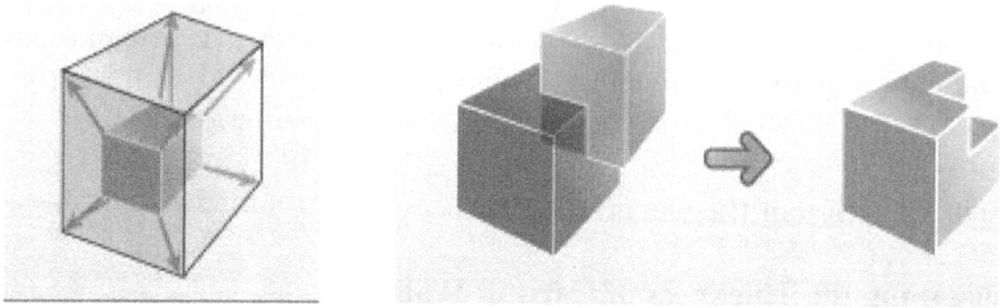

Fig. 4. The schematic diagrams of 3D extension and Boolean operation

3 Result and Discussion

With the high resolution MRI, we obtained the raw images of the carotid artery. After the 3D entity reconstruction of the carotid blood through Mimics, we successfully get the model of carotid wall with the help of Magics. The final result is shown in figure5.

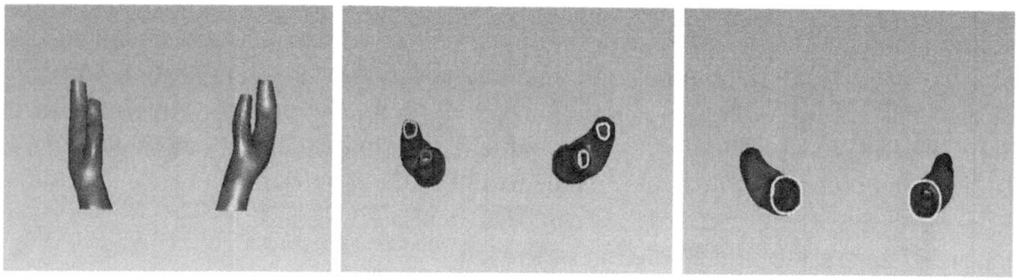

Fig. 5. The 3D model of carotid wall

The 3D model of carotid blood and wall will put foundations for the further study of carotid artery. One point we show pride on is the combination of 3D extension and Boolean operation, which Magics should absolutely take credit for.

However, one we should clarify is that in determining the IMT, we neglected the local difference of IMT as well as the change of IMT after the carotid artery bifurcation. This is where the weakness exists and what cannot be solved by software. Besides, the fact that we have replaced the thickness of carotid wall with IMT is more likely to arouse controversy. Thus, our model has no choice but to be the approximate model for the qualitative analysis, and the further optimization scheme should be proposed.

Acknowledgment

The Supplementary Class-based Program of Capital Medical University in 2010*; Basic and Clinical Cooperation Fund of Capital Medical University, No. 10JL51.

References

1. Zhang, C.G., Zhang, H.Q., Xie, J., et al.: Relationship between carotid atherosclerosis and ischemic cerebrovascular disease. Chinese Journal of Neurology 39(12), 832–835 (2006)
2. Zhang, Z., Xing, Y.: Carotid artery affection and cerebral stroke. Chin J. Geriatr Heart Brain Vessel Dis. 11(9), 645–648 (2009)

3. Ma, H., Han, Z.D., Li, Y.W., et al.: Image segmentation based on reduction of rough ret attributes. Fujian Computer (9), 128–129 (2006)
4. Liao, X.X., Liang, L.J.: Three-dimensional medical image reconstruction technology. China Medical Equipment 6(2), 21–23 (2009)
5. Chang, S.J., Shan, X.Z., Zhai, X.Y.: Serial section-based three-dimension reconstruction of kidney tissue. China J. Biomedical Engineering 16(1), 33–37 (2010)
6. Yang, L.L., Sun, W.L., Zhao, Q.: Study on CT model reconstruction technology of skull based on rapid prototyping. Modular Machine Tool and Automatic Manufacturing Technique (1), 41–45 (2007)
7. Qin, H.Q., Wang, Y.J.: Comparative study of predicting the clinical events caused by carotid plaques by high resolution MRI and ultrasonic test. In: Tiantan International Stroke Conference (2010)
8. Fu, M., Li, L., He, Y.S.: Mimics and three-dimensional medical image reconstruction. China Journal of Modern Medicine 20(19), 3030–3031, 3035 (2010)
9. Gu, F., Cui, Y.Q., Zeng, B., et al.: Three-dimensional reconstruction of craniofacial vascularity based on the data of CT strengthening scanning. Journal of Clinical Rehabilitative Tissue Engineering Research 14(9), 1531–1534 (2010)
10. Chen, H., Hong, H.S.: Vascular remodeling and carotid artery remodeling under hypertension. Journal of Clinical Rehabilitative Tissue Engineering Research 11(14), 2724–2728, 2740 (2007)
11. Zhu, J.W., Fan, L., Dong, Q.R., et al.: Computer-assisted design of individualized femoral prosthesis according to 3D reconstruction of CT images. Journal of Clinical Rehabilitative Tissue Engineering Research 14(35) (August 27, 2010)
12. Xu, X., Ju, H.Y., Wang, X.J., et al.: Quantitative evaluation of superficial calcification and stability of carotid atherosclerotic plaque by high-resolution 3T MRI. Academic Journal of Second Military Medical University 29(12), 1483–1486 (2008)
13. Han, J., Cai, J.M., Cai, Y.Q.: Study on the carotid atherosclerotic plaque on high-resolution MRI. Chinese Journal of Medical Imaging 14, 218–221 (2006)
14. Chen, W.C.: Exploitation of visual post-processor software system about the hemodynamic analysis by ANSYS. Beijing University of Technology, Beijing (2008)
15. Wang, L.: Relationshiop between carotid intima-media wall thickness and cerebral stroke. Chinese Journal of Cerebrovasc Disease 14(2), 73–75 (2010)
16. He, X.Y., Zhu, J.Q.: Ultrasound in detecting intima-media thickness and plaque development of carotid artery in essential hypertension. Journal of Shanxi Medicine 37(8), 981–982 (2008)
17. Liu, F., Yang, H.Y., Li, J.R., et al.: Correlation of carotid arterial intima-media thickness with cardiovascular disease assessed by ultrasound. Chinese Journal of Ultrasound Medicine 19(1), 30–32 (2003)
18. Liu, J.W., Zhang, X.Y., Li, N.F.: orrelation among homocysteine content and carotid artery thickness in hypertensive patients. Chinese Journal of Cardiovascular Rehabilitation Medicine 18(1), 32–35 (2009)
19. Bi, L., Wang, L.G., Chen, J.H., Feng, X.L.: Special Boolean operations of 3D mesh model. Journal of Huazhong University of Science and Technology (Nature Science Edition) 36(5), 82–85 (2008)
20. Guo, K.B., Zhang, L.C., Wang, C.J., et al.: Implementation of Boolean operations on STL models. Journal of Huazhong University of Science and Technology (Nature Science Edition) 34(7) (2006)

D&B: Two Additional Workflow Patterns

Yusheng Xu, Hongxin An, Zhixin Ma, and Li Liu

School of Information Science and Engineering of Lanzhou University,
Lanzhou, 730000, China
{xuyusheng,mazhx,liulnd}@lzu.edu.cn, an.hx@163.com

Abstract. Workflow system is one of the most popular applications for enterprise business processing and collaborating. With stable workflow engineering and mature design tool, workflow systems can be designed and maintained flexibly and economically. During the development of workflow systems, workflow specification is the most primary design task. Workflow pattern is a main technique for modeling workflow control flow. Based on real projects implement, two new workflow patterns, D&B (**D**eactivate and **B**y-pass patterns), are proposed. The semantic of D&B are not covered by other known workflow patterns. D&B patterns enrich the workflow model method and make workflow specifying in a more natural way.

Keywords: workflow system, business processing, workflow specification, workflow pattern, workflow language.

1 Introduction

Transaction processing are the primary application systems for enterprises, which produce millions of data records every day and host a large number of business transactions. These systems are mainly developed with navigation-driven models [10]. But most of them are designed based on the business of one department. And, it is a difficult task to exchange information among departments. The reason is that they were developed by different investors and can not be integrated. Each of them depicts only a part of the overall enterprise business logical picture. Currently, most of existing systems are designed according to their business processes, which should incorporate user and machine actives [5]. Workflow technology is an effective prescription and a mass of research attention are attracted. As to F. Leymann et al [4], workflow-based applications have many benefits such as removal of data dependency, removal of flow dependency, flexibility, reusability, integration, scalability etc. Business process modeling, workflow modeling and workflow management are the primary methods for workflow system development. Generally, workflow systems are complicated for different reasons, which include: (i) they are implemented manually in small-scale and large-scale organizations and may be more complicated with respect to the constraints imposed by the workflow. (ii)Workflows have many business rules which constraint business processing. (iii)Business rules may change frequently. (iv)Workflow engineering is mixed with user interfaces which add the designing difficulty. (v)Security is another factor that effects system implementation.

H. Tan and M. Zhou (Eds.): CSE 2011, Part I, CCIS 201, pp. 434–445, 2011.

As to Workflow Management Coalition, workflow is defined as "the automation of a business process, in whole or part, during which documents, information or tasks are passed from one participant to another for action, according to a set of procedural rules". During a workflow system development, workflow specification, workflow model, tools and workflow engine selection and designing of related task processing modules are the crucial design tasks. Previous research mainly focused on following directions: workflow modeling technique, workflow management systems/workflow engines, workflow data or user interface modeling and workflow security. And substantial fruit have been obtained. Several workflow modeling methods and according modeling language have been proposed, such as SCXML [15] (state machine notations), the Petri Nets [14] and colored Petri Nets [17], Business Process Modeling Notation (BPMN) [9], UML Activity Diagrams [8]. Influential workflow management systems that have been developed include Progression Model [12], Action Port Model [2], State Chart XML [15], etc. Based on these modeling methods, workflow system development platforms are designed accordingly. Usually, the development platforms are also called workflow engines. At the same time, user interface is another factor that affects applicability of workflow applications. Some user interface models have also been proposed, such as UsiXML [6], ExWM [1], ect. UsiXML [6] proposed an effectively user interface modeling method, which includes three main steps. By user interface pattern defining, task model incorporating and final user interface defining, concrete user interfaces can be gotten. Unlike other workflow model method, ExWM [1] models workflow as an information flow rather than a control one. Based on the information that each business object state displayed, captured and processed, the logical user interfaces are obtained. Workflow user interface is built upon these logical user interfaces and characteristic of concrete devices. At the same time, several workflow security modeling strategies emerged, such as Separation of duty (SoD) [11], Workflow Authorization Model (WAM) [13], Workflow Role Based Access control (W-RBAC) [7], etc. With these workflow modeling methods, commercially available workflow management systems (WFMS) and security strategies, high-quality workflow application systems have been developed in more and more domains.

Although, there are so many workflow modeling methods as previous mentioned, there is no a universal workflow theory or modeling concept. The absence of standard workflow concept leads to a formidable workflow specification process. Workflow patterns [16] proposed a uniformed way for workflow specification and defined 20 classical patterns. In this abstract patterns method, a workflow can be modeled as a graphics form with accurate syntax and semantic from the control flow view. In the implement of real workflow project, we find that there are still other cases that 20 classical ones can not cover up. And these particular situations inspired us to search for new workflow patterns. D&B (Deactivate and By-pass patterns) are the special patterns which are different from the 20 classical ones.

The rest of the paper is organized as follows. Section 2 introduces the basic concepts related to the workflow model and workflow patterns. Section 3 discusses the detailed D&B patterns. The comparison of D&B with similar patterns is depicted in section 4. Finally, conclusions can be found in section 5.

2 Primary Concepts

This section gives a basic formal workflow concept for the follow-up discussion. And then, 20 classical workflow patterns proposed in [16] are overviewed and some related patterns are described in more detail.

2.1 A General Formal Workflow Model

Workflow can be modeled in several ways, such as control flow, data or information flow, duties flow, etc. As previously mentioned, the control flow method is the general way for workflow modeling. Among these workflow models, the *LTS* tuple [10] is a formal representative.

Formally, a workflow *W* can be defined as a *LTS* tuple [10],

$$W =< S, E, G, \rightarrow, S_0, S_t, T_s, T, \tau > \tag{1}$$

where S is a set of states in W. E is a set of transition labels in W which mean events. G is a set of Boolean expressions to guard events condition. $\rightarrow \subseteq S \cdot S \cdot E \cdot G$ is a set of transition relations triggered by events if guarding statements are satisfied. $S_0 \subseteq S$ and $S_t \subseteq S$ are the sets of initial and terminal states respectively. T_s, T are the set of system tasks and non-system tasks. And, $\tau \subseteq S \cdot (T_s \cup T)$ is a set of relations mapping states to tasks.

The *LTS* tuple is just a formal model for depicting the control flow of workflow systems. For capturing workflow specifications, there are still other things that to be defined in more details. For example, the time each task is invoked, the relationship among two or more transitions that from same system state. Workflow patterns provide an accurate way for capturing workflow characteristics at design time.

2.2 Overview of Workflow Patterns

As to [16], a workflow pattern is defined as a way for indicating workflow requirements. Workflow pattern is an abstract from a concrete form which keeps recurring in specific nonarbitrary contexts and is independent from the workflow languages or implementation solutions.

In [16], six categories are proposed which include basic control flow patterns, advanced branching and synchronization patterns, structural patterns, multiple instances patterns, state-based patterns and cancellation patterns. Table I is the overview of the 20 classical workflow patterns and the six categories are detailed as follows.

1. Basic control flow patterns are used to depict the basic constructs that model sequential, parallel and conditional routing.
2. Advanced branching and synchronization patterns allow for more advanced types of splitting and joining behaviors such as **AND-join** or **XOR-join** depending on the context.
3. Structural patterns include patterns that allow for a less rigid structure.

4. Patterns involving multiple instances describe the situations that several instances must to be instantiated in the context of a single case.
5. State-based patterns are the patterns that capture both of states and activities or events.
6. Cancellation patterns are about the situation that the occurrence of an event may lead to the cancellation of activities

Table 1. Overview of the 20 classical workflow patterns

Category	Workflow patterns
Basic control flow patterns	P1-Sequence, P2-Parallel split, P3-Synchronization, P4-Exclusive choice, P5-Simple merge
Advanced branching and synchronization patterns	P6-Multi-choice, P7-Synchronizing merge, P8-Multi-merge, P9-Discriminator
Structural patterns	P10-Arbitrary cycles, P11-Implicit termination
Multiple instances patterns	P12-Multiple instances without synchronization P13-Multiple instances with a priori design time knowledge, P14-Multiple instances with a priori runtime knowledge P15-Multiple instances without a priori runtime knowledge
State-based patterns	P16-Deferred choice, P17-Interleaved parallel routing, P18-Milestone
Cancellation patterns	P19-Cancel activity, P20-Cancel case

2.3 Related Workflow Patterns

D&B patterns are the relationships between two transitions, events, tasks or paths. In order for following comparison, the similar workflow patterns are described in more details. For their definition, please reference to [16].

P2 parallel split or named AND-split is a point in the workflow process where a single thread control splits into multiple threads of control which can be executed in parallel or in any order. The multiple split threads of control may or may not have corresponding guard conditions. Fig1(a) depicts the case which split has no guard condition.

P4 exclusive choice or named XOR-split is a point in the workflow process where, based on a decision or workflow control data, one and only one of several control flow branches is chosen. Fig1(b) is the simplest XOR-split case. The split decision may be made in state S1, where exclusive transition condition is calculated. At the other side, the XOR-split may be realized by the guard conditions corresponding to each transition. In the second case, workflow designers should ensure that only one guard condition is satisfied for every workflow instances.

P6 multi-choice or named OR-split is a workflow process point where, based on a decision or workflow control data, a number of branches may be chosen. Fig1(c) shows the OR-split situation. The decision making is similar to XOR-split, but multiple branches may be chosen this time.

P16 Deferred choice pattern is a point in the workflow process where one of several branches is chosen, but the choice is not made explicitly and several alternatives are offered to the environment. That is to say the choice is delayed until the processing in one of the alternative branches is actually started, and once the environment activates one of the branches the other alternative branches are withdrawn. Fig1(d) depicts the semantic of deferred choice pattern.

P19 Cancel activity pattern is a workflow process in which an enabled activity may be disabled, i.e. a thread waiting for the execution of an activity is removed.

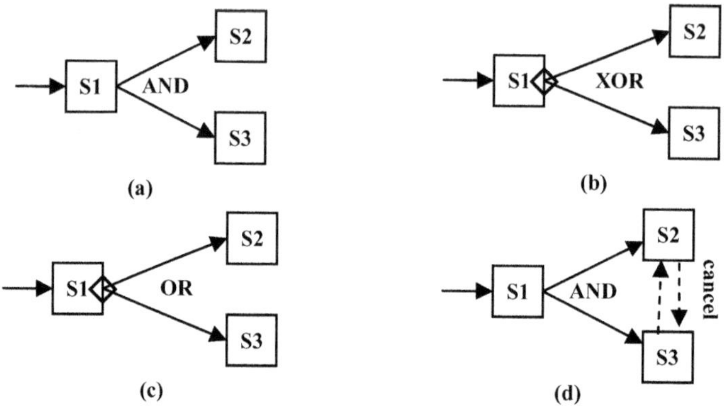

Fig. 1. Related workflow patterns

3 D&B Workflow Patterns

This section expatiates upon deactivate pattern and by-pass pattern. They are described through their semantic, applicable conditions, examples of business situations and implementation solutions.

3.1 The Deactivate Pattern

Semantic. Let s_s be a state of a workflow *W* and S_n be the set of states that follow the state s_s. That is to say, for every state $s \in S_n$, there is a transition *t* that transform from s_s to s. $s' \in S_n$ is a special state that once s' is active or executing, all other states in S_n should be deactivated. Here $s'' \in S_n$ is deactivated by s' means that for the same workflow instance: 1) if s'' has not been activated, it can not be activated for ever even its guard condition is satisfied; 2) if s'' is just in activated situation, it must be deactivated or stopped executing and its unfinished processing may or may not be cleared; 3) if s'' has already been activated and finished its execution process and some processing result has been produced, it must be flagged as deactivated and its result is unreadable. Once s'' is deactivated, its result is useless if it has in situation 2) and 3), just like it has not been activated. Fig2 shows the semantic of deactivate pattern.

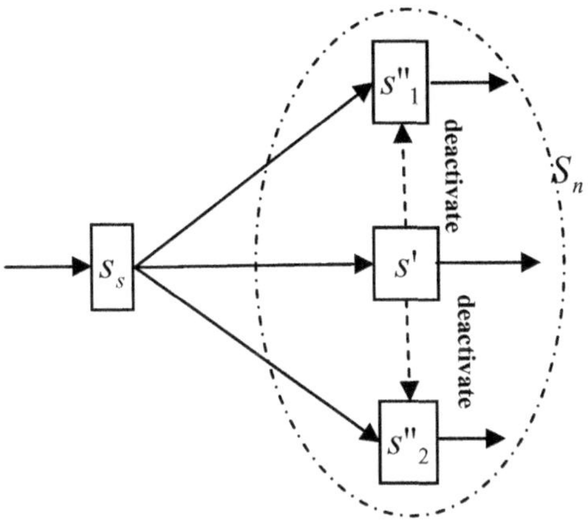

Fig. 2. The semantic of deactivate workflow pattern

Similar workflow patterns: P2 parallel split, P4 exclusive split, P6 multi-choice and P16 deferred choice.

Applicable situations and business examples. As previous description, s' is a state that has highest priority in S_n. Once s' has the control of executing, it takes over all other states in S_n, and their executing results may be overcastted by s'. All workflow systems that have similar situation may be modeled by the deactivate pattern. Some business examples may include:

- In the tax counting workflow system, the sum of tax for an ordinary enterprise is counted by tax code with according counting rules. The counting process is executed by several parallel threads each of which have an according workflow state. But for a special enterprise, whose tax sum should be derated according tax policies, the counting process is executed by high priority thread which deactivates all other parallel ones. Even when all other parallel threads have finished, their results can not be readable, that is to say, they are covered over by the high priority thread.
- In a public bidding of constructing project application, the tenderee of the project should pay for the bidding procedure. The fee is calculated according to the attributes and total cost of the project. But in special condition, for example, the project is supported by the government, the fee may be reduced. In this situation, a high priority state is needed to model the reducing behavior, and it is an applicable situation for the deactivate pattern.
- A business trips approval application, which comes from [16], is another example. In this example, there are two ways to approve a business trip. Generally, the approval is made by both the project manager (activity A11) and the financial manager (activity A12). The other selection is the department manager makes the trip approval (activity A2). But the department manager has higher priority, he may deactivate the trip approval made by the project manager and the financial manager. The activities A11 and A12 are executed sequentially and the choice between A2

on the one hand and A11 and A12 on the other hand is implicit, i.e., at the same time both activity A2 and activity A11 are offered to the department head and project manager respectively. At this moment, each activity can be selected. But, once the department manager starts to approve, he deactivates the other selection even the trip approval has been made by the project manager and financial manager. At the other side, if A11 is selected (the project manager makes the approval), A2 can not be deactivated by A11 or A12.

Implementation of the deactivate pattern. There are three possible implementation solutions, which are described as follows:

- Since activity (*A1*) of s' has higher priority than other states in S_n (whose activities denoted as $\{Ai\}$), change *A1* and $\{Ai\}$ into a sequent flow pattern. In this case, s' has the selection chance earlier than all the other states in S_n. Once s' is active (*A1* is executed), all other states in S_n has no chance to be active ($\{Ai\}$ can not be executed), thus all other states in S_n are deactivated. At the other side, if s' decides not to be activated or a given length of time passed, all other states in S_n get their chance to be activated. Fig3(a) shows this implementation solution, where the mark ***B*** and the arrow near state s' mean the by-pass of control flow.
- Similar to the previous solution, changes the deactivate pattern into a sequent one. This time, let all other states in S_n occur before s'. That is to say, let all $\{Ai\}$ to execute firstly. Then passes the control to s', whose active can decide to be activated or not. If *A1* executes, it overwrites the results of all $\{Ai\}$, thus all other states in S_n are invalidated and *A1* is the last process thread. Fig3(b) depicts this solution. In this picture, there is a dashed arrow from s' to s_1, which means the control flow by-pass. This solution makes s' as an auditing node. If all things are right, s' makes no changes. Otherwise, it will process business logic in its own way and A1 is executed. The semantic is same as that of the deactivate pattern.
- All the previous two solutions implement the deactivate pattern by reconstructing the workflow model. Thus the performance of the workflow system may be debased. The reason is that there may be a period of waiting time before s' forwards the control flow. The third solution implements the deactivate pattern through a primitive named *Deactivate()*. Fig3(c) describes the pseudocode of *Deactivate()*. The meanings of all statements is clear, no more explaining is needed. The choice statement withdraws the results of all other states (through the *API Withdraw()*) or informs all other states (with the *API Flag()*) that state s' has already processed the business and there is nothing to be done for all other states. The noticeable things is that the *API Deactivate()* can be invoked either before or after the business processing logic of state s'.

In the first two implement solutions, a dashed line arrow with a mark ***B*** is used. This symbol means by-pass control flow. And this is the semantic of the by-pass pattern, which is described in details in the following part.

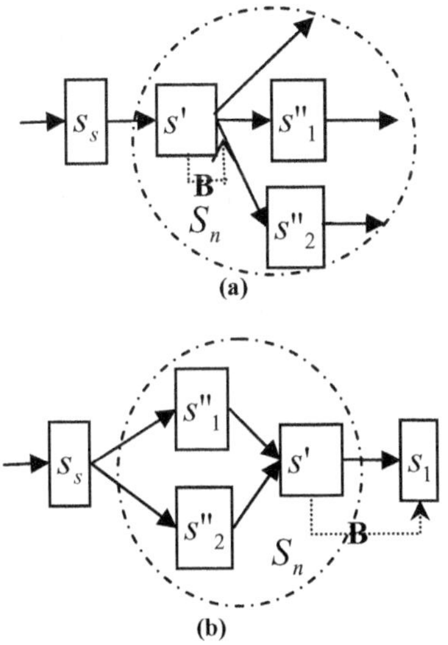


```
# Deactivate all other states
# Input: S_n and s'
# Name: Deactivate

Void Deactivate( S_n , s' )
  FOR ALL s'' IN S_n \ s'
    IF Active( s'' )OR actived( s'' )
      Withdraw( s'' )    (*)
    ELSE
     Flag( s'' )      (**)
```

(c)

Fig. 3. Implementation solutions for the deactivate pattern

3.2 The By-Pass Pattern

Semantic. Suppose s be a state of workflow W , and u is a user who has the authority to interact with the state s . The by-pass pattern is a workflow node s whose activity is optional, but the control flow is necessary. Whether the activity is chosen may depend on several independent conditions as followings: 1) the user u , who takes charge of the node, decides to give up the activity; 2) for a long period of time, the activity has not been initialed, thus its chance is lost; 3) some other nodes inform it to by-pass its activity. No matter which condition occurs, the node forwards the control flow to the next node directly without its own activity executing. Fig 4 depicts the graphic symbols to model these three conditions.

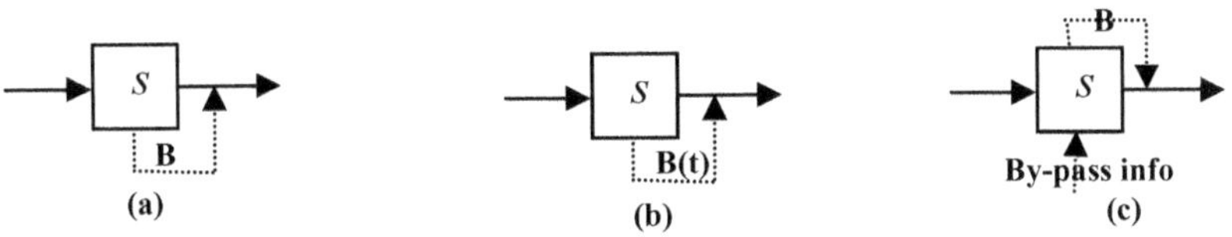

Fig. 4. Semantic of by-pass pattern

Similar workflow patterns: P19 the cancel activity pattern.

Applicable situations and business examples. The by-pass pattern is a useful pattern for modeling the case in which a node may give up its business processing while forwarding workflow control flow of the same instance. Following are several applicable business examples:

- In the review process of a scientific paper submitted to an international conference, the activity review paper is instantiated several times depending on the content of the paper, and the availability of referees. Only if all reviews have been returned, processing is continued. This is a similar example as in [16]. But in reality, for some reasons, referees may not review the paper. The next processing is waiting for the returning of all reviews while one of them may not be returned for ever. In this case the by-pass pattern is a good solution in which each activity of reviewing has a separate state. After waiting for a long time, the state can be by-passed if there is no reviewing is returned.
- Another example comes from construction drawings reviewing. Once the design finishes, a construction drawing is submitted to the professional organization for reviewing. The reviewing process, which may continue until all design flaws are improved for the same review instance, consists of structure reviewing, architecture reviewing, electric reviewing, heating & ventilating reviewing, water supply reviewing and investigation reviewing. After the first round of review, the design is improved according to the review results. In the second round of review, not all six professional reviewing are needed. In this case, some of review activities must be by-passed, and the by-pass pattern is an applicable modeling method.

Implementation of the by-pass pattern. Unlike others, the by-pass pattern can not be re-constructed through existent ones. One possible way is to separate the by-pass node s into manage and business parts, which are denoted as $s.manage$ and $s.activity$ respectively. The by-pass strategies are implemented in the manage part while the business process logic are in the business part. Once the node s gets the control, it checks for whether it has received the decision from user u or for by-pass command from other nodes. If the status has by-pass signal by-pass takes place immediately, otherwise the control flow is forwarded to $s.manage$. $s.activity$ can only get control under the node s is not by-pass. Once $s.manage$ gets of control, it waits for decision from user u or for by-pass command from other nodes. And at the same time, it initializes a timer to set up the waiting time parameter.

4 Comparation

As previous mentioned, there several similar patterns. Among these patterns, P2 parallel split, P4 exclusive split and P6 multi-choice just have similar fork structure to the deactivate pattern and the semantic between them are very different. Thus they are ignored. This part only describes their semantic similarity.

4.1 Deactivate Pattern and Deferred Choice Pattern

With semantic analysis, deactivate pattern and deferred choice pattern have key similarities:

- They have same structures. Both of these two patterns have a fork structure in workflow model and withdrawing activity occurs among these forks.
- Their choices are all delayed. In the fork structure, which branch is chosen not depends upon forked node but upon the fork branches. The choice is not made explicitly and several alternatives are offered to the environment. The choice is delayed until the processing in one of the alternative branches is actually started.
- There may be withdrawn states. In both of the two patterns, once one branch is chosen, all the other branches may be withdrawn or canceled and may not have control flow for ever for the same workflow instance.

At the other side, the two patterns have distinctly different semantic meanings.

- The relationship among the branches is different. In the deactivate pattern, one branch has higher priority than others. Which branch is chosen depends on the activity of the high priority workflow node. In the deferred choice pattern, each branch may make the choice decision. There are no different priorities among the branches therefore.
- Whether the deactivate activity occurs is different. In deactivate pattern, there may be two and more parallel branches which perform their business logic as long as the higher priority branch is not activated. The same thing can not be occurred in the deferred choice pattern. Once one of the alternative branches is actually started, all the other branches are canceled.
- Which branch can send deactivate or cancel command is different. In the deactivate pattern, only the higher priority branch can deactivate or cancel other branches. All other branches can not send deactivate or cancel command. On the contrary, every branch may deactivate all other branches in the deferred choice pattern.
- Which time deactivate or cancel activity can occur is different. In the deactivate pattern, the deactivate activity may occur at any time before the next merge node getting control flow. Even if all the activities of other nodes have been completed, the higher priority node can deactivate them. Unlike this, the cancel can only occur before all the activities start of other nodes in deferred choice pattern. All the branches compete to start their activities, and the first one becomes a winner and all other branches must be cancelled.

4.2 By-Pass Pattern and Cancel Activity Pattern

The most obvious similarity between by-pass pattern and cancel activity pattern is that both of their activities contribute nothing to workflow instances, no matter whether the activity is started. At same time, these two workflow patterns have plenty of differences in their semantic.

- The inducement factors are different. As previously described, the by-pass pattern has three types of possible inducement factors which include giving up business

logic actively, overtime of timer or receiving a by-pass command. Unlike by-pass-pattern, the node in cancel activity pattern can only passively wait for cancel signal from the environment.
- Whether their activities are started is different. In by-pass pattern, the activity has not started when the according node is by-passed. On the contrary, when the node receives the cancel command in cancel activity pattern, its activity may have been started, or even it has been finished its activity.
- How to pass control flow is different. When by-pass occurs, the corresponding node forwards the workflow control to the next node directly without its own activity executing. Different from by-pass pattern, how to process control flow is not defined in cancel activity pattern. The cancel activity pattern just defines that the node's activity must be cancelled, and just that.

5 Conclusions

Workflow system is one of the most popular applications for enterprise business processing and collaborating. Even having stable workflow management systems and mature design tools, workflow application development is still an untoward task. During the development of workflow systems, workflow specification is the most primary design task. Workflow pattern is a main technique for modeling workflow control flow. Based on experience of real projects implement, two new workflow patterns, D&B (Deactivate and By-pass patterns), are proposed in this paper. The semantic of D&B patterns are not covered by other known workflow patterns. D&B patterns enrich the workflow model method and make workflow specifying in a more natural way.

Acknowledgements

This work is supported by the Fundamental Research Funds for the Central Universities under grant No. lzujbky-2010-92.

References

1. An, H., Xu, Y., Ma, Z., Liu, L.: Integrating User Interfaces by Business Object States. In: The 2nd International Conference on Information Science and Engineering, Hangzhou, China, December 4-6, vol. 4, pp. 2900–2903 (2010)
2. Carlsen, S.: Conceptual modeling and composition of flexible workflow models, PhD thesis, Norway: Norwegian University of Science and Technology (1997)
3. Stohr, E.A., Leon Zhao, J.: Workflow Automation: Overview and Research Issues. Information Systems Frontiers 3(3), 281–296 (2001)
4. Leymann, F., Roller, D.: Workflow-based Applications. IBM Systems Journal 36(1), 102–123 (1997)
5. Guerrero García, J., Vanderdonckt, J., González Calleros, J.M.: FlowiXML: a step towards designing workflow management systems. Int. J. Web Engineering and Technology 4(2), 163–182 (2008)

6. García, J.G., Vanderdonckt, J., Calleros, J.M.G., Winckler, M.: Towards a Library of Workflow User Interface Patterns. In: Graham, T.C.N. (ed.) DSV-IS 2008. LNCS, vol. 5136, pp. 96–101. Springer, Heidelberg (2008)
7. Wainer, J., Barthelmess, P., Kumar, A.: W-RBAC: A Workflow security Model Incorporating Controlled Overriding of Constraints. International Journal of Cooperative Information Systems 12(4), 455–485 (2003)
8. Dumas, M., ter Hofstede, A.H.M.: UML Activity Diagrams as a Workflow Specification Language. In: Gogolla, M., Kobryn, C. (eds.) UML 2001. LNCS, vol. 2185, pp. 76–90. Springer, Heidelberg (2001)
9. Object Management Group. Business process modeling notation specification, final adopted specification (February 6, 2006)
10. Barna, P., Frasincar, F., Houben, G.-J.: A workflow-driven design of web information systems. In: Proceedings of the 6th International Conference on Web Engineering, vol. 263, pp. 321–328 (2006)
11. Sandhu, R.S.: Separation of duties in computerized information systems. In: The Proceedings of IFIP WG11.3 Workshop on Database Security, Halifax, UK, pp. 179–190 (September 1990)
12. Stavness, N., Schneider, K.: Supporting flexible business processes with a progression model. In: The Proceedings of the First International Workshop on Making Model-based User Interface Design Practical: Usable and Open Methods and Tools MBUI 2004, Funchal, January 13. CEUR Workshop Proceedings, vol. 103 (2004)
13. Atluri, V., Huang, W.K.: An Authorization Model for Workflows. In: Martella, G., Kurth, H., Montolivo, E., Hwang, J. (eds.) ESORICS 1996. LNCS, vol. 1146, pp. 44–64. Springer, Heidelberg (1996)
14. Van der Aalst, W., van Hee, K.: Workflow Management. Models, Methods, and Systems, March 1. The MIT Press, Cambridge (2004) ISBN-10: 0262720469
15. W3C, Working draft, World Wide Web Consortium (July 5, 2005), `http://www.w3.org`
16. Van Der Aalst, W.M.P., Ter Hofstede, A.H.M., Barros, A.P.: P Barros, Workflow Patterns. Distributed and Paralled Databases 14, 5–51 (2003)
17. Lu, Y., Zhang, L., Sun, J.: Using colored Petri nets to model and analyze workflow with separation of duty constraints. Int. J. Adv. Manuf. Technol. 40, 179–192 (2009), doi:10.1007/s00170-007-1316-1

CEA Programming Based on Jbeam Software for Automobile Measurement Data Processing

Aimin Du[1], Zhongpan Zhu[1], Yajie Zhang[1], and Rui Liang[2]

[1] Tongji university, 201804 Shanghai, China
[2] AMS GmbH China, 201203 Shanghai, China
{duaimin1971,zzpan2006,rayrocket1023}@yahoo.com.cn,
rui.liang@jbeam.com

Abstract. Standard of Component based model for Evaluation and Analysis of measurement data(CEA) founded by ASAM is introduced in this paper, and then some flexible CEA assemblies of measurement and evaluation applications based on JBEAM software is analyzed and reviewed before the process of CEA programming is expounded. At last, combined the study and programming of CEA application in automobile industry, the meaning of CEA application is summarized and further study on CEA application and programming is prospected.

Keywords: CEA programming, automobile industry, foreign standard specification, measurement data processing.

1 Introduction

As the increasing automobile market and stricter environment legal protection, automobile products upgrade and vehicle functionality improvement requirements are increasing quickly, which lead to an exponential increase in technology research and testing functionality improvement. In order to fulfill these requirements, different kinds of Computer Aided Testing (CAT) cells made up of equipment and software from multiple suppliers are widely used in automobile manufacturers. ASAM sets up standardizations which can dramatically reduce the amount of time and money required to develop the interfaces among all these different equipments and software products and to maintain these interfaces even while testing requirements continue to expand [1, 2].

The ASAM-CEA standard was founded in October 1998 in order to define a framework as well as basic functions which enable a flexible assembly of measurement and evaluation applications based on different functional components. The main technical objective is combining the components of several different manufacturers to a specific application which means that the software based on different technology could be easily customized and smoothly integrated for different application.

2 CEA Architecture

The CEA architecture focuses on the usage which includes running tests, gathering and evaluating measurement data and producing plots, reports etc. from it – of

H. Tan and M. Zhou (Eds.): CSE 2011, Part I, CCIS 201, pp. 446–453, 2011.

desktop-based applications usually equipped with a comfortable graphical user interface (GUI). The basic composition of the CEA architecture contains CEA components, CEA bus, CEA items and CEA services which are illustrated in Figure 1 and Figure 2 [1, 3].

Importer, worker, viewer and exporter all belong to CEA component, and they can be divided into two categories by data flow, producer and consumer. Producer component can get and produce measurement data and send them in forms of items to CEA bus while consumer component can get appropriate input items from CEA bus for analysis and review.

The CEA bus works as a "backbone" of an individual CEA application decoupling the single functional CEA components from each other. CEA standardization enables those individually and independently developed components work together via such a bus.

CEA services offer functionality fundamental to components and test tools. For example, the help service gives standardized access to help information with regard to a component. The item factory service allows a component to create new, empty data objects that can be used for inter-component communication.

CEA item is defined as interfaces access data as well as services which are communicated between respectively CEA components. When a CEA application is used, some data is imported by importer, and the data is registered to the bus as an item, then the bus informs all the consumer components of the event, so the consumer components can seek available items from the bus. Generally worker component which is both consumer and producer can get items sent from importer to bus for data processing and create new items to the bus, the bus sent a listener event to viewer or exporter, the viewer or exporter can get the items created by worker for data visualization and further analysis by test engineer. After all the available CEA items are gotten by the suitable components, the communication takes place between items directly without the bus, the measurement data flow can be seen in figure 2.

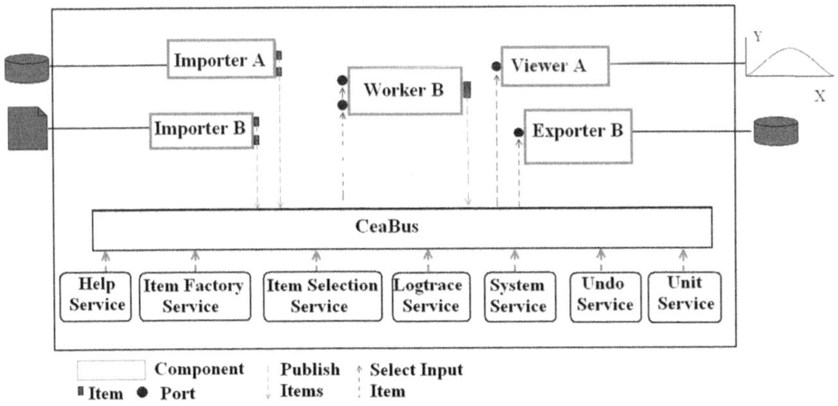

Fig. 1. CEA overall architecture [1]

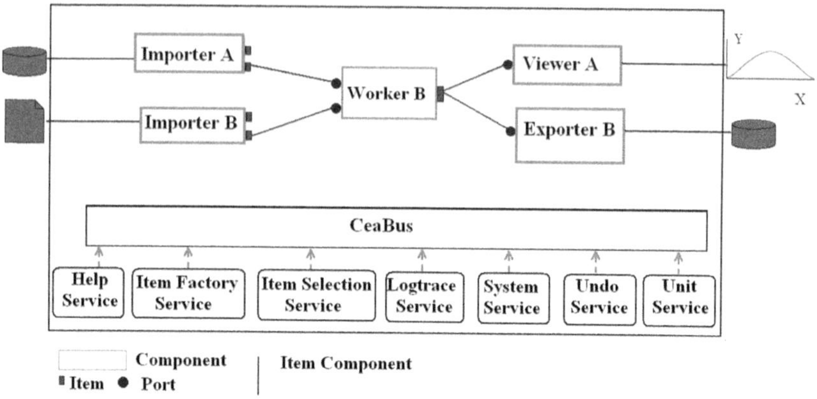

Fig. 2. CEA overall architecture (running time) [1]

3 CEA Application in Automobile Industry

AMS is the specialist for measurement and analysis of engineering data, especially data from test and simulation. Their data processing software JBEAM, a platform independent tool for data acquisition, analysis and visualization, is also a CEA Framework for desktop usage which can integrate other CEA components provided by other software vendors or users. CEA applications based on JBEAM in the abroad automobile industry have been taken and definitely show many advantages [4].

1) MDM system of Volkswagen R&D metrology department, as shown in figure 3
There are almost 100 different measurement types of data for Volkswagen to handle which means a multitude of different measurement data import modules and corresponding graphical display modules should be created, In the long run, the number of needed evaluation modules may even be increased. For this, a measuring data management (MDM) system was created with JBEAM embedded to solve this problem. JBEAM works as a CEA engine to create all import modules as CEA data producers and create all display components as the CEA viewer and connect them together via the ASAM CEA bus, so the MDM system can offer the option to evaluate certain data types and when some new types are added, the number of available evaluation modules would increase accordingly.

2) TestXplorer of Kratzer [5]
During the testing process huge amounts of digital data are generated, which have to be stored safely over long periods of time. Kratzer Automation provides the test management solution testXplorer, designed for data and information handling in test

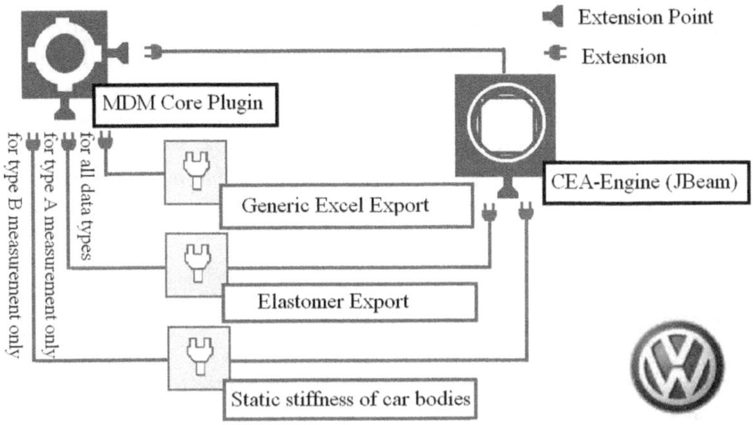

Fig. 3. A look on how the MDM plug in approach [5]

facilities. The CEA based client-server architecture of JBEAM is integrated directly into the testXplorer application window, and testXplorer and JBEAM exchange data through a shared caching area, where duplicates of the test data objects are copied for evaluation. Hence, the original fixed content data stay unchanged and safely managed in the testXplorer data store. Based on the CEA components, the two software products are easily and smoothly integrated for either efficient data processing or long term storage of test data, measurements, images, information and documents.

3) Multi-device data acquisition system of Magna Auteca, as shown in figure 4

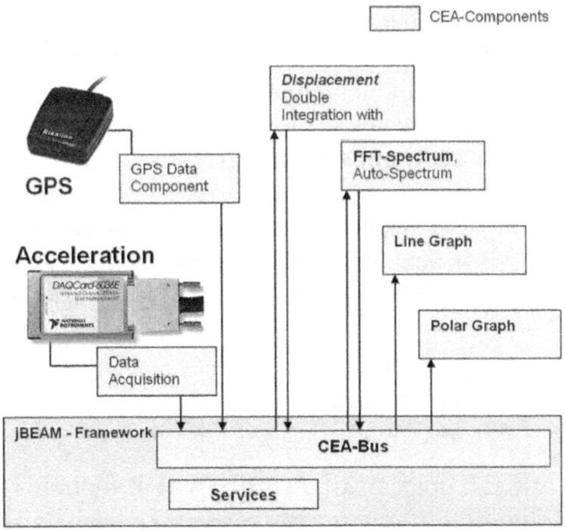

Fig. 4. Multi-device data acquisition system of Magna Auteca [5]

Low vibration of outside mirrors of cars is essential for good backward visibility, so vibrations is usually need to be measured with small acceleration sensors on the moving cars. Magna Auteca, one of the mirror suppliers for automobile manufactures, together with AMS designed a multi-device data acquisition a system based on JBEAM to solve the complete working process from data acquisition to data analysis and finally to measurement reporting.

As JBEAM software is completely written in java language, it is much better to build CEA components in java programming environment. The process of CEA programming is expounded in the next section.

4 CEA Programming

CEA programming uses the technology of object-oriented programming (OOP) and Java's basic control mechanisms [4]. The software Eclipse is chosen for CEA programming environment, CEA files have the suffix ". cea" and contain several files compressed with the zip algorithm. The structure of CEA files is shown in table 1.

Table 1. The structure of CEA files

Files	Description
Compiled Java class file (*.class)	A main component class contains all methods to do the main work of the CEA component, implenents the CEA interfaces or extends Jbeam class. A editor class called by the main components "cea2Customize" method provides the ability to edit the components input values (e.g. parameters for import / calculation)
Xml file(*.xml)	Describing the CEA component (e.g. the menu location, name of the component, manufacturer information and localized component information)
MANIFEST.MF	Containing Java specific information about this component (e.g. the main class although this component must not be executable as a standalone Java application)
Resource files	Some resource files like images, icons or language resources etc.

The specification of CEA consists of 7 CORBA IDL modules each contains certain interfaces comprising the definitions for the respective basic concept of CEA's architecture: Cea2Component, Cea2Bus, Cea2Items, Cea2Services, Cea2Events, Cea2Types, Cea2Excertions. Those modules define a number of interfaces and functions with certain grammars necessary to build up CEA applications. Figure 5 shows a part code of the main class implementing CEA interfaces in a CEA programming example, TongjiImporter.java.

```
/**
 * @author zhuzhongpan
 *
 */
package com.tongji.importer;

import java.io.BufferedReader;

public class TongjiImporter implements Cea2ProducerIF,
Cea2BusEventListenerIF {
    private Cea2BusIF cea2Bus;
    private String componentName = "Tongjiimport";
```

Fig. 5. TongjiImporter.java

Besides, AMS provided JBEAM as CEA framework and several JBEAM class to help customers to create CEA components without implementing each CEA interface, in less code and less defect possibilities. Figure 6 shows a part code of the main class extending Jbeam class in a programming example, TongjiImporter2.java. Either TongjiImporter2.java or TongjiImporter.java builds up the same importer components into JBEAM software as shown in figure 7.

```
/**
 * @author zhuzhongpan
 *
 */
package com.tongji.importer;

import java.io.BufferedReader;

public class TongjiImporter2 extends AbstractCea2Producer {

    private File importFile = null;
    private boolean inputvalid = false;
```

Fig. 6. TongjiImporter1.java

The Function of TongjiImporter component is to import a given text file which contains cam profile parameters (cam revolution, the damping part wrap angle, valve lift at the end of the damping part) in special former. To design a good lift curve of the damping part, three basic parameters should be selected carefully: the damping part wrap angle, valve lift at the end of the damping part and the final velocity. So another CEA component is built up to calculate the value of the final velocity, whose editor dialog box embedded in JBEAM is shown in figure 8.

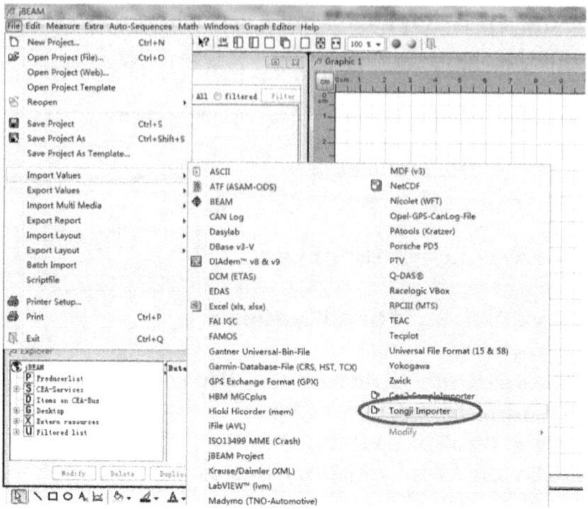

Fig. 7. Importer components

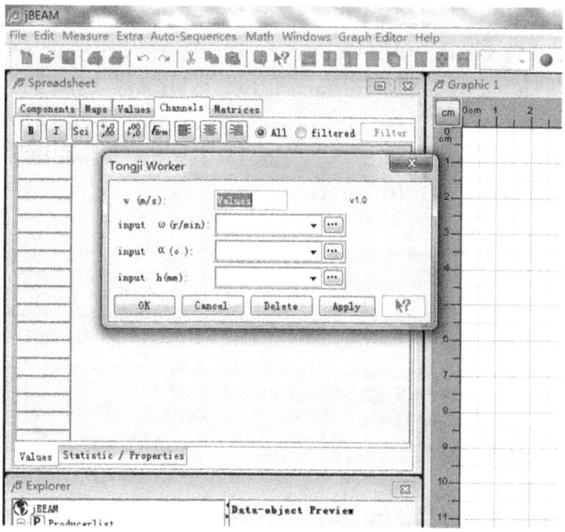

Fig. 8. TongjiWorker Component

5 Conclusions and Future Work

In a conclusion, the CEA applications bring great convenience to the whole process from measurement data acquisition to the data processing and visualization, and finally to the data storage. Using open CEA based software guarantees an easy adoption to new situation by only adding new components as plug-ins. The composition of different CEA components allows the quick development of new, highly, flexible applications that reduce maintenance and administration cost. CEA components can be produced by many different suppliers which mean that the special projects of different enterprises can easily integrate third party components, thus improving development time and economic cost.

CEA standard specification has not been widely used in the domestic automobile industry. Further study should be taken on developing some special CEA assemblies of measurement and evaluation applications for automobile technical research and testing functionality improvement.

References

1. Göhler, I.: ASAM CEA Components for Evaluation and Analysis Programmer's Guide.s. ASAM (December 2009)
2. Wang, Y., Wang, Z.: The Introduction of ASAM ODS standard (Chinese). In: Academic Symposium of Aviation Test Measurement Technology, pp. 181–184. Urumqi (2007)
3. New software version addresses ASAM standard. J. EE 49(5) (2010)
4. Flachenecker, C.: The development and use of common software interfaces in test bed environments. J. International Journal of Vehicle Design 1(2) (1999)
5. Electronic Documents, http://www.asam.net

Improving Teaching Efficiency with Heuristic Teaching Method in Information Technology

Shaoxi Wang[1], Ru Han[2], Meng Zhang[2], Xiaoya Fan[2], and Shenbin Zhang[2]

[1] College of software and microelectronics,
Northwestern Polytechnical University, Xi'an, 710072, China
shxwang@nwpu.edu.cn
[2] Department of computer, Northwestern Polytechnical University, Xi'an, 710072, China

Abstract. Heuristic teaching method is one of the most important teaching methods nowadays. In the paper, the existing problems using tradition teaching method in information technology have been analyzed. Then, paper shows the procedure of applying heuristic teaching in information technology, which includes searching close relationship, explaining definition, creating problem and teaching problem solving idea. Finally, the specific application in information technology is given. Results shows the teaching efficiency and effectiveness has been improved.

Keywords: Heuristic teaching method, information technology, effectiveness, efficiency.

1 Introduction

Information technology is an international recognized important subject and the key to the national development in economy and technology. It has a wide application in most cases. For students who majored in information technology and computer, they are necessary to master the basic concepts in information technology, the basic principles, the basic methods and techniques, to familiar with the design procedure. Moreover, the most important thing is that student must have known how to use the basic knowledge and methods to solve practical application problems. All the abilities of students have been reached with course-listening and project-working ways in and after classes.

Western heuristic teaching method was originated from Socrates who initiated the teaching mode of "teachers ask, students answer". A distinctive feature of this mode was that teachers were the decisive factor in the process of teaching and learning, who raised the questions at the very beginning and gave conclusions in the end. On the contrary, oriental style of heuristic teaching method based itself on the principle that students put forward their puzzles and then asked the teachers for advice. Heuristic teaching method is one of the most important teaching methods nowadays, which has been widely applied in area of foreign language, history, mathematics, computer experiments, etc. And it has been proved of great success in the teaching process abroad.

In the paper, the reason that students have low learning efficiency had been analyzed in traditional teaching method. Then the heuristic teaching method was introduced to show how to improve the efficiency. In the rest part, the paper has been organized

H. Tan and M. Zhou (Eds.): CSE 2011, Part I, CCIS 201, pp. 454–458, 2011.

below. Part 2 will give the analysis of present information technology courses teaching methods and problems. Part 3 describes heuristic teaching method. Part 4 demonstrates using heuristic teaching method in teaching information technology courses. Part 5 makes a conclusion.

2 Traditional Teaching Method and Problem

In China, there is an ancient great educator named Confucius, who was greatly respected by a lot of Chinese people, especially ancient Chinese people. More than 2000 years ago, Confucius had a lot of things to say about how to teach and how to study. Another Chinese educator Han Yu said, "A teacher is to propagate the doctrines of the ancient sages, give academic instructions, and remove doubts in life". Traditional teaching is the learning process, in which the teachers will explain clearly the main content of the materials, make sure students understand the concepts, principles, methods and ideals of information technology. Students can only complete the process in a passive position; however, the process will be useful for student to master the important points. What's more, many teachers begin to assign several projects or case study which will be finished after class by students alone or in a group, which is a very popular and effective teaching way, and can promote students to review in-class contexts and to familiar with its application.

However, many problems exist in practice for Chinese students who are taught by traditional teaching method nowadays. First, students may feel boring in class when teaching process last long time. In the case, students will may doze during listening when teaching give more and more concepts or principle according to teaching materials. Especially for class arranged in the first or last class in a day, students are more prone to drowsihead and cannot pay their attention to the teaching. Second, not all case study or projects can be enough supported in university. For information technology courses in computer science, finishing projects need setup lab for students with some lab sets, such as SUN workstation, FPGA broad, etc. Moreover, some students always are lazy and have no positive action to work on the projects after classes. Therefore, case study or projects method cannot bring promising effect on those students' study. Last, there are some other problems in teaching of the course, such as unreasonable curriculum design, insufficient preparation, lack of passion and so on, all of these will lead a decline in student interest in learning. All of these problems have affected the teaching effectiveness and the enhancement of the students' quality.

3 Heuristic Teaching Method

The word heuristic comes from the same Greek root as "eureka", which means "I have found", an exclamation of triumph at any discovery. Heuristic teaching refers to "a particular method of teaching allowing the students to learn by discovering things by themselves and learning from their own experience, rather than by telling them things". Students will be encouraged to propose any idea to try to solve the problems through critical thinking and reasoning. After that, students will think carefully after communicated with classmates or teacher to get the answer. Heuristic teaching is a kind of art and science for discovery and invention. A problem-solving approach will be applied in heuristic teaching method. The method encourages students to learn, to discover, to understand, or to solve problems on his or her own.

The core of Heuristic teaching is inspiration, focusing on the teachers "issue awareness", which is thought to be the key open the thought. Teachers should build situations or cases in accordance with the teaching content and materials, setting up interesting and relative questions to guide and inspire students to think and desire for knowledge so that students can consciously involved in the teaching process. On the other hand, teachers should remember to protect students 'curiosity. Curiosity can enhance the sensitivity of students to the outside world, and also trigger the desire to explore ideas and activities, cultivate the spirit of the doubt. The spirit of the suspect can question the issue; in addition, it spurs the students to find the difference in new ground, resulting in innovation.

4 Using Heuristic Teaching Method in Information Technology Course

In traditional teaching method, teachers will explain knowledge from teaching materials step by step, and someone may give additional illustrations on this key points. However, for information technology, most knowledge has certain relationship with others. For example, the case that point A has been demonstrated should have happened after students have known point B and point C. Then teachers must arrange schedule to teach point B, point C and point A in sequence. It will need long time teaching and listening activity and make students boring. Therefore, in heuristic teaching method, we have shorten the time used for teaching and listening activity and offered limited time for students' creativity. In the case, teachers interpret point B and point C clearly, at the same time, tell students the definition of point A and(or) the idea how to get point A with point B and point C. In following, students need to draft their simple design for point A. At last teachers make a conclusion and give more explanation. A specific application in information technology course is showed as follows.

When teaching digital fundamentals, flip-flop is a quite important logic unit. According to all teaching materials, students must have learned latch first, then flip-flop and last master slave flip-flop in sequence. In traditional teaching method, teachers will teach latch, flip-flop and master slave flip-flop step by step, give their definitions, constructions and work states. At last teachers analyze their similarity and difference. During whole period, students act as listeners and try their best to understand all information.

However, when using heuristic teaching method, we change the teaching schedule. Firstly, we explain what the bi-stable device is, which is the common of latch and flip-flop. Then, the latch and flip-flop including RS, JK, T and D type have been introduced carefully. Third, we don't illustrate and teach the master slave flip-flop then but conclude the definition and design idea of master slave flip-flop and set a problem for students to design according to latch, flip-flop and its definition which have been taught former. Last we have analyzed and concluded the students' workout and offered more explanation of master slave flip-flop. During the period, students need to concern all their attention on the listening then actively draft the solution. The heuristic teaching process is shown in Figure 1.

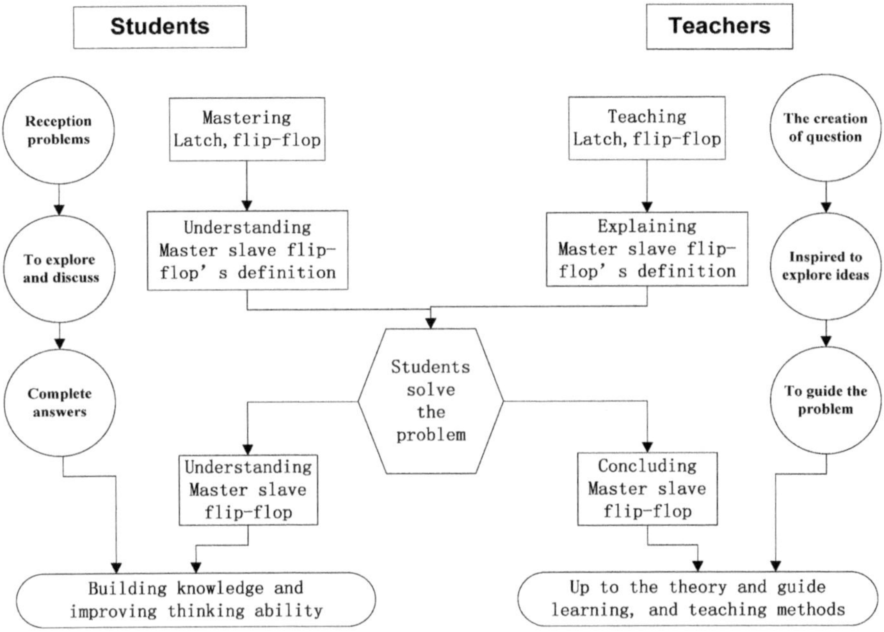

Fig. 1. The heuristic teaching process

After the heuristic teaching method was used in the information technology course, the teaching efficiency has been improved. First, students can focus their attention in the class to listen what teachers taught. Second, when students have finished the draft and received feedback from teachers, they not only can understand all knowledge required in teaching materials, but their solving problem ability has been increased. Moreover, more interactive activities can harmony teacher-student relationship. Harmonious relationship will be conducive to maintain order in the class and improve student learning, and also be favorable for teachers to use heuristic teaching in classes improving the effectiveness and the quality of teaching. At the same time, feedback from students is positive. Most students are more interested in the learning and solving procedure, and their understanding is more clarity than before.

5 Conclusion

The heuristic teaching method is the main trend of the world. It has been adopted widely in variety of courses. Due to close relationships are available in different parts considering information technology courses. It is easy to explore the relationship and build specific problems, which can be used to practice students' problem-solving ability and master knowledge effectively. Its application demonstrates that the using heuristic teaching method in the information technology course is effective. Although teachers need to cost more time for preparing, the results is promising. For students, they can build knowledge distinct and increased thinking ability. In contrast, teachers will improve the teaching efficiency.

References

1. Zhang, J.W., Mo, R.: Reconsider Confucius' enlightening reflection: Implications on heuristic teaching. Sino-US English Teaching 4(43), 32–38 (2007)
2. Zhang, X.P.: The Combination of Traditional Teaching Method and Problem Based Learning. The China Papers 10(1), 30–36 (2002)
3. Li, C.B., Zhang, Q.: A Research on Application of Heuristic Teaching Methods in the Teaching of Management. In: International Workshop on Education Technology and Computer Science, Washington, vol. 3, pp. 762–766 (2009)
4. Li, L., Chen, Z.A., Jiang, Y.H.: Strategy, style, attribution: Learning to learn English. Shanghai Foreign Language Education Press, Shanghai (2006)
5. Zhang, S.Q.: Heuristic Teaching and Classroom Questions. Teaching and Research Forum 1 (2001)
6. Zhao, H.Q.: Teaching Art. Teaching of China University 1 (2003)
7. Gardner, D., Miller, L.: Establishing Self-access. Shanghai Foreign Language Education press, Shanghai (2002)

The Research on Banking Cluster System Based on Linux Virtual Server

Zhisong Hou, Xiangang Zuo, Yukun Ma, and Zhou Yu

School of Information Engineering,
Henan Institute of Science and Technology, 453003 XinXiang, China
forhouor@gmail.com, zuoxg2002@163.com,
yukuner@126.com, yyuzhou@tom.com

Abstract. Considering the present situation of the online banking business, on the foundation of the traditional load balancing technology, passes through researching Linux virtual server and puts forward a kind of banking cluster system based on Linux virtual server. This system uses a distributed selfsche- duling mechanism and multi-process multi-threaded concurrent processing mode. It can achieve the goals of high-availability, high performance and low cost.

Keywords: Cluster, Load Balancing, Virtual Server; Banking.

1 Introduction

With the development of network infrastructure, especially that Internet technology is widespread, the service process mode and management mode in financial system are going to be 'human- computer' mode based on network, instead of 'human- human' mode based on counter; the movements of funds is turning to electronic voucher mode from entity voucher mode, namely, more and more banking business is dealt on network virtual bank, not on traditional entity bank. At the moment, more and more transaction is dealt on network virtual bank, and it's obvious that transactions on network bank will replace transactions on traditional counter. That will be a stricter requirement to banking business system, and people look forward to that banking servers have high ability of dealing with concurrent service to make banking business more quickly. The operational capability of independent server and storage equipment cannot meet the traffic requirement generated by banking business. Then, it will be the bottleneck of banking system. On the other hand, influenced by financial crisis, bank systems have to decrease operation cost, so it had better be higher performance price ratio. Considering this situation, this paper puts forward a new way of network service: Banking Linux Virtual Server (BLVS). This cluster system includes of any parallel servers, among of which network traffic and business load can be shared equally. It provides for banking service system a solution which is high performance, loose coupling, easy to extend and low cost.

The aim of researching and realizing this banking cluster system are: one the one hand, increase usability. BLVS can realize node redundancy. By detecting the failure of hardware, software and service process, BLVS can assign the task of the failure

H. Tan and M. Zhou (Eds.): CSE 2011, Part I, CCIS 201, pp. 459–464, 2011.

node to a certain live node, which achieves the purpose of shielding the single point of failure. On the other hand, increase service capability. In the premise of that quality of service can be satisfied, as much as people can be serviced by cluster system.

2 Research of Pivotal Technology

Considering the present situation of the banking business, BLVS accepts the thought of clustering and load balancing of Linux Virtual Server (LVS), and then brings forward a banking cluster system. The architecture of BLVS is shown in figure 1.

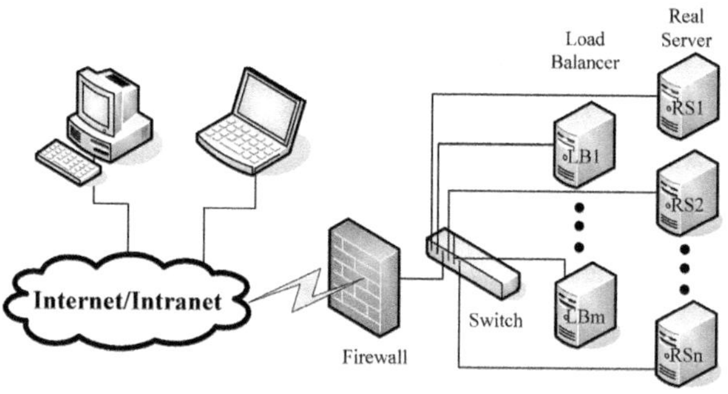

Fig. 1. Architecture of Banking Linux Virtual Server

2.1 Distributed Load Balancing of Automatic Self-scheduling

Load balancing of LVS concentrates on load balancer. If the server node which client connected on is failed, the task of client cannot migrate to another live server node. The advantage of distributed load balancing of automatic self-allocating is that real server also can collect status of server cluster to balance load. Through real-time monitoring the quality of service and resource utilization of local server node and other real servers, real server automatically recommend a new real server for the client, which is called automatic self-allocating. At the same time, from the point of view of cluster scheduling control, the cluster control center locates in the back-end real server. Automatic self-allocating implies the meaning of the distributed scheduling.

To the algorithm of IP load balancing in LVS, server load is expressed by the number of connections, which can not indicate the status of real server. BLVS combines advantages of the algorithm of IP load balancing, and uses the algorithm of least-connection min-load weighted empirical parameters, which takes into account both connection number and system load. In order to promptly capture the connection number and load status of every server, all servers will run load status collection module. The module can collect connection number and load status of local host, and then regularly send the information to load status collection modules on others real server.

In the least-connection min-load scheduling algorithm, the server load index is indicated by concurrent connections ration and CPU utilization. Concurrent connection ratio is defined as the number of concurrent connections accounted for the maximum number of concurrent connections which the server can support. The maximum number of concurrent connections is set respectively by the capability of real server. Because the server load index is the ratio of the number of concurrent connections, the weight of the server capability is also considered. At runtime, the number of maximum of connections of front scheduling node should be set smaller, because it is responsible for scheduling. CPU utilization is defined as the time used by user process and kernel process in one unit of time.

Suppose that there is a server group $S = \{S_0, S_1, \ldots, S_{n-1}\}$ in a cluster system. *C(Si)* is the number of concurrent connections in server S_i and *MC(Si)* is the number of maximum connections of this server. *U(Si)* is CPU utilization of server *Si*. New connection request will be send to server *Sm*, only if server *Si* meets the condition:

$$p\times(\frac{C(S_m)}{MC(S_m)})+U(S_m)=\min\left\{p\times(\frac{C(S_i)}{MC(S_i)})+U(S_i)\right\},0\leq i<n$$

The factor p is the empirical factor, which can be obtained in real running and adjusted dynamically.

2.2 Multi-front Non-forwarding Scheduling

The existing load scheduling techniques are mainly divided into non-front scheduling node and front scheduling node. The advantage of the former is no bottleneck in structure, and simple to realize; the disadvantage is low reliability and balancing performance. The latter can obtain additional security, but in the case of surge in network traffic, front scheduling node will be the bottleneck of system.

BLVS has several front scheduling nodes. Besides scheduling, these nodes also can work as real server. All back-end real servers have an IP address which can access directly by client. When a client logs, first of all, it will chooses a front scheduling node which has public IP addresses to connect, however, its data packets will not be forwarded through or changed by this node. According to the given load balancing algorithm, scheduling node chooses a server node from real server (which may include the scheduling node itself and the other nodes), and send the IP address of the server node to the client. Then, the client reconnects the real server according to the new IP address. This technology will not increase the pressure of the scheduling node and will decrease network delay. More important, there are several scheduling nodes in cluster which can shield single point of failure. However, every real server in the cluster must have an IP address which can be access directly.

2.3 Multi-process Multi-threaded Concurrent Processing Mode

The processing mode of server-end software can be divided into three categories:

Multi-process mode. The server creates several processes to service. Many applications in Unix or Linux use this way, such as CGI. This mode can offer good stability, because if a process is failed or blocked, others still can service. But there are so many processes that the consumption of system resource is excessive.

Multi-threaded mode. The server creates several threads to service. Many applications in Windows Operation System use this way. Its disadvantage is lower stability. The crash of a piece of thread can lead to the collapse of the whole process.

Multi-process multi-threaded mode. The server creates several processes, and then, each of the processes creates several threads. This mode can not only increase performance but also increase stability.

In BLVS cluster, a single real server must support thousands of long-term stable concurrent connections which accessed by client, so using multi-process multi-threaded parallel processing mode is an appropriate choice.

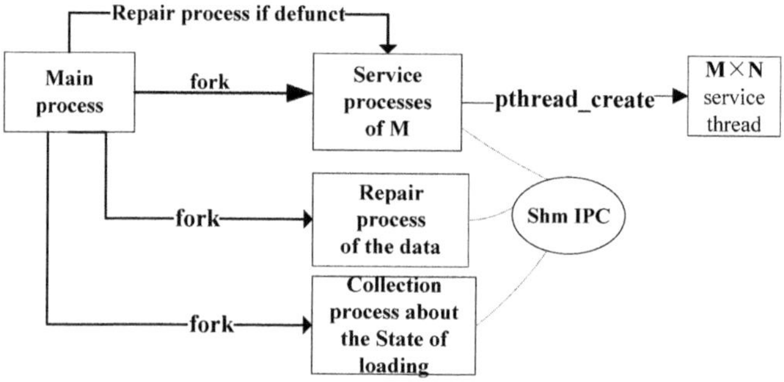

Fig. 2. Multi-process multi-threaded mode

After starting to service, server program creates *m* pieces of processes and several assistant processes in advance using by the function of fork(), and every processes create *n* pieces of threads with the pthread_create() function call. As a result, there are $m \times n$ threads which can concurrently access by the users. All *m* pieces of processes are listening on the service interface simultaneously for competing user's connections. After obtaining a connection, the process sends it to a idle thread. The main process inspects status of these service processes regularly. When a certain process cannot service normally or become Zombie process, main process will reclaim the resource occupied by the process, and supply a new process to service. Simple data exchange between processes use Shared memory IPC mechanism, and complicated data exchange and date sharing will be done by assistant processes.

3 System Work Flow

Client finds appropriate front scheduling node by automatically searching the front scheduling nodes of BLVS, then log in the selected scheduling node (① in figure 3). According to the load status of server group, scheduling front node recommends a real server which has the minimum load, and gives the real server's IP address and service interface to client (②). If client finds that the real server is not the scheduling node itself, it will release the connection to the scheduling node, and reconnect the real server using the new IP address and service interface got from the scheduling node (③). If the new real server cannot accept this connection, it will recommend other real server to client again, then client try to connect to the new real server (④⑤). According to the network setting, a client can reconnect *n* times at most, and after *n* times reconnection it will be connected to the last real server, otherwise it will be prompted that server is busy.

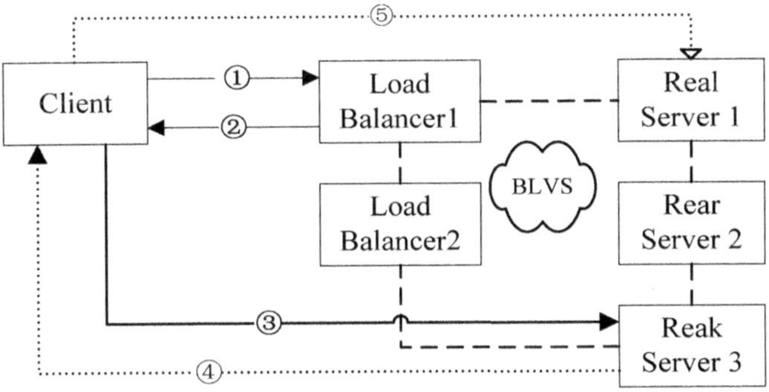

Fig. 3. Work flow of BLVS

Status information exchange between the load status collection modules are realized by UDP broadcast packet. Servers that switch in or out are found automatically. Status information of live servers is broadcasted over the whole cluster server through a certain UDP port, including public IP address, service port and load status (concurrent connections ration and CPU utilization). Every live server maintains a status table which restores the status information received from other servers and the status information will be added into the status table when the server receives a piece of status information. The status information will be deleted from the status table if the server cannot receive the same status information for a certain period of time (Maybe the server is failed). When live server schedules the load among the servers, it carries out load balancing according to the status information in status table.

4 Conclusion

In BLVS, distributed load balancing of automatic self-allocating can get better performance of load balancing; multi-front non-forwarding scheduling can resolve the single point of failure and bottleneck in scheduling node; multi-process multi-threaded concurrent processing mode can increase usability and performance in service. In actual run time, the cluster is running stable and convenient to maintain. Furthermore, it can gain a better performance of response and flexibility. With further research, BLVS will be more and more important in network banking business.

References

1. Bryant, R.M.: A stable distributed scheduling algorithm. In: Proceedings of International Wire and Cable Symposium, pp. 314–323. Comput. Soc. Press, Los Alamitos (1981)
2. Barak, S.: Distributed load-balancing policy for a multicomputer. Software-Practice and Experience 15(9), 901–913 (1985)
3. Stankovic: Adaptive bidding algorithm for processes, clusters and distributed groups. In: Proceedings-International Conference on Distributed Computing Systems, pp. 49–59. IEEE, New York (1984)
4. Legrand: Mapping and load-balancing iterative computations. Parallel and Distributed Systems 6(3), 546–558 (2004)
5. Barker, K.: A load balancing framework for adaptive and asynchronous applications. Parallel and Distributed Systems 2(1), 183–192 (2004)

Strengthening the "Power Electronics" Course Teaching, Focusing on Students' Capacity-Building

Xiumin Yang[1], Guanjin Chen[2], Bo wan[1], Yongshu Guo[1], and Lei Zhang[2]

[1] Department of Automatic Controls,
Shenyang Institute of Engineering, Shenyang 110004, China
[2] School of Mechanical Engineering & Automation,
Northeastern University, Shenyang 110036, China
yxiumin@tom.com

Abstract. According to "Power Electronics" course features, it respectively from training students' learning, anglicizing and engineering practicing those three kinds of capacity to discuss the methods such as motivating the intrinsic studying motivation of students, enhancing the circuit analysis and improving the efficiency of practical application teaching and so on. making full use of multimedia teaching methods and elaborating courseware, it Constantly explore and practice in the terms of student training and establish a effective teaching system through Succinctly and training of classroom teaching and practical teaching. And it also was named as excellent course of Higher Vocational in Liaoning Province in 2008.

Keywords: Capacity training, Learning capacity, Circuit analysis, Engineering capacity.

1 Introduction

Power Electronics is a subject that using electronic device to control and transform energy on voltage, current, frequency and waveform ect, which also is a cross-disciplinary among three electrical engineerings including Electricity, electronics and control. It has been widely used in various fields such as industry, power, transportation, household appliances, new energy ect. Many disciplines of Shenyang Institute of Vocational Education, such as Electronic automation, Power Generation, Power Relay, Power Supply, Application of Electronic, Integrated Control ect, have set up "power electronics" course, which is positioned as a basic course in the corresponding Professional training program and a main courses of Electrical Automation Technology.

We have constantly explored and practiced how to training students' learning ability, analytical skills and engineering capacity in the "Power Electronics" teaching, and achieved some success.

2 Stimulate Intrinsic Motivation and Focus on Learning Ability

Learning Ability is defined as that students master scientific methods of learning through the guidance of teachers, also known as the 'will to learn' Only Students are

H. Tan and M. Zhou (Eds.): CSE 2011, Part I, CCIS 201, pp. 465–471, 2011.

willing to 'learn', can they achieve "learning", in order to continuously improve the learning ability. Therefore, that the teachers how to effectively guide the students to improve their learning ability is the key, that is also the question that every teacher should think about.

2.1 Initiate the Firstclass – Introduction

Motivation to learn is to guide the learning behavior of the students. It's a state of mind which maintain the learning behavior and make sure it develops towards a certain target behavior toward .Initiating first class well is the initial momentum to stimulate students to learn well and carry on.

What is Power Electronics? What is the prospect of development of the power electronics technology disciplines? What is the basic content of courses- "Power Electronics"? What's the use of learning "Power Electronics" well? How to learn "Power Electronics" well? This series of issues which students are most interested in need to be answered well in the first class during the introduction by teachers and try to make it perfect as much as possible. This can inspire the enthusiasm and curiosity of students and induce the students to learn the knowledge initiatively.

2.2 Optimization and Integration of Course Content

Power Electronics is a main course of the electrical automation major (course with the requirement to pass the test, 60 hours or so). It's a required professional course for the major including power generation, power relay and power supply (course with the requirement to submit a term paper, 30 hours or so), and optional for the students from applied electronic and centralized control of professional electives (30hours or so) .For different majors, different hours required, we make a optimization and integration for the main lessons with many hours and non-main course with fewer hours in the teaching content. Main courses emphasize on the integrity of the curriculum greatly and we focus on the basic curriculum in order to lay a solid foundation for subsequent specialized courses. Non-main courses emphasize on the independence of the curriculum. "Power Electronics" course is divided into several modules including 'power electronics', 'Controlled Rectifier', 'DC chopper', 'AC power switch and AC voltage regulation circuit', 'Inverter circuit and inverter circuit', 'rigger circuit with the drive circuit', 'PWM control techniques', 'soft-switch technology'. For different major, each module can have a different focus and pay more attention to curriculum Applicability. For example, the major of power generation, power relay, power supply can focus on the application of 'AC power switch' in the reactive power compensation device. The applied electronic should focus on the application of "DC chopper circuit "in switching power supply.

2.3 Elicitation Method

The prerequisite for 'power electronics' courses are 'circuit based ', 'Electronic Technology ', 'Motor and Drag' and so on. During the classroom teaching, when it comes to the knowledge point mentioned in previous course, the teachers should set a reasonable doubt to inspire and guide students to think, recalling what they learn to break the 'calm 'in the minds of students, so that students generate desire to learn knowledge in the search to better understand and grasp the new knowledge points in context. For example, when teaching Controlled Rectifier charged inductive loads, you can ask: 'what is the kind of inductance device in the basic circuit class? "As the load for controlled rectifier, what if the current flow through the inductor? "What's the difference in contrast to the resistance of the load?' Set up question to discuss and finally guide the students to draw the right conclusions. In this way, students gain knowledge, inspired thinking and stimulate interest in the process of questioning and doubting. This can cultivate the student's ability to learn and think.

3 Explaining the Method Thoroughly and Focusing on Capacity-Building of Analysis

Power Electronics is a subject that using electronic device to control and transform energy on voltage, current, frequency and waveform ect. "Power Electronics" course include two kinds of electric power, alternating current and direct current, and four categories of conversion circuit, AC/DC conversion circuit, DC / AC conversion circuit, AC / AC conversion circuit and DC / DC conversion circuit. We use a controlled rectifier circuit teaching (i.e., AC / DC conversion circuit) as an example to introduce the process of training students' circuit analysis capacity in following parts.

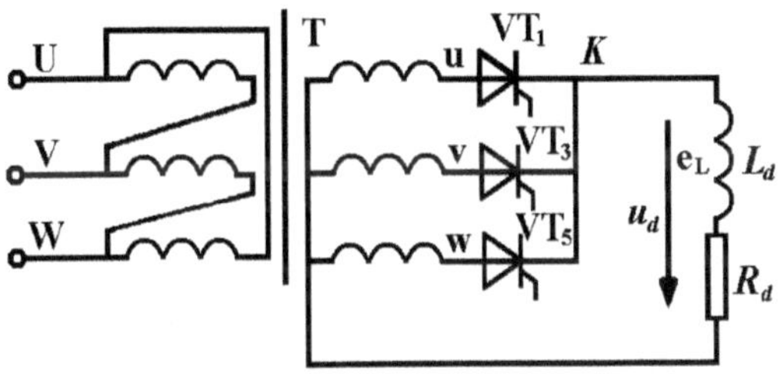

Fig. 1. Three-phase half-wave controlled rectifier circuit

3.1 Explaining the Method of Circuit Analysis Thoroughly

The analycal method of Controlled Rectifier circuit is : According to circuits—drawing the waveforms of work— derivationing the basic quantitative relationship.

Analysis of circuit's structure. Rectifier circuit converse AC to DC, so it's input is AC (single phase, three phase ect), which is usually connected to rectifier circuit through the rectifier transformer. The output of rectifier circuit is DC, two ends of DC is connected to the load (which commonly including resistive load, inductive load and EMF load). The power electronic devices used in the middle rectifier circuit are mainly thyristors, which forming the controlled rectifier circuit. According to the structure of rectifier circuit, it can be divided into zero rectifier circuit (such as half-wave) and bridge rectifier circuit. According to the principle of that composition, it is easy to understand the classification of rectifier circuit. And then we make use of Specific circuit to train students' ability of interpreting drawings, ultimately achieve the desired effect that students can easy name any given rectifier circuit. For example, shown in Figure 1, the name of the circuit -- three-phase half-wave controlled rectifier circuit, connecting with inductive load.

Analysis of working waveforms. After understanding the configuration of circuit, we use the analycal method of working waveforms to teach how to analyze the circuit work? How to understand the principle that controlled rectifier transform alternating current into adjustable direct current to supply the load to use? So the key point and difficult point is drawing the working waveforms of controlled rectifier circuits, needed to explain thoroughly.

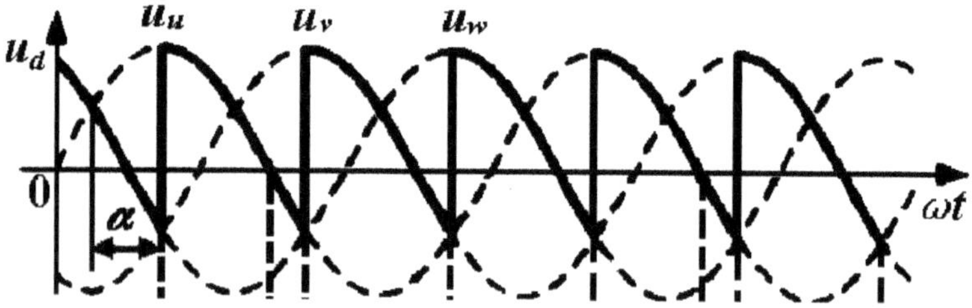

Fig. 2. The output voltage waveform of the three-phase

According to the waveform and control conditions (control angle α) of input AC, we can determine the working status of SCR (conduction or cut-off), find out the corresponding equivalent circuit, and draw the corresponding working waveforms (such as waveform of output DC voltage u_d). Shown in the figure 2, it is the output half-wave controlled rectifier circuit connecting DC voltage waveform of a three-phase with inductive load half-wave controlled rectifier circuit, connecting with inductive load, when $\alpha = 60^o$. The dashed shown in figure 2 is the waveform of the input three-phase symmetrical AC, u_u, u_v and u_w . The output voltage u_d is pulsating DC,and the circuit output three pulsating waves,which respectively belonging to some part of phase voltage, u_u, u_v and u_w, in 2π, a cycle of AC. So, the greater value of α, the smaller positive area of output palsating waves, and the lower average of DC , and that qualitatively and intuitively show the working principle of controlled rectifier transforming AC to adjustable DC. And as long as changing the control conditions, the value of the control angle α, it can be very convenient to control the output of DC .

Derivationing the basic quantitative relationship. The working waveform just intuitively reflect the qualitative relationship between output and input, so we need to do the formula derivation in order to get the quantitative relationship. And the process of derivation is : according to working waveforms and circuits — using mathematical tools — derivationing the basic quantitative relationship. For example, the formula derivation of the average outputing DC voltage and current of the three-phase half-wave controlled rectifier circuit, when connected to inductive load is following:

According to the output voltage ud waveform shown in Figure 2, the derived average value of the output DC voltage U_d is ：

$$U_d = \frac{3}{2\pi}\int_{\frac{\pi}{6}+\alpha}^{\frac{5\pi}{6}+\alpha} \sqrt{2}U_2 \sin\omega t d(\omega t) = \frac{3\sqrt{6}}{2\pi}U_2 \cos\alpha = 1.17U_2 \cos\alpha \qquad (1)$$

According to the circuit shown in Figure 1, the derived average value of the output DC current I_d of the load is ：

$$I_d = \frac{U_d}{R_d} = 1.17\frac{U_2}{R_d}\cos\alpha \qquad (2)$$

3.2 Picking Out Typical Questions, Seriously Teaching Exercise Lesson

In order to train students' analycal ability of circuit in the exercise lesson , we pick out typical questions for them ,which are explained thoroughly, teach them more about ideas and methods, less about the specific knowledge, and guide them to extend their mind. For example, when teaching the three-phase half-wave controlled rectifier circuit connected to inductive load shown in Figure 1, we ask student questions such as, "what is the difference of the output in the same circuit refer to different control conditions? ", "what will the output change to after inductive load parallelled to the Freewheeling diode ? ", " what will the output change to, when the load change to the resistive load?", " what will the output change to, when the load change to back-EMF load and series connect to a large smoothing reactor ? " ect. students are asked to think each raised question firstly ; and then we give up the idea and method to solve the problem and let them practice, we give the correct answer at last.

4 Teach with a Combination of Training While Focus on Cultivating Engineering Ability

Power Electronics Technology is a comprehensive technical disciplines, it is closely linked with the actual production application. In order to meet the requirement of engineering, practice and application, we established a knowledge-based teaching system in connection with practical applications to focus on cultivating the ability of practice, which is with the guidance of the theory "integration of theory and practice ". We have done the following work.

4.1 Make Full Use of Multimedia Teaching Methods and Elaborate Courseware

The power electronics mainly includes power electronic devices, power electronic conversion circuits and power electronic devices. Power electronic devices is not a basic component in "Power Electronics " course content, but in order to combine devices, circuits and devices can organically, reflect the application of courses, and cultivate students engineering application capabilities, we make full use of multimedia teaching methods to increase the power electronic device image (see Figure 3 below) in the classroom. It enables students to build awareness of engineering applications and enhance the students' enthusiasm to learn knowledge.

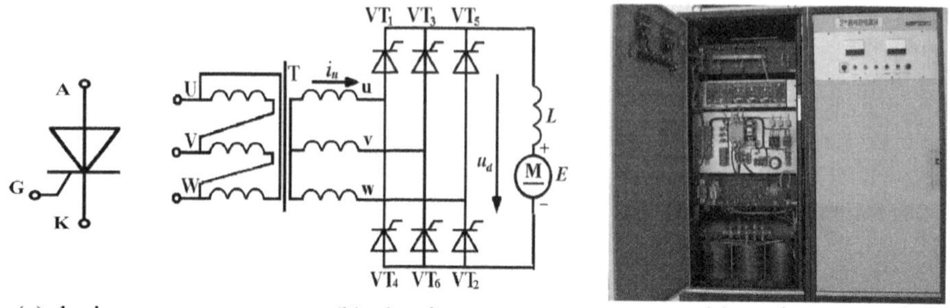

(a) device (b) circuit (c) equipment

Fig. 3. Devuce,circuit,equipment

4.2 Increase the Intensity of Practice

Practice teaching is an important means to cultivate engineering capabilities, in order to take full advantage of experiments, training and practical terms and train students on engineering skills and help them develop into good professional habit, we have increased the intensity of practice teaching.

First, during experimental teaching, we emphasize on achieving "integration of theory and practice", in order to cultivate progressive spirit of innovation, stimulate the creative potential of students, cultivate the ability to identify problems, analyze problems and solve problems, better connect theory with practice. We change experimental instructions to the experimental tasks book. We make it available to students on the network teaching platform after "power electronics" course set up, let students to become the main body of the experiment. Secondly, during the training in school, we add the training content power electronic devices; During the off-campus internship in industries and enterprises, power electronics technology is taught with connection to the application.

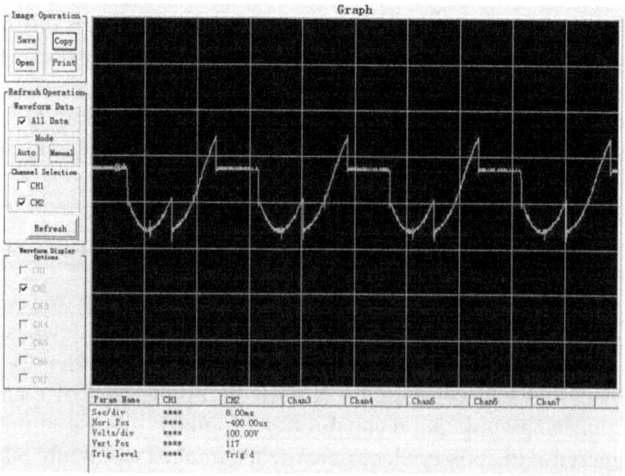

Fig. 4. Experimental Waveforms

4.3 Reform Test Methods and Content

According to the requirement for different majors of "Power Electronics" course, different test methods have been utilized for professional examinations and the reform varies. "Power Electronics" course is the main course fro electronic automation, the professional program stipulate that the course is for exam. According to characteristics of the course, from 2005, we change the form from closed book examination to the form of a one-page open-book exam including the experimental aspects (eg. questions from 2008/2009 second semester final exam, a experimental waveforms is shown in Figure 4 answer the question: The experimental measured three-phase bridge full-controlled pressure drop u_{T1} wave rectifier circuit is shown in Figure 4, how many degrees that control angle α is at this time ?) in order to assess students' ability to analyze problems and solve problems. The final scores consist of three parts: book results, experimental results and daily results.

5 Conclusion

In the curriculum teaching, how to improve students' ability in training is a long-term work, and is the ultima goal of development and reformation. Over years hard working, "Power Electronics"course was named as excellent course of Higher Vocational in Liaoning Province in 2008. We still need to constantly think, explore and practice how to continue to strengthen curriculum construction after become a provincial excellent course? how to avoid become lockstep and lack of the power of innovation which many other couse being after named as excellent couse? and how to maintain and develop our created teaching mode of "integration of theory and practice",which have been proven to be effective? Next , we will still focus curriculum building on capacity training : (1) we figure out the social and business needs through research to integrate and refine the content of teaching ,and finish the practical material library building of theoretical teaching . (2) we strengthen theoretical instruction in practical teaching to make sure studets "to know truly is to know by cause",and to train them to get the ability of sustainable development .

References

1. Li, X., Yang, X.M., Li, Y.P.: Power electronics. China Electric Power Press, BeiJing (2007)
2. Jiang, W., Duan, Z.M., Li, H.: Implement educational reformation, improve the quality of basic circuit course teaching. In: ETT 2010, Wu Han (2010)
3. Zhang, L., Lu, J.J., Quan, Z., Liu, Z.R., Li, Y.: Sustainable development strategy of numerical control technology (application) for self-study examination. In: ETT 2010,Wu Han (2010)

Using Piecewise Hashing and Lagrange Interpolation Polynomial to Preserve Electronic Evidence

Xiuli Song[1], Hongyao Deng[2], and Zhihai Xiong[3]

[1] Institute of Computer Science and Technology,
Chongqing University of Posts and Telecommunications,
400065, Chongqing, China
songxl@cqupt.edu.cn
[2] College of Mathematics & Computer Science,
Yangtze Normal University,
408100, Chongqing, China
[3] School of Law, Chongqing University of Posts and Telecommunications,
400065, Chongqing, China

Abstract. Electronic evidence has some characteristics, such as it is easily deleted, modified, and fabricated, so it is presented to use piecewise hashing and Lagrange interpolation polynomial to preserve electronic evidence. On local computer, the electronic evidence is converted into the values of polynomials, and then these values are hided into images, finally they are uploaded to server. For finding erroneous pieces in electronic evidence, piecewise hashing techniques were used twice to verify the integrity of the evidence itself and the values of polynomials. On server side, the values of polynomials are extracted from the images, and all electronic data are recovered using Lagrange interpolation polynomial. Experiment results show that the method could reconstruct electronic evidence and guarantee its integrity, authenticity and validity even if the parts of evidence were destroyed or lost in network transmission.

Keywords: Evidence preservation, Piecewise hashing, Lagrange interpolation polynomial, Image hiding.

1 Introduction

Nowadays, with the rapid development of network and information technology, electronic information activities such as electronic commerce, electronic affairs, and virtual assets transferred, etc, are gradually penetrated into daily life of people. Electronic file, e-mail, electronic chat record, and electronic signature have replaced traditional contract, insurance policy, invoice and information in writing. These materials are used as evidence in electronic form is called electronic evidence[1].

H. Tan and M. Zhou (Eds.): CSE 2011, Part I, CCIS 201, pp. 472–480, 2011.

Electronic evidence preservation is to fix and store the evidence, the purpose is prevent specific evidence from being destructed by nature and man. Generally, the investigators fix the evidence in specific form as they collect them before the filing of a lawsuit [2]. If electronic evidence can be sanctified by law, it must be true, reliable, integrated, in accord with legal requirements. But electronic evidence has some digital characteristics, so it is easily to be deleted, forged, modified and removed marks. There are some new challenges to evidence acquisition and preservation.

At present, the research on preservation of electronic evidence is still in its infancy. The researchers use data copy, data recovery, encryption& decryption, and digital signature technology to preserve the evidence [2]. This paper presents a new method on preservation of electronic, which uses piecewise hashing and Lagrange interpolation polynomial to ensure integrity of the evidence.

2 Traditional Hashing and Piecewise Hashing

2.1 Traditional Hashing

Hash functions transform arbitrary-length input into fixed-length output, and the output is called hash value or message digests. In hash function, MD5 and SHA-1 algorithm are now widely used in daily life, in order to distinguish them from piecewise hashing, they are considered as traditional hashing. Traditional hashing can verify the integrity of files, if a document has a little alteration, its hash value would completely change [3]. For example, we take an original document as the input of SHA-1 algorithm in traditional hashing, and calculation result is hash value H_1. When the document has a small change, now use SHA-1 algorithm to produce hash value H_2, and two hash values are very different.

2.2 Piecewise Hashing

Piecewise hashing is proposed by Harbour[4], which divide a document into several pieces, and compute separately hash value for each piece. When all pieces are stored and transmitted in Internet, if the hash value of one piece is mistake, and other hash values are no change, it can be proved that only this piece has been damaged, other pieces are integrate and no be damaged [5].

In Figure 1(a), we use piecewise hashing techniques to divide document A into three pieces, then take SHA-1 algorithm to calculate separately hash value for each piece, finally, we get three different hash values H_3, H_4 and H_5. It can be seen from Figure 2(b), document A has been slightly damaged during transmission and storage. We calculate again hash value for each piece and get H_6, H_7 and H_8. Comparing them with H_3, H_4 and H_5, we find hash value of the second piece is only changed, and hash values of other two pieces are no changes, they are complete.

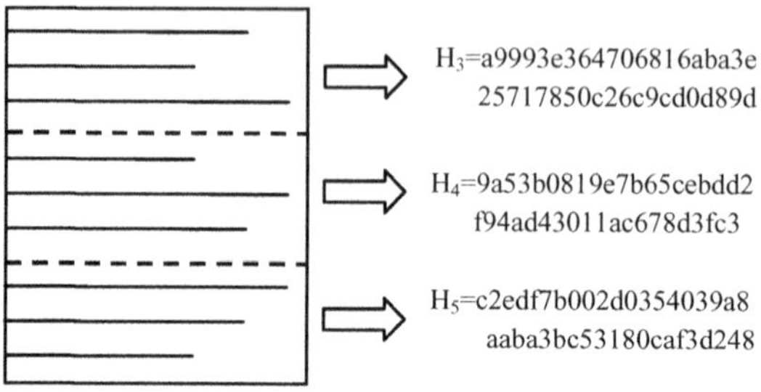

(a) Document A has been divided into 3 pieces

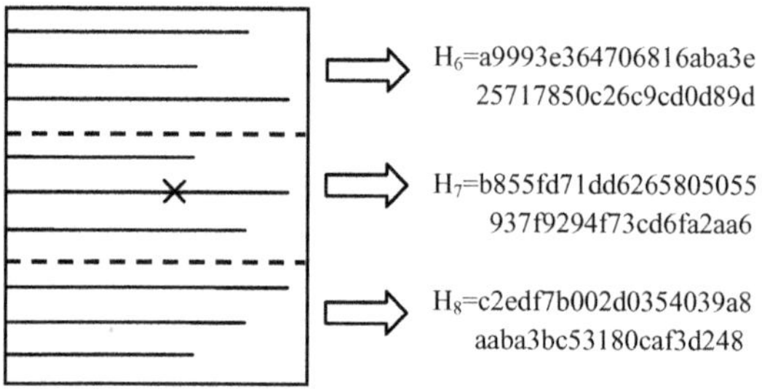

(b) The second piece has been slightly damaged in document A

Fig. 1. Using piecewise hashing to verify the integrity of document A

3 The Threshold Scheme Based on Lagrange Interpolation Polynomial

In 1979, Shamir proposed a threshold scheme based on Lagrange interpolation polynomial for preserving private key [6]. The scheme divided one initial key K into sub-keys $y_1, y_2, \cdots, y_n$, and distributed secretly to n participants. The scheme satisfied the following two conditions:

- If any combination of $s (s < n)$ or more than s sub-keys were known, initial key K was easily figured out.
- If any combination of $s-1$ or less than $s-1$ sub-keys were known, initial key K couldn't be figured out.

In the scheme, the points on polynomial $g(x)$ were denoted as (x_i, y_i), s points could uniquely work out polynomial $g(x)$ of s -1 degree. Finally, $g(x)$ could be constructed, and K could be figured out. And the other way round, if the number of points on polynomial $g(x)$ is less than s, $g(x)$ couldn't be constructed.

4 Preservation and Reconstruction of Electronic Evidence

The electronic evidence comes from hard disks, the cache, and Internet information logs in suspicious computer. E-mail, chat sessions, electronic signatures and monitoring data may all be took as digital evidence, which is easily deleted, modified, and fabricated, and it is difficult to ensure the integrity of electronic evidence.

To ensure the integrity, authenticity and validity of electronic evidence, in this paper, if the investigators have collected some valuable electronic evidence, they will promptly deal with them on local computer. They not only use piecewise hashing to figure out each hash value of the evidence, but also hide the values of polynomials into the images, and transmit them to remote server. The investigators extract the values of polynomials from the images on the server, and they use Hash algorithm to verify the integrity of the evidence. If a small part of the evidence has lost, they would use Lagrange interpolation polynomial to reconstruct the evidence to ensure the content of evidence in the sender must be same as in the receiver.

4.1 Preservation of Electronic Evidence

Electronic evidence including system security log, intrusion detection log, temporary file and caches data of important process, etc, can transiently disappear. Even if the evidence has been preserved at the time, later it may also be wiped out or deleted directly by criminal suspects. So the key to evidence preservation is copying as soon as possible and transferring safely important information can ensure them to be true and complete. From figure 3, we can see that electronic evidence is divided into t pieces, hided into the images and uploaded to the remote server.

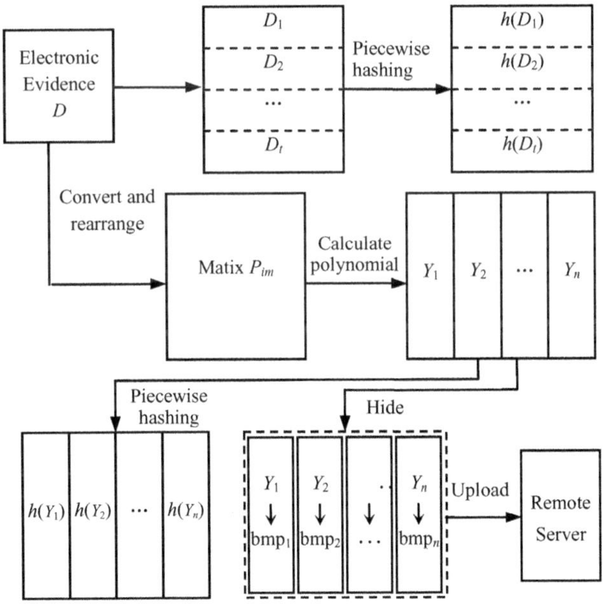

Fig. 2. Preservation process of electronic evidence

On the local computer, the concrete steps of preserving electronic evidence are shown below:

1) Divide evidence file D into t picecs: $D_1, D_2, \cdots, D_t$;
2) Figure out hash value to every piece of the evidence, and get $h(D_1), h(D_2), \cdots, h(D_t)$, then store all the hash value for the public;
3) Convert every character in evidence file D into decimal elements of matrix P_{im}, and let $w = i \times m$. where w is the number of characters, i is the number of rows in matrix P_{im}, and m is the number of columns in matrix P_{im};
4) Take every row $p_{i,1}, p_{i,2}, \cdots, p_{i,m}$ of matrix P_{im} as coefficient to construct the polynomial of degree $m-1$ $f_i(x) \equiv (p_{i,1}x^{m-1} + p_{i,2}x^{m-2} + \cdots + p_{i,m}) \bmod q$, $(1 \le i \le w/m)$;
5) Let $x_{i,1} = 1, x_{i,2} = 2, \cdots, x_{i,n} = n$, then calculate polynomial $f_i(x)$ to get the values $y_{i,1}, y_{i,2}, \cdots, y_{i,n}$, $(1 \le i \le w/m)$;
6) All columns of matrix Y_{in} are $Y_1 = [y_{1,1}, y_{2,1}, \cdots, y_{i,1}]$, $Y_2 = [y_{1,2}, y_{2,2}, \cdots, y_{i,2}]$, $\cdots$, $Y_n = [y_{1,n}, y_{2,n}, \cdots, y_{i,n}]$ .Now, Figure out their hash values to get $h(Y_1), h(Y_2), \cdots, h(Y_n)$, then store all the hash value for the public;
7) Hide respectively $Y_1, Y_2, \cdots, Y_n$ into the images $Bmp_1, Bmp_2, \ldots, Bmp_n$;
8) Upload the images $Bmp_1, Bmp_2, \ldots, Bmp_n$ to remote server through security network.

4.2 Reconstruction and Recovery of Electronic Evidence

On server side, the investigators extract all columns of matrix Y_{in} from the images, then use hash algorithm to verify their integrity. When the parts of them were destructed or lost in network transmission, the investigators can reconstruct electronic evidence and recover their content. The concrete steps of reconstructing and recovering electronic evidence are as follows:

1) Extract all columns of matrix Y_{in} from the images $Bmp_1, Bmp_2, \ldots, Bmp_n$ to get $Y_1', Y_2', \cdots, Y_n'$;
2) Calculate the hash values of $Y_1', Y_2', \cdots, Y_n'$ to get $h(Y_1), h(Y_2), \cdots, h(Y_n)$. Compare $h(Y_j)$ with $h(Y_j')$, $(1 \le j \le n)$, If all $h(Y_j) = h(Y_j')$,it can be confirm $Y_j = Y_j'$, $(1 \le j \le n)$ and all columns of matrix Y_{in} are complete. If the hash values of one or or several columns are $h(Y_j) \ne h(Y_j')$ $j \in [1, 2 \cdots n]$, it shows one or several columns have been destructed or lost in network transmission;
3) Arrange the points $(x_{i,1}, y_{i,1})$, $(x_{i,2}, y_{i,2})$, $\cdots$, $(x_{i,n}, y_{i,n})$ to get matrix Y_{in} .In these points, $x_{i,1} = 1, x_{i,2} = 2, \cdots, x_{i,n} = n$,and $y_{i,1}, y_{i,2}, \cdots, y_{i,n}$ are the i th row of matrix Y_{in} .Get rid of the points that have been destructed or lost, select m

points (x_r, y_r) $(1 \le r \le m)$ from the remainder of n points, and use Lagrange interpolation method to reconstruct ($g_i(x)$)polynomial of degree($m-1$) is shown below[8].

$$g_i(x) = \sum_{r=1}^{m} y_r \prod_{\substack{s=1 \\ s \ne r}}^{m} \frac{x - x_s}{x_r - x_s}$$

The number of correct points must more than m, if they are less than m, the investigators will not liable to reconstruct the polynomial of degree $m-1$;

4) Recover the coefficients of ($g_1(x)$)polynomial to get $p_{1,1}, p_{1,2}, \cdots, p_{1,m}$. The every row of matrix Y_{in} can construct a polynomial of degree($m-1$), i rows of matrix Y_{in} can construct the number of polynomial are i $(1 \le i \le w/m)$. Now, all $p_{i,1}, p_{i,2}, \cdots, p_{i,m}$ $(1 \le i \le w/m)$ can be recovered.
5) Convert every element of matrix P_{im} to characters, and get electronic evidence D' ;
6) Divide the evidence D' into pieces $D_1', D_2', \cdots, D_t'$, then calculate their hash values to get $h(D_1'), h(D_2'), \cdots, h(D_t')$, and compare $h(D_i)$ and $h(D_i')$ $(1 \le i \le t)$. If all $h(D_i) = h(D_i')$,where $(1 \le i \le t)$, It would prove all pieces of evidence are complete.

5 The Operating Processes and Results in the Experiment

Now, we give a example to describe the steps of preserving and reconstructing electronic evidence. This example has debugged satisfactorily in matlab7.0 programming environment based on Windows Xp. The operating processes and results in the experiment are as follows:

If you manage or administer information systems and networks, you should understand computer forensics. Forensics is the process of using scientific knowledge for collecting, analyzing, and presenting evidence to the courts. (The word forensics means "to bring to the court.") Forensics deals primarily with the recovery and analysis of latent evidence. Latent evidence can take many forms, from fingerprints left on a window to DNA evidence recovered from blood stains to the files on a hard drive.

We assume that above passage is electronic evidence will be preserved. Firstly, we divide the passage into four pieces D_1, D_2, D_3, D_4 , and take "." as the end of each piece. Then we use SHA-1 algorithm to calculate hash values of each piece to get $h(D_1), h(D_2), h(D_3), h(D_4)$, and store all the hash values in public, the values of ($h(D_1), h(D_2)$) are listed below:

>>hash ('If you manage or administer information systems and networks, you should understand computer forensics.','SHA-1')
ans = 2afd5df59f5c34070c9d1a959a2fcc0e146f5921 %--h(D1)--%
>>hash('Forensics is the process of using scientific knowledge for collecting, analyzing, and presenting evidence to the courts.','SHA-1')
ans = bb829918a73410ea8160040c6ba7bce2e7a4687d %--h(D2)--%
……

The electronic evidence has 500 characters including blank character. To ensure the number of characters are integer multiple of 3, we add a character "x" to the end of original message. Then, we change 501 characters into ASCII codes to get 501 integers, and a part of ASCII codes are listed below :

>>uint8('If you manage or administer information systems and networks, …….')
ans =
73 102 32 121 111 117 32 109 97 110 97 103 101 32 111 114 32 97 100 109 105 110 105 115 116 101 114 32 105 110 102 111 114 109 97 116 105 111 110 32 115 121 115 116 101 109 115 32 97 110 100 32 ……

We divide 501 integers into 167 groups and each group has 3 integers. In the *i*th group, the integers are $p_{i,1}, p_{i,2}, p_{i,3}$ $(1 \le i \le 167)$, we take them as coefficient to construct polynomial:

$$f(x) \equiv (p_{i,1}x^2 + p_{i,2}x + p_{i,3}) \bmod q, \quad (1 \le i \le 167, q = 97)$$

When i =1, three integers of first group are

$$p_{1,1} = 73, \quad p_{1,2} = 102, \quad p_{1,3} = 32$$

The polynomial that be constructed is

$$y_1 = f_1(x) \equiv (73x^2 + 102x + 32) \bmod 97$$

Also let $x_{1,1} = 1$, $x_{1,2} = 2$, $x_{1,3} = 3$, $x_{1,4} = 4$, $x_{1,5} = 5$

The operating processes in matlab7.0 programming environment are shown below:

```
>>P = [73 102 32];
>>X = [1,2,3,4,5];
>>Y = polyval(P,X);
>>mod (Y,97)
ans =13 43 25 56 39
```

Here $y_{1,1} = 13$, $y_{1,2} = 43$, $y_{1,4} = 56$, $y_{1,5} = 39$

When all polynomials are constructed, we get $y_{i,1}, y_{i,2}, y_{i,3}, y_{i,4}, y_{i,5}$ $(1 \le i \le 167)$ and rearrange them in column, finally, we obtain Y_1, Y_2, Y_3, Y_4, Y_5 , Where $(1 \le j \le 5)$

We calculate hash values of (Y_1, Y_2, Y_3, Y_4, Y_5)and store openly all hash values. Then we hide (Y_1, Y_2, Y_3, Y_4, Y_5) respectively into 5 images (Bmp_1, Bmp_2,…,Bmp_5) and transmit them to remote server in secure path.

On the server, the investigators extract $Y_1^{'}, Y_2^{'}, \cdots, Y_5^{'}$ from the bitmaps and calculate their hash values. In order to verify that all Y_j $(1 \le j \le 5)$ were not be modified, and damaged in the course of being hided, transmitted, and extracted, the investigators compare all $h(Y_j)$ and $h(Y_j^{'})$ $(1 \le j \le 5)$. If only $h(Y_2) \ne h(Y_2^{'})$ and other four pairs of hash values are equal, it shows $Y_1 = Y_1^{'}$, $Y_3 = Y_3^{'}$, $Y_4 = Y_4^{'}$, $Y_5 = Y_5^{'}$. Further, the investigators can recover $y_{i,1}, y_{i,3}, y_{i,4}, y_{i,5}$ $(1 \le i \le 167)$, and reconstruct $f_i(x)$ to find out $p_{i,1}, p_{i,2}, p_{i,3}$ $(1 \le i \le 167)$. For example, if $y_{1,1} = 13$, $y_{1,3} = 25$, $y_{1,4} = 56$, $y_{1,5} = 39$ have been recovered, they choose 3 from 4 values, the 3 values are $y_{1,1}, y_{1,3}, y_{1,5}$. Then they use the points $(1,13)$, $(3,25)$, $(5,39)$ to reconstruct $f_1(x) \equiv (73x^2 + 102x + 32) \bmod 97$ and recover $p_{1,1} = 73$, $p_{1,2} = 102$, $p_{1,3} = 32$.

When all $p_{i,1}, p_{i,2}, p_{i,3}$ $(1 \le i \le 167)$ have been recovered, the investigators change them into characters to obtain electronic evidence $D^{'}$, then divide $D^{'}$ into 4 pieces $D_1^{'}, D_2^{'}, D_3^{'}, D_4^{'}$ and treat "." as their separator. Further calculate $h(D_1^{'}), h(D_2^{'}), h(D_3^{'}), h(D_4^{'})$ and compare $h(D_i)$ and $h(D_i^{'})$ $(1 \le i \le 4)$ to verify the integrity of electronic evidence.

6 Conclusion

This paper provides a new method to preserve electronic evidence, which is suitable for the evidence transmission in network but not large bulk. In the method, to find out error pieces of electronic evidence through network transmission, piecewise hashing is used twice. First time, it is used to verify the integrity of evidence itself. For the second time, it is used to verify the integrity of the values of polynomials.

The electronic evidence is divided into several pieces, and each piece does not mean anything. If these pieces are put together, the evidence will be reconstituted. We hide the values of polynomials into images and transmit them separately, not only enhance the double confidentiality of the evidence, but also when among them several are modified, lost, delete, there will have no effect on whole recovery of electronic evidence. So that the method can ensure the evidence is complete, true and valid, when it is uploaded to remote server on the networks.

Acknowledgment

This paper is partially sponsored by National Social Science Foundation of China and by Natural Science Foundation of Chongqing University of Posts and Telecommunications in China (No.A2009-59).

References

1. Zhao, X., Zheng, H.: Secure Protection Policy for Electronic Evidence Supporting Computer Forensic. Computer Engineering 34(21), 161–163 (2008)
2. Ding, L., Wang, Y.: Study on Relevant Law and Technology Issues about Computer Forensics. Journal of Software 16(2), 260–275 (2005)
3. Stallings, W.: Cryptography and Network Security: Principles and Practice, 4th edn. Prentice Hall, Englewood Cliffs (2005)
4. Piecewise Hashing, `http://www.forensicswiki.org/wiki/Piecewise_hashing`
5. Kornblum, J.: Identifying Almost Identical Files Using Context Triggered Piecewise Hashing. Digital Investigation 3, 91–97 (2006)
6. Shamir, A.: How to share a secret. Communications of the ACM 22(11), 612–613 (1979)
7. Bo, Y.: Modern Cryptography, 2nd edn. Tsinghua University Press, Beijing (2007)
8. Chen, G., Wang, L., Li, Y.: Color Image Sharing Method Based On Lagrange's Interpolating Polynomia. Computer Measurement& Control 16(7), 1030–1032 (2008)

Non-destructive Line Detection of Salted Egg Based on Image Processing and BP Neural Network

Zhongqiang Chen, Qiaohua Wang*, and Tao Zhu

College of Engineering, Huazhong Agricultural University,
Wuhan, 430070, P.R. China
wqh@mail.hzau.edu.cn

Abstract. This paper proposed a method to detect the quality of salted duck eggs based on image processing and artificial neural network. Fourier transform was employed after pre-processing for the images of eggs. It was found that the texture of phase spectrum images of four kinds eggs ("non-well pickled", "well-pickled", "over-pickled" and "spoilt" eggs), varied from clear and ordered to vague and disordered, while the corresponding entropies of images gradually decreased. Through the brightness statistics of images with wavelet reconstruction, it was found that in terms of brightness, the "well-pickled eggs" ranked the first, and the "spoilt eggs" being the last. Color, texture, and statistical moment parameters were selected as image parameters, and BP neural network was created with three-layer feedforward structure (10-18-4). Then the network was tested and the correct ratio of the model amounted to about 92%, certifying the feasibility of this method.

Keywords: Salted egg, Non-destructive Detection, Image Processing, BP Neural Network.

1 Introduction

Salted duck eggs (namely duck eggs pickled by salt), as a traditional Chinese food with a long history, are greatly enjoyed by Chinese people. However, the quality of duck eggs will change during the time of salting away. Some eggs, with good quality, are pickled for proper time, which are called "well-pickled eggs"; some, pickled for too short time, are called "non-well pickled eggs"; some are pickled for too long time, and these eggs are called "over-pickled eggs"; some even become spoilt [1]. Thus, the quality of salted eggs must be detected before they are packaged and sold in the market. The "non-well pickled eggs", the "over-pickled eggs" and the "spoilt eggs" need to be picked out, leaving the "well pickled" eggs to be packaged and put on the market.

Nowadays, the quality test of salted duck eggs in Chinese egg processing industry mainly relies on man-made test. The work is laborious with low efficiency and high error ratio. Thus, there is a necessity to search for methods and mechanisms to test the quality of salted duck eggs efficiently with no destruction. This paper combined computer vision techniques with artificial neural network, proposing a non-destructive

* Corresponding author.

H. Tan and M. Zhou (Eds.): CSE 2011, Part I, CCIS 201, pp. 481–488, 2011.

method to detect the inner quality of salted eggs. And the paper proved that this method performed well.

2 Materials and Methods

2.1 Salted Duck Egg Samples

The samples for experiments were offered by Hubei Jiaolong Egg Company, including 70 "well-pickled eggs", 70 "non-well pickled eggs", 70 "over-pickled eggs" and 70 "spoilt eggs".

2.2 Experimental System

The detection equipment consisted of transmission mechanism, photographing mechanism, computer, egg moving mechanism, egg unloading mechanism, optoelectronic sensor, and passages for sorted eggs. The testing equipment was showed in Fig. 1

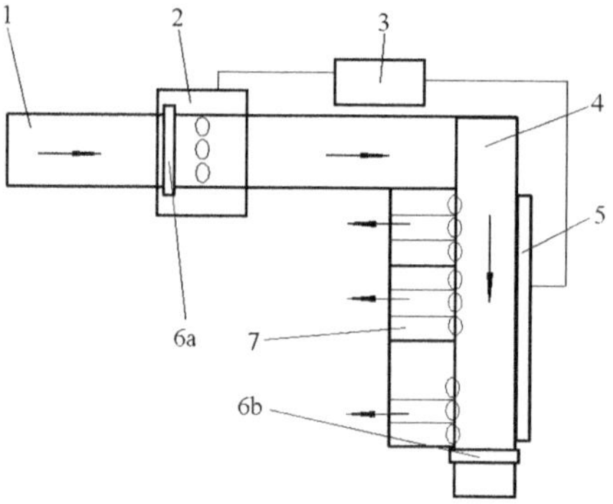

Fig. 1. Detection Equipment (1-Transmission mechanism, 2-Photographing mechanism, 3-Computer, 4-Egg moving mechanism, 5-Egg unloading mechanism, 6a & 6b-Optoelectronic sensor, 7-Passages for sorted eggs)

2.3 Experimental Procedure

First of all, every kind of eggs was assigned a number, and this number was marked on the small side of the egg. The "well-pickled" were assigned number "1"; the "non-well pickled" were assigned number "2"; the "over-pickled" were assigned number "3"; the "spoilt" were assigned number "4".

Secondly, the computer vision equipment was adjusted and all preparations for photographing were done.

Thirdly, all eggs were photographed. Eggs were put on the transmission mechanism with three in a row. When eggs to be tested came into the lighting box of the photographing mechanism and just faced the light directly, the optoelectronic senor would sense the arrival signal of eggs, and trigger the camera. Then the images of eggs were obtained and saved respectively in accordance with their sorts.

3 Results and Discussion

3.1 Image Processing

Distinguishing the four kinds of eggs from their original images obtained in the experiments, except the "spoilt eggs", there was almost no difference among the other three. Thus, there was a necessity to implement image processing to find the differences. Initially, the images were denoised. Median filter was a non-linear method to restrain noise. The original images were treated with median filter [2], and the results were showed in Fig. 2. It was found that there was still little difference among these three kinds of eggs.

In order to find the difference among these four kinds of eggs, more image processing was necessary.

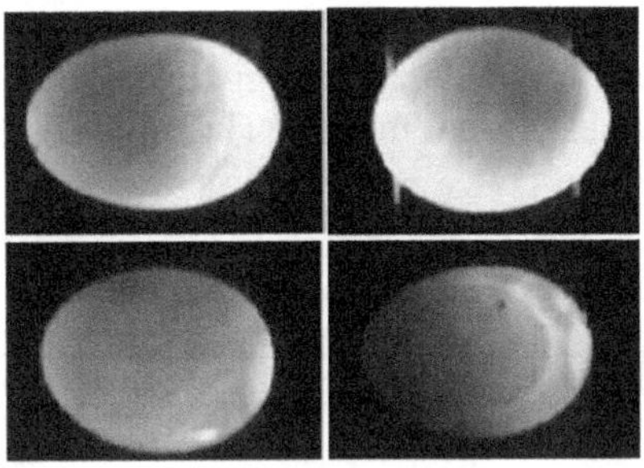

Fig. 2. Images processed by Median filter (From left to right and from up to down: the "non-well pickled egg", the "well-pickled egg", the "over-pickled egg", the "spoilt egg")

3.1.1 Wavelet Transform of Images

Decomposing algorithm and reconstruction algorithm were important applications of wavelet transform.

Decomposition and reconstruction algorithm are the following [3].

Decomposition algorithm:

$$\begin{cases} c_{k;n,m} = \sum_{l,j} a_{l-2n,j-2m} c_{k+1;l,j} \\ d^i_{k;n,m} = \sum_{l,j} b^i_{l-2n,j-2m} c_{k+1;l,j} \end{cases} \tag{1}$$

Reconstruction algorithm:

$$c_{k+1;n,m} = \sum_{l,j} (p_{n-2l,m-2j} c_{k;l,j} + \sum_{i=1}^{3} q^i_{n-2l,m-2j} d^i_{k;l,j}) \tag{2}$$

Where, i=1, 2, 3

c and d are decomposing series, a, b, p, q are decomposing coefficients.

According to the algorithms above, the denoised images of four kinds of eggs were decomposed and reconstructed by wavelet, and the results were showed in the Fig. 3 [4].

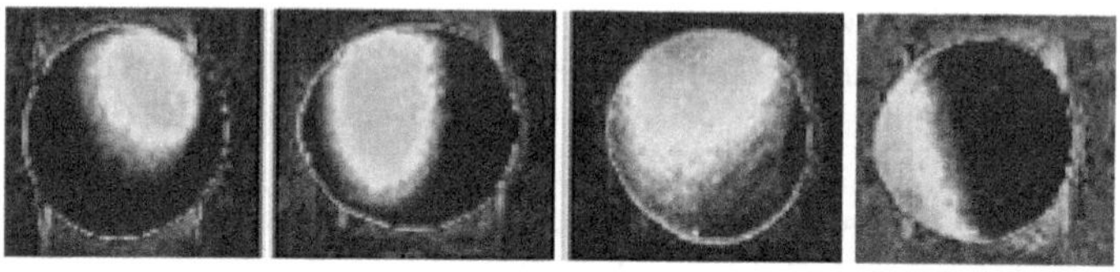

Fig. 3. Pretreated Images processed by Wavelet Reconstruction (From left to right: The "well-pickled egg", the "non-well pickled egg", the "over-pickled egg", the "spoilt egg").

Brightness statistics of the approximately synthesized images after reconstruction were showed in Table 1. In this table, it was found: the brightness of the "well-pickled egg" ranked the first; the "non-well pickled egg" came second; the "over-pickled egg" came third; the "spoilt egg" stayed the last. This result matched the judgment of vision testing.

Table 1. Brightness Statistics of All Eggs

Sort	*Mean*	*Standard Deviation*
"Well-pickled"	89.91	85.79
"Non-well pickled"	84.91	79
"Over-pickled"	70.15	62
"Spoilt"	53.44	51.14
"Well-pickled"	89.91	85.79

3.1.2 Fourier Transform of Images

Fourier transform offered another aspect to observe images. It could transfer images from grey distribution to frequency distribution to contribute to the observation of images.

In computer vision system, images always appear in the form of discrete two dimensional matrixes, and there is a necessity to implement two dimensional Fourier transform. The continual function *f(x, y)* of two dimensional real variables- *x* and *y* are turned into matrix with the length of *M*×*N*, and the corresponding discrete Fourier transform is the following [5]:

Positive Transform:

$$F(u,v)=\sum_{x=0}^{M-1}\sum_{y=0}^{N-1} f(x,y)e^{-j2\pi(\frac{ux}{M}+\frac{vy}{N})} \tag{1}$$

Reserve Transform:

$$f(x,y)=\frac{1}{MN}\sum_{u=0}^{M-1}\sum_{v=0}^{N-1} F(u,v)e^{j2\pi(\frac{ux}{M}+\frac{vy}{N})} \tag{2}$$

Two dimensional discrete Fourier transform was applied to the four kinds of eggs respectively, and the corresponding phase spectrum images were showed in Fig. 4 [6]. From the figure, it was found that the phase spectrum stripes of the "well-pickled egg" were clear and ordered, and the stripes of the "non-well pickled egg" were relative vague. The stripes of the "over-pickled egg" were broken and laid disorderedly, while the stripes of the "spoilt egg" almost could not be found.

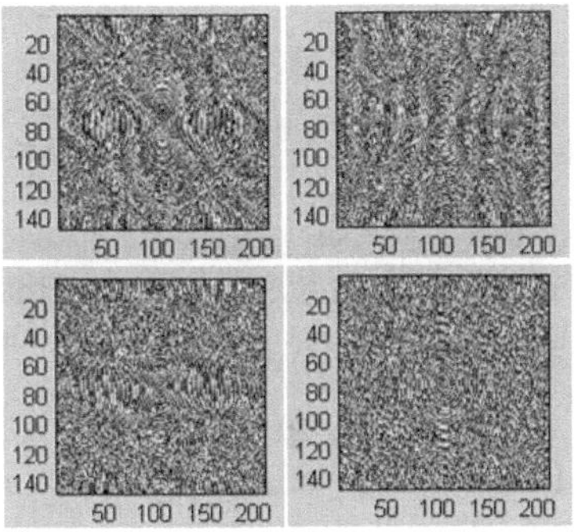

Fig. 2. Phase Spectrum (From left to right and from up to down: the "well-pickled egg", the "non-well pickled egg", the "over-pickled egg", the "spoilt egg")

To reflect these differences in terms of values, MATLAB was employed to calculate the statistical moment of four kinds of eggs' phase spectrum obtained through Fourier transform. The results were showed in Table 2, and it was found that the entropies in the statistical moment gradually increased as the following sequence: the "well-pickled egg", the "non-well pickled egg", the "over-pickled egg" and the "spoilt egg".

Table 2. Statistical Moment of Phase Spectrum

Sort	*Entropy*
"Well-pickled"	0.051771
"Non-well pickled"	0.063222
"Over-pickled"	0.063
"Spoilt"	0.074629
"Well-pickled"	0.051771

3.2 Feature Extraction

3.2.1 Color Feature Parameters Extraction

Color feature parameters (including *R*, *G*, *B*, *H*, *S* and *V*) were extracted from all the images. For the images of each kind of eggs, 51 were selected stochastically. Then scatter diagrams were drew for these six parameters respectively.

Fig. 5 showed that four color parameters (*R*, *G*, *B* and *V*) with marked variance and less overlapping regions. Thus, these four parameters were kept for the later test.

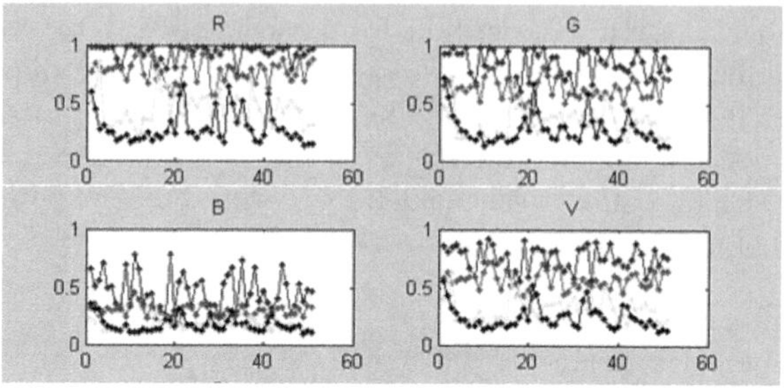

Fig. 3. Color Parameters Scatter Diagrams

3.2.2 Textural Feature Parameters Extraction

Textural features based on co-occurrence matrix are multiple, and four of them were chosen in this paper: Angle secondary moment, inertial moment (contrast), reverse difference moment and entropy.

Textural feature parameters (including *RW1, RW2, RW3, RW4, GW1, GW2, GW3, GW4, BW1, BW2, BW3* and *BW4*) were extracted from all the images. For the images of each kind of eggs, 51 were selected stochastically. Scatter diagrams were drew for these twelve parameters respectively.

Fig.6 showed three textural parameters (*GW1, BW1* and *BW4*) with marked variance and less overlapping regions. Thus, these three parameters were kept for the later test.

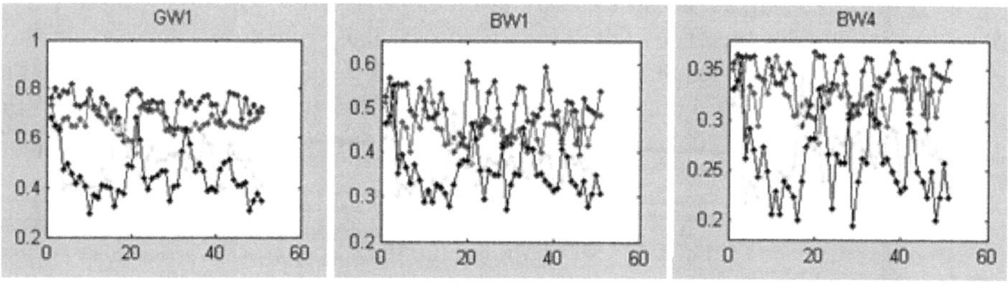

Fig. 4. Textural Parameters Scatter Diagrams

3.2.3 Textural Feature Parameters Extraction

The mean values of statistical moment parameters of all the images were calculated and the results were in the following Table.3.

Table 3. Statistical Moment of Real Color Images

	"Well-pickled"	*"Non-well pick-led"*	*"Over-pickled"*	*"Spoilt"*
Mean Brightness	23613.22	15350.63	7196.747	2389.956
Mean Contrast	27108.51	20393.72	10706.49	5271.957
R	0.999903	0.999828	0.999188	0.981476
The Third Level Moment	95678999	104000000	26681774	11887343
Consistency	0.342996	0.401242	0.484668	0.760306
Entropy	3.374802	3.480725	2.682251	1.215876

From the table above, it was found that the mean values of brightness, contrast and entropy gradually decreased as the following order: the "well-pickled egg", the "non-well pickled egg", the "over-pickled egg" and the "spoilt egg". Therefore these three parameters, "Mean Brightness", "Mean Contrast" and "Entropy" were kept for the later test.

3.3 Modeling

BP algorithm is one of the most widely used neural network learning algorithms at present. It could realize the discretional non-linear mapping of the input and the output, and is endowed with the function of generalization.

The sorting test of salted duck eggs was also a kind of pattern recognition. Therefore this study chose the BP algorithm as the designed algorithm.

3.3.1 Network Structure

Fig. 7 showed a basic structure of artificial neural network. The neural network consisted of three parts: Input layer, Output layer, and Hidden layer. The hidden layer may contain one layer or many layers.

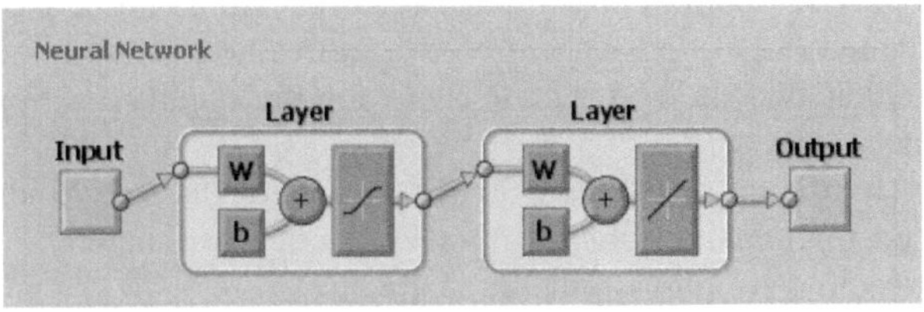

Fig. 5. Diagrammatic Drawing of Neural Network

For this BP network, three-layer feedforward structure (namely Input layer, Output layer and one Hidden layer) was taken [7]. The nodes in the Input layer was 10, namely the number of the selected parameters including color, texture, and statistical moment; there were four nodes in the Output layer, and these four nodes were corresponding to the different sort codes of eggs; according to empirical equations, the number of the nodes in the Hidden layer was set as 18.

3.3.2 Network Training

The total number of the sample (including four kinds of eggs) was 279; among them, 160 made up the training sample and the rest made up the testing sample [8]. Prior to the neural network training, the data were normalized to avoid data saturation and to increase the velocity of convergence. The function for normalization was "premnmx". The training sample was used to train the BP network. The input and output data of the training sample matched the structure of the network. The training ended when the total error value decreased to a level that was lower than the set value.

3.3.3 Model Test

To test the reliability of the network, the testing sample was employed. The input and the output principles were the same as those in the training. Among the 119 testing sample, about 9 eggs were sorted incorrectly and the corrective ratio amounted to about 92%. Besides, there were no cases that the "over-pickled eggs" and "spoilt eggs" were regarded as the "well-pickled egg". This result satisfied the requirement of industrial production.

3.3.4 Result Analysis

From the above result, it was found that the error ratio of this neural network was about 8%. The reasons for the incorrect judgments may be the following:

First of all, workers sorted some eggs mistakenly.
Second, the eggs for the experiment may transform and turn bad in the transportation.
Thirdly, the light of the photographing mechanism was unstable in the experiment.

4 Conclusions

This paper proposed a method based on image processing and neural network to test the quality of salted duck eggs. The corrective ratio amounted to about 92%, and this result certified that this method was feasible for the quality testing and sorting of salted duck eggs.

There were significant differences for the images of the four kinds of salted duck eggs in the color, texture and statistical moment feature parameters.

Images of salted duck eggs with good quality were with the highest values of brightness and entropy.

References

1. Chen, L.: Processing Technology of Soft Yolk Preserved Egg and Red Yolk Duck Egg, in the first version, the second print in February, pp. 86–92. Jindun Press, Beijing (2005)
2. Gonzalez, R.C., Woods, R.E., Eddins, S.L., translated by Qiuqi Ruan and others: Digital Image Processing Using MATLAB, in the ninth print, pp. 179–210, 252-284, 321-363. Electronic Industry Press, Beijing (November 2009)
3. Cheng, Z.: Wavelet Analysis and Application Cases, pp. 78–107. An Jiaotong University Press, Xi'an (2007)
4. Zheng, Z., Shen, P., Yang, X., Wan, Y.: Wavelet Transform and MATLAB Tool Application, pp. 35–42, 87-110. Earthquake Press, Beijing (2001)
5. Ying, Y., Han, D.: Non-destructive Testing Technology of Agricultural Product, pp. 68–146. Chemical Industry Press, Beijing (2005)
6. Misiti, M., Misiti, Y., Oppenheim, G., Poggi, J.-M.: Wavelet Toolbox^{TM} 4 User's Guide
7. Wang, Q., Wen, Y.: Egg Freshness Detection Based on BP Neural Network, pp. 29–34. Huazhong Agricultural University Graduate Thesis, Wuhan, China (2004)
8. Neural Network Theory and Its Realization through MATLAB, Feisi Science and Technology Study Center, pp. 44–59, 99–1. Electronic Industry Press, Beijing (2005)

Depth Calculation and Object Detection Using Stereo Vision with Subpixel Disparity and HOG Feature

Weilong Song, Guangming Xiong, Linlang Cao, and Yanhua Jiang

Intelligent Vehicle Research Center, Beijing Institute of Technology, Beijing, China,100081

Abstract. Object detection using image processing mainly includes single-camera based detection and stereo vision based detection. Stereo vision-based object detection approaches need to find correspondences from the left to the right image. In this paper, we proposed to detect the region of interest (ROI) of objects like cars, people, bikes using HOG descriptors and make correspondence matching only in ROI. Moreover, we used 3D reprojection method to calculate the depth and employed the subpixel disparity technology to increase the depth range resolution. By the proposed approach, the corresponding is only needed to be done for special features in the special region which improves the accuracy.

Keywords: Stereo vision, depth calculation, subpixel disparity.

1 Introduction

Object detection using image processing mainly includes single-camera based detection and stereovision based detection. The monocular approach uses techniques such as object model fitting [1], color segmentation [2], or detection of specific characteristics such as texture [3] or symmetry axes [4]. The stereovision-based approaches have the advantage of directly estimating the 3D coordinates of an image feature [5]. It is a technique that analyzes the foreground and background information and extracts objects by means of computer without human supervision, and also a closer simulation to the human perception. Recently, stereo vision which is able to overcome many of monocular vision's problems has been studied. Especially, many stereo algorithms which extract 3-dimensional information, namely the disparity map, are proposed. For these reasons, many obstacle localization algorithms are also proposed [6].

It is worth mentioning that all these stereovision-based object detection approaches need to find correspondences from the left to the right image. In this paper, we proposed to find the region of interest (ROI) of objects like cars, people, bikes using HOG descriptors and to detect corner features in ROI only in the left image and then to make correspondence matching for these features in the right image. By this approach, the matching is only needed to be done for special features in the special region which increases the accuracy and saves the computation time.

The rest of this paper is organized as follows. The framework of the system is briefly introduced in Section II. Section III describes the depth calculations method including subpixel disparity technology. Section IV presents ROI detection using

H. Tan and M. Zhou (Eds.): CSE 2011, Part I, CCIS 201, pp. 489–494, 2011.

HOG descriptors followed by corner detection in ROI in Section V. Finally, Section VI gives the results of the experiment.

2 Framework of the System

We constructed a framework to calculate depth distances of objects in combination with ROI detection using HOG, features matching and subpixel disparity technology. The flowchart is illustrated in Fig.1.

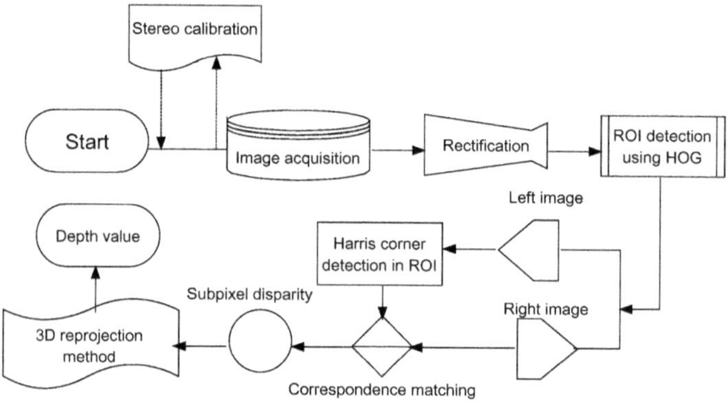

Fig. 1. Flowchart

3 Depth Calculations Using Stereo Vision

3.1 Triangulation of Stereo Vision

Assume that we have a stereo rig as shown in Figure 2: two cameras whose image planes are exactly coplanar with each other, with exactly parallel optical axes that are a known distance apart, baseline T and with equal focal lengths f. Also, assume for now that the images are row-aligned and that every pixel row of one camera aligns exactly with the corresponding row in the other camera. And then we can find a point $P(x,y,z)$ in the physical world in the left and the right image views at $P_l=(x_l,y_l)$ and $P_r=(x_r,y_r)$.

We can easily derive the depth Z by using similar triangles from Fig.2.

$$\frac{T + x_l - x_r}{Z - f} = \frac{T}{Z} \tag{1}$$

The disparity is defined simply by $d = x_r - x_l$, so we can obtain

$$Z = f\frac{T}{(x_r - x_l)} = f\frac{T}{d} \tag{2}$$

The depth is inversely proportional to the disparity between these views

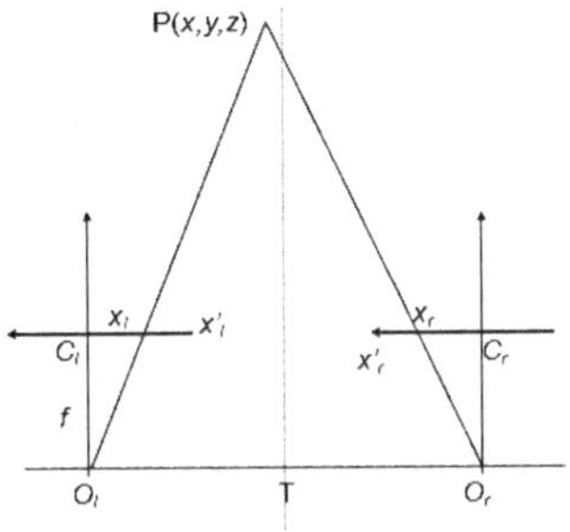

Fig. 2. Stereo rig

3.2 Depth Computation

3D reprojection method can be used to calculate the depth. Given a two-dimensional homogeneous point (x,y) and its associated disparity *d*, we can project the point into three dimensions using [7]:

$$Q\begin{bmatrix} x \\ y \\ d \\ 1 \end{bmatrix} = \begin{bmatrix} X \\ Y \\ Z \\ W \end{bmatrix} \tag{3}$$

Here, the 3D coordinates are (X/W, Y/W, Z/W).

Given the rotation matrix and translation (R, T) between the stereo images and the camera intrinsic matrix, Bouguet algorithm [8] for stereo rectification can be used to obtain the reprojection matrix Q.

In the real test, we found that the calculated depth value is different from the real distance, and the differences are increased gradually along with depth. Thus, it needs to fit the calculated value to real value using fitness method.

3.3 Subpixel DisparityTechnique

Consider the case of a stereoscopic vision system used in this work, Table 1 shows depth values for image disparity range of 3 to 7 pixels.

It can be concluded that a certain disparity value computes to a one depth value. For example, a disparity of 3 pixels would give depth of exactly 27.7947 m, while a pixel disparity of 4 would work out to a depth value of 20.8460 m. Without considering the subpixels between 3 and 4, it is not possible to obtain depth values between 27.7947 m and 20.8460 m.

Table 1. Comparison between disparity and depth

Disparity (pixels)	Depth (m)
3	27.7947
4	20.8460
5	16.6768
6	13.8973
7	11.9120

On the other hand, given the smallest allowed disparity increment Δd, we can determine smallest achievable depth range resolution ΔZ by using the formula [7]:

$$\Delta Z = \Delta d \frac{Z^2}{fT} \tag{4}$$

From Equation (4), the depth range resolution will be increased sharply along with depth value if the minimum disparity increment is 1. Thus, we need smaller disparity increments which are less than 1.

The disparity map is obtained through stereoscopic matching. The subpixel disparity technique [9] was integrated into this work. New disparity is calculated and sent to the depth estimation algorithm for further processing.

4 ROI Detection Using HOG

Histogram of oriented gradient (HOG) descriptor counts occurrences of gradient orientation in localized portions of an image. This method is similar to that of edge orientation histograms, scale-invariant feature transform descriptors, and shape contexts, but differs in that it on a dense grid of uniformly spaced cells and uses overlapping local contrast normalization for improved accuracy [10].

HOG algorithm implementation includes some steps: gradient computation, orientation binning, descriptor blocks, block normalization and SVM classifier. Dalal and Triggs presented results on applying Histogram of Oriented Gradient descriptors to image objects including human beings, cars, buses, and bicycles, as well as common animals such as dogs, cats, and cows [11]. They included with their results the optimal parameters for block formulation and normalization in each case. Therefore, we can use HOG descriptors to detect cars, bicycles or pedestrians in front of our mobile robot. The detected region can be seen as a region of interest (ROI) for the next step.

5 Feature Detection in ROI Using Harris Corner Detector

The Harris corner detector is a popular interest point detector due to its strong invariance to: rotation, scale, illumination variation and image noise [12]. The Harris corner detector is based on the local auto-correlation function of a signal; where the local auto-correlation function measures the local changes of the signal with patches shifted by a small amount in different directions. Compared to other detection operators, the Harris corner detector is simple and suited for many situations.

Although we obtained the ROI using HOG descriptors, there are a lot of pixels belonging to different objects in the region. We proposed to detect corner features using Harris corner detector in ROI of the left image and then make correspondence matching in the right image for these corner features.

And then we can calculate the subpixel disparities of these corner features using subpixel disparity technology after ROI detection and features matching. Finally, the depth values of these corner features can be calculated using 3D reprojection method. Then we can determine which corner features belonging to the same object using certain clustering method.

6 Experiments

Fig.3 shows the stereo sensors (Point Grey Bumblebee) used for the experiments. After configuration and calibration, the image planes are parallel and the epipolar geometry is rectified. The parameters of the stereo sensors are T_x = 120.3608 mm, f = 692.7840 pixels. The resolution of each image is 1024 x 768 pixels. 1394 Driver were used for grabbing images on a laptop computer with Pentium® 4 CPU 1.6GHz and 0.99GB of RAM running under Microsoft Windows XP.

According to the proposed approach, we grabbed the stereo images and made rectification. Fig.4(a) and (b) are the rectified left and right image. And we detected the object like people and car in this case using HOG descriptor only in the left image shown in Fig.4(c). Then, we found corner features using Harris detector in ROI shown in Fig.4(d). We found the matched pixels in the right image for these features and obtained the subpixel disparities of these features and calculated their depth values. Finally, we used an appropriate clustering method to distinguish the car and person and output their distances.

Fig. 3. Stereo sensors

Fig. 4. (a) and (b) the rectified left and right images, (c) ROI detection using HOG for left image, (d) corner detection in ROI

References

1. Gavrila, D.M.: Pedestrian Detection from a Moving Vehicle. In: Vernon, D. (ed.) ECCV 2000. LNCS, vol. 1843, pp. 37–49. Springer, Heidelberg (2000)
2. Ulrich, I., Nourbakhsh, I.: Appearance-Based Obstacle Detection with Monocular Color Vision. In: Proc. of the AAAI National Conference on Artificial Intelligence, Austin, TX (July/August 2000)
3. Kalinke, T., Tzomakas, C., von Seelen, W.: A Texture based Object Detection and an Adaptive Model-based Classification. In: Procs. IEEE Intelligent Vehicles Symposium 1998, Stuttgart, Germany, pp. 341–346 (October 1998)
4. Kuehnle, A.: Symmetry-based vehicle location for AHS. In: Procs. SPIE Transportation Sensors and Controls: Collision Avoidance, Traffic Management, and ITS, Orlando, FL, vol. 2902, pp. 19–27 (November 1998)
5. Nedevschi, S., Danescu, R., Frentiu, D., Marita, T., Oniga, F., Poco, C.: High Accuracy Stereo Vision System for Far Distance Obstacle Detection. In: IEEE Intelligent Vehicles Symposium, June 14-17. University of Parma, Parma (2004)
6. Lee, C.-H., Lim, Y.-C., Kwon, S., Lee, J.-H.: Obstacle localization with a binarized v-disparity map using local maximum frequency values in stereo vision. In: International Conference on Signals, Circuits and Systems (2008)
7. Bradski, G., Kaehler, A.: Learning OpenCV – Computer Vision with the OpenCV Library. O'Reilly Media, Inc., Sebastopol (2008)
8. Bouguet, J.-Y.: Visual methods for three-dimensional modeling, PhD Thesis (1999)
9. Morgan, G.L.K., Liu, J.G., Yan, H.: Precise Subpixel Disparity Measurement From Very Narrow Baseline Stereo. IEEE Transactions on Geoscience and Remote Sensing 48(9), 3424–3433 (2010)
10. `http://en.wikipedia.org/wiki/Histogram_of_oriented_gradients`
11. Dalal, N.: Finding People in Images and Videos, PhD thesis, France (2006)
12. Schmid, C., Mohr, R., Bauckhage, C.: Evaluation of interest point detectors. International Journal of Computer Vision 37(2), 151–172 (2000)

Research on Course System Construction on Computer Science & Technology Specialty

Huanli Pang, Lianzhe Zhou, and Xin Chang

College of Computer Science & Engineering,
ChangChun University of Technology, 130012 Changchun, China
panghuanli@mail.ccut.edu.cn

Abstract. Expounded the specially of computer science & technology specialty, bring up reformation strategy of development on computer science & technology specialty , and designed course system excogitation set with three basic conduct course teach, three conjoin to construct course system frame, three grades platform to complete student's comprehensive diathesis fossilize and release subjective motile nature and creative nature, achievement feeling molds successful life experience, vocation role play to experience engineering practical requirement. By these to improve student's applied ability of computer, engineering practice ability and technological innovate ability.

Keywords: computer science & technique, course system, creativity, profession role.

1 Introduction

Engineering kinds of profession educate engineers. It's an Engineering mode of training talents. The word "Engineer" being used in many meaning. Its function concludes design, plan, mastermind and direct etc. So, being a computer Specialty Engineer should have ADIT that is Analysis, Design, Implementing and Troubleshooting.

How to form satisfactory computer science & technology Specialty education system through rational set up the course in training scheme to carry through engineering talent and training Life-long Education, self adopt ability to adopt future social need seemed extremely important.

2 Present of Computer Science and Technology Specialty Training Scheme

Ministry of Education has promulgated "Ordinary college undergraduate subject catalogues" in 1998 and combined the former computer software and computer application to computer science & technology. Computer science & technology specialty shows the principle of "solid academic foundation with high quality and flexible adaptation to new changes and profound potential capacity". It demands the students to hold systematically the basal knowledges, basal theoretics and basal technologies of

H. Tan and M. Zhou (Eds.): CSE 2011, Part I, CCIS 201, pp. 495–499, 2011.

computer science & technology. The collage offered specialized core courses add facultative courses pattern. It is a kind of vertically course scheme. With the subdivide need of graduate, course design evolve to specialized core course add Specialty direction course add selected course. These cannot satisfy the need of innovative talents training for "twelfth five-year" plan. We need to establish innovative education thought to training innovative talent.

3 Basis for Curriculum System

This paper reference the five kinds of talent with IEEE/ACM CC2005[1] course system: CS (Computer Science), CE (computer Engineering), SE (Soft Engineering), IS (Information System) and IT (Information Technology). Also combine literature [2] and literature [3].

CC2005 gives requirement of every kind of talent; reinforce engineering practice ability and profession character.

Literature [2] requires Engineering Practice occupies certain on a percentage. It also said to lead certain industrial specifications and norm into occupation Accomplishment training.

4 Scheme for Curriculum System

Undergraduate education educates learning ability and team cooperation ability. For the cultivation of the talent innovation, we need to build a dynamic course system to avoid ossified template.

The implementing of personnel training scheme of the undergraduate courses would training self-study ability self-accommodate to social requirement ability. Through building personal Professional Accomplishments in the campus teach surrounding we can make student fitting employment environment. According to the need of different professional role for theories, practice technical abilities to formulate corresponding education proposal of personnel training. The teacher and student each other enter into respective roles to finish teaching and learning process, really training direct available engineers.

Through design several training scheme according to profession role, we can realize pluralistic, multidirectional training mode. Four years training make students have firmer theories and practice foundation, they can rapid into real work.

Based on literature [1], literature [2] and literature [3], this paper bring up the curriculum system schema with building three-basis to guide class teaching; three-in-one combinations to build Course System framework; three-level platform to raising student integrated quality. By these to release student's subjective activity and creativity, mold successful life experience with a sense of accomplishment, experience engineering practice with vocational role transform.

4.1 Three-Basis to Guide Class Teaching

Three-basis (basal knowledges, basal theoretics and basal technologies) is the kernel of a course. It is the main line for training three-basis. Only through teaching to invert theories to knowledge, knowledge convert to technical ability that student can really understand, grasp and use with facility.

To implement three-basis during class teaching we must combine theory with practice; combine knowledge with innovation; combine professional technical ability training with overall quality.

4.2 Three-in-One Combinations to Build Course System Framework

Theory combines with practice. Without the evolving route of ascendant helix through theories into practice again theories can not have real cognition to the objective world. Only with rich and real practical teaching theory teaching can really become the self knowledge of the student.

Combine theory class system with practice teaching system; theory teaching with inner-curricular experiment, Course Design and integrated design construct a complete learning chain.

Knowledge combines with innovation. A college graduate demands interdisciplinary talents with innovative consciousness and innovative abilities. By using college student's innovation investment fund and creation base, we can realize the cultivation of innovative. In the specific implement period we can: Innovative subject with student by himself, 2 divide sub subject from teacher.

Teaching combines with employment. In-class teaching content always differs with engineering practice and the enterprise actual demand. How to combination professional teaching activities with employment, shorten the transition time each other is worth researching. We can through the enterprise personnel come in - understanding enterprise way of thinking, engineering practical and theoretical gap, clear enterprise needs, strengthen the understanding of engineering; Students go out – interactive with enterprise, finish graduation design in enterprise, achieve organic combination of learning and employment. For example, in software engineering course introducing economic evaluation content, combining with engineering projects.

4.3 Mold Successful Life Experience with a Sense of Accomplishment

Today, it's very important of the education of learning interest and achievement in the university education. In the high school stage of learning for years of study life make some students without learning intention after entering university. By setting up innovation credits, which enables students must receive the credits, must attend all kinds of competitions, write academic papers, take part in scientific research activities, obtain vocational skills certification, application and finish college students' innovative programs, etc. Through one or more of the results obtained make the student experience scientific research and academic activities of the joy of success, find there own interests.

4.4 Three-Level Platform to Release Students Subjective Activity and Creativity

Through the formation of professional foundation courses cluster to build professional foundation platform. Construct professional theory foundation to form knowledge module; Set professional direction, fusion professional roles, establish professional direction curses cluster, constitute independent assemble module to form technology module; Fusion engineering training in the course content to match engineering practice; Each professional direction set depth series courses to incarnate professional direction research, application route, and form application modules. By construct innovative practice platform to form students' free play platform. So, form professional platform - direction module - professional prestige - the cultivation of innovative platform route.

Construct professional foundation platform, set professional direction, build a specialist path. Constructing computer science & technology professional basic theoretical platform as a basic theoretical support, form the base of the discipline, achieve broad caliber, strengthening the quality of talent cultivation mode. In professional foundation platform set professional direction. Constitute a professional multi-direction module course cluster with backbone course of every direction. Class advisor give student guide of study and guide students to choose their own areas of interest. Students consist interest/venture group to compose there individuation interest.

Construct practice teaching platform to realize the combination of theory with practice. Through constructing practice teaching system with point, line, plane to combine the practice teaching platform with theory teaching and personnel train together.

Point: that is specialized courses experimental, curriculum design to completion basic knowledge verification and integrated use of course;

Line: that is professional direction synthesis experiment to realize the Integrated Application of professional direction domain knowledge;

Plane: that is production practice, graduation design, course contests, and enterprise practice. With these we can complete the comprehensive use of professional knowledge, achieve the employment role preview with enterprise resources.

Constructing innovation platform, improve the students' innovative thinking and effective employment. The training of engineering technology and skills can not go without innovation. Innovative education needs to guide students to think, analyzing and solving problems actively. In order to mobilize students' enthusiasm, it is a good method in which enables students to get a sense of achievement in the process. By cultivating student community, and guide students to participate in the mathematical modeling competition, ACM programming contest, web design contest etc, in the process of challenges to complete learning process actively. And then guide the student to summarize the technology, tips and form scientific papers. Through such innovation platform can promote students' innovative thinking credits.

During the concrete implementation, setting elective course such as mathematical modeling and ACM competition analyze to give students theoretical guidance; Organizations to improve students' participation with school competition. These allow students to active learning, and improve work efficiency.

4.5 Experience Engineering Practice with Vocational Role Transform

According to professional fields and combined with vocational character to design several training scheme to construct course system which blend profession role. Through the well-defined career role positioning, guides the student to study domain knowledge view.

In undergraduate teaching, put employment into the curriculum system Settings. In professional course constitution, professional direction is the basic division. With the employment as the guidance, design course system vocational character, through the teaching content evaluation and employment simulation assessment to complete student's career play, thus make students have specific learning goals and accomplishment, make study with passively to positive, fully mobilize students' subjective initiative. For example, According to programmer, senior programmer, system analyst, database administrator, project manager position to design Professional direction course arrangement such as software engineering, database application technology etc. In the course arrangement and the course content, such as the course content of database administrator we can use Oracle product as example to explain, combining DBA Certification to improve students' employment levels.

5 Conclusion

Establish of computer science & technology professional curriculum system, which embodies the formulation of the engineering makers in the understanding of the essence. Its implementation need the entire teacher's sincerely work. On enrollment mobilization, establisher needs to discuss the core thinking of the curriculum system to student. In the process of implementing, teachers need to implement makers guidance and intention. Class advisor guide students understand the essence of curriculum system. The cooperation between teachers and students can truly reflect the value of curriculum system.

References

1. Computing Curricula 2005 – The Overview Report, ACM IEEE Computer Society (September 30, 2005)
2. Ministry of Education Computer Science & Technique Specialty Teaching Subcommittee. Computer Specialty Undergraduate Education assessment criterion of Higher Education, Beijing (2007)
3. Ministry of Education Computer Science & Technique Specialty Teaching Subcommittee. Chinese Computer Undergraduate Specialty Devemopment Strategic Research Report, Beijing (2010)

Self-Organizing Polynomial Neural Network for Forecasting Chaotic Time Series: Comparison Results

Jui-Yu Wu*

Department of Business Administration,
Lunghwa University of Science and Technology, Taiwan
jywu@mail.lhu.edu.tw

Abstract. While lacking previous knowledge, general users often have difficulty in using nonlinear statistical time series methods (e.g., bilinear model, threshold autoregressive model, smoothing transition autoregressive model, autoregressive conditional heteroscedastic model and generalized autoregressive conditional heteroscedastic model) and spectral analytical approaches. Moreover, standard back-propagation neural networks (BPNNs) using the steepest descent algorithm have the disadvantage that they converge to local optima. To overcome the above limitations, this work develops a self-organizing polynomial neural network (SOPNN) based on the group method of data handling (GMDH) algorithm, which is a statistical learning network. The proposed SOPNN scheme can create an optimal network topology by using an evolutionary process and is easily to be used. Performance of the proposed SOPNN scheme is also measured by using the Mackey-Glass chaotic time series problem. Additionally, numerical results of the proposed SOPNN scheme are compared with those of conventional BPNN, cerebellar model articulation controller NN (CMAC NN), advanced simulated annealing-based BPNN (ASA-BPNN) and artificial immune algorithm-based BPNN (AIA-BPNN). Experimental results indicate that the optimum training and test capabilities of the proposed SOPNN are superior to those of a conventional BPNN. Furthermore, the generalization capability and computational CPU time of the proposed SOPNN scheme are competitive for those of CMAC NN, AIA-BPNN and ASA-BPNN.

Keywords: group method of data handling, cerebellar model articulation controller, back-propagation neural network, artificial immune algorithm, chaotic time series.

1 Introduction

Sales prediction [1, 2], demand forecasting [3] and stock price forecasting [4, 5] can be considered as time series prediction problems. Traditional analytical methods of time series prediction can be categorized into statistical and spectral analytical approaches. Statistical methods such as exponential smoothing and autoregressive

* Corresponding author.

H. Tan and M. Zhou (Eds.): CSE 2011, Part I, CCIS 201, pp. 500–510, 2011.

integrated moving average (ARIMA) approaches assume that the future value of time series linearly depends on observed values of history, and have the advantages that are easily used and interpreted. Unfortunately, such statistical methods based on linear models have difficulty in solving real world problems with nonlinear behavior. Therefore, among the many nonlinear time series models developed include bilinear, threshold autoregressive, smoothing transition autoregressive, autoregressive conditional heteroscedastic and generalized autoregressive conditional heteroscedastic models. However, the parameter settings of these models depend on solving specific problems, explaining the difficulty that general practitioners have in applying conventional spectral analytical methods. For instance, prior signal processing knowledge is required to adjust specific parameters for these spectral analytical methods [6].

As quantitative modeling tools, Neural networks (NNs) hold several advantage over traditional statistical approaches. For instance, NNs exhibit good learning and generalization capabilities in data-rich environments. Recent decades have witnessed the successful application of many NNs to time series forecasting problems. For instance, Zhang et al. [7] surveyed NNs to solve prediction problems. Wu [8] introduced an efficient cerebellar model articulation controller (CMAC) NN for chaotic time series forecasting. Bodyanskiy and Popov [9] presented a novel NN method for financial time series forecasting. Balestrassi et al. [10] used a NN for forecasting a nonlinear time series. Faruk [11] presented a hybrid back-propagation NN (BPNN) and ARIMA approach to predict a water quality time series. Unfortunately, the standard BPNN using the steepest descent algorithm has the disadvantage that converges to local optima. Many stochastic search optimization methods have been used to overcome the limitation of conventional BPNNs. For example, Wu [12] used an artificial immune algorithm to optimize the weights of a BPNN (AIA-BPNN). Wu [13] employed an advanced simulated algorithm to find the weights of a BPNN (ASA-BPNN). Lee and Kang [14] optimized the network topology and parameter settings for a BPNN, including the number of hidden layers, number of neurons in a hidden layer and weights of the network topology.

Ivakhnenko [15] developed a group method of data handling (GMDH) algorithm, which is a statistical learning network, to identify nonlinear relationships between input and output variables. Many enhanced NNs based on the GMDH algorithm have been developed and applied to time series forecasting [16-18]. Moreover, data mining methods based on the GMDH algorithm have been presented and used to solve prediction and classification problems [19].

This work presents a self-organizing polynomial NN (SOPNN) scheme based on the GMDH algorithm. Performance of the proposed SOPNN scheme is evaluated by using a benchmark chaotic time series problem, i.e. Mackey-Glass time series [20, 21]. This work also compares the numerical results of the proposed SOPNN scheme with those of CMAC NN [8], AIA-BPNN [12], and ASA-BPNN [13].

2 GMDH Algorithm

Figure 1 shows the network topology of a GMDH scheme, which is a multi-layered feed-forward NN. GMDH algorithm creates an optimal network topology of the model through successive generations of neurons regarded as quadratic regression polynomials with two input variables, as follows:

$$y_{d,j} = \hat{\beta}_0 + \hat{\beta}_1 x_{v,j} + \hat{\beta}_2 x_{w,j} + \hat{\beta}_3 x_{v,j}^2 + \hat{\beta}_4 x_{w,j}^2 + \hat{\beta}_5 x_{v,j} x_{w,j}, \quad j = 1, 2, \ldots, n_{\text{tr}} \tag{1}$$

where

$y_{d,j}$ = desired output of input pattern j

x_v and x_w = input variables

n_{tr} = the number of input patterns for training

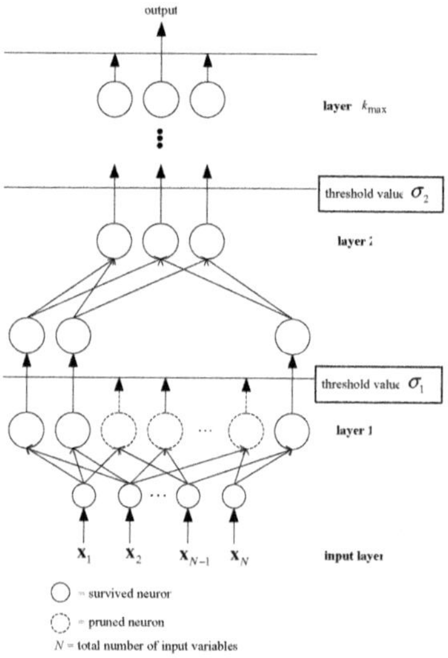

Fig. 1. Network topology of GMDH scheme

Given that these variables $y_{d,j}$, $x_{v,j}$ and $x_{w,j}$ are known, parameters $\hat{\beta}_0$, $\hat{\beta}_1$, $\hat{\beta}_2$, $\hat{\beta}_3$, $\hat{\beta}_4$ and $\hat{\beta}_5$ can be estimated using Eq. (2), as follows:

$$\hat{\boldsymbol{\beta}} = (\mathbf{X}^T \mathbf{X})^{-1} \mathbf{X}^T \mathbf{Y}_d \tag{2}$$

where

$\mathbf{Y}_d = [y_{d,1}, y_{d,2}, \cdots, y_{d,n_{\text{tr}}}]^T$, matrix of a desired output

$$\mathbf{X} = \begin{bmatrix} 1 & x_{v1} & x_{w1} & x_{v1}^2 & x_{w1}^2 & x_{v1}x_{w1} \\ 1 & x_{v2} & x_{w2} & x_{v2}^2 & x_{w2}^2 & x_{v2}x_{w2} \\ \vdots & \vdots & \vdots & \vdots & \vdots & \vdots \\ 1 & x_{vn_{\text{tr}}} & x_{wn_{\text{tr}}} & x_{vn_{\text{tr}}}^2 & x_{wn_{\text{tr}}}^2 & x_{vn_{\text{tr}}}x_{wn_{\text{tr}}} \end{bmatrix}, \text{ design matrix}$$

For each layer, the total number of generated neurons N_t can be defined as follows:

$$N_t = \frac{N(N-1)}{2} \tag{3}$$

where

N = total number of input variables

An output j of neuron m in layer k ($y_{o,j}^{k,m}$) can be expressed by

$$\begin{aligned} &y_{o,j}^{k,m} = \hat{\beta}_0 + \hat{\beta}_1 x_{v,j} + \hat{\beta}_2 x_{w,j} + \hat{\beta}_3 x_{v,j}^2 + \hat{\beta}_4 x_{w,j}^2 + \hat{\beta}_5 x_{v,j} x_{w,j}, \\ &j = 1,2,\ldots,n_{\text{tr}}, \quad k = 1,2,\ldots,k_{\max}, \quad m = 1,2,\ldots,N(N-1)/2 \end{aligned} \tag{4}$$

$k_{\max}$ = the maximum number of evolutionary layers

2.1 Learning Algorithm of GMDH Scheme

The learning algorithm of GMDH consists of the following three steps:

Step 1: estimate $\hat{\boldsymbol{\beta}}$

To avoid over-learning of GMDH scheme, a whole training dataset is divided into two subsets, i.e. training and checking subsets. The values $\hat{\boldsymbol{\beta}}$ described in Eq. (2) is estimated using the training subset, and some strong neurons described in Step 2 are selected using the checking subset.

Step 2: select neurons

GMDH algorithm uses a regularity criterion to prune neurons, as follows:

$$r_{k,m}^2 = \frac{\sum_{j=n_{\text{tr}}+1}^{n_{\text{tr}}+n_{\text{ch}}} (y_{d,j} - y_{o,j}^{k,m})^2}{\sum_{j=n_{\text{tr}}+1}^{n_{\text{tr}}+n_{\text{ch}}} y_{d,j}^2}, \quad k = 1,2,\ldots,k_{\max}, \quad m = 1,2,\ldots,N(N-1)/2 \tag{5}$$

where

$r_{k,m}^2$ = the criterion value obtained from neuron m in layer k

n_{ch} = the number of input patterns for checking

If $r_{k,m}^2$ is smaller than the predefined threshold value in layer k (σ_k), the neuron m in layer k can survive as an input variable for the next layer; if $r_{k,m}^2$ is larger than or equals σ_k, the neuron m in layer k is deleted.

Steps 1 and 2 are repeated to create an optimal network topology. The self-organizing network topology can be viewed as a natural evolution process.

Step 3: terminate learning

A situation in which the lowest $r_{k,m}^2$ is smaller than the lowest $r_{k-1,m}^2$ implies that the network topology can be further improved. If an improvement is achieved, return and repeat Steps 1 and 2; otherwise, terminate the learning iteration.

3 Method

Figure 2 shows the pseudo-code of the proposed SOPNN scheme, which is described as follows.

Training stage:

Step 1: Split the dataset and normalize desired outputs $y_{d,j}$

A dataset is divided into two subsets: a whole training dataset and a test dataset. A whole training dataset is composed of 80 % training and 20% checking patterns.

Each desired output $y_{d,j}$ ($j = 1, 2, \ldots, n_{\text{total}}$) undergoes Min-Max normalization, as follows:

$$y'_{d,j} = \frac{y_{d,j} - y_d^{\min}}{y_d^{\max} - y_d^{\min}}(E_{\max} - E_{\min}) + E_{\min}, \quad j = 1, 2, \ldots, n_{\text{total}} \tag{6}$$

where

$y'_{d,j}$ = normalized desired output j

$\mathbf{Y}_d = [y_{d,1}, y_{d,1}, \ldots y_{d,D_{\text{total}}}]^T$, desired output vector

$y_d^{\min}$ = minimum value of $\mathbf{Y}_d$

$y_d^{\max}$ = maximum value of $\mathbf{Y}_d$

$E_{\min}$ = minimum value of expected output

$E_{\max}$ = maximum value of expected output

According to Yeh [22], the values [$E_{\min}$, $E_{\max}$] are set to [0.2, 0.8].

Step 2: Determine threshold value σ_k

The proposed SOPNN scheme uses a threshold value σ_k to select strong neurons in layer k . The σ_k is in the interval [0, 1]. A large σ_k implies that weak neurons are eliminated. The initial threshold value σ_0 is 0.5.

Step 3: Create neurons from two input variables

For each layer k , N_t is computed using Eq. (3) and $\hat{\boldsymbol{\beta}}$ is estimated for each neuron by using Eq. (2). The outputs of each neuron can be obtained using Eq. (4).

```
Procedure SOPNN scheme
  Begin
    Training stage
    k ← 1
    Step 1  Split the dataset and normalize desired outputs
    Step 2  Determine threshold value σ_k
     While  k ≤ k_max  do
        Step 3  Create neurons form two input variables
        Step 4  Select strong neurons
              if  R²_{k,m} > σ_k  then
                 maintain  neurons
              else
                 eliminate neurons
              endIF
        Step 5  Terminate the learning process
              if max[R²_{k,m}] ≥ 0.999 then
                   break
              endIF
        Step 6  Evaluate the training accuracy
        Step 7  update threshold value σ_{k+1}
           σ_{k+1} ← σ_k × 1.05
           if  σ_{k+1} > 1.0  then
               σ_{k+1} = 1.0
           endIF
         k ← k + 1
     endWhile
    Test stage
        Step 8  Measure the test accuracy
  End
End
```

Fig. 2. The pseudo-code of SOPNN scheme

Step 4: select strong neurons

The proposed SOPNN scheme uses a polynomial regression model. A coefficient of multiple determination is thus used as a selection criterion, as follows:

$$R_{k,m}^2 = \frac{\sum_{j=n_{tr}+1}^{n_{tr}+n_{ch}} (y_{o,j}^{k,m} - \bar{y}_d')^2}{\sum_{j=n_{tr}+1}^{n_{tr}+n_{ch}} (y_{d,j}' - \bar{y}_d')^2}, \quad k = 1, 2, \ldots, k_{max}, \quad m = 1, 2, \ldots, N(N-1)/2 \tag{7}$$

where

$R_{k,m}^2$ = the coefficient of multiple determination obtained from neuron m in layer k

$\mathbf{y}_d'$ = the normalized desired vector

$\bar{y}_d'$ = the mean of y_d'

k_{max} = the maximum number of evolutionary layers

Notably, $R_{k,m}^2$ is used to represent the fitness of a regression model for a neuron and is in the interval [0, 1]. Additionally, $R_{k,m}^2$ is closest to 1, implying that the regression model has a high interpretation capability for input patterns. A situation in which $R_{k,m}^2$ is larger than the value σ_k suggests that the related neuron survives. Moreover, a situation in which $R_{k,m}^2$ is smaller or equal to σ_k implies that the related neuron is dead. To reduce the number of evolutionary layers, an elitist strategy is used to select three strong neurons with a high value of $R_{k,m}^2$ as input variables for the next layer, since the GMDH algorithm does not create a highly versatile structure when input variables are less than three input variables [18].

Step 5: Terminate the learning process

A situation in which $\max[R_{k,m}^2]$ obtained from Step 4 is larger than or equals 0.999 implies that the learning process is terminated.

Step 6: Evaluate the training accuracy

A neuron with the $\max[R_{k,m}^2]$ is defined as the best neuron in layer k. The outputs of best the neuron $y_{o,j}^*$ can be obtained using Eq. (4). The root mean square error (*NRMSE*) is used as a performance index to determine a training accuracy, as follows:

$$NRMSE = \sqrt{\frac{\sum_{j=1}^{n_{\text{tr}}} (y_{d,j}^{'} - y_{o,j}^{*})^2}{n_{\text{tr}}}}, j = 1, 2, \ldots, n_{\text{tr}} \tag{8}$$

Step 7: Update threshold value σ_{k+1}

To overcome the limitation that creates highly complex polynomial regression models, the proposed SOPNN updates threshold value σ_{k+1}, as follows:

$$\sigma_{k+1} = 1.05 \times \sigma_k \tag{9}$$

Repeat steps 3–7 until the termination criterion $k_{\max}$ is met.

Test stage:

Step 8: Measure the test accuracy

The test *NRMSE* can be evaluated using Eq. (8) from a test dataset.

4 Results

The proposed SOPNN scheme was applied to the Mackey-Glass time series problem [20, 21]. For this case, a dataset of 1100 input patterns was generated based on the Mackey-Glass equation, as follows:

$$y(t+1) = (1-\eta)y(t) + \frac{\kappa y(t-\tau)}{1 + y(t-\tau)^{10}} \tag{10}$$

where

$y(t+1)$ = output at time $t+1$
$y(t)$ = output at time t

The series becomes chaotic for $y(0) = 1.2$ and $\tau = 17$ when parameters η and κ are set to 0.1 and 0.2, respectively. Initial conditions were assumed as $y(t) = 0$ when $t < 0$. This series has been used in many studies [23, 24], which used four measurements $y(t)$, $y(t-6)$, $y(t-12)$ and $y(t-18)$ to predict the value at $t+\Delta t$ ($\Delta t = 85$). In financial time series forecasting (such as stock index forecasting), the previous day's closing cash price is often used as a forecasting variable to predict today's closing cash price [5]. Therefore, this work uses measurements $y(t)$, $y(t-6)$, $y(t-12)$ and $y(t-18)$ to forecast the value at $t+\Delta t$ ($\Delta t = 1$).

The dataset was then divided into two datasets, i.e. a whole training dataset with 1000 input patterns and a test dataset with 100 input patterns. The proposed SOPNN scheme was coded using MATLAB software and was run on a Pentium D 3.0 (GHz) personal computer. For each run, parameter settings $\sigma_0 = 0.5$ and $k_{max} = 20$ were used. The best training *NRMSE* = 0.0051 and test *NRMSE* = 0.0056 were found using the proposed SOPNN scheme using 13 evolutionary layers.

Figure 3 shows the best training results obtained by SOPNN scheme for this case. Figure 3(a) plots the number of training patterns against $y'_{d,j}$ ($j = 1, 2, \ldots, 1000$). Figure 3(b) shows the number of training patterns against modelling errors $y'_{d,j} - y_{o,j}$ ($j = 1, 2, \ldots, 1000$). The finding reveals that these errors were in the interval [−0.01, +0.02].

Figure 4 displays the test results. Figure 4(a) plots the curves of $y'_{d,j}$ and $y_{o,j}$ (j = 1001, 1002,..., 1100), indicating that these two curves correlated well with each other. Also, Fig. 4(b) displays the number of test patterns against generalization errors $y'_{d,j} - y_{o,j}$ (j = 1001, 1002,..., 1100). This finding suggests that these errors were in the interval [−0.01 +0.01].

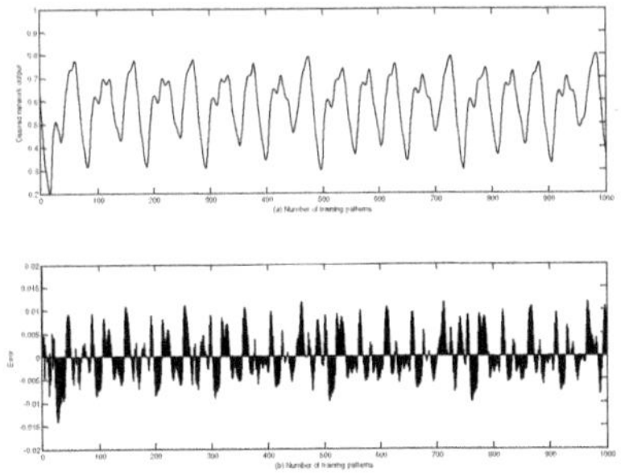

Fig. 3. The best training results obtained using the SOPNN scheme

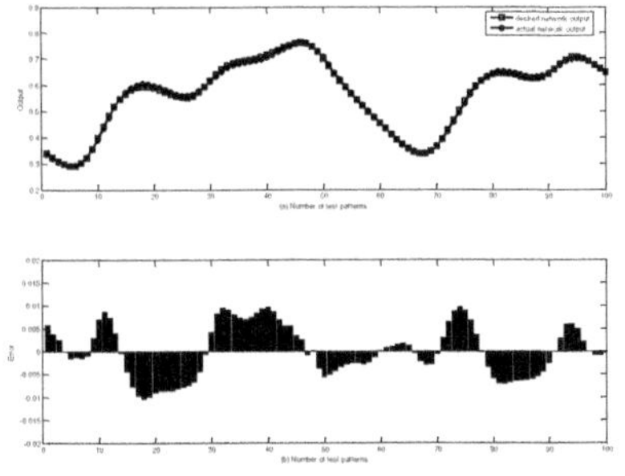

Fig. 4. The best test results obtained using the SOPNN scheme

4.1 Comparison

Table 1 lists the mean training, test *NRMSE*s and mean computational CPU time (MCCT) for CMAC NN [8], AIA-BPNN [12] and ASA-BPNN [13]. All methods were run on Pentium D 3.0 (GHz) personal computer. In Table 1, the '–' indicates that information is unavailable and the "#" represents that the number of neurons in a hidden layer for a BPNN. By using a deterministic learning algorithm, the proposed SOPNN scheme can obtain unique training and test *NRMSE*s by using only one execution. According to this Table, the mean training *NRMSE*s of the CMAC NN and AIA-BPNN are superior to those of ASA-BPNN (#4), standard BPNN (#3), standard BPNN (#4) and standard BPNN (#5), and that the AIA-BPNN (#4) obtained the best mean test *NRMSE*.

Table 1. Comparison results of the CMAC NN, ASA-BPNN, AIA-BPNN and standard BPNN

	mean training *NRMSE*	mean test *NRMSE*	MCCT (sec.)
CMAC NN	0.0085	0.0103	51.21
ASA-BPNN (#4)	0.0107	0.0100	42.03
AIA-BPNN (#4)	0.0085	0.0085	70.56
standard BPNN (#3)	0.03134	0.0283	31.29
standard BPNN (#4)	0.0248	0.0226	36.69
standard BPNN (#5)	0.0225	0.0205	42.65
the proposed SOPNN	–	–	–

Table 2 summaries the best training *NRMSE*, the best test *NRMSE* and the computational CPU time for the proposed SOPNN, CMAC NN, ASA-BPNN (#4), AIS-BPNN (#4) and standard BPNN (#5) schemes. Experimental results indidate that the training and generalization accuracies of the proposed SOPNN, CMAC NN, ASA-BPNN (#4) and AIS-BPNN (#4) are better than that of standard BPNN (#5); in addition, the generalization accuracy and computational CPU time of the proposed SOPNN scheme are competitive for those of CMAC NN, ASA-BPNN (#4) and AIA-BPNN (#4).

Table 2. Comparison results of the CMAC NN, ASA-BPNN, AIA-BPNN, standard BPNN, and SOPNN schemes

	the best training *NRMSE*	the best test *NRMSE*	computational CPU time (sec.)
CMAC NN	0.0034	0.0058	56.52
ASA-BPNN (#4)	0.0069	0.0067	63.31
AIA-BPNN (#4)	0.0066	0.0068	71.64
standard BPNN (#5)	0.0145	0.0135	37.75
the proposed SOPNN	0.0051	0.0056	2.03

5 Conclusion

This work has developed a SOPNN scheme based on GMDH algorithm. The proposed SOPNN scheme can create an optimal network topology through an evolutionary process. Performance of the proposed scheme is evaluated using the Mackey-Glass time series problem and compared with a conventional BPNN, CMAC NN and stochastic search optimization-based BPNNs. Numerical results demonstrate that the training and generalization accuracies of the proposed SOPNN scheme are superior to standard BPNN. Furthermore, the proposed SOPNN scheme is competitive in terms of generalization capability and computational CPU time for those of CMAC NN, ASA-BPNN and AIA-BPNN schemes.

Acknowledgements

The author would like to thank the National Science Council of the Republic of China, Taiwan for financially supporting this research under Contract No. NSC 97-2218-E-262-002- and NSC 98-2221-E-262-014-.

References

1. Ni, Y., Fan, F.: A Two-Stage Dynamic Sales Forecasting Model for the Fashion Retail. Expert Systems with Applications 38, 1529–1536 (2011)
2. Thomassey, S., Happiette, M.: A Neural Clustering and Classification System for Sales Forecasting of New Apparel Items. Applied Soft Computing 7, 1177–1187 (2007)
3. Liu, H., Wang, P.: Bullwhip Effect Analysis in Supply Chain for Demand Forecasting Technology. Systems Engineering - Theory & Practice 27, 26–33 (2007)
4. Lu, C.J., Lee, T.S., Chiu, C.C.: Financial Time Series Forecasting Using Independent Component Analysis and Support Vector Regression. Decision Support Systems 47, 115–125 (2009)
5. Lu, C.J., Wu, J.Y.: Forecasting Financial Time Series via an Efficient CMAC Neural Network. In: The 7th International Symposium on Neural Networks. Lecture Notes in Electrical Engineering, pp. 73–82. Springer, Heidelberg (2010)
6. Rigozo, N.R., Echer, E., Nordemann, D.J.R., Vieira, L.E.A., de Faria, H.H.: Comparative Study between for Classical Spectral Analysis Methods. Applied Mathematics and Computation 168, 411–430 (2005)
7. Zhang, G., Patuwo, B.E., Hu, M.Y.: Forecasting with Artificial Neural Networks: The State of Art. International Journal of Forecasting 14, 35–62 (1998)
8. Wu, J.Y.: Cerebellar Model Articulation Controller for Predicting Chaotic Time Series. In: The 12th Conference on Artificial Intelligence and Applications, pp. 508–515 (2007)
9. Bodyanskiy, Y., Popov, S.: Neural Network Approach to Forecasting of Quasiperiodic Financial Time Series. European Journal of Operational Research 175, 1357–1366 (2006)
10. Balestrassi, P.P., Popova, E., Paiva, A.P., Marangon Lima, J.W.: Design of Experiments on Neural Network's Training for Nonlinear Time Series Forecasting. Neurocomputing 72, 1160–1178 (2009)
11. Faruk, D.Ö.: A Hybrid Neural Network and ARIMA Model for Water Quality Time Series Prediction. Engineering Applications of Artificial Intelligence 23, 586–594 (2010)

12. Wu, J.Y.: Forecasting Chaotic Time Series Using an Artificial Immune System Algorithm-Based Bpnn. In: The 2010 Conference on Technologies and Applications of Artificial Intelligence, pp. 524–531 (2010)
13. Wu, J.Y.: Advanced Simulated Annealing-based BPNN for Forecasting Chaotic Time Series. In: The 2010 International Conference on Electronics and Information Engineering, pp. 38–43 (2010)
14. Lee, J., Kang, S.: GA based Meta-Modeling of BPN Architecture for Constrained Approximate Optimization. International Journal of Solids and Structures 44, 5980–5993 (2007)
15. Ivakhnenko, A.G.: Polynomial Theory of Complex Systems. IEEE Transactions on Systems, Man, and Cybernetics SMC-1, 364–378 (1971)
16. Nikolaev, N.Y., Iba, H.: Polynomial Harmonic GMDH Learning Network for Time Series Modeling. Neural Networks 16, 1527–1540 (2003)
17. Oh, S.K., Pedrycz, W.: The Design of Self-Organizing Polynomial Neural Networks. Information Sciences 141, 237–258 (2002)
18. Oh, S.K., Pedrycz, W., Park, B.J.: Polynomial Neural Networks Architecture: Analysis and Design. Computers and Electrical Engineering 29, 703–725 (2003)
19. Muller, J.A., Lemke, F.: Self-Organising Data Mining - an Intelligent Approach to Extract Knowledge from Data. Dresden, Berlin (1999)
20. Mackey, M.C., Glass, L.: Oscillation and Chaos in Physiological Systems. Science 197, 287–289 (1977)
21. Moody, J., Darken, C.J.: Fast Learning in Networks of Locally-Tuned Process Units. Neural Computation 1, 281–294 (1989)
22. Yeh, I.C.: Structural Engineering Applications with Augmented Neural Networks. Computer-Aided Civil and Infrastructure Engineering 13, 83–90 (1998)
23. Omidvar, A.E.: Configuring Radial Basis Function Network Using Fractal Scaling Process with Application to Chaotic Time Series Prediction. Chaos, Solitons and Fractals 22, 757–766 (2004)
24. Roy, A., Govil, S., Miranda, R.: A Neural-Network Learning Theory and a Polynomial Time RBF Algorithm. IEEE Transactions on Neural Networks 8, 1301–1313 (1997)

Integrated Real-Coded Genetic Algorithm and Particle Swarm Optimization for Solving Constrained Global Optimization Problems

Jui-Yu Wu*

Department of Business Administration,
Lunghwa University of Science and Technology, Taiwan
jywu@mail.lhu.edu.tw

Abstract. This work presents an integrated real-coded genetic algorithm and particle swarm optimization with a penalty function method (RGA-PSO) to solve constrained global optimization (CGO) problems. An outer RGA is used to optimize the parameter settings of an inner PSO algorithm, which includes the constriction coefficient, cognitive parameter, social parameter, penalty parameter and mutation probability. To increase the diversity of particles, the inner PSO method uses a multi-non-uniform operator. Performance of the proposed RGA-PSO algorithm is evaluated using a set of benchmark CGO problems. Additionally, this work compares the numerical results obtained using the proposed RGA-PSO algorithm with those of GAs and artificial immune algorithms (AIAs). Experimental results indicate that the proposed RGA-PSO algorithm converges to a global optimum solution to a CGO problem, and that the performance of the proposed RGA-PSO algorithm is competitive with those of GAs and AIAs. Although a hybrid method increases the complexity of an algorithm, the proposed RGA-PSO algorithm can obtain the optimum parameter settings for the inner PSO algorithm by using the outer RGA and can find a global optimum solution to a CGO problem by using the inner PSO algorithm, simultaneously. Hence, the proposed RGA-PSO algorithm can be considered as an alternative stochastic global optimization method for solving CGO problems.

Keywords: real-coded genetic algorithm, particle swarm optimization, nonlinear programming, constrained global optimization.

1 Introduction

Many scientific and engineering problems can be expressed as constrained global optimization (CGO) problems, as follows:

$$\text{Minimize} \quad f(\mathbf{x}) \tag{1}$$

$$s.t. \quad g_m(\mathbf{x}) \le 0, \quad m = 1, 2, \ldots, M \tag{2}$$

* Corresponding author.

H. Tan and M. Zhou (Eds.): CSE 2011, Part I, CCIS 201, pp. 511–522, 2011.

$$h_k(\mathbf{x}) = 0, \quad k = 1, 2, \ldots, K \tag{3}$$

$$x_n^l \le x_n \le x_n^u, \quad n = 1, 2, \ldots, N \tag{4}$$

where $f(\mathbf{x})$ is an objective function; $g_m(\mathbf{x})$ represents a set of m nonlinear inequality constraints; $h_k(\mathbf{x})$ is a set of k nonlinear equality constraints; $\mathbf{x}$ represents a vector of decision variables which take real values, and each decision variable x_n is constrained by its lower and upper boundaries $[x_n^l, x_n^u]$.

Global optimization approaches for solving CGO problems can be categorized as deterministic or stochastic [1]. Many stochastic global optimization methods have been successfully used to solve CGO problems. For instance, Sun et al., [2] presented an improved vector particle swarm optimization (PSO) algorithm with a constraint-preserving method to solve CGO problems. Tsoulos [3] developed a real-coded genetic algorithm (RGA) with a penalty function approach for solving CGO problems. Deep and Dipti [4] presented a self-organizing GA with tournament selection method for solving CGO problems. Wu [5] developed RGA with a static penalty function approach for solving non-convex optimization problems. Wu presented [6] an artificial immune algorithm (AIA) with an adaptive penalty function method to solve CGO problems.

Zadeh [7] presented the term "soft computing", which refers to the synergistic power of 2 or more fused computational intelligence schemes, such as GAs, PSO algorithms and AIAs [8]. Based on this concept, this work focuses on the co-ordination of an RGA and a PSO algorithm. This work develops a RGA-based PSO (RGA-PSO) algorithm. The specific parameters of an inner PSO algorithm are optimized using an outer RGA. The inner PSO algorithm is used to solve a CGO problem. Performance of the proposed RGA-PSO algorithm is evaluated using a set of benchmark CGO problems.

2 Related Work

2.1 Genetic Algorithm

GAs are stochastic global optimization methods oriented using both the concepts of natural selection as well as genetics and use three genetic operators i.e. selection, crossover and mutation, to explore and exploit the solution space. In solving continuous function optimization problems, RGA is superior to binary-coded GA [9]. Thus, this work describes operators of a RGA [10].

(1) Selection

A Selection operator picks up some strong individuals based on their fitness function values from a current population and, then, reproduces these individuals into a crossover pool. Among the several selection developed include the roulette wheel method, ranking method and tournament technique [9, 10]. Normalized geometric ranking method is a rank-based scheme, as follows:

$$p_j = q'(1-q)^{r-1}, \quad j = 1, 2, \ldots, ps_{\text{RGA}} \tag{5}$$

p_j = probability of selecting individual j

q = probability of choosing the best individual (here q = 0.35)

$$q' = \frac{q}{1-(1-q)^{ps_{\text{RGA}}}}$$

r = individual ranking based on fitness value, where 1 represents the best, $r = 1, 2, \ldots, ps_{\text{RGA}}$

ps_{RGA} = population size of RGA

(2) Crossover

While exploring the solution space by creating new offspring, the crossover operator randomly selects two parents from crossover pool and, then, uses these two parents to generate two new offspring. This operator is repeated until the $ps_{\text{RGA}}/2$ is satisfied. The whole arithmetic crossover is easily implemented, as follows:

$$\mathbf{v}_1' = \beta \times \mathbf{v}_1 + (1-\beta) \times \mathbf{v}_2 \tag{6}$$

$$\mathbf{v}_2' = (1-\beta)\mathbf{v}_1 + \beta \times \mathbf{v}_2 \tag{7}$$

where

$\mathbf{v}_1$ and $\mathbf{v}_2$ = parents

$\mathbf{v}_1'$ and $\mathbf{v}_2'$ = offspring

β = uniform random number in the interval [0, 1.5]

(3) Mutation

Mutation operator can increase the diversity of individuals to exploit the solution space. Multi-non-uniform mutation is described as follows:

$$x_{\text{trial},n} = \begin{cases} x_{\text{current},n} + (x_n^u - x_{\text{current},n})A(g) & \text{if } U_1(0,1) < 0.5 \\ x_{\text{current},n} - (x_{\text{current},n} - x_n^l)A(g) & \text{if } U_1(0,1) \geq 0.5 \end{cases} \tag{8}$$

where

$$A(g) = \left[U_2(0,1)\left(1 - \frac{g}{g_{\max,\text{RGA}}}\right)\right]^2$$

$U_1(0, 1)$ = uniform random variable in the interval [0, 1]

$g_{\max,\text{RGA}}$ = maximum generation of RGA

$x_{\text{current},n}$ = current decision variable x_n

$x_{\text{trial},n}$ = trial candidate solution

2.2 PSO

Edward and Kennedy [11] first presented a standard PSO algorithm, which is inspired by the social behavior of bird flocks or fish schools. Similar to GAs, a PSO algorithm is a population-based algorithm. A population of candidate solutions of is called a particle swarm. Operators of a PSO algorithm are introduced as follows.

(1) Update particle velocities

The particle velocities can be updated by Eq. (9), as follows:

$$\begin{aligned} v_{j,n}(g+1) &= v_{j,n}(g) + c_1 r_{1j}(g)[p_{j,n}^{lb}(g) - x_{j,n}(g)] \\ &\quad + c_2 r_{2j}(g)[p_{j,n}^{gb}(g) - x_{j,n}(g)] \\ j &= 1,2,\ldots,ps_{\text{PSO}},\ n = 1,2,\ldots,N \end{aligned} \tag{9}$$

$v_{j,n}(g+1)$ = particle velocity of decision variable x_n of particle j at generation $g+1$

$v_{j,n}(g)$ = particle velocity of decision variable x_n of particle j at generation g

c_1 = cognitive parameter

c_2 = social parameter

$x_{j,n}(g)$ = particle position of decision variable x_n of particle j at generation g

$r_{1,j}(g), r_{2,j}(g)$ = independent uniform random numbers in the interval [0, 1] at generation g

$p_{j,n}^{lb}(g)$ = best local solution at generation g

$p_{j,n}^{gb}(g)$ = best global solution at generation g

(2) Compute particle positions

The particle positions can be computed using Eq. (10), as follows:

$$\begin{aligned} x_{j,n}(g+1) &= x_{j,n}(g) + v_{j,n}(g+1) \\ j &= 1,2,\ldots,ps_{\text{PSO}},\ n = 1,2,\ldots,N \end{aligned} \tag{10}$$

(3) Inertia weight

Shi and Eberhart [12] presented a modified PSO algorithm, in which an inertia weight (ω) was incorporated into Eq. (11) to control the exploration and exploitation abilities of a PSO algorithm, as follows:

$$\begin{aligned} v_{j,n}(g+1) &= \omega v_{j,n}(g) + c_1 r_{1j}(g)[p_{j,n}^{lb}(g) - x_{j,n}(g)] \\ &\quad + c_2 r_{2j}(g)[p_{j,n}^{gb}(g) - x_{j,n}(g)] \\ j &= 1,2,\ldots,ps_{\text{PSO}},\ n = 1,2,\ldots,N \end{aligned} \tag{11}$$

(4) Constriction coefficient

Moreover, a constriction coefficient (χ) has been inserted into Eq. (12) to balance the exploration and exploitation trade-off [13-15], as follows:

$$\begin{aligned} v_{j,n}(g+1) &= \chi\{v_{j,n}(g)+\rho_1(g)[p_{j,n}^{lb}(g)-x_{j,n}(g)] \\ &\quad +\rho_2(g)[p_{j,n}^{gb}(g)-x_{j,n}(g)]\} \\ j &= 1,2,\ldots,ps_{\text{PSO}},\ n=1,2,\ldots,N \end{aligned} \tag{12}$$

$$\chi=\frac{2U_3(0,1)}{\left|2-\rho-\sqrt{\rho(\rho-4)}\right|}$$

$$\rho=\rho_1+\rho_2,\ \rho_1=c_1r_{1j},\ \rho_1=c_2r_{2j}$$

This work considers the parameters ω and χ to update the velocities of particles, as follows:

$$\begin{aligned} v_{j,n}(g+1) &= \chi\{\omega v_{j,n}(g)+c_1r_{1j}(g)[p_{j,n}^{lb}(g)-x_{j,n}(g)] \\ &\quad +c_2r_{2j}(g)[p_{j,n}^{gb}(g)-x_{j,n}(g)]\} \\ j &= 1,2,\ldots,ps_{\text{PSO}},\ n=1,2,\ldots,N \end{aligned} \tag{13}$$

where

$\omega=\left(\dfrac{g_{\max,\text{PSO}}-g}{g_{\max,\text{PSO}}}\right)$, increased g reduces the ω

$g_{\max,\text{PSO}}$ = maximum generation of PSO algorithm

According to Eq. (13), the optimal values of the parameters c_1, c_2 and χ are difficult to obtain when using a trial and error approach. Therefore, this work uses a RGA to optimize these parameter settings.

2.3 Penalty Function Methods

Stochastic global optimization, such as GAs, AIAs and PSO algorithms, are naturally unconstrained optimization methods. Penalty function methods, which are constraint handling approaches, are commonly used to create feasible solutions to a CGO problem and transform it into an unconstrained optimization problem. Exterior penalty functions use an infeasible solution as a starting point, and the direction of convergence is from the infeasible region to the feasible region. Many exterior penalty functions have been developed, such as static, dynamic, adaptive and death penalty functions [16]. This work uses a static penalty function, as follows:

$$\text{Minimize} \quad f_{\text{pseudo}}(\mathbf{x},\rho) = f(\mathbf{x}) + \rho\left\{\sum_{m=1}^{M}\left\{\max\left[0, g_m(\mathbf{x})\right] + \sum_{k=1}^{K}\left[h_k(\mathbf{x})\right]\right\}^2\right\} \tag{14}$$

where

$f_{\text{pseudo}}(\mathbf{x},\rho)$ = pseudo-objective function obtained using an original objective function plus a penalty term
ρ = penalty parameter

Unfortunately, penalty function schemes are limited in that the penalty parameter ρ has to be fine-tune [4]. To overcome this drawback, this work uses an RGA to find the optimum ρ for each CGO problem. Additionally, to obtain an RGA-PSO solution with high quality that is an accuracy of at least five decimal places for the violation of each constraint to a specific CGO problem, the parameter ρ is within the search space $[1\times10^9, 1\times10^{11}]$.

3 Method

Figure 1 shows the pseudo-code of the proposed RGA-PSO algorithm, in which the outer RGA searches for the best parameter settings of the inner PSO algorithm and the inner PSO algorithm optimizes CGO problems.

Outer RGA:

Step 1: Initialize the parameter settings

Parameter settings such as ps_{RGA}, crossover probability p_c, mutation probability of the outer RGA $p_{\text{m,RGA}}$ as well as lower and upper boundaries of these parameters c_1, c_2, χ, ρ and the mutation probability of the inner PSO algorithm $p_{\text{m,PSO}}$ for a PSO algorithm are given. The candidate solution (individual) of the outer RGA represents the optimized parameters of inner PSO algorithm. Figure 2 illustrates the candidate solution of the RGA.

Step 2: Compute the fitness function value

The fitness function value $fitness_j$ of the outer RGA is the best objection function value $f(\mathbf{x}^*_{\text{PSO}})$ obtained from the best solution $\mathbf{x}^*_{\text{PSO}}$ of each inner PSO algorithm execution, as follows:

$$fitness_j = f(\mathbf{x}^*_{\text{PSO}}),\ j = 1, 2, \ldots, ps_{\text{RGA}} \tag{15}$$

The candidate solution j of the outer RGA is incorporated into the inner PSO algorithm and, then, the inner PSO algorithm is employed to solve a CGO problem. The inner PSO algorithm is executed as follows.

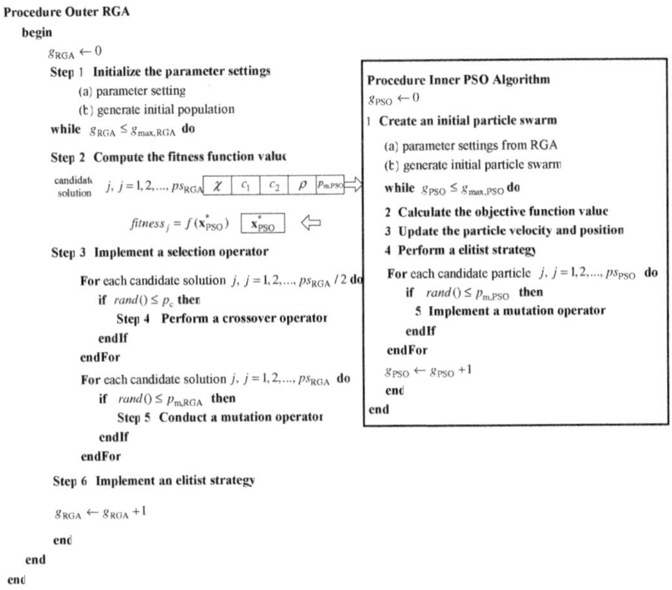

Fig. 1. The pseudo-code of the proposed RGA-PSO algorithm

candidate solution j

χ	c_1	c_2	ρ	$p_{m,PSO}$	$fitness_j$

Fig. 2. Candidate solution of the RGA

Inner PSO algorithm:

1. Create an initial particle swarm

An initial particle swarm is created based on the population size of particles ps_{PSO} from [x_n^l, x_n^u] of a CGO problem. A particle represents a candidate solution of a CGO problem.

2. Calculate the objective function value

According to Eq. (14), the pseudo-objective function value of the inner PSO algorithm is defined by

$$f_{\text{pseudo},j} = f(\mathbf{x}_{\text{PSO},j}) + \left\{ \rho \times \sum_{m=1}^{M} \left\{ \max\left[0,\ g_m(\mathbf{x}_{\text{PSO},j})\right] \right\}^2 \right\},\quad j = 1, 2, \ldots, ps_{\text{PSO}} \tag{16}$$

3. Update the particle velocity and position

Equations (10) and (13) can be used to update the particle position and velocity, respectively.

4. Perform a mutation operator

Standard PSO algorithm lacks evolution operators of GAs such as crossover and mutation. To maintain the diversity of particles, this work uses the multi-non-uniform mutation operator defined by Eq. (8).

5. Implement an elitist strategy

A new particle swarm is create from inner step 3. Notably, $f(\mathbf{x}_{\text{PSO},j})$ of a candidate solution j (particle j) in the particle swarm is evaluated. This work makes a pair-wise comparison between the $f(\mathbf{x}_{\text{PSO},j})$ of candidate solutions in the new particle swarm and that in the current particle swarm. A situation in which the candidate solution j ($j = 1, 2, \ldots, ps_{\text{PSO}}$) in the new particle swarm is better than candidate solution j in the current particle swarm implies that the strong candidate solution j in the new particle swarm replaces the candidate solution j in the current particle swarm. The elitist strategy guarantees that the best candidate solution is always preserved in the next generation. The current particle swarm is updated to the particle swarm of the next generation.

Inner steps 2 to 5 are repeated until the maximum generation number of the inner PSO $g_{\max,\text{PSO}}$ of the inner PSO algorithm is satisfied.

Step 3: Implement a selection operator

Equation (5) is used to select the parents into a crossover pool.

Step 4: Perform a crossover operator

In GAs, the crossover operator performs a global search. Thus, the crossover probability p_c usually exceeds 0.5. Additionally, candidate solutions are created Eqs. (6) and (7).

Step 5: Conduct a mutation operator

In GAs, the mutation operator implements a local search. Also, a solution space is exploited using Eq. (8).

Step 6: Implement an elitist strategy

This work uses an elitist strategy to update the population. A situation in which the $fitness_j$ of candidate solution j in the new population is larger than the $fitness_j$ of candidate solution j in the current population suggests that a replacement of the weak candidate solution j takes place. Additionally, a situation in which the $fitness_j$ of candidate solution j in the new population is equal to or worse than that in the current population implies that the candidate solution j in the current population survives. In addition to maintaining the strong candidate solutions, this strategy effectively eliminates weak candidate solutions.

Outer Steps 2 to 6 are repeated until the maximum generation number of the outer RGA $g_{\max,RGA}$ of the outer RGA is satisfied.

4 Results

The proposed RGA-PSO algorithm, as described in Section 3, was applied to a set of CGO problems taken from other studies [17-20]. The proposed RGA-PSO algorithm was coded in MATLAB software and executed on a Pentium D 3.0 (GHz) personal computer. Fifty independent runs were conducted to solve each test problem. Numerical results were summarized. They include the best, median, mean, worst, standard deviation (S.D.) of objective function values obtained using RGA-PSO solutions, mean computational CPU times (MCCT) and mean absolute error MAE (mean absolute value of the gap between the objective function values obtained using RGA-PSO solutions and the known global minimum value). The RGA-PSO algorithm used the following parameter settings; $p_c = 1$, mutation probability of the outer RGA $p_{m,RGA} = 0.15$, lower and upper boundaries of parameter χ ($[\chi^l, \chi^u] = [0.1, 1]$), lower and upper boundaries of parameter c_1 ($[c_1^l, c_1^u] = [0.1, 2]$), lower and upper boundaries of parameter c_2 ($[c_2^l, c_2^u] = [0.1, 2]$), lower and upper boundaries of parameter ρ ($[\rho^l, \rho^u] = [1\times10^9, 1\times10^{11}]$), lower and upper boundaries of mutation probability for the inner PSO algorithm $p_{m,PSO}$ ($[p_{m,PSO}^l, p_{m,PSO}^u] = [0.1, 0.5]$), $ps_{RGA} = 10$, $g_{\max,RGA} = 3$, $ps_{PSO} = 100$ and $g_{\max,PSO} = 3000$ for solving each test problem (TP).

Table 1 lists the numerical results obtained from the proposed RGA-PSO algorithm for TPs 1–4. Numerical results indicate that the RGA-PSO algorithm can obtain the global minimum solution to each test CGO problem and the difference among the RGA-PSO solutions is small, since each MAE and S.D. of objective function values obtained using RGA-PSO solutions is very close to "0".

Table 1. Numerical results of the proposed RGA-PSO algorithm

TP NO.	Global Optimum	*MAE*	Best	Median	mean	Worst	S.D.	MCCT (sec.)
1	24.306	0.270	24.341	24.565	24.573	24.886	0.13	359.14
2	−30665.539	0.004	−30665.539	−30665.539	−30665.539	−30665.538	0.00	294.19
3	680.630	0.012	680.632	680.642	680.642	680.655	0.01	330.81
4	−15.000	0.000	−15.000	−15.000	−15.000	−15.000	0.00	376.77

4.1 Comparison

Table 2 compares the numerical results of the proposed RGA-PSO algorithm with those obtained using published GAs and an AIA. In Table 2, the '–' indicates that information is unavailable; GA-1 is a GA with a penalty function methods, as used by Michalewicz [18]; and GA-2 represents a GA with a penalty function, but without any penalty parameter, as employed by Deb [19], and AIA-1 is an AIA that is based on an adaptive penalty function, as developed by Wu [6]. GA-1 was run ten times as well as GA-2 and AIA-1 were executed 50 times, to obtain the best, median and worst solutions to each test CGO problems. According to Table 2, the best, median and worst values obtained using the proposed RGA-PSO algorithm are superior to those obtained using GA-1 for TP 1; the worst value yielded from the RGA-PSO algorithm is better than those obtained using GA-2 and AIA-1 for TP 1; the worst value obtained using the RGA-PSO algorithm is greatly superior to those obtained using GA-2 for TP 2; the median and worst values of the RGA-PSO algorithm are better than those of GA-1 for TP 3, and the worst value of the RGA-PSO algorithm is superior to those of GA-2 and AIA-1 for TP4.

Table 3 compares the results of the proposed AIAs with those of the alternative AIA that was presented by Wu [6] (here called AIA-1), the alternative AIA that was (herein as AIA-2) developed by Coello Coello and Cruz-Cortés [17] and the alternative AIA that was (here called AIA-3) proposed by Cruz-Cortés *et al.* [20]. According to Table 3, the best, mean and worst values of the proposed RGA-PSO algorithm are superior to those of AIA-3 for TP 1; the worst value obtained using the RGA-PSO algorithm is better than that obtained using AIA-2 for TP 2; the best and worst values of the RGA-PSO algorithm are superior to those of AIA-2 for TP 3, and the mean and worst values obtained using the RGA-PSO algorithm are better than those obtained using AIA-2 and AIA-3 for TP 4.

Table 2. Comparison of results of the proposed RGA-PSO algorithm and those of the published GAs and an AIA

TP No.	Global Optimum	Methods	Best	Median	Worst
1	24.306	GA-1 [18]	24.690	29.258	36.060
		GA-2 [19]	24.372	24.409	25.075
		AIA-1 [6]	24.377	24.663	24.988
		the proposed RGA-PSO	24.341	24.565	24.886
2	−30665.539	GA-1 [18]	–	–	–
		GA-2 [19]	−30665.537	−30665.535	−29846.654
		AIA-1 [6]	−30665.543	−30665.524	−30665.500
		the proposed RGA-PSO	−30665.539	−30665.539	−30665.538
3	680.630	GA-1 [18]	680.642	680.718	680.955
		GA-2 [19]	680.634	680.642	680.651
		AIA-1 [6]	680.632	680.640	680.651
		the proposed RGA-PSO	680.632	680.642	680.655
4	−15.000	GA-1 [18]	−15.000	−15.000	−15.000
		GA-2 [19]	−15.000	−15.000	−13.000
		AIA-1 [6]	−14.997	−14.993	−14.988
		the proposed RGA-PSO	−15.000	−15.000	−15.000

Table 3. Comparison of results of the proposed RGA-PSO algorithm and those of the published AIAs

TP No.	Global Optimum	Methods	Best	Mean	Worst	Performance index: Number of objective function evaluations
1	24.306	AIA-1 [6]	24.377	24.663	24.988	350,000
		AIA-2 [17]	–	–	–	–
		AIA-3 [20]	24.506	25.417	26.422	350,000
		the proposed RGA-PSO	24.341	24.573	24.886	9,000,000
2	−30665.539	AIA-1 [6]	−30665.543	−30665.522	−30665.500	300,000
		AIA-2 [17]	−30665.00	−30662.32	−30652.21	150,000
		AIA-3 [20]	−30665.539	−30665.539	−30665.539	350,000
		the proposed RGA-PSO	−30665.539	−30665.539	−30665.538	9,000,000
3	680.630	AIA-1 [6]	680.632	680.641	680.651	500,000
		AIA-2 [17]	680.750	681.666	683.258	150,000
		AIA-3 [20]	680.631	680.652	680.697	350,000
		the proposed RGA-PSO	680.632	680.642	680.655	9,000,000
4	−15.000	AIA-1 [6]	−14.997	−14.993	−14.988	300,000
		AIA-2 [17]	−14.998	−14.820	−12.993	150,000
		AIA-3 [20]	−14.987	−14.726	−12.917	350,000
		the proposed RGA-PSO	−15.000	−15.000	−15.000	9,000,000

According to Tables 2–3, performance of the proposed RGA-PSO algorithm is competitive with those of GAs and AIAs, although the RGA-PSO algorithm is more complex than an RGA or a PSO algorithm and takes a large number of objective function evaluations to find the solutions.

5 Conclusion

This work exhibits the synergistic power of an RGA and a PSO algorithm in solving CGO problems. This work has developed an RGA-PSO algorithm that incorporates an outer RGA and an inner PSO algorithm. Performance of the proposed RGA-PSO algorithm is evaluated using four CGO problems. Numerical results indicate that the proposed RGA-PSO algorithm can converge to a global minimum for each test CGO problem and obtain the best parameter settings of the inner PSO algorithm. Moreover, the numerical results obtained from the RGA-PSO algorithm are superior to some of other alternative stochastic global optimization methods such as GAs and AIAs. The RGA-PSO algorithm can thus be considered as an alternative stochastic optimization approach for solving CGO problems.

References

1. Xu, P.: A Hybrid Global Optimization Method: The Multi-Dimensional Case. Journal of Computational and Applied Mathematics 155, 423–446 (2003)
2. Sun, C.I., Zeng, J.C., Pan, J.S.: An Improved Vector Particle Swarm Optimization for Constrained Optimization Problems. Information Sciences 181, 1153–1163 (2011)
3. Tsoulos, I.G.: Solving Constrained Optimization Problems Using a Novel Genetic Algorithm. Applied Mathematics and Computation 208, 273–283 (2009)
4. Deep, K.: Dipti: A Self-Organizing Migrating Genetic Algorithm for Constrained Optimization. Applied Mathematics and Computation 198, 237–250 (2008)
5. Wu, J.Y., Chung, Y.K.: Real-Coded Genetic Algorithm for Solving Generalized Polynomial Programming Problems. Journal of Advanced Computational Intelligence and Intelligent Informatics 11, 358–364 (2007)
6. Wu, J.Y.: Solving Constrained Global Optimization Via Artificial Immune System. International Journal on Artificial Intelligence Tools 20, 1–27 (2011)
7. Zadeh, L.A.: Fuzzy Logic, Neural Networks, and Soft Computing. Communications of the ACM 37, 77–84 (1994)
8. Konar, A.: Computational Intelligence-Principles, Techniques and Applications. Springer, New York (2005)
9. Michalewicz, Z.: Genetic Algorithms + Data Structures = Evolution Programs. Springer, New York (1999)
10. Houck, C.R., Joines, J.A., Kay, M.G.: A Genetic Algorithm for Function Optimization: A Matlab Implementation. North Carolina State Univ, Raleigh (1995)
11. Kennedy, J., Eberhart, R.: Particle Swarm Optimization. In: IEEE International Conference on Neural Networks, pp. 1942–1948 (1995)
12. Shi, Y., Eberhart, R.: A Modified Particle Swarm Optimizer. In: The 1998 IEEE International Conference on Evolutionary Computation, pp. 69–73 (1998)

13. Clerc, M.: The Swarm and the Queen: Towards a Deterministic and Adaptive Particle Swarm Optimization. In: The IEEE Congress on Evolutionary Computation, pp. 1951–1957 (1999)
14. Clerc, M., Kennedy, J.: The Particle Swarm-Explosion, Stability, and Convergence in a Multidimensional Complex Space. IEEE Transactions on Evolutionary Computation 6, 58–73 (2002)
15. Engelbrecht, A.P.: Fundamentals of Computational Swarm Intelligence. John Wiley & Sons, Chichester (2005)
16. Coello Coello, C.A.: Theoretical and Numerical Constraint-Handling Techniques Used with Evolutionary Algorithms: A Survey of the State of the Art. Computer Methods in Applied Mechanics and Engineering 191, 1245–1287 (2002)
17. Coello Coello, C.A., Cruz-Cortés, N.: A Parallel Implementation of an Artificial Immune System to Handle Constraints in Genetic Algorithms: Preliminary Results. In: Proceedings of the Congress on Evolutionary Computation, pp. 819–824 (2002)
18. Michalewicz, Z.: Genetic Algorithm, Numerical Optimization, and Constraints. In: Proceedings of the Sixth International Conference on Genetic Algorithms, pp. 151–158 (1995)
19. Deb, K.: An Efficient Constraint Handling Method for Genetic Algorithms. Computer Methods in Applied Mechanics and Engineering 186, 311–338 (2000)
20. Cruz-Cortés, N., Trejo-Pérez, D., Coello Coello, C.A.: Handling Constraints in Global Optimization Using an Artificial Immune System. In: The 4th International Conference on Artificial Immune Systems, pp. 234–247. Springer, Berlin (2005)

ECE Undergraduate Computer Engineering Education Mode Analysis

Wenxia Ding[1], Hao Wang[2], and Xishu Ku[1]

[1] School of Electronic Science and Engineering, NUDT, Yanwachistr, 137, 410073 Changsha, China
[2] School of Information Science and Engineering, CSU, LushanSouthroad, 932, 410083 Changsha, China
wenxiading@Gmail.com, whdave@163.com, kuxishu@126.com

Abstract. The Edward S. Rogers Sr. Department of Electrical and Computer Engineering (ECE) is one of the important departments in the Faculty of Applied Science and Engineering of the University of Toronto. The Computer Engineering of ECE consistently ranks among the top in North America, even in the world, so its education mode analysis is very meaningful for us. The academic research areas, the undergraduate teaching program information and the training mode of the students' engineering practical experiences of the Computer Engineering in ECE department of U of T are analyzed mainly in this paper.

Keywords: Computer Engineering Education, Academic Research Groups, Undergraduate Teaching Program, Curriculum Matters Committee, engineering practical experience training.

1 Introduction

The University of Toronto (U of T), founded in 1827, has degree-granting authority from the Province of Ontario, Canada. It is the Canada's largest university and leading research institution. According to the Times Higher Education Supplement, 2008, the University of Toronto is one of only five universities world-wide ranked in the top 16 for all fields – the other four are UC Berkeley, Cambridge, Oxford and Stanford. The Edward S. Rogers Sr. Department of Electrical and Computer Engineering (ECE) is one of the important departments in the Faculty of Applied Science and Engineering, which was founded in 1909 and located in the St. George (Downtown) Campus of U of T.

On Feb 15th, 2011, we landed on Toronto, the biggest city of Canada, and registered to the department of ECE the next day as a visiting professor for half a year. We have been auditing several undergraduate courses: Computer Hardware, Software Engineering, Analog Electronics, Digital Electronics, etc. for about two months. At the same time, we collected and analyzed a lot of teaching and research resources in electrical engineering and computer engineering fields through the wonderful website of the ECE department. Through these studies we know that the

H. Tan and M. Zhou (Eds.): CSE 2011, Part I, CCIS 201, pp. 523–529, 2011.

ECE department is a leading research institution in the areas of computer, electronics, communications, electromagnetics, biomedical, energy systems, photonics and systems control, which are all the research focuses in IT and Energy fields. It has a new flexible undergraduate degree curriculum and an outstanding funding program for graduate students and research, and it attaches great importance to the training of students' engineering experiences as well.

Let's analyze the academic research situations of the ECE department firstly.

2 ECE Department Academic Research Groups Introduction

Electrical and Computer Engineering is a broad field encompassing many areas of study. So ECE sits at the core of most technical advances made today as its fields include IT and energy. ECE is truly the engine that powers the technology of the 21st century. So research is an integral part of the ECE department mission and activity. Their focus is to provide state-of-the-art training for 450 graduate students in MEng, MASc, and PhD programs. With an annual research budget of about $16M, 21 named research chairs, and approximately 36 PhDs awarded annually, the department literally buzzes with innovative research ideas and projects. This creative energy, in turn, benefits their undergraduate program enormously, enriching the course content and providing valuable research experiences.

As a result, ECE is engaged in the pursuit and dissemination of knowledge across a wide range of areas of engineering and applied science-from the fabrication of atomic level structures with special optical properties, through to the technologies that have revolutionized the world. As to facilitate this research, members of the department are organized into 8 groups: the Computer Engineering Group, the Electronics Group, the Biomedical Engineering Group, the Communications Group, the Biomedical Engineering Group, the Energy Systems Group, the Photonics Group and the Systems Control Group. All the groups are outstanding in every area. In 2009, The Times Higher Education World University Rankings placed engineering at U of T eighth worldwide, and fifth in North America alongside MIT, Berkeley, Stanford, and Caltech.

As to the Computer Engineering Group, which began in ECE department in about 1965, has now grown to include over half of undergraduate students and to have a degree bearing its own name. It is internationally recognized for its state-of-the-art research activity in the design, implementation, and use of both computer software and hardware. Today, computer engineering is offered by the ECE department of the Faculty of Applied Science & Engineering at U of T. Its research areas focuses on the hardware and software of computers, the computer architecture, the Human Computer Interaction, the computer architecture, the compilers, the VLSI CAD and how computers can be used in industry, medicine and other systems, like communications or a transit system, and so on. So all these indicate the Computer Engineering Group of the ECE department has its solid basis for theoretical study.

3 ECE Undergraduate Teaching Program Information Analysis

The four year undergraduate teaching program of department ECE is divided into two parts: the Electrical Engineering program and the Computer Engineering program. The first two years of study provide the essential background in basic science and mathematics and also introduces the student to the important concepts in Electrical and Computer Engineering such as circuits, digital systems, electronics, and communication systems. These two years of study are identical for both the Electrical Engineering and Computer Engineering programs.

In third and fourth year, the curriculum allows flexibility in a student's course selection, subject to program and accreditation requirements. A student has a greater choice from a broad array of courses in several areas of study that would appeal to their individual strengths and interests. A number of streams or course packages (public profiles) have been developed by the CMC (Curriculum Matters Committee) members to serve as course selection examples. These can be used as inspiration for a student to help develop more concrete decisions on their own. A student is also free to use one of the public profiles as their template.

The curriculum streams [1] of department ECE are showed in Fig.1. Through it we can know that the curriculum streams arrangement of the ECE department is solely on the basis of its academic research areas. So the teaching program and the academic research can be combined perfectly.

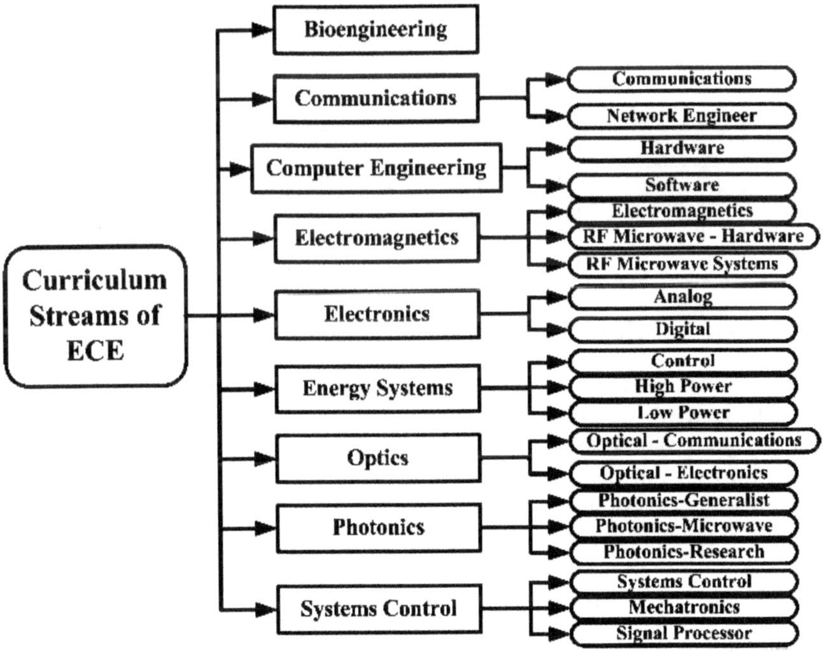

Fig. 1. The undergraduate curriculum streams structure of department ECE

Next, let's highlight two curriculum streams: Computer-Hardware and Computer–Software curriculum stream which we are most concerned about as below.

3.1 Computer-Hardware Curriculum Stream

The computer hardware stream includes the basics of digital design at the gate and system/architectural level. Most people will spend their entire life no more than one meter away from some type of digital system (e.g. laptop, cell phone, PDA, iPod, GPS, auto, controllers, etc.) Digital hardware surrounds us all and affords many interesting careers. Students of the ECE department in this stream will study computer hardware, computer architecture, VLSI systems, and digital systems design, and so on.

Sample Profile for Computer-Hardware stream [2] focused only on the third and fourth year - provided by Curriculum Matters Committee (CMC) member of U of T is showed in Table 1.

Table 1. Sample profile for Computer-Hardware curriculum stream in the 3rd and 4th Year

Session	Course Selections- Computer-Hardware Area				
3F	ECE302H1F Probability & Random Processes	ECE344H1F Operating Systems	ECE345H1F Algorithms & Data Structures	ECE361H1F Computer Networks I	CS3F undecided
3S	ECE318H1S Fundamentals of Optics	ECE334H1S Digital Electronics	ECE342H1S Computer Hardware	PHY335H1S Introduction to Quantum	CS3S undecided
4F	CSC444H1F Software Engineering I	ECE454H1F Computer Systems Program	ECE461H1F Internetworking	ECE496Y1Y Design Project	CS4F undecided
4S	CSC343H1S Introduction to Database	ECE450H1S Software Engineering II	ECE472H1S Engin. Econ. Analysis & Entrepreneurship	**ECE496Y1Y Design Project**	CS4S undecided

3.2 Computer - Software Curriculum Stream

In the computer software stream students of the ECE department learn the basics of operating system structures, memory management, compilers, middleware, etc. Computers today are designed in conjunction with compiler technology and almost all make use of an operating system – this includes laptops, cell phones, and PDAs. Students will also study the basics of data structures, programming languages, databases, security, software engineering, and so on.

Sample Profile for Computer-Software Stream[3] - provided by Curriculum Matters Committee (CMC) member of U of T is showed in Table 2.

Through the analysis of the two curriculum streams above we know that the Computer Engineering undergraduate teaching program of the ECE department is broad coverage, strict, orderly, and very flexible. So it can lay a solid theoretical foundation for the cultivation of students' engineering practice experiences.

Table 2. Sample profile for Computer- Software curriculum stream in the 3rd and 4th Year

Session	Course Selections- Computer-Software Area				
3F	ECE302H1F Probability & Random Processes	ECE344HF Operating Systems	ECE345H1F Algorithms & Data Structures	ECE361H1F Computer Networks I	CS3F undecided
3S	ECE318H1S Fundamentals of Optics	ECE334H1S Digital Electronics	ECE342H1S Computer Hardware	PHY335H1S Introduction to Quantum	CS3S undecided
4F	CSC444HF Software Engineering I	ECE454H F Computer Systems Program	ECE461H1F Internetworking	ECE496Y1Y Design Project	CS4F undecided
4S	CSC343H1S Introduction to Database	ECE450H1S Software Engineering II	ECE472H1S Engin. Econ. Analysis & Entrepreneurship	**ECE496Y1Y Design Project**	CS4S undecided

4 ECE Engineering Experience Training Mode Analysis

According to the Canadian Engineering Accreditation Board (CEAB) of the Canadian Council of Professional Engineers [4], the practice of engineering is regulated, by statute, in all Canadian provinces and territories. To become a professional engineer the students of U of T must satisfy the requirements of the licensing bodies. These requirements include a degree from an accredited program, successful completion of a professional practice examination in engineering law and ethics, and suitable experience.

There are two ways to acquire the engineering practical experience for the students in ECE department: one is the project design, as the course ECE496Y, which is showed in Tab.1 and Tab.2, just like the Graduation Project Design called in most universities; the other way is to participate in the 600 Hours Practical Work Experience program, which includes two programs: the Engineering Summer Internship Program (eSIP) and the Professional Experience Year (PEY) Program. The contents of each way are introduced as follows.

4.1 Course ECE496Y Introduction

ECE496Y[5] is a full-year umbrella course for all fourth-year design projects in ECE department of U of T. It is a requirement for all fourth-year electrical and computer engineering students, allowing them to integrate the knowledge acquired over the first three years of study in the context of project proposed either by the student or by a supervisor.

Students coming into this course will have developed:

- the basic theoretical tools to solve a wide range of technical problems;
- a basic understanding of the Design Process based on experience of a structured design problem would have been developed in earlier years;

- the ability to express their ideas in writing to the extent that thoughts are developed in a structured way and expressed in coherent paragraphs with proper grammar, spelling and punctuation.

In this course, the students will develop skills that allow them to identify a problem given a brief description its context. Given that many real problems are solved by teams, it is essential that students learn how to work in teams and how to plan a project so that all team members become responsible for specific tasks.

4.2 600 Hours Practical Work Experience Program Introduction

Every student in the U of T must complete a minimum of 600 hours of practical work before graduation. The nature of the work should form an integral part of a student's education and career development. It therefore must contain a good measure of responsibility (e.g., management of programs, systems, equipment, personnel, or finances), sound judgment and effective communication, and be supportive of the professional career of the student after graduation. Work in many facets of industry, government or public service of Canada would be acceptable for this requirement.

This experience of student may be obtained at any time during the program or through the Engineering Summer Internship Program (eSIP) or Professional Experience Year (PEY) Program, but work done before entering the Faculty may also meet the requirement. Participation in the Professional Experience Year or the Engineering Summer Internship Program automatically satisfies the practical experience requirement, provided that students complete and submit the requisite reports.

eSIP PROGRAM. The Engineering Summer Internship Program (eSIP) is a paid 4month summer co-op program available to 2nd & 3rd year engineering students. The value of the eSIP program is that it acts as an introductory career development program, particularly for the 2nd year students that make up the majority of applicants. Students are introduced to concepts and tools to prepare them for the workplace and understand the dynamics therein. This is critical as the knowledge gained from the eSIP 4month placement makes them competitive and further applied in their participation in the PEY 12-16month Program after their 3rd year of study.

PEY INTERNSHIP PROGRAM. Students wishing to participate in an internship program, which formally integrates a student's academic studies with a concentrated period of engineering experience in an employer organization, may with the approval of the Director of the PEY Internship Program and the Department concerned, register in the Professional Experience Year (PEY) Internship Program.

The Professional Experience Year (PEY) Internship Program is available to engineering students who have completed the second or third year of academic studies and wish to obtain industrial experience and wish to earn a good salary between their second and third year, or between third and fourth year. The individual's cumulative average in their previous engineering sessions should be a minimum of 65%.

Normally, the Professional Experience Year (PEY) is not only a University of Toronto's co-op program, but also a facilitated bridge for students' smooth transition to the community. Every year, there are over two thirds of ECE students participate in the PEY program excitedly; through it they can enrich their engineering practical experiences effectively.

5 Conclusion

In this paper, we have mainly analyzed the academic research areas, the undergraduate teaching program information and the training mode of the engineering experience about Computer Engineering in the Edward S. Rogers Sr. Department of Electrical and Computer Engineering (ECE) of U of T. Through these analyses we learned that the ECE department of U of T has a new flexible undergraduate degree curriculum and an outstanding funding program for the students and research, and it attaches great importance to the training of students' engineering experience. So, it can consistently ranks among the top in North America, even in the world till now.

References

1. EEC Current Undergraduate Students Program Information Curriculum Streams, http://www.ece.utoronto.ca/Current_Undergraduate_Studies/program/Curriculum_Streams.htm
2. EEC Current Undergraduate Students Program Information Computer Hardware Stream, http://www.ece.utoronto.ca/Current_Undergraduate_Studies/program/Curriculum_Streams/Computer_Hardware.htm
3. EEC Current Undergraduate Students Program Information Computer Software Stream, http://www.ece.utoronto.ca/Current_Undergraduate_Studies/program/Curriculum_Streams/Computer_Software.htm
4. The 2010 Curriculum & Programs of the University of Toronto - Faculty of Applied Science and Engineering. pdf (2010), http://www.ece.utoronto.ca/research.htm
5. ECE496Y Design Project Course, https://internal.ece.toronto.edu/ece496.1011/

On the Training Path of Compound Talents for E-Business in China

Zhao Jingfeng

School of Management and Economics,
North China University of Water Resources and Electric Power, Zhengzhou, P.R.C.

Abstract. As a brand new mode of business operation, the E-business has brought about a new industrial revolution. The Net Economy has exerted a tremendous impact on talents knowledge structure and the traditional economic theory, causing the change in the personnel training mode. Starting with the status quo of E-business development in China and based on the requirements of E-business education, the thesis analyzed talents demand and training mode for E-business and put forward diverse compound talents training path.

Keywords: E-business, Talents, Compound.

As a brand new mode of business operation, the E-business has brought about a new industrial revolution. Compared with the E-business in the developed countries, the development of China's E-business remains immature but the development speed is overwhelming. The transformation from traditional enterprises to information will give rise to the extensive demand for E-business talents. Starting with the status quo of E-business development in China and based on the requirements of E-business education, the thesis analyzed talents demand and training mode for E-business and put forward diverse compound talents training path.

1 The Status Quo of E-Business Development in China

The internet usage of Chinese netizens is featured with the increased commercialization, entertainment trend, deeper communication and more valuable information tool.

1.1 Shopping Online

By the time of June, 2010, the number of China's shopping online users had reached 142 million, the usage rate increased to 33.8%, and rose by 5.7%, in addition, the increase rate was 31.4% in half a year. Relatively rapid growth of the number of online shopping users shows the strong development trend of E-business market. With the normalized trend of SMEs E-business applications, the routine of online retail business, online shopping market becomes increasingly powerful. Meanwhile, the first half of 2010 saw some new models and opportunities in the online shopping market. First, the advent of group purchase indicates the trend of the regional E-business services development; Second, shopping sites moves to the platform of mobile phone, which makes mobile commerce thrive; Third, with the mainstream development of B2C

H. Tan and M. Zhou (Eds.): CSE 2011, Part I, CCIS 201, pp. 530–536, 2011.

mode, online shopping more focus on users' experience and security, etc.; Fourth, shopping sites accelerate the pace of self-logistics or cooperation-supply logistics and actively lay a solid foundation for the off-line service. In addition, with the breaking out of free shipping price campaign again, media campaigns and promotional activities have sped up the penetration of online shopping to the public.

1.2 Online Payment

By June 2010, the utilization rate of China's online payment had reached 30.5% the size of net users 12.81 million, rising by 36.2% in six months, and it is still the net application with the fastest growing. Rapid growth of online payment for several reasons: There are several main reasons: for one thing, the rapid growth of online shopping drives that of online payment. In half a year, the size of online shopping users increased by 33.96 million, while the rate of online payment users on shopping online reached 72.8%. For another thing, more and more enterprises put online payment into operation, such as water, electricity rate, which makes the support range wider for online payment. Geographically, not only in the eastern cities, but in many mid-western cities online payment is also developed. Third, online payment among enterprises becomes more extensive as well. Deeper level of enterprise information, the upgrade of software and hardware facilities have accelerated the upgrade of the enterprise information flow, which causes more and more capital flows to be conducted by the means of online payment.

1.3 Travel Reservation

Country travel reservation is relatively low, but it has showed the growth trend acceleration. By June 2010, the utilization rate of travel reservation was 8.6%, the users' size will reach 36.12 million people, rising by 19.4% in six months. The user communities that make the travel reservation through the Internet platform have been growing. Meanwhile, China's mobile E-business is also accelerating the pace of entering into the online travel reservation. In the first half of 2010, domestic travel reservation website began to be assigned to mobile terminals, which launched the phone reservation function, opening mobile website to realize the service function of hotel and air ticket reservations. From the client side of travel reservation, potential users of mobile phone travel reservation are a large group. Among mobile phone users, travel reservation users have a relatively higher proportion. The products standardization of travel reservation is suitable for display through mobile phone platform, therefore travel reservation will usher in the faster growth in the future.

By June 2010, most network applications become more popular among netizens, the users' size in a variety of network applications continues to grow, especially the business application. By June 2010, the utilization rate of online shopping, online payment and online banking were 33.8%, 30.5% and 29.1% respectively, the increase rate of the users' size were 31.4%, 36.2% and 29.9 % respectively. The users' growth rate in various applications ranked the top three places, far surpassing those of other types of network applications, such as, users social networking sites, network literature and search engine etc.

The rapid development of E-business will inevitably bring a substantial increase in the corresponding demand for talent. Thus, the demand for talent in E-business industry the study and practice on education modes are quite essential and impending.

2 The Practice of E-Business Talents Training

As for E-business education, there is a distinctive discrepancy between China and western developed countries in development history and research level. In western developed countries, starting from the master, E-business took MBA as an important object, and then extended to undergraduate and community college levels. the development path is giving priority to the high-level quality and then extending to low level skill. In addition, There are diversified educational modes including independent profession, special projects, curriculum modules, courses infiltration ect. However, large-scale construction of Chinese E-business specialty began from junior college and then the undergraduate. At present, E-business also set up research direction in master's and doctoral levels. Development path is opposite to that of western developed countries (A few key universities are exceptional, such as Xi'an Jiaotong University, similar to the development path of western developed countries.). This educational method is relatively simple, relying mainly on independent junior college and undergraduate education while vocational skills training program subsidiary to develop teaching activity an specialist, primarily undergraduate, to start teaching, supplemented by activities (such as E-business series certification conducted by Ministry of Labour and Social Security).

E-business training goal is determined, mainly based on the demand for talent in modern business activities under the environment of modern information technology. Talent training is supposed to make a target of practical problems to be solved in terms of business management under the conditions of modern information technology. Besides, in the different training stages, the level of personnel training is expected to be different (Table 1).

Table 1. Talent training goal & knowledge structure

<table>
<tr><td rowspan="2">Decision level</td><td rowspan="3">Compound talents</td><td>proficient in business mode , laws and regulations</td></tr>
<tr><td>skillful at business operation management</td></tr>
<tr><td rowspan="2">Management level</td><td>Good at information application and business management</td></tr>
<tr><td rowspan="3">Applica-tion-oriented talents</td><td>Familiar with information technology application and business management</td></tr>
<tr><td rowspan="2">Operational level</td><td>Familiar with business management</td></tr>
<tr><td>Familiar with information technology</td></tr>
</table>

As a dynamic combination of modern information technology and business activities E-business has influenced and changed existing business models, management systems, conventional law etc., therefore, those who are able to master the use of E-business theories and technology are obliged to be compound talents having good command of modern information technology, modern business theory and practice, modern management means and methods and relevant laws. Obviously, it is unrealistic to train an all-round person mastering three or four subjects mentioned above. Therefore, so-called "E-business talent " is a collective noun, with a common knowledge and expertise in E-business activities.

Overall, E-business business, in a reasonable personnel structure, needs the following four talent types: operational support personnel, technical support personnel, technical service personnel, business services personnel, business service, specific characteristics shown in Table 2.

Table 2. Characteristics of demand for E-business talent

Talent types	Characteristics of demand for talent ability
operational support personnel	They have Good command of rich business skills and the knowledge of internet and other information technologies; they are in charge of closely cooperating with information department and develop new system when they conduct routine business.
technical support personnel	They need master rich skills and have a knowledge of business; Many information departments set up new business skills and regard business department as customers and appoint professionals to provide internet technology support to meet the needs of business department.
technical service personnel	Information departments need outstanding net and software expertise; Though some professionals have a good knowledge of business, they can't tackle complex work in design, implement and operation of net systems。 Among these professional, some provide extremely important skills in network operating system, and others develop complex software systems.
business services personnel	They need more business skills than knowledge and experience related to information technology.

Demand for E-business Talent itself is diverse and compound, and its common mode criteria are supposed to be E-business knowledge plus computer network knowledge plus innovation ability, enterprise e-business needs diversified and compound talent, which bought the challenge to the current E-business training Mode.

3 Environmental Requirement of Compound E-Business Talent Training

In the process of E-business talent training, colleges and universities are supposed to deliberately take into consideration curriculum system construction, mould a sound practical environment and keep a good relationship with enterprises to cultivate talent according to practical needs of enterprises in reality,

3.1 Facility Preparedness Level

At present, most of universities or vocational institutions have set up E-business professional. Schools that have set up or is establishing E-business professional make sure that leaders attach importance to it, and offer strong support in the material and financial resources. In the hardware, it is essential to establish the hardware facilities with high quality and technology, simultaneously conduct the large-scale transformation of the Internet accelerating the network speed, and increasing bandwidth to provide a good internship environment for E-business; In the software, it is necessary to purchase e-business simulation software, such as E-business division ECP software used by electronic business division professional unified national laboratory training.

3.2 Teachers' Construction Level

Composition of e-business educational teachers is expected to be a synthesis and teachers come from the professionals of e-business enterprises or business elites in line with E-business division practitioners. And what's more, it is essential that part of these teachers know about business and trade modes in the areas of industry, commercial, distribution, foreign trade, consumption, can evaluate E-business trade time based on the accurate cost-benefit analysis, know how to sign trade contract supporting E-business, learn how to create support for building E-business financial accounting; and be proficient in business management and technology. The other part of teachers are supposed to be familiar with and master computer technology, know about and construct E-business systems on sales and service , and know how to evaluate E-business tools. Only such a synthesis can catch up with time to ensure that the actual E-business education and the real development keep synchronous and teachers grasp the latest developments in E-business, conducive to train a large number of e-business applications talent adapting to future E-business..

3.3 Professional Training Goal and Knowledge System Level

E-business training goal is supposed to be confirmed based on the enterprises' requirements of work ability. Because E-business profession is comprehensive, involving disciplines of technology, economy, trade, and management etc., it is vital for universities and vocational institutions to comprehensively take into account knowledge system, As for how to construct their professional, how to set up curriculum, there has been no an accepted model yet. Domestic and abroad scholars are actively exploring the setting up of curriculum system and construction of E-business professional. Its knowledge system is composed of business operations, information technology, network technology and network technology aspects of composition. In the implementation process, study is combined with practice to improve students' learning ability, practical ability and innovative ability.

4 The Training Path of Compound E-Business Talents

To promote the combination of network economy and traditional economy, strengthen the construction of talent groups, E-business talent training are supposed to start with the following levels:

4.1 Government Level

4.1.1 Strengthening the Construction of Enterprise E-Business Talents

Taking concept innovation, policy innovation, institutional innovation and mechanism innovation as a breakthrough, Government is obliged to actively create a social environment beneficial to the healthy growth of E-business talents, build the growth mechanism of talent in line with the modern requirements of network economic development, strengthen E-business education and training, enhance the quality of E-business personnel, perfect the incentive and restraint mechanism and accelerate the process of enterprise e-business talent professionalization and marketization.

4.1.2 The Specification of Education and Use of Information Talent

Government departments may provide materials of the status quo of the talents use and enterprise development by employing their own advantages for colleges and universities as reference, subsidize universities to actively develop E-business training activities to train talents for the society, who meet the needs of enterprise development at the current stage, and finally carry out corresponding policies and regulations to standardize the education and use of information talents.

4.1.3 Establishing and Perfecting the Training System of Business Operation Management Talent

Government is obliged to guide and standardize the training institutions of enterprise E-business talent and the construction of educators' team and further strengthen the enterprises' dominant position in the E-business talent training. Making the most of institutional training, online education, distance education, special lecture ect., combining job training and off-job training, theoretical training and practice, growing E-business training, government constantly strengthens pertinence and efficiency of E-business training.

4.2 School Level

4.2.1 Implementing Curriculum Integration and Dimensional Talent Training

At present, specialized talents are more in technology and information while E-business itself is a multi-discipline integration. Therefore, when the schools carry out and implement teaching plan, they must attach importance to the goal of "high-quality compound talents" by introducing cross-disciplinary, implementing curriculum integration, and conducting dimensional, multi-angle talent training. On the one hand, according to levels and types of E-business talent training, disciplines should be comprehensively developed with respective characteristic towards integration to realize arts, science, engineering cross.. On the other hand, based on their respective characteristics of E-business, the school should recombinate relevant disciplines, and establish margin course of interdisciplinary.

4.2.2 Paying Attention to the Update of Knowledge and Improving the Quality of Teachers

E-business teachers must pay attention to the update of their own knowledge structure, reform the traditional teaching methods by using modern teaching methods and strengthen the study for new problems and new situations so that they can keep up with the pace of scientific development. In addition, the university is supposed to take effective measures to actively encourage and support teachers to make in-depth theoretical study on E-business, so that theory is prior to practice, correctly guiding E-business work to achieve the gradual and steady development

4.3 Enterprise Level

4.3.1 Changing the Traditional Concept to Promote the Flow of Talent

For talent "owns", Enterprises should get out of the traditional concept, because the most fundamental is to have human intelligence. The traditional concept of the flow is called "job-hopping", the development of the network economy proves that flow of talent benefits the development of enterprises. If talent does not flow, enterprises are not active. Digging up persons promotes the flow of talent, enhances the status of talent and reflects the value of talent.

4.3.2 Establishing Development Mechanism

E-business talent is the determinants of high-tech industry development. In order to meet the economic development of the network, enterprises must establish a mechanism of human resource development as the core of market competition to create conditions for the emergence of outstanding E-business talent. The establishment of talent development mechanisms includes talent training mechanism, flow mechanisms and competition mechanisms.

4.3.3 Innovative Distribution System

Whether enterprise could insist on a fair and reasonable distribution system is the key to mobilizing and bring into the initiative of E-business talent. Nowadays, many local enterprises encourage E-business personnel to make technology investment, accounting for more than 35% of the total capital stock, which provides the evidence that intellectual resource and human capital are transformed to material capital in the system. From the actual situation of high-tech industry development, enterprises' innovations in the system bring the tremendous space for E-business development.

References

1. Liqi, Zhangli, Penglifang: The Thinking of Diversification Compound E-business Talents Training Mode. Economic Management 14 (2007)
2. Fanglingyu: Training posts and E-business Talents. E-business World 07 (2005)

The E-Business Development Trends in China Online Shopping Industry

Zhao Jingfeng

School of Management and Economics,
North China University of Water Resources and Electric Power, Zhengzhou, P.R.C.

Abstract. Selecting the fastest growing online shopping industry and basing on the analysis of current situation in the industry, this paper focuses on online shopping industry relying on electronic commerce innovates forms of traditional market transactions, and predicts prospect of online shopping industry in China.

Keywords: Online Shopping Industry; E-business; Market Transaction.

As the Internet industry's most important and soundest branch, the E-business platform have relied on the global network, with its low transaction cost, high efficiency, wide coverage, strong coordination, high transparency and many obvious other advantages, have extensively penetrated into various aspects of China industrial economy, life shopping and E-government. In the development of E-business in recent years, online shopping has showed strong potentiality. According to statistics data in 2009, the scale of online shopping market[1] in China has reached 238.8 billion with its growth rate of 86.3%. This paper analyzes the online shopping industry on the basis of the status quo, and focuses on the achieved innovation which has applied by E-business in the industry.

1 Development Status Quo of China's Online Shopping Industry

1.1 E-Business Services Corporations in China

The growth of E-business services companies in China have experienced roughly five phases as following: the start-up phase in 1997 to 2000, the stagnation and adjustment phase in 2001 to 2004, the recovery phase in 2005 to 2006, he rapid development phase in 2006 to 2007, and since 2008 E-business services companies have come into phase of transformation and upgrading in business model, products services and so on. As the transaction platform of online shopping, the number of E-business service corporations with B to C model and C to C model has skyrocketed, and has risen rapidly from 1997 to 2009, in 1997 just a few, however, there is nearly 7,000 in 2008, as shown in figure 1.

According to the China B to B Research Center survey data, the number of China E-business website have reached 12,282 in July 2009, among which B to C, C to C business models and other non-mainstream model businesses have showed rapid growth trends since 2008, and in figure 1 shows it amounts to 6962 in 2009. In recent

[1] Refer to the sum of B to C market transaction scale and C to C market transaction scale.

H. Tan and M. Zhou (Eds.): CSE 2011, Part I, CCIS 201, pp. 537–547, 2011.

years, the number of China E-business service providers has experienced a "geometric" growth. Geographically, China E-business and E-services companies mainly situate in the Yangtze River Delta, Pearl River Delta and Beijing[2], and other more developed provinces and cities.

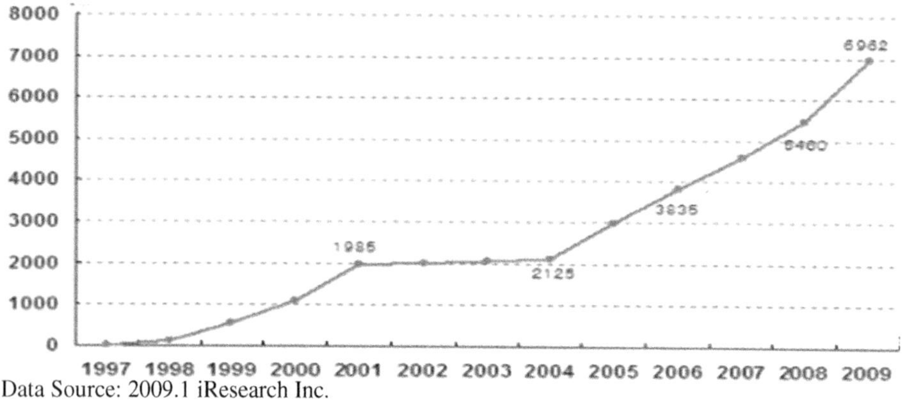

Data Source: 2009.1 iResearch Inc.

Fig. 1. Chart of B to B and C to C E-business Services Corporation Number (1997-2009)

1.2 China Online Consumption Having Bright Future

During 2007 and 2009, the number of Chinese internet users accelerates drastically, so does the proportion of Internet users shopping. Such E-business, which increases with its scale of potential consumer groups, is rapidly changing the traditional consumption model, consumer ideas, and influencing mass's lifestyle. Relevant data have showed that China online shoppers reach 110 million for the first time in 2009 (Figure 2). China's B to C overall user scale have reached 60 million with the growth rate of 50% in 2009; C to C overall user scale have reached 81 million with growth rate of 25.6%. From the user's age structure of online shopping, the mainstream age group is 18-30-year-old. In 2008, the composition of China's online shopping users is: the ages of 18-24 accounting for 33.3%, 25-30-year-old of 24.1%, 31-35- years-old of 12.8%, 29.8% of other people.

1.3 Online Shopping Transactions Scale Expanding

With the rapid development of E-business, China E-business transactions scale have high record, according to statistical data analysis, China E-business market turnover have reached 3.15 trillion yuan in 2008, among which B to C and C to C business online shopping transactions have amounted to 150 billion, which shows that online shopping market size have make up considerable part of the entire E-business transaction. China online shopping market transaction scale is 238.8 billion yuan in 2009, with its total transaction scale growth rate of 86.3%; of which B to C transaction scale is 31.8 billion

[2] Among which Yangtze River Delta accounted for 33.52%, Pearl River Delta 32.04%, Beijing 8.86%, other regionof the country 25.58%.

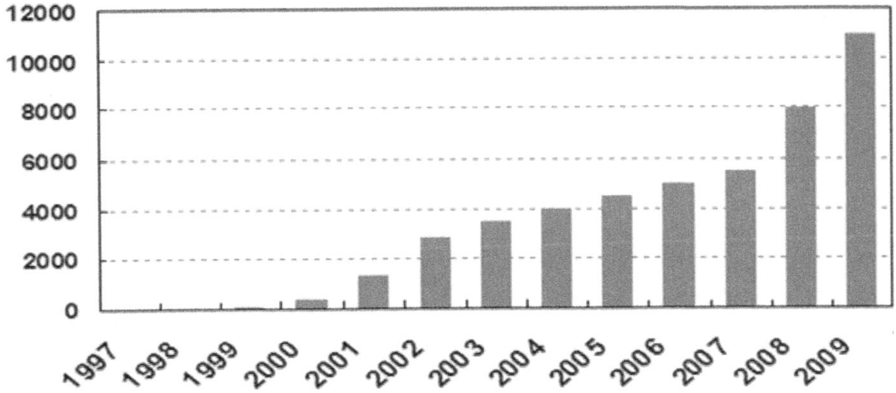

Data Source : 2009.1 iResearch Inc.

Fig. 2. China Online Shopping Users Growth Chart (1997-2009)

with the growth rate of 26.5%, and C to C transaction is 207 billion yuan with growth rate of 73.3%. Especially in the first six month of 2009, online shopping market scale break through 100 billion yuan, and amount to 103.46 billion, with increase of 94.8% year growth and chain growth of 37.8%. It is shown in Figure 3, the online shopping of have reached as high as 190 billion yuan in 2009, and the scale of online shopping market transactions have showed rapid upward trend. At the same time, the per capita of online shopping amount has showed gradually rising trend during the period of 2003-2008, from 127.6 yuan of 2003 to 1602.3 yuan of 2008.

According to related studies, the online shopping market is composed of B to C model and C to C models basing on the E-business. According to Table 1, China major B to C E-business operator transaction volume scale distributed in a balanced way in 2008. However, it can be analyzed from the Table 2 that the major C to C E-business operator transaction volume scale distributed unbalanced in the in 2008. Based on the China B to B Research Center survey data, the number of China E-business website have reached 12,282 in July 2009, among which B to C, C to C business models and other non-mainstream model businesses have showed rapid growth trends since 2008, and in figure 1 shows it amounts to 6962 in 2009. In recent years, the number of China E-business service providers has experienced a "geometric" growth. Geographically, China E-business and E-services companies mainly situate in the Yangtze River Delta, Pearl River Delta and Beijing[3], and other more developed provinces and cities.

As the data in 2008, among China B to C E-business operators, Taobao.com, Jing-dong Mall, Joyo Dangdang.com are on the top list, which have accounted for 60% of China B to C market transactions scale; however in 2008, among China major C to C E-business operators, Taobao.com's transaction scale have achieved absolutely advantage. According to relevant survey data, the B to C online shopping market made a bright spot in transaction volume of China online shopping market. Comparing to the earlier year, C to C market structure keep stable, the Taobao.com's transaction scale

[3] Among which Yangtze River Delta accounted for 33.52%, Pearl River Delta 32.04%, Beijing 8.86%, other regionof the country 25.58%.

have accounted for 82.2% of transaction volume, and the eBay.com, Paipai.com have increased steadily with a steady rising market share.

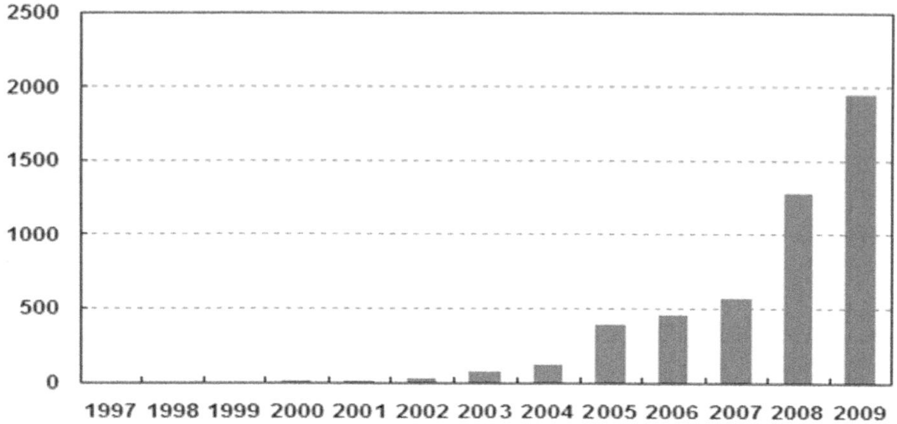

Data Source：2009.1 iResearch Inc.

Fig. 3. China Online Shopping Online Transaction Growth Chart (1997-2009)

Table 1. China Major B2C E-business Operator Transaction Scale (2008) Unit: Billion yuan

Operator	**Taobao.com**	**Jingdong Mall**	**Joyo.com**	**Dangdang.com**
Transaction Volume	17.60	14.05	10.50	9.81
Operator	**M18.com**	**Vancl**	**139 shop.com**	**Redbaby.com**
Transaction Volume	6.9	3.72	3.65	3.04

Table 2. China Major C2C E-business Operator Transaction Scale (2008) Unit: Billion yuan

Operator	Taobao.com	Paipai.com	Eachnet.com
Transaction Volume	98.2	11.87	9.4
Market Share (%)	82.2	9.9	7.9

1.4 China Online Shopping Commodity Composition Diversifying

According to relevant data each year, Taobao.com's market transactions scale take an absolute ratio in overall online shopping. Therefore, this paper chooses commodity trading of Taobao.com in 2008 to analyze China's commodity composition of goods online shopping.

Table 3. Top10 of Goods Categories in Taobao.com Transactions (2008)

sequence	First Half of 2008	Whole Year	sequence	First Half of 2008	Whole Year
1	clothing	clothing	6	cosmetics	PC& accessory
2	mobile	mobile	7	pre-paid card	jewelry
3	daily neces-sities	cosmetics	8	outdoor sports equipment	laptop
4	PC& accessory	daily necessities	9	jewelry	home appliance
5	laptop	outdoor sports equipment	10	home appliance	pre-paid card

Data Source: 2008.12 iResearch Inc

As can be seen from the table 3, online shopping have penetrated into daily lives of Internet users in deep way. According to the Taobao.com's ranking list of product classification, the sales of daily necessities such as clothing, appliances, furniture food and merchandise sales are at the front of the list. Related statistics data showed that China's clothing online shopping market scale is 7.521 billion yuan in 2007, accounting for 3.6% of overall clothing retail market transactions; clothing online shopping market transaction scale is 17.11 billion yuan in 2008, accounting for 6.3% with growth rate of 127.6%; Chinese clothing online shopping market scale is 30.52 billion yuan in 2009, accounting for 9.2% with growth rate of 78.4%. As the largest transaction volume in commodity groups, clothing's growth rate has skyrocketed and has showed strong development potentiality.

With the gradual completion of logistics and payment system, China online shopping market is becoming more and more perfect. The online shopping transactions volume amounted to 56.1 billion yuan in 2007, accounting for 0.63% of the total social retail sales; the transactions volume amounted to 121.88 billion yuan in 2008, accounting for 1.2% of the total social retail sales; online shopping transactions amounted to 238.8 billion yuan, accounting for 1.96% of total social retail sales in 2009, which have showed steady-speed growth trend. The global financial crisis does not affect the growth of online shopping potentiality, which has already become powerful supplement for the traditional retail market.

2 Analysis on E-Business Applications

The introduction of E-business in shopping industry triggers tremendous changes in traditional shopping industry, which make online shopping favored by the consumers. From the perspective of market structure, online shopping market have is the monopolistic competition market , which bases on the traditional shopping market, and takes advantage of E-business platform to innovate in line with the technology development. The industry value chain of online shopping market is shown as following:

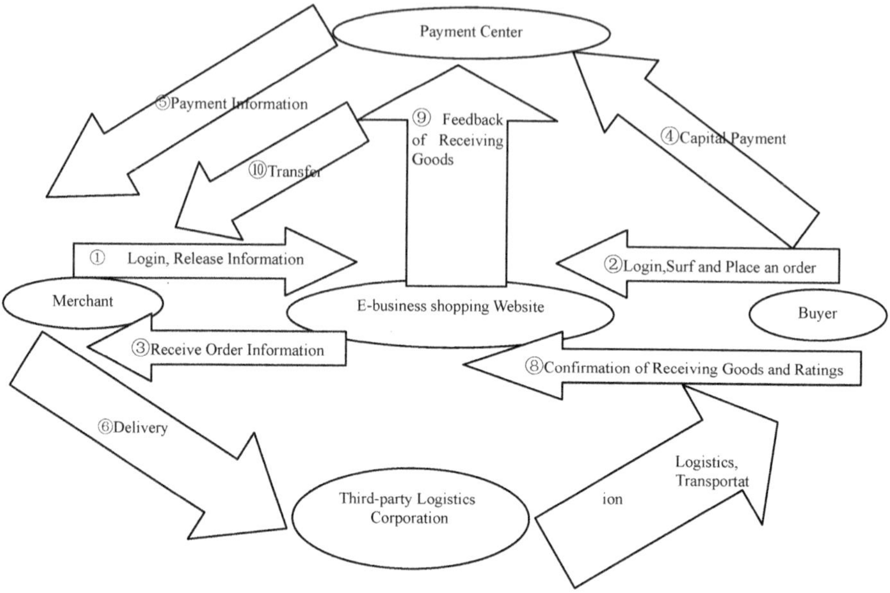

Fig. 4. Online Shopping Industry Value Chain Structure

In online shopping industry, E-business run through the whole process from placing order to completing transaction. The whole value chain is made up of three elements: information flowing, capital flowing and logistics. The convenient E-business platform simplifies traditional shopping transaction process, and largely saves social resources. Information flowing is the base of online shopping, which mainly including goods' characteristics, consumers' placing orders, confirmation of receiving goods and rating information. Online shopping justly bases on these information communications. In Graphic 4, these steps such as ①、②、③ and ⑧ are the major composition of online information flowing. Capital flowing refers to processes of the consumer's placing order and paying expenditures to the appointed payment center, then the sellers receive information of payment and delivering goods, at last the payment intermediary transfers money to the sellers after consumer's confirmation of receiving goods. In Graphic 4, the steps ④、⑤、⑩indicate capital flowing process. Logistics refers to the transportation process of the third-party corporation for transporting the goods to consumers, which is shown as in ⑥ and ⑦. As it can be showed that the emergence of E-business integrate information flowing, capital flowing, logistics in online shopping market into complete system. Under the joint efforts of the triple, the online shopping overcome the limitation of time and spaces and renovate traditional transaction processes, and bring unprecedented convenience to online consumers.

2.1 Simplifying Market Transaction Procedures and Shortening Product Value Chain

The Emergence of online shopping industry has changed value chain of traditional retail industry fundamentally. The online shopping industry converts the goods transportation processes from "manufacturer→distributer→retailer→consumer" to "manufacturer→consumer(B to C model) or manufacturer→broker→consumer(C to C model)", and it also forms benign interactive process of "information flowing→capital flowing→logistics" and effective activity management model of "zero inventory"(supply trailer demand). Customization overcomes various shortcomings brought by Ford line's batch production since 20 century; then releases corporation's accumulating value, and largely saves social wealth.

2.2 Renovating Market Transaction Methods and Saving Market Transaction Cost

The emergence of online shopping industry have simplified traditional transaction processes such as consumer shopping, choosing category and pattern of goods, bargaining with sellers. The consumers just take advantage of internet online shopping platform, choose satisfactory goods by comparing several sellers' without stepping outside, then make payment through E-business transaction platform and get the purchased goods in short time via the convenient third-party logistics, which largely save social resources. Comparing to traditional goods transaction needing land, human and financial resources in traditional fixed market, E-business transaction ask for few resources. In fact, E-business platform transfer traditional visible market into virtual invisible market, so as accelerate the flowing of capital, resources and manpower, and largely improve goods transaction efficiency. Statistics data shows that the application in E-business reduces shopping transaction cost by 75%

2.3 Breaking through the Limitation of Time and Spaces

Basing on third-party logistics, characterized convenient air-service and taking full advantage of convenient information, the online shopping triggers tremendous changes in goods transaction method. In traditional market transaction, the sellers and consumers must make great effort to overcome limitation of spaces in to make a market deal, and even take long arduous travel. However, in the modern online shopping, time and spaces are no longer the factors to restrict the deal-making. Firstly, the consumers browse sufficiently on electronic transaction platform; secondly, choose goods; thirdly, transfer payment to appointed account through some methods; fourthly, the sellers deliver goods after receiving payment information, at last, goods reaches consumer through appointed third-party logistics. During the process, consumers have access to goods arrival time information, which enhance goods transaction scale inter-region. Consumers enjoy various goods from different part of the country without stepping outside. Online shopping industry improves consumer's welfare significantly.

2.4 Driving Development of Third-Party Payment and Boosting Modern Logistics

Supported by information flowing, capital flowing and logistics, online shopping industry does not only base on internet technology, but also develops by the joint effort of third-party payment system and third-party logistics. In other words, without third-party payment system and third-party logistics, online shopping would become air castle, losing its reliable route. In recent years, with the rapid development of online shopping industry, third-party payment business and third-party logistics corporations emerge quickly and become crucial component of social development, which as well as support facilities closely relating to online shopping industry, then refresh whole social development, and perfect social credit system and infrastructure.

2.5 Online Shopping Industry's Advantages and Drawbacks

After years of market fostering, China E-business steps such as supporting infrastructure, payment, logistics have already established, with accelerating penetration rate[4] and maturate user habit. Therefore, the whole steps are favorable. At the same time, in development of online shopping industry, some competitive E-business platform have emerged, which have accumulated years of user resources and technology experience in operation, so as to undoubtedly become basic conditions of online shopping industry rapid development. In addition, the emergence of online shopping brings consumers great convenience and satisfactory of fashion-pursuing. It integrates with payment system and third-party logistics, and provides convenient, quick, great service, which is the crucial condition of online shopping's rapid development. Most importantly, online shopping shortens goods' value chain and creates superior price advantage, which is the source of its competitiveness.

Online shopping bases on the system payment and sound logistics system, therefore, its development is seriously restricted by infrastructure of country and region. The online shopping geographic structure in China, which due to the hardware limitations such as infrastructure and degree of popularization level, the most developed cities are developing fast than other, and the E-business corporations mainly locate in Yangtze River Delta, Pearl River Delta and Beijing.

Table 4. China Online Shopping Users Geographic Distribution of 2008 Unit: Million

Province	Guangdong	Shanghai	Zhejiang	Jiangsu	Beijing	Shandong	Hubei	Sichuan	Fujian	Hunan
Number	917.6	745.8	728.5	705.5	640.4	409.5	314.9	314.8	308.3	251.9

Data source: Department of Commerce http://eb.mofcom.gov.cn

According to the data, the online shopping users in Beijing, Guangzhou and Shanghai account for 28.8% of all users, 33.1% of all transactions and other cities account for71.2%, 66.9% respectively. From the region penetration rate of online shopping, Shanghai is highest with the ratio of 67.2%, and Beijing is 65.3%. Therefore, China region imbalance economic growth rate is the major factor restricting the online

[4] Penetration rate refers to ratio of online shopping users to netizens in half year.

shopping development. In the process of online shopping, the transaction security and credit-loss are the main problems which have prevented online shopping industry from further advanced development. Without meeting the counterpart, consumer's knowledge about goods was directly influenced by electronic shopping website. For example, the distortion of goods information brings loss to consumers, the problem about credit-loss relating to goods quality results in high consumer cost in right maintenance, which not only to confine increase in online shopping users, and as well as to restrict development of online shopping industry.

3 China's Online Shopping Industry Development Trends

3.1 B to C and C to C Showing Convergence Trend

In recent years, many traditional industries constantly entered into B to C area, at the same time, many website of operating pure online business have emerged. However, C to C platform have also realized that goods provided by B to C platform have absolute advantage in quality, brand, after-sale service of these key steps. Therefore, the C to C platform launch B to C business in succession, especially service of COD (cash on delivery) provided by B to C website, which is consistent with Internet users transaction habit of "cash on delivery, goods on delivery". With gradually adding B to C business to C to C platform, in addition to traditional manufacturer and maker attaching great importance to E-business, as well as reduction in technology and operating management cost, all of which have jointly derived convergence of B to C and C to C. Data showed that in 2008, B to C model users in Dangdang.com accounted for 24.3% of transactions, B to C model users in Joyo-Amazon.com for 17%. As far as 2009, only users in Taobao.com participated in transaction of Taobao.com maintaining at ratio of 70%, other website only has ratio of 20%. Two models respectively seek possibility and spaces to develop towards opposite side. Model convergence not only realizes mutual-supplement, but also provides new profit model for each other. Especially, the searching becomes entrance of shopping and community becomes shopping viscous source after B to C's function of searching and community converging to C to C. In the condition of interactive and mutual-supplement of two models, existing operators as well as start-up will promote mew model development and advancement.

3.2 Manufacturers Founding Their Own Online Mall and Entering Online Shopping Industry

The rapid development in online shopping industry makes the new source of profit growth becomes possible for manufacturer. Due to online shopping consumer's high elasticity for goods price, many manufacturers establish their own online mall to conduct online direct marketing, such as home appliances manufacturer of Skyworth and Hisense. The new selling method further shortens value chain of goods from production to consumer, which saves profit gained by middleman, shortens product circulating time, promotes product liquidity and largely reduces product cost. Reduction in product cost reflects in price change, and which is beneficial for consumers. Therefore, the new online shopping model have favored by online shopping consumer.

Meanwhile, consumers can directly order products from manufacturer via convenient information flowing, which realizes “zero-inventory” and saves resources. Statistics data shows that home appliance online shopping users increases from 24.32 million in 2008 to 42.46 million in 2009, with growth rate of 74.6%. At the same period, the scale of home appliance grows from 770 million yuan in 2008 to 2.12 billion yuan in 2009, with growth rate of 177.0%. As it can be seen that with E-business develop fast, online selling channel’s strength have showed itself, and have promoted home appliance online shopping scale with constantly increasing growth rate and have attracted more home appliance manufacturer to devote to construction of online retail channel.

3.3 Security, Credit and Legislation

China market has huge potential for transaction, but also has some issues which need to be solved, such as online transaction security, credit-loss and laws on electronic contract. Responding to these issues, the authority launches more than 10 laws and regulations relating to E-business. “Internet Trading Platform Specification” was launched in 2005, which have purposed to protect parties’ legal right, foster fair environment and boost E-business development. In order to assist and encourage online transaction parties conduct transaction, guard and prevent transaction risk, the Department of Commerce released “Guidance on Online Transaction (Interim)” in March, 2007. In October 1, 2009, the implementation of new "Postal Law" clearly expressed legal status of delivery companies. On base of new "Postal Law", “National Post Office’s Implementation Advice on Implementation of Restructuring and Revitalization in Logistics Industry” was launched to promote development of E-business distribution. At present, Department of Commerce is listing systematically the draft on coming “E-business Model Specification” and “Online Shopping Service Specification”, and People's Bank of China is consummating “Management Methods on Payment and Settlement”. The implementation of these laws and regulations will play positive role in consummating China E-business legislation, third-party safekeeping transaction capital, transaction dispute mediation and other issues. The consummating of these mechanisms will effectively safeguard online shopping industry’s development.

Table 5. Online Shopping Scale and Penetration Rate in Beijing, Guangzhou, Shanghai of 2009

City	Netizen (Million)	NPR (%)	OSU (Million)	(OSPR) (%)
Beijing	10.37	60.7	5.32	51.3
Shanghai	11.67	61.8	6.13	52.6
Guangzhou	6.34	62.3	2.23	35.2

Data source: Department of Commerce http://eb.mofcom.gov.cn

Table 6. OSPR (Online Shopping Penetration Rate) in Several Cities of China

City	OSPR	City	OSPR
Beijing	51.3%	Tianjing	31.8%
Shanghai	52.6%	Chengdu	29.0%
Guangzhou	35.2%	Luoyang	27.0%
Wuhan	38.9%	Zigong	24.0%
Xiamen	36.7%	Dongguan	23.3%
Hangzhou	34.7%	Handan	22.0%
Shenzhen	34.1%	Haerbin	19.9%
Xi'an	33.3%	Cangzhou	19.0%
Jiujiang	32.3%		

Data source: Department of Commercehttp://eb.mofcom.gov.cn

4 Concluding Remarks

China current online shopping users have centered on developed area, such as Beijing, Shanghai, Guangzhou and some developed cities. In these areas, the number of online shopping users is increasing rapidly with accelerating online transaction volume and penetration rate. As shown in Table 5, the above-mentioned areas have online shopping users (OSU) no less than 1 million, especially Guangzhou with number of 6.13 million. And online shopping penetration rate (OSPR) of these areas are 51.3%、52.6%、35.2% respectively in Beijing, Shanghai and Guangzhou. In undeveloped central and western regions, due to limitations of infrastructure and degree of network popularization, the degree of online shopping popularization is low, which restricts the online shopping's development. As shown in table5.

Online shopping penetration rates (OSPR) in Xi'an, Chengdu are respectively 33.3% and 29%, Haerbin merely 19.9% and Handan 19.9%. However, with the deepening of network using, online shopping market in developed areas gradually saturated and infrastructure in all parts of country continuously consummated, which makes exploitation of undeveloped online shopping market become new engineer of online market.

References

1. iResearch-China Online Shopping Industry Development Report of 2008-2009
2. iResearch: 12-year Development Report of China E-business(1997-2009)
3. Song, w., Xu, H.: New Development of Comparative Advantage Theory in E-business economics Contemporary Manager (2005)
4. Sun, R., Hui, H., Yang, L.: Study on New Model of C2C E-business Logistics Development. Logistics Sci-tech 12 (2009)

The Use of DOSXYZnrc to Simulate a Voxel Phantom in Radiation Protection

Changran Geng[1], Xiaobin Tang[1], Feida Chen[1], Yunpeng Liu[1], Qin Xie[1,2], Ding Ding[1], and Da Chen[1,*]

[1] Department of Nuclear Science and Engineering, Nanjing University of Aeronautics and Astronautics, Nanjing 210016, China
[2] School of Nuclear Science and Technology, Lanzhou University, Lanzhou 730000, China
gengchr@nuaa.edu.cn

Abstract. Very significant advancements were presented during the years with computational phantom, passing from stylized analytical human models to realistic voxel models based on computed tomography scans or MRI scans ,and finally to advanced surface-geometry models. This paper presents an investigation on the description of phantom based on the DOSXYZnrc code using ICRP reference voxel models. Several modifications have been made in the DOSXYZnrc source code and macro parameters. Irradiations from broad parallel beams in antero-posterior, postero-anterior directions and eight energies both of male and female have been performed numerically by the Monte Carlo transport code EGSnrc. Comparison was also done between the result of this method and ICRP 74 report. While the effective dose conversion coefficients calculated were little discrepancy with ICRP 74, generally speaking, we believe this edited version of dosxyznrc code together with computational phantoms is a suitable method to determine organ and tissue doses from various radiation exposures.

Keywords: ICRP reference phantom, EGSnrc, DOSXYZnrc, Effective dose.

1 Introduction

Three mile island and chernobyl, Hiroshima atomic bomb events have been deeply embedded in people's mind, the radiation hazards to human beings by all have also deeply shocked the human heart. Recently the earthquake induce to radioactive leaks from nuclear power plant at fukushima, that is also deeply alarming people all over the world .Meanwhile, the radiation hazards of human understanding become more and more objective and comprehensive, the importance of the radiation protection should be paid more and more attention. Also there are various reasons necessitating patient dose assessment in diagnostic radiology and radiotherapy procedure.Radiation phantom has widely used in these problems for years.

The first heterogeneous anthropomorphic model used for dosimetry, the Fisher-Snyder phantom (Snyder et al. 1969, 1978), was devised at the Oak Ridge National Laboratory (ORNL) for the Medical Internal Radiation Dose (MIRD) Committee of

[*] Corresponding author.

H. Tan and M. Zhou (Eds.): CSE 2011, Part I, CCIS 201, pp. 548–554, 2011.

the Society of Nuclear Medicine[1,2]. Its exterior shapes and internal structures are defined by planar, cylindrical, elliptical, and spherical surfaces that present simplified representations of the human anatomy. With great advancement of computers and medical imaging techniques, researchers have recently been able to develop anatomically realistic phantoms of the human body[3].To date, more than 121 computational phantoms have been reported in the literature for ionising and non-ionising radiation dose calculations[4]. A more advanced type of geometry, boundary representation (BREP), has been demonstrated since the 2000s by several groups of researchers for simulating organ motions and for adjusting organ or body size and shape while preserving anatomical realism[5-7]. In supervision by the ICRP(International Commission on Radiological Protection) ,Rex and Regina as a member of voxel phantoms were developed by M. Zankl etc in order to cover several features important to external and internal dosimetry[8]. They will be used as the standard human models for some applications ,such as in radiation protection and for the protection of the patient also in the protection of the aviation fields.

Most of the general Monte Carlo codes, including EGSnrc and DOSXYZnrc, are written with user-friendly interfaces that require minimal modification of the source code. Even this is convenient for users who do not want to do programming, but the lack of flexibility in specifying geometry in the DOSXYZnrc code can be a problem when the system needs to be optimized for special problems involving the description of the computation phantom.

2 Material and Method

2.1 Monte Carlo Method(EGSnrc and dosxyznrc)

The EGSnrc system is a package for the Monte Carlo simulation of coupled electron-photon transport [9]. Its current energy range of applicability is considered to be 1 keV to 10 GeV. The EGS acronym stands for Electron Gamma Shower, and EGSnrc is an extended and improved version of the EGS4 package originally developed at Stanford Linear Accelerator Center (SLAC).

BEAMnrc is based on the EGSnrc code system for modeling radiotherapy sources coupled electron and photon transport. It may use couples of CM(component module) to simulate the accelerator. And it also can generate a phase-space file to be used in dosxyznrc to simulate a therapy procedure or other applications. DOSXYZ is used for three-dimensional(3D) dose calculations, which simulates the transport of photons and electrons in a Cartesian volume and scores the energy deposition in the designated voxels [10]. DOSXYZ is "stand alone" in the usual EGSnrc someway in that it is controlled by scripts, which explicitly refers to the .pegs4dat and .egs4inp files, and is capable of writing out ASCII formatted dose distribution arrays. The geometry described in it is a rectilinear volume with the X–Y plane on the page, X to the right, Y down the page and the Z-axis into the page. Density and material in every voxel may vary with you need. A variety of geometries may be incident on the phantom, including full phase-space files from BEAMnrc and beams characterized using Beam Characterization models.

Their simulation geometry is an integrative geometry consisting of several beam modifiers and a 3D rectilinear voxel (volume elements) human geometry model. The voxel dimensions are variable in all three directions. Every voxel can be assigned to a different material, and the cross-section data for the materials used are available in a preprocessed PEGS4 cross-section data file. Because of so many voxels and too many organs be used in this calculation, we have to modified several macro parameters with DOSXYZnrc and recompile it with another way to read in defined files.

2.2 ICRP Reference Phantom

From the two individual segmented data sets to the reference computational phantoms, Three steps were performed: (1) adjustment of the body height and the skeleton mass of the original model to the reference values by voxel scaling; (2) adjustment of the organ masses to the reference values by adding or subtracting the required number of organ voxels; and (3) adjustment of the whole-body mass to the reference values by adding or subtracting an appropriate number of adipose tissue voxels. The major property of the reference phantom is list by table 1[11].

Table 1. The major property of the reference phantom

Property	Male	Female
Height (m)	1.76	1.63
Mass (kg)	73.0	60.0
Number of tissue voxels	1,946,375	3,886,020
Voxel volume (mm^3)	2.137*2.137*8.0=36.54	1.775*1.775*4.84=15.25
Voxel Number	254*127*220 (+2)	299*137*346 (+2)

2.3 Dose Calculation Procedures

2.3.1 Effective Dose, E

Average dose of each organ and tissue was calculated by equation(1):

$$D_{T,R} = \overline{D_T} = \frac{\int_V D(x,y,z)\rho(x,y,z)dV}{\int_V \rho(x,y,z)dV} \tag{1}$$

Where V is the volume of the organ or tissue, $D(x,y,z)$ is the absorbed dose of voxel(x,y,z), $\rho(x,y,z)$ is the density of voxel(x,y,z).

As ICRP 103 recommend, the tissue-weighted sum of the equivalent doses in all specified tissues and organs of the body, given by the expression:

$$E = \sum_T w_T \left(\frac{H_T^M + H_T^F}{2}\right) = \sum_T w_T \frac{(\sum_R w_R D_{T,R})_M + (\sum_R w_R D_{T,R})_F}{2} = \frac{E_M + E_F}{2} \tag{2}$$

Where E_M,E_F means effective dose of male and female respectively, H_T or $w_r D_{T,R}$ is the equivalent dose in a tissue or organ, T, and w_T is the tissue weighting factor. The unit for the effective dose is the same as for absorbed dose (J/kg), and its special name is sievert (Sv).

2.3.2 ICRP 103 Weighting Factors

In this study, the newest tissue weighting factors, which were released in 2007 with recommended values in ICRP 103, were used to calculate the effective dose. There were some modifications in the tissue weighting factors to take into account the new information on health effects of radiation [12].Such as an increase in breast tissue weighting factor from 0.05 to 0.12 and a reduction in gonad tissue weighting factor from 0.2 to 0.08. The remainder tissues in table 2 include: Adrenals , Extra thoracic (ET) region, Gall bladder, Heart, Kidneys, Lymphatic nodes, Muscle, Oral mucosa, Pancreas, Prostate(male), Small intestine, Spleen, Thymus, Uterus/cervix (female), etc.

Table 2. Recommended tissue weighting factors

Tissue	w_T	Tissue	w_T
Bone-marrow (red)	0.12	Esophagus	0.04
Colon	0.12	Liver	0.04
Lung	0.12	Thyroid	0.04
Stomach	0.12	Bone surface	0.01
Breast	0.12	Brain	0.01
Remainder tissues*	0.12	Salivary glands	0.01
Gonads	0.08	Skin	0.01
Bladder	0.04	Total	1.00

2.3.3 Monte Carlo code

Create input file

First of all, we should construct an .egsphant file to describe the computational phantoms. It includes the coordinate information, material and density information. This procedure was accomplished by the help of Visual C++ program. The program first read in the organ ID number for each voxel, and then convert into plain text format that is required by DOSXYZnrc input file. The density convert process was completed by the way. This program is very flexible and other functions can be easily added. For example, it calculated the total number of voxels and mass for each organ during this study. Source and some other parameters to transport particles were defined in the .egsinp file.

Modifications to DOSXYZnrc code

Seven or less media was always used in some situation of the dosxyznrc code before [10]. But in computational voxel phantoms simulation more media will be used, so the MXMED can be modified to 150 or more. Also the voxel limits was changed for more voxels may have in radiation model. But on account of the memory or other factors, the maximum of voxel number can only be set to about 100 million. During running of dosxyznrc, the way to read the .egsphant file was rewritten in order to running properly in this study.

Result of dosxyznrc
The dose as the result of the dosxyznrc is always normalized by the incident particle fluence, ainflu

$$\text{ainflu} = \frac{\text{NCASE} + \text{ncaseold} - \text{nmissm}}{\text{xcol} * \text{ycol}} \tag{3}$$

where NCASE is the number of histories in this run, ncaseold is the number of histories from previous runs (if this is the first run then this will be 0) and nmissm is the total number of particles from the source that missed the geometry, including in any previous runs, xcol*ycol is the area of the incident beam.

So we always call this dose value as dose per unit fluence, the unit is Gy*cm2.

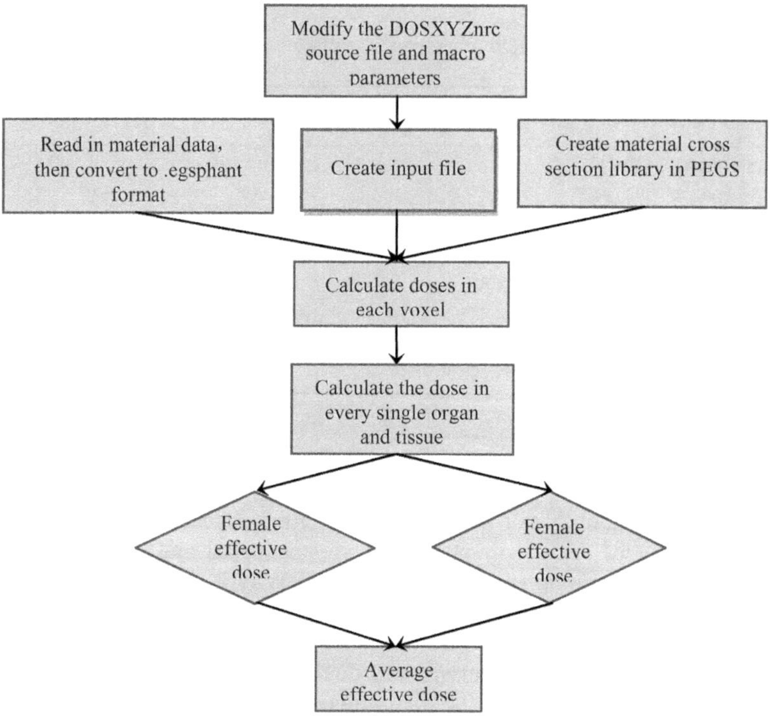

Fig. 1. Schema to calculate the effective dose in DOSXYZnrc

3 Conclusion

Two geometries and eight energies of both phantoms were simulated in this study. The main schema of calculate effective dose in DOSXYZnrc is shown in figure 1. In order to ensure enough accurate, 1E9 histories were used to calculate the result.

The coefficients of variance of every voxel dose in this study is below 10%.And the result of this research is compared with ICRP 74 was list in figure 2 and figure 3.The difference will be mostly put down to the anatomical structure difference, the ICRP draft recommendations of weighting factors, or the uncertain in the simulation of Monte Carlo. As everyone knows, the enormous power to simulate the transport of electron by EGSnrc can't be ignored. Generally speaking, the changes in the effective dose conversion coefficients are small, the results of calculation prove this edited version of dosxyznrc code together with computational human models are a suitable method for determining organ and tissue doses from various radiation exposures in both radiation protection or medical physics. In future, we will combine with the BEAMnrc do something like second cancer risk estimation during radiation therapy and also the radiation protection in aviation field.

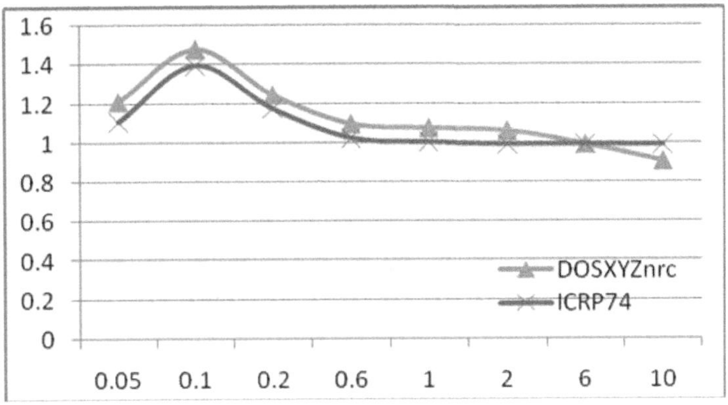

Fig. 2. Effective dose per unit air kerma free-in-air, E/Ka, for monoenergetic photons incident in AP geometry

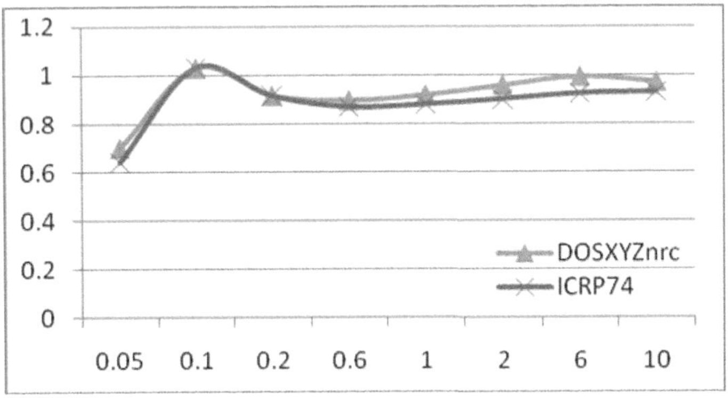

Fig. 3. Effective dose per unit air kerma free-in-air, E/Ka, for monoenergetic photons incident in PA geometry

References

1. Snyder, W.S., et al.: Estimates of specific absorbed fractions for photon sources uniformly distributed in various organs of a heterogeneous phantom. MIRD Pamphlet 5(1), C67 (1978)
2. Snyder, W.S., et al.: Estimates of absorbed fractions for monoenergetic photon sources uniformly distributed in various organs of a heterogeneous phantom: Society of Nuclear Medicine (1969)
3. Zankl, M.: Methods for assessing organ doses using computational models. Radiation Protection Dosimetry 80, 207 (1998)
4. Xu, X.G., Eckerman, K.: Handbook of anatomical models for radiation dosimetry. Taylor & Francis, Abington (2009)
5. Kramer, R., et al.: Female and male adult human phantoms based on polygon mesh surfaces: II. Physics in Medicine and Biology 55, 163–189 (2010)
6. Cassola, V., et al.: FASH and MASH: female and male adult human phantoms based on polygon mesh surfaces: I. Development of the anatomy. Physics in Medicine and Biology 55, 133 (2010)
7. Zhang, J., et al.: RPI-AM and RPI-AF, a pair of mesh-based, size-adjustable adult maleand female computational phantoms using ICRP-89 parameters and their calculations for organ doses from monoenergetic photon beams. Physics in Medicine and Biology 54, 5885 (2009)
8. Zankl, M., et al.: The ICRP Reference Computational Phantoms. In: Handbook of Anatomical Models for Radiation Dosimetry, p. 377 (2009)
9. Kawrakow, I., Rogers, D.: Report PIRS-701-The EGSnrc Code System: Monte Carlo Simulation of Electron and Photon Transport, National Research Council of Canada, Ottawa (2006)
10. Ma, C., et al.: DOSXYZ users manual (2010)
11. ICRP, Adult Reference Computational Phantoms, ICRP Publication 110 (2009)
12. ICRP, The 2007 Recommendations of the International Commission on Radiological Protection, ICRP Publication 103 (2007)

Effects of Information and Communication Technology and Relationship Network on International Trade*

Yinghua Meng

Open Economy and Trade Research Center,
Shanghai Lixin University of Commerce
Shanghai, P.R. China
mymgy@yahoo.com.cn

Abstract. We argued that the there exists information cost in international trade. Information and communication technology, relationship network play an important role in decreasing the information cost of international trade, thus facilitating trade as a result. We use Asian overseas Chinese network to test our assumptions. We found that the role of relationship network is more important than information and communication technology, in addition, the improvement of information and communication technology will worsen the positive effect that the Asian overseas Chinese network on China's import, but has no obvious effect on China's export.

Keywords: International Trade, Information and Communication Technology, Information Cost.

1 Introduction

With new technology broke out in 20th 90s, more and more information and communication technology has been used in international trade, such as the establishment of cyber transaction centers of ebay.com, taobao.com and amazon.com, these transaction centers decrease the information cost in international trade, make the buyers and sellers more easily match together and complete a deal. But in realistic world, it will cost more time and money to find the suitable trade partner.

In addition, during the 20th 90s, economics have been investigating the role of business and social network in international trade, they tried to find that if the business and social network can conquer the informal trade barriers and promote the international trade. Rauch E. (2002) believed that international trade is a searching and matching process between buyer and seller, and inevitably will be influenced by the problem of information and contract cost. But in business and social network, much of the problems of information and contract cost can be solved, and it can be a tool for facilitating international trade. In related empirical literatures, because

* Supported by Leading Academic Discipline Project of Shanghai Municipal Education Commission: International Trade (J51702).

H. Tan and M. Zhou (Eds.): CSE 2011, Part I, CCIS 201, pp. 555–562, 2011.

overseas Chinese distribute around the world and many overseas Chinese are traders, then, much attention has been given to the overseas Chinese network to investigate this issue.

With those considerations above, we can imagine that information and communication technology and relationship network can decrease the trade barrier and facilitate the international trade. But Curtin (1984) argued that emergence of E-Commerce, searching engine, and improvement of information sorting technology can have a negative effect on demand of relationship network in international trade, in addition, innovation of communication method, such as email, may destroy the existing traditional relationship network depending on face to face communication. So, in order to have a more clear imagination and test the above assumptions, we use econometric method to run the regression.

There are some difference between our research and other literatures: first, instead of cross-section regression method, we use the panel data regression method to test our opinions; second, because overseas Chinese in different countries are doing different business, for example, overseas Chinese around Asian are prone to doing trade, finance, and manufacturing; overseas Chinese around European are prone to doing restaurant service, and overseas Chinese in USA are prone to investing in property, IT and electricity industry, so we will focus our study on overseas Chinese around Asian; third, we pay attention to the China's export and import at the same time.

2 Literature Review

In the past, economics usually pay their attention on the issues of the effects of migration on factor endowment between the source country and host country. But in recent year, more and more economics are devoting their effort on the issue of migration on trade. Table 1 lists some of the distinguished papers in this field. In these literatures, we can see that most researchers investigated English spoken countries, only Rauch E. and Trindade V. (2002) investigated overseas Chinese network. In their research, Rauch E. and Trindade V. (2002) used maximum likelihood method to run the econometric regression, and estimated differentiated goods, referenced goods and homogeneous goods separately, but their research did not classify export and import elasticity coefficient.

Most of the research results from table 1 are overseas migration network can have a positive effect on international trade. Gould (1994), Dunlevy and Hutchinson (1999, 2001) found that migration relationship network have a more obvious effect on trade in consumer goods than trade in inputs. Rauch E. and Trindade V. (2002), Wager, Head and Ries (2002) found that the regression coefficient of differentiated goods is bigger than homogenous goods. Ching and Chen (2002) considered that the migration of entrepreneurs have a more positive effect on trade than the migration of investors. Gould (1994) thought that with the increasing of migration numbers, the coefficient of trade elasticity will decrease. Girma and Yu (2000) believed that the coefficient of trade elasticity is bigger when there is no colonial relationship between source country and host country of migration.

Table 1. Literatures on effects of migration on international trade

Literatures	Sample	Export Elasticity	Import Elasticity
Gould(1994)	US and 47 trade partner: 1970-1986	0.02	0.01
Dunlevy, Head and Ries (1998)	Canada and 136 trade partner:1980-1992	0.10	0.31
Hutchinson(1999,2001)	US and 17 trade partner:1870-1910	0.08	0.29
Girma and Yu(2000)	UK and 48 trade partner:1981-1993	0.02	-0.04
Combes et al(2002)	France:1993	0.25	0.14
Rauch and Trindade(2002)	Mainland China and 63 trade partner	0.21/0.47	0.21/0.47
Wagner, Head, and Ries(2002)	Canada and 160 trade partner:1992-1995	0.08	0.25
Blanes-Cristobal(2003)	Spanish and 40 trade partner:1991-1998	0.23	0.03
Ching and Chen(2000)	Canada and Taiwan	-0.06	0.30

Data from: John Bryant, David Law.: Trade and Migration to New Zealand. Research Paper, 45th Congress of the Regional Science Association in Amsterdam, 23-27 August (2005)

3 Data and Model

The gravity model is the workhorse model for empirical analysis of the relationship between trade costs and trade flows. The gravity model explains bilateral trade as a function of the trading partner's market size, and bilateral trade costs relative to all other trading partners. Trade costs in turn include transport, tariffs and a host of administrative costs related to crossing the border, translating information to a foreign language and cultural context and entering and enforcing contracts with foreign suppliers. Commonly used measures of such costs are the distance between the trading partners, whether or not they have a common border, whether or not they share a common language and whether or not one or both are members of a regional trade agreement. In the following, in order to emphasis on the variable of relationship network, we construct the gravity model as follows:

$$Log(EXijt)=Cijt+a1*Log(GDPit*GDPjt)+a2*Log(POPit*POPjt)+a3*Log(DISTij)+a4*Colonyij+a5*Overseasijt+uijt \quad (1)$$

$$Log(IMijt)=Cijt+a1*Log(GDPit*GDPjt)+a2*Log(POPit*POPjt)+a3*Log(DISTij)+a4*Colonyij+a5*Overseasijt+uijt \quad (2)$$

$$Log(EXijt)=Cijt+a1*Log(GDPit*GDPjt)+a2*Log(POPit*POPjt)+a3*Log(DISTij)+a4*Colonyij+a5*Overseasijt+a6*Log(ICTit*ICTjt)+uijt \quad (3)$$

$$Log(IMijt)=Cijt+a1*Log(GDPit*GDPjt)+a2*Log(POPit*POPjt)+a3*Log(DISTij)+a4*Colonyij+a5*Overseasijt+a6*Log(ICTit*ICTjt)+uijt \quad (4)$$

The indicators' meaning in the gravity equation (1)-(4) are presented below: GDPit: GDP of country i in year t; GDPjt: GDP of China in year t; POPit: population of country i in year t; POPjt :population of China in year t; DISTij: distance between country i and China's economic zone; Colonyij: If country i and China have colony relationship in history, then=1, else=0; EXijt: China' export value to country i in year t; IMijt: China's import value from country i in year t; Overseasijt: the relationship between overseas Chinese merchant in country i and merchant in mainland China in year t; ICTit: information and communication technology in country i in year t; ICTjt: information and communication technology in China in year t; Cijt: intercept; uijt: white noise.

In our model, variable Overseasijt refers to the intensity of relationship network between overseas Chinese merchant in country i and Chinese merchant in mainland China. But in fact, this data is very hard to find, and in this paper, we use the method of Rauch E. and Trindade V. (2002), in their paper, they use the product of people proportion of overseas Chinese in country i in year t and people proportion of Chinese in mainland China in year t (98%).

In addition, we consider the following three factors: rate of telephone and mobile phone users, popularization of computers, and application of internet, and the computation equation is: ICTit= $(Xi1t*Xi2t*Xi3t)^{1/3}$, ICTit refers to information and communication technology in country i; Xi1t refers to the total numbers of telephone and mobile phone users/ per 100 persons in year t; Xi2t refers to the total numbers of computers/ per 100 persons in year t;Xi3t refers to internet users / per 100 persons in year t. In addition, considering the data of application of internet is available after 1990, and there is a lag effect of information and communication technology on international trade, so we use the data of 1990, 1993 and 1998 accordingly, we use 0.01 replace the zero value. The above data comes from the UN stat. database.

In this paper, we use the data of overseas Chinese from 1980, 1985, 1990, 1994, 1999, and the host country of migration is Japan, Burma, Korea, India, Thailand, Singapore, Malaysia, Philippine, Indonesia, Saudi Arabia, Pakistan, and Vietnam. The data of 1980, 1990 from Rauch E. and Trindade V. (2002); data of 1985 comes from "Overseas Chinese Yearbook"; data of 1994 comes from Huang runlong(2003); data of 1999 comes from overseas Chinese statistics from Taiwan Province of China.

Data of China's Export and China's import comes from "CHINA EXTERNAL ECONOMIC STATISTICAL YEARBOOK", data of population, GDP comes from UN stat. database, the distance between host country's capital and Shanghai comes from the "distance calculator" in web www.indo.com.

We use Eviews 5.0 to run the regressions of equations above.

4 Estimates Results

This section applies the gravity model for estimating the impact of information and communication technology and relationship network on international trade.

First, we use the data of five years (1980, 1985, 1990, 1994 and 1999) and equation (1), equation (2) to run the regression. The results are as follows:

Table 2. The Regression results of Gravity Equation[1]

Variable	Equation(1)	Equation(2)	Equation(1')	Equation(2')
Cijt	3.852 (5.167)	-2.888 (7.171)	5.1088 (4.317)	3.501 (6.113)
Log(GDPit*GDPjt)	1.044*** (0.081)	1.203*** (0.105)	1.064*** (0.064)	1.161*** (0.088)
Log(POPit*POPjt)	-0.368*** (0.146)	-0.300 (0.206)	-0.465*** (0.129)	-0.444*** (0.186)
Log(DISTij)	-0.559*** (0.217)	-0.562*** (0.263)	-0.325*** (0.195)	-0.553*** (0.239)
Overseasijt	2.038** (0.881)	2.106* (1.106)	1.899** (0.833)	1.566 (1.050)
Colonyij	-0.522 (0.515)	-0.818 (0.635)	--	--
R2	0.992	0.975	0.994	0.976
D.W.	1.906	2.119	1.909	2.133
N	60	60	60	60

The results are presented in Table 2 by and large support our hypothesis, almost all the variable coefficients get their expected values and are significant at the 5% level: 1% increasing of bilateral economic size will increase 1%-1.2% of China's export and China's import. As to the effects of bilateral population on international trade, there exist two opposite opinions, on one hand, if a country is supplied by itself, so its population will have a negative effect on its export, on the other hand, more people will promote labor specialization, thus facilitating the international trade. In the regression results above, we can see that the bilateral population has a negative effect on China's export and China's import (even if the coefficient is not obvious), it means that first effect is stronger than the latter effect, 1% increasing of bilateral population will decrease 0.3%-0.37% of international trade. In addition, distance has a negative effect on China's export and import.

As to our interested variable, the overseas Chinese network has a positive effect on China's international trade, 1% increasing of intensify of overseas Chinese network will increase 2.11 %(2.04%) of China's import (export). As we can see in the table, the variable of colony is not significance, so we delete the variable and run the regression of equation (1) and (2) again, the results are seen in the column 4 and 5 of table 2, after deleting the colony variable, the positive effects of overseas Chinese network on international trade decrease as a result, the coefficient of trade elasticity of import (export) fall from 2.11%(2.04%) to 1.57%(1.9%).

In order to compare the effects of information communication technology on China's international trade, firstly, we use the data of three years (1990, 1993 and 1998) and equation (1), equation (2) to run the regression, the results are showed in table 3.

[1] The t-value is presented in parentheses. Values marked (***) , (**) and (*)are significant at the 1% and 5% and 10% levels, respectively.

Table 3. The Regression results of Gravity Equation

Variable	Equation(1)	Equation(2)	Equation(3)	Equation(4)
Cijt	7.469* (1.774)	-1.056 (-0.145)	5.675 (1.455)	5.916 (1.085)
Log(GDPit*GDPjt)	0.752*** (12.458)	1.116*** (11.356)	0.787*** (9.218)	0.706*** (5.762)
Log(POPit*POPjt)	-0.270*** (-2.077)	-0.248 (-1.190)	-0.256*** (-2.152)	-0.143*** (-1.101)
Log(DISTij)	-0.553*** (-4.112)	-0.766*** (-3.559)	-0.497*** (-3.782)	-0.812*** (-6.027)
Overseasijt	1.622** (2.223)	2.077* (1.765)	1.564** (2.129)	1.409* (1.682)
Colonyij	-0.278 (1.029)	-0.854*** (-2.229)	--	-0.179 (-0.469)
Log(ICTit*ICTjt)	--	--	0.028 (0.960)	0.195*** (5.147)
R2	0.99	0.99	0.99	0.99
D.W.	1.852	2.013	1.842	2.101
N	36	36	36	36

Regression results of equation (1) in table 3, except for colony variable is not significance, all other variables are significance at the 5% level and get their expected values. 1% increasing of intensify of overseas Chinese network will increase 1.622% of China's export, and this figure is less than the figure of regression results of equation (1) in table 2, and this is because with the development of information communication technology and improvement of law after 20th 90s, it decrease the promoting effect of overseas Chinese network on overcoming information barriers in international trade, and the regression in table (3) does not include the data before 1990.

When we use the equation (3) to run the regression, we can see that the coefficient does not pass the test of significance, 1% increasing of intensify of information communication technology will increase 0.02% of China's export, this effect is much less than the effects of overseas Chinese network on China's export (1.564%); at the same time, when we add the variable of information communication technology, the positive effect of overseas Chinese network on China's export reduce at a slow rate, from 1.622% to 1.564%, and this means the improvement of bilateral information communication technology has little effect on the influence of overseas Chinese network on China's export.

From the regression result of equation (2) in table 3, we can see that all variables have passed the significance test except for population variable.1% increasing of overseas Chinese network will promote 2.077% increasing of China's import. When we add the variable of information communication technology into the equation (2), and we found that the coefficient of information communication technology have passed the significance test, 1% increasing of information communication technology will increase China's import by 0.195%, and it is much less than the effects of overseas Chinese network on China's import, at the same time, when we add the variable of information communication technology, the positive effect of overseas

Chinese network on China's import decrease from 2.077% to 1.409%, and it means that the improvement of bilateral information communication technology restrain the positive effects of overseas Chinese network on China's import.

5 Conclusions and Policy Implications

Through using the gravity model, this paper has quantified the effects of information communication technology and overseas Chinese network on China's international trade. We found that above two factors have positive effects on China's international trade, but these the effects of these two factors are different, the positive effects of overseas Chinese network is much larger than the effects of information communication technology on China's international trade. In addition, there also exist interactions between these two factors: improvement of information communication technology restrains the positive effects of overseas Chinese network on China's import, but does not influence the positive effects of overseas Chinese network on China's export.

Because of externality, Rauch E. (2002) believed that the network membership lack the motive to enlarge or retain their network relationship. Like Sogo Shosha in Japan or Chaebol in Korea, if Chinese government wants to utilize the overseas Chinese network to facilitate international trade, it is necessary to establish a law to support the communications between overseas Chinese and mainland China, and can not depend on the overseas Chinese network itself. For example, the government can invest in establish the communication center to increase trust between overseas Chinese.

At the same time, we also should be aware the importance of improvement of information communication technology on the development of international trade, it change the trade pattern to a large extent. Even if information communication technology can restrain the positive effects of overseas Chinese network on China's import, but this effect can be reduced by the government's policies.

Acknowledgments

Supported by Leading Academic Discipline Project of Shanghai Municipal Education Commission: International Trade (J51702).

References

1. Bryant, J., David, L.: New Zealand's Diaspora and Overseas-born Population. Wellington, New Zealand Treasury, Working Paper (2004)
2. Ching, H.S., Chen, L.-L.: Links Between Emigrants and the Home Country: The Case of Trade Between Taiwan and Canada. In: Kohno, H., Nijkamp, P., Poot, J. (eds.) Regional Cohesion and Competition in the Age of Globalization, pp. 185–198. Edward Elgar, Cheltenham (2000)

3. Dunlevey, J.A., Hutchison, W.K.: The Impact of Immigration on American Import Trade in the Late Nineteenth and Early Twentieth Centuries. Journal of Economic History, 1043–1062 (1999)
4. Girma, S., Yu, Z.: The Link between Immigration and Trade: Evidence from the UK. Nottingham, University of Nottingham, Centre for Research on Globalization and Labour Markets, Research Paper No 23 (2000)
5. Gould, D.M.: Immigrant Links to the Home Country: Empirical Implications for US Bilateral Trade flows. Review of Economics and Statistics 76(2), 302–316 (1994)
6. Greif, A.: Contract enforceability and Economic Institutions in Early Trade: the Mghribi Tades' Coalition. American Economic Review 83(3), 525–548 (1993)
7. Keith, H., Ries, J.: Immigration and Trade Creation: Econometric Evidence from Canada. Canadian Journal of Economics 31(1), 47–62 (1998)
8. Kohli, U.: Migration and Foreign Trade: Further Results. Journal of Population Economics 15, 381–387 (2002)
9. Rauch, J.E.: Networks Versus Markets in International Trade. Journal of International Economics 48(1), 7–35 (1999)
10. Rauch, J.E., Watson, J.: Entrepreneurship in International trade.National Bureau of Economic Research, Working Paper (2002)
11. Rauch, J.E., Trindade, V.: Ethnic Chinese Networks in International Trade. Review of Economics and Statistics 84(1), 116–130 (2002)
12. Wang, H.: Weak State, Strong Networks: The Institutional Dynamics of Foreign Direct Investment in. Oxford University Press, Oxford (2001)

Comparative Advantage Analysis on the Modes of Supply of Trade in Service*

Yinghua Meng

Open Economy and Trade Research Center,
Shanghai Lixin University of Commerce
Shanghai, P.R. China
mymgy@yahoo.com.cn

Abstract. There exists four modes of supply of trade in service, and they affect the comparative advantage of trade in service in different ways. At present, because of lacking of appropriate evaluation methods and indexes, we can not fully analyze the comparative advantage of trade in service. By constructing revealed comparative advantage index for supply modes 1(2,4) of trade in service, competitive advantage index for supply mode 3 and FDI comparative advantage index, we empirical study the comparative advantage of modes of supply of trade in service

Keywords: Modes of Supply, Comparative Advantage, Trade in Service.

1 Introduction

Now lots of literatures have showed that the law of comparative advantage can be used for analyzing of trade in service (Sapir and Lutz, 1981; Hindley and Smith, 1984; Deardoff, 1985), and empirical studies on comparative advantage of trade in service usually used the traditional methods and indexes that used for trade in goods. But we have to admit that services can be traded through four different modes of supply, namely, Cross Border Supply, Consumption Abroad, Commercial Presence, and Movement of Natural Persons, termed modes 1, 2, 3, and 4, respectively, and there is only one mode of supply for trade in goods: Cross Border Supply, so we may ignored many traits of trade in service if we use the same way of analyzing trade in goods.

First, we can not judge that there is comparative advantage only by the trade surplus or deficit of the service sector. For example, there may be comparative advantage in supply mode of Commercial Presence, but lacking of comparative advantage in supply mode of Cross Border Supply, so even if the service sector get trade surplus in supply mode of Commercial Presence, but it still may get trade deficit in supply mode of Cross Border Supply.

* Supported by Leading Academic Discipline Project of Shanghai Municipal Education Commission: International Trade (J51702).

H. Tan and M. Zhou (Eds.): CSE 2011, Part I, CCIS 201, pp. 563–569, 2011.

Second, there exists interaction between four modes of supply of trade in service. Then if adverse transition of comparative advantage has occurred in one supply mode of supply, it may influence the comparative advantage of the other mode of supply of trade in service.

Third, when service is supplied by mode of Commercial Presence, the transaction is occurred between residences and non- residents in one country, and service transaction does not provided cross the border, so the statistics data base on balance of payment does not include this kind of mode of supply, and traditional comparative advantage indexes can not be used to analyze as a result.

Fourth, from our analysis above, we can conclude that the traditional means of analyzing the comparative advantage can not fully reflect the real comparative advantage of trade in service. In our paper, we try to construct new indexes to realize this goal.

2 Influence Mechanism of Modes of Supply on Comparative Advantage of Trade in Service

Services trade through different supply mode means crossing the border of different endowment and services supplier, we try to analyze and conclude this issue as the following mechanisms.

2.1 Influence Mechanism of Cross Border Supply on Comparative Advantage of Trade in Service

When service is traded through Cross Border Supply, service provider and service receiver do not go across the border to complete the deal, instead, service is traded through the internet, for example, call center and data processing center can provide the communication service or data processing service to the demanding country, by this way, capital intensive country can get the labor intensive service from labor abundant country, and labor intensive country can get the capital intensive service from capital abundant country (like doctor consultant service). That is to say, under this condition, comparative advantage of trade in service depends on the immobile factor endowment and the related restriction policy on cross border service.

2.2 Influence Mechanism of Commercial Presence on Comparative Advantage of Trade in Service

Mode of Commercial Presence means the transnational corporations establish affiliated companies in other countries and provide the services to the domestic people. In this situation, we classify transnational corporations into two types: transnational corporations of manufacturing that investing in service sector and transnational corporations of service that investing in service sector. The comparative advantage of the first kind comes from the cooperation between parent company and affiliated companies, and the comparative advantage of the latter comes from the capabilities of the company, such as the management and professional ability.

2.3 Influence Mechanism of Consumption Abroad on Comparative Advantage of Trade in Service

Mode of Consumption Abroad means that the consumers go to the other country and receive the service. It is impossible for consumer to cost so much money and time to buy the foreign service only because it's price. So cost can not fully reflect the comparative advantage of trade in service in this condition. For example, tourism service is attractive because it's difference and culture and other reasons. So we can conclude that difference of the service can explain most of the comparative advantage under this supply mode.

2.4 Influence Mechanism of Movement of Natural Persons on Comparative Advantage of Trade in Service

On this mode, except for professionals, comparative advantage of trade in service depends on the restricted policies on migration and temporary movement of professionals. At present, because most developed countries are afraid of rigid domestic employment losing because of lots of non technical immigrations from developing countries, so they set up many restrictions to limit the temporary movement of the people.

3 Empirical Study of Comparative Advantage of Supply Mode 1, 2, 4 of Trade in Service

RCA index is usually used in analyzing the comparative advantage of trade in goods, and it means that the rate between proportions of specified export goods to total export goods of a country and proportion of specified export goods to total export goods of the world:

$$RCA=(Xik/Xi)/(Xk/X) \quad (1)$$

RCAj: Revealed Comparative Advantage in goods k; Xik: export value of k of country i; Xi: total export value of country i; Xk: total export value of k of the world: total export value of the world.

In order to use this index to analyze the comparative advantage of services mode, we revise the RCA index as follows:

$$RCAj=(Xij/Xi)/(Xj/X) \quad (2)$$

RCAj: Revealed comparative advantage of trade in services mode j (j=1, 2, 4); Xij: export value by service mode j of country i; Xi: total export value of country i; Xj: total export value by service mode j of the world; X: total export value of the world.

In addition, we use the data of China, USA and Japan to analyze the comparative advantage of supply mode of trade in service between these countries.

Because data of trade in service are not available in many countries, especially in FATS (Foreign Affiliates Trade Statistics), so we can not get the whole integrated data of trade in service base on the modes of supply classification directly. Base on the Statistics Manual of Trade in Service (IMF, OECD, UN, UNCTAD, WTO, EU,

2002), we define and compute the data of supply mode 1, 2, 4 as follows: Cross Border Supply=transportation+ insurance+ telecommunications+ financial services+ computers information+ royalties and license fees+ other commercial services other than personal, entertainment, and government services. Consumption Abroad=travel. Movement of Natural Persons=personal services and entertain services.

Base on our statistics method above, we use the data of China, US and Japan to compute the RCAj index. China's data is from the table of balance of payment; USA's data is from Beau of Economic Analysis, Japan's data is from the table of balance of payment. And the results are showed in table 1.

Table 1. Revealed Comparative Advantage of Trade in Services in Supply Mode j (j=1, 2, 4)

		1998	1999	2000	2001	2002	2003	2004	2005	2006
	Mod1	0.54	0.56	0.55	0.55	0.58	0.6	0.61	0.6	0.62
USA	Mod2	1.62	1.56	1.62	1.55	1.49	1.48	1.5	1.56	1.55
	Mod4	3.17	3.73	3.96	4.84	4.86	4.82	4.75	4.9	4.82
	Mod1	0.35	0.32	0.39	0.36	0.38	0.51	0.5	0.5	0.54
China	Mod2	2.22	2.28	2.24	2.26	2.22	1.91	1.96	1.87	1.78
	Mod4	1.51	1.74	1.24	2.02	2.46	3.04	3.07	4.36	4.68
	Mod1	1.28	1.32	1.33	1.32	1.31	1.22	1.19	1.18	1.21
Japan	Mod2	0.19	0.18	0.16	0.17	0.18	0.4	0.42	0.42	0.28
	Mod4	3	2.51	2.56	2.26	2.12	1.8	2.21	2.1	2.47

From the table 1, we can conclude that:

For mode of Cross Border Supply, Japan's index RCA1 is near to 1.3, indicated that there is strong comparative advantage in supply mode 1, and China and USA's index RCA1 are both below 0.6, indicated that there is weak comparative advantage in supply mode 1in these two countries, in addition, it is worth noting that even if USA's service trade value by supply mode 1 is large, but trade value by supply mode 2 is also large, then it reduced the importance role of mode 1 in service transaction.

For mode of Consumption Abroad, USA and China's index RCA2 retain 1.4 to 2.2, it means that USA and China have strong comparative advantage in supply mode 2 of trade in service, but China's index show a descending trend. Japan's index RCA2 is below 0.5, shows that Japan have a weak comparative advantage in supply mode 2 of trade in service.

In addition, USA, China and Japan have a very strong comparative advantage in supply mode 4 of trade in service. USA and China's index RCA4 shows an ascending trend.

4 Empirical Study of Comparative Advantage of Supply Mode 3 of Trade in Service

Because there is not an integrated data on foreign affiliate's statistics in the world, so we can not compute and compare the comparative advantage index of supply mode 3 in a large scale, we can only compute USA, Japan, Hungary and China's index base on these country's available data.

Trade competitive index (TC) refers to the proportion of trade net flow value to total trade value (export plus import).

$$TCij=(Xij-Mij)/(Xij+Mij) \quad (3)$$

TCij: Trade competitive index of country i in goods j; Xij: export value of country i in goods j; Mij: import value of country i in goods j. In order further fully investigate the comparative advantage of supply mode 3, we revise the above TC index as:

$$TCi3=(Xi3-Mi3)/(Xi3+Mi3) \quad (4)$$

TCi3: Trade competitive index of country i in supply mode 3; Xi3: export value of country i in supply mode 3; Mi3: import value of country i in supply mode 3.

With index TCi3, we compute and compare the comparative advantage of USA, Japan and Hungary in supply mode 3 of trade in service. The results are showed in table 2.

Table 2. Trade competitive index of country i in supply mode 3 (USA, Japan and Hungary)

	1997	1998	1999	2000	2001	2002	2003	2004	2005	2006
USA	0.067	0.076	0.092	0.091	0.069	0.071	0.095	0.117	0.152	n.a.
Japan	0.730	0.739	0.661	0.658	0.680	0.673	0.634	0.671	0.682	0.716
Hungary	n.a.	n.a.	n.a.	n.a.	n.a.	n.a.	n.a.	0.330	0.293	n.a.

Data source: USA's data from BEA; Japan's data from METI(Japan); Hungary's data fromEurostat.

From table 2, we know that USA has a slight comparative advantage in supply mode 3 of trade in service (the index value is below 0.15), but showed an ascending trend in recent years; on the contrary, Japan has a strong comparative advantage in supply mode 3 of trade in service (the index value is over 0.6), even if the value has decreased since financial crisis in 1997, but began to increase again from 2004; Hungary's index shows a little comparative advantage in supply mode 3 of trade in service (the index value is around 0.3).

There is close relationship between supply mode 3 (Commercial Presence) and FDI in service, so when the data of foreign affiliates of trade in service is not available, we usually use the data of FDI in service to substitute. Here we revise the index TCi3 and construct the FDI Competitive Advantage index to evaluate comparative advantage in supply mode 3 of trade in service.

$$FCAi=(OUTFDIi-INFDIi)/ (OUTFDIi+INFDIi) \quad (5)$$

FCAi: FDI Competitive Advantage index of country i; OUTFDIi: outflow foreign direct investment of country i; INFDIi: inflow foreign direct investment of country i. By using this index, we compare the results of FDI Competitive Advantage of USA, Japan and China, the results are showed in table 3.

Table 3. FDI Competitive Advantage index (USA, Japan and China)

	1997	1998	1999	2000	2001	2002	2003	2004	2005	2006
USA	-0.08	0.50	-0.12	-0.38	-0.15	0.33	0.46	0.3	-3.02	0.04
Japan	0.82	0.56	0.31	0.27	0.08	0.32	0.13	-0.29	n.a.	n.a.
China	n.a.	n.a.	n.a.	n.a.	n.a.	n.a.	-0.88	-0.69	-0.28	-0.32

Data source: USA's data from BEA; Japan's data from Jetro (Japan).

From table 3, we can see that the FDI Competitive Advantage index of USA fluctuating between -0.5 and 0.5, it shows an instable condition; the FDI Competitive Advantage index of Japan has decreased since 1997, from 0.82 to -0.29 in 2004; the FDI Competitive Advantage index of China has showed an improvement since 2003, from a comparative disadvantage to a strong comparative advantage.

In addition, we compare the results of FDI Competitive Advantage index and Trade Competitive index of supply mode 3, and found that there existed a difference when we substitute FATS data with FDI data, the results show completely dissimilarity in comparative advantage: even if FDI Competitive Advantage index of USA showed a obvious fluctuation, but this does not influence the comparative advantage of supply mode 3 of trade in service, the comparative advantage of supply mode 3 of USA still retain at a weak comparative advantage condition; after the financial crisis broke out in 1997, The capability of Japan's transnational corporation in investment abroad has decreased, it indicated a decreasing trend of FCA index, but it did not mean that Japan has lost its comparative advantage in supply mode 3, it has still retained comparative advantage at a high level.

5 Conclusions

Four modes of supply of trade in service affect the comparative advantage of trade in service in different ways. By constructing revealed comparative advantage index of modes 1(2, 4), competitive advantage index in supply mode 3, FDI Competitive Advantage index, we empirical study the comparative advantage of modes of supply of trade in service. We found that:

On mode of Cross Border Supply, Japan has a strong comparative advantage, and USA and China have a weak comparative advantage;

On mode of Consumption Abroad, China and USA have strong comparative advantage, but it reflected a descending trend in China; Japan have a weak comparative advantage.

On mode of Movement of Natural Persons, USA, China and Japan also show a strong comparative advantage, and it showed a ascending trend in USA and China, Japan's comparative advantage retain a stable condition.

On mode of Commercial Presence, it showed a weak comparative advantage in USA, Japan has a strong comparative advantage, but Hungary has a weak comparative advantage, there is no comparative advantage in China.

Acknowledgments

Supported by Leading Academic Discipline Project of Shanghai Municipal Education Commission: International Trade (J51702).

References

1. Deardoff, A.: Comparative Advantage and International Trade and Investment in Services. In: Stern, R.M. (ed.) Trade and Investment in Services, Canada/US Perspectives, Toronto, Ontario Economic Council (1985)
2. Hindley, B., Smith, A.: Comparative Advantage and Trade in Service. World Economy 7(4), 369–389 (1984)
3. Hisanaga, M.: Comparative Advantage Structure of US International Service. KIER Disscussion Paper, No.633 (2007)
4. Sapir, A., Lutz, E.: Trade in Service: Economic Determinants and Development Related Issues. World Bank Staff Working Paper, 410 (1981)
5. Chanda, R.: Inter-Modal Linkages in Services Trade. OECD Trade Policy Working Paper No.30, Working Party of the Trade Committee (2004)
6. Walmsley, T., Winters, L.A.: Relaxing the Restrictions on the Temporary Movement of Natural Persons: A Simulation Analysis. CEPR Discussion Paper, 3719 (2002)

Finite Element Numerical Simulation for 2-D Ground Water Groundwater Movement in Confined Aquifer

Mengling Zhao

School of Science, Xi'an Scientific and Technical University, Xi'an, 710054, China
zhaomengling@26.com

Abstract. According to the plane suppose of groundwater movement in confined aquifer, the numerical model of 2-D ground water flow in confined aquifer with variable h was established and was calculated by the finite element numerical simulation method. For a instance is validated by using matlab.the numerical simulation shows that the calculated results of the finite element numerical simulation method is in good agreement with the calculated result of the finite difference method.

Keywords: Groundwater, Numerical Simulation, Finite Element Method, Matlab.

Aquifer located between two impervious layer and no exisingt free surface called confined aquifer. According to the permeability coefficient of space and the direction of the mutation characteristics, can be divided into homogeneous and aquifer heterogeneity, isotropic and anisotropic aquifers. In this paper , For the homogenizing, isotropic, the flow movement problems of groundwater in two-dimensional confined aquifer is calculated by finite element numerical simulation .

1 Mathematical Model

1.1 Assumption of Plane of Groundwater Movement in Confined Aquifer

Natural groundwater flow, especially, under the condition of the regional groundwater flow, Aquifer thickness comparing with groundwater flow in horizontal space scale is very small. Therefore, for regional groundwater flow can be thought to flow mainly on the planar region of in parallel to the horizontal plane, vertical flow speed can be ignored, in fact, in vertical direction gradient $\left(\frac{\partial h}{\partial z} \approx 0\right)$ of measure pressure head is ignored. This kind approximate method of ignoreing vertical flow , called assumption of groundwater movement plane .

1.2 The Equation of Motion of the Flow Movement Problems of Groundwater in Two-Dimensional Confined Aquifer[1-4]

In assumption of plane flow, the equations of motion of the problems of groundwater flow in two-dimensional confined aquifer with variable h can be described as eq.1

H. Tan and M. Zhou (Eds.): CSE 2011, Part I, CCIS 201, pp. 570–577, 2011.

$$\frac{\partial}{\partial x}\left(T\frac{\partial h}{\partial x}\right)+\frac{\partial}{\partial y}\left(T\frac{\partial h}{\partial y}\right)+\varepsilon=\mu_e\frac{\partial h}{\partial t} \qquad (x,y\in\Omega) \tag{1}$$

In eq.1, T guide water coefficient. μ_e is storage water coefficient. ε is Pumping flow. Ω is the calculating regionas shown in fig.1. There is lateral supplied runoff of single wide flow being q_1 in the border of AB.BC boundary for water-barrier boundary.The rest of the both sides CD and AD are set head boundary.

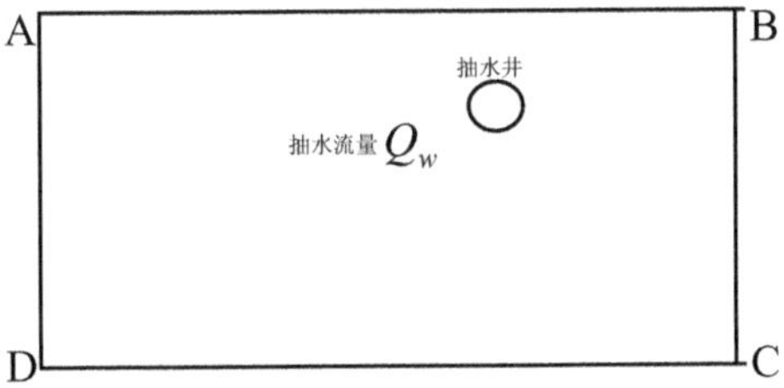

Fig. 1. Sketch map of repion Ω seepage bearing press

1.3 The Initial and Boundary Conditions[5-6]

(1) The initial conditions $(t=0)$

$$h(x,y,0)=h_0 \quad (x,y\in\Omega,t=0)$$

Where h_0 is initial pressure measuring head.

(2) The boundary conditions

$$h(x,y)|_{AD}=h_a \quad (x,y\in\overline{AD},t>0)$$

$$h(x,y)|_{CD}=h_c \quad (x,y\in\overline{CD},t>0)$$

$$T\frac{\partial h}{\partial n}|_{AB}=q_1 \quad (x,y\in\overline{AB},t>0)$$

$$T\frac{\partial h}{\partial n}|_{BC}=q_2 \quad (x,y\in\overline{BC},t>0)$$

$$\varepsilon=Q_w \quad (x,y\in(x_w,y_w))$$

Where n **is** the outside normal direction. q_1 is the single wide flow of AB boundary. q_2 is the flow of BC boundary.

2 The Numeric Moel[7-11]

2.1 The Dividing of Computing Region

As shown in fig.2,the computing region will be divided into N_e isosceles right triangle units, the apex of triangle is named node .Each triangle units e_n($n=1,2,\ldots,N_e$)is corresponding with three nodes. The three nodes are prescribed as i,j,k according to the counterclockwise.So each node is corresponding with a coordinate value.

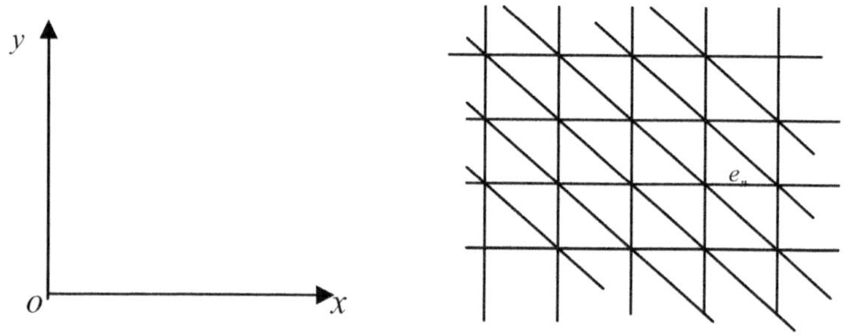

Fig. 2. Sketch map of trianglation ofcalaulated

2.2 The Establishment of Numeric Model

By using the numerical simulation method of galerkin finite element, eq.2 is the equation of galerkin corresponding with two-D groundwater solute transport eq.1.

$$\iint_{\Omega}\left[\mu_e\frac{\partial h}{\partial t}-\frac{\partial}{\partial x}\left(T\frac{\partial h}{\partial x}\right)-\frac{\partial h}{\partial y}\left(T\frac{\partial h}{\partial y}\right)-\varepsilon\right]\cdot N_m dxdy=0\text{,}m=1,2,3,\ldots E \tag{2}$$

Where Ω is calculating region, E is the number of the nodes, the serial numbers of node are ($1,2,3,\cdots,E$) according to from down to up and left to right, N_m is shape function.So

$$h=\left(N_1(x,y)\ N_2(x,y)\ \cdots\ N_{E-1}(x,y)\ N_E(x,y)\right)\cdot\left(h_1(t)\ h_2(t)\cdots h_{E-1}(t)\ h_E(x,y)\right)^T$$

($h_1(t),h_2(t),\cdots,h_{E-1}(t),h_E(t)$) are the values of the functions for C in every node.

By using Green formula , Eq.2 can be Simplified as eq.3.

$$\begin{aligned}&\iint_{\Omega}\mu_e\frac{\partial h}{\partial t}N_m dxdy+\iint_{\Omega}\left(T\frac{\partial h}{\partial x}\cdot\frac{\partial N_m}{\partial x}+T\frac{\partial h}{\partial y}\cdot\frac{\partial N_m}{\partial y}\right)dxdy\\&=\iint_{\Omega}\varepsilon N_m dxdy+\int_{AB}q_1N_m dxdy+\int_{BC}q_2N_m dxdy\end{aligned} \tag{3}$$

Considering the first n triangle unit, the nodes of according to counterclockwise are desigated i, j, k, the coordinate of the three points followe (x_i, y_i), (x_j, y_j), (x_k, y_k), So there is eq.4. in e_n.

$$h(x,y,t) = N_i(x,y)h_i(t) + N_j(x,y)h_j(t) + N_k(x,y)h_k(t) \tag{4}$$

Where $(N_i(x,y), N_j(x,y), N_k(x,y))$ is linear basis function in e_n.

$$N_i(x,y) = \frac{1}{2\Delta_e}\begin{vmatrix} x & y & 1 \\ x_j & y_j & 1 \\ x_k & y_k & 1 \end{vmatrix}, \quad N_j(x,y) = \frac{1}{2\Delta_e}\begin{vmatrix} x & y & 1 \\ x_k & y_k & 1 \\ x_i & y_i & 1 \end{vmatrix}, \quad N_k(x,y) = \frac{1}{2\Delta_e}\begin{vmatrix} x & y & 1 \\ x_i & y_i & 1 \\ x_j & y_j & 1 \end{vmatrix}.$$

Order

$$N = (\ N_i(x,y), N_j(x,y), N_k(x,y)\ ),\quad h_e = (h_i\ \ h_j\ \ h_k)^T \tag{5}$$

By using the nature of integral , eq.3 can be turned into eq.6.

$$\begin{aligned}&\sum_{n=1}^{N_e}\iint_{e_n}\left(T\frac{\partial h}{\partial x}\cdot\frac{\partial N}{\partial x} + T\frac{\partial h}{\partial y}\cdot\frac{\partial N}{\partial y}\right)dxdy + \sum_{n=1}^{E_n}\iint_{e_n}\mu_e\frac{\partial h}{\partial t}\cdot Ndxdy \\ &= \sum_{n=1}^{N_e}\iint_{e_n}\varepsilon Ndxdy + \int_{AB} q_1 N_m dxdy + \int_{BC} q_2 N_m dxdy\end{aligned} \tag{6}$$

Set

$$[A_n] = \iint_{e_n}\left(T\frac{\partial h}{\partial x}\cdot\frac{\partial N}{\partial x} + T\frac{\partial h}{\partial y}\cdot\frac{\partial N}{\partial y}\right)dxdy = T\iint_{e_n}\left(\frac{\partial h}{\partial x}\cdot\frac{\partial N}{\partial x} + \frac{\partial h}{\partial y}\cdot\frac{\partial N}{\partial y}\right)dxdy$$

$$[D_n] = \iint_{e_n}\mu_e\cdot\frac{\partial h}{\partial t}\cdot Ndxdy = \mu_e\frac{dh_e}{dt}\iint_{e_n}N^T\cdot Ndxdy,$$

$$[E_n] = \iint_{e_n}\varepsilon Ndxdy = \varepsilon\iint_{e_n}Ndxdy$$

The gradient vector of the $h(x,y,t)$ can be denoted by

$$\nabla h = \begin{bmatrix}\frac{\partial h}{\partial x} & \frac{\partial h}{\partial y}\end{bmatrix}^T = Bh_e,\quad B = \begin{bmatrix}\frac{\partial N_i}{\partial x} & \frac{\partial N_j}{\partial x} & \frac{\partial N_k}{\partial x} \\ \frac{\partial N_i}{\partial y} & \frac{\partial N_j}{\partial y} & \frac{\partial N_k}{\partial y}\end{bmatrix}$$

By $\frac{\partial h}{\partial t} = N\cdot\frac{dh_e}{dt}$, get to $[A_n] = \iint_{e_n}h_e TB^T Bdxdy = Th_e\iint_{e_n}B^T Bdxdy$

Similarly, the matrixs $[A_i]$ $(i = 1,2,3,\ldots,n-1,n+1,\ldots,N_e)$ of other units e_i can be gotten. Then the $[A_i]$, $(i = 1,2,3,\ldots,n-1,n,n+1,\ldots,N_e)$ are expanded and overlaid . The guide water matrix $[A]$ can be gotten. The storage water matrix $[D]$ and matrix $[E]$ can also be gotten by using the same way.

Set $G_{i1} = \int\limits_{AB} q_1 N_i dxdy$, $G_{i2} = \int\limits_{BC} q_2 N_i dxdy$, $(i = 1,2,\cdots,E)$

Where G_{ij} $(i = 1,2,\cdots,E.),(j = 1,2)$ is the item of boundary flow,only when i lies in the second boundary nodes, will only have this item,for other nodes are zero.

Order $G_i = G_{i1} + G_{i2}$, $[G] = [G_i]_{E\times 1}$ $(i = 1,2,\cdots,E)$

So we get water matrix $[F] = [E] + [G]$. For the matrix $[A],[D],[F]$ is carried on transformation of the row or column. $[h(t)],\left[\frac{dh(t)}{dt}\right]$ is also carried on transformation a corresponding transformation. Such, we can get a set of linear equations about h.

$$[A]\times[h(t)] + [D]\times\left[\frac{dh(t)}{dt}\right] = [F] \tag{7}$$

Where $[A] = [A_1 \quad A_2 \quad \cdots \quad A_G \quad \cdots \quad A_G]^T$, $\left[\frac{dh}{dt}\right] = \left[\frac{dh_1}{dt} \quad \frac{dh_2}{dt} \cdots \frac{dh_G}{dt} \cdots \frac{dh_E}{dh}\right]^T$, E is the total node number, G is the first boundary node numbers.

Thus, the original mathematical model has been discreted in the space. Remainder problem is how to make calculating time discretization.In this paper,the discretization of the time uses the central differencing method.So eq.7 can be changed into eq.8.

$$\left(\frac{[A]}{2} + \left[\frac{D}{\Delta t}\right]\right)\times[h(t_{k+1})] = [F] - \left(\frac{[A]}{2} - \left[\frac{D}{\Delta t}\right]\right)\times[h(t_k)] \tag{8}$$

By using the iterative method solves the $(E-G)$ elements system of quations. First, to set the control standard e, then to adopt the initial values $h^{(0)}$ as the first iterative values , $h^{(1)}$ can be gotten. So, and so on,until iteration results meet $\max\left|\frac{h_j^{(p)} - h_j^{(p-1)}}{h_j^{(p-1)}}\right| \le e$. p is number of iterations.So can enter the next time calculating.

3 Simulation Example [12-16]

There is a confined aquifer seepage area Ω, Its shape approximate the rectangle of $500m\times 400m$ being showed in fig.3. There is lateral supplied runoff of single wide flow being $q_1 = 0.6m^3/(d\cdot m)$ in the border of AB. BC boundary for water-barrier boundary.The rest of the both sides CD and AD are set head boundary. There's a pumping Well at area $(200,100)$. Pumping flow $Q_w = 1080m^3/d$, the initial head of every point is 100m. Seepage are homogeneous isotropic aquifers, its water transmetting coefficient $T = 120.0m^3/d$,its storage water coefficient $\mu_e = 0.0003$. For this insance is carried on finite element numerical simulation by using the method of this paper.

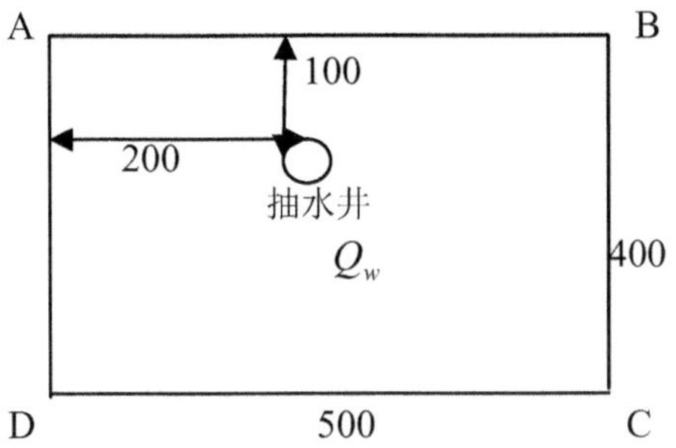

Fig. 3. Sketch map of repion Ω seepage bearing press

The following is the calculate tresults contrast by using finite difference method and finite element method.

Table 1. Distributing sheet request about h by using finite difference method

j \ i	1	2	3	4	5	6
		$k=1$	$\Delta t=0.200$	$t=0.200d$		
1	100.000	99.051	97.487	98.933	99.734	99.910
2	100.000	98.428	96.241	97.911	98.836	100.752
3	100.000	99.130	97.918	98.843	99.356	100.417
4	100.000	99.613	99.075	99.486	99.714	100.185
5	100.000	100.000	100.000	100.000	100.000	100.000
		$k=2$	$\Delta t=0.200$	$t=0.400d$		
1	100.000	99.089	97.973	98.777	99.484	99.893
2	100.000	98.420	96.355	97.795	98.608	101.040
3	100.000	99.138	98.187	98.683	99.079	100.607
4	100.000	99.621	99.243	99.344	99.520	100.199
5	100.000	100.000	100.000	100.000	100.000	100.000
		$k=3$	$\Delta t=0.200$	$t=0.600d$		
1	100.000	99.092	97.921	98.823	99.590	99.731
2	100.000	98.430	96.116	97.856	98.635	101.311
3	100.000	99.138	98.111	98.695	99.061	100.791
4	100.000	99.632	99.195	99.360	99.523	100.292
5	100.000	100.000	100.000	100.000	100.000	100.000
		$k=10$	$\Delta t=0.200$	$t=2.000d$		
1	100.000	99.135	98.148	99.189	100.689	96.549
2	100.000	98.383	96.135	97.135	97.209	104.937
3	100.000	99.132	98.232	98.725	99.217	100.196
4	100.000	99.622	99.261	99.362	99.581	100.016
5	100.000	100.000	100.000	100.000	100.000	100.000

Table 2. Distributing sheet request about h by using finite element method

j \ i	1	2	3	4	5	6
		$k=1$	$\Delta t = 0.200$	$t = 0.200d$		
1	99.662	98.880	97.701	98.590	99.246	99.456
2	100.000	98.591	96.107	98.201	99.006	99.226
3	100.000	99.201	98.449	98.876	99.227	99.339
4	100.000	99.666	99.419	99.487	99.590	99.594
5	100.000	100.000	100.000	100.000	100.000	99.805
		$k=2$	$\Delta t = 0.200$	$t = 0.400d$		
1	99.468	98.503	97.128	98.012	98.716	98.948
2	100.000	98.267	95.546	97.650	98.502	98.741
3	100.000	98.980	98.069	98.470	98.837	98.954
4	100.000	99.556	99.231	99.275	99.373	99.353
5	100.000	100.000	100.000	100.000	100.000	99.657
		$k=3$	$\Delta t = 0.200$	$t = 0.600d$		
1	99.409	98.396	96.966	97.818	98.509	98.739
2	100.000	98.181	95.399	97.470	98.309	98.545
3	100.000	98.918	97.959	98.334	98.687	98.798
4	100.000	99.524	99.173	99.201	99.288	99.254
5	100.000	100.000	100.000	100.000	100.000	99.629
		$k=10$	$\Delta t = 0.200$	$t = 2.000d$		
1	99.491	98.544	97.192	98.096	98.812	99.046
2	100.000	98.299	95.603	97.726	98.590	98.834
3	100.000	99.003	98.111	98.528	98.905	99.027
4	100.000	99.568	99.253	99.306	99.411	99.399
5	100.000	100.000	100.000	100.000	100.000	99.706

Through the table 1 and 2 can see the results of finite element method with finite difference method calculation results change trend being good consistency.Generally speaking, the finite element method has higher precision.

4 Summary

In this paper,by using matlab for an insance is verified. First, the equations of motion of the problems of groundwater flow in two-dimensional confined aquifer with variable h was established.Then, by using the finite element method to discretize it and to get the finite element model of underground water movement in confined aquifer.Finally, by using the gotten numerical model carried on numerical simulation for an insance. Through the comparison with distribution table of originally with finite difference method,can see that there are good consistency between the both results.

Acknowledgments

This work was supported by technology innovation fund of Small and medium-sized enterprise from National Scientific and Technology department in 2009——Intrinsically Safe Industrial Ethernet equipment for mine (09C26226115674); Applied Materials Innovation Fund of Xi'an city in 2008——HDV (high definition video) Acquisition Platform for Low Illumination Environment based on the Optical MEMS (XA-AM-200813).

References

1. Lei, Z., Yang, S., Xie, S.: Soil Water Dynamics. Tsinghua university press, Beijing (1988)
2. Zhang, W.: Groundwater and Soil Water Dynamics. China Water Conservancy and Hydropower Press, Beijing (1996)
3. Li, Y., Li, B.: Soil Solute Transport. Science Press, Beijing (1998)
4. Zhu, X., Xie, C.: Groundwater migration model. China architecture & building press, Beijing (1990)
5. Lu, W.: Discussion of Boundary Condition Problems for Numerical Simulation of Groundwater Movement. Journal of Hydraulic 03 (2003)
6. Luo, H., Chen, Y.: The Numerical Simulation of the Groundwater Movement. China Architecture & Building Press, Beijing (1988)
7. Zhu, C., Hao, Z., Li, S., Zhou, J., Liu, D.: Application of Two Dimensional Gray Water Quality Model in Goundwater Pollution Simulating. Journal of Liaoning Engineering and Technology University 06 (2007)
8. Varni, M.R., Usunoff, E.J.: Simulation of Regional-scale Groundwater Flow in the Azul River Basin, Buenos Aires Province, Argentina. Hydrogeology Journal 7(2) (1999)
9. Chen, Z., Wang, Y.: Standard lumen with boundary conditions on the C ~ r binary spline space. Journal of Applied Mathematics and Computational Mathematics 01 (1993)
10. Guan, Z., Lou, J.: Numerical Analysis. Science Press, Beijing (1998)
11. Hu, J., Tang, H.: Differential Equation Numerical Method. Science Press, Beijing (1999)
12. Wang, B.: Fem Program Design, pp. 134–171. Beijing polytechnic university press, Beijing (1991)
13. Hanks, R.J., Bowers, S.B.: Numerical Solutions of the Diffusion Equation for the Movement of Water in Soils. Soil Sci. Soc. Am. Proc. 26, 530–534 (1962)
14. Bruch Jr, J.C., Zyvoloski, G.: Solution of Equation for Vertical Unsaturated Flow of Soil Water. Soil Science 116(6), 417–422 (1974)
15. Qin, X., Ma, Y., Zhang, Y.: Convection Diffusion Equation the Two-fold Characteristic Finite Element Grid Algorithm. Journal of Xi 'an Jiaotong University 38(2), 208–211 (2004)
16. Komatsu, H., Yoshida, N., Takizawa, H., Kosaka, I., Tantasirin, C., Suzuki, M.: Seasonal Trend in the Occurrence of Nocturnal Drainage Flow on a Forested Slope Under a Tropical Monsoon Climate. Boundary - Layer Meteorology 106(3), 145–149 (2003)

Examining Student Ability Using KIDMAP Fit Statistics of Rasch Analysis in Excel

Tsair-Wei Chien[1], John M. Linacre[2], and Wen-Chung Wang[3,*]

[1] Researcher, Chi Mei Medical Center, Taiwan
[2] Director of Winsteps.com and formerly Director of the MESA Psychometric Laboratory at the University of Chicago
[3] Professor, Assessment Research Center, The Hong Kong Institute of Education, Hong Kong
wcwang@ied.edu.hk

Abstract. It is very common that examinees have identical test scores. In such a case, some subjective procedures are often used to determine admission priority for those examinees with identical scores. This study proposed an objective procedure to do so. In Rasch analysis, the fit statistics are used to assess the difference between expected and observed responses and thus can be used to determine the priority: the smaller the MNSQ, the higher the priority. If OUTFIT MNSQs are identical across persons with identical test scores, INFIT MNSQs can then be used to determine the priority. In this study, we implemented an Excel-VBA KIDMAP that provides detailed response pattern and fit statistics for each individual examinee. A real data set of 37 multiple-choice items and 500 examinees was analyzed and two students having identical test scores were selected to illustrate the KIDMAP and the procedure in determining priority. In addition, the Excel-VBA KIDMAP provides instant feedback to respective examinees, their teachers and parents.

Keywords: Rasch analysis, identical score, KIDMAP, fit statistics, item response theory.

1 Introduction

It is very common that examinees have identical test scores, especially in short tests or large samples. In such a case, some subjective procedures are often used to determine admission priority for those examinees with identical scores. It is of great importance to propose an objective procedure to help determine the priority, which is the major purpose of this study.

1.1 Rasch Model's Fit Statistics

Consider two examinees with identical test scores in an admission test. Who should be admitted when there is a single place? It has been argued that the priority should be given to the examinee who answers difficult items correctly rather than to the examinee who answers easy item correctly. This seems to be a plausible argument, because the

* Corresponding author.

H. Tan and M. Zhou (Eds.): CSE 2011, Part I, CCIS 201, pp. 578–585, 2011.

former examinee should receive a higher measure than the latter examinee. However, given they have the same total score, the former examinee must at the same time answer easy items incorrectly and the latter must answer difficult items incorrectly. If correct responses to difficult items can receive a higher credit, then incorrect responses to easy items must receive a penalty so that they are cancelled out. It is thus more reasonable to give equal credits to examinees who have the same total scores.

In reality, spaces are often so limited that not all examinees with identical total scores can be admitted. Under such a case, we propose to use person fit statistics in Rasch analysis [1-11] to determine priority. Person fit statistics describe the relationship between observed response pattern and expected response patterns for a give examinee (person). A smaller mean square error (MNSQ) of person fit statistics indicates not only a better fit between observed and expected response patterns, but also a more predictable response to other items that are not included in the current test. As a result, the first priority should be given to the examinee who has the smallest mean square error of person fit statistics [12].

There are two kinds of MNSQ: OUTFIT and INFIT. OUTFIT is dominated by unexpected outlying, off-target, low information responses and so is outlier-sensitive. INFIT is dominated by unexpected inlying patterns among informative, on-target observations and so is inlier-sensitive. An MNSQ greater than 2.0 indicates an aberrant response pattern [16, 17]. MNSQ can be transformed to a statistic called ZSTD, which follows approximately the standard normal distribution [15]. OUTFIT is often more powerful than INFIT [13, 17]. Table 1 illustrates common response patterns to dichotomous items and their person fit statistics. In general, an MNSQ greater than 1.5 shows a great deal of noise and a large standard error in the person measure, whereas an MNSQ close to zero indicates a high discrimination [14].

Table 1. Various types of person responses diagnosed by fit statistics

Person Responses: Easy -- Items -- Hard	Diagnosis Pattern	OUTFIT MNSQ	INFIT MNSQ
111¦0110110100¦000	Modelled/Ideal	1.0	1.1
111¦1111100000¦000	Guttman/Deterministic	**0.3**	**0.5**
000¦0000011111¦111	Miscode	**12.6**	4.3
011¦1111110000¦000	Carelessness/Sleeping	**3.8**	1.0
111¦1111000000¦001	Lucky Guessing	**3.8**	1.0
101¦0101010101¦010	Response set/Miskey	**4.0**	**2.3**
111¦1000011110¦000	Special knowledge	0.9	**1.3**
111¦1010110010¦000	Imputed outliers *	**0.6**	1.0
111¦0101010101¦000	Low discrimination	**1.5**	**1.6**
111¦1110101000¦000	High discrimination	**0.5**	**0.7**
111¦1111010000¦000	Very high discrimination	**0.3**	**0.5**

Note. Extracted from reference [14]

1.2 KIDMAP Diagram Developed in Excel Module

In investigating person fit, one may use the visual diagram KIDMAP, which can be implemented in Excel [18,19]. KIDMAP provides thorough information about observed and expected response patterns, and MNSQ and ZSTD for OUTFIT and INFIT, which can be used to determine priority for examinees with identical total scores.

2 Methods

2.1 Data

A real data set of 37 multiple-choice items and 500 examinees was extracted from sample1.dat of the Quest software [20]. A module was programmed using Excel VBA (visual basic for applications) to plot KIDMAP that is exactly identical to the commercial software such as Quest and WINSTEPS. KIDMAP helps teachers examine performances of students. The parameter estimation procedures are described below.

2.2 Rasch Model's Attribute

In classical test theory (CTT), raw scores (or their linier transformation scores, e.g., T-score) are usually adopted to represent students' measures. However, raw scores are not additively interval so that parametric statistical analyses, such as ANOVA, Pearson's correlation, and Cronbach's alpha [21, 22] are problematic [23]. To resolve this problem, the item response theory (IRT) based Rasch measurement [5] was developed. The log odds with additive and interval attributes for persons and items are placed on an identical underlying continuum. Item and person fit statistics are used to evaluate the quality of items and persons [9, 10].

In the Rasch model (Eq.1), person n's measure (B_n) and item i's difficulty (D_i) are connected as:

$$\ln\left(P_{ni1} / P_{ni0}\right) = B_n - D_i , \tag{1}$$

where P_{ni1} and P_{ni0} are the probabilities of scoring 1 and 0 for person n on item i, respectively; and ln is the natural logarithm. The larger the value of B_n, the higher the level of the latent trait (e.g., ability); the larger the value of D_i, the more difficult the item. P_{ni1} is greater than 50% when $B_n > D_i$, equal to 50% when $B_n = D_i$, and less than 50% when $B_n < D_i$.

2.3 OUTFIT and INFIT Statistics

In Rasch analysis the χ^2 test is used to examine MNSQs of OUTFIT and INFIT. OUTFIT is based on the unweighted mean of squared standardized residuals. Let X_{ni} be the observed score for person n on item i, E_{ni} be its expected value based on Rasch parameter estimates:

$$E_{ni} = \sum_{k=0}^{M_i} k \times P_{nik} , \tag{2}$$

where P_{nik} is the probability of scoring k, and M_i is the maximum score of item i (M_i =1 for dichotomous items). Let Y_{ni} be the residual:

$$Y_{ni} = X_{ni} - E_{ni} . \tag{3}$$

The standardized residual is:

$$Z_{ni} = Y_{ni} / \sqrt{W_{ni}} , \tag{4}$$

where W_{ni} is the variance of residual:

$$W_{ni} = \sum_{k=0}^{M_i} (k - E_{ni})^2 \times P_{nik} . \tag{5}$$

Then the squared standardized residual Z_{ni}^2 follows approximately the χ^2 distribution with one degree of freedom. OUTFIT MNSQ for person n is defined as:

$$\text{OUTFIT MNSQ}_n = \sum_{i=1}^{L} Z_{ni}^2 / L , \tag{6}$$

where L is the number of items [14]. INFIT MNSQ is an information-weighted mean of squared standardized residuals:

$$\text{INFIT MNSQ}_n = \frac{\sum_{i=1}^{L} Z_{ni}^2 W_{ni}}{\sum_{i=1}^{L} W_{ni}} = \frac{\sum_{i=1}^{L} (X_{ni} - E_{ni})^2}{\sum_{i=1}^{L} W_{ni}} . \tag{7}$$

OUTFIT and INFIT MNSQs have an expected value of 1, when the model-data fit is perfect. A value great than 1.5 is often treated as too much noise in response patterns. A value close to zero suggests over-fit (muted) to the model and high discrimination in response patterns [2,24,25].

2.4 ZSTD Statistics

OUTFIT and INFIT MNSQs can be transformed to ZSTDs, which follow approximately the standard normal distribution [9,10]. A value greater than 2.56 suggests statistically under fit; a value smaller than -2.56 suggests statistically over fit, at the .01 nominal level. The OUFIT ZSTD is computed as follows [9]. Let the fourth moment of person n on item i be:

$$C_{ni} = \sum_{k=0}^{M_i} (k - E_{ni})^4 \times P_{nik} , \tag{8}$$

the variance of OUTFIT MNSQ be:

$$s_n^2 = \sum_{i=1}^{L} (C_{ni} / W_{ni}^2) / L^2 - 1/L , \tag{9}$$

and the variance of INFIT MNSQ be:

$$q_n^2 = \sum_{i=1}^{L} (C_{ni} - W_{ni}^2) / (\sum_{i=1}^{L} W_{ni})^2 . \tag{10}$$

Thus, OUTFIT ZSTD is:

$$\text{OUTFIT ZSTD}_n = (\text{OUTFIT MNSQ}_n^{1/3} - 1)(3/s_n) + s_n/3\,, \tag{11}$$

and INFIT ZSTD is:

$$\text{INFIT ZSTD}_n = (\text{INFIT MNSQ}_n{}^{1/3} - 1)(3/q_n) + q_n/3\,. \tag{12}$$

2.5 Excel-VBA Model Plotting KIDMAP and Wright Map

We used Microsoft Excel to establish KIDMAP to increase its feasibility and applicability. Together with INFIT and OUTFIT MNSQ and ZSTD, KIDMAP reveals both the strength and weakness of each student. Such valuable information can be delivered to teachers and parents through automatically email function in real time.

3 Results

3.1 KIDMAP Reports for Individual Students

Two students (persons) have identical raw scores and measures (= -1.21 logits) but different INFIT MNSQs (0.83 for the first person, Fig. 1; and 1.23 for the second person, Fig. 2). According to the above basic rational: the more predicable the responses, the more reliable the measure, and thus the higher the priority should be. We would thus give the first priority to the first person.

As shown in the two figures, an asterisk (*) indicates the observed response was statistically different from the expected response (a large residual) at the .05 nominal level. For example, the items with an asterisk in the 2nd quadrant suggests that hard

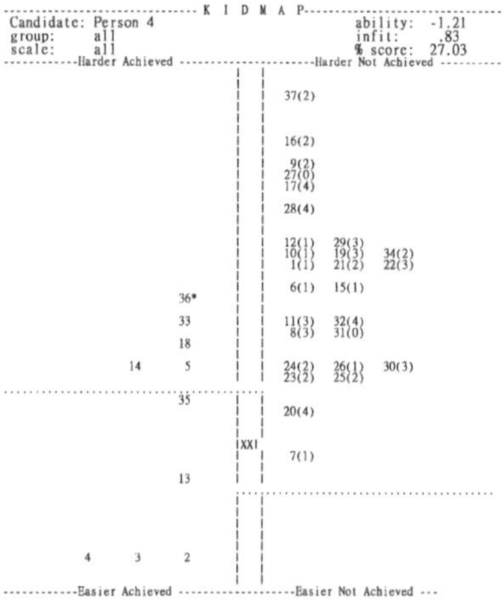

Fig. 1. Student with INFIT=0.83

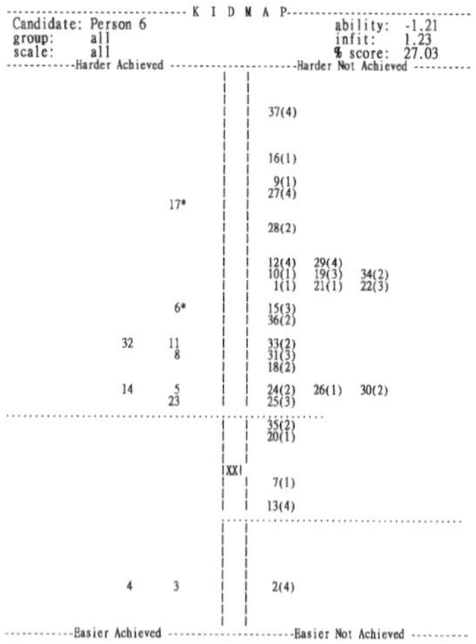

Fig. 2. Student with INFIT=1.23

items were unexpectedly and correctly achieved. Actually, the person (-1.21 logits marked with XX in the middle of KIDMAP) had a very low chance to achieve an item located above 2 standard errors (SE) above (e.g., see the top-left corner in Fig. 1 and 2). These unexpected responses are worth noting, because they may indicate the person's strength, luck, or cheating. The INFIT MNSQs in Fig. 1 and 2 are critical in identifying which response pattern is more reliable [26,27].

3.2 KIDMAP Generated in Excel

The KIDMAP of Fig.3 was generated with Excel, which reveals information for (a) inter-person comparison (by inspecting performance levels along the logit scale and the distribution on the right-hand side), (b) intra-person comparison (by inspecting response patterns in the four quadrants), and (c) model-data fit checking (by inspecting MNSQ and ZSTD).

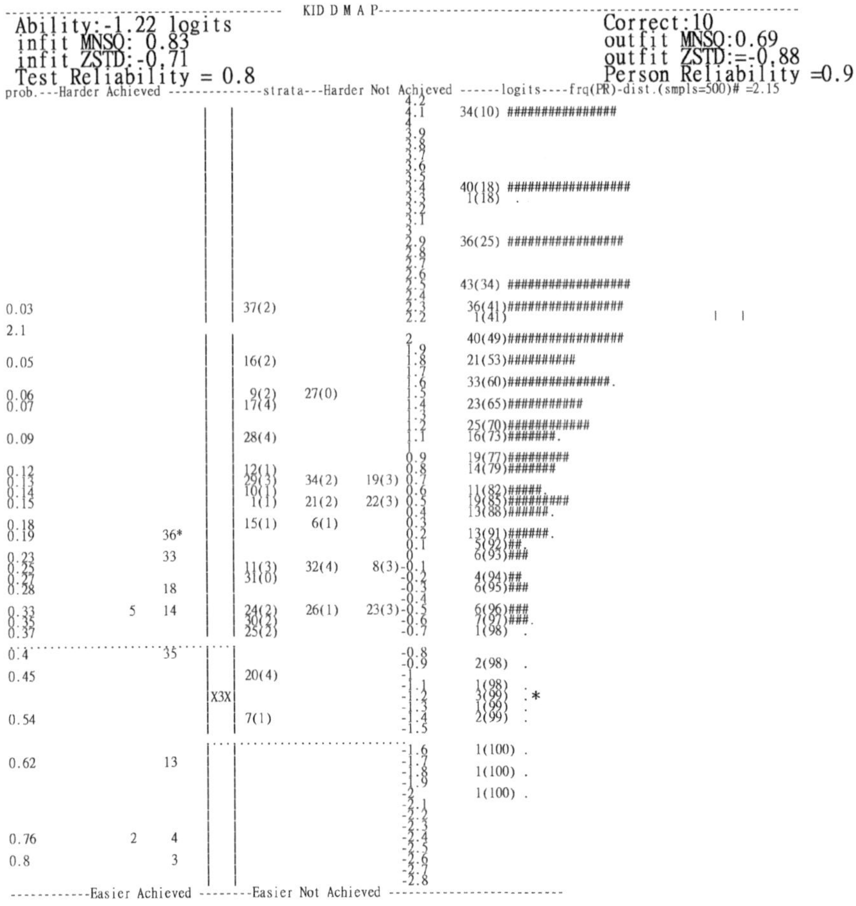

Fig. 3. KIDMAP with much more information than traditional KIDMAP generated in Excel

4 Conclusion

KIDMAP are released in commercial software like Quest or WINSTPS (Version 3.71.0.1). In this study, we adopted Excel-VBA module to create KIDMAP that provides more information than that given by commercial software. Information about inter-person and intra-person differences and model-data fit statistics is provided. Furthermore, it can be automatically emailed to individual students, teachers or parents for instant feedback.

OUFIT and INFIT MNSQ statistics describe model-data fit. A value greater than 1.5 indicates a great deal of noise in responses whereas a value close to zero indicates a highly predictable pattern in responses. With this property, we recommend to use MNSQ to determine the priority for examinees with identical raw scores, the smaller the MNSQ, the higher the priority. Since OUTFIT is more powerful than INFIT, one may consider OUTFIT to determine priority. If OUTFIT MNSQs are identical across persons, INFIT can then be used to determine priority [28].

References

1. Andrich, D.: Rasch models for measurement. Sage, Beverly Hills (1988)
2. Bond, T.G., Fox, C.M.: Applying the Rasch model: Fundamental measurement in the human sciences. Erlbaum, Mahwah (2001)
3. De Boeck, P., Wilson, M. (eds.): Explanatory item response models: A generalized linear and nonlinear approach. Springer, New York (2004)
4. Fischer, G.H., Molenaar, I.W. (eds.): Rasch models: Foundations, recent developments, and applications. Springer, New York (1995)
5. Rasch, G.: Probabilistic models for some intelligence and attainment tests. University of Chicago Press, Chicago (1960)
6. Smith, E.V., Smith, R. (eds.): Introduction to Rasch measurement. JAM Press, Chicago (2005)
7. von Davier, M., Carstensen, C.H. (eds.): Multivariate and mixture distribution Rasch models: Extensions and applications. Springer, New York (2007)
8. Wilson, M.: Constructing measures: An item response modeling approach. Erlbaum, Mahwah (2005)
9. Wright, B.D., Masters, G.N.: Rating scale analysis, p. 100. MESA Press, Chicago (1982)
10. Wright, B.D., Stone, M.H.: Best test design: Rasch measurement. MESA, Chicago (1979)
11. Wright, B.D., Stone, M.H.: Making measures. Phaneron Press, Chicago (2004)
12. Wright, B.D.: Who is awarded first prize? Rasch Measurement Transactions 12(2), 629 (1998)
13. Smith, R.M.: Fit analysis in latent trait measurement models. Journal of Applied Measurement 1, 199–218 (2000)
14. Linacre, J.M., Wright, B.D.: Chi-square fit statistics. Rasch Measurement Transactions 8(2), 360 (1994)
15. Linacre, J.M.: Size vs. significance: Standardized chi-square fit statistic. Rasch Measurement Transactions 17(1), 918 (2003)
16. Linacre, J.M.: Optimizing rating scale category effectiveness. J. Appl. Meas. 3(1), 85–106 (2002)

17. Linacre, J. M.: WINSTEPS [computer program], Chicago (2011), http://www.Winsteps.com, http://www.winsteps.com/winman/diagnosingmisfit.htm
18. Masters, G.N.: KIDMAP - a history. Rasch Measurement Transactions 8(2), 366 (1994)
19. Wright, B.D., Mead, R.J., Ludlow, L.H.: Kidmap. Research Memorandum Number 29. Chicago: Statistical Laboratory, Department of Education, University of Chicago (1980)
20. Adams, R.J., Khoo, S.-T.: Quest, Version 2.1: The interactive test analysis system. Rasch Measurement Transactions 11(4), 598 (1998)
21. Crocker, L., Algina, J.: Introduction to classical and modern test theory. Harcourt Brace Jovanovich, Fort Worth (1986)
22. Nunnally, J.C., Bernstein, I.H.: Psychometric theory. McGraw-Hill, New York (1994)
23. Wright, B.D., Linacre, J.M.: Observations are always ordinal; measurements, however, must be interval. Arch. Phys. Med. Rehabil. 70, 857–860 (1989)
24. Wright, B.D., Linacre, M.: Reasonable mean-square fit values. Rasch Measurement Transactions 8(3), 370 (1994)
25. Smith, R.M., Schumacker, R.E., Bush, M.J.: Using item mean squares to evaluate fit to the Rasch model. Journal of Outcome Measurement 2, 66–78 (1998)
26. Chien, T.-W., Wang, W.-C., Lin, S.-B., Lin, C.-Y., Guo, H.-R., Su, S.-B.: KIDMAP, a Web based system for gathering patients' feedback on their doctors. BMC Med. Res. Methodol. 9(1), 38 (2009)
27. Chien, T.-W., Wang, W.-C., Wang, H.-Y., Lin, H.-J.: Online assessment of patients' views on hospital performances using Rasch model's KIDMAP diagram. BMC Health Serv. Res. 9, 135 (2009)
28. Chien, T.-W., Li, O.L., Wang, W.-C.: Determining admission priority for examinees with identical test scores using Rasch analysis. Psychological Testing 56(2), 129–151 (2009)

Usages of 2D Digital Sketching in Industrial Design Sketching Education Mode

Li Gong

University of Shanghai for Science & Technology
Department of Industrial Design
College of Art & Communication, USST
Shanghai, China
juliesnoopyli@yahoo.com.cn

Abstract. This essay describes the meaning of the sketching in industrial design, and analyzes the advantages of 2D digital sketching in design process which can solve the problems in hand sketching, and how to utilize it in industrial design education for the students of different classes with an example. The discussion on hand sketching and digital sketching is about their relationships for serving the design and their efforts in design respectively. New techniques are expected to be exploited to improve design process efficiency for more progress.

Keywords: 2D digital sketching, hand sketching, industrial design education.

1 Introduction

Nowadays, computer technology is penetrating to industries of all sorts, forming a new field called as CAD/CAM, and it is affected industrial design obviously because it covers many related fields, such as: arts, crafts, materials, dynamics and manufacturing, which all have tight links with digital technologies. It can be concluded that the development of Industrial Design sticks with the continuously revolutions on CAD/CAM, meanwhile, the rapid development of industrial design has more requirements to CAD/CAM as well. In this situation, how to make full use of CAD/CAM to promote the design efficiency should be taken into consideration in modern design education mode. This essay aims at the cad/cam used in a foundational course-sketching.

2 The Meaning of Sketching for Industrial Design

Sketches based on different technologies have the same purpose-describe the design in a direct and right way, and all techniques are used to assist to realize the purpose. Pursuing the techniques is meaningless if the skill is separated with design, but any techniques which can help present the design are acceptable.

According to William Buxton, sketching is quickly working up product concepts into a concrete form sufficient to serve as the basis for discussion, evaluation and questioning. From the perspective of quality, the metric is in terms of concept and speed, not refinement of execution [1].

H. Tan and M. Zhou (Eds.): CSE 2011, Part I, CCIS 201, pp. 586–592, 2011.

3 The Shortages of Hand Sketching

Hand sketching skill, from the view of traditional education, is considered as one of the most important standards for a designer, because traditional design education was set when the computer technology was immature and the design purpose could be presented via the only way of hand sketching at that time. Then, the skill had to be practiced adequately to describe the design clearly. But this mode was not updated throughout even the computer technology has developed. Many today's students are still absorbed in studying the techniques so that the real meaning of sketching is ignored. Moreover, the hand sketching skill testing is still a big part of the examination of entering colleges.

However, hand sketching reveals its shortages in today's society, which can be listed as below, and these problems can be solved with the help of 2D graphic design software.

- detailed sketching costs too much time and needs many tools
- not easy for amending
- low accuracy
- hard for storage

4 How to Choose Appropriate 2D Graphic Software

The comments on different pieces of software should never be "good" or "no good", because every piece of software is designed for coping with some special problems, so the students should distinguish their respectively characteristics and make full use of them for products sketching, normally, fair comments on these pieces of software is helpful to selection. Usually, Digital technology used for sketching can be divided into two ways- sketches made by computer and sketches made by the combination of hand and computer, which are determined by the level of using the computer.

There are abundant pieces of 2D software available for different usages in design fields. First of all, these pieces of software should be grouped by their characteristics correspondingly. Then, rank them as their relationships with product design. At last, select the ones that can be operated conveniently. What should be considered is that the rest ones should not be rejected but for spare use because it is well likely that these ones can have great impact on some special occasions which can be learnt later. Today, the most popular software for sketching are Coreldraw or Illustrate for outlines of the forms, Photoshop or Painter for coloring and rending.

5 Advantages of Digital Technology for Sketching

The first requirement of modern industrial design to digital sketching is efficiency, because today's product exploiting process is much shorter than before. The time of every phase must be fully used. The days of making detailed sketches by hand which cost long time have gone. What is needed today is the sketches to be used for design communication and revised by following the feedbacks as soon as possible. These sketches are made quickly, but not scrabbled sloppily. So, digital sketching can be considered to play an important role for industrial design.

Some problems in hand sketching can be solved easily and rapidly with the help of 2D software, such as, drawing the complicated light and shadow existing on the curved surfaces of variety sorts, which costs much time but ends up with probably unsatisfied results. Moreover, the software can revise the mistake happened in drawing process at any time easily that improves the efficiency. On the other hand, any revise work will not lead to the mess on the pages which frequently happens in hand sketching process, such as vestige or marks after using the rubber or pastels.

The digital sketching can be saved easily and will never be discolored or unsaturated, and can be saved and searched quickly in hard disks, totally or partly printed easily with printers. Today, WACOM and light pen are launched to simulate the hand sketching process with digital technique (see figure1). The user even can draw on the screen directly with light pen, which has the similar way of sketching on the paper, but without other tools, and the sketch can be printed unlimitedly when done.

The last but not least, mark pens or spraying glue that needed for hand sketching are composed of chemical elements, which is unhealthy for people but this problem does not exist in digital sketching.

Fig. 1. WACOM equipments

6 How to Use the Software Appropriately

Before practicing, the students of junior class should not pursue so called "visionary efforts" techniques, but reference some clear and simple works to understand and summarize the merits from them and meditate how to use these merits flexibly in further work. Then, the students can start with sketching some simple geometric objects to get a general idea about the digital techniques, and the simple beginning can generate the students' interests on using the software. Moreover, this stage is a basis of sketching some simple products in next stages and students can enrich their experiences of digital sketching techniques gradually.

Students can practice sketching some products with details after a period of time of beginning training, In this stage, the products can be presented from some normal views, such as top, left and front views, moreover, the students should study how to plan the sketching process with —computer thinking || (see fig2). The next step for the student of senior class is to sketch some complicated products to improve their digital sketching techniques, which requires good digital sketching plans and enough patience.

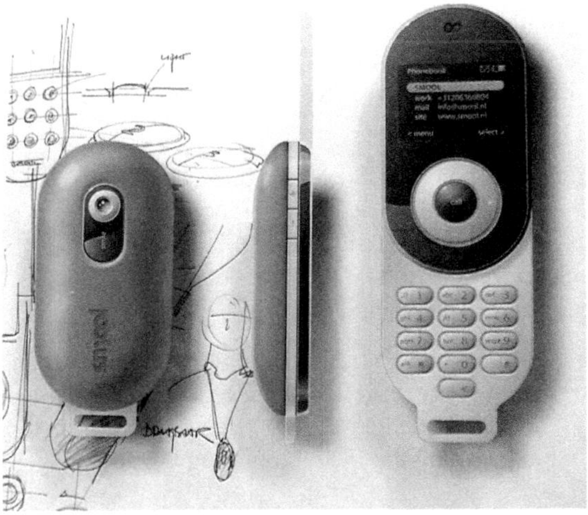

Fig. 2. Side view for presenting a design

7 Combination of Hand Sketching and Digital Techniques

Surely, the digital sketching also has some shortages, such as, it is limited by the using environments, it can be only run at a place where are equipped with computer, at least, access to electricity, for example, an idea is difficult to be recorded immediately on a bus. But hand sketching can even happen anywhere, because a piece of paper and a pencil are enough to capture the aspirations sparkling in the brain, and no details are needed at that time. So, designers are used to drawing some rough drafts at some places where they cannot use the computers and bring them to the office for refining with digital software.

Designers will make a detailed sketch for presenting the designs, once the schemes are confirmed by refining the drafts. Then, designers can adjust the curves, proportion, perspective, and graphic design that are wanted with the help of 2D graphic design software. The students can study the whole process which can be concluded as:

- Complexity level 1: Monochrome line drawing, no shading or color, uniform line thickness
- Complexity level 2: Monochrome line drawing, no shading or color. Line thicknesses vary to give emphasis, may include brief annotation.
- Complexity level 3: Monochrome with rough shading to suggest form, may be annotated.

- Complexity level 4: Line and shading, may include color and graduation.
- Complexity level 5: Color illustration to show what the product looks like [2].

What should be taken into consideration is that the original curves can be kept for artful feeling as well, but the hand-drew curves should be combined with digital colors naturally, and both for serving the design description. The contrast efforts of two sorts of techniques make the picture more vivid compared to the original sketches (Fig3).

This process needs rich experience of sketching and enough patience, which can be only got from meditating and practicing, because adjustment of details is a process of continuous comparison with unadjusted status.

To give a direct idea about the whole process, an example finished in PHOTOSHOP is showed below:

- hand sketching with pencil and scan the draft
- put the draft as the basis layer as the reference of form
- make some sections for different coloring
- adjust the light and shade tone
- give the details and adjust the picture(Fig4)

The process of combining the two sketching ways is not unchangeable, but flexible to meet the requirements of the sketches. A lot of studios have reconsidered the use of drawing done by hand to gain renewed attention- both as method on its own and, more especially, mixed with digital media ,utilizing the advantages of both world[3].

Fig. 3. Hand drawing curves with digital colors

Fig. 4. Digital sketching example- SUV design

8 Discussions about Product Design Sketching Education Mode

The paragraphs above focuses on the digital techniques used for product design sketching and related educational methods. However, what should be emphasized is that the part above is not used to prove that hand sketching will be eliminated by the fast developing digital skill, on the contrary, the digital drawing must be based on hand sketching, and the advantages of traditional hand sketching should be realized as well, such as, the quick draft- drawing needs simple tools, which can help designers to capture their aspirations promptly, and what is more important is that hand sketching brings random factor, such as a casual curve, which was even not at the place where it was expected to be, but result in new idea of designer.

Moreover, the skill of controlling perspective and proportion in hand sketching is still the basis of making digital sketching as well. The students should build a notion that digital sketching is not substitution for hand sketching, but development and extension, and they co-exist in industrial design and they can be employed simultaneously to increase design efficiency.

Another point should be emphasized is that either sketching sort is a beginning part of whole design process, though it is important, but neither of them is equal to design, which contains more parts, such as, 3D models, rapid prototyping, and manufacturing, and each of these parts relies on different software. Many students think that sketching a "beautiful" picture is all the missions for an industrial designer, but it is incorrect. Mission of a designer is about whole design process, including communication with clients, manufacturers, and product users. A "beautiful" sketch used for showing off the techniques but split with the design purpose is meaningless. Illegible sketches are those which can present the final product design and this is the information that the students should know.

In these days, well visualized digital sketches can be seen easily on line, so that the students who are lack of real design experience think these ornate sketches mean good designs, hence they put all of their attention on digital techniques rather than traditional sketching techniques. Actually, the students should be encouraged to study the foundational knowledge gradually. It is not a wise behavior to pursue digital techniques and have bias to hand sketching techniques, and vice versa. On the other hand, the sketches only for entertaining the eyes called as "styling" are not suitable for students of junior class, because the essence of industrial design can be ignored.

CAD/CAM technology is continuously developing so there are varieties of sketching software and sketching techniques. Today, some 3Dsoftware can convert the frame of the forms into 2D curves to be rendered within 2D graphic design software (Fig5). It seems that the problems of perspective or proportion can be solved easily. However, the sequences are disorder because the product should be designed from 2D sketching to 3D modeling, and adjusting the forms in 3D software is inefficient and inconvenient for design communication.

9 Further Development

It can be concluded that the 2D graphic digital technologies are tend to boom in near future. The new software or redeveloped ones will bring industrial design new sketching methods. "Convenient and efficient operations" must be the tenet of digital techniques development. The new technologies are expected to make the sketching closer to design purpose with efficient ways. However, hand sketching techniques will always be the foundational capacity for a designer, and it is the source of all advanced 2D digital sketching.

Recently, some pieces of 2D digital sketched based 3D software has been employed in industrial design, which means digital models can be created with some adjusted curves rapidly [4]. It should be believed sketching will bring more convenience to industrial design.

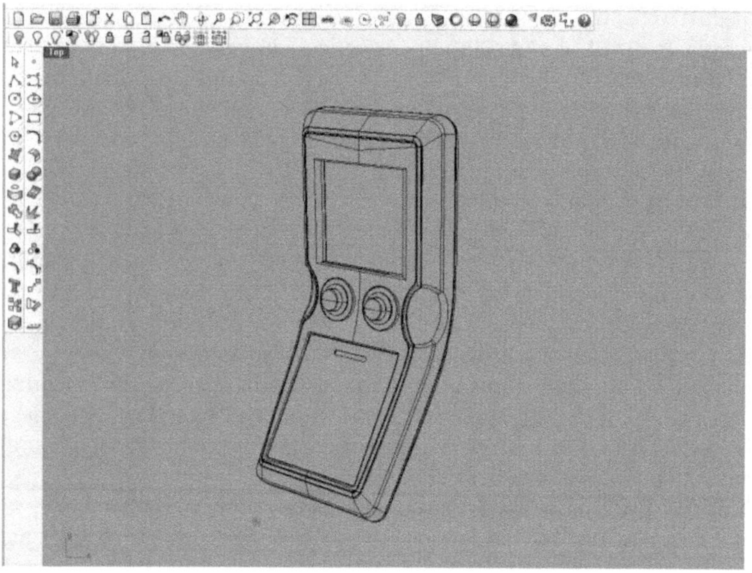

Fig. 5. The curves converted from 3d Software-Rhinocero

References

1. Buxton, W.: Performance by design: The Role of Design in Software Product Development. In: Proceedings of the Second International Conference on Usage-Centered Design (October 2003)
2. McGown, A., Green, G., Rodgers, P.: Visible ideas: information patterns of conceptual sketch activity. Design Studies 19(4), 431–453 (1998)
3. Eissen, K., Steur, R.: Sketching. Page One Publishing Private Limited, Singapore (2007)
4. Kare, D.L.B., Shimada, K.: Supporting Early Styling Design of Automobiles Using Sketch-based 3D Shape Construction. Computer-Aided Design & Applications 5(6), 867–876 (2008)

Research on a Kind of Web Based Distributed Forest Remote Sensing Parallel Processing Service

Deng Guang[1], Huang Zhenchun[2], Qin Xianlin[1], Zhang Xu[1], and Li Zengyuan[1]

[1] Institute of Forest Resource Information Techniques, Chinese Academy of Forestry,
[2] Department of Computer science, Tsinghua University
dengg@caf.ac.cn

Abstract. Nowadays, many scientists only use desktop EO data processing software to do their specifically algorithms. These useful algorithms cannot to adapt the fast huge computing area and to be used by others expediently. Sharing the EO algorithms and taking clear of the "information lonely island" need newly information and communications technologies such as software as a service. The goal of this research is to put up web based distributed remote sensing parallel processing services for forest researchers and educators. These services use SaaS conception to provide an uniform man-machine interface for user's data uploading and result spreading over the web quickly. The geo computing services in HPC environment are integrated in a grid based infrastructure by using SIRGE middleware and SIGApp middleware. The workflow of this experiment system and some service results are be set out and discussed.

Keywords: SaaS, Geo-computation grid, Distributed computing, MODIS, Forest remote sensing, HPC, PIPS.

1 Introduction

Recent years public can easily access the earth observation (EO) data from Google map and other Internet site. Although navigation service is prolific but the EO data has other more deeply usage in disaster early warning, environment monitoring, resources management, city management, science research, military applications and so on. These services depend on the professional remote sensing processing systems. Remote sensing processing systems need to deal with the collection, processing, and distribution of large amounts of EO data, which often require massive computing resources to generate the data of interest for their users. Nowadays, many scientists only use desktop EO data processing software to do their specifically algorithms. These useful algorithms cannot to adapt the fast huge computing area and to be used by others expediently. Sharing the EO algorithms and taking clear of the "information lonely island" need newly information and communications technologies such as software as a service.

Parallel processing strategies have applied in remote sensing area. For example, NASA is maintaining two massively parallel clusters of the Top500 list of supercomputer sites for remote sensing applications. [1] HPC resources and specialized software often needs more

H. Tan and M. Zhou (Eds.): CSE 2011, Part I, CCIS 201, pp. 593–600, 2011.

remote computing than local computing. Software as a service (SaaS) is a potential technology for EO HPC application. SaaS, sometimes referred to as "software on demand," is software that is deployed over the internet or is deployed to run behind a firewall on a local area network or personal computer. [2]

The goal of this research is to put up web based distributed remote sensing parallel processing services for forest researchers. These services use SaaS conception to provide a uniform man-machine interface for user's data uploading and result spreading over the web quickly. The geo computing services in HPC environment are integrated in a grid based infrastructure to the web information publishing. Through a dedicated web portal users can have easy and fast access to the different data regardless the place where they are physically located.

After a short introduction of the research objective, the paper gives the main architecture of this distributed service environment, and then outlines the remote sensing HPC environment. We present the forest remote sensing parallel processing service in this system and describe the encapsulation by web service technology. In the fourth part, we give an example to lay out the workflow of this experiment system. In the end, some discussions of this work are being put forward.

2 Main Architecture of Distributed Forest High Performance Service Environment

The architecture of forest remote sensing service environment is a distributed parallel processing one. This environment has four layers which presented in Fig1.Distributed nodes means data node, processing node and publishing node are not in one machine. Users upload data and download result from the web portal. All the computing resources can be distributed, discovered, and matched astronomically by a runtime environment shortly named SIGRE (full name is the Spatial Information Grid Runtime Environment) by deployed SIGRE instance on the resource nodes conveniently. SIGRE is founded based on the following components: JVM and JRE , web server, and servlet container and they should be downloaded and in-stalled separately for the sake of the user's free choice on them. SIGRE provides a basic job framework and make it possible to create, run, monitor, and manage a job through web service interface. [3, 4]

When the resource node is built, the static information of the resources must be registered to the resource registry and discovery service. When the services are invoked executed, the status information about them will be probed and collected by the node monitor. And the information organized and analyzed by the service monitoring service and node monitor will be provided to the resource registry and discovery service for service discovery and matching. [3, 4]

SIGRE can only manage the job or web service separately, and that SIGApp is a tools to put the unattached web service working together for the specifically target. The geo-computation web services are arranged in a XPDL file which means a workflow definition document. SIGApp middleware reads the XPDL file information and puts them in a web graphic mode to end user. SIGApp is built with Java and run in java servlet container. With these tools, the forest fire detection application can be set up easily. [3, 4]

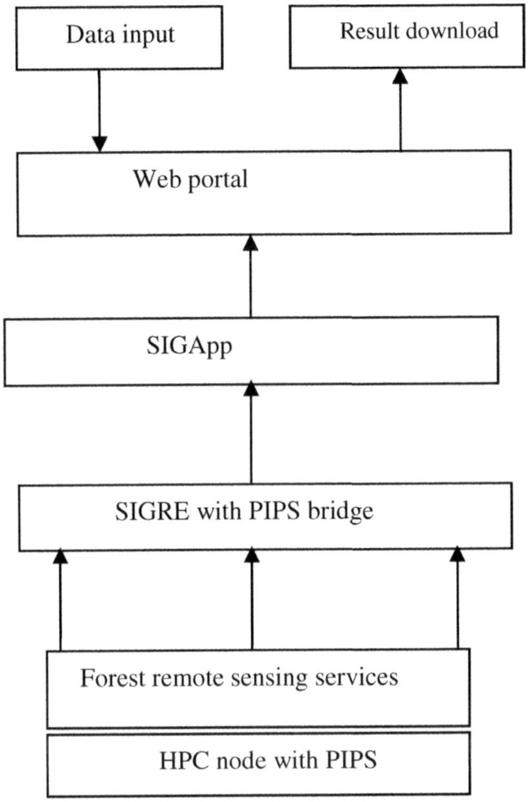

Fig. 1. Main architecture of forest fire detection service application

Jetspeed is an Open Portal Platform and Enterprise Information Portal, written entirely in open source under the Apache license in Java and XML and based on open standards.[5] We use Jetspeed 2.1.3 as the application portal. Through the provided robust portal security policy, the parameter input and running monitoring of individual forest remote sensing parallel processing service can be as portlets to aggregate to the portal by creating a page. Each portlet is an independent application with Jetspeed acting as the central hub making information from multiple sources available through a single web site to use manner. [5]

3 Forest Remote Sensing Parallel Processing Service and Gridification

PIPS2010 is a cluster-based parallel computing system for remote sensing processing by the Center for Earth Observation and Digital Earth, CAS. PIPS2010 uses MPICH standard message passing model embedding in the OpenCV based remote sensing image processing environment. PIPS2010 is deployed in a 4 nodes HPC machines, which is installed CentOS 5.3. One node is master, the others are slaves. [6]

The present research develops a set of forest fire detecting algorithms and assistant forest type classification algorithms based MODIS data. The forest fire point detecting algorithm uses 22 channel and 31 channel to distinguish the fire radiation and background earth radiation.[7]The assistant forest type classification algorithms cover the earth cloud masking algorithm, Savitzky-Golay filtering algorithm based on the time series MODIS NDVI data and so on.

From the beginning, all these algorithms are behaved as a function of a Windows based software from different research institutes. Some are running in IDL language running environment, some are in C language running environment. The procedures to put these programs to the parallel processing service are divided in two steps. First is to use PIPS parallel programming specification rewriting the above programs. (See Fig2) Then uses PIPS bridge to encapsulate these programs to service. The service can be registered in SIGRE as a job with some descriptions. In the end, the web based distributed forest remote sensing parallel processing service can use these jobs to construct the application with facility.

PIPS provides OMS Web Service of their parallel workflow jobs. SIGRE must put these services as its jobs and then to manage the PIPS web services. The steps of above work are as follows. First, we import the OMS Web Service packages in SIGRE. Then, the java class corresponding the PIPS workflow must be needed by creating SIGRE job instance. In this way, the parameters are sending to the PIPS workflow by web page. In the end, the web service can be submitted to the PIPS and be managed. [8, 9]

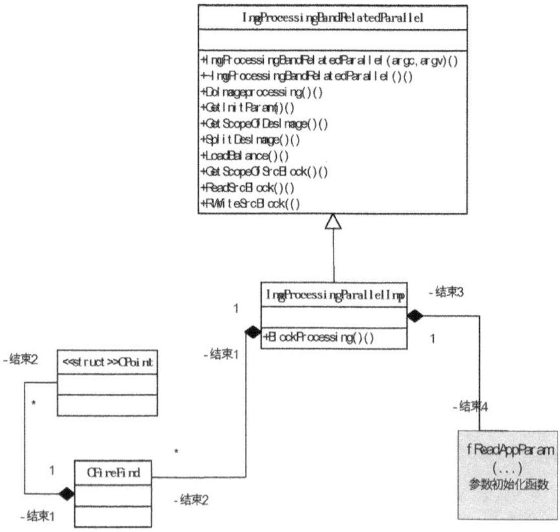

Fig. 2. Parallel Programming of the Forest Fire Point Detecting Algorithm

4 Workflow and Implement Results

Every geo computation service must have the input EO data. The input data has many existing modes. In this paper, users can upload their data by the web portal interface following the requirements of the specialty algorithm. After using distributed HPC resources, the user can get result data from web interface.

The workflow of the application is to input the parameters of the service, data upload, data select, submit the PIPS service and data download. The steps of data source upload and data select has user interference. The SIGApp middleware with XPDL file defined workflow can control this kind user interface by waiting and pause the workflow running.

Fig 3 shows the research result of implement cloud mask application on the web. In Fig3a is web portal interface of the service and waiting for the parameters input by users. Fig3b is the data uploading. Fig3c shows the time after data uploading and the workflow of cloud mask model starting. The yellow mark means this step is running and the grey one means it does not start yet. In Fig3d, the workflow is finished and the result can be downloading from a URL. The green mark means this step is finished correctly. The right part of the web shows some management function of the job. Fig3e shows the image of the result, in which the white one is cloud and the black one is not cloud.

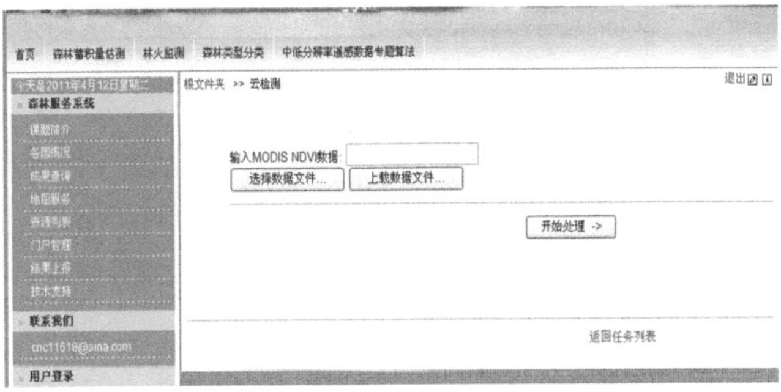

a. Waiting for the parameters input

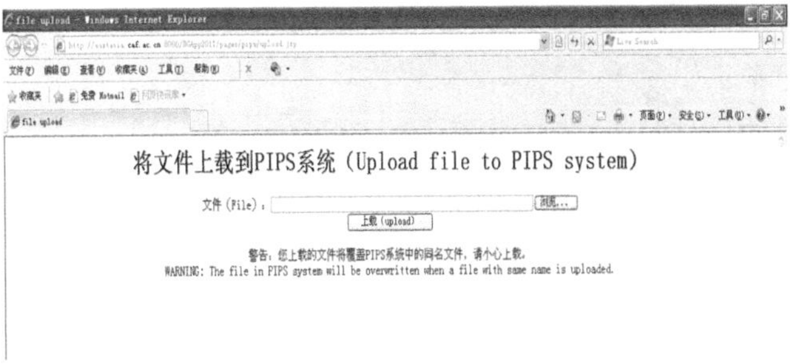

b. Data uploading

Fig. 3. Snapshots of the Implement Application

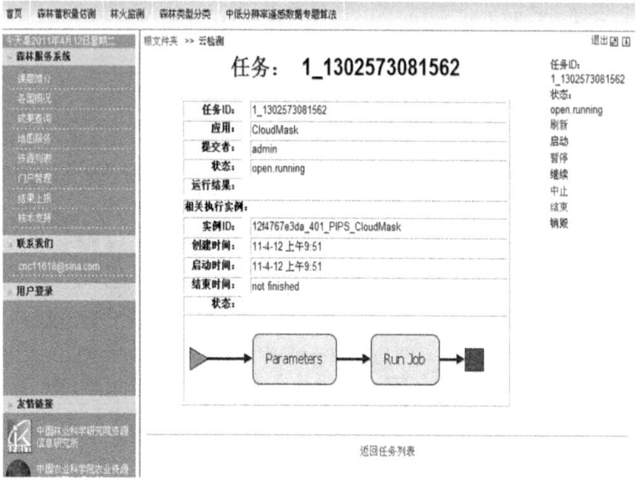

c. Workflow of cloud mask model starting

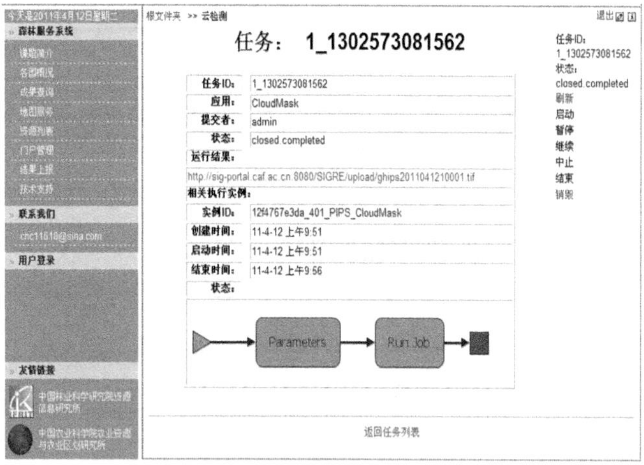

d. The workflow is finished

Fig. 3. *(Continued)*

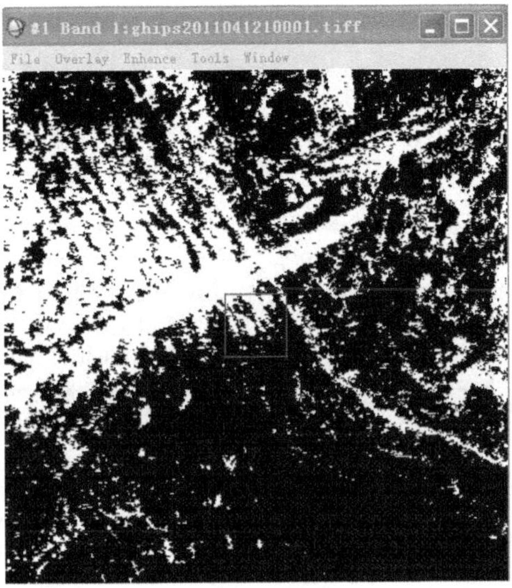

e. The image of the result

Fig. 3. (*Continued*)

5 Discussions and Conclusions

This paper releases a new of framework for distributed forest remote sensing parallel processing service using SaaS technology to integrate the remote user's data, HPC geo computing service for forest researchers, teachers and students. This paper gives the validation by constructing some forest remote sensing HPC service application with MODIS data. This work proves that using SaaS tools, the traditional forest remote sensing program can be rebuilt in parallel and service way to needs a coordinated web based observing network for disaster early warning system. The main achievement of this paper is using gird technology and web portal for a community of users contributing and consuming specialty geo information in web information resources management and web information integration area. The transparence of the workflow can be improved by integrating the data source searching and service matching in later work. For this purpose, the architecture of the system must be reformed by using new information technology.

Acknowledgment. Above work is supported by some of funded projects, such as CAF projects (IFRIT200905) and Chinese MOST 863 projects. The authors thank to Professor Liu Dingsheng , Professor Li Guoqing and their research team of Center for Earth Observation and Digital Earth Chinese Academy of Sciences. The authors thank to Dr.Wu Wenbin, Dr. Denghui and Dr. Zhang Mingwei from Institute of Agricultural Resources and Regional Planning, CAAS.

References

1. Petcu, D., Panica, S., Neagul, M., Frîncu, M., Zaharie, D., Ciorba, R., Dinis, A.: Earth Observation Data Processing in Distributed Systems. Informatica (Slovenia) 34(4), 463–476 (2010)
2. Software as a service, `http://en.wikipedia.org/wiki/Software_as_a_service`
3. Huang, Z., Li, G., Du, B., Zeng, Y., Gu, L.: SIGRE – an autonomic spatial information grid runtime environment for geo-computation. In: Xu, M., Zhan, Y.-W., Cao, J., Liu, Y. (eds.) APPT 2007. LNCS, vol. 4847, pp. 322–329. Springer, Heidelberg (2007)
4. Huang, Z., Li, G.: Building data grid for spatial information applications by meta-data adapters. In: 2008 International Conference on Computer Science and Software Engineering (CSSE), pp. 87–92 (2008)
5. `http://portals.apache.org/jetspeed-2.1.3/`
6. Li, G., Liu, D.: Key technologies research on building a cluster-based parallel computing system for remote sensing. In: Sunderam, V.S., van Albada, G.D., Sloot, P.M.A., Dongarra, J. (eds.) ICCS 2005. LNCS, vol. 3516, pp. 484–491. Springer, Heidelberg (2005)
7. Jiang, Y.: A Trial Discussion on Forest Fire Monitoring Using EOS-MODIS Data. Forest Fireproofing 4 (2002) (in Chinese)
8. Foster, I.: Globus Toolkit Version 4: Software for Service-Oriented Systems. Journal of Computer Science and Technology 21(4), 513–520 (2006)
9. Institute of Forest Resource Information Techniques,Chinese Academy of Forestry, Synopsis of building web based distribued forest remote sensing parallel processing service, Technology report (in Chinese)

Author Index

GPSR Compliance

The European Union's (EU) General Product Safety Regulation (GPSR) is a set of rules that requires consumer products to be safe and our obligations to ensure this.

If you have any concerns about our products, you can contact us on ProductSafety@springernature.com

In case Publisher is established outside the EU, the EU authorized representative is:

Springer Nature Customer Service Center GmbH
Europaplatz 3
69115 Heidelberg, Germany

Batch number: 10844611

Printed by Printforce, the Netherlands